THE NEW LATINO STUDIES READER

THE NEW LATINO STUDIES READER

A Twenty-First-Century Perspective

EDITED BY

Ramón A. Gutiérrez and Tomás Almaguer

 UNIVERSITY OF CALIFORNIA PRESS

University of California Press, one of the most distinguished university presses in the United States, enriches lives around the world by advancing scholarship in the humanities, social sciences, and natural sciences. Its activities are supported by the UC Press Foundation and by philanthropic contributions from individuals and institutions. For more information, visit www.ucpress.edu.

University of California Press
Oakland, California

Library of Congress Cataloging-in-Publication Data

Names: Gutiérrez, Ramón A., 1951–   editor. | Almaguer, Tomás, editor.
Title: The new Latino studies reader : a twenty-first-century perspective / edited by Ramón A. Gutiérrez and Tomás Almaguer.
Description: Oakland, California : University of California Press, [2016] | Includes bibliographical references and index.
Identifiers: LCCN 2016017311|
    ISBN 9780520284838 (cloth : alk. paper) |
    ISBN 9780520284845 (pbk. : alk. paper) |
    ISBN 9780520960510 (e-edition)
Subjects: LCSH: Hispanic Americans.
Classification: LCC E184.S75 N49 2016 | DDC 973/.0468—dc23
LC record available at https://lccn.loc.gov/2016017311

Manufactured in the United States of America

25 24 23 22 21 20 19 18 17 16
10 9 8 7 6 5 4 3 2 1

CONTENTS

FIGURES AND TABLES

FIGURES

TABLES

INTRODUCTION

The New Latino Studies Reader is a textbook offered as an act of pedagogy and one of alchemy, conjuring *Latinidad* as a political project that cultivates a broad cultural sense of belonging to a grander community that is created through ancestral links to Latin America. As a teaching tool, this volume is designed to introduce students, teachers, and interested readers to the recent emergence of Latino studies as an interdisciplinary field of research, with all of its complex themes, preoccupations, and intellectual challenges. Gathered here is a broad-ranging collection of essays focused on the sense of group belonging brought into self-awareness, and potentially political mobilization, by naming this sentiment of affiliation as "Latina" or "Latino." Calling oneself "Latino" and feeling a member of this group unites individuals of different nationalities from throughout Latin America, but it does not erase racial, class, gender, and sexual differences, which the all-inclusive word "Latina" or "Latino" all too often obscures. The readings presented here thus focus not only on individuality, personal sentiments, and self-fashioning, but just as importantly on group cohesion and coalition building, whether simply imagined, aspired to, or concrete and real. The collective aspirations of group empowerment captured by the word *Latinidad* often are dashed by social and national differences, levels of assimilation and adaptation to life in the United States, political beliefs, and a sense of belonging to other groups that may be just as important, say to one's religion, to one's town of birth, or to one's gender as an ardent feminist. All of these cleavages hold the possibility of tearing apart that potent political possibility of a collectivity named *Latinidad*. Indeed, in a 2013 report of the Pew Research Center on Latino self-identification, only 20 percent of its nationwide random sample of 5,103 adults explicitly called themselves "Hispanic" or "Latino"; 54 percent said they most often thought of themselves as "Mexicans," "Puerto Ricans," "Cubans," and so forth, and 23 percent proclaimed themselves to be "Americans."[1] This landscape of group membership becomes even more complex and differentiated if we include immigrants from different Latin American indigenous groups who feel oppressed and marginalized in their native states of origin, such as the Maya of Mexico and Guatemala, the Quechuas of the Andean republics, and the Mixtec and Zapotecs of Oaxaca, Mexico. For them, while the denomination as "Latino" theoretically fits, it is not a comfortable one.

That residents of the United States at present imagine themselves to be tied to some hemispheric Latin American unity, calling themselves "Latinas" and "Latinos" and referring to this sense of coherence as *Latinidad*, is of rather recent origin. The history of that sense of unity rooted in human action is perhaps only forty years old. While earlier linguistic antecedents, such as the term "Hispanic," which is now used rather interchangeably with "Latino," had been in circulation since the eighteenth century in English-language texts, it was only in the 1940s that both "Hispanic" and "Latino" entered into American scholarly discussions as a way of describing larger aggregations of peoples of Latin American origin in the United States. "Hispanic" was often used to describe the descendants of the original Spanish colonial territories that became part of the United States in the nineteenth century (Florida, New Mexico, Arizona, California), while "Latino" was more aptly used to describe immigrants from Latin America, of course with some geographic and temporal exceptions. *Hispanidad* and *Latinidad* remained categories that were used to describe groups of people for many years before either of these words were embraced for self-description and group membership rooted in collective discussion and action. As far as can be surmised, this first occurred in Chicago in the early 1970s. There, Mexican Americans and Puerto Ricans temporarily suspended their group differences and came together to forge a coalition of civil rights organizations with the goal of petitioning the city of Chicago for bilingual education, employment opportunities, and the extension of affirmative action policies to their newly found alliance as members of a "Latino" community.[2] Since then, other groups, be they from public or private life, from the public sphere, from the academy, or from government, have chosen "Latinas" and "Latinos" as the categories that best describe their behavior, aspirations, sense of belonging, and community membership.

"Latino" is now included in most American English–language dictionaries as an English word, and etymologically explained as the abbreviated form of the Spanish *latinoamericano*, which simply means "Latin American." The idea that a place called "Latin America" existed on the face of the globe was itself a mid-nineteenth-century geographic invention, created out of thin air by intellectuals from Spain's former New World colonies who were living in Paris in the early 1850s, seeking to redraw the broad cultural boundaries that emerged in the aftermath of the American, Spanish American, and Haitian Revolutions. Looking for a way to describe the emergent political order that had succeeded Spain's sharply reduced colonial empire, they called it "Latin America" and its residents *latinoamericanos*.[3] Thus "Latinos" was birthed.

How the word "Latino" emerged in the United States among a wide swath of distinct national-origin groups is a much more complicated story. For introductory purposes here, suffice it to say that just as Mexican Americans and Puerto Ricans came together in Chicago's Pilsen neighborhood to claim benefits they felt their collective due as "Latinos," so too members of other institutions, organizations, corporations, and state agencies have seen it in their interest to deploy the word "Latino" for purposes of simplification, political advantage, and monetary profit. Take the case of the Southwest Council of La Raza. When it was formed in 1968, the Southwest Council of La Raza had as its goal mobilizing and politically empowering the Mexican American and Chicano populations of Texas and California. Seeking to become the representative for this numerically ascendant population that was then being increasingly called "Hispanic," the organization changed its name to the "National Council of La Raza," moved its headquarters to Washington, DC, and developed a broader public policy agenda that included not only Mexican Americans but immigrants from many Latin American countries as well. The organization was soon recognized by philanthropic foundations and the United States Census Bureau as the organization they had to engage when they were trying to address broad issues of importance to Hispanics, much as the National Association for the Advancement of Colored People (NAACP) did for African Americans.[4] Corporations producing products to satisfy the ethnic appetites and consumption desires of Hispanics and Latinos were equally involved, working symbiotically with advertising agencies and media conglomerates to reach their intended targets, who if properly understood and pitched to, might indeed consume the beer, cheese, and host of consumables being intentionally produced to embody *el sabor latino*, that unique flavor they imagined as "Latino."[5]

According to the most recent population estimates generated by the United States Census Bureau and the Pew Research Center, as of July 1, 2014, the Latino or Hispanic population numbers roughly 54.4 million individuals, representing approximately 17 percent of the country's total. In previous decades Hispanics and Latinos were first counted by the census as "Spanish surnamed" individuals, then as "Spanish-speaking" persons, and now, as the result of increasing political pressure and numeric importance, they have emerged as "Latinos" and "Hispanics" in government statistics. Demographers predict that if current population trends continue, by the year 2060 Latinos will number 128.8 million, composing 31 percent of the country's population. By 2048 the country will become "majority-minority," with Latinos, African Americans, and Asian Americans numerically overwhelming the country's historically majority white population. In certain states this change has already occurred. California and New Mexico became majority-minority states in 2014; Texas and the District of Columbia should shortly follow. By 2020 Arizona, Florida, Maryland, and Nevada are expected to reach this milestone too.[6]

The Latino population in the United States comes from many Latin American countries. Historically, since the 1880s, Mexicans have been the largest group. By 2013 estimates, ethnic Mexicans constitute 64 percent of the 54 million total. Puerto Ricans follow, with 9.4 percent of the total, Salvadorans 3.8 percent, Cubans 3.7 percent, Dominicans 3.1 percent, Guatemalans 2.3 percent, Colombians 1.9 percent, Spaniards 1.4 percent, Hondurans 1.4 percent, Ecuadorians 1.2 percent, Peruvians 1.1 percent, Nicaraguans 0.8 percent, Venezuelans 0.5 percent, Argentineans 0.5 percent, with the remaining 4.9 percent coming from other Latin American countries. Immigrants from Brazil, Latin America's largest country, figure into this mix but represent only 0.1 percent of all Latinos.[7]

Latinidad has emerged potently in the academy in recent years because of the increasing ethnic complexity that now characterizes high schools, colleges, and universities. Those institutions of higher learning that once had distinct Mexican American and Puerto Rican studies departments, centers, and programs have met the challenge of increasing Dominican, Salvadoran, Cuban, and Guatemalan student enrollments by expanding into larger units of Latino studies. Increasing interest in intersectional analyses led to the first international conference on Latina and Latino studies, which was held in Chicago on July 17–19, 2014. Nearly seven hundred scholars, activists, and artists gathered for the event. As Raúl Coronado, one of the conference organizers and now the first president of the newly founded Association of Latina/o Studies explained, "We know so much about the history and culture of Mexican Americans, Puerto Ricans, [and] Cubans, for example, but we know so little about the similarities and differences between these various communities." The association's goal is to "promote research and effect policy change related to US Latinas/os. . . . We hope our work will help transform school curriculums and make a larger impact in national politics and culture."[8] We thus hope that this book addresses the pedagogical needs of teachers intent on designing courses that show the complexity of America's Latinos and educating the next generation of students about the complexity of their divergent pasts and collective future in the United States.

This anthology is organized into seven parts that are devoted to mainly social science themes. In part 1, "Hispanics, Latinos, Chicanos, Boricuas: What Do Names Mean?" we have essays by Ramón A. Gutiérrez, Frances R. Aparicio, and Frances Negrón-Muntaner that delve into the complexity of *Latinidad* in history, social networks, and memory. In chapter 1 Gutiérrez offers us a genealogy of the politics of group naming at three historical moments: the Spanish colonial period, after the territorial acquisition of Mexico's north by the United States at the end of the U.S.-Mexico War (1846–1848), and in the midst of the civil rights movement of the 1960s, when young Mexican Americans and Puerto Ricans began calling themselves "Chicanos" and "Boricuas" in opposition to the dominant society. In chapter 2 Aparicio explores the complex ways in which women and men of various national origins, distinct sexual preferences, and various class and regional locations speak about and imagine their *Latinidad* at the most intimate and personal levels of daily interaction. In chapter 3 Negrón-Muntaner illuminates the role of memory, evoking the images we saw on television and the musical tunes we heard on the radio and record player to interrogate how celebrities such as Celia Cruz conjure up a sense of feeling connected to a larger *Latinidad* born of exile and abandonment of the homeland.

In part 2, "The Origins of Latinos in the United States," chapter 4 by Ramón A. Gutiérrez, traces the nineteenth-century territorial expansion of the United States, and the processes by which it annexed more than half of Mexico's national territory at the end of the U.S.-Mexico War in 1848. Mexican citizens who resided in the conquered territory were given one year to remove themselves back to Mexico. If they remained, they automatically became American citizens. These Latinos often sarcastically quip that "we did not cross the border; the border crossed us." The other essays in part 2 study the economic and political impulses that continually fueled and renewed distinct Latino immigration patterns, based primarily on labor needs and geopolitics. David G. Gutiérrez's essay in chapter 5 is a comprehensive history of Latino immigration, which Lillian Guerra extends in chapter 6 with her focus on emigration from the Caribbean and Central America since the 1959 Cuban Revolution. The disparities created by U.S. Cold War politics toward different national groups is Guerra's primary concern, explaining why Cubans were, and still are, welcomed as refugees from totalitarian Communism, while those fleeing revolutionary and counterrevolutionary violence propagated and funded by the United States in Central America are not.

"The Conundrums of Race" is the title of part 3, which comprises essays by Jorge Duany, Ginetta E. B. Candelario, and Tomás Almaguer. In chapter 7 Duany studies racial formation in Puerto Rico to contest the U.S. ideology of hypodescent and the black/white racial binary that its notion of the "one drop rule" produced historically. He argues that racial understandings among Puerto Ricans are quite complex and particularly situational, depending on whether race is being evaluated on the island or mainland. On the island many think of themselves as white despite phenotypes that most would recognize as evidence of extensive racial mixing. On the mainland these same individuals deem themselves neither black nor white, but one of a host of other racial categories the U.S. Census Bureau has never comprehended or fully captured statistically in its inquiries about race. Candelario's contribution, chapter 8, takes us to the most elemental level, to women's hair and its quality, texture, and look as the central organizing principle of how Dominican women living in New York City imagine race. In the Dominican Republic there is no strict racial binary but a host of physical color graduations, with whiteness and blackness at opposite ends of a continuous spectrum. Whiteness itself is far from pure and instead is imagined as a mixture between *lo indio* (i.e., the Taino indigenous people that once inhabited the island but were wiped out during the early colony) and *lo hispano* (the white somatic look of the Hispanics who first colonized the island). To distance themselves from blackness in the present, which they equate with the African slave past and with the Haitians whom they disdain, who reside on the western half of the island of Hispaniola, Dominican women spend considerable time and money self-fashioning a mixed racial look that is appropriately demonstrated in wavy, flowing hair with no traces of African kink. Almaguer's essay in chapter 9 studies the categories the U.S. Census Bureau uses to understand Hispanics and Latinos racially, and how these two groups describe themselves. He then compares the racial lexicon of Mexicans and Puerto Ricans living in the United States with the categories that are used to describe persons of African and indigenous ancestry in Puerto Rico and Mexico. He concludes that the national cultures of origin profoundly shape how people think about racial formations in their homeland and how they "reracialize" themselves and others once they become residents in the United States.

Most of the women and men who emigrated from Latin America to the United States over the past century have come seeking well-paid work, so part 4 explores the theme of "Work and Life Chances." In essays by Patricia Zavella, Nicholas de Genova and Ana Y. Ramos-Zayas, and Manuel Pastor Jr., we learn the raw details of the work process, its hierarchical organization, and its meager levels of compensation, which naturally result in poverty for the majority of Latino immigrants. In chapter 10 Zavella surveys the rural and urban worlds of workers in Northern California, with their gender hierarchies, levels of sexual harassment that women especially experience, and linguistic barriers that routinely result in low wages. These conditions have been made all the more difficult by the economic recession of 2008 and the increasing reality of capital flight. Throughout this book we highlight instances of Latino unity, but also the conditions under which national groups feud when they compete for the same spaces, occupations, and compensation. In part 4 we read about the racial stereotypes Mexicans have of Puerto Ricans and vice versa, and of the racial tensions between these Latino populations. Here we turn to Chicago, where Mexican immigrants and Puerto Ricans live side by side and compete for the poorly paid unskilled work the city offers. While many Mexicans in the Humboldt Park neighborhood are older immigrants who have regularized their status and become citizens, the majority are unauthorized immigrants. Puerto Ricans by law have been citizens since 1917. This fact troubles the relationships between these two national groups. In chapter 11 de Genova and Ramos-Zayas explore the competing ideologies of work and worth that allow Puerto Ricans to lampoon Mexicans as "illegal aliens" who undercut wages and fail to invoke their rights as workers, and thus are caricatured as timid because of their ever-present fear of deportation. The retort Mexicans sling at Puerto Ricans is that they are lazy, that they have become dependent on government benefits because of their citizenship, particularly the women who have become "welfare queens." In Pastor's essay in chapter 12, we have a recent analysis of the levels of poverty among ethnic Mexicans in California, the state with the largest number of Latinos. What is particularly startling is that in 2012 two out of every five Mexicans in the state lived in conditions of working poverty, a ratio that significantly surpasses that for every other ethnic group in California. These Mexicans are not part-time workers. Instead, they are fully employed, indeed overemployed, with some toiling daily at two and sometimes three jobs to make ends meet. The pathways to upward mobility for these workers are limited, with education and skills acquisition offering the surest possible route, but an improbable one. The improbability is due to their all-consuming work routines that leave little time for vocational training.

Social mobility, always measured generationally from the immigrant cohort forward to assess how they have integrated or assimilated into American life over decades, is the theme of part 5, "Class, Generation, and Assimilation." Here we have gathered essays by Luis Fraga and a number of Latino political scientists, Edward Telles and Vilma Ortiz, and Richard L. Zweighenhaft and G. William Domhoff. In chapter 13 Fraga and his colleagues study how powerful the American dream of upward mobility and economic success has been in shaping Latino aspirations and reality. Most Latino immigrants have arrived intent on fulfilling this iconic dream, but many have failed because of limited educational opportunities and outright discrimination. How Mexican Americans have improved their lot or remained socially, culturally, and economically stagnant is the focus of Telles and Ortiz's chapter 14, in which they study the long course of Mexican immigrant integration into American society. Mexicans are the oldest Latino immigrant group in the United States, having begun migrating northward shortly after the end of the U,S,-Mexico War in 1848. Because of the number of years that have passed since their immigrant entry, it is easiest to measure this group's progress toward assimilation, or an embrace of American identity and an acceptance of the values and norms of the dominant culture. Telles and Ortiz characterize the Mexican immigrant experience as "generations of exclusion," noting that by the fourth generation in the United States, there has been upward mobility only for some. Terms such as "segmented assimilation" or "bumpy road assimilation" have been used recently to reflect the difficulties Latinos have experienced advancing socioeconomically over the course of several generations. When Latinos are studied as a whole with group-level data, it is often difficult to detect what is happening with the very rich and powerful at the top of society, and what is happening with those at the bottom. In Pastor's essay we survey the bottom of society, and in Zweighenhaft and Domhoff's contributions in chapters 15 and 16, we focus on the top, or what they call the "Latino power elite." There are few rags-to-riches stories, because most wealthy Latinos were already rather rich when they arrived in the United States and simply parlayed what they had into much more by attending elite schools and exploiting their social connections.

Gender and sexuality are powerful forces in the daily lives of Latinos. In part 6, "Gender and Sexualities," we have essays by Ramón A. Gutiérrez, Robert Courtney Smith, Lorena García, and Tomás Almaguer that illustrate the impact of these themes on personal lives in the past and present. When Latina and Latino immigrants come to the United States, among the many things they bring with them as parts of their cultural baggage are a set of gender and sexual ideologies that are deeply imprinted, shaping their behavior for generations wherever they go. These gender ideals and norms mostly privilege men and masculinity over women and femininity, and they are spoken about and understood through the idiom of male honor and female shame, which if properly reproduced result in respect for one's family and the honoring of its head. Gutiérrez's essay in chapter 17 traces the long history of honor and shame in Spain and its American colonial empire. He shows how the hierarchical secular evaluations of personal and familial honor were understood and deployed, and how these ideals constantly conflicted with the more egalitarian kinship ideology of the Catholic Church, which had as its intended goal the weakening of familial and patriarchal power that it saw as accumulating and evolving into the formation of kingdoms and states capable of challenging the authority of the Church. Ultimately, a family's honor was an evaluation of its social standing. How that judgment was rendered had much to do with the comportment of its females, particularly their *vergüenza*, or their "sexual modesty" or "shame." Men had to protect the shame of their womenfolk until they married, for if that sexual integrity was lost, it could never be restored or regained. A man's honor, his very sense of manliness and self-worth, was dependent on his capacity to protect his women. Men who did not safeguard their women were seen as unworthy of respect; disrespected men often became the easy prey of powerful men.

The essays in part 6 by Smith and by García move from history to ethnography, exploring how gender ideologies among conservative, former rural peasants from Mexico and Puerto Rico are lived and experienced in New York City and Chicago. In chapter 18 Smith studied a group of Mexican immigrants who made their way from the rural village of Ticuani, in the state of Puebla, to work legally in New York City's restaurants. Daily, in this new environment, the Ticuani men have to negotiate their "*ranchero* masculinity," donning aprons and working as cooks—considered women's work—while demonstrating their virility and manhood by economically supporting their families and maintaining order within them, which includes ensuring that their wives reproduced their own "*ranchera* femininity" amid astounding cultural pressures to change. Among some immigrants these pressures strengthened and redefined gender norms; among others Mexican gender ideals eroded, producing significant conflict among family members.

From New York we move back to Chicago and to the negotiation of gender comportment among Mexican immigrant mothers who are often seen by their daughters as having "old school" ways of thinking about gender and sexual ideals and norms, values they clearly carried from Mexico. As García's essay in chapter 19 shows, these mothers are quite concerned about the shame (*vergüenza*) and reputation of their daughters who have started having premarital sex, something quite taboo according to Mexican ideals of honor and shame, mainly because conservative men would never think of marrying a woman who is known to have lost her virginity. Mothers thus constantly warn their daughters to respect themselves, even as the daughters negotiate gender ideologies that are more egalitarian in the United States around issues of educational opportunities, dating patterns, the use of contraceptives, and partner selection. These topics become sources of immense give-and-take between mothers and daughters, particularly when fathers are drawn into the equation concerning the family's social standing in the community, or its reputation, which is the putative source of the respect it is due. Finally, in Almaguer's essay in chapter 20, we turn to the homoerotic fantasies and sexual behavior of ethnic Mexican men who have sex with other men in the San Francisco Bay Area. Some of these men are openly gay, others bisexual, and still others are heterosexuals peeking out of the closet to experiment with their desires. In the oral histories Almaguer has collected, he focuses on childhood socialization, on the memories of the relationships these boys had with their fathers, and on the grander sexual scripts that define ideal Latino masculine sexuality as *activo* and insertive, while the *pasivo* and receptive sexual partner in oral or anal sex is equated with the feminine. The men Almaguer interviewed described playing out childhood fantasies in their adult erotic lives, seeking out older masculine men for passive receptive sex, and thus playing the feminine role with them.

Part 7 is devoted to "Latino Politics." In this part of the book, we look at formal politics at the institutional level through elections, political parties, and legislation, and then to popular manifestations of politics, from the fear some exhibit toward young Latino immigrants, to the limited social horizons those who are incarcerated experience, to the ways immigrants have organized and mobilized to protest the conditions of unauthorized immigrants. Lisa García Bedolla's essay in chapter 21 delves into the demographic complexity of the Latino electorate, disaggregating its national and class dimensions, differentiating between the native and foreign born and between the political behavior of women and men, and pointing to the low levels of voting by the working classes as compared to wealthier Latinos, who give the ballot box much more importance. García Bedolla instructs us on how majority rule functions in our system of government, often disempowering Latino elected officials at the federal level unless they can enter into larger coalitions within and between parties over converging interests.

In chapter 22 and an update in chapter 23, David E. Hayes-Bautista, Werner Schink, and Jorge Chapa carefully study California's demography, proposing the possibility of rebellion that pits young Latinos against aging whites. As Hayes-Bautista, Schink, and Chapa explain, Latinos are increasingly young, undereducated, and poor, and their numbers are increasing. Through their taxes they will be expected to support older retired whites, even as the numbers of whites are shrinking. Given that Latinos increasingly see their future prospects as bleak, what options will they have? Some imagine that rebellion is certainly a possibility. Today in California, for every one hundred Latinos who enter elementary school, only forty-seven will graduate from high school; the other fifty-three will face grim prospects. Statistics and state expenditures clearly show that their likeliest career pathway will be into prison. Since 1980 the state of California has constructed eight new prisons and only one university, which at present enrolls fewer than 2,000 students. Martin Guevara Urbina's essay in chapter 24 thus explores the difficulties Latina women and Latino men have when they leave prison, either upon serving their sentences or upon parole.[9]

While the essays by Hayes-Bautista, Schink, and Chapa anticipated that intensifying social inequality would soon pit young, poor Latino men against elderly, wealthier, white men, the Southern Poverty Law Center, in its September 2009 report in chapter 25 on conditions in Suffolk County, New York, describes a war waged by young white men against Latino immigrants. These thugs constantly harassed, beat, maimed, and even murdered Latino immigrants in the area.

Pierrette Hondagneu-Sotelo and Angelica Salas's essay in chapter 26 takes us to the spring of 2006, when across the United States major rallies were staged supporting the rights of authorized and unauthorized immigrants. This massive mobilization did not just happen spontaneously out of thin air; it was the product of a number of factors that were first catalyzed by the introduction of the Border Protection, Antiterrorism and Illegal Immigration and Control Act of 2005, authored by Congressmen James Sensenbrenner (R-WI) and Peter King (R-NJ), which proposed making entry into the United States without review a felony. To protest such draconian anti-immigrant legislation, labor unions, religious leaders, and civil rights organizations came together using social media and successfully blocked approval of the bill. Finally, in Ann Louise Bardach's essay in chapter 27, we take a closer look at Cubans. Since the Cuban Revolution of 1959, Cubans have been seen as "good immigrants" fleeing Castro's Communist regime, welcomed with open arms and given immediate assistance in ways that have never been extended to other Latino immigrants, especially not to those deemed "bad," such as the Mexican and Salvadoran "illegal aliens." The Cuban Refugee Program extended resettlement funds, welfare benefits, health services, job training, adult education opportunities, aid to public schools attended by immigrants, and foster care for unaccompanied children. Cubans were given unprecedented opportunities to integrate themselves into American society. This quickly resulted in upward mobility and entry into the country's political elite, with three Cuban Americans now serving as U.S. senators: Ted Cruz (R-TX), Marco Rubio (R-FL), Robert Menéndez (D-NJ); Cruz and Rubio are candidates for the Republican Party's 2016 presidential nomination. Bardach argues that Cubans no longer need special privileges, particularly as relations between Cuba and the United States are rapidly being normalized. All immigrants seeking entry into the United States should be treated equally, but they are not.

We began this introduction by discussing the excitement that surrounds the political and cultural possibilities of *Latinidad*, the demographic expansion of Hispanics and Latinos as an ethnic group, and the emergence of the field of Latino studies as an interdisciplinary and transnational field of study. As the co-editors of this anthology, we have labored intensely to accomplish three things: to make this work as current and cutting-edge as possible in its survey of the theoretical and empirical literature; to reproduce here the wide diversity of national, regional, class, racial, gender, and sexual differences that constitute the Latina and Latino population in the United States; and to honor the scholarship of women and men alike. We have chosen in most instances to refer to

"Latinos" generically, inflecting gender when appropriate, but generally avoiding symbols such as "Latina/o" and "Latin@" to acknowledge differential gendered experiences.

We hope you will enjoy the essays gathered here, which are organized as a course syllabus would be, systematically introducing themes with progressive levels of complexity. Because of space limitations, we have not been able to address the rich complexity of Latino cultural expression, which merits a volume of its own. Nor have we been able to traverse the terrain of language difference in Latinos who often speak not only English but also Spanish, Portuguese, and a host of indigenous languages.

NOTES

1. Mark Hugo López, "Three-Fourths of Hispanics Say Their Community Needs a Leader: Most Latinos Cannot Name One," *Pew Center Report*, October 22, 2013.

2. Felix M. Padilla, *Latino Ethnic Consciousness: The Case of Mexican Americans and Puerto Ricans in Chicago* (Notre Dame, IN: Notre Dame University Press, 1985).

3. Walter Mingnolo, *The Idea of Latin America* (Malden, MA: Blackwell, 2005); Arturo Ardao, *Génesis de la idea y el nombre de América Latina* (Caracas: Consejo Nacional de la Cultura, 1980).

4. G. Cristina Mora, *Making Hispanics: How Activists, Bureaucrats, and Media Constructed a New American* (Chicago: University of Chicago Press, 2014).

5. Arlene Dávila, *Latinos Inc.: The Marketing and Making of a People* (Berkeley: University of California Press, 2001).

6. Centers for Disease Control and Prevention, "Minority Health: Hispanic or Latino Populations," http://www.cdc.gov/minorityhealth/populations/REMP/hispanic.html (accessed May 30, 2015).

7. Ibid.; Mark Hugo López, Ana Gonzalez-Barrera, and Danielle Cuddington, "Diverse Origins: The Nation's 14 Largest Hispanic-Origin Groups" (Washington, DC: Pew Research Center, June 19, 2013), http://www.pewhispanic.org/2013/06/19/diverse-origins-the-nations-14-largest-hispanic-origin-groups/ (accessed May 30, 2015).

8. "An International Latina/o Studies Conference: Imagining the Past, Present, and Future," press release, Inaugural Conference on U.S. Latinas/os, Chicago, July 5, 2014, http://www.chicano.ucla.edu/files/events/ILSC%20Press%20Release.pdf.

9. Armida Ornelas and Daniel G. Solórzano, "Reaffirming Affirmative Action: An Equal Opportunity Analysis of Advanced Placement Courses and University Admissions," in *Mexicans in California: Transformations and Challenges*, eds. Ramón A. Gutiérrez and Patricia Zavella (Urbana: University of Illinois Press, 2009), pp. 77–93, dropout statistics on p. 78.

PART 1

HISPANICS, LATINOS, CHICANOS, BORICUAS

What Do Names Mean?

. . .

Who is a Latino? Who is a Hispanic? What should we call them? What do they call themselves? What are the politics of choosing a particular ethnic label? This section addresses these nettlesome questions and explores the contemporary origins of Latino identities in a historical, sociological, and biographical way. It surveys the broad outlines of Latino diversity and how individuals are assigned or choose personal identities based on their respective nationalities (as Mexicans, Puerto Ricans, Salvadorans, Cubans, etc.) as well as collective panethnic labels such as "Latino" or "Hispanic." In so doing, we draw upon the work of historian Ramón A. Gutiérrez and cultural critics Frances Aparicio and Frances Negrón-Muntaner to illuminate the complex ways Latino identity has been forged and evolved over time as well as experienced individually and collectively.

In chapter 1 Ramón A. Gutiérrez's essay, "What's in a Name? The History and Politics of Hispanic and Latino Panethnicities," delves into the history of naming in what is now the American West as various groups have sought to forge collective ethnic identities both internally from below and through imposition from above by state institutions. Looking at how particular panethnic identities were born, Gutiérrez examines three moments in the history of what became the United States—the Spanish conquest of the indigenous peoples of Mexico's north (which started in 1598), the military takeover of the West by the United States at the end of the Mexican War of 1846–48, and the mobilization by racialized minorities during the civil rights movement in the mid-1960s and early 1970s.

His essay reminds us that contemporary debates over terms like "Latino" or "Hispanic" have long, deep, and convoluted historical roots, which constantly shift, are abandoned, return with new meanings, and have lives of creative human makings. Gutiérrez focuses our attention on the complex ways that the three largest Latino populations—Mexicans, Puerto Ricans, and Cubans—have each contended with their subjugation under the cataclysmic colonial project initiated by Spain and then later by the United States. Their political, economic, and social subordination under the Spanish regime helped ignite status hierarchies and identity categories based on religion, region, race, property, and legitimacy of birth. Gutiérrez shows that personal identities were and remain complex bundles of status categories. What allowed Mexicans, Cubans, and Puerto Ricans to first think of themselves as "Hispanics" and later as "Latinos" was a shared language, until quite recently a shared religion, and natal attachments to geographies that were once claimed as Spain's colonial empire.

The contemporary use of the term "Latino," and its political invocation of a collective sense of *Latinidad,* was initially forged in the 1970s. It emerged as a sign of the combined assertion of the dignity and worth of Puerto Ricans and Mexicans in Chicago in their common struggle for collective political goals. In tracking the crystallization and evolution of this oppositional consciousness and the militant assertion by these nationalities for collective social justice, Gutiérrez reminds us that

> *Latinidad*, that communal sense of membership in a group tied to Latin America through ancestry, language, culture, and history, emerged from below precisely out of such nationalist sentiments. Individuals first start calling themselves "Latinos" in cities like Chicago and New York, largely to advance political agendas not easily achievable by small, isolated, and distinct national origin groups. By coming together as Latinos, their numbers swelled, and their political clout expanded, demanding inclusion in the polity through affirmative action, fair housing, voting rights, and bilingual education. In time *Latinidad* was also championed from above by ethnic specific civil rights organizations seeking grander nationwide influence and larger membership rolls. Eventually, government bureaucrats, foundations, and corporate marketers recognized the unity of *Latinidad*.

A shared common language, religious culture, residential proximity, and sense of oppression animated the emergence of Latino panethnicity from below, which in time got imposed by the state from above. This is most evident when both "Latino" and "Hispanic" are interchangeably used as the official nomenclature of the U.S. Census Bureau for the more than twenty different nationalities that are now collectively aggregated under these two designations. Gutiérrez's essay charts this process over time and documents the varied roles that the state, the media, corporations, and community-based organizations have played in how these categories of belonging and group consciousness initially emerged. And the essay describes how it has been continually expanded and sustained with the arrival of an increasingly diverse Latino population that has immigrated to the United States in the past fifty years.

We move from this broad historical sweep of the way Latino identity emerged to an analysis of how that category functions in the daily lives of the diverse Latino population. Frances R. Aparicio's essay in chapter 2, "(Re)constructing *Latinidad*: The Challenge of Latina/o Studies," focuses on the complex intersection of Latino identity with a range of other social identities forged by unique personal histories. Like Gutiérrez, Aparicio challenges us to critically consider the question: Who is a Latina/o? In answering this question, she shows us that one's replies are not always simple and easy but are born of local, regional, national, panethnic, and global forms of being and knowing. These attachments and associations are profoundly socioeconomic, linguistic, racial, generational, gendered, and sexual. The processes that shape Latino identities are rooted in ethnic conflicts and struggles, in the movement of peoples and cultures across large spaces, in the imposition of force by the powerful, and in resistance by the weak, who develop an oppositional consciousness and deploy various strategies of existence that are given form in names like "Boricua" (an identity embraced by Puerto Ricans) and "Chicano" (an identity embraced by Mexicans).

When Aparicio takes us to a Latino music venue in Chicago and introduces us to her friends, she helps us appreciate how people who call themselves "Latinos" come from different nationalities, class backgrounds, generational cohorts, immigrant statuses, racial identities, genders, sexualities, and linguistic skills. Despite everyone being of Latin American descent, they each simultaneously embody complex and often contradictory identities and experiences. These personal selves, Aparicio notes, are "contingent, fluid, and relational, used strategically and structurally depending on the context." It is from such complex collectivities that Latinas and Latinos are formed. According to Aparicio the mapping of this diversity remains the central challenge of Latino studies as it gains prominence as a discipline and field of study. "Latina/o studies can become the space in which these diverse experiences, identities, and power dynamics can be accounted for in the construction of a new social imaginary that transcends the old paradigms and nationality based conflicts." And she submits that "heterogeneity challenges scholars to find new, interdisciplinary approaches that can address our multiple and shifting realities."

In chapter 3 Frances Negrón-Muntaner explores these multiple and collective identities as they are individually experienced in "Celia's Shoes." Her biographical essay explores the life of the late Afro-Cuban singer Celia Cruz and delves into issues of memory, diaspora, and identity. Negrón-Muntaner begins her essay marveling at the collection of Cruz's platform shoes in the permanent collection of the Smithsonian National Museum of American History in Washington, DC. The shoes are part of the Smithsonian's Latino history and culture collection and its Caribbean music artifacts section. Negrón-Muntaner describes Cruz's life from her beginnings in one of the poorest neighborhoods in Havana to her becoming lead singer for La Sonora Matancera—Cuba's most popular orchestra—to her exile in Mexico after the Cuban revolution in 1959 and eventual permanent settlement in the outskirts of New York City.

Through the course of Cruz's life, she was celebrated with one cultural title after another, from national musical icon in Cuba, *"la guarachera de Cuba"* (the Cuban reveler), to pan-Latino, global status as the "Queen of Salsa." This evolution was accompanied by a continual renegotiation and refashioning of her appearance. Celia Cruz became notorious because of her distinctive raspy voice, her high-heeled shoes, her outrageously colored and designed wigs, her multicolored dresses, her long painted nails, and her very expensive jewelry.

Negrón-Muntaner's essay charts the challenging path Celia Cruz navigated to celebrity and stardom. Often standing on shoes as high as eight inches, Cruz had a collection of platform shoes that numbered in the thousands, many of them extravagantly adorned with simulated diamonds or ruby material and custom-made to fit perfectly. According to Negrón-Muntaner, "Celia's footwear seemed to defy gravity itself, as they did not rest on a conventional heel but on the thinnest of soles. By appearing physically unfeasible, Celia's trademark shoes offer the illusion of walking on air, a magical attribute that again elevates the queen above mere mortals." This regal status was a far cry from Cruz's humble, "undistinguished" class origins in Cuba of African ancestry that was evident in her appearance. Wigs covered her coarse, kinky African hair. Flowing dresses draped her large, voluptuous body. And Cruz's shoes elevated her stature above her adoring fans when she held court. These accoutrements helped to position her on a "good footing" as she climbed up from her impoverished background to the heights as an international Afro-Cuban female star. Celia Cruz's high-heeled shoes symbolically depict her rise in social status and the difficult path she traversed to stardom and musical immortality after her death in 2003.

Cruz's shoes also registered the unique fashioning of her gender presentation as an Afro-Cuban woman. As Negrón-Muntaner notes, "while high heels made Celia a woman, she did not want to be just any kind of woman. She wished to be seen as a Cuban, Latina, and Afro-Caribbean woman, but also as *mujer decente,* a decent woman." Not being blessed with the European features that culturally might have marked her as pretty, Cruz herself said that she was *"fea de cara pero bella de alma"* (with an ugly face but beautiful soul). Indeed, she became a "decent woman," who knew the meaning of *vergüenza* (shame), and negotiated that reputation carefully in public and private. Celia Cruz's "unique style allowed her to project an illusion of abundance, dignity, talent, Cubanness, beauty, femininity, and, toward the end of her life, eternal youth," writes Negrón-Muntaner. Celia Cruz's shoes thus offer us a complicated way to think about how Latino and Latina identity travels in disaporic ways, and intersects with and illuminates other existential dimensions of our identities in the United States.

1

WHAT'S IN A NAME?

The History and Politics of Hispanic and Latino Panethnicities

Ramón A. Gutiérrez

There is an apocryphal tale of recent popular vintage that circulates along the Mexico/United States border. It tells of an act of miscommunication, born of a mistranslation, between a Mexican immigrant traveling north and an officer of the U.S. Border Patrol trying to stem that flow. The Mexican woman named Molly was waiting in line to cross over to the American side. Finally, after hours of waiting, her interview moment with the U.S. Border Patrol agent arrived. The officer asked: "Are you Latina?" She replied: "*No, no, no señor. Yo no soy la Tina. Yo soy la Molly. La Tina ya cruzó.*" ("No, no, no sir. I am not Tina. I am Molly. Tina already crossed.") The border agent was asking the woman about her ethnicity as a Latina. Molly, who was clearly unfamiliar with this U.S.-based ethnic category, interpreted the question as best she could. She heard "Latina" not as one word but as two—*la* and *Tina*—interpreting "*la*" as "the," and "*Tina*" as her friend's name. Indeed, her name was not Tina; it was Molly.

This story of miscommunication across national borders, when repeated, frequently provokes nervous laughter among Spanish/English bilingual speakers in the western United States. It shows how the ethnic groups and categories that are known and operate in one national space often make no sense when transported just a few miles north or south. When national regimes categorize populations, the very act of naming gives them a living reality.

Ethnic groups, whether deemed minorities in nation-states or simply identified as members of a subordinated and marginalized group in a given polity, have always resisted and defied the easy classifications of their oppressors. They generate the names they use to refer to themselves as a collectivity, often in their own native language, thus underscoring their linguistic resistance to domination. Such group names are often rooted in religious and communal conceptions of personhood and kinship, as well as in history, language, and culture. Institutions such as the Catholic Church, professional guilds, even merchants hoping to monopolize markets for ethnic goods, have long had vested interests in naming, generating, and sustaining national understandings of group collectivity. My goals in this essay are several. At the theoretical level, I want to examine three moments in the history of what became the United States, looking at the contexts of power that produced particular understandings of social boundaries and group membership: the Spanish conquest of the indigenous peoples of Mexico's north, which started in 1598; the United States military's takeover of what became the American Southwest at the end of the Mexican War in 1848; and the mass decolonization civil rights movement undertaken by racialized minorities in the United States during the mid-1960s and early 1970s. At the lexical level, I want to show how a small set of ethnic labels, whether tied to self-understandings of group membership, to actual social behavior, or merely as text, emerged, evolved, and disappeared, only to reappear again with new meanings generations later. The emergence of ethnic labels that demarcate social boundaries occurs in different temporal registers, sometimes quite rapidly and other times more slowly.

.   .   .

Since the early 1970s, sociologists in the United States have been particularly fascinated by the emergence of panethnicities, which are confederations created when several distinct ethnic groups come together in alliance for social, economic, or cultural advantage, thereby augmenting their numeric power and influence around issues of common concern. During the late 1960s and early 1970s, for example, indigenous peoples such as the Cherokee, the Apache, and the Menominee came to be understood sociologically as "Native Americans." For several centuries conquering states had lumped them together as "Indians" in punitive ways that marked their subordination and marginalization. They had resisted such leveling, homogenization, and the eradication of their ancestral group differences, cleaving to their own internal ways of being and knowing, and defending their language and culture from the influence of those they labeled as outsiders and whites. But indigenous peoples in the United States had many common experiences. They had long histories of genocide and domination, of wars aimed at their eradication, of territorial segregation on reservations, and of similar structural relationships to the federal government. Calling themselves "Native Americans" made sense not only as a way of consolidating their factionalized power but also of maximizing their use of civil rights, voting rights, and affirmative action policies.

Immigrants and long-time residents hailing from such divergent places as Mexico, Puerto Rico, and the Dominican Republic began celebrating their unity as "Latinos" in the 1970s, just as persons from such distinct places as China, Japan, and Korea came to call themselves "Asian Americans" in the United States. As new panethnic groups, they protested their marginalization and the toxic legacies of racism, militated for political recognition, and petitioned the state for compensatory remedies, demonstrating not only broader levels of interaction among their different national groups but also a heightened sense of oppositional consciousness in relationship to the state.

The rise of such new nationalisms is not an entirely unique or new sociological process. Historian Eric J. Hobsbawm reminds us in *Nations and Nationalism since 1870,* how emerging nation-states, through a process he calls "nationalism from above," transformed the residents of the ancient kingdoms of Castile, Aragón, Asturias, and León into Spaniards through mandatory language instruction, compulsory public schooling, and military service, just as the United States forged Polish, Italian, and German immigrants into Americans using these same institutions and techniques for similar ends.[1] What is new and distinct about panethnicities is that they can emerge not only from above through the actions of states and elites, but they also percolate upward from below, as acts of popular mobilization and consciousness in direct opposition to state actions.[2]

·   ·   ·

Many of the people of European ancestry who first colonized and settled what eventually became the American Southwest migrated there from the Iberian Peninsula, from what we now call Spain, but which in the fifteenth and sixteenth centuries was a series of independent kingdoms that were gradually aggregated, most definitively by the 1469 marriage of King Ferdinand of Aragón and Queen Isabella of Castile, which laid the foundation for the emergence of modern Spain. Several decades before the English founded Jamestown in 1607 or the Pilgrims landed at Plymouth colony in 1620, residents of Spain's medieval kingdoms had already established a permanent settlement in Saint Augustine in Florida (1565) and begun colonizing the kingdom of New Mexico, which by 1598 encompassed roughly the current states of New Mexico and Arizona. Texas's first Spanish settlements date from 1691, and those of Alta California began with the founding of San Diego in 1769. The kingdom of New Mexico and the provinces of Texas and Alta California were all situated at the northern edge of Spain's American empire, isolated from one another, surrounded on all sides by mostly hostile indigenous groups, and too distant from the major centers of Spanish culture in central Mexico and Cuba for frequent or rapid communication. What developed in each of these provinces over the centuries were distinct regional subcultures that were Spanish in name and form, but thoroughly hybrid in culture due to prolonged contact with local indigenous groups.

National consciousness, by which I mean a sense of membership as a resident or citizen of a particular nation-state, did not exist as a well-developed sentiment among the colonists who initially left the Iberian Peninsula, migrated to Cuba and Puerto Rico, and then moved on to Mexico, eventually settling New Spain's north. What affinity they most shared and expressed was religious; they were Christians first and foremost. The fervor of their religious sentiment was forged during the Crusades and particularly strengthened over nearly eight centuries of warfare during the Iberian Reconquest between AD 711 and 1492, when the Christian monarchs rallied their populations behind the standard of the cross, vanquishing the Moors and pushing the influence of Islam south. What victories the Christian kings won in those years were won in the name of their one true God. The year 1492 marked the acme of the Reconquest with the fall of the last Moorish stronghold in Granada, the underwriting of Christopher Columbus's voyage of discovery westward, and the intensification of religious orthodoxy, leading to Jewish and Muslim forced conversions to Christianity, and eventually to their expulsion. From 1492 onward, Spain's public culture was Christian to the core. The first and most distinct sense of group membership among the residents of Spain's enormous empire was as *cristianos viejos,* or "old Christians." Men and women who were firm in their faith stood ready to defend it from neophytes, from infidels and heretics, and from *cristianos nuevos,* or "New Christians," which in Spain was made up of recently and forcibly converted Moors and Jews, and in the Americas of equally recent indigenous converts to the faith.[3]

The *patria chica,* the "small fatherland," or the region of origin, was next in importance to these colonists. By the sixteenth century, each of Spain's kingdoms had a well-developed *conciencia de sí,* or "self-consciousness." After men and women proclaimed themselves Christians, they boasted of their rootedness in local affairs as Aragonese, Catalans, Galicians, and Castilians. Indeed the word the indigenous peoples of the southwestern United States first used to describe their new Spanish overlords was *Castillas,* meaning a person from the kingdom of Castile. Though initially the native peoples understood very little of what soldiers told them in Spanish, they did repeatedly hear them call themselves *castellanos,* announcing that the natives were now subjects of *Castilla* and that a king in *Castilla* was their new lord. Gaspar Peréz de Villagrá, who participated in the 1598 conquest of New Mexico and in 1610 commemorated the feats in his book *Historia de la Nueva México,* reported that the residents of Acoma Pueblo "called to me, crying, Castilian! Castilian! . . . Zutacapan [their chief] asked me if more Castilians followed me and how long before they would arrive."[4]

Identification with Spain's various regions persisted in the Americas into the nineteenth century, whether in Cuba, Hispaniola, Puerto Rico, or Mexico. Residents of the kingdom of New Mexico called themselves *nuevo mexicanos* and *neomexicanos,* those in California referred to themselves as *californios,* and those in Texas as *tejanos.* Throughout Spanish America loyalty and a sense of attachment to the *patria chica,* to one's natal place, persisted and remains strong even to this day.

The Spanish conquest and colonization of the Americas brought together men from different regions, and through their common experiences of warfare, established them as a victorious colonizing class. The men who marched into the Aztec capital at Tenochtitlán in 1519 most likely had never before thought of themselves as Spaniards, or *españoles.* This was so because a unitary nation-state had only begun to emerge recently, as a result of the unification of the kingdoms of Aragón and Castile, born of the 1469 marriage of King Ferdinand and Queen Isabella, and because these men were more deeply invested in their Christianity and regional loyalties to place. It was in the Americas that they came to think of themselves as "Spaniards," particularly when confronting indigenous peoples as overlords. This is how the emerging Spanish nation-state, from above, forged a panethnic sense of group membership. By calling themselves *españoles* the colonists acknowledged that their culture and social institutions were of Iberian origin and thus quite different from those of the indigenous peoples they called *indios*, or "Indians." Three hundred years of contact between these two groups through intermarriage and cohabitation would radically transform what it meant to be *español* and *indio*, but about that there will be much more to say below.[5]

Just as *españoles* were forged in the foundry of warfare through their battlefield victories as Christian soldiers in Mexico, Central America, and Peru, so too the vanquishment of their enemies transformed America's native peoples into *indios*, or "Indians." In 1491, on the eve on the Columbian voyages, there were some 123 distinct indigenous language families spoken in the Americas, with more than 260 different languages in Mexico alone. Perhaps as many as 20 million people were living in the Valley of Mexico in 1519, in hierarchical, complexly stratified theocratic states.[6] But there were no Indians. Christopher Columbus invented them in 1492 by mistakenly believing that he had reached India, and thus calling them *indios* producing the lexical distinction we now use to refer to the Caribbean as the West Indies and to India as the East Indies. Inventing Indians was to serve an important imperial end for Spain, for by calling the natives *indios*, the Spaniards erased and leveled the diverse and complex indigenous political and religious hierarchies they found. Where once there had been many ethnic groups stratified as native lords, warriors, craftsmen, hunters, farmers, and slaves, the power of imperial Spain was not only to vanquish but also to define, largely reducing peoples such as the mighty Aztecs into a defeated Indian class that soon bore the pain of subjugation as tribute-paying racialized subjects.

Militant Christian *españoles* colonized Hispaniola, Cuba, Puerto Rico, Mexico, and New Mexico in the name of Spain's Christian monarchs. As conquering soldiers they carried writs of incorporation (*capitulaciones*) for the formation of towns, which included aristocratic titles, land grants, and tributary *indios* they could exploit mercilessly, but whom they were also expected to Christianize and protect. The Catholic priests who accompanied these colonists carried all the symbols in which their ethnicity was rooted: the sacred texts and stories of the Bible; the altars, crosses, and statuary that connected the terrestrial community to the celestial one; and all the religious ritual formulas that conjoined the sacred and profane, and which ordered time and space.

Yearly in Santa Fe, New Mexico, the city's founding is still routinely remembered by reenacting the submission of the Pueblo Indian chiefs before Don Juan de Oñate, the area's conquistador, as it was done and described in 1598.[7] This is the occasion for the staging of didactic dramas such as "The Christians and the Moors," which in the late 1600s was marked by "loud acclamations from the soldiers, with a salvo of harquebuses, and by skirmishes and horse races." Wooden lanterns known as *luminarias,* which are still lit on important dates of the Christian calendar, were meant to evoke memories of the heat of battle, the fire and destruction the *españoles* used to establish their supremacy over the *indios* and the imposition of their Christian God and culture. Even the bedecked and bejeweled statue of *La Conquistador,* Our Lady of the Conquest, is taken annually from her venerated perch in church and processed through the streets, unifying and sanctifying the space she traverses. The messages encoded in all of these ritual acts are not lost on observers of Santa Fe's fiesta, for as a Taos Pueblo Indian woman recently pronounced, the skirmishes, the bonfires, the dramas all symbolized "the brute force the Spanish used" to conquer the land.[8]

The Pueblo Indians, of course, have long resisted such chauvinistic celebrations. In 1998, someone from the northern Pueblos severed the right foot of the large bronze equestrian statue of Don Juan de Oñate, the Spanish conqueror of the kingdom of New Mexico, which sits in front of the Oñate Monument and Visitors Center near Española, New Mexico. The vandal's explicit political goal was to force everyone to recall the collective punishment Oñate meted out to the residents of Acoma Pueblo in 1600 for resisting his tributary demands: every man over the age of twenty-five had one of his feet cut off, the women and children over the age of twelve were condemned to twenty years of slavery, and the children were distributed to serve as servants in Spanish households. As Andrés Lauriano, of Sandía Pueblo noted of the foot severed from the Oñate statue, "When I think of what Oñate did . . . I have a vision of Indian men lined up to have one foot cut off. I see the blood pouring from their legs as they crawled or hopped away. I see the bloody pile of feet left behind."[9]

The *españoles* who settled Mexico's north were extremely status conscious and viewed society as hierarchically ranked by religion, property ownership, occupation, race, and legitimacy of birth. Whenever anyone came before a state official, whether civil or ecclesiastical, between roughly 1600 and 1760, the first fact recorded in the legal documents was a person's *calidad,* literally his or her "quality" or "social status." Social privileges and corporal punishment were based on such standing. Thus petitions, denunciations, even routine investigations of any sort always began with a formulaic statement that established one's status and group membership. For example: Pedro López *"es de calidad mestizo, obrero, hijo legítimo de María Sánchez y Fabián López, y cristiano nuevo"* (Pedro López's quality is *mestizo,* a laborer, the legitimate son of María Sánchez and Fabián López, and a New Christian).

Starting in the 1760s, and stretching all the way into the 1820s, explicit discussions of race took on a greater importance in the establishment of one's *calidad.* Though legal color categories had been widely known and codified as the *régimen de castas* since the founding of Spain's colonies in the Americas, these were not broadly invoked by church or state functionaries at the local level until the middle of the eighteenth century, when more-extensive racial mixing began taking place. Access to marital partners and honorific posts, to desirable occupations, and even to the Roman Catholic priesthood was based on one's ability to prove one's genealogical racial purity according to the categories of the code.[10]

The *régimen de castas* defined precisely every possible biological mixture that could occur when Spaniards, Indians, and Africans mated and reproduced. A Spaniard and an Indian produced a *mestizo*. A *mestizo* and a Spanish woman begot a *castizo*. The mating of a Spanish man and a mulatto woman produced a *morisco*, and so on. The code spelled out for six generations of descent the exact level of biological mixing from an original set of ancestors, yielding racial categories that were quite difficult for individuals to perceive or to recognize in phenotype, much less for church and state officials to reconcile the personal declarations they were given with their own physical observations of the person who stood before them. Theoretically, this classificatory system visually fused notions of blood, ancestry, and lineage so that without reference to baptismal certificates, family histories, or personal genealogies one could quickly glance at a person's physique and just as rapidly conclude if a person was of pure blood, of gentle birth, and of an honorable past. In Spain even remotely impure blood derived from mixing with Jews, Moors, and heretics disqualified a person from high honorific posts. In the Americas contact with Indians and African slaves was deemed equally polluting. Physical color or appearance, what today we call "phenotype," became the basis by which state and church officials praised and reviled their subjects and privileged or punished the racial groups society deemed most inferior.

The *españoles* in Mexico's north in the 1760s began to imagine colonial society and themselves in much more complicated ways than the original conquest dichotomy between Spaniards and Indians allowed, precisely because the *régimen de castas* provided them with a more capacious lexicon for understanding racial difference. The reality on the ground after several generations of miscegenation was that only at the polar extremes of the racial classification system did the categories actually fit any visible physical types. The *régimen de castas* was intended to protect the privileges of local nobilities. But as the quickening of the economy undertaken by the Bourbon Reforms in the second half of the eighteenth century took hold, status increasingly became based on enterprise and personal achievement, thus displacing notions of aristocracy and social standing rooted in memory of the by then remote facts of conquest. When the crown began selling writs of whiteness, known as *gracias al sacar*, to anyone who could afford them in the 1760s, the system of racial classification was doomed, and indeed was abolished with Mexico's independence in 1821.[11]

Racial status was of grand importance because it was intimately associated with one's legitimacy or illegitimacy at birth. The legal scholar Juan de Solórzano y Pereira in his *Política Indiana* (1648) maintained that illegitimates were "Those born of adulterous or other illicit and punishable unions, because there are few Spaniards of honor who marry Indian or negro women; this defect of birth makes them infamous, at least *infama facti*, according to the weighty and common opinion of serious scholars; they carry the stain of different colors and other vices."[12] Throughout the colonial period, illegitimacy was deemed an indecent and shameful mark because of its association with mixed racial unions and the generation of race.

The multiple categories that defined a person's *calidad* were intricately tied to one another. A person's reputation was a summation of these various measures of social standing, made particularly clear in social action. The fiercest fighting words one could utter were slurs that impugned a person's total social personality—his or her race, ancestry, and position in the division of labor. The fight that occurred in Albuquerque, New Mexico, on June 3, 1765, between Eusebio Chávez and his father-in-law, Andrés Martín, illustrates this point. Chávez beat Martín with a large stick and dragged him by his hair, leaving Martín's arm badly bruised, his chest covered with black and blue welts, his scalp swollen out of shape, and his hair completely tangled and caked in blood. The reason: Martín had called Chávez a *"perro mulato hijo de puta"* (a mixed-blood dog son of a bitch). One insult, perhaps, would have been enough, but by calling Chávez a dog, Martín implied that he was less than human, a habit well understood by Spaniards who often referred to the Indians as dogs. He added that Chávez was of mixed blood, and if truly a son of a bitch, he was undoubtedly illegitimate. Martín had thus combined three statuses to insult Chávez.[13]

Functionaries of the Catholic Church and the Spanish state often used the same racial and ethnic categories because these were the ones that had been generated initially through the process of Christian expansion into new territories. One exception widely used in Mexico's north during the colonial period, particularly in California, was the racialized category *gente de razón*, literally "people of reason," or rational beings. Its meaning in social life is best understood through its opposite, or *gente sin razón*, "people lacking reason," as irrational persons. The Holy Office of the Inquisition concocted this legal distinction to protect the Indian from prosecution for heretical ideas. The inquisitors reasoned that the Indians were *gente sin razón*, mere children lacking the rational faculties to understand the dogmas of faith and the errors of their ways. Everyone deemed a rational person was punishable for exercising his or her knowledge and will in the commitment of evil acts. With the demise of the Inquisition in the early 1800s, the term *gente de razón* remained in circulation in Mexico's north as a way of differentiating individuals who were culturally "Spanish" from those who lived by their more traditional "Indian" ways; more infrequently it was used to differentiate fluent Spanish speakers from those who were not.

Indian slavery was a significant social institution throughout Mexico's north and accordingly generated the stigmatized *genízaro* ethnic category, which first appeared in New Mexican documents at the beginning of the eighteenth century and from there spread outward to Texas and California, where it was also recorded in the documentation of social life. The *genízaros* were Apache, Navajo, Ute, and Comanche Indians, enslaved during raids the Spaniards provoked to profit from the lucrative trade in captives. In time, Pueblo Indian foundlings abandoned by their indigenous mothers as the products of rape, as well as adults exiled from Indian towns because of some transgression, came to be referred to as *genízaros*. Approximately 4,000 person of indigenous ancestry called *genízaros* entered New Mexican society during the eighteenth century. By the 1750s they composed about one-third of New Mexican society. They were considered marginal because of their slave, ex-slave, or outcast status.[14] *Genízaros* did not own land, spoke a distinctive broken form of Spanish, were residentially segregated, married endogamously, and shared a corporate sense, living together, said Fray Carlos Delgado in 1744, in great unity *"como si fueran una nación"* (as if they were a nation).[15] Fray Atanasio Domínguez described the *genízaros* he met in New Mexico in 1776 as "weak, gamblers, liars, cheats, and petty thieves." This caricature survived for centuries. Mischievous and unruly children today are still ridiculed in the American Southwest with the saying *"genízaro, genízaro, puro indio de rescate"* (genízaro, genízaro, pure bartered Indian). When New Mexicans now say *"no seas genízaro,"* or "don't be a *genízaro*," they mean "don't be a liar." Anthropologist Florence Hawley Ellis was told by the villagers of Tomé in the 1950s that the *genízaro* residents in the adjacent village of Belén were "semi-slave, low class, and without ability." Anthropologist Frances Swadesh encountered the same stereotypes in the 1970s in northern New Mexico. When someone was referred to as *genízaro* there, it meant crude, low class, and "indiado" (Indian-like).[16]

Some ethnic classifications still used in the American Southwest originated in the legal categories of the *régimen de castas* but took on significant new meanings. In the colonial period, Spaniards did not hesitate to dehumanize Indians and those they deemed half-breeds by barking the epithet "dog" at them, usually in combination with some other expletive: dirty dog, Indian dog, half-breed dog. Half-breeds were thus frequently called *lobos* and *coyotes*, denoting an unspecific mixture between a Spaniard and an Indian. With both of these categories, the mixed-blood individual was portrayed as a low species close to an animal. *Lobo* and *coyote* are still used in common parlance to refer to persons of any racial mix between Anglo and Mexican.

Colonized subjects always develop rich vocabularies to describe their colonizers. This was the case among the native peoples the Spaniards conquered. How ethnicity was described, both then and now, depended on the language used, whether it was in the tongue of the colonizers or the colonized, thus giving different valances to the utterances of outsiders versus those of insiders, or members of one's own group. The Pueblo, the Yaqui, and the Mayo Indians all had insider terms in their native languages for the *españoles* and *castillas* based on the most dominant aspect of their religion. Among the Pueblo Indians, the Spaniards were called "wet-heads" because of the water poured on a person's head at baptism. The Yaqui and Mayo Indians called the Spaniards "water-fathers" for similar reasons.[17]

.   .   .

We move now from Mexico's colonial far north to what was to become the American Southwest, where we will explore a similar territorial conquest and the ethnic categories that were used to define and describe the conquerors and the conquered in the new regime. To understand how the United States came to exercise sovereignty over what had previously been Mexico's far north, let us recall the anticolonial revolutions that engulfed England (American independence in 1776), France (Haitian independence in 1804), and Spain (Spanish American independence 1807–1821). In 1700 the last Spanish Hapsburg king died without an heir, leading to the War of the Spanish Succession and ushering in the French Bourbon monarchs, who became known for the economic, political, and cultural reforms they undertook in Spain's vast empire. The reforms, collectively known as the Bourbon Reforms, had several goals: to streamline the administrative structure of Spain's overseas empire, to boost the colonial economies through free trade and heightened communication, to increase silver extraction and taxation, and to neutralize the extensive indigenous warfare that had plagued Mexico's north. If Spain's first colonization was directed at exploiting the native peoples of the Americas, the Bourbon Reforms were viewed as a second colonization, aimed this time at undermining the power of wealthy regional elites and focused mostly on the interests of local *españoles* and *mestizos* who had been born, reared, and assimilated in the New World.

Under the Bourbon Reforms, local *criollo* or creole bureaucrats in America were increasingly replaced by *peninsulares,* men born in Spain who were assumed loyal to the king and thus more deeply moored to metropolitan interests and affairs. Free trade policies were intended to destroy local industries (and did), which had taken centuries to develop, forcing Americans to again become more dependent on the goods Spain produced and exported. Taxes and silver bullion were needed to finance European wars and conspicuous consumption at home. What remained in America were heavily taxed colonial subjects with long lists of grievances and deep resentments toward the monarchy and its metropolitan agents.

At the beginning of the nineteenth century, the only persons in Mexico's far north who could genuinely claim that they were *peninsulares* were colonial bureaucrats and priests, and it was between them and the local *criollo* elites that intense struggles emerged in New Mexico, Texas, and California. Further south, in the urban centers of Mexico and Peru, by the early 1800s the creole elite began looking beyond Spain for their redemption, finding models for the overthrow of monarchy and the creation of popular self-governance in the United States and France. Between 1807 and 1821, all of Spanish America, save for a few regions, gained independence, inspired by liberal political theorists. Spanish Americans mostly chose republican forms of government, the exception being Mexico, where independence began with the short-lived constitutional monarchy of King and Emperor Agustín de Iturbide, who reigned from 1821 to 1823. Cuba, Puerto Rico, Hispaniola, and the Philippines all began independence movements at roughly the same time, but only the Dominican Republic succeeded, in 1844.

When Mexican independence arrived in 1821, a host of categories based on property, race, gender, age, and legitimacy were still being used to describe the social stratification that had been imposed by the Spanish conquerors over the indigenous peoples. Thus, when news of Mexico's independence reached New Mexico, Texas, and California, the residents did not immediately call themselves *mexicanos* or Mexicans, probably because the authority of the newly established Mexican nation-state remained fragile until 1857, torn as it was politically by conflicts among centralists and federalists, liberals and conservatives. The term *mexicano* began to appear in legal documents and census records only in the 1830s, and then, for only a small percentage of the population. In New Mexico only about 5 percent of all individuals who married legally between 1830 and 1839 claimed that they were *mexicanos*. The rest continued calling themselves *españoles*. As the newly established Mexican nation-state bestowed large land grants on individuals willing to settle the north, particularly in those poorly protected frontier areas coveted by England, the United States, France, and Russia, and under constant attack by the Apache and Comanche Indians, the category *vecino* took on increasing import, differentiating these propertied citizen males from landless peasants.[18]

Mexico was faced with numerous challenges between 1821 and 1880, which the wars of independence left it ill prepared for. The new state emerged weak and remained fragile because of the constant wars and invasions Mexico experienced in this period. It waged a century-long war against the Comanches and Apaches in the north. Texas rebelled and gained its independence in 1836. The French invaded and occupied Mexico in 1838–1839, and again in 1861–1867. The United States invaded Mexico in 1846, and at war's end in 1848, seized its northern provinces. Throughout all of this, Mexico was at war with itself, ripped apart by conflicts between liberals and conservatives over what form of government and whose interests would be advanced and protected. Mexico's precarious state of affairs in this period is best reflected by the fact that between 1821 and 1857, on average, there was a new head of state every year.

While Mexico struggled, Spain, France, England, and the United States were themselves locked in intense rivalries precisely over their national boundaries. In 1803 Thomas Jefferson negotiated the purchase of the Louisiana Territory from Napoleon, a transfer Spain refused to recognize until 1819. That year, too, John Quincy Adams, President James Monroe's secretary of state, signed the Transcontinental Treaty with Spain, purchasing Florida for $5 million. Spain thus acknowledged U.S. ownership of Louisiana; the United States conceded Spain's sovereignty over all of Texas west of the Sabine River. In the midst of these diplomatic negotiations, the United States was monetarily aiding the independence movements of Spain's colonies. In 1823 President Monroe pronounced what became known as the Monroe Doctrine, warning European powers that any foreign intervention in the hemisphere would be deemed a bellicose act that would provoke intervention by the United States.

It was in this contentious context over Mexico's eventual shape and form that Mexican *tejanos*, and the Anglo immigrants who settled in Texas, declared their independence in 1836 as the Republic of Texas. A decade later, in 1846, the United States fabricated a border dispute to provoke war with Mexico. What for decades the United States had attempted to purchase with cash, it then took by force in the name of its "Manifest Destiny." The Treaty of Guadalupe Hidalgo, which ended the war in 1848, ceded close to two-thirds of Mexico's national territory. The United States thus emerged as a nation that reached from coast to coast, with ports on the Pacific Ocean from which it could exploit the lucrative trade with Asia.

U.S. sovereignty over the ceded Mexican territories and over Texas, which was simultaneously annexed and became a state in 1845, created a new political order for the longtime residents of what became the American Southwest. Much as *españoles* had established their military dominance over the indigenous peoples of Mexico after 1521, and marked that subjugation through a number of demeaning legal categories, so too citizens of the United States arrived in the Southwest vaunting their superiority, establishing structures of domination, and asserting that their primacy was rooted in their Protestant God, in their laws and constabularies, in the purity of their whiteness, and in their very way of life. Whereas in 1521 the colonists who arrived in the Americas from the Iberian Peninsula transformed their notions of group belonging to become *españoles* with lordship over *indios,* so the soldiers and settlers who ventured westward after 1848 defined themselves as "Anglos" and "Anglo-Americans," calling the longtime residents "Mexicans," which as we saw above, was not particularly germane, given the recentness of Mexico's national independence. The process of linguistic erasure Christopher Columbus undertook by naming "Indians" where none had existed before likewise was used by the Americans to flatten Mexican class and ethnic distinctions, calling all locals "Mexicans" despite the fact that this denomination had never really developed roots.

The resident ethnic Mexican population used a number of Spanish-language words to describe their new Americans lords. When speaking Spanish the *mexicanos* called the outsiders *extranjeros,* or "foreigners," labeling themselves *nativos,* or "natives."[19] As the number of migrants increased, the ethnic lexicon became more complex. They were called *anglos, anglosajones,* and *americanos;* with *americanos* or Americans becoming and remaining the most popular over time.[20] But there were also a slew of other ethnic categories that were employed in the Spanish language that more acutely described the cultural politics of domination. *Mexicano* polychromatic sensitivities to race and color focused on the peculiarities of *americano* skin, eye, and hair color, and to the size of their feet. Accordingly, in newspapers and songs, in insults and expletives are found *canosos* (gray-haired), *colorao* (red-faced), *bolillo* (doughy faced), *cara de pan crudo* (bread dough face), *ojos de gato* (cat eyes), and *patón* (big foot). Other Mexican ethnic labels for the Americans were the result of misunderstandings of the English language. The word *gringo,* for example, comes from a linguistic corruption of a song the Mexican soldiers heard the Texas rebels singing at the Alamo in 1836. The first two words of the prairie song "Green Grows the Grass of Kentucky" were heard by Mexicans as *"grin gros"* and, finally, as one word, *gringos,* which remains the most common way Americans are referred to when *mexicanos* want to express contempt and derision toward them as a dominant class. Because the *americanos* allegedly loved eating cabbage, or at least those of Irish origin were said to, they were often called *repolleros,* or "cabbage eaters."

And because of their penchant for chewing tobacco, rather than the Mexican custom of smoking it, they became known as *masca tabacos*.[21]

Some of the negative ethnic categories used to describe the Americans originated farther south as insults first used by Mexicans to describe their French invaders. So was the case for the derogatory term *gabacho*. Its etymology is the Provençal word *gabach*, which means "foreigner" but also "froggy" and "Frenchy." As is apparent from this etymology, *gabacho* was used in Spain and Mexico to express contempt for the French. The word *güero* (blond) was similarly born in diplomatic relations with Mexicans describing the skin color of their French occupiers as devoid of color, as "empty," or *huero*.[22]

Anglo-Americans were equally adept at name-calling. The Mexican diet was the source of much inspiration. Most histories of the use of the word "greaser" to refer to Mexicans offer a utilitarian explanation noting the *mexicano*'s penchant for cooking with lard, which can be heated to high temperatures to rapidly cook food. The word was also used to describe Mexican oily skin, the logical result of cooking with and eating lard. These primal etymologies became more complex when referring to the labor Mexicans performed, particularly the dirty work of greasing the wheels of the carts on which they carried people and goods to markets. By the 1850s "greaser" had taken on overtly racist and segregationist meanings. One American passing through El Paso offered the following definition: "A 'greaser' was a Mexican—originating in the filthy, greasy appearance of the natives."[23] Contempt for Mexicans produced California's infamous 1855 "Greaser Act," which authorized authorities to arrest "all persons who are commonly known as 'Greasers' or the issue of Spanish and Indian blood . . . who go armed and are not known to be peaceable and quiet persons, and who can give no good account of themselves."[24] Subsequently, Mexicans are described as living in a segregated California town called "Greaser Gulch." From "greaser" other insults eventually emerged, such as "grease-ball" and "goo-goo." From the Mexican diet came "pepper-belly," "taco-choker," "frijole guzzler," "chili picker," and, for a woman, "hot tamale."[25]

When Americans entered the Southwest as a conquering caste, they reacted to the ethnic geography much as the Spaniards had in 1598; they saw few cultural distinctions and lumped everyone into large panethnic groups. Certainly long-standing cleavages and status differentiations on the basis of race, occupation, legitimacy, property ownership, and even religion existed among the area's newly denominated *mexicanos*, who themselves had only become *mexicanos* with independence in 1821. In addition, the older, long-established Spanish residents of the area clearly deemed themselves superior and different from the Mexican immigrants who had started to cross the border into the United States in large numbers during the gold rush, and particularly after the 1880s as Mexico's modernization displaced many peasants northward, creating the conditions for Mexico's 1910 revolution. But through the eyes of Americans, the residents of the area all looked alike, dressed alike, spoke Spanish, and were fanatical Catholics. They were all Mexicans, pure and simple. The deep-seated racial prejudice among some *americanos* toward blacks was easily transferred to persons of Spanish origin due to their darker skin color.[26]

Calling someone a "Mexican" in 1850 was deeply insulting to a *mexicano* because the English word "Mexican" signified a dominated population, stigmatized by defeat and subordination. "Mexican" rapidly became the insulting expletive hurled to hurt its auditors as "mex," "meskin," "skin," and "skindiver," or modified with adjectives such as "dirty," "stinking," "greasy," "lazy," and "ugly." *Mexicano* responses to such insults came in two forms. First, they crafted distinctions in Spanish that were understood only within their linguistic community, and, second, they created larger imagined communities of belonging that were hemispheric and global in reach, far beyond the boundaries of the national geography of the United States in which they found themselves subordinated and marginalized. Although I have found no good example from 1850–1900 to illustrate the politics of language in such a colonial situation, the larger theoretical point here can be made with an example from the 1950s. Arthur L. Campa, a linguist who spent most of his career studying the nuances of Spanish use in the United States, in the 1950s asked long-time residents of New Mexico in Spanish what their ethnicity was. Most responded, "*Soy mexicano*" (I am Mexican). When he asked the same individuals what they liked to be called in English, they responded, "Spanish American." Campa then again asked in Spanish, "What do you call a person from Mexico?" The response was "*mexicano de México*" (Mexican from Mexico). One informant remarked that in English such a person was simply a Mexican because "Mexican . . . is the most used when someone is being rude. . . . Example—dirty Mexican." Another echoed this sentiment. "I'd rather not be called Mexican because of the stereotype remarks that are associated with it. Such as lazy, dirty, greaser, etc."[27]

To understand the ethnic categories *mexicanos* chose for themselves or bore the brunt of, bear in mind that the effective sociopolitical conquest of the Southwest occurred in different temporal registers. Gold was discovered in California in 1848, six months after the Mexican War ended. It was thus here that we first find the *californios* invoking ethnic categories they would use as *mexicanos* to resist domination throughout the Southwest. As the world swept into California with the gold rush, the population quickly swelled, attracting Spaniards, Chileans, Peruvians, Panamanians, even Mexicans who had vast experience mining. In 1848 California had approximately 7,500 resident Mexicans. By 1850, the population had grown to 92,598; by 1860 it had reached 379,994.[28] Similar demographic transformations occurred in Texas in the 1860s and 1870s, and in New Mexico in the years preceding and following the arrival of the railroad in 1879.

The *californios* referred to prospectors of Mexican nationality as *mexicanos* when speaking among themselves in Spanish, for they were indeed Mexicans. But when speaking English, they called these same miners "Mexicans," a label the *californios* fiercely resisted when it was used to refer to them. Anglos saw no apparent physical or cultural difference between the *californios* and Mexicans; both were alike. To counter being stereotyped as a conquered population, to insist that they were unlike Mexican nationals, and to imagine membership in larger, liberatory spaces, *californios* began insisting that they were either *latinoamericanos,* or *hispanoamericanos.* Here, then, are the first Spanish-language invocations by the former *españoles* of Mexico's far north, calling themselves in shortened form *hispanos* and *latinos,* which when translated into English circulated in print as "Latins," "Latin Americans," "Hispanics," and "Spanish Americans."[29]

Readers with a contemporary understanding of the emergence of the word "Hispanic" as a U.S. census category in 1980, and "Latino" as an emergent panethnicity in the early 1970s, may justifiably wonder how this occurred. To understand this development, let us imagine the circumstances of the former creole elite in California, buffeted by the war and the gold rush, seeing their land fraudulently seized, their language denigrated, their schools closed, and their religion mocked. These were men and women who started patriotic societies, who were literate and who began to write, publish, and circulate their sentiments broadly, informing their communities and compatriots around the world how *la raza hispana* (the Hispanic race), how *el pueblo latinoamericano* (the Latin American people) of California were faring miserably under the rule of the United States. The capacious scope of their geographic horizons is apparent even in the names of the newspapers they published in Spanish. In San Francisco there was *La Voz de México* (*The Voice of Mexico*), *El Nuevo Mundo* (*The New World*), *La Voz de Chile y de las Républicas Americanas* (*The Voice of Chile and of the American Republics*), and *El Éco del Pacífico* (*The Echo of the Pacific,* which was the Spanish-language insert in the French daily *L'Echo du Pacifique*); in Los Angeles was *El Amigo del Pueblo* (*The Friend of the People*) and *El Clamor Público* (*The Pubic Outcry*).

Why did "Hispanic" and "Latino" emerge as words of collective self-description in the 1850s, given the many lexical alternatives that could have been used to describe the older-still resident Spanish colonial population? "Hispanic" is easier to explain simply because of the area's genealogical origins as a Spanish colony. Living by then under U.S. sovereignty, the creole elites recalled nostalgically their former mother country, claimed they spoke *castellano,* ordered books and merchandise from Spain, and even had a *Tienda Española* (Spanish store) in San Francisco, where they could indulge themselves in memories of the good old days they hoped might return.[30] Newspapers regularly called out their countrymen to employment opportunities and events with the headline "*Aviso a los Hispano-Americanos*" (An Announcement for Hispanic Americans). *Nativos* (natives) rallied against *estranjeros* (foreigners), referring to themselves as *la raza Hispano Americana* (the Hispanic American race), noting that a new bilingual school in Los Angeles sought students "*de raza Española*" (of the Spanish race) in 1856. Writing in English, Francisco Ramírez, the owner of the Los Angeles newspaper *El Clamor Público,* praised "the young and rising generation" as "Spanish-American."[31] Disgruntled by the race relations they faced in California after 1848, in 1856 a group consisting of "*mexicanos, hispano-americanos y californios*" (Mexicans, Hispanic Americans, and Californians) formed a colonizing party for the purpose of emigrating from California southward to Sonora, Mexico, where they hoped they would thrive.

The word *latinoamericano* emerged in the years following the wars of independence in Spain's former colonies. Creole intellectuals from these newly independent nations turned to France for inspiration, finding in its revolutionary articulation of rights, liberty, and citizenship ways to think about their own freedom, emancipation, and autonomy. Residing in Paris and congregated around a young French intellectual named Michel Chevalier, in 1851 they discussed alternative modernities and subsequently invented "Latin America" as a way to map a new geography for the postcolonial global order. In the political ideology that birthed *latinoamerica* and *latinidad,* creole and mestizo elites imagined a hemispheric unity that would supersede and perhaps thwart the political and cultural impact of European imperialisms, and, most importantly, envisage Latin America as part of a world order. As Torres Caicedo, the Colombian intellectual who was catalytic in advancing the idea, noted, "There is Anglo-Saxon America, Danish America, Dutch America, etc.; there is also Spanish America, French America and Portuguese America; and therefore to this second group what other scientific name applies but Latin?"[32] Earlier in the century, Simón Bolívar had attempted to weld northern South America into a Gran Colombia, and from that to forge a larger "Confederation of Spanish American Nations." By 1850, Bolívar had been dead for twenty years. The space he denominated "Spanish America" was forgotten, its glimmer revived as "Latin America," and at century's end, José Martí fleetingly reimagined it anew as *Nuestra América,* or "Our America."

By the late 1850s, *californios* were writing in newspapers about their membership in *América latina* (Latin America) and *latinoamerica,* calling themselves *latinos* as the shortened name for their hemispheric membership in *la raza latina* (the Latin race). Reprinting an 1858 opinion piece by a correspondent in Havana on race relations in the Americas, *El Clamor Público* of Los Angeles surmised that "two rival races are competing with each other . . . the Anglo Saxon and the Latin one [*la raza latina*]."[33]

Hispano and *latino,* as abbreviated versions of *Hispano-Americano* and *latinoamericano,* flourished in California's Spanish-language discourse during the second half of the nineteenth century but had virtually disappeared by the 1920s. The explanation for this appears to be found in the increasing number of Mexican immigrants fleeing the violence and displacement of the 1910–1917 Mexican Revolution and finding employment in California. From 1911 to 1920, 219,000 Mexican immigrants formally entered the United States; from 1921 to 1930, this number more than doubled reaching 459,287. In the face of this demographic increase, "Mexican" and "Mexican American" became prominent ways of describing the numerically ascendant immigrants and *hispano, latino,* in all of their Spanish-language forms virtually disappeared, only to reemerge to the east fifty years later, in Chicago in the 1970s.

Tejanos, like the *californios,* called themselves *mexicanos* and *latinoamericanos* in Spanish-language discourse during the last half of the nineteenth century, but I have found no textual evidence of the use of *Hispano-Americano.* When the *tejanos* joined forces in 1836 with the Anglo settlers of Texas to form an independent republic, they decisively rejected their Mexican citizenship and membership in the Mexican nation, only to be constantly reminded in the language of their oppressors that whatever their wealth or rank, they were still nothing but dirty, stinking Mexicans. In the 1920s, faced with the same discrimination and prejudice Mexican immigrants suffered in California, the old-time *tejanos* insisted on being called "Latin Americans" (*latinoamericanos*) in polite, English-speaking company. Indeed, this was the self-referential English word they chose in 1929 when *tejano* community leaders established the first major Mexican American civil rights organization in the United States, calling it the League of United Latin American Citizens, or LULAC for short.[34]

The pace of demographic change was much slower in New Mexico because the monetization of land there did not reach a fevered pitch until the arrival of the railroad in 1879 and because statehood was not won until 1912. Unlike in California and Texas where Mexican immigrants quickly outnumbered the *nativos*, few Mexican peasants who had been displaced by modernization arrived in New Mexico in the last quarter of the nineteenth century, and fewer refugees of the Mexican Revolution found safety and employment there, so *nuevomexicanos* were able to hold on to their older identities as *españoles* and *hispanoamericanos* much longer. *Hispanoamericano* was often translated into English as "Spanish American." A. Gabriel Meléndez and Doris Meyer, historians of the New Mexico nineteenth-century Spanish-language print culture explain that the word *hispanoamericano* was used frequently to resist Anglo-American racism while simultaneously asserting their membership in a larger transnational, global community that existed to protect their liberty and rights. The editors of Spanish-language newspapers formed La Asociación de la Prensa Asociada Hispano-Americana in Las Vegas, New Mexico, in 1892, to serve as "the trustee and defender of the race it represents." Writing on March 31, 1892, in *El Sol de Mayo*, which was published in Las Vegas, New Mexico, Manuel C. de Baca wrote that the press association would "take up . . . its duty . . . so that *hispano-americanos* will bring to an end the repeated injuries that all too frequently are directed at them."[35] For as the publisher of the Taos, New Mexico, *La Revista de Taos* announced in the "Himno del Hispano" (the Hispanic's Hymn) in 1915,

We do not want racial law,
We do not want discord
We want unity and peace
With equal rights and rewards.
We want to be free men
Who enjoy freedom,
Without the shackles and chains
That come with tyranny . . .
We want the schools
Both primary and secondary
Not to be used like matches
To inflame exclusion.
We want free men, not intruders,

We were born on this land,
Not to endure abuses
That cry for almighty justice.[36]

By the 1920s Mexican immigrants had arrived throughout the Southwest in large numbers; New Mexico was by then no exception, recruiting cheap labor for agriculture and mining. New Mexico's *nativos* reacted to these numbers by distancing and differentiating themselves as *hispanoamericanos*, or as "Spanish Americans," when speaking or writing in English, not wanting to be lumped together with Mexican nationals, whom they viewed as rough and uncouth members of the lower class. New Mexico had long been historically marginal to New Spain, to central Mexico, even to the Republic of Mexico once it gained independence. This fact prompted one man to state, "My identity has always been closer to Spanish as an ethnic group and for that reason I consider myself Spanish. . . . Being from northern New Mexico the only connection I have with anything Mexican is as a tourist and not as my national origin."[37] Novelist Erna Fergusson proposed that the ethnic category "Spanish American" came into popular use in New Mexico after World War I to counter the Anglo-American perception that soldiers who called themselves *mexicanos* when speaking in Spanish were aliens from another country. Anthropologist Nancie González largely concurred. The term "Spanish American" emerged in response to an upsurge of prejudice and discrimination against Spanish speakers in New Mexico during the 1920s.[38]

Arizona too had a core of original settler *españoles* who had been residing there since the 1690s. On January 14, 1894, Carlos Velasco, Pedro Pellón, Mariano Samaniego, and some forty-six other men gathered in Tucson to establish the Alianza Hispano-Americana, which announced as its motto "*Protección, Moralidad, e Instrucción*," or "the protection of *Hispano-Americanos* (Hispanic Americans)" through mutual aid and fraternalism, through a morality that focused on the common good, and through the acquisition of knowledge that would lead to self-improvement and communal advance.[39] By 1930 the Alianza Hispano-Americana had become the largest ethnic Mexican fraternal organization in the United States, with more than 17,000 members scattered throughout the Southwest. It did this by rallying *españoles* and *mexicanos* in Arizona, and then in New Mexico and California, to the effects of Anglo-American racism on their daily lives, the need for the development of a group consciousness to resist and thwart it, and a cultural solidarity across the class divide that then existed among Mexicanos. But the massive levels of Mexican immigration into Arizona that started during the 1910 revolution and accelerated in the 1920s produced similar tensions between Spanish and Mexican group membership. Whereas in New Mexico the local *españoles* differentiated themselves from the immigrants at that moment by calling themselves "Spanish Americans," and in Spanish *hispanos*, in Arizona *hispano-americano* disappeared from print, along with the Spanish-language newspapers that had kept it alive, and one can only speculate that it also eventually fell out of use in conversation.[40]

As should be obvious from these examples of ethnic categories fashioned in the American Southwest, first in response to Anglo-American conquest and then to massive levels of Mexican immigration, the longtime local populations called themselves *hispanos* and *hispano-americanos* to assert their racial whiteness. They claimed European origins as Spaniards, and by so doing, doggedly resisted being labeled "nonwhite" and thus presumed to be of the same lowly status as blacks. Whenever Anglo-Americans have wanted to depict the Spanish origins of the ethnic Mexicans in the United States positively and affirmatively, they have referred to them as "Spanish," "Spanish Americans," "Spanish speakers," and "individuals of Spanish surname," thereby declaring them ancestrally tied to European civilization and racial whiteness. Identifying someone as Spanish immediately signaled membership in a set of overlapping groups—religious, linguistic, legal, and cultural—that through Spain could be tied back to Rome. In *Racial Faultlines: The Historical Origins of White Supremacy in California*, sociologist Tomás Almaguer argues that in the racial order in which *californios* found themselves after 1848, they invoked Spanish and Hispanic origins to establish the de jure whiteness they had been accorded by the 1848 Treaty of Guadalupe Hidalgo but that rarely materialized de facto. In the racial hierarchy Anglo-Americans imposed throughout the Southwest, the cultural connection to European and Roman origins, as remote as it might be, was what made the *californios* superior to Indians, Asians, and African Americans, who had no comparable claims to whiteness.[41]

·   ·   ·

Thus far we have discussed two instances of military conquest—the Spanish colonization of the indigenous peoples who resided in Mexico's far north that began in 1598, and the annexation of this same territory by the United States in 1848 at the end of the Mexican War—to illustrate how ethnic labels and emergent nationalisms were named and imposed from above, but equally resisted from below, employing code switching into a different language to demarcate "us" and "them." We turn now to a third example of the conjuring of national aspirations and their ideal ordering through the process of naming. Above, we discussed the mid-nineteenth century origins of the word "Latino" as an English-language panethnicity that brings together, from below, Mexican, Puerto Rican, Cuban, and a range of Latin American–origin immigrants in the United States. In this section we will also turn to the word "Hispanic," which likewise entered our vocabulary as an English-language word imposed from above, by the U.S. Census Bureau in 1980, to aggregate Latin American–origin peoples as a panethnic group.

The *Oxford English Dictionary* (OED) defines a "Latino" (note that it is now an English word found in most American English dictionaries) as "A Latin-American inhabitant of the United States." According to the OED, the word's etymology is *latinoamericano*, which in Spanish means "Latin American." The OED offers several historical uses of the word, starting in 1945 and running to 1974, when "Latino" entered popular parlance among English speakers. The first recorded use of the word "Latino" in print appeared in 1946, in a book entitled *San Antonio,* which describes a musical performance by a group of Latin American exchange students that took place at the University of Texas. G. Peyton, the book's author, snidely remarks, "That in itself would be a fresh intellectual experience for Texas, where Latinos are usually looked on as sinister specimens of an inferior race." Next came Lady Bird Johnson's *White House Diary,* which contained an entry for April 2, 1970, noting that "Six young girls, all Latinos, had encased themselves in cardboard boxes" during a White House lawn party for the Latin American diplomatic corps. Finally, *The Black Panther,* the Black Panther Party's newspaper, reported on March 17, 1973: "A program was drawn up . . . by an . . . action group composed of Blacks, Latinos, and Whites."[42]

The first two recorded references to "Latinos" in English were tied geographically to ethnic understandings of group membership and belonging in Texas, where calling someone a "Mexican" in the 1940s was extremely insulting. In polite English-speaking company, if the intention was to praise or honor ethnic Mexicans, they were called "Latin Americans." If the intent was to ostracize and humiliate, they were simply "Mexicans." As we have seen, the first Mexican American civil rights organization in the country was named the League of United Latin American Citizens by its Texas founders.[43] What should also be highlighted in the above-cited OED passages from G. Peyton's book and *The Black Panther* newspaper is that "Latino" referred to an "inferior race." In the late 1960s members of minority communities began recognizing three distinct races—black, white, and Latino—to signal that American society had moved beyond its simple black/white racial dichotomy, which no longer adequately described the racism persons of Latin American origin experienced in the United States.

Sociologists Alejandro Portes and Rubén G. Rumbaut tell us that when immigrants and their progeny enter American society and are largely greeted with hostility, segregation, and overtly racist acts, they react negatively, often gathering defensively and collectively to assert their own dignity and self-worth. *Latinidad,* that communal sense of membership in a group tied to Latin America through ancestry, language, culture, and history, emerged from below precisely out of such nationalist sentiments. Individuals first started calling themselves "Latinos" in cities like Chicago and New York, largely to advance political agendas not easily achievable by small, isolated, and distinct national-origin groups. By coming together as Latinos, they swelled their numbers, and expanded their political clout as they demanded inclusion in the polity through affirmative action, fair housing, voting rights, and bilingual education. In time *Latinidad* was also championed from above by ethnic specific civil rights organizations seeking grander nationwide influence and larger membership rolls. Eventually, government bureaucrats, foundations, and corporate marketers recognized the utility of *Latinidad.* Its broadest diffusion has been at the hands of media conglomerates and advertising companies.[44]

Ethnic Mexicans are the largest, best documented, and most regionally dispersed of the immigrant groups that hail from Latin America whose members often call themselves "Latinos." They are now the largest ethnic group in the United States, having surpassed African Americans in numbers and proportion of the country's total population. According to the U.S. Census Bureau, as of July 1, 2013, the country had a Latino population of 54 million, representing approximately 17 percent of the country's total. Of these 54 million, 34.6 million are of Mexican ancestry. Their sustained presence in areas that eventually were incorporated into the United States dates back to the 1598 establishment of a Spanish colony in New Mexico. Their numbers were increased by the annexation of the Republic of Texas (1845) and the acquisition of northern Mexico's provinces (1848), and grew exponentially with the flight northward of refugees during the Mexican Revolution (1910–1917) and the development of agricultural production in the Southwest that relied on a guest worker program (the Bracero Program) between 1942 and 1964, which recruited millions of workers both legally and illegally.

Today, the majority of Mexican Americans are relegated to the lowest rungs of the economy, working as unskilled laborers in service industries, agriculture, and construction. The history of discrimination against them is well known and extensively chronicled. Their work has been valued differentially at lower rates and afforded few legal protections, and, in cases of superexploitation, they have been left with few remedies, even through recourse to courts of law. Their segregation in barrios, or ghettos, has been marked by substandard housing with little access to public transportation and commerce, and even fewer bridging ties to earning and learning opportunities. Their children historically have been systematically denied quality education by restricting their access to schools reserved for whites, by refusing to employ bilingual and bicultural instructors to facilitate the transition to English-language mastery, by tracking them into lower-paid trades rather than college preparatory courses, and by assigning underprepared and derelict teachers to their dilapidated, underfunded schools. Despite the fact that the majority of ethnic Mexicans were born in the United States, are naturalized citizens, or are here legally on work visas, their phenotype is equated with the stigma of "illegality," which frequently results in racial profiling and harassment by the police, thus robbing them of the equal protection the law guarantees. When accused of crimes in past times, they were rarely judged by their peers, were handed stiffer sentences than whites, and were constantly surveilled, trends that have continued to the present.[45]

A similar history of discrimination and marginalization can be recited concerning the 5 million Puerto Ricans who currently live on the U.S. mainland. They are the second-largest Latino group, and together with Mexican Americans account for 73 percent of all Latinos. Puerto Rico was originally explored by Christopher Columbus on his second voyage to the Americas in 1493 and was settled by Spanish colonists soon after. For most of its Spanish colonial history, Puerto Rico was largely a military fort and entrepôt for commerce between Mexico and Spain. In the early part of the nineteenth century, as Spanish America's various regions won their independence, only Cuba, Puerto Rico, and the Philippines failed to break Spain's colonial grip. Though there has been plenty of sentiment and activity for the proclamation of Puerto Rican independence since 1810, it has been repeatedly thwarted by Spain, and then by the United States. The latter had long coveted the island as a way of achieving its own larger geopolitical visions of hemispheric empire and repeatedly asserted such claim, at various times offering to buy the island from Spain. In 1898 the United States provoked war with Spain over the Philippines, which quickly spread to the Caribbean as well. When the Spanish-American War ended with the Treaty of Paris in 1898, the United States emerged as the victor and took possession of Cuba and Puerto Rico, quickly smashing Puerto Rico's independence movement, establishing its sovereignty over the island with the 1900 Foraker Act, and declaring Puerto Ricans citizens of the United States through the Jones Act of 1917.

Puerto Rico's population remained largely confined to the island between 1900 and 1930, with approximately 1,800 individuals migrating to the mainland yearly during this period. This trend accelerated in the years before World War II, when increasing numbers migrated to New York City to take its unskilled jobs and to enter military rolls. In 1940 there were 69,967 Puerto Ricans living on the mainland, the vast majority in New York City. By 1950 that number had increased to 226,110, by 1970 to 1,391,464, by 2000 to 3.4 million, and by 2013 to 5 million. While in 1940, 88 percent of all Puerto Ricans on the mainland lived in New York state, by 1980 they were much more dispersed, with only 49 percent in New York, 12 percent in New Jersey, 6.4 percent in Illinois, and approximately 4.5 percent in California, Florida, Pennsylvania, and Connecticut. By 2010, only about 20 percent of mainland Puerto Ricans resided in New York City.[46]

The problems Puerto Ricans faced in the United States were not unlike those of Mexican Americans. While the presence of Mexicans in the United States had long been suspect and equated with illegality, Puerto Ricans have been de jure citizens since 1917, but rarely treated so de facto. Their life chances on the mainland have been limited, despite repeated scholarly studies proclaiming that they too eventually would be integrated into the American body politic as other immigrant groups had. If they learned English, took American brides, accepted the Protestant work ethic, and persevered in school, they too would move out of their ghettos and gain political representation and upward mobility. In 1976 the U.S. Commission on Civil Rights issued a report entitled *Puerto Ricans in the Continental United States: An Uncertain Future* that concluded that the majority of Puerto Ricans were living in substandard housing, were unemployed and living in poverty, had poor access to education and health care, and inordinately suffered from racial discrimination. Ten years after the United States declared a "War on Poverty," Puerto Ricans remained in the ranks of the war-scarred poor.[47]

I recite this history of inequities Mexican Americans and Puerto Ricans have experienced to help explain what led them to abandon older forms of political activism rooted in self-help associations, in mutual aid societies, in labor unions, and in ethnic churches, for the militant, reactive nationalism they forged in the late 1960s. Mexican Americans then announced themselves "Chicanos" as a colonized nationality demanding self-determination and national autonomy, much as Puerto Ricans started to call themselves "Boricuas" and advocated similar forms of nationhood. Both eschewed any association with racial whiteness, something civil rights organizations had invoked since the 1920s to distance themselves from the stigma of blackness. Both Chicanos and Boricuas found inspiration in the aspirations and organizational structures of the Black Panther Party. Chicanos accordingly founded the Brown Berets and Boricuas, the Young Lords, heralding racialized brown and black pride. Whereas their parents and grandparents had eschewed the color categories of their oppressors, now the young embraced them with gusto as oppositional badges of authenticity.

Those who identified as Chicanos and Boricuas gave territorial dimensions to their nationalist sentiments, seeking succession and national sovereignty as the antidote to their histories of segregation and marginalization in the United States. Chicanos proclaimed that they would unite, as the nation of Aztlán, the states of California, Arizona, Texas, New Mexico, Colorado, and Nevada, returning to Mexican control these territories lost in 1845 and 1848.[48] Boricuas deemed Puerto Ricans living on the island and mainland a "divided nation." If liberation was to occur for mainland Puerto Ricans, they had to bring national liberation to the island first. In early 1971 the Young Lords began their "Ofensiva Rompecadenas" (Break-the-Chains Offensive), asking for unity in their attempt to gain Puerto Rican independence. Though such a territorial ambition had been pursued militantly since the 1950s, its embrace by the Young Lords ultimately weakened their organization, spread its resources thin, and caused considerable factionalism between themselves and the island's political groups. By late 1972 the Young Lords repudiated this strategy, arguing instead that Puerto Ricans were an "oppressed national minority" in the United States, that Puerto Rico was a nation, and that mainland Puerto Ricans had to focus their energies on their compatriots in the United States.[49]

Besides such dreams of national autonomy and self-determination, Chicanos and Boricuas both espoused an ideology of self-help, seeking the improvement of their co-ethnics. Inspired by César Chávez, they supported his unionization campaign for better wages and working conditions for farm workers of every nationality. Reies López Tijerina's movement to regain lands fraudulently stolen from *mexicanos* in New Mexico, Colorado, and Texas similarly heightened their understanding of the importance of land ownership to economic well-being. In places like New York City, Denver, Albuquerque, and Los Angeles, they protested police brutality. In New York, Texas, New Mexico, and California, the states with the densest Mexican American and Puerto Rican populations, they launched legal challenges against discriminatory schooling, housing, employment practices, policing, and the exercise of justice by the courts.

Equally important to both Chicanos and Boricuas was their assault on racism in its material, psychic, and institutionalized forms. Heralding their personal beauty and pride both movements affirmed the beauty of their art, language, culture, and skin color as a way to corrode the toxicity of racism. Pedro Pietri captured this sense of pride in his now famous book of poems, *Puerto Rican Obituary*.

Here lies Juan
Here lies Miguel
Here lies Olga
Here lies Manuel
Who died yesterday today
And will die again tomorrow
Always broke
Always owing
Never knowing
That they are beautiful people
Never knowing
The geography of their complexion
PUERTO RICO IS A BEAUTIFUL PLACE
PUERTORIQUEÑOS ARE A BEAUTIFUL RACE[50]

Rodolfo "Corky" Gonzales's poem "I Am Joaquín," similarly was meant to incite Chicano rebellion and cultural pride. The poem, excerpted here, begins and ends as follows:

Yo soy Joaquín,
perdido en un mundo de confusión:
I am Joaquín,
lost in a world of confusion,
caught up in the whirl of a gringo society,
confused by the rules, scorned by attitudes,
suppressed by manipulation, and destroyed by modern society . . .
in all the fertile farmlands,
the barren plains,
the mountain villages,
smoke-smeared cities,
we start to MOVE.
La raza!
Méjicano!
Español!
Latino!
Chicano!
Or whatever I call myself,
I look the same
I feel the same
I cry
And
Sing the same.
I am the masses of my people and
I refuse to be absorbed.
I am Joaquín.

The odds are great
But my spirit is strong,
My faith unbreakable,
My blood is pure.
I am Aztec prince and Christian Christ.
I SHALL ENDURE!
I WILL ENDURE![51]

The "Plan Espiritual de Aztlán," the 1969 document that birthed the Chicano student movement, offered a capacious blueprint for how national unity and political empowerment would be achieved. It called for unity among all racially oppressed groups, for community control over local institutions and the communitarian management of its resources through responsible capitalism, for culturally relevant educational curricula with community control of schools, for the development of institutions that would protect Chicano civil and human rights and guarantee fair wages, for community self-defense through humanitarianism, for a contestational cultural politics "to defeat the gringo dollar value system," and for the rejection of the two-party system for a more equitable pluralist politics.[52]

In the forty-seven years since the plan was issued, many have questioned the nationalism it spawned as crude because it fractured the liberal civil rights coalition that was being forged, and because it celebrated a culture of violence, hypermasculinity, sexism, and homophobia that was on display not only in boardrooms but in bedrooms too. The plan nevertheless created an alternative vision of cultural incorporation and membership in a body politic, challenged unbridled capitalism, and framed the local in relationship to the global, simultaneously linking local struggles for self-determination with global anti-imperialist ones. It created organizations for community policing, food cooperatives, and educational campaigns for safer food, healthier bodies, and sharper minds.

The thirteen-point platform of the Puerto Rican Young Lords made almost identical demands:

We want community control of our institutions and land. We want control of our communities by our people and programs to guarantee that all institutions serve the needs of our people. People's control of police, health services, churches, schools, housing, transportation, and welfare are needed. We want an end to attacks on our land by urban renewal, highway destruction, and university corporations. LAND BELONGS TO ALL THE PEOPLE![53]

The oppositional consciousness and militant nationalism Chicanos and Boricuas articulated established the groundwork for the emergence of *Latinidad*. As far as I have been able to ascertain, Chicago was the place an explicit sense of group membership as Latinos emerged into public visibility, precisely out of older coalitional politics. Mexican Americans and Puerto Ricans there understood that if they were to enhance their material lives, they had to come together to advance collective goals. In the early 1970s, this took the form of the La Coalición Latinoamericana de Empleos. Instead of translating the group's name literally as "The Latin American Jobs Coalition," they chose "The Spanish Coalition for Jobs." Composed of twenty-three Puerto Rican and Mexican American community organizations, the coalition explicitly militated for the improvement of "Latinos'" lives though work, demanding first that Illinois Bell Telephone and Jewel Tea Company honor federal affirmative action policies. As the coalition's foundational document explained, they had united because "the racist attitude of employers triggered us into utilizing our consumer power as a tool or bargaining device . . . to compete in the job market."[54]

Illinois Bell was their first target. In 1971 coalition representatives repeatedly met with the company's management to question why its workforce of 44,000 included only 300 Latinos, demanding that 3,000 new Latino workers be hired. Illinois Bell's retort was an offer of 115 jobs. What followed was the first mass action organized in the name of Latinos, and the group picketed the company's headquarters in Chicago starting in mid-September 1971. On June 14, 1972, a settlement was reached. Illinois Bell agreed to hire 1,323 Latinos and two top-level executives by the end of 1976, and would form a community review committee to chart the company's progress toward these goals.[55]

The coalition next targeted Chicago's Jewel Tea Company, presenting it with similar demands in March 1972. The company had received more than $250,000 from the federal government to train minority workers for work in their stores, yet only 140 Latinos had been hired. The coalition cited statistics about Jewel's workforce and the underrepresentation of Latinos. After almost a year of picketing, in the summer of 1973, Jewel agreed to hire more Latinos through an independent job placement agency.[56]

These initial successes intensified the coalition's sense of unity, and on March 16, 1973, it convened a "Latino Strategies for the 70s" conference. The press release for the event announced: "The brown skin Latino has awakened and he will never be the same again . . . because he knows that to live is to enjoy freedom. He has learned that to be a Latino is good."[57] Among the many conference outcomes was the formation of the "Latino Institute" to bring into constant contact the coalition's initial constituent groups. The Latino Institute took as its first major goal the education of Latino parents about bilingual education, teaching parents how to advocate for it, how to choose from the range of bilingual education models, and how to evaluate a school's progress in educating their children in their native Spanish language.

Since the emergence of *Latinidad* as a panethnic form of consciousness that emphasized an antiracist coalitional politics among Chicago's Latinos in the early 1970s, a number of studies have appeared chronicling different aspects of it in other American cities. What makes it difficult to compare these works is that when they articulate the contours of *Latinidad*, they have very different notions of its embodiment and deployment in mind. Two well-regarded studies of *Latinidad* take a bottom-up perspective

for the emergence of panethnicity, arguing that the daily experiences of social interaction on neighborhood streets, in residences, in markets, in houses of worship, and
in workplaces foster a sense of commonality among immigrants from many Latin
American countries. Two books maintain that women are the active agents who diffuse
and cement *Latinidad* as lived experience: Carol Hardy-Fanta's *Latina Politics, Latino
Politics: Gender, Culture, and Political Participation in Boston,* which focuses on language
politics surrounding bilingual education and campaigns to elect Latino candidates to
political posts, and Milagros Ricourt and Ruby Danta's *Hispanas de Queens: Latino Panethnicity in a New York City Neighborhood,* which studies how women in Corona and
Queens interact.[58] When women gather in the stairwells of their apartment buildings
to gossip about local affairs, when women commiserate about the poor education their
children receive, when they gather at the local laundromat, when they wrangle over
the price of tomatoes and potatoes with a local vender, and when they chat about their
personal worlds and commiserate over their life challenges, they interact in the Spanish
language, connect with Latin Americans from different places, and by doing so give
Latinidad tangible meanings. Of course, immigrants from Ecuador, the Dominican
Republic, Mexico, and Guatemala do not quickly or easily lose their natal nationalites,
but by constantly interacting, or so these female authors contend, women are creating
the behavioral, interactional foundation for *Latinidad.*[59]

Open up any newspaper, listen to any talk radio show, or watch the television pundits, and what they repeatedly announce is that Latinos are an emerging majority that
every day is becoming more potent in politics, commerce, and the very racial makeup
of the United States. How much unity exists among Latinos? How operative and decisive is *Latinidad* in the lives of people who claim it or among the individuals who are
lumped into this imagined community? The simple demographic fact is that the Latino
population of the United States is large and diverse, encompassing more than twenty
nationalities, and numerous languages that include a complex tapestry of indigenous
ones. Latinos occupy various class locations and span the entire spectrum of race and
color. Nothing specifically unites Latinos. In the past Roman Catholicism was such
a glue for many, but even here Protestant evangelical churches and indigenous religions factionalize that unity, if indeed it ever existed. In places where the two largest
Latino groups—Mexican Americans and Puerto Ricans—have been in close contact
for long periods, relationships of affiliation and trust exist, as well as relationships of
chauvinism and suspicion. As Nicholas de Genova and Ana Y. Ramos-Zayas make clear
in their study of relations between Mexicans and Puerto Ricans in Chicago during
the late 1990s, a period only twenty years after the exuberance of Latino unity in the
1970s chronicled above, relations between the two groups were tense and were often
marked by antagonism. Mexicans resented Puerto Ricans because of their citizenship
status, which entitled them to welfare and government assistance, and thus constantly
demonized them as lazy, welfare dependent, and abusers of state benefits for the poor.
Mexicans suffered the stigma of illegality, of being unauthorized immigrants in the

United States, and thus were seen by Puerto Ricans as persons who allowed themselves to be exploited easily, accepting minimal wages and operating in an underworld of illicit drugs, prostitution, and gangs to make their way in the United States.[60] Thus, whatever unity and political cohesion *Latinidad* provided these two groups in Chicago in the 1970s, by 2000 that sentiment had evaporated into fractious relations, largely because of the growth of the unauthorized Mexican immigrant population that began competing with Puerto Ricans for low-paying jobs.

By now, attentive readers may be wondering about the place of Cuban Americans in this history of the radicalization of Mexican Americans and Puerto Ricans in the United States. The Cuban Revolution occurred in 1959, but it was not until the early 1960s that significant numbers of Cubans fled the island for residence ninety miles away, concentrating mostly in Miami and more generally in Florida. The Cubans who arrived in the United States as political refugees fleeing Communism were of a much higher class (mostly elites and middle-class professionals), carried immensely more money and cultural capital with them, often already had homes and businesses in the United States, and quickly became beneficiaries of affirmative action programs meant for persons who had had fewer privileges and opportunities in American life. What radicalism Cuban refugees did express was focused on the regime of Fidel Castro, on their return to Cuba to overthrow the Cuban Revolution, and was entirely anti-Communist in nature.

Cuban Americans did not actively participate in claiming or shaping *Latinidad* because of their class positions and their laser-like focus on the overthrow of Castro's regime. They were nevertheless instrumental in domesticating and naturalizing *Latinidad*, transforming it from an oppositional and reactive sentiment to a media and marketing one primarily focused on the consumption of Latin American panethnic services and goods. In the 1950s much of the advertising by American firms that took place in Latin America was designed and purchased in Havana, Miami, and New York. After the Cuban Revolution, many of the Cuban advertising executives immigrated to New York and Miami, whence they resumed their activities. In the 1970s and 1980s, these mostly Cuban Americans started a process of combining Latin American national groups into a larger marketing sector, which they also called "Latino." If they could create a clearly larger Latino market than was represented by individual national groups, and identify its needs and desires, they stood to profit enormously as individuals and as the advertising firms that knew precisely how to pitch products to this group. With that expertise they stood ready to persuade the large corporations producing food, beverages, and a host of domestic goods that Latinos constituted a significant mass market that needed special ad campaigns that only their advertising agencies were expertly prepared to create. This is exactly what happened, argues Arlene Dávila in *Latinos Inc.: The Marketing and Making of a People*. These advertising people began educating the manufacturers of products about what the Latino market wanted and would consume. The producers then purchased advertising campaigns targeted to the Latino market the ad agencies had invented. Quickly, then, beer, soda pop, cooking oil, even bleach came to embody *lo latino*, that unique Latino essence that only the Coors Brewing Company, PepsiCo, General Foods, and Clorex could deliver.[61]

The power of the advertising dollar and the reach of global media were also, in part, responsible for the popularization of the fiction that another word, "Hispanic," best described the putative sense of unity that existed among immigrants from Latin America residing in the United States. The U.S. Census Bureau introduced "Spanish/Hispanic origin" as a panethnic category for purposes of official data gathering and analysis in 1980. But the movement toward its codification and use was complicated, the product of negotiations with community representatives, elected officials, and state functionaries. The mobilization of ethnic communities for civil rights in the 1960s, the emergence of massive social unrest in cities across the country, and the radical nationalism young men and women began to expound as Chicanos and Boricuas all gained the attention of the Congress and of the administrations of Presidents Lyndon B. Johnson and Richard Nixon. Seeking to defuse and moderate the increasingly radical segments of these groups, in 1967, through executive order, Johnson established the Inter-Agency Committee on Mexican American Affairs (IMAA). The committee held hearings and funneled federal resources to potentially incendiary spots, increasing employment and manpower training and making the government aware of the militancy percolating in the streets. When Nixon entered the White House, he equivocated on what to do with the committee, and left it to the Congress to extend its life. It did. On December 31, 1969, President Nixon signed the bill creating the Cabinet Committee on Opportunities for Spanish Speaking People (CCOSSP). The morphing of the IMAA into a vastly expanded CCOSSP had been the result of congressional and representative politics. Among the complainants were Puerto Ricans and Cubans who felt that their grievances had been ignored by the government's almost exclusive focus on African Americans and Mexican Americans. By expanding the purview of CCOSSP to the three ethnic groups, then calling this aggregation "Spanish speakers," the Congress and the Nixon administration were simultaneously lancing a number of boils. Congressman Edward Roybal (D-CA), explained the reasons for his authorship of the bill creating CCOSSP:

> The militants in our community are on our backs almost every moment of the day. And the question that is being asked of me, members of Congress, and other elected officials is, "Is it necessary for us to riot? Is it necessary for us to burn down a town before the government looks at our problems objectively? What are we to do if our community is not recognized?" Those of us who represent the Spanish-speaking communities have quite a problem on our hands. We do not want to see the violence of Watts erupt in East Los Angeles or anyplace else, and I hope that this will never come about. But the answers must be found, and I believe that one of the answers is the establishment of the [CCOSSP].[62]

Senator Joseph M. Montoya (D-NM), the co-author of the legislation creating CCOSSP, wanted the panethnic aggregation of Mexican Americans, Puerto Ricans, and Cubans to be called "Hispanic," and by 1980 it was.

The same activists who had lobbied Congress and gotten the federal government to create CCOSSP realized that if Mexican American issues were to receive the same level of national attention African American issues got, they needed a nationwide organization to advance their cause. In *Making Hispanics: How Activists, Bureaucrats, and Media Constructed a New American*, G. Cristina Mora studies such a transformation for the Southwest Council of La Raza. Founded in 1968 as a local, grassroots organization to fight poverty and discrimination with a regional focus primarily in Texas and California, by 1972 the Southwest Council of La Raza had become the National Council of La Raza, modeled after the National Association for the Advancement of Colored People (NAACP). Hoping to serve as the interlocutor for the entire Hispanic population of the United States, it opened a headquarters office in Washington, DC, and began to advocate not only for Mexican Americans, but on behalf of the social, political, and economic concerns of all Hispanics. As Mora argues, the organization's transformation occurred by first recognizing and harnessing popular identification with Hispanics, then developing a national vision and mission that included the issues of all persons of Latin American origin in the United States. With an organization, a national office, and an emergent political identity, the National Council of La Raza created the infrastructure and authority to get philanthropic groups to recognize it as the interlocutor for all Hispanics, and accordingly generously fund its work, as indeed the Ford and Rockefeller Foundations did. Finally, it gained such national visibility and economic support that the federal government sought its advice as well, calling on it to help the U.S. Census Bureau craft the ethnic categories that would be used in subsequent decennial counts. While in 1980 the U.S. household census had first asked "Is this person of Spanish/Hispanic origin or descent?" by the 2000 count "Latino" was used as equal to "Spanish/Hispanic origin." Mora argues that for "Latino" to emerge as a panethnicity, it needed not only ideological and institutional foundations, which were quickly harnessed, but it also needed a source of diffusion, which it got from Univision, the Spanish-language television network in the United States that generated its own programming aimed to appeal to American Hispanics, supplemented by programming the network purchased from other countries in the Hispanophone world.[63]

·   ·   ·

The scholarly literature suggests that for panethnicity to emerge, one first needs a population that is significantly marginalized and exploited, and one that comes to see itself as such, in opposition to the group it deems the dominant, oppressive one. Once such a reactive ethnicity is in place, demography and geographic isolation through segregation has brought together ethnic groups that previously had no common history or mutual interests. Much of the world's ethnic politics are language politics; that

Mexican Americans and Puerto Ricans, or for that matter any other combinations of Latin American national groups, shared a common language and sometimes also a common religious culture, made it easier for panethnicity to emerge, get propagated, and get institutionalized from above through such things as the boundary-making national census, or from below through interactions, commiseration, and mobilization. Evidence from Chicago over a period of forty years also shows that state action, a changing demographic balance between immigrants and the native born, between citizens and noncitizens, and more intense competition between national/ethnic groups over local resources can just as easily breed antagonisms and hatreds where once mutuality and common understanding were deemed necessary for sociality and communal advancement. Reflecting on why the 1960 count had not included a panethnic category that encompassed Mexican Americans, Puerto Ricans, and Cuban Americans, one census official stated that back then they "didn't really identify [with one another, and] didn't really know what Hispanic meant." This essay has tried to show how group relations evolve over time, how state and institutional actors, journalists and media executives, as well as community organizations, all have played a role in how categories of belonging and group consciousness emerge, are sustained, and, just as often, disappear to be replaced by others.

NOTES

Note: I wish to thank my colleagues Mauricio Tenorio and David Ayón for their careful readings of this essay and for their helpful comments.

1. Eric J. Hobsbawm, *Nations and Nationalism since 1870: Programme, Myth, Reality* (New York: Cambridge University Press, 1990).

2. Yen Le Espiritu, *Asian American Panethnicity: Building Institutions and Identities* (Philadelphia: Temple University Press, 1992); Milagros Ricourt and Ruby Danta, *Hispanas de Queens: Latino Panethnicity in a New York City Neighborhood* (Ithaca, NY: Cornell University Press, 2003); Jonathan Daniel Rosas, "Looking Like a Language, Sounding Like a Race: Making Latina/o Panethnicity and Managing American Anxieties" (PhD diss., University of Chicago, 2010); G. Cristina Mora, *Making Hispanics: How Activists, Bureaucrats, and Media Constructed a New American* (Chicago: University of Chicago Press, 2014).

3. Américo Castro, *The Spaniards: An Introduction to Their History* (Berkeley: University of California Press, 1971), pp. 1–94. See also María Elena Martínez, "The Black Blood of New Spain: *Limpieza de Sangre*, Racial Violence, and Gendered Power in Early Colonial Mexico," *William and Mary Quarterly*, 3rd Series, 61, no. 3 (July 2004), pp. 479–520.

4. Gaspar Pérez de Villagrá, *History of New Mexico*, trans. Gilberto Espinosa (Acalá, 1610; reprinted, Los Angeles: The Quivira Society, 1933), p. 173. See also Aurelio M. Espinosa, "El desarrollo de la palabra Castilla en la lengua de los indios Hopis de Arizona," *Revista de Filología Española* 22 (1935): 298–300.

5. The details of contact between Spaniards and Indians can be found in Ramón A.

Gutiérrez, *When Jesus Came, the Corn Mothers Went Away: Marriage, Sexuality and Power in New Mexico, 1500–1846* (Stanford, CA: Stanford University Press, 1992).

6. Fredrich Katz, *The Ancient American Civilizations* (New York: Praeger, 1972); Eric R. Wolf, *Sons of the Shaking Earth* (Chicago: University of Chicago Press, 1966); Sherburne R. Cook and Woodrow W. Borah, *The Indian Population of Central Mexico, 1531–1610* (Berkeley: University of California Press, 1960).

7. Ronald L. Grimes, *Symbol and Conquest: Public Ritual and Drama in Santa Fe, New Mexico* (Ithaca, NY: Cornell University Press, 1976).

8. France V. Scholes, "Documents for the History of the New Mexican Missions in the Seventeenth Century," *New Mexico Historical Review* 10 (1929): 195–99, quotation on pp. 196–97.

9. James Brooke, "Oñate's Missing Foot," http://pages.ucsd.edu/~rfrank/class_web/ES-112A/Onate.html (accessed May 8, 2014). The most complete description of the vandalization of the Oñate statue can be found in Michael P. Carroll, *The Penitente Brotherhood: Patriarchy and Hispano-Catholicism in New Mexico* (Baltimore: The Johns Hopkins University Press, 2002) pp. 1–6.

10. The history of the *régimen de castas* can be studied in Magnus Mörner, *Race Mixture in the History of Latin America* (Boston: Little, Brown and Company, 1967); Claudio Esteva-Fabregat, *Mestizaje in Ibero-America* (Tucson: University of Arizona Press, 1995); Silvio Zavela, *Las instituciones jurídicas en la conquista de América* (Madrid: Imprenta Helénica, 1935); Magali M. Carrera, *Imagining Identity in New Spain: Race, Lineage, and the Colonial Body in Portraiture and Casta Paintings* (Austin: University of Texas Press, 2003); Illona Katzew, *Casta Painting: Images of Race in Eighteenth Century Mexico* (New Haven: Yale University Press, 2004).

11. Magnus Mörner, *Race Mixture in the History of Latin America* (Boston: Little, Brown, 1967); Ann Twinam, *Public Lives, Private Secrets: Gender, Honor, Sexuality, and Illegitimacy in Colonial Spanish America* (Stanford: Stanford University Press, 1999).

12. Quoted in Verena Martínez-Alier, *Marriage, Class and Colour in Nineteenth-Century Cuba* (London: Cambridge University Press, 1974), pp. 83–84.

13. Spanish Archives of New Mexico, microfilm edition, Reel 9: frames 789–820.

14. Fray Angélico Chávez, "Genízaros," in *Handbook of North American Indians*, vol. 9, ed. William C. Sturtevant (Washington, DC: Smithsonian Institution, 1979), pp. 198–201; Steven M. Horvath, "The Social and Political Organization of the Genízaros of Plaza de Nuestra Señora de los Dolores de Belén, New Mexico 1740–1812" (PhD diss., Brown University, 1979); David M. Brugge, *Navajos in the Catholic Church Records of New Mexico 1694–1875*, Research Report no. 1 (Window Rock, AZ: The Navajo Tribe, 1968), p. 30.

15. Fray Carlos Delgado, Historia, Tomo 25, expediente 25, folio 229, Archivo General de la Nación (México).

16. Frances Leon Swadesh, *Los Primeros Pobladores: Hispanic Americans of the Ute Frontier* (Notre Dame, IN: Notre Dame University Press, 1974), p. 45; Florence Hawley Ellis, "Tomé and Father J. B. R.," *New Mexico Historical Review* 30 (1955): 89–114, quotation from p. 94.

17. Elsie C. Parsons, "Tewa Mothers and Children," *Man* 24 (1924): p. 149; Edward H. Spicer, *The Yaquis: A Cultural History* (Tucson: University of Arizona Press, 1980), pp. 22–

23; N. Ross Crumrine, *The Mayo Indians of Sonora: A People Who Refuse to Die* (Tucson: University of Arizona Press, 1977), p. 69.

18. Gutíerrez, *When Jesus Came, the Corn Mothers Went Away*, pp. 193–94.

19. A. Gabriel Meléndez, *So All Is Not Lost: The Poetics of Print in Nuevomexicano Communities, 1834–1958* (Albuquerque: University of New Mexico Press, 1997), p. 59.

20. Ibid., p. 59.

21. Américo Paredes, "The Problem of Identity in a Changing Culture: Popular Expressions of Culture Conflict along the Lower Rio Grande Border," in *Views Across the Border: The United States and Mexico*, ed. Stanley R. Ross (Albuquerque: University of New Mexico Press, 1978), pp. 68–94.

22. Ibid.

23. Arnoldo de León, *They Called Them Greasers: Anglo Attitudes toward Mexicans in Texas, 1821–1900* (Austin: University of Texas Press, 1983), p. 16.

24. Tomás Almaguer, *Racial Faultlines: The Historical Origins of White Supremacy in California* (Berkeley: University of California Press, 1994), pp. 57, 228; on Greaser Gulch see David E. Hayes-Bautista, *El Cinco de Mayo: An American Tradition* (Berkeley: University of California Press, 2012) p. 62.

25. Paredes, "The Problem of Identity," pp. 72–75.

26. Raymund A. Paredes, "The Mexican Image in American Travel Literature, 1831–1869," *New Mexico Historical Quarterly* 1 (1977): 5–29; Deena Gonzáles, "The Spanish-Mexican Women of Santa Fe: Patterns of Their Resistance and Accommodation, 1820–1880" (PhD diss., University of California, Berkeley, 1986); John R. Chávez, *The Lost Land: The Chicano Image of the Southwest* (Albuquerque: University of New Mexico Press, 1984); Phillip A. Hernández, "The Other Americans: The American Image of Mexico and Mexicans, 1550–1850" (PhD diss., University of California, Berkeley, 1974); Susan R. Kenneson, "Through the Looking Glass: A History of Anglo-American Attitudes Toward the Spanish-Americans and Indians of New Mexico" (PhD diss., Yale University, 1978); Jack D. Forbes, "Race and Color in Mexican-American Problems," *Journal of Human Relations* 16 (1968): 55–68; Manuel Gamio, *Mexican Immigration to the United States* (Chicago: University of Chicago Press, 1930), pp. 129, 209.

27. Joseph V. Metzgar, "The Ethnic Sensitivity of Spanish New Mexicans: A Survey and Analysis," *New Mexico Historical Review* 49 (1974): 52.

28. U.S. Census Bureau, "California Resident Population," https://www.census.gov/dmd/www/resapport/states/california.pdf (accessed May 11, 2014).

29. Leonard Pitt, *The Decline of the Californios: A Social History of the Spanish-Speaking Californians, 1846–1890* (Berkeley: University of California Press, 1966), pp. 53, 157, 174, 188, 204, 259, 267, 309; Arthur L. Campa, *Hispanic Culture in the Southwest* (Norman: University of Oklahoma Press, 1979), p. 5.

30. Hayes-Bautista, *El Cinco de Mayo*, p. 20

31. Hayes-Bautista, *El Cinco de Mayo*, p. 208, note 141.

32. Torres Caicedo, as quoted in Walter Mingnolo, *The Idea of Latin America* (Malden, MA: Blackwell, 2005), p. 59. See also Arturo Ardao, *Génesis de la idea y el nombre de América Latina* (Caracas: Consejo Nacional de la Cultura, 1980).

33. Hayes-Bautista, *El Cinco de Mayo*, pp. 41–42.

34. Richard Norstrand, "Mexican American and Chicano: Emerging Terms for a People Coming of Age," *Pacific Historical Review* 42, no. 3 (1973): 396.

35. A. Gabriel Meléndez, *So All Is Not Lost: The Poetics of Print in Nuevomexicano Communities, 1834–1958* (Albuquerque: University of New Mexico Press, 1997), pp. 60–66.

36. "Himno del Hispano," December 3, 1915, as quoted in Doris Meyer, *Speaking for Themselves: Neomexicano Cultural Identity and the Spanish Language Press, 1880–1920* (Albuquerque: University of New Mexico Press, 1996), pp. 172–73.

37. Mingnolo, *The Idea of Latin America*, p. 60.

38. Erna Fergusson, *New Mexico: A Pageant of Three Peoples* (New York: Knopf, 1964), p. 218; Nancie González, *The Spanish-Americans of New Mexico: A Heritage of Pride* (Albuquerque: University of New Mexico Press, 1969), pp. 80–81.

39. Olivia Arrieta, "La Alianza Hispano-Americana, 1894–1965: An Analysis of Collective Action and Cultural Adaptation," in *Nuevomexicano Cultural Legacy: Forms, Agencies, and Discourses*, eds. Francisco Lomelí, Victor A. Sorell, and Genaro M. M. Padilla (Albuquerque: University of New Mexico Press, 2002), pp. 109–126; Tomás Serrano Cabo, *Las Crónicas de la Alianza Hispano Americana* (Tucson: Alianza Hispano-Americana, 1929); Thomas Sheridan, *Los Tucsonenses: The Mexican American Community in Tucson 1854–1941* (Tucson: University of Arizona Press, 1986), esp. pp. 108–9.

40. Gamio, *Mexican Immigration to the United States*, p. 133.

41. Almaguer, *Racial Faultlines*, pp. 46, 54–57, 73–74.

42. Oxford English Dictionary, s. v. "Latino," www.oed.com (accessed September 2, 2020).

43. Benjamin Marquez, *LULAC: The Evolution of a Mexican American Political Organization* (Austin: University of Texas Press, 1993).

44. Alejandro Portes and Rubén G. Rumbaut, eds., *Legacies: The Story of the Immigrant Second Generation* (Berkeley: University of California Press, 2001), p. 248; Mora, *Making Hispanics*; Arlene Dávila, *Latinos Inc.: The Marketing and Making of a People* (Berkeley: University of California Press, 2001).

45. Ian Haney López, *Racism on Trial: The Chicano Fight for Justice* (Cambridge, MA: Harvard University Press, 2003).

46. Carmen Teresa Whalen and Víctor Vásquez-Hernández, eds., *The Puerto Rican Diaspora: Historical Perspectives* (Philadelphia: Temple University Press, 2005), pp. 2–3.

47. U.S. Commission on Civil Rights, *Puerto Ricans in the Continental United States: An Uncertain Future* (Washington, DC: Government Printing Office, 1976), p. 5.

48. Rodolfo Anaya and Francisco Lomelí, eds., *Aztlán: Essays on the Chicano Homeland* (Albuquerque: Academia/El Norte Publications, 1989).

49. Iris Morales, "¡Palante, Siempre Palante! The Young Lords," in *The Puerto Rican Movement: Voices from the Diaspora*, eds. Andrés Torres and José E. Velázquez (Philadelphia: Temple University Press, 1998), pp. 221–22.

50. Pedro Pietri, *Puerto Rican Obituary* (New York: Monthly Review Press, 1973), p. 3.

51. Rodolfo Gonzalez, "I am Joaquín," http://www.latinamericanstudies.org/latinos/joaquin.htm.

52. "El Plan Espiritual de Aztlán," in *Testimonio: A Documentary History of the Mexi-*

can American Struggle for Civil Rights, ed. F. Arturo Rosales (Houston: Arte Público Press, 2000), pp. 361–63.

53. Young Lords Platform, as quoted in Cristina Beltrán, The Trouble with Unity: Latino Politics and the Creation of Identity (New York: Oxford University Press, 2000), pp. 33–34.

54. "History of the Spanish Coalition for Jobs," as quoted by Felix M. Padilla, Latino Ethnic Consciousness: The Case of Mexican Americans and Puerto Ricans in Chicago (Notre Dame, IN: University of Notre Dame Press, 1985), pp. 89–90.

55. Ibid., pp. 96–97.

56. Ibid., pp. 96–97.

57. "Latino Strategies for the 70's—Report," as quoted in Padilla, Latino Ethnic Consciousness, p. 105.

58. Carol Hardy-Fanta, Latina Politics, Latino Politics: Gender, Culture, and Political Participation in Boston (Philadelphia: Temple University Press, 1993).

59. Milagros Ricourt and Ruby Danta, Hispanas de Queens: Latino Panethnicity in a New York City Neighborhood (Ithaca, NY: Cornell University Press, 2003).

60. Nicholas de Genova and Ana Y. Ramos-Zayas, Latino Crossings: Mexicans, Puerto Ricans, and the Politics of Race and Citizenship (New York: Routledge, 2003).

61. Arlene Dávila, Latinos Inc.: The Marketing and Making of a People (Berkeley: University of California Press, 2001).

62. Congressman Edward Roybal, Establishing the Cabinet Committee on Opportunities for Spanish Speaking People: Hearings before a Subcommittee of the Committee on Government Operations, House of Representatives, 91st Congress 18 (1969), as quoted in Mora, Making Hispanics, p. 35.

63. Mora, Making Hispanics; and G. Cristina Mora, "De Muchos, Uno: The Institutionalization of Latino Panethnicity, 1960–1990" (PhD diss., Princeton University, 2009).

2

(RE)CONSTRUCTING *LATINIDAD*
The Challenge of Latina/o Studies

Frances R. Aparicio

WHO IS A LATINA/O?

One evening last year in Chicago, I attended a Latino concert at a local music venue downtown with some friends and colleagues. Around the table we were all Latino, yet each of us embodied very different social, class, cultural, linguistic, gendered, and racial experiences. We were all of Latin American descent; some were born and raised in Chicago, others were more recent immigrants, having arrived to the U.S. five years ago, and others, like me, had been in the United States for most of their lives as adults. Most outsiders would have grouped us all together as Latinas/os, minorities, foreigners, and Spanish-speaking. But a closer look at the complex and contradictory identities and experiences among us all reveals a much more complicated picture about Latino America. This is, indeed, one of the most central challenges that Latina/o studies faces as a field of study.

Who is a Latina/o? What constitutes a Latina/o identity? When does a Latin American become a U.S. Latina/o? How do regional, national, and political identities—Chicano, Boricua, Tejano, Central American—intersect with the larger rubric of "Latino"? How do we account for socioeconomic, linguistic, racial, generational, and gender differences? How can we explore the mutual interactions, transculturations, conflicts, and power struggles among the 54.4 million Latinas/os in the United States, not to mention the power asymmetries between Latinas/os and dominant society? As a multi- and interdisciplinary site of academic inquiry, Latina/o studies examines the multiple factors that affect the everyday lives of U.S. Latinas/os. Such heterogeneity challenges scholars to find new, interdisciplinary approaches that can address our multiple and shifting realities.

Since the early 1990s, Latina/o studies has produced cutting-edge knowledge that responds to the historical shifts witnessed by our communities: colonialism and subordination, border crossing and transnationalism, racism and racialization, gendered identities and sexualities, stereotypes and representations, and the constitution of hybrid identities. These areas of inquiry are also located at the intersections between individual selves, collective groups, and the institutions of civil society, the media, and the state. If identity is defined by the dialogic struggles between notions of the self and the constructions imposed from the outside (other individuals, institutions, and discourses), then Latina/o identities need to be understood at the interstices of both.

Scholars have debated the usefulness of the term "Latino" as a rubric that incorporates or fails to account for the heterogeneous experiences of U.S. Latinas/os. Because it is an umbrella term that erases our cultural specificities, or that mostly foregrounds the conflicts and segmentations among the various national groups—what has been called the "Latino Cultural Wars" (Kugel 2002)—the term itself has been the object of suspicion and debate within the field. Yet now it is becoming a site from and around which to discuss the implications of the demographic diversification of the Latina/o population in the United States. Let us go back to the circle of my Latina/o friends in Chicago in order to explore the complexities behind Latina/o identities.

A middle-class immigrant from Venezuela, Sarita came to the United States to study English originally in the late 1990s, but decided to stay in Chicago and brought her children over at the beginnings of the Hugo Chávez turmoils. Yet she also stayed because she fell in love with a Chilean man. Sarita and her children are undocumented, but their lives are informed by the middle-class values and aspirations that were part of her life in Venezuelan society. Their preoccupations range from being deported anyday to maintaining their social status through consumerism and social circles. José, a gay, Puerto Rican professor, has been in the United States since he was a graduate student, yet he is still very connected to Puerto Rican Island culture, to Spanish, and to Latin America. His long-term partner is an Anglo man who doesn't speak Spanish. They live in the suburbs and attend the Chicago opera and theater after work when they can. José grew up very poor on the Island, yet he is perceived as an Anglo because of his light skin color and blond hair. His gay identity, however, makes him vulnerable to homophobia and exclusion. Rosario, a Mexican woman in her fifties, a single mother of two young men, has not found full-time employment in years because she does not have a degree, yet she doesn't have enough money to pay for her tuition to complete her bachelor's degree in a continuing education program in the city. She is a citizen, but she cannot afford to pay her gas bills. She has no medical insurance, but she owns a small home in the south side of the city. Her car is always breaking down, and she is constantly struggling to make ends meet. Yet her cultural life is very rich. She has been an active participant of various Latino arts and theater organizations in the city for more than twenty years and she possesses a particular social capital in terms of her knowledge about the community. David, half Puerto Rican, half Mexican, was born in Chicago but raised in the suburbs by his Mexican mother, who wanted to escape life in the inner city after her divorce. Despite his suburban identity, he grew up poor, lacking any sort of luxury and having to work since he was a child. Like many native-born Latinas/os, he speaks English and feels uncomfortable speaking Spanish. Many of his acquaintances assume he is privileged and assimilated because of his suburban, Anglophone identity. Yet he is deeply connected to his biological father and his family, who live in a very poor area of the city. His identity integrates the suburbs and the inner city, for he has been a part of these two worlds, cultures, and families. He knows about gang violence, about inner city high schools, and about unemployment through the experiences of his half brothers. He also knows about middle-class lifestyles, an individualist work ethos, and Anglo families and neighbors. And I, a Puerto Rican *blanquita*, have lived in the United States for thirty years, been married to two working-class Chicanos, and have felt less and less connected to the Island as the years go by. A single mother of two Puerto Rican/Mexican daughters, and having lived in most regions of the United States, my own experience has connected me to both U.S. Puerto Rican and Chicano/Mexicano cultures. I have in-laws in El Paso, Texas, and sisters in Boston and New York. Chicago is now my home. I call my girls *niñas* (the Mexican term) instead of *nenas* (the Puerto Rican term), I spend more time with my Mexican mother-in-law than with my own mother, but I definitely love to dance salsa and merengue more than cumbias or nortenas. In my case, class, gender, and cultural identities have all been marked by my personal connections to the Mexican American community.

This small group of individuals represents a small slice of the heterogeneous identities and experiences that constitute today what we call Latino. First, the different experiences among economic immigrants, political refugees, exiles, and native-born historical and racial minorities structure Latino lives, yet they do not determine them. Indeed, the contradictions in the lives of Sarita, Rocio, José, David, and myself reveal that individuals' multiple and contradictory identities unfold differently and lead to divergent results in terms of material and social survival. Sarita's undocumented status has made it very difficult for her to purchase a home, while Rocio's citizenship has not significantly improved her living conditions. Yet this past summer Rocio was able to travel to Mexico with a school tour and Sarita and her daughter were not able to go. While David's suburban upbringing may be seen as the most privileged experience in the group, this has not shielded him from poverty nor from witnessing the challenges and social problems of the inner city. In turn, José and I have been in the United States as part of the brain drain that has significantly robbed the Island of the talents and resources of young professionals. Yet gender issues, more than salaries, have kept José and me from returning to the Island.

Despite the fact that Spanish has been repeatedly hailed as the common denominator among Latinas/os, the linguistic diversity within this sector continues to be hybrid, fluid, and politically contingent. That evening, José refused to speak in English to David, asserting the dominance of Spanish at the table. If David has been privileged socially and in educational institutions for his knowledge of English and for not having an accent, contrary to José's heavily accented English despite his many years in the United States, that evening David became a linguistic minority, silenced by the dominance of Spanish among the group, an experience of exclusion that he has faced multiple times. This moment of linguistic conflict represented the inverse of language politics in the United States, whereby Spanish is usually subordinated and racialized. In this case, José's Latin American subjectivity and linguistic power exerted dominance over a U.S.-born Latino.

Elements of socioeconomic status and class also become significant in accounting for the Latino experience. While most U.S. Latinas/os are working class or working poor, there is an emerging middle class and professional sector that has become an intermediary between institutions and those with less power and social capital. The case of Rocio is interesting in this regard. While she considers herself an upper-class venezolana, in the United States she has been struggling to maintain that lifestyle while earning much less than what she made in her country. Simultaneous to this shift in her own class experience, she has become an activist and advocate for immigrant and refugee rights. She has used her skills in networking, communications, media, and marketing to speak publicly for the undocumented. This differs from the more common phenomenon of middle-class Latin American immigrants being privileged over U.S. Latinas/os in the workplace, given their levels of education in their home countries and their native skills in Spanish. In Chicago, for instance, the Spanish-language media—television and newspapers—recruit professionals directly from Latin America rather than U.S. Latinas/os because of a perceived deficiency in the use of Spanish among the latter. It is not a coincidence that Rosario, despite her citizenship, has not found a decent, full-time job in the city. While Latin American professionals are displacing U.S. Latinas/os from particular jobs, some U.S. Latinas/os, like Sarita, are also using their skills and resources to advocate for the larger community.

The term "Latino" carries with it internal semantic tensions that reflect the multiple sites from which it has emerged. Most scholars and many community members have embraced the term because it has represented a more organic alternative to the government-imposed term "Hispanic," coined and used since the 1970s (Oboler 1995). Yet this acceptance has not precluded the recognition that the term itself homogenizes the diverse power locations among U.S. Latinas/os. As an umbrella term, it can be used strategically to indicate the oppositional location of Latinas/os versus, or outside of, dominant society. Likewise, it can be used to erase the specificities of the various national groups and historical experiences outlined above. Many second-generation Latinas/os use the term to identify themselves vis-à-vis Anglos (Flores-González 1999), yet they also use their national identity to identify themselves in relation to other Latino groups. It is also increasingly common for hybrid Latinas/os, that is, those who are descendants of two national groups, to use the label Latino in order not to erase either of their identities. Thus, the use of labels is contingent, fluid, and relational, used strategically and structurally depending on the context. I define myself as a Puerto Rican professor among other Latina/o colleagues, but I also define myself as a Latina cultural critic in the larger context of my university colleagues. The term "Latino" then does not necessarily displace the significance of the national identifiers, but is used to signal the multiple and relational selves of colonized subjects.

Many Latina/o scholars have argued against the use of the term "Latino" because the media has deployed it historically to homogenize and lump us all together as one undifferentiated mass. This media discourse has had egregious consequences for the communities involved. For instance, the literary market sells Latin American literature as part of their Latino market. This conflation has less to do with the mutual influences or literary continuities between these two canons than with the economic benefit of attracting additional readers and buyers. The Puerto Rican feminist writer Rosario Ferré acknowledged some years ago that she wrote her last two novels in English because she wanted to be part of the very visible group of Latina writers in the United States. This controversial posturing triggered not only an attack against her by the purists and linguistic nationalists on the Island, but also a debate about the more delicate and fragile issue of who can be identified as a Latina writer and who cannot. The experience of confronting racial, cultural, and linguistic marginalization and subordination in the United States as a result of the colonized status of our communities is a strong argument that distinguishes U.S. Latino writers from their Latin American counterparts. Yet, what about the literature written by the Cuban exiles during the 1960s and 1970s? What about the literature that is now being produced in Spanish by Latin American émigrés and recent immigrants? Do we consider these texts a part of the Latino canon? Do we read them as a displaced national literature or as the literature of an ethnic, historical minority? In the musical sphere, Shakira's relocation from being a Colombian rock singer to a U.S.-based Latina rock/pop singer has been achieved not only through marketing but also through her stage performances, musical arrangements, the interpellation of audiences, and use of English (Cepeda 2003). These are all questions that arise as we continue to witness the diversification of the identities and historical experiences of our writers, artists, and entertainment figures.

REDEFINING *LATINIDAD*

In Chicago, as in the other major Latino urban centers in the United States, communities from all Latin American countries live, work, dance, and interact throughout the cities that they are also transforming. Chicago is the third largest city in the United States and home to the second largest Mexican and Puerto Rican communities nationwide. It is also home to a growing Guatemalan sector that has become the third largest Latino group in this urban area. As of the 2000 Census, Latinas/os constitute 26 percent of Chicago's total population. Of that, Mexicans constitute 70.4 percent, Puerto

Ricans 15 percent, Guatemalans 1.8 percent, Ecuadorians 1.2 percent, and Cubans 1.1 percent. The fact that the Guatemalans and Ecuadorians have outnumbered the Cubans suggests that the traditional trinity of the three major historical minorities—Mexican American, Puerto Rican, and Cuban American—is shifting, creating a much more complex mosaic of Latin American national encounters. Indeed, recent Census figures show that Chicago ranks ninth in the metropolitan areas receiving large numbers of South American immigrants. Certainly, Peruvians have long made Chicago their home. In addition, the so-called new Latinas/os—Dominicans, Colombians, Ecuadorians, and other South and Central Americans—are all represented in the growing Latino demographics of the city.

As Juan Flores has stated, the demographic shifts since the 1990s have created urban spaces in which Latinas/os of various nationalities will interact with each other. Flores (1996) points to the increasing presence of Mexicans in New York City, a new sector that is growing as the numbers of Puerto Ricans, historically the predominant group, decrease or remain the same. This social mosaic leads to new forms of interaction, affinities, and power dynamics between and among Latinas/os from various national groups. It is interesting that media and journalism seem to zero in on the ensuing cultural conflicts and national tensions that have arisen from these new social spaces.

Yet we are also witnessing different forms of affiliations, solidarity, identifications, desire, and intermarriage among Latinas/os. This is not necessarily new, for Chicago and the Midwest have witnessed similar interactions between Puerto Ricans and Mexicans, particularly since the 1940s. Yet the growing numbers and the dimensions of this demographic revolution call for a recognition that the term "Latino" is a real thing, an emerging social and cultural experience and experiment, and not just a label or construction imposed from the outside. If in the past decades, paradigms of national identity served to understand and produce a sense of collectivity grounded in particular geocultural locations and regions—the Chicanos in the West and Southwest, the Puerto Ricans in New York and the Northeast, the Cuban Americans in Miami—nowadays national identities are still significant, but they are not the exclusive axis of reference from which to understand Latino lives. In fact, national identities are restructured and reorganized as a result of these increasingly hybrid spaces. New interlatino subjectivities are emerging and we need to examine them at various levels.

Angie Chabrám Dernersesian coined the term "domestic transnationalism" to refer to the multiple power dynamics that emerge as a result of interlatino interactions. First, there are myriad examples of mutual transculturations among different Latino nationals. From the impact of Afro-Caribbean music in Mexican culture (Carlos Santana's music), to the linguistic borrowings and influences, let's say, between Cubans and Nicaraguans in Miami, to the ways in which new Latino cuisine fuses Mexican ingredients with Caribbean ones, Latinas/os from various nationalities are creating new cultural objects and practices that are the result of two or more national influences. (The combined Puerto Rican and Mexican hanging flags for the car sold in Chicago is another evidence of these transculturations.) Secondly, there are outright cultural conflicts among Latinas/os, most of which stem from the ways in which we racialize each other. These negative constructions of the national other are usually fueled and informed by stereotypes and racializations that have been historically shared and internalized, but that also point out differences in behavior that may result from gender and racial subordination and from the larger forces of colonization. For instance, for some Mexican women, Puerto Rican women are "rencorosas" and aggressive; from the perspective of the latter, the Mexicanas seem too submissive and "sufridas" (Pérez 2003). There are also instances in which perceived differences of power inform the disidentification or the gesture toward differentiation from our national others. For instance, public figures in the Cuban American community have rejected any comparisons or analogies to Mexican economic immigrants. This is partly a way of protecting the privileges that the Cuban exile generation has held as political refugees escaping a communist regime. In their case there are also racial (white) and class identities (middle-class, professional sector) that need to be protected and reclaimed. For undocumented Latinas/os, Puerto Rican U.S. citizenship is seen as a privilege, while many Puerto Ricans consider it another reminder of their colonial and second-class status within the United States. At the same time, Puerto Ricans are continuously racialized by many other Latinas/os for their Caribbean Spanish, for their darker skin color, and for their high poverty rates. Many Latinas/os also refuse to be confused for a "Mexican," an attitude that reveals their fear of being racialized themselves as much as their internalization of that very same dominant discourse. Many of these disavowals and discourses of subordination, then, are rooted in larger structural forces rather than in individual prejudices.

The term "domestic transnationalism" can also refer to the hybrid Latino subjects who are the offspring of Latinas/os of two different national groups. These hybrid Latino subjects, who populate our classes at UIC, De Paul, and Northeastern in Chicago, negotiate their identities in ways that differ from the Anglo-Latino power dyad that has structured most of our understandings about Latinas/os in the United States. These younger Latinas/os may identify with each national culture in more relational ways and in more specific contexts, rather than in the linear ways in which we tend to think about national awareness or cultural reaffirmation. Mérida Rúa's (2001) research about the MexiRicans and PortoMex subjects in Chicago suggests that, in fact, hybrid Latinas/os make strategic decisions about national differentiation based on a variety of contextual, family, and social factors. Thus, their identity constructions tend to be more concentric, multiple, and diffused than what we are accustomed to. Rúa proposes the term "colando-ing" to refer to the negotiations that interlatino subjects make in specific social contexts, in family, neighborhood, or with friends. Colando can mean passing for one identity while erasing the other; choosing from a repertoire of transculturated elements; or making oneself part of a larger group, by either cutting in line or with the assistance of others.

Like interlatino racializations, these forms of passing for a national other are likewise informed structurally by the political positions and cultural presence of specific nationalities. For instance, factors such as the power and visibility of each group in relation to the others, or the mainstream acceptance of some identities over others, or the political rights and citizenship accorded to some, have an impact on the ways in which hybrid Latinas/os foreground one identity over another. For David, who is half Puerto Rican and half Mexican, it is easier to identify with the Mexican culture, partly because he was raised by his Mexican mother, but also because, according to him, he has been keenly aware of the fact that Mexico and Mexican history—iconized through its pyramids and the epic grandeur of its Aztec culture—have been much more visible in the U.S. imaginary than its Puerto Rican counterpart. This canonization of particular national groups reveals the uneven ways in which our specific histories have been integrated as part of the U.S. official knowledge. Given his suburban upbringing and his U.S. citizenship by birth, David has not had to take into account the racialization of Mexicans in the context of U.S. labor and immigration policy, nor the privilege of Puerto Rican citizenship. In general, the need to avoid racialization, to be perceived as an agent with social power or cultural capital, and to belong, definitely influence the forms of strategic essentialism that hybrid Latinas/os perform when choosing one identity over another. While these forms of passing are strategic and relational, hybrid Latinas/os can never totally avoid or erase the subordinated identities that they embody in each of their nationalities. Colao identities transcend the national/regional segmentation of our fields as well as of the identity paradigms that have traditionally informed our way of thinking. Because our fields of study have developed in such segmented ways and because cultural nationalism and Cuban exceptionalism have informed the boundaries of our research and thinking, this epistemological segmentation has prevented us from exploring these other very significant hybrid Latino sites, moments, and identities.

The history of interlatino relations in Chicago dates back at least to the 1940s when, as Elena Padilla (1947) documented, Puerto Rican newcomers were welcomed, housed, and offered social and economic support by the Mexican community. Given this social history, Puerto Rican/Mexican marriages, like marriages between Latinas/os of various nationalities, are quite common in this Midwest city. While the diversification and increasing internal hybridity of the Latino communities is now coming to the fore as a result of the great migration of the 1980s, the fact is that this hybridity is not altogether new, but rather increasing as a result of these demographic changes. Yet these sites of *Latinidad* do not necessarily imply a utopian, egalitarian dynamic, nor do they suggest altogether that power differentials are decreasing, but rather, that new power relations emerge from these encounters.

CONCLUSION

What are the implications of this increasing *Latinidad* for Latina/o studies as a field of study? Rather than reproducing the national and geographical segmentation that has structured the way we organize knowledge in teaching and research, Latina/o studies can become the space in which these diverse experiences, identities, and power dynamics can be accounted for in the construction of a new social imaginary that transcends the old paradigms and nationality-based conflicts. By studying and reflecting on interlatino dynamics through interdisciplinary approaches we can produce more nuanced knowledge that moves even beyond comparative studies. The demographic changes also call for the establishment of new programs in areas where Latinas/os are new communities in the making. For instance, the Southeast faces new challenges in terms of incorporating Latino communities in discussions about race, culture, language, and labor that have been historically informed by Anglo–Black relations. At the University of North Carolina, Chapel Hill, a new Latina/o studies minor has been initiated precisely to prepare students for this task. Likewise, approaches to *Latinidad* will enhance current discussions about internal diversity and power differentials within national groups. The increasing hybridity of younger Latina/o subjects who embody and constitute two national groups, or a Latino and other racial group, will inevitably force us to transform the existing identity paradigms that still inform our thinking. PortoMexes, Cubolivians, Mexistanis (Mexican and Pakistani) are but a few of the possible hybrid identities that populate our urban centers. Will a new Latino melting pot develop as a result of this internal *mestizaje*, or will we continue to use national identities as the dominant criterion for exclusion and inclusion in the community? Redefining *Latinidad* from this point of view, rather than rejecting it altogether, will yield meaningful knowledge for the future of both Latino and non-Latino sectors in the United States.

REFERENCES

Arias, Arturo. 2003. "Central American–Americans: Invisibility, Power and Representation in the US Latino World." *Latino Studies* 1: 168–87. London: Palgrave.

Cepeda, Maria Elena. 2003. "Shakira as the Idealized, Transnational Citizen: A Case Study of Colombianidad in Transition." *Latino Studies* 1: 211–32. London: Palgrave.

Chabrám Dernersesian, Angie. 1994. "Chicana! Rican? No, Chicana-Riqueña! Refashioning the Transnational Connection." Pp. 269–95 in D. T. Goldberg (ed.), *Multiculturalism: A Critical Reader*. Oxford: Blackwell.

Flores, Juan. 1996. "Pan-Latino/Trans-Latino: Puerto Ricans in the 'New Nueva York.'" *Centro: Journal of the Center for Puerto Rican Studies* 8 (1–2): 171–86.

Flores-González, Nilda. 1999. "The Racialization of Latinos: The Meaning of Latino Identity for the Second Generation." *Latino Studies Journal* 10 (3): 3–31.

Kugel, Seth. 2002. "The Latino Cultural Wars." *New York Times*, February 24, 7–8F.

Oboler, Suzanne. 1995. *Ethnic Labels, Latino Lives: Identity and the Politics of (Re)presentation in the United States*. Minneapolis: University of Minnesota Press.

Padilla, Elena. 1947. "Puerto Rican Immigrants in New York and Chicago: A Study in Comparative Assimilation." MA thesis, Anthropology, University of Chicago.

Pérez, Gina. 2003. "Puertorriqueñas rencorosas y mejicanas sufridas: Gendered Ethnic

Identity Formation in Chicago's Latino Communities." *Journal of Latin American Anthropology* 8 (2): 96–124

Rúa, Méroda. 2001. "Colao Subjectivities: PortoMex and MexiRican Perspectives on Language and Identity." *Centro: Journal of the Center for Puerto Rican Studies* 8: (2): 117–33.

3

CELIA'S SHOES

Frances Negrón-Muntaner

Shoes can tell us where a person has been and where she wants to go.

—ERIN MACKIE[1]

I held a pair of Cuban singer Celia Cruz's most famous shoes long enough to marvel at the seven-inch razor-thin platform that had lifted her up in the air for decades. I had barely touched the shoes when I felt compelled to put them down as fast as possible, to not completely erase the awe of the object, the fact that they belonged to a queen. Hand-carved by Mexican artisan Miguel Nieto, known as *el zapatero de los sueños* (the shoemaker of dreams),[2] the one-of-a-kind shoes felt heavy, as if in their long stage life they had carried not only the memories of salsa music's most important female star but also of Cubanness itself.

Since 1997, Celia's shoes have been part of the permanent collection of the Smithsonian National Museum of American History in Washington, DC. The shoes found their way there at the initiative of Marvette Pérez, the Smithsonian's Latino history and culture curator. Early on, Pérez became interested in acquiring Caribbean music artifacts for the museum, which, despite having a rich collection of objects belonging to African-American music greats, such as the Supremes and Ella Fitzgerald, had few Latino items. While at the Smithsonian, Celia's shoes have been exhibited four times to large and appreciative audiences. To find her shoes off season, however, I had to be led through the Smithsonian's back rooms by Marvette's hand, a hesitant if generous Virgil, who could not help but to continuously ask, "Why do you want to see Celia's shoes?"

The year that I made the journey into the singer's displaced closet, in 1998, I was not entirely sure of the answer. But it came to me soon enough. Shortly after returning home, I mentioned my impulsive visit to a distinguished Cuban who had been a diplomat under Fidel Castro's government and still considers himself a socialist. To my surprise, the former ambassador held only the deepest contempt for what he called the Smithsonian's "pedestrian" taste. Insisting that the museum's exhibition of Celia's finery was a way of humiliating Cuban exiles in the United States, he asked, "Couldn't the Smithsonian choose something more *elevated* to represent the Cuban people? . . . A poem by patriot José Martí? A portrait of Father Varela, the nineteenth century priest called the 'first Cuban'? A uniform worn by the pro-independence general Antonio Maceo?"

Although depending on how you look at it, the difference between Maceo's pants and Celia's shoes might be only a matter of accessories, the Cuban diplomat did see one thing straight. In displaying Celia's shoes, the Smithsonian was choosing to represent Cuban exiles through the lowliest of cultural and corporeal signs as imagined by elite culture, whether in the Caribbean or on terra firma. For how much "lower" can one possibly go, socially speaking, than under the feet of an old, salsa dancing, Afro-Cuban woman?

Seen from below, however, Celia's shoes are so much more than footwear. They bear the mark of endless negotiations with the trappings of upward mobility, *Latinidad*, the eternal feminine and the body's inevitable decline over time. Furthermore, that some of us may be inexplicably drawn and others passionately repulsed by Celia's shoes implies that these are part of a larger signifying web, one which, to paraphrase psychoanalyst Jacques Lacan, "catches" spectators in their desire to be seen and identified in a specific fashion. This is why, with (if not entirely in) Celia's shoes it is possible to walk through her career as a Cuban female singer in the nearly all Puerto Rican male club of salsa, and thread the ways that shoes told stories of hardship and triumph differently enjoyed—and sometimes disowned—by Latinos as part of their public "ethnic" body in the United States.

OYE COMO VA (HEY, HOW GOES IT)

Born Úrsula Hilaria Celia Caridad Cruz Alfonso on October 21, 1924, the singer began her unlikely rise to stardom in Santos Suárez, one of Havana's poorest neighborhoods. Although Celia's class origins prompted official biographer Ana Cristina Reymundo to suggest that "nothing in her background gave any indication of the heights she would reach,"[3] a sense that this girl had a special gift became evident early on. According to Cruz lore, reproduced in countless published accounts in the popular press, young Celia began to sing to put her siblings to bed, attracting the attention of her neighbors and cousins, one of whom registered her to participate in an amateur singing contest called *La hora del té* (*The Tea Hour*). Already a university student, the twenty-three-year-old Celia won the competition by singing the tango "Nostalgia," a prophetic choice in light of her eventual and permanent exile from Cuba.

Before considering a career in music, Celia studied to be a schoolteacher, a relatively low-paid profession that nevertheless connoted a certain level of respect for blacks in Cuba, who had historically been excluded from educational opportunity. But it was not meant to be. By 1951, and only four years after her debut on the radio, Celia had become the lead singer for La Sonora Matancera, Cuba's most popular orchestra. Even if fans initially rejected Celia because she was virtually unknown and had replaced the wildly popular Puerto Rican singer Myrta Silva, she quickly consolidated her own following, eventually earning the first in a succession of cultural titles: *la guarachera de Cuba*.

After more than a decade of touring and recording with La Sonora, Celia responded dramatically to the 1959 Cuban revolution and its swift restructuring of the entertainment industry. She first moved to Mexico and then settled permanently outside New York City. This turn of events was to have contradictory consequences. On the one hand, Celia experienced exile as a great loss: she would never see her parents or set foot in Havana again. On the other hand, exile provided the conditions for her to ascend from the nationally bound musical identity as *la guarachera de Cuba* to a pan-Latino and global one as the Queen of Salsa. While Celia seems to have rationalized this loss of identity by arguing that salsa was but a variation of the Cuban *son* (a long and exhausted debate among musicians and scholars), she had little trouble incorporating the new accents that came to define "Latin" music over the next forty-three years. True to form, the last major hit of her career, "La negra tiene tumbao," combined elements of salsa, reggae, and hip-hop.

In retrospect, Celia's legendary ability to fuse a wide range of sounds undoubtedly contributed to her longevity as a star. Yet, in an era where looks and not vocal ability tend to sell records, Celia had to also creatively *resolver*, that is, deal with a small problem to ensure long-term success as a salsa diva: that of not "looking good" as a performer.

At the height of her global fame, for instance, Celia was not beautiful in a conventional sense, slim, or young. She was also hailed as a "nice" person in a context in which gossip sells newspapers and a racy personal life defines iconicity. "The collective question," declared television producer Cristina Saralegui after she pitched Celia's story to Hollywood studios, was: "How do you write a compelling screenplay about somebody whose life had no apparent Tina Turner tragedy, no *Behind the Music* crash and burn, no tabloid-worthy scandal?"[4] What Hollywood executives may have missed, however, was precisely what her fans saw in her, and, I would argue, was the open secret of the *salsera*'s long-term success. For whatever Celia may have lacked in typical celebrity ways, she made up for by other means, through what many came to refer to as the "unique and unmistakable Celia Cruz look."[5]

Different from other Latina singers, Celia's most recognized performative excess was not how she moved her body—the queen was at times as regal as her title—but how she fashioned it. From the start of her career, Celia showed a great interest in style, and as a starving young singer in Havana, admittedly "spent all her money on clothes."[6] Yet it was in exile, living in a racially polarized country where Latinos remain expendable, that Celia became as famous for her distinctive voice as for her shoes, wigs, and gowns. In the words of music critic Ramiro Burr, Celia wore lavish dresses made up of "feathers, spangles, lace, and yards upon yards of multi-colored fabrics."[7] Topping the dresses, were often outrageously designed wigs, complemented by hands "featuring long painted nails and expensive jewelry" that, according to one observer, made it "quite obvious that she's never had to do the dishes."[8]

But although wigs, gowns, and nail polish constitute an important part of the singer's public anatomy, shoes were considered "Celia's signature"[9] and bear the greatest weight in narrating her public persona. Eveningwear designer Julian Asion was perhaps the most succinct when he wrote, "On top of these heels, you have this voluptuous body moving around, dancing around. Those heels are her."[10] The question that remains is why did this load fall so heavily on Celia's shoes and to what effect?

ESA NEGRITA QUE VA CAMINANDO (THAT BLACK GIRL WALKING BY)

As has been noted by journalists and other observers, Celia had a formidable collection of shoes. The collection included thousands of pairs kept at home and in New Jersey warehouses that were worn "for photo shoots and to perform on stage or on the red carpet."[11] Significantly, despite the collection's size, the vast majority of these shoes were of only one style: high heels, a type of footwear originally linked to the aristocracy since it was considered to be "highly impractical for women who had to perform menial labor."[12] Although Celia may or may not have been aware of this historical detail, the fact that her shoes were often made of glittery, simulated diamond or ruby materials references the style's origins. It also seeks to confirm her status as a queen—*la reina de la salsa*—at the same level with, if not a cut above, that other voracious collector of high-heeled shoes, the French queen Marie-Antoinette.[13]

Celia's signature shoes, however, went beyond being elaborately decorated high heels. They were *very* high heels, some standing as high as nine inches off the ground. Perhaps because shoes worn by the poor tend to be ill fitting due to coarse material and design,[14] Celia's shoes were handmade, too costly to mass produce and fitted exclusively for her. These attributes not only point to affluence and luxury, but also uniqueness and difference, a way to, in the words of journalist Colin McDowell, "signal clearly who and what their wearer is and why he is different from (and superior to) the rest of mankind."[15] Even further, Celia's footwear seemed to defy gravity itself, as they did not rest on a conventional heel but on the thinnest of soles. By appearing physically unfeasible, Celia's trademark shoes offer the illusion of walking on air, a magical attribute that again elevates the queen above mere mortals.[16]

Part of the explanation therefore rests on the ways that the shoes themselves connoted wealth, luxury, and enchantment. Given the singer's "undistinguished" class origins and membership in a racial and ethnic group rarely afforded the dignity of individuality, Celia's shoes insisted on her uniqueness as a person and a performer—a one of a kind brand. Moreover, if as theorist Maureen Turim has written, feet are the "most abject part of the body . . . the body part in direct contact with the dirt and assigned the role of support,"[17] Celia's heels literally raised her from the soil—away from her lowly social origins—onto a stage where reality appears to be free and self-fashioned. In this regard, Celia's "wildly stylish"[18] shoes "dressed up" her struggle of upward mobility while insisting that a black woman born in poverty on a small Caribbean island can reach the heights of a transnational star.[19]

Accordingly, in her hagiographic story of upward mobility, Celia's social location is almost always narrated in relation to shoes. For instance, Celia was one of thirteen children "as shoeless as her" who managed to finish her education by going to school with "torn shoes."[20] This state of poverty only began to change when as a teenager "Celia got her first pair of quality shoes singing for a tourist on the street."[21] Toward the end of Celia's career, it was said more than once that no one, including her handpicked successor La India, could possibly fill her shoes.[22] And even when her high place in popular music history was completely assured, Cuban journalist Norma Niurka wrote that, after finally recording an album with a major label in 2000, Celia felt as "a girl with new shoes."[23]

Although on various occasions Celia disputed the anecdote that she sang to tourists for shoes, saying, "I was very poor but never a beggar,"[24] this tale with *ribetes de leyenda*[25] (streaks of legend) stands as her founding myth. "Not only had my singing made them happy," Celia recalls in her autobiography, "but those white patent-leather shoes, which meant so much to me, initiated my lifelong fascination with fashion."[26] Shoes, then, refer to and incorporate what literary scholar Erin Mackie has called an "originary event," one that "fixes together previously disparate, heterogeneous elements into a novel identity,"[27] in this case, that of an Afro-Cuban female star. A step further, they made Celia not simply a singer of humble origins who became famous, but a "Black Cinderella," a girl who, like in a fairy tale, went from a "poor neighborhood of Havana to a queen's burial in New York."[28]

DE CUBA VENGO (I COME FROM CUBA)

The idea that shoes denote social status is evident across many cultural contexts, including the United States and Latin America. In this regard, Celia's shoe fetishism—that is, her tendency to invest shoes with non-inherent meanings—was widely shared with her Caribbean and Latino peers. Since the (sometimes shoeless) native peoples encountered the (often well heeled) Europeans, shoes have become a significant social concern for everyone who lives in the Americas. As Turim reminds us, "The opposition of shoes to bare feet is central . . . to significations of wealth, public space, and civilization itself."[29]

Puerto Rican history, for example, is full of references to shoes as a means to narrate national life. The Spanish priest and historian Iñigo Abad y Lasierra described the eighteenth-century *criollos* or "native-born" as not only promiscuous and lazy, but also prone to going barefoot.[30] Over a century later, U.S. President McKinley requested an 1899 report on the state of Puerto Rico that measured the island's poverty in part by the size of its shoeless population: "child labor was common practice, unemployment was widespread, and out of a population of nearly a million people some seven hundred thousand were without shoes."[31] Not surprisingly, when after the Second World War the Puerto Rican and U.S. elites embarked on a modernization effort to curb extreme poverty on the island, the project was known in English as "Operation Bootstrap." And this is probably why, toward the end of the 1980s, writer Luis Rafael Sánchez concluded that since Bootstrap could only deliver on higher levels of consumption by setting off mass migration and excessive debt, Puerto Ricans still belonged to *la América descalza* (barefoot America) of the south and not the wealthy North America exemplified by the United States.[32]

Among Cubans, shoes are also tied to national narratives, and perhaps with a tighter bow. In his memoir from the independence war of 1868, *A pie y descalzo, de Trinidad a Cuba, 1870–1871 (Recuerdos de campaña),*[33] Ramón Roa measures the *mambises'* enthusiasm for the war in terms of their willingness to fight without shoes, and urgently defines his own situation—shoeless and horseless, *a pie y descalzo*—as the most abject and dehumanizing of all social conditions.[34] In Roa's words, "[with] my feet cracked and swollen due to the stones and bushes . . . I began for the first time in life to suffer the moral horrors that can only be suffered when one sees oneself, above all, barefoot and hatless, something like abandoned by mankind and at the enemy's mercy."[35]

Even though writer and pro-independence advocate José Martí harshly criticized Roa's book in his speech "Los pinos nuevos" because it could discourage Cubans from embracing the cause, several of his texts further elaborated on the relationship between shoes, class, and national struggle. In his 1891 classic essay "Our America," Martí represents U.S. imperial power as "giants in seven-leagued boots,"[36] and authentic Latin Americans as those who wear not "epaulets and professor's gowns" but "hemp sandals and headbands."[37] Arguably, Martí uses shoes as a trope to maximum effect in his broadly anthologized modernist poem "Los zapaticos de rosa" ("The Little Pink Shoes"), in which a well-off girl offers her pink shoes to another who is ill and poor in order to temper the shame of class privilege.[38]

Far from ending with the nineteenth century's independence struggles, the allusion to shoes in Cuban cultural production continued well into the twentieth century and without ideological distinctions. While pro-revolutionary writer Lourdes Casal criticized those who left Cuba during the Mariel exodus and ridiculed Western "democratic normalcy" as an "office full of shoe boxes,"[39] the dissident writer and *marielito* Reinaldo Arenas, who once called Casal's journal *Areíto* "the official organ of the Cuban state police in New York," launched his own career with a short story titled "Los zapatos vacíos" (The Empty Shoes). Here, Arenas alludes to a peasant boy's pair of torn shoes left unfilled on Three Kings' Day, to suggest that despite living in great poverty, the child had access to something grander than mere presents: the infinite wealth of nature's bounty.[40]

In the United States, high heels have also been linked to Latina feminine identity. As literary critic Tace Hedrick has observed, "the connection of heels with the exotic beauty of certain Latin American and Hispanic American women has been part of the United States' collective imaginary for decades."[41] For Cuban-American women of the post-war period, high heels were explicitly associated with ethnic difference, autonomous sexuality, and validation of a different body type presumed to be below "average" height, meaning "inferior" to (white) Americans. According to Cuban-American columnist Liz Balmaseda, during the 1970s "it was the heels that distinguished the Latinas from the Americanitas. We were the chicks in the seven-inch, custom-designed platforms, the ones unconcerned by details such as dwarfing our dates."[42]

Since Celia would never have been confused with the white girls Balmaseda calls "Americanitas," her fashion choices were more linked to a desire to be seen as a Latina rather than as an "American" black woman, a common response for Afro-Caribbean people living in the United States who reject the country's rigid racial binary and overt exclusion of blacks as full citizens. Yet, while stepping up her *Latinidad* did not imply a denial of her black identifications, evident in her recordings of African diaspora rhythms and her display of pan-African style, Celia's "Latin thing" tended to rule over her "black power" in public discourse. Her success in using style as a means to assert Cubanness and *Latinidad* above other identities is evident when designer Julian Asion makes Celia's shoes the litmus test of Latino identity. Referring to a pair of Celia's signature shoes, Asion states: "If you don't know whose shoes these are, you're not Latino."[43]

Celia's shoe fetish was therefore not just a personal choice or private affectation. If, for Celia, shoes stand in for her achievements as a black working-class woman, a Cuban exile, and a Latina icon, for her fans, many of whom were female, black, Latino, poor, and/or queer, they offered the possibility of reaching a similar stature and of unsettling the social hierarchies that keep them down. This partly explains why, despite the extravagance inherent in Celia's shoes and the affluence implicit in acquiring a sizable collection, fans did not resent these displays of wealth. On the contrary, Celia's overt love for shoes struck a chord with many fans (including those in the mainstream media), who saw in the popular singer a person who, despite adversity, "never allowed her dreams of liberty and dignity to be stepped on."[44] The importance of Celia's shoes to telling her story makes evident that, in contrast to the common definition of fetishism as an individual sexual perversion, a fetish is, as psychoanalyst Robert J. Stoller once put it, "a story masquerading as an object."[45]

CABALLERO Y DAMA (GENTLEMAN AND LADY)

Celia's buying into the stereotype of the high- (and well-) heeled Latina helped her to maintain ethnic and national specificity, and accentuate a different way to be a black star, not to be confused with African-American divas. But to the extent that in Western culture shoe styles are gender coded, and high heels in particular signify "universal" femaleness and sexuality,[46] Celia's love of shoes is also about standing up for femininity itself. In fact, Celia pointed to shoe style as a fundamental marker for gender differentiation, irrespective of ethnicity and race. In responding to her husband, Pedro Knight, on the subject of stars who wear sneakers along with tuxedos, Celia vehemently argued, "[T]hey're men, Pedro . . . Women can't do that."[47]

At the same time, while high heels made Celia a woman, she did not want to be just any kind of woman. She wished to be seen as a Cuban, Latina, and Afro-Caribbean woman, but also a *mujer decente*, a decent woman. Celia, for instance, rarely failed to tell interviewers about the contrast between her and the singer she replaced at La Sonora Matancera, the Puerto Rican Myrta Silva, who was known for projecting a sexually unconventional and mischievous public persona captured in nicknames such as *la gorda de oro* (the golden fat lady) and *la vedette que arrolla* (the vedette that will run you over).[48] In Celia's words, "[Silva] would come out in *Bohemia* magazine wrapped in just a towel. I was very serious."[49]

Celia's need to be perceived seriously and as a serious woman reached panic levels in 1949. During an engagement in Venezuela, one of the women dancing in the troupe that accompanied Celia, Las Mulatas del Fuego, became ill. On a whim, Celia offered to replace the fallen dancer on the show. Although Celia dressed in the customary *mulatas* bikini and made it to the edge of the curtain, she could not go forward: "I froze: I couldn't go on. I just couldn't . . . I felt naked. There were so many people out there looking at us."[50]

In Celia's narrative, the resistance to expose herself in this way was explicitly linked with the shame of being looked upon as an "easy" woman by her father, who viewed her entry into show business as tantamount to declaring that she was a prostitute. "When he saw the path that I was on as an entertainer," recalled Celia, "he feared that I would disregard my teaching aspirations and fall prey to the *mujeres de la vida* (prostitute) culture . . . My father was ashamed of me and he wouldn't even tell anyone I even existed. Fortunately, all of that changed one day."[51] The fear of being taken for a *mujer de la vida* may also explain Celia's confessed inability to dance or move her body while she lived in Cuba. At times, Celia's physical stiffness was so pronounced that her Aunt Ana repeatedly advised her to loosen up and "shake a little": "You have to understand that you have to let the public feel everything you're carrying inside through your entire body. Not just your voice."[52]

Whereas Celia eventually loosened up as she became increasingly successful, a second, and more pervasive, bodily shame came to constitute her public persona: the shame of being "ugly." In fact, "ugliness" appears in Celia's narrative of self as the one major liability that she had to deal with, rather than those explicitly associated with race, ethnicity, sexuality, or gender. For example, when things got rocky early on at La Sonora, Celia stated that she compensated by hard work and good values: "God may have not given me a pretty face, but He gave me many gifts."[53] Celia further claims that, during her early years, she was unable to hire an agent because, "I was ugly. Yes,

I did have a pretty voice, but I didn't have the look many agents wanted to represent."[54] In a succinct declaration, Celia described herself as "fea de cara pero bella de alma"[55] (having an ugly face but beautiful soul) underscoring the height of spirituality over the lowliness of her body.

In this regard, Celia's shoes carried the burden of a shamed femininity, one that dare not be revealed in the flesh. Accordingly, Celia fashioned her body away from "natural" conceptions of beauty. Apart from her spectacular shoes, most of her wigs were dyed with colours not found in nature. Even though Celia argued that wigs were good because they were practical and easy to use since the natural hair did not have to be worked on,[56] the kind of hairstyle (straight), color (blue, red), and other features of most of her wigs underscore that Celia's general aesthetic was against regimes of representation that signified beauty as part of a woman's "nature." And while it is true that Celia experimented with a spectacular "Afro" style in the 1980s, not only was this look equally unnatural, but her own hair was rarely seen and when it was, it was in the chemically "relaxed" style. Not surprisingly, the wig she donated to the Smithsonian was blonde, and so was the one that she was buried in.[57]

That Celia bore masks, however, did not mean that she did not want to be seen. On the contrary, Celia wanted the audience to both listen and take note of her body, particularly as she aged. "If I can't call attention on my own," Celia asserted, "I will do so through my clothes."[58] In this sense, it is important to underscore that Celia did not hide but rather covered up to avoid being perceived in ways that black women are assumed to signify available and "hot" sexuality. This move protected Celia against two discriminating looks, one that consumed her as a vulnerable object—female and dark—as well as one that may not have found her to embody black "beauty" in acceptable terms.

To cover up was then more than a simple matter of accessories. It was also a style of struggle, deployed by a woman who was aware of the forces that aimed to limit her possibilities as an "unattractive" black female singer. This may be why Celia threw a big mantle over all details about her life. She always insisted, for example, that she had an idyllic sentimental life with her husband and manager, Pedro Knight, and avoided the spectre of scandal at all costs. She linked her body's hard fought ability to dance not as a sign of her sensuality, but as part of the "joy of singing," an offering and a plea not to be excluded from cultural exchange because of race, class, sexuality, or gender. As Celia observed on more than one occasion, "Music is the only gift that God has given me. Unless he takes it away from me, I will continue to share that gift."[59] With great skill, Celia protected this gift—and her hard won social privilege—by always appearing as a "black Latin woman, who achieved greatness through a lot of hardships that she always kept to herself."[60]

Celia's strategy of looking good of course had a price: accepting the stereotype of the maternal and asexual black woman. She has been called charming, generous, affectionate, motherly, and gracious by many musicians, writers, and television personalities, but in very rare instances sexy or attractive.[61] According to novelist Oscar Hijuelos, "Celia was the kind of gracious lady that we would love to have for an aunt, a fairy godmother whose tender-heartedness works a healing magic on even the most troubled souls."[62] Celia was also frequently represented as a guardian angel, not unlike the matronly black nannies and cooks that populate canonical hemispheric American fiction, characters that exhibit, in novelist Toni Morrison's words, great "benevolence, harmless and servile guardianship and endless love."[63]

Yet, it was the fusion of *seriedad* (seriousness) and extravagance that allowed Celia to be seen both as a spectacle worth looking at and as a decent woman, impossible to confuse with the *mujeres de la vida* her father worried about.[64] In this way, Celia was able to become an icon without engaging in the sexual ambiguities of her handpicked successor, La India, nor proclaiming the erotic disconformity performed by her relative contemporary, the Queen of Soul, Guadalupe Victoria Yolí Raymond, also known as "La Lupe," who took off her shoes and threw them at the audience.[65] If Celia was going to sing salsa—that is, black music—and was not deemed beautiful enough to be appreciated by the eyes of strangers, her unique style allowed her to project an illusion of abundance, dignity, talent, Cubanness, beauty, femininity, and, toward the end of her life, eternal youth.

MI VIDA ES CANTAR (SINGING IS MY LIFE)

There is, however, a second important reason why Celia required a style that accentuated her femininity: the kingdom of salsa—like the nation—is almost universally associated with men and male ideologies of gender.[66] Salsa's virility is reiterated in multiple ways, including the fact that, as scholar Wilson Valentín-Escobar has commented, top *salseros* are often baptized with names calling attention to their particular kind of masculinity. In this canon, the mellow Gilberto Santa Rosa is "el caballero de la salsa" (meaning "salsa's gentleman") and the *muy macho* Tito Rojas is "el gallo de la salsa" (meaning "salsa's cock"). Moreover, the salsa that Celia was part of was considered *salsa dura* (hard) versus more recent incarnations such as the *salsa sensual* or *monga* (limp), that is characterized by the bolero's "feminine" discourse of courtly love[67] and a softer sound that "contain[s] little or no brass and percussive sounds and/or improvisational swing."[68] Within this context, any woman that attempted to crown herself as the queen of salsa had to artistically situate herself on the genre's hard side without losing her feminine look. And this is precisely what Celia did.

From a musical point of view, Celia always succeeded in being perceived by critics, audience members, and peers alike in the best of terms, that is, in masculine terms. For instance, Celia is frequently represented as a woman who "entered" the salsa world and "had the gallantry of incurring in this genre."[69] In addition, Celia's voice itself was repeatedly described with adjectives that underscore its masculinity: "tough," "raspy,"[70] "powerful contralto,"[71] and projecting "a mature *marimacho* punch."[72] Her impressive talent to *sonear*, an improvisational skill that is assumed to separate not only the men from the women but the boys from the men, also earned her the admiration of other singers. As *salsero* Cheo Feliciano famously observed, Celia was different from other female singers because, unlike most women who were confined to singing boleros and ballads—"girl stuff"—she "understood and assimilated the masculine way of singing and feminized it . . . that is why there will be never be any other woman who can wear her shoes and do what she did."[73]

At the same time that Celia was widely praised for her masculine "way" of singing salsa, her male peers also valued her feminine "discretion" in personal matters. In Feliciano's terms: "[s]ince she was the only woman in the group, she was always very discreet touring. You know . . . men things, she never said a word."[74] Equally important, Celia never crossed the line that distinguished singers from true musicians. She followed the "feminine" tradition of interpreter, and did not participate in arranging, producing, or distributing her music. A clear example of the ways that musicianship is gendered in salsa can be appreciated in the filmed 1989 Fania concert in Zaire, available on DVD and currently marketed as *Celia Cruz and the Fania Allstars in Africa.*[75] Whereas Celia opened the concert, sang, and was arguably the most compelling performer to the audience, she was clearly different than the rest of the participants. In contrast to every other musical or vocal performer on stage—which included Santana, Ray Barreto, Hector Lavoe, Johnny Pacheco, and Roberto Roena—that Celia was literally not a boy in the band underscored the fact that the business of salsa essentially remained a Latin and male thing.

The importance of successfully managing gender codes for women aspiring to stardom in Caribbean music can be confirmed by comparing Celia to other major female stars. The Puerto Rican Ivy Queen, otherwise known as "the queen of reggaeton,"[76] has also been able to stay on top of a male-dominated musical genre. In contrast to Celia, Ivy Queen initially became famous for a hard masculine look of oversized jackets, caps, and overalls. But once reggaeton went global, she polished her hard gender edges with a formula similar to that of the Cuban queen. Known for her "raspy vocals"[77] that according to journalist Gavin Mueller sound "less feminine than a lot of male reggaeton MCs,"[78] Ivy Queen reminded fans that she was a real woman through a "flaming style" that includes high heels, long hair, nails up to four inches long, platinum accessories, and plastic surgery to enhance bust size. Furthermore, she insisted that "in contrast to other divas she does not come to sell her *nalgas* [buttocks] but her lyrics."

Ivy Queen's and Celia's successful incorporation into their respective genres contrasts to other female stars in Latin music. Despite her importance, La Lupe continues to be ignored in the salsa canon due to her excessive "feminine" performance style—desiring, hysterical, impossible to contain—even if, as Frances R. Aparicio argues, she also "gave voice to the urban, warlike, and male-gendered modulations of salsa."[79] Similarly, La India's voice is often described in gendered terms as having an "androgynous style rather than a soft, melodious tone,"[80] and her ambiguous sexuality has made many see her as not a lady in the midst of a male world but as "the industry's Tomboy, who likes to play with the big boys and knows how to hold the pants better than they ever will."[81] Although La India's women-centred lyrics and self-fashioning have won her hardcore fans among women and gays, who claim her as the "Princess of Salsa and underground dance music,"[82] the fact that she has been rumoured to be a lesbian—even if her publicists counter that she is married and is the mother of two children—marginalizes her in relation to the salsa family. The difference then lies in what kind of masculinity is invoked and to what ends. While La India's imagined lesbianism and La Lupe's feminine irreverence make some uncomfortable, Celia's masculine vocal range and feminine sensibility constituted the perfectly gendered arrangement for salsa success.

In other words, given the likely dire consequences of a style misstep, Celia's hyper feminine costuming can also be understood as a means to both "hide anxieties about being perceived as masculine"[83] and insist on her image as a "real" (decent) woman. In this sense, it is revealing that although in some classic studies about Latin music such as *The Latin Tinge* by John Storm Roberts and *Salsa, sabor y control* by Ángel Quintero Rivera she is largely neglected, when Celia is addressed at length, the excessive style of her star persona takes precedence over her male relationships. Perhaps because she was aware that style was an important strategy to hold her place, Celia encouraged female impersonators and drag queens to "perform" and never forget her. In doing so, Celia seemed to know that her immortality—a critical concern for any queen—came from being constantly remembered as a public woman, bound by the "feminine" discourse of fashion while singing "like a man."

EPILOGUE: *YO VIVIRÉ* (I WILL SURVIVE)

Even if unthinkable to many salsa fans, *la reina de la salsa* passed away at her home in Fort Lee, New Jersey, on 16 July 2003 after a relatively short battle with brain cancer. News that Celia had died travelled fast throughout Latino communities in the United States. In Miami, the capital of Cuban exiles and the home of over a million Latinos, emails, phone calls, and street chatter celebrated the singer as a dignified representative of Latino America. For several months before her death, as she struggled with illness yet continued to release hit songs, one could spot scribbled messages on cardboard on the front entrances of *cafetines* and other modest gathering places. One in front of the Latin American Restaurant in Coral Gables said: "Celia te queremos" ("Celia, we love you").

But while many fans cherished her, Celia's popularity among Latinos, including Cubans, was far from universal. If the donation of her shoes to the Smithsonian had provoked a rumble of discontent from those who felt that the shoes did not adequately represent Cuban culture, perhaps no other event of her public life brought to light so many internal racial and national tensions among Cuban exiles as her funeral.

Envisioning her funeral as a grand finale, Celia herself desired nothing short of making a spectacle of her dead self. "Laid out in a platinum-blonde wig, a sequined gown and flashy jewelry, her nails painted white, her lips hot pink," Celia had requested public viewings in Miami and New York.[84] In her own words, "I want a wake and a funeral home where a lot of cars can park and everybody attends."[85] And they did—over half a million people stood in interminable lines to get a last glimpse. But, as is often the case, the wake revealed as much—if not more—about the mourners than the departed. If New York was to be the final resting place in lieu of Cuba, Miami was the showcase, the surface upon which Cubans contemplated the state of their transnational selves.

Respecting her wishes as communicated to her family and circle of influential friends, Celia occupied the signs of Cuban exile politics as well as those of the New York elite. Her viewing was held in Torre de la Libertad, a processing centre in Miami for Cuban exiles during the 1960s. In New York, the city closed Fifth Avenue so she could be carried along before her mass at St. Patrick's Cathedral. Then she was flown to Frank E. Campbell's funeral home, where viewings for both Jacqueline Kennedy and Judy Garland were held, although according to "funeral directors who handled the historic Judy Garland wake in 1969 . . . it could not compare to Celia's."[86] She was buried at Woodlawn Cemetery; her mausoleum rests between the tombs of music legends Miles Davis and Duke Ellington.

Yet, if in Miami and New York Celia's funeral was televised by the Spanish language media and her life heralded as a symbol of Latino achievement in the United States, another story was unfolding on the pages of Miami's newspapers. Scores of angry letters to the editor indicated that the bitterness that I had originally encountered with the Cuban diplomat was neither idiosyncratic nor isolated. In the words of Efraín Hernández, a reader of *Street*, a Miami cultural weekly, Celia

> did nothing useful in this society except jiggle around on stage and scream. She is an embarrassment to all Cubans who are trying not to be the laughing stock of the American community . . . Did you ever take the time to listen to her talk? She was dumber than two boxes of rocks, and she represents the Cuban people? No way! We have many successful Cuban doctors, educators, politicians, businessmen . . . Thanks to Celia Cruz, every person in the modern world thinks Cubans are nothing but Salsa dancing, banana eating idiots . . . Let's move on.[87]

At this moment, after death, it became clear that if Celia played it safe as a "good" black, a "good" wife, and a "good" exile, she had her reasons. For Efraín was not alone.

In the letters section of Miami's main cultural weekly, the *Miami New Times*, mail poured in in response to an article by Celeste Fraser Delgado in which the journalist underscored how race played a role in Celia's life and death. During the first week, two letter-writers expressed offense at Delgado's "foolishness": "What an idiot Celeste Fraser Delgado is . . . as a Cuban woman I was quite offended by her constant mention of Celia Cruz being black. First and foremost, Celia was Cuban."[88] But the real fireworks went off a week later. In the 14–20 August edition, five letters were printed. Of these, three found the suppression of a discussion on race and racism to be the insulting part. "What I find offensive," wrote Maggie Urrely, "is to hear cries of racism, and once backs are turned, hearing racist remarks blurted out."[89] And from Doris Fernández: "I know from first-hand experience that white Cubans are just as bigoted as their American counterparts, so they can try that rhetoric on other Cubans because we Americans know better."[90]

The crudeness of the racism of some exiles seemed to contrast with Celia's standing with the white Cuban elite. In writing about the virtues of the past versus a mediocre present, historian Luis Aguilar León, for instance, commented that Celia herself was a symbol of better times, specifically times of "mulatta laughter," "the narrow streets of Havana," "the smell of coffee." In sum: "Celia Cruz is living Cuba, present, flaming, seminal and eternal," a performer capable of offering "class, hierarchy, elegance."[91] Significantly, this type of assessment was not limited to those Cubans of Celia's own generation. For Richard Pérez-Feria, the "ñ generation" editor of *People en Español*, "Celia Cruz . . . always made herself felt in my home. Not so much her music, to be honest, but her spirit, her energy, her cubanía, which was [what] my parents wanted me and my siblings to emulate."[92]

In addition to her status as one of the most famous bodies of exile—"estandarte del pueblo cubano y del exilio patriótico" (banner of the Cuban people and its patriotic exile)[93] through which "vibra en ella Cuba entera" (all of Cuba vibrates)[94]—Celia's acceptance also rests in her having the right line concerning Fidel.[95] According to popular accounts, the only topic that made Celia lose her habitual composure and dignified stance was her hatred of Castro, who she once allegedly called, "hijo de la gran . . . pura y sincera" ("son of a . . . pure and sincere", that is, son of a bitch).[96] If in private Celia was in constant communication with relatives in Cuba and sent money to them, in public, she was represented as a queen who was never seduced by the tyrant, and was made to suffer when Fidel did not allow her to bury her mother in Cuba. For influential segments of the exile community, Celia was an acceptable symbol, one who never embarrassed them politically, cherished pre-socialist Cuban culture, preached the importance of hard work and success so essential to the myth of Cubans as a model Latino minority, and, although "proud of being black,"[97] sang to harmony and good humor in the face of adversity.

In this sense, publicly loving Celia was a way to camouflage the pain of exile itself. While most of her fashion choices had pan-Latino appeal, some elements of style, such as dresses inspired by the traditional *bata cubana* and *rumbera* outfits, directly evoked Cuba and spoke to exiled Cubans. An example of this is the much-photographed Cuba flag outfit that Celia wore in a May 2002 concert in Miami to commemorate Cuban Independence Day. The idea that by dressing up as Cuba one could literally remain there was a strategy to minimize the political defeat of Cuban exiles and never accept exile as final or definitive. In other words, if being an exile is to suffer a break between time and space, to be suspended, Celia lived for (and on) the stage, a trope for home and a site for memory. "The stage, my performances, and my audience," Celia noted, "have always been my refuge."[98]

The defense of exile as an in-between space is also evident in that Celia never attempted to cross over into the English-language market. Her famous refusal to speak English because her *inglés* was not "very good-looking,"[99] articulated not only a resistance to accept exile as permanent but a rejection of "Anglo" ways of fashioning the public self in the United States. By always insisting that she had left her heart in Havana, her feet took her all over the world in a frenzied pilgrimage to not lose her place.

Celia's final crossing, which paradoxically underscored to what extent and in what ways many Latinos have become part of America, likewise heralded the end of the *Cuba de ayer* that Celia represented to so many, as well as the Cuba of Fidel, its necessary inverse. In the words of Marta Cabrera, a Cuban exile employed as a domestic worker in Washington: "Cuba is leaving us. The good ones are leaving us and Fidel doesn't even fall off the bed."[100] Meantime, Celia's passing in style left all salsa lovers with a complex icon who navigated the treacherous constraints of subalterity with caution, creativity, and intelligence. Perhaps a significant part of Celia's legacy is precisely her particular style of *taconeo*, the distinct way that she clicked her heels while moving through deep waters. For, as her curator Marvette Pérez once said, "The men, when they have died, have left behind other men who could take their place. But Celia left no woman who could step into her shoes."[101]

ACKNOWLEDGMENTS

In writing this essay, I was fortunate to receive the support of colleagues and friends. I would like to thank writer Celeste Fraser Delgado for her editorial acumen, Marvette Pérez for her scholarly generosity, and Kairos Llobrera and Katerina Seligmann for their exceptional research assistance. I would also like to thank Myra Mendible, Ifeona Fulani, James McGirk, and Erin MacLeod for their editorial suggestions.

NOTES

1. Erin Mackie, "Red Shoes and Bloody Stumps," in *Footnotes: On Shoes*, ed. Shari Benstock and Suzanne Ferris (New Brunswick, NJ: Rutgers University Press, 2001), 233.

2. Juan Soto Meléndez, "Pelucas y vestidos," *PROFROGUI*, http://www.prfrogui.com/caribenet/celiatributoze.htm.

3. Celia Cruz with Ana Cristina Reymundo, *Celia: My Life* (New York: HarperCollins, 2004), 3.

4. Lydia Martin, "Adiós to the Queen of Salsa," *Miami Herald*, 17 July 2003, http://www.puertorico-herald.org/issues/2003/vol7n29/AdiósQueen-en.shtml.

5. Cruz with Reymundo, *Celia*, 5.

6. Marvette Pérez, telephone interview with author, 25 September 2003.

7. Ramiro Burr, "La primera en su clase," *El Nuevo Herald*, 28 December 2000, 39D. Original Spanish: "Celia generalmente usaba trajes con plumas, lentejuelas, encajes y yardas y más yardas de telas de colores."

8. Julian Asion, "Style by Celia," *Latino*, September 1957, 85.

9. Ibid.

10. Ibid.

11. Dario Mendez, "Celia Cruz, ¡Unica!," http://www.mipunto.com/foros/foros.jsp?forum=2.66&start=51.

12. Toby Fischer-Mirkin, *Dress Code: Understanding the Hidden Meanings of Women's Clothes* (New York: Clarkson Potter, 1995): 196.

13. Shari Benstock and Suzanne Ferris, introduction, in *Footnotes: On Shoes*, ed. Shari Benstock and Suzanne Ferris (New Brunswick, NJ: Rutgers University Press, 2001), 1.

14. Colin McDowell, *Shoes: Fashion and Fantasy* (New York: Rizzoli, 1989).

15. Ibid., 118.

16. Asion, "Style by Celia," 85.

17. Maureen Turim, "High Angles on Shoes," in *Footnotes: On Shoes*, ed. Shari Benstock and Suzanne Ferris (New Brunswick, NJ: Rutgers University Press, 2001), 62.

18. Cruz with Reymundo, *Celia*, 181.

19. Dick Hebdige, *Subculture: The Meaning of Style* (London: Routledge, 2003), 78.

20. "Una guarachera con aché," *Letralia*, no. 96 (21 July 2003), http://letralia.com/96/ar02-096.htm.

21. "Adiós Celia," *People*, 4 August 2003, 71.

22. Maria Friedler, "India Upon Her Grammy Nomination," http://www.salsaweb.com/features/indianew.htm.

23. Norma Niurka, "Celia Cruz: La armada invencible de la salsa," *El Nuevo Herald*, 26 October 2000, 27D. Original Spanish: "se siente como niña con zapatos nuevos."

24. "Biografía no autorizada de Celia Cruz," 11 November 2003, http://cronica.com.ar/article/articleprint/1060646710/1/27/.

25. Javier Zerolo, "Adiós a la ceniciente negra," 27 September 2003, http://diariodeavisos.com.

26. Cruz with Reymundo, *Celia*, 19.

27. Mackie, "Red Shoes," 236.

28. Zerolo, "Adiós a la ceniciente negra."

29. Turim, "High Angles," 62.

30. Hugo Rodríguez Vecchini, "Foreword: Back and Forward," in *The Commuter Nation: Perspectives on Puerto Rican Migration*, ed. Antonio Carlos Torre, Hugo Rodríguez Vecchini, and William Burgos (Rio Piedras: Editorial de la Universidad de Puerto Rico, 1994), 75–76.

31. Thomas Aitken Jr., *Poet in the Fortress* (New York: Annual World Book, 1994), 38.

32. Luis Rafael Sánchez, *La Importancia de llamarse Daniel Santos* (Hanover: Ediciones del Norte, 1988), 3.

33. Ramón Roa, *A pie y descalzo, de Trinidad a Cuba, 1870–71 (Recuerdos de campaña)* (Havana: Establecimiento Tipográfico de O'Reilly, 1890). Reproduced as part of Ramón Roa, *Pluma y machete* (Havana: Instituto del Libro, 1969).

34. Roa, *Pluma y machete*, 55. Original Spanish: "se dirigían hambrientos, casi desnudos y descalzos a la ambicionada meta."

35. Ibid., 33. Original Spanish: "agrietados los hinchados pies por las piedras y zoquetes de los arbustos . . . empecé a sufrir por primera vez en la vida los horrores morales que sólo

se experimentan cuando se ve uno, sobre todo, descalzo, y luego sin sombrero, algo así como abandonado de los hombres y a merced del enemigo."

36. José Martí, "Nuestra América," in *Nuestra América* (Caracas, Venezuela: Biblioteca Ayacucho, 1977), 26. Original Spanish: "los gigantes que llevan siete leguas en las botas . . . charreteras y togas . . . alpargatas en los pies y la vincha en la cabeza."

37. Ibid. Translation, Jeffrey Belnap, "Headbands, Hemp Sandals, and Headdresses: The Dialectics of Dress and Self-Conception in Martí's 'Our America,'" in *José Martí's 'Our America': From National to Hemispheric Cultural Studies*, ed. Jeffrey Belnap and Raúl Fernández (Durham, NC: Duke University Press, 1998), 198.

38. Jose Martí, "Los zapaticos de Rosa," in *Páginas escogidas*, ed. Roberto Fernández Retamar (Havana: Editorial de Ciencias Sociales, 1971), 124–29.

39. Lourdes Casal, *Palabras Juntan Revolución* (Havana: Ediciones Casa de las Américas, 1981), 25.

40. Reinaldo Arenas, "The Empty Shoes," *Mona and Other Tales* (New York: Vintage, 2001), 3.

41. Tace Hedrick, "Are you a Pure Latina? Or, Menudo Every Day: Tacones and Symbolic Ethnicity," in *Footnotes: On Shoes*, ed. Shari Benstock and Suzanne Ferris (New Brunswick, NJ: Rutgers University Press, 2001), 135.

42. Liz Balmaseda, "Seduction by Spikes," *Latina*, September 1997, 82.

43. Asion, "Style by Celia," 85.

44. Dario Mendez, "Celia Cruz, ¡Unica!," http://www.mipunto.com/foros/foros.jsp?forum=266&start=51.

45. Robert J. Stoller, *Observing the Erotic Imagination* (New Haven: Yale University Press, 1985), 15.

46. Benstock and Ferris, introduction, 5.

47. Lydia Martin, "Salsa Queen Celia Cruz Is Praying for a Special Heeling," *Miami Herald*, 31 October 2001, 2E.

48. Frances R. Aparicio, *Listening to Salsa: Gender, Latin Popular Music, and Puerto Rican Cultures* (Middletown, CT: Wesleyan University Press, 1998), 177.

49. Martin, "Adiós."

50. Cruz with Reymundo, *Celia*, 47

51. Ibid., 50.

52. Ibid., 34.

53. Ibid., 62.

54. Ibid., 67.

55. Merce Beltrán, "Azúuucar," *La Vanguardia: Cuba News*, http://64.21.33.164/Cnews/y01/dec01/1707.htm.

56. Leila Cobo, "Azúcar para toda una época," *El Nuevo Herald*, 28 December 2000, 31D.

57. Hebdige, *Subculture*, 3.

58. "Sin Celia," *People en español*, October 2003, 81. Original Spanish: "Si yo no llamo la atención, que la llame mi vestuario."

59. Cited in "Celia Cruz," 27 September 2003, http://geek.musicasdelmundo.org.

60. Lydia Martin, "Salsa Star Celia Cruz Is Recuperating in N.Y. from 'Delicate Surgery,'" *Miami Herald*, 6 December 2002, 4A.

61. One such instance is Ernesto Montaner's song, "Un son para Celia," where he calls Cruz "muñequita de café" ("coffee-colored doll") and "negra linda" ("beautiful black woman"). In Cruz with Reymundo, *Celia*, vii, viii.

62. Oscar Hijuelos, "A Song of Love for Cuba," *New York Times*, 23 August 2003.

63. Toni Morrison, ed. *Race-ing Justice, En-gendering Power: Essays on Anita Hill, Clarence Thomas, and the Construction of Social Reality* (New York: Pantheon, 1992), 207.

64. Martin, "Salsa Star Celia Cruz," 4A.

65. *People*, 4 August 2003, 69–78, 75.

66. Aparicio, *Listening to Salsa*, 144.

67. For further commentary on this distinction, please see Frances R. Aparicio, "La Lupe, La India, and Celia: Toward a Feminist Genealogy of Salsa Music," in *Situating Salsa: Global Markets and Local Meanings in Latin Popular Music*, ed. Lise Waxer (New York and London: Routledge, 2002), 135–60.

68. Wilson Valentín-Escobar, "Nothing Connects Us All but Imagined Sound," in *Mambo Montage*, ed. Agustín Laó-Montes and Arlene Dávila (New York: New York University Press, 2001), 207–33.

69. Javier Santiago, "Celia: La perseverante de la salsa," *Claridad/En Rojo*, 22–28 June 1990, 25. Original Spanish: "se distingue como una de las pocas mujeres que se han atrevido a cantar salsa . . . [que] han tenido la gallardía de incursionar en este género."

70. Jon Pareles, "Celia Cruz, Petite Powerhouse of Latin Music, Dies at 77," *New York Times*, 17 July 2003.

71. Martin, "Adiós."

72. Celeste Eraser Delgado, "Over Her Dead Body," *Miami New Times*, 24 August 2003, http://miaminewtimes.com/issues/2003-07-24/music.html/l/index.html.

73. Estela Pérez, "Celia Cruz triunfó en un mundo de hombres," http://holahoy.com/lunes/internet.nsf/All/pg003798.htm.

74. Ibid.

75. *Celia Cruz and the Fania Allstars in Africa*, director Leon Gast (Geneon Entertainment, 2001, DVD).

76. http://www.musicofpuertorico.com/en/queen_ivy.html.

77. Patricia Meschino, "Ivy Queen," *Miami New Times*, 18 November 2004.

78. Jonpito, "India," http://www.stylusmagazine.com/feature.php?ID=1326.

79. Aparicio, *Listening to Salsa*, 179.

80. Aparicio, "La Lupe," 148.

81. "India," http://www.freestylemusic.com/Interviews/india.htm.

82. Howard Pérez, "India Loves the Nightlife: The Princess of Salsa Talks about Her Music and Her Love for the Gay Community," *qvMagazine*, www.qvmagazine.com/qv6/latinospotlight.html.

83. Lorraine Gamman, "Self-Fashioning, Gender Display, and Sexy Girl Shoes: What's at Stake—Female Fetishism or Narcissism?" in *Footnotes: On Shoes*, ed. Shari Benstock and Suzanne Ferris (New Brunswick, NJ: Rutgers University Press, 2001), 98.

84. "Adiós Celia," *People*, 4 August 2003, 70.

85. Ana Cristina Reymundo, "Celia Cruz: La bella época de una diva," *Nexos* (January–March 2003): 73. Original Spanish: "Yo quiero que me velen y quiero una funeraria donde quepan muchos carros y que todo el mundo vaya."

86. Lydia Martin, "Queen of the People," in *Presenting Celia Cruz*, ed. Alexis Rodríguez-Duarte (New York: Clarkson Potter, 2004), 79.

87. "Not His Queen," *Street*, 8 August 2003, www.miami.com/mld/screetmiami/entertainment/6480646.htm.

88. Rebecca Díaz, "We Cubans Found It Offensive," *Miami New Times*, 7–13 August 2003, 7.

89. "Celia: I'll Tell You What's Offensive," *Miami New Times*, 14–20 August 2003, 7.

90. "Celia Racial Rhetoric," *Miami New Times*, 7–13 August 2003, 7.

91. Luis Aguilar León, "Hay que refugiarse en Celia Cruz," *El Nuevo Herald*, 8 October 2000.

92. Richard Pérez-Feria, "Mi tía cubana," *People en español*, October 2003, 12. Original Spanish: "siempre se hacía sentir en mi hogar. No tanto su música, para serles sincero sino su espíritu, su energía, su cubanía, que era lo que más mis padres querían que mis hermanos y yo emuláramos."

93. Olga Connor, "Tributo a Celia Cruz: de Santos Suárez para el mundo," *El Nuevo Herald*, 23 July 2003.

94. Ernesto Montaner, "Un son para Celia," in Cruz with Reymundo, *Celia*, v.

95. For further analysis concerning Celia Cruz's politics, see Frances R. Aparicio's essay, in *Archipelago of Sound*, op.cit. 2–27.

96. Beltrán, "Azúuucar."

97. Cruz with Reymundo, *Celia*, 211.

98. Ibid., 211.

99. Ibid., 102.

100. Francisco Ayala-Silva, "De Celia, Compay, Cuba y otras hierbas," *ElSalvador.com*, 19 July 2003, http://www.elsalvador.com/noticias/2003/07/19/escenarios/escen1.html.

101. Lydia Martin, "Capital Museum Mounting Show on Celia Cruz," *Miami Herald*, 30 October 2004.

PART 2

THE ORIGINS OF LATINOS
IN THE UNITED STATES

In part 1 we delved into the complexity of *Latinidad*, looking at the ways in which ethnic and national identities are forged historically, sometimes of one's own making, but, just as often, imposed from above by dominant groups and thus either accepted or resisted at the personal level. In part 2 we turn to the history of how Latin Americans first entered the sovereign space of the United States. Wars of territorial conquest explain much of the initial process, which Ramón A. Gutiérrez chronicles in chapter 4, "The Latino Crucible: Its Origins in Nineteenth-Century Wars, Revolutions, and Empire." In this essay he advances two major points. The first is that Spain and then Mexico were once sovereigns of most of the territory that became the western half of the United States. As the descendants of the Mexicans who were living in this vast terrain in 1848 still explain, "We did not cross a border. The border crossed us." By saying this they renew their memory of the territorial annexation that occurred at the end of the U.S.-Mexico War in 1848 and the treaty that ended the Spanish American War of 1898. When the U.S.-Mexico War ended in 1848, the United States took nearly half of Mexico's national territory, along with the roughly 100,000 Mexicans who chose to stay in the conquered territory. Within a year these people were granted American citizenship. Spain met an almost identical fate in 1898, losing Cuba, Guam, the Philippines, and Puerto Rico, with the latter eventually becoming an American territory. In 1800 the territorial boundaries of the United States did not stretch much beyond the initial thirteen colonies. By 1900 the United States extended from the Atlantic to the Pacific, southward into the Caribbean, and westward across the Pacific Ocean, with control over the Philippines.

Territorial conquest was the first force that incorporated Latinos into the polity. In chapter 5, "A Historical Overview of Latino Immigration and Demographic Transformation of the United States," David G. Gutiérrez traces the complexity of the second force—immigration. The economic development of the American West, which was spurred by the Gold Rush of 1848 and accelerated by the building of the transcontinental railroad in the 1870s, and which was in need of an alternative cheap labor source after Chinese exclusion in 1882, led American enterprises to recruit Mexican immigrants. Initially, this labor stream was small, unregulated, and mostly legal. By 1900 the Mexican immigrant population in the United States had grown to about 100,000. In the decades that followed, the numbers grew rapidly, with Mexicans pushed northward by the violence and displacements that accompanied the 1910–1917 Mexican Revolution and pulled by American labor needs during the First and Second World Wars. In 1924 immigration from Southern and Eastern Europe was severely restricted, again accelerating the need for Mexican immigrant laborers in agriculture, construction, and mining, the leading economic engines of the development of the American West. Eventually, a guest worker program known as the Bracero Program was put in place in 1942, putatively to alleviate labor needs during the Second World War, but which lasted much longer, until 1964. This guest worker program brought some 5 million Mexican laborers to the country legally, with an almost equal number entering illegally, allowing employers to skirt the fiscal and administrative requirements necessary to officially contract braceros.

Puerto Ricans were granted American citizenship in 1917, with the right to travel and reside where they chose in the United States. Puerto Rican movement from the island to the mainland is not formally a topic of immigration history but a migration circuit between two American spaces. Before World War II the tempo of this migration was slow, but the numbers increased considerably in the 1940s as Puerto Ricans sought a way of escaping rural poverty wrought by the island's reliance on sugar as its main export. In the 1940s and 1950s, Puerto Ricans found work in New York City's service sector, in clothing manufacturing, and in the military.

In Lillian Guerra's essay, we find evidence for the second Latino maxim that explains Latinos' origins in the United States: "We are here because you were there." The logic here is that American foreign policy in Latin America has been responsible for fomenting violent civil wars and regime changes in the Caribbean and Central America that have sent populations packing to neighboring countries and to the United States seeking protection as refugees. Gutiérrez summarizes the numeric, geographic, and ideological origins of these; Guerra's essay in chapter 6, "Late-Twentieth-Century Immigration and U.S. Foreign Policy: Forging Latino Identity in the Minefields of Political Memory," provides a deeper historical analysis of the relationship between American foreign policy in Latin America and the refugees born of these policies over the past fifty years.

The successful 1959 Cuban Revolution led by Fidel Castro was the juncture at which the United States intensified its anti-Communist foreign policy in the hemisphere, fearing that other nations might also opt for socialist regimes. Thus, soon after Castro set about nationalizing industries and limiting capital flight, the United States rabidly opposed the revolution and did everything in its power to destabilize it through an embargo and covert military campaigns, among them the botched 1961 Bay of Pigs invasion. Having failed to install a new government in Cuba, the United States granted elite Cubans seeking to flee the island asylum status as political refugees, providing unprecedented benefits and readjustment programs. Cuban refugees came in class-inflected temporal waves. First, in the 1960s came the elites and entrepreneurs; then, in the 1970s, members of the middle class; and, finally, in 1980, the some 125,000 Cubans, to Florida, in the Mariel Boatlift. Castro willingly dispatched this last cohort northward, deeming them criminals, degenerates, petty thieves, and homosexuals he wanted to be rid of. The U.S. government initially greeted the Marielitos warmly and generously with financial assistance and relocation programs, but as time went on and the true nature of who had arrived became known, President Jimmy Carter felt duped by the exit visas Castro had so generously given the Marielitos.

During Ronald Reagan's presidency, from 1981 to 1989, a muscular American foreign policy set out to eradicate potential Communist governments in the hemisphere, establishing friendly relations with brutal authoritarian dictators and providing them military aid to achieve this aim. Numerous coups, civil wars, and incidents of mass violence followed, the most notorious being the attempt to overthrow the popularly elected government of José Daniel Ortega in Nicaragua because of its socialist land reform, wealth redistribution, and literacy policies. The United States waged a covert war against Nicaragua, funding a group of mercenaries who became known as "Contras," to overthrow the government with the maximum amount of terror and disruption to the country's economy. President Reagan underwrote similar anti-Communist campaigns in El Salvador and Guatemala, which were equally lethal, producing mass genocide against indigenous peoples and silencing most critics though assassinations and disappearances. Those who fled the violence that gripped Central America in the 1980s and 1990s arrived at America's borders fearing for their lives and seeking refuge. It was largely denied, Guerra explains, because the United States did not want to acknowledge its covert policies in Latin America or the repercussions of those policies on human lives. Unable to enter the United States legally as political refugees, these people did what they could, entering surreptitiously without inspection and thus becoming "illegal aliens."

4

THE LATINO CRUCIBLE

Its Origins in Nineteenth-Century Wars, Revolutions, and Empire

Ramón A. Gutiérrez

The people who now reside in the U.S. and call themselves Latinos, have long and complex historical genealogies in this country. Many of them entered the U.S. willingly as immigrants in the 20th century, but just as many were territorially incorporated through America's wars of imperial expansion in the 19th century. As many ethnic Mexican residents of the Southwest correctly explain, "We did not cross a border; the border crossed us." Or as others often remark, "We are here because you were there." To understand how and why Mexicans, Cubans, and Puerto Ricans, the three groups that today constitute the bulk of American Latinos, first entered the U.S., let us imagine two very separate zones of imperial concentration in the Americas that were born in 1492 with the voyages of Christopher Columbus.

The first area of Spanish imperial settlement in the Americas was in the Caribbean, with Cuba, Puerto Rico, and Hispaniola as its principle sites. The native inhabitants of these islands were few in number at contact, were quickly decimated by European diseases and labor demands, and their labor was just as rapidly replaced by African slaves. This is why the Spanish Caribbean has long had such a strong African cultural tradition and such a distinct racial legacy around issues of blackness. Cuba is by far the largest Caribbean island, almost eleven times bigger than Puerto Rico. For four centuries, Cuba was one of the most productive and prosperous of Spain's colonies. It was the staging point for the early Spanish expeditions of exploration and conquest in the Americas, and it was through the port of Havana that most trade flowed between Europe and Spanish

America. Florida and Louisiana by virtue of their geographic proximity and trade were closely tied to Cuba in the colonial period and have remained in its cultural orbit ever since. Of the 54.5 million Latinos now living in the U.S., 13.1 percent or 7.1 million trace their ancestry back to these initial Spanish settlements in Cuba and Puerto Rico.

The largest group of Latinos in the U.S. is from Mexico, representing about 64 percent of the group's total and numbering 34.8 million by the 2014 census count. In the early 16th century, expeditions of exploration originating in Cuba learned of the wealthy Aztec Empire in the Valley of Mexico with its immense population of some 20 million and its streets putatively paved in gems, silver, and gold. The Spanish conquest of the Aztecs followed in 1521, and when that was completed expeditions of conquest radiated out from Mexico, eventually subjugating the Inca Empire in Peru in 1532. This zone of Hispanic presence in the New World was centered in Mexico City and had a dense indigenous population that supplied its labor needs under both Aztec and Spanish rule. Since relatively few African slaves were ever imported into this colony, its racial politics have focused on *mestizaje*, or racial mixing between whites and Indians, while largely ignoring its African heritage.

Mexico was tied to Europe through established trade routes between Havana and Veracruz, and connected to Asian markets by the convoys that regularly sailed between Mexico's Pacific port at Acapulco and Manila Bay in the Philippines. For our story about the devolution of Spain's American colonial empire and the genesis of Latinos, we focus only on Mexico's attempts to settle its far north, what became the states of California, Arizona, New Mexico, and Texas. In the 18th century, the mines of northern Mexico were producing the bulk of the world's silver. The settlement of New Mexico, Texas, and California became an imperative for Spain as a way of protecting these operations and thwarting English, French, American, and Comanche threats.

Many Latinos date their origin as subjects or citizens of the U.S. to the period between 1800 and 1900. This essay roughly takes these dates as its temporal beginning and end. The U.S. began 1800 as 13 colonies with no major territorial possessions. It ended 1900 having fulfilled a continental ambition, with sovereignty over Louisiana, Texas, New Mexico, Arizona, California, Colorado, Utah, Nevada, Oregon, and Alaska, and with an overseas empire that included Cuba, Puerto Rico, the Philippines, Guam, and Hawaii. This rapid expansion gave rise to a legitimating nationalist myth of empire that became popularly known as Manifest Destiny. In its most elemental form, Manifest Destiny asserted that God providentially had chosen the Anglo-Saxon race of the U.S. to bring civilization to inferior, dark peoples, to sweep away monarchy and replace it with democracy, to establish republican forms of government premised on Protestantism, generously helping benighted pioneers and people who occupied the spaces America coveted. Manifest Destiny was a complex time/space matrix of ideas variously inflected, but unitarily evolutionary and racialist, explaining America's need for new lands, ports, and markets, for secure national borders, and most of all, for its god-ordained destiny to greatness.

REVOLUTIONARY STIRRINGS

At the end of the 18th century, Europe and the Americas were overcome by a number of revolutions that profoundly transformed the colonial empires England, France, and Spain had built. First England's 13 colonies declared independence in 1776 as the United States of America. Then, influenced by America's republican creation embodying many French Enlightenment ideals, France too underwent a revolution in 1789. With *liberté, égalité, fraternité* as their motto, the revolutionaries swept away feudal, aristocratic, and religious privileges, issuing a Declaration on the Rights of Man and of the Citizen, and ultimately beheading both King Louis XVI and his wife Marie Antoinette.

News of the French Revolution rapidly spread to Saint-Domingue, France's most profitable colony in the Caribbean, which was then producing with African slave labor much of the sugar and coffee consumed in England and France. From 1788 to 1791, as the ties of empire weakened and the French monarchy was swept aside, the island's white planters and settlers mainly fought among themselves divided as royalists and separatists but united in wanting self-rule, the continuation of slavery, and their racial privileges as whites. As the revolution became more radical in France, extending in 1791 full legal equality to all free men, whatever their color, this proclamation inspired slaves to seek their own freedom too, sparking revolts on Saint-Domingue, which quickly left many of the island's plantations destroyed and some 2,000 whites dead. Spain and England came to the aid of the planters on Saint-Domingue, but just as they did France abolished African slavery in 1794, the first country in the world to do so, sparking slave revolts in Spain's and England's colonies. What began as an independence movement in Saint-Domingue in 1791, quickly devolved into a genocidal racial war against whites and French power, ending in 1804 with the creation of the Republic of Haiti.

Enlightenment ideals about equality, citizenship, and inalienable rights similarly infected Spain's colonies. These ideas proved particularly incendiary when compounded by local grievances about heavy taxation, the over-regulation of trade, the unity of church and state, and the place of the Indian in the colonial scheme. Napoleon's invasion of Spain and his removal of the Bourbon dynasty from its throne in 1807 provoked a crisis of royal authority both in Spain and in the Americas, quickening independence in the latter, as one region after another declared themselves independent states. By 1825, only Cuba, Puerto Rico, and the Philippines remained under Spanish rule.

CONTESTING MANIFEST DESTINY

The victors of war always control the writing of history, forging and fixing exactly how events will be represented, remembered, and studied. This is particularly the case in American historiography because the narratives of the nation's development have been so thoroughly interested in denying empire and erasing the resistance of those peoples who were swept aside by conquest. Indeed, many American history books still attest that the nation's territorial expansion was motivated by benevolence, by an Anglo Protestant civilizing mission to rescue and uplift racialized savages, even denying genocide, calling it by a more genteel name "Indian removal," and asserting that there was little opposition to American rule.

American history textbooks still largely narrate the 19th century as a series of pivotal wars, from the Texas Revolution (1836), to the U.S.-Mexico War (1846), to the Spanish American War (1898). When American history is told and taught this way Latinos all but disappear. Mexican Texans and Anglos united during the Texas Revolution against a Mexico they deemed tyrannical. When we as modern Americans are urged to "Remember the Alamo," however, it is a call to remembrance not of this unity but of the butchery Mexico unleashed to crush Texan self-rule. The popular names we still use to refer to America's expansionistic wars intentionally erase many of the major actors, certainly all of the vanquished, particularly those who became subjects and second-class citizens of the U.S. by virtue of their race and subjugation. Mexicans, *Tejanos*, and Comanches are often missing from the imperial narratives of the Texas Revolution. Comanches, Navajos, and the old Spanish/Mexican residents in New Mexico, Arizona, and California are rarely mentioned in accounts of the U.S.-Mexico War. Cubans, Puerto Ricans, and Filipinos are absent from the title of the Spanish American War, and even more so missing from the narratives of their independence struggles. My goal here is to re-inscribe these missing groups, consciously shifting the optic from war names to war dates to incorporate more fully the histories of forgotten groups.

THE WAR OF 1836

At the beginning of the 19th century Spain's settlements east of the Mississippi River in Louisiana and Florida changed hands a number of times. In 1803, the U.S. paid France 15 million dollars for the Louisiana Territory, an area that stretched from New Orleans all the way north to portions of the Canadian provinces of Alberta and Saskatchewan, encompassing some 828,000 square miles. When Spain ceded Florida and Louisiana, it encouraged its subjects to move westward into Texas offering them virtually free, tax-exempt land.

Who exactly owned Texas was a question of considerable contestation after 1803. The U.S. claimed it as part of the Louisiana Purchase, something Spain patently denied. In 1805, the Viceroy of New Spain commissioned a boundary study, which resulted in Father José Antonio Pichardos' 3,000-page *Treatise on the Limits of Louisiana and Texas*, issued in 1808. The report arrived too late. In 1807, Napoleon Bonaparte invaded Spain, placed his brother Joseph on the throne and, lacking now a legitimate monarch, accelerated the popular momentum for declarations of independence, including Mexico's in 1810. The future of Texas was now something Mexico would have to resolve.

Anglo colonists from Louisiana, who had rapidly seen the boundaries of political authority under which they lived shift from Spain to France, to the U.S., began moving into Texas where land was abundantly cheap and slavery could be maintained. Moses Austin, then a resident of Missouri, petitioned the town council of San Antonio de Béjar for an *empresario* grant in 1819, to settle 300 families, taking it upon himself as the agent or *empresario* to fulfill all the conditions of the contract. The Governor of Coahuila and Texas approved it, but before possession could take place, Moses Austin died. It fell to his son, Stephen F. Austin, to settle the families. Each immigrant family was granted one section of land (640 acres) with the clear understanding that the settlers had to be former residents of Spanish Louisiana, had to swear allegiance to the monarchy, had to honor the language and culture of Texas, and had to be Roman Catholic in faith. They agreed. They never really complied.

In the years that followed, the Mexican government awarded many more *empresario* grants. Why Spain and then Mexico eagerly welcomed Anglo settlers into Texas is best understood with a short digression to include another set of powerful historical actors in the region, Native Americans. In 1706, New Mexico's Spanish authorities reported that a group of Indians known as Comanches had entered the grasslands south of the Rio Grande. Though the observation was made in passing and seemingly without alarm, by the middle of the century the Comanches had become the major force in the southern plains, amassing contingents of armed and mounted warriors that often reached the thousands, significantly outnumbering anything Spain, France, England, or the U.S. could muster to resist their advances. Known to the Spanish as the *indios bárbaros*, these "barbaric Indians" were indeed formidable opponents. Remembered fearfully by the Spanish for their plundering and killing and for their looting and enslaving, they were, in fact, nimble political actors who often consciously played the local functionaries of European empires against each other to expand their own commercial trade networks in livestock, hides, and slaves. From the 1780s on the territory of their effective control expanded rapidly because of their acquisition of horses and arms, their development of remarkable equestrian skills, and their unflinching humiliation of their competitors. By the 1840s, their lands reached from the eastern border of Texas at the Nueces River westward to New Mexico's western border, eventually extending to encompass the southern half of Colorado all the way south to the Mexican states of Zacatecas and San Luis Potosi, which were home to Spain's most lucrative silver mines. In this area the Comanches cut a swath of trade and terror few could match, prompting historian Pekka Hämäläinen to call it a Comanche Empire.

Spain began opening Mexico's northern provinces to rapid settlement, offering arms and large land grants, even to foreign immigrants after 1803, to stem Comanche raiding and American and English encroachments. Softening its highly restrictive trade policies to heighten communication and protection of its settlements, merchants from various countries were also allowed to enter Mexico's north. Soon they were traversing the Camino Real, which provisioned the silver mines in Zacatecas and San Luis Potosí, linking from south to north Mexico City, Zacatecas, Durango, Chihuahua, and Santa Fe, now connecting the Royal Road to Kansas City and Chicago.

In 1821, the Kingdom of New Mexico, which then encompassed what became New Mexico, Arizona, Colorado, and Utah, was by far the most densely populated place in northern Mexico, with some 28,500 residents who called themselves Spaniards and 10,000 Pueblo Indians. California was second with a populace of 3,400 Spaniards and 23,000 mission Indians. Arizona counted about 700 Spaniards and 1,400 congregated Indians and Texas had roughly 4,000 Spaniards and 800 Indians in its mission settlements.

What Mexican settlers, Anglo immigrants, and merchants under the protection of various flags found as they entered to settle the northern Mexican provinces of Chihuahua, Nuevo Mexico, Coahuila, Nuevo León, and Tejas in the early 19th century were large ranches, dispersed farming settlements, and small towns. Many of them had begun as *colonias*, or colonies, intended to fortify the frontier. By the 1820s, however, they were being increasingly attacked by the Comanches and were rarely able to defend themselves, leaving many of their settlements abandoned.

Foreign immigrants from the U.S. flocked into Texas, quickly outnumbering the older Mexican *tejanos*. From 1823 to 1830, roughly 1,000 Anglo Americans arrived per year; in the 1830s the pace quickened to some 3,000 yearly, recruited mostly from Kentucky, Arkansas, and Louisiana. On the eve of the War of 1836, there were roughly 30,000 Anglo Americans residents, 5,000 black slaves, 3,470 Mexicans, a settled Indian population of 14,200, and a surrounding nomadic Indian population of 40,000 Comanches.

From the moment Anglo American colonists arrived in Texas, four issues dominated their relations with *tejanos*, with local authorities, and with the Mexican state: slavery, religion, Comanche raids, and representative government. Since the early 1800s, Spain had maintained that any slave who fled the U.S. and crossed the Sabine River into Texas would be considered free. In 1810, at the start of Mexico's independence war, Miguel Hidalgo y Costilla, the movement's first leader, abolished slavery as a way of gaining broader support. The revolution was crushed and slavery remained intact. Stephen F. Austin insisted that slavery was legal in Texas, which indeed it still was. The Mexican Constituent Congress of 1824 tried to abolish slavery hoping that by doing so it would curtail the Anglo immigrant onslaught. It failed. In 1827, the state Constitution of Coahuila and Texas declared: "No one is born a slave in the state from the time this Constitution is published in the seat of each district; and after six months the introduction of slaves is prohibited under any pretext." Stephen F. Austin persisted in defending slavery but to no avail. Finally, on September 15, 1829, Mexico's President Vincent Guerrero emancipated all slaves and prohibited all commerce in them, immediately heightening tensions with Texans who owned them and who began concocting various ruses to keep them.

Anglo Americans were also patently violating the terms of their settlement grants around issues of religion. A few Anglo American men married Texas Mexican women and converted to Catholicism. The majority did not. The federal Constitution of 1824 declared Roman Catholicism as the only sanctioned religion in the republic, immediately heightening conflict between Mexican Catholics and Anglo Protestants. In 1825, when the state legislature of Coahuila and Texas debated the colonization law that would soon govern settlements, Stephen F. Austin lobbied to get this requirement changed from "Catholic" to "Christian." Again, he failed.

If slavery and religion profoundly pitted *tejanos* against Anglo Americans, the Comanche threat they faced bound them together, but mostly in collective impotence. The national government's forces had been left too weakened by the wars of independence and could scarcely be marshaled to protect them. The Comanches effectively controlled most trade in the southern plains, sometimes peacefully trading their livestock, bison hides, and captives for iron works, guns, and ammunition, but just as often raiding and taking what they wanted. What solidarity existed between Mexicans and Anglos in Texas had been forged through mixed marriages and common defense against Indian enemies who limited their movements and constrained their commerce.

Since its foundations in the early 1700s, Texas had been a region far removed from the centers of political power. Under Spanish rule, Texas was one of New Spain's Internal Provinces (*Provincias Internas*) governed by an intendant in Mexico City. With the Constitution of 1824, Mexico became a federal republic with Texas and its neighbor province Coahuila united as one state. Texas had minimal representation at the state capitol in Saltillo, constantly bristled about this fact, and regularly petitioned state and federal governments for more local control. They wanted the creation of more town councils (*cabildos*), trial by jury, the ability to use English in all legal and administrative matters, exemption from state taxes, the right to own slaves, religious tolerance, and a state-sponsored educational system.

Texas' first, but short-lived, attempt at self-government came in 1826, when the Cherokee and Anglo residents of east Texas allied as the Republic of Red and White Peoples, most commonly known as the Republic of Fredonia. Calls for independence were again voiced in January 1832, when General Antonio López de Santa Anna staged a military coup in Mexico City, ushering in a centralist government. Texans, by far the most militant defenders of federalism in Mexico, again felt disenfranchised. Stephen F. Austin immediately traveled to Mexico City to make the case that Texas should be an independent state. Before learning that Santa Anna had rejected his proposal, however, he wrote the *cabildo* of San Antonio saying that they could begin the process. Austin's letter was intercepted. He was quickly imprisoned. While awaiting trial in Mexico City he penned and published his *Exposition to the Public about Texas Affairs* (1835) demanding Mexican statehood.

Fearing that Austin's detention might spark rebellion, the authorities quickly set him free. He found his compatriots in Texas fuming and badly divided on a course of action. Would it be Mexican statehood, autonomy in the form of an independent republic, or annexation by the U.S.? Even before Austin reached Texas, the settlers of Nacogdoches conscripted a militia eager to demand U.S. annexation. Meanwhile, back in Mexico City, the centralist government pointed to Texas as one of the problems federalism had created. Greater central control from Mexico City over this increasingly renegade province was what was needed.

Texans bolted. They did so on November 3, 1835. What they envisioned for themselves was still not clear. Stephen F. Austin assumed leadership over the military defenses of Texas, while Sam Houston turned to the recruitment of volunteers, money, and arms. On March 2, 1836, just after General Santa Anna's troops arrived to crush the rebellion, Texas finally declared its independence, elected David G. Burnet as president and Lorenzo de Zavala as vice president. Their Declaration of Independence recited anew their well-known grievances, most of which were already moot due to federal reforms. Elite *tejanos* were themselves divided on succession. Some of the prominent merchants and landowners—José Asiano, José Antonio Navarro, Juan Nepomuceno Seguín—supported it, while such powerful men as Carlos de la Garza and Vicente Córdova opposed it, wishing to remain loyal Mexicans and confident that succession was yet another Anglo ploy to continue slavery. They were correct. *Tejanos* immediately became apprehensive as they heard Anglo Texans openly declaring that Mexicans were unfit for self-government and republican rule. Mexicans were a cruel and cowardly breed of mongrels. They were indolent and ignorant, the Anglos maintained. Mexicans naturally had grave forebodings about such incipient racial conflict, which indeed would rapidly intensify after independence.

General Santa Anna and the Mexican Army moved quickly against the rebels. The first major defeat of the Texas patriots came on March 6 at the mission garrison of the Alamo. All 187 Texan defenders died; between 600 and 1,600 Mexican soldiers were killed. Santa Anna's troops next marched on Goliad, where another major contingent of Texans had gathered in defense of their revolution. Here too Texans were quickly overpowered, taken as prisoners of war, and on March 26, 1836, all 303 of them were executed. These defeats emboldened the Texans and attracted numerous volunteers from the U.S. "Remember the Alamo, Remember Goliad," became their battle cry. Sam Houston sallied forth with his troops and on April 21 captured Mexico's president General Santa Anna, decimating his forces at the Battle of San Jacinto. When General Santa Anna and David Burnet signed the peace treaty on May 14, 1836, Mexico promised to compensate Texas for destroyed property, release all prisoners, and vow never to wage war against Texas again. Texas was independent at last.

Though victorious, Texas was left impoverished by the war. Its principal irritant, the Comanches, had only been strengthened by the retreat of the Spanish and the defeat of the Mexicans. Texas could not pay its troops. Food was in short supply. Much of the arable land lay fallow and what had been planted had been destroyed. On learning of Texas independence, however, support poured in from the U.S. for reasons the editor of New York's *Courier and Enquirer* made clear: "War will now be carried into the enemy's country, where gold and silver are plenty, there will be fine picking in the interior. The war will never end until Mexico is completely our own and conquered."

In the decades that followed 1836, Anglo immigrants and their slaves rapidly flocked to Texas. *Tejanos* were increasingly outnumbered, so much so that by 1850 they were only five percent of the state's population. The American newcomers knew little of the area's history and quickly vaunted opinions that they were white and Mexicans were not. As Oscar M. Addison put it in the 1850s, Mexicans were "a class, inferior to common nigers [*sic*]." Anglos asserted that they were superior and Mexicans were inferior, that *tejanos* should toil for the benefit of Anglos, but not the inverse. During the second half of the 19th century, *tejanos* faced blatant discrimination, were segregated in limited social spaces, and encountered mostly abuse and neglect from government offices and officers, the most brutal coming from the Texas Rangers. Even elite status proved of little protection, as many Anglo newcomers seized their lands, claiming them as compensation for the destruction and bloodshed Mexican nationals had inflicted on whites during the revolution.

Tejano responses to the new racial order were various. In places where the two communities were sufficiently separated they retreated and accommodated, but remained resentful and suspicious of their fellow citizens. A few of the *tejano* elite assimilated and took up political posts in the new order, their loyalties always suspect, particularly whenever the harassment of *tejanos* broke out in violence and rebellion. Anglo rustling of *tejano* livestock became a daily fact of life, which was met with exact retaliation. Many *tejanos* dreamed of life free from Anglo control and consequently joined the failed movement to create the Republic of the Rio Grande in 1840, which would have united that portion of Texas lying west of the Nueces River with Nuevo León, Zacatecas, Durango, Chihuahua, and Nuevo Mexico. Here too their hopes were dashed. *Tejanos* joined local rebellions against Anglo domination, like those initiated by Juan Nepomuceno Cortina in Brownsville in 1859, and by Gregorio Cortez in Kenedy in 1901.

What almost a century of Anglo domination in Texas produced was an etiquette of race relations by which *tejanos* understood their subordination, and at least in public, accepted it and respectfully observed its rules. In the 1920s, one sociologist observed that *tejanos* always had to approach Anglos with "a deferential body posture and respectful voice tone." One also used the best polite forms of speech one could muster in English or Spanish. One laughed with Anglos but never at them. One never showed extreme anger or aggression towards an Anglo in public. Of course the reverse of this was that Anglos could be informal with Mexicanos; "they could use '*tú*' forms, '*compadre*' or '*amigo*' and shout 'hey, *cabrón*' or 'hey, *chingado*' (son of a bitch) in a joking, derogatory way. Anglos could slap Mexicanos on the back, joke with them at their expense, curse them out, in short, do all the things people usually do only among relatively familiar and equal people."

THE WAR OF 1846

In the years following Texas independence, its annexation into the U.S. became a cause célèbre. During his presidential campaign in 1845, James Knox Polk made the annexation of Texas, Oregon, and California his central promise. Before his election, however, Congress approved the annexation on March 1, 1845. Mexico lodged a protest. It deemed annexation an act of war and immediately broke off diplomatic relations with the U.S. In a strange twist of irony, General Antonio López de Santa Anna's main campaign promise for the Mexican presidential election in 1843 was that he would re-annex the rebellious Texas province and defend California. Santa Anna won, soon learned of the annexation of Texas, and prepared for war. That President Polk dispatched John Slidell to Mexico with an offer to purchase California, New Mexico, and a western border for Texas at the Rio Grande for $30 million only made matters worse.

A contrived border dispute provoked hostilities between Mexico and the U.S. in 1846. Since Spanish colonial times the western boundary of Texas had been the Nueces River. The Congressional resolution annexing Texas listed no western border precisely because a previous bill listing it as the Rio Grande had been defeated. With Texas now annexed President Polk ordered General Zachary Taylor's 3,500 troops into the disputed territory between the Rio Grande and the Nueces, simultaneously sending Commodore John D. Sloat and the Pacific Squadron with instructions that if Mexico declared war Sloat should immediately seize California's ports. On April 25, 1846, General Taylor wrote President Polk saying, "hostilities may now be considered as commenced," reporting on a brief skirmish between Mexican and American troops in the disputed territory. In his May 11 message to Congress requesting a declaration of war, Polk contended, "after reiterated menaces, Mexico has passed the boundary of the U.S., has invaded our territory and shed American blood on American soil." Senate Whigs ridiculed Polk's assertion saying that he had intentionally invaded Mexico to provoke a war. It was during the public debates over this contentious war that the notion of Manifest Destiny gained a name and tangible form. John O'Sullivan, editor of the *Democratic Review* and a great supporter of the war reasoned in 1846 that it was "Our manifest destiny to overspread the continent allotted by Providence for the free development of our yearly multiplying millions."

The war against Mexico really had begun six months before its formal declaration. In December 1845, President Polk commissioned John C. Frémont for a "scientific" expedition to California. His arrival there with a band of armed men provoked local anxieties. They were quickly ordered to leave. Frémont feigned that he was simply headed to Oregon and needed supplies. On June 14, 1846, his intention became clear when a group of Americans arrested Sonoma, California's Mexican commander, General Mariano Vallejo, and declared their independence. On July 5, Frémont was elected the head the Republic of California and five days later, on July 9, Commodore John D. Sloat's forces marched inland to Sonoma, having previously taken San Francisco. Sloat declared California a U.S. possession, lowered the bear flag, and hoisted the stars and stripes.

The U.S. waged war against Mexico on four fronts. The Pacific Squadron took the ports of northern California by July 9, 1846. The Army of the West, under the command of General Stephen W. Kearny, took Santa Fe on August 15, 1846, and from there proceeded westward to southern California. Part of Kearny's company was dispatched south into Chihuahua. Under the command of Colonel Alexander Doniphan, Chihuahua was occupied by early February of 1847.

The American strategy for the conquest and occupation of California was to take the northern ports first, then sail south to Los Angeles, where Robert F. Stockton's naval forces would reconnoiter with Kearny's army to take control of southern California. Both Kearny and Stockton encountered significant resistance from the local Californios, but by January 13, 1847, the invasion was secure.

With New Mexico and California nominally under American control by early 1847, President Polk next dispatched General Winfield Scott to occupy Mexico City. Arriving at the port of Veracruz with an armada on March 7, Scott proceeded to bombard the city until its residents surrendered on March 27. From there his troops advanced on Puebla, and then on Mexico City, which they occupied on September 15, 1847. Though Mexican President Santa Anna had led his troops bravely and had fought valiantly through tough battles and guerrilla skirmishes, they were fighting a professional army that was well equipped and rigorously trained, and thus no match.

Nicholas P. Trist, the U.S. Peace Commissioner, arrived in Mexico City shortly after to negotiate the war's end. The Mexican government was in shambles. No one was prepared to negotiate with Trist the unfavorable terms he wanted to impose. The treaty called for Mexico to acknowledge the Rio Grande as the border with Texas, to surrender 55 percent of its national territory—New Mexico, Colorado, Arizona, Utah, and California—for which Mexico was indemnified $15 million. Signed on February 2, 1848, in the town of Guadalupe Hidalgo and thus bearing its name, the treaty was negotiated under extreme duress. Mexico City was militarily occupied. President Polk let it be widely known that he had popular support to annex all of Mexico if necessary.

The treaty consisted of 23 articles, most of which dealt with military logistics, prisoner exchange, property disposition, commercial rights, and arbitration procedures that would govern all subsequent disputes between the two countries. Article VIII gave Mexican citizens residing in conquered territory one year to leave. Those who remained would become American citizens and their "property of every kind . . . [acquired by] contract . . . shall be inviolably respected . . ." Article IX guaranteed that the ceded territories eventually would be incorporated into the U.S. Until that moment Mexican residents would enjoy American federal citizenship, "their liberty and property, and secured in the free exercise of their religion without restriction." Article XI recognized that because "a great part of the territories . . . are occupied by savage tribes," the U.S. vowed to police the Comanches and Apaches to curtail their raiding and sale of hostages, arms, and livestock on both sides of the border.

Article X stated, "All grants of land made by the Mexican Government or by the competent authorities . . . shall be respected as valid, to the same extent that the same grants would be valid, if the said territories had remained within the limits of Mexico." The U.S. Senate excised this article from the treaty precisely because it gave too much protection to Mexican land grants. The Mexican treaty negotiators understood that without this protection Mexicans in the ceded territories would quickly lose their land, which indeed they did, though at different speeds in California and New Mexico. The discovery of gold in California in 1848 hastened the process there. U.S. courts, usually based on flimsy justifications, failed to honor many of the land grants the Mexican government had awarded its citizens between 1821 and 1846. Those grants it did recognize were much reduced in size, stripped of the use of the commons that formed most grants, thereby guaranteeing that they would be inadequate for farming or ranching.

One of the persistent myths of American historiography has been that Mexicans happily greeted American soldiers as liberators, offered no overt resistance to military occupation, and allowed the conquest to occur without spilling a drop of blood. The facts attest otherwise. There was significant resistance in both California and New Mexico to American rule. In 1847, New Mexicans assassinated Charles Bent, the occupational governor imposed on them by the U.S. military. They fought vigorously and died valiantly in various theaters of the war. When they were eventually overpowered, they militarily resisted colonial domination and the dispossession of their lands through guerrilla activity. Tiburcio Vásquez and Joaquín Murieta in California are but two of the men disparaged by the American press simply as "bandits." In New Mexico those resisting occupation banded secretly creating organizations such as *La Mano Negra* and *Las Gorras Blancas*. They formed political parties, such as *El Partido del Pueblo Unido*, and joined anarchist and syndicalist groups. If Mexico's north is now remembered as having been easily conquered, it was because Comanche raids had so weakened the area's defenses and had so depleted its essential resources that locals were poorly animated and even less so equipped to mount a major defense.

THE WAR OF 1898

Having annexed half of Mexico in 1848, American foreign policy discussions naturally turned to Cuba, which the U.S. had coveted and repeatedly tried to purchase since colonial times. As the U.S. had warned in its 1854 Ostend Manifesto, no country would be allowed sovereignty over Cuba except Spain and if she persisted in her refusal to sell the island, the U.S. would take it by force: "The Union can never enjoy repose, nor possess reliable security as long as Cuba is not embraced within its boundaries."

The War of 1898 is often explained as the result of a number of national developments, most notably industrialization and extensive material progress, followed in 1893 by the most severe economic depression the country had then witnessed. Between 1803 and 1898, the U.S. saw massive geographic and demographic growth. The country was now continental in scope, with a score of colonized subjects, particularly in the West. The Indian threat had been eradicated through genocidal wars and forced confinement on reservations. Between 1870 and 1910, the U.S. absorbed 20 million immigrants. By 1898 many of them—the Chinese, Japanese, and Jews—were being increasingly denigrated as unworthy of national membership. This was a period of technological advances in transportation and communication, with many people abandoning subsistence agriculture in the countryside for wage labor in cities. Frequent labor unrest sought socialist solutions, while populists agitated against unbridled capitalist corporations and unregulated trusts. Indeed, it was in 1893 that historian Frederick Jackson Turner declared the American frontier closed. In the minds of elites and perhaps the popular masses as well, America had reached its limits at precisely the moment other empires were scrambling to claim one-quarter of the globe as their colonies. If American dynamism and economic vitality were to be maintained, new lands had to be conquered.

The territorial spoils of the War of 1898 were Cuba, Puerto Rico, the Philippines, Guam, and Wake Island. It was really Cuba, however, that the U.S. most coveted because of its proximity, its strategic location, its natural resources, and because of the extensive investments Americans already had in the island. Cuba was a paradise for agricultural production, abundantly yielding sugar and its by-products, molasses, and rum. Since the cultivation and processing of sugar cane was undertaken mostly by free blacks and African slaves, by the early 19th century planters in the American South began militantly promoting Cuba's annexation, fearing that black insurgency there might infect the mainland with racial war, as it had in Haiti in 1791. Cuba was slavery's last haven in Spain's empire, not abolished until 1884. After Barcelona, Havana was Spain's second busiest port. After Mexico City and Lima, Havana was the third largest city in Spanish America in 1821 and one of its richest.

American interest in Cuba was expressed quite early and doggedly sustained. President Thomas Jefferson sent agents to Cuba in 1805 with offers to purchase it from Spain. President James Monroe had his eye sharply focused on Cuba when in 1823 he forcefully announced the "Monroe Doctrine," warning European powers that any intervention in the Americas would be deemed an act of aggression that would provoke immediate U.S. response. At the end of the War of 1846, President Polk again offered to buy Cuba for $100 million; President Pierce upped the ante by $30 million but failed still.

The majority of Spain's colonies were independent by 1825. There had been a number of scattered attempts to gain Cuban and Filipino independence since the 1860s but all of them were easily foiled or rapidly faded. Finally, on February 24, 1895, a group of rebels in Cuba's *Oriente* province issued a call to arms—the *Grito de Baire*—against Spain, which proved more successful. Led by José Martí, Máximo Gómez, and Antonio Maceo, with broad popular support from every sector of Cuban society, by August 1896, the insurgents had amassed a fighting force of some 50,000 widely distributed across the island. The Cuban rebels quickly mired Spain in a guerrilla war in which she simply slogged along. War-weary, facing army mutinies, draft riots, and antiwar demonstrations at home, Spain was further weakened by the eruption of a second major independence movement in the Philippines in August of 1896. Since 1892, Filipinos had been secretly organizing an independence movement. Now it had broken out in armed rebellion, creating an autonomous government headed by Andrés Bonifacio.

Spain tried to blunt the Cuban independence movement on January 1, 1898, by conceding to political reforms and home rule. The rebels demanded complete independence. As Spain's soldiers mutinied and refused to fight, many of them wilting under the heat of the tropical sun, sickened by yellow fever and other diseases, it became clear to Cuban rebels and American observers that Spain had lost its will and ability to fight. Seeing a vulnerable Spain and unwilling to fathom an independent Cuba, the U.S. dispatched the warship *Maine* to Havana to protect American interests. On February 15, the ship exploded and sank, killing 266 sailors and wounding at least 100 more. To this day, the cause of the explosion remains unclear. At the time, the sinking was attributed to a Spanish mine. Quickly the calls for war against Spain intensified in the U.S. "Remember the Maine, to Hell with Spain!" became an oft-shouted, frequently reprinted, jingoistic refrain.

The U.S. feared an independent Cuba largely because of racial anxieties. Cuba had an immense free black population that had grown enormously with emancipation in 1884. What would happen if the island nationalists won? Would this racially riven polity be able to establish a stable government? President McKinley's government thought not, refused to sell the Cuban insurgents arms, and consistently intercepted Free Cuba volunteers before they could set foot on the island. Steward L. Woodford, McKinley's minister to Spain, summarized American worries and ambitions well when he stated, "I see nothing ahead except disorder, insecurity of persons, and destruction of property. The Spanish flag cannot give peace. The rebel flag cannot give peace. There is one power and one flag that can secure peace and compel peace. That power is the U.S. and that flag is our flag."

The spring of 1898 found the U.S. attempting to broker a peace with Spain, simultaneously asking the rebels to disarm and accept an armistice. Both refused. On April 11, President McKinley asked Congress for a declaration of war to subordinate Spain. The U.S. would enter the fray as a neutral broker, McKinley explained, who, at war's end, would become plenipotent over Spain's former possessions. The war declaration never mentioned the active struggles the Cuban, Puerto Rican, and Filipino independence movements were waging on the ground or the provisional governments they had established. Instead, McKinley emphasized, "Our trade has suffered, the capital invested by our citizens in Cuba has been largely lost, and the temper and forebearance of our people have been so seriously tried as to beget a perilous unrest among our citizens . . ."

Cuban rebels and their American Congressional supporters balked, finally approving a war resolution on April 25 only if it included the Teller Amendment in which the U.S. "disclaims any disposition or intention to exercise sovereignty . . . [and once Spanish rule is ended] to leave the government and control of the island to its people." As we will see shortly, this was a promise that would hauntingly constrain the U.S. when the war ended.

The War of 1898 was short. Hostilities began on May 1 when American naval forces steamed into Manila Bay in the Philippines, engaged Spain's naval forces, destroyed all of their ships, and within seven hours had silenced most of the fire from land batteries. That same day the major ports of Cuba were blockaded; on May 11 American ground troops invaded. By July 16, Spain's naval forces in Cuba surrendered. American forces then advanced to Puerto Rico and occupied it on July 26. Spain and the U.S. suspended hostilities on August 12, announced a general armistice, and on December 10, 1898, signed the Treaty of Paris ending the war.

The treaty was drafted entirely by Spanish and American representatives. No Filipinos, Cubans, or Puerto Ricans participated. For $20 million, Spain relinquished its claim and sovereignty over Cuba, Puerto Rico, the Philippines, Guam, a number of small Spanish-controlled Caribbean Islands, and part of the Samoan archipelago. Spain's Queen-Regent María Christina accepted the terms of the treaty noting bitterly that her country "resigns itself to the painful task of submitting to the law of the victor, however harsh it may be, and as Spain lacks the material means to defend the rights she believes hers, having recorded them, she accepts the only terms the U.S. offers her . . ."

The U.S. rapidly overwhelmed Spain's forces largely because in the 1880s America's military strategy had been reshaped from national to global in scope, shifting its focus from the defense of national borders and the protection of its merchants, to the creation of mobile, offensive forces that were variously embedded abroad in areas of import to the U.S. This required the construction of military bases on foreign soil, the creation of a "New Navy" with a large number of modern, steel battleships, and a highly trained military, which was accomplished by creating the Naval War College in 1884. When Spain battled the U.S. in 1898, it lacked such modern ships and had organized its navy to defeat internal insurrections in Cuba and the Philippines, but had not prepared itself for naval assaults from without or at sea. When these two highly unequal armadas and personnel met, Spain was easily outflanked.

Cuba was allowed to declare its own independence in 1902, but only after the American Congress saddled it with the 1901 Platt Amendment, which formally replaced the Teller Amendment. The Platt Amendment created a neocolonial relationship between the U.S. and Cuba whereby it striped Cuba of most of its sovereign powers and prohibited it from entering foreign treaties or assuming foreign debt. In addition, it required Cuba to cede territory to the U.S. in perpetuity for the Guantánamo naval base and grant the U.S. the right to intervene in Cuban affairs to guarantee "a government adequate for the protection of life, property and individual liberty." The Platt Amendment governed U.S.-Cuban relations until 1934.

Puerto Rico did not fare as well. Spain had always imagined it as one of its lesser colonies, as a minor military base in which it invested little but extracted all it could. Whereas Cuba prospered with the cultivation of sugar cane in the 19th century, Puerto Rico remained relatively stagnant and sparsely populated, without a major export crop. Its agriculture was devoted mainly to subsistence farming and coffee production, which were worked by relatively few African slaves, a majority white population (the largest of any of the major islands in the Caribbean), and a colored population that was mainly free.

Puerto Rico, like most of Spain's American colonies, briefly sought but failed to gain independence in the 1820s and 1830s. Another attempt was made on September 23, 1868, with the Grito de Lares, inspired by Ramón Betances, a French-trained physician who had lived in exile most of his adult life. On that day over a thousand rebels declared the birth of the Republic of Puerto Rico, hoisted their flag, abolished slavery, and named a new town council for Lares. The movement failed rather rapidly, lacking popular support, composed as it was mostly of planter and merchant elites who wanted to end the economic grip Spanish merchants and large landholders held over the island. Such sentiments erupted in the 1880s, and again on the eve of American invasion. When Betances learned that the Americans were about to invade Puerto Rico on July 25, 1898, he urged his fellow countrymen to rise en masse, forcing the Americans to acknowledge a fait accompli. "It's extremely important," Betances wrote, "that when the first troops of the U.S. reach shore, they should be received by Puerto Rican troops, waving the flag of independence . . ." That did not occur. Instead, Spain granted Puerto Rico autonomy in November of 1898, several months after Spain and the U.S. had signed an armistice ending hostilities, but before a peace treaty had been ratified. Puerto Rico's independence was ever so brief.

For the U.S. the spoils of the War of 1898 were Cuba and the Philippines. Robert T. Hill, an American geologist who just before the war wrote a book on the West Indies noted that Puerto Rico was more unknown to the U.S. "than even Japan or Madagascar. . . . The sum total of the scientific literature of the island since the days of Humboldt would hardly fill a page of this book." The American Congress debated what to do with Puerto Rico precisely because it was too small, too poor, too thinly populated, and for some, too racially dark to merit statehood. Its colored population in 1899 was 40 percent.

From October 18, 1898 to May 1, 1900, Puerto Rico was administered by the U.S. as a colony, ruled successively by three military governors: Maj. Gen. John R. Brooke, Maj. Gen. Guy V. Henry, and Brig. Gen. George W. Davis. Puerto Rico's elites, wearied by four centuries of Spanish exploitation, were hopeful that American rule would be a radical improvement, based as it was on ideals of democracy and progress. They soon learned otherwise. Puerto Rico was now an American colony and would remain so. One of the first acts Governor Brooke took was to rename the island Porto Rico, its official spelling until 1932.

The transition from military to civilian rule occurred on May 1, 1900, when the Foraker Act was put into effect, setting out the terms of the island's governance. Puerto Rico was declared an unincorporated territory. Neither the U.S. Constitution would apply nor would its residents be deemed American citizens. The island would be under the authority of a civilian governor, appointed by the President of the United States and approved by Congress. An Executive Council (*Consejo Ejecutivo*) would be similarly appointed to serve as the governor's cabinet and a 35-member House of Delegates (*Cámara de Delegados*) would be elected to two-year terms, but all of their decisions were subject to veto by the governor or Congress. Most other officials—the attorney general, the treasurer, the court's justices, the commissioner of education—would likewise be presidential appointees. The *San Juan News* on May 29, 1901 well captured Puerto Rican frustration, "We are and we are not an integral part of the U.S. We are and we are not a foreign country. We are and we are not citizens of the United States. . . . The Constitution covers us and does not cover us . . . it applies to us and does not apply to us." Americans considered Puerto Ricans to be ill prepared for self-government, backward and uncivilized, and in need of paternal tutoring. Or, as Governor Henry stated in 1899, "I am . . . giving them kindergarten instruction in controlling themselves without allowing them too much liberty."

The Foraker Act was also an economic instrument of blunt force to advance American interests on the island and to thwart local ones. The act imposed a monetary system based on the dollar, devaluing the local *peso*, thus creating cheap access to land for sugar companies that would soon transform the island's exports to one. The native capitalist development Puerto Rico had established before 1898 in sugar, coffee, and urban manufacturing, was quickly destroyed. Although the U.S. did invest in eradicating tropical diseases, in educating the population, and constructing an extensive system of roads, most of these infrastructural expenditures were undertaken to improve the climate for U.S. businesses, providing them with healthier workers, minimally educated consumers, and routes to export their goods.

The Foraker Act of 1900 was replaced by the Jones Act, Puerto Rico's Second Organic Act, on March 2, 1917. The new constitution's changes were minimal and mostly cosmetic, offering lexical changes in the island's governing bodies, calling for a higher proportion of Puerto Rican election to these, and finally declaring the island's residents as U.S. citizens. Jurisdiction over Puerto Rico remained in the hands of the U.S. Congress, and Puerto Ricans ever since have demanded more autonomy; some have wanted statehood, and still others have maintained the dream of independence.

When Spain and the U.S. signed the Treaty of Paris ending the War of 1898, Filipinos resisted American occupation, declaring themselves independent on June 12, 1898. For the next forty-eight years, the Filipinos doggedly fought the American invaders. On July 4, 1946, the U.S. finally recognized an independent Republic of the Philippines. The treaty provisions in the Bell Trade Act were akin to those neocolonial strictures imposed on Cuba through the Platt Amendment. Filipinos were not allowed to make or trade any item that would compete with similar American products, nor could they nationalize natural resources in which U.S. citizens had ownership stakes. In addition, the U.S. was given sovereignty over its military bases in the Philippines in perpetuity.

CODA

In the 100 years between 1800 and 1900 the U.S. created two empires—one continental and one oceanic—utimately extinguishing the imperial ambitions France, Spain, England, and the Comanches once had. The human and natural resources annexed by the continental empire augmented the nation's industrial capitalist production. The maritime empire was built by establishing sovereignty over a series of islands that assured America easy movement to global markets, with permanent military bases from which they could easily launch attacks. All of this was done and justified in the name of a God-chosen nation destined to greatness. If suffering occurred, if peoples had to be "removed," if innocents lost all of their possessions, so be it. It was the duty of a superior U.S. to uplift and civilize weaker savages. If they refused, noted an 1846 article in the *Illinois State Register* then, like "reptiles in the path of progressive democracy . . . they must either crawl or be crushed." Never mind what territorial rights of anteriority existed. Never mind what rules of international law existed. For as John O'Sullivan proclaimed in 1845: "Away, away with all these cobweb tissues of rights of discovery, exploitation, settlement, contiguity. . . . The God of nature and of nations has marked it for our own; and with His blessing we will firmly maintain the incontestable rights He has given, and fearlessly perform the high duties He has imposed."

This, then, is a history of how residents of Spain, Mexico, Cuba, and Puerto Rico entered the U.S. through wars of territorial expansion during the 19th century. In the 20th century, both Mexico and Cuba would experience major social revolutions that would propel their citizens to the U.S. in search of liberty, refuge, and work. Puerto Ricans would make similar treks but as American citizens, seeking to better their lives on the mainland. And it was in the U.S. in the 1980s that these and other immigrants of Latin American origin coalesced politically as Latinos.

REFERENCES

Chávez, Ernesto. 2008. *The U.S. War with Mexico: A Brief History with Documents*. New York, NY: Bedford/St. Martins.

Conway, Christopher, ed. 2010. *The U.S.-Mexican War: A Binational Reader*. Indianapolis: Hackett Pub. Co.

DeLay, Brian. 2008. *War of a Thousand Deserts: Indian Raids and the U.S.-Mexican War*. New Haven: Yale University Press.

Friend, Theodore. 1965. *Between Two Empires: The Ordeal of the Philippines, 1929–1946*. New Haven: Yale University Press.

Gómez, Laura E. 2007. *Manifest Destinies: The Making of the Mexican American Race*. New York: New York University Press.

Gómez Núñez, Severo. 1899–1902. *La Guerra Hispano-Americana*. Madrid: Imprenta del Cuerpo de Artillería.

Greenberg, Amy, S. 2012. *Manifest Destiny and American Territorial Expansion: A Brief History with Documents*. Boston: Bedford/St. Martin's.

Hämäläinen, Pekka. 2008. *The Comanche Empire*. New Haven: Yale University Press.

Kramer, Paul Alexander. 2006. *The Blood of Government: Race, Empire, the United States and the Philippines*. Chapel Hill: University of North Carolina Press.

Limerick, Patricia Nelson. 1987. *Legacies of Conquest: The Unbroken Past of the American West*. New York: Norton.

Merk, Frederick. 1995. *Manifest Destiny and Mission in American History: A Reinterpretation*. Cambridge, MA: Harvard University Press.

Miller, Bonnie M. 2011. *From Liberation to Conquest: The Visual and Popular Cultures of the Spanish-American War of 1898*. Amherst: University of Massachusetts Press.

Miller, Stuart Creighton. 1982. *"Benevolent assimilation": The American Conquest of the Philippines*. New Haven: Yale University Press.

Navarro, José-Manuel. 2002. *Creating Tropical Yankees: Social Science Textbooks and U.S. Ideological Control in Puerto Rico, 1898–1908*. New York: Routledge.

Remesal, Agustín. 1998. *El enigma del* Maine: *1898: el suceso que provocó la guerra de Cuba: accidente o sabotaje?* Barcelona: Plaza & Janés Editores.

Ruiz, Ramón Eduardo. 1963. *The Mexican War: Was it Manifest Destiny?* New York: Holt, Rinehart and Winston.

Thomas, Evans. 2010. *The War Lovers: Roosevelt, Lodge, Hearst, and the Rush to Empire, 1898*. New York: Little, Brown and Co.

Traxel, David. 1998. *1898: The Birth of the American Century*. New York: A. A. Knopf.

Watterson, Henry. 1898. *History of the Spanish-American War: Embracing a Complete Review of Our Relations with Spain*. New York: Werner Co.

5

A HISTORIC OVERVIEW OF LATINO IMMIGRATION AND THE DEMOGRAPHIC TRANSFORMATION OF THE UNITED STATES

David G. Gutiérrez

Immigration from Latin America—and the attendant growth of the nation's Hispanic or Latino population—are two of the most important and controversial developments in the recent history of the U.S. Expanding from a small, regionally concentrated population of fewer than 6 million in 1960 (just 3.24 percent of the U.S. population at the time), to a now widely dispersed population of well more than 54 million (or 17 percent of the nation's population), Latinos are destined to continue to exert enormous impact on social, cultural, political, and economic life of the U.S.[1] Although space limitations make it impossible to provide a comprehensive account of this complex history, this essay is intended to provide an overview of the history of Latino immigration to the U.S. with particular emphasis on issues of citizenship and non-citizenship, the long-running political controversies over immigration policy, and the global economic context in which regional migration and immigration have occurred. The essay suggests that the explosive growth of the nation's pan-Latino population is the result of the intricate interplay of national, regional, and global economic developments, the history of U.S. military and foreign policy in the Western Hemisphere, the checkered history of international border enforcement and interdiction efforts, and, not least, the aspirations of Latin American migrants and potential migrants themselves.

FOUNDATIONAL POPULATION MOVEMENTS: MEXICO

The history of Latino migration to the U.S. has complex origins rooted in the nation's territorial and economic expansion. Technically, the first significant influx of Latino immigrants to the U.S. occurred during the California Gold Rush, or just after most of the modern boundary between the U.S. and Mexico was established at the end of the U.S.-Mexican War (1846–48). Under the terms of the Treaty of Guadalupe Hidalgo (signed outside of Mexico City in February 1848), the Republic of Mexico ceded to the U.S. more than one-third of its former territory, including what are now the states of California, Nevada, Utah, Arizona, New Mexico, Colorado, Texas, and parts of several other states. In addition, the treaty also offered blanket naturalization to the estimated 75,000 to 100,000 former citizens of Mexico who chose to remain north of the new border at the end of the war.[2]

With exception of the approximately 10,000 Mexican miners who entered California during the Gold Rush, migration from Mexico was very light during most of the 19th century, averaging no more than 3,000 to 5,000 persons per decade in the period between 1840 and 1890.[3] This changed dramatically at the beginning of next century. As the pace of economic development in the American West accelerated after the expansion of the regional rail system in the 1870s and 1880s, and as the supply of labor from Asian nations was dramatically reduced by a series of increasingly restrictive immigration laws beginning in 1882, U.S. employers began to look to Mexico to fill a dramatically rising demand for labor in basic industries including agriculture, mining, construction, and transportation (especially railroad construction and maintenance). Drawn to the border region by the simultaneous economic development of northern Mexico and the southwestern U.S. (largely facilitated by the eventual linkage of the American and Mexican rail systems at key points along the U.S.-Mexico border), at least 100,000 Mexicans had migrated to the U.S. by 1900. The outbreak of the Mexican Revolution in 1910 greatly intensified the movement of people within Mexico and eventually across the border, a trend that continued for the first three decades of the 20th century.

Historical migration statistics for this period are notoriously inaccurate because of inconsistent enumeration techniques, changing methods of ethnic and racial classification in the U.S., and the fairly constant movement of uncounted thousands of undocumented migrants into and out of U.S. territory. Extrapolation from both U.S. and Mexican census sources, however, provides a sense of the magnitude of population movement over this period. In 1900, the number of Mexican nationals living in the U.S. reached 100,000 for the first time and continued to rise dramatically thereafter, doubling to at least 220,000 in 1910, and then doubling again to 478,000 by 1920. In 1930, at the beginning of the Great Depression, the number of resident Mexican nationals is conservatively estimated to have increased to at least 639,000. When combined with the original Mexican American population (that is, the descendants of the former citizens of Mexico who lived in the Southwest at the end of the U.S.-Mexican War), the total Mexican-origin or heritage population of the U.S. in 1930 was probably at least 1.5 million, with the largest concentrations in the states of Texas, California, and Arizona, and a smaller yet significant number working in industrial jobs in the Midwest, especially in the metropolitan areas of Chicago, Detroit, and Gary, Indiana.[4]

Despite a brief reversal of migration flows during the Great Depression, when an estimated 350,000 to 500,000 Mexican immigrants and their children were pressured or compelled to leave the country in a mass repatriation campaign coordinated by local, state, and federal officials, Mexican migration trends seen earlier in the century quickly resumed after the U.S. entered the Second World War in 1941.[5] Facing a significant farm labor shortage as a result of conscription and war mobilization, U.S. employer lobbies convinced the Federal Government to approach Mexico about the possibility of implementing an emergency bilateral labor agreement. Still stinging from the humiliation suffered by Mexican nationals and their children during the repatriation campaigns of the previous decade, Mexican government officials were at first reluctant to enter into such an agreement, but after securing guarantees from U.S. officials that contract workers would be provided transportation to and from Mexico, a fair wage, decent food and housing, and basic human rights protections, the two governments signed the Emergency Farm Labor Agreement in the summer of 1942.[6]

Soon dubbed the Bracero Program (from the Spanish colloquial word for manual laborer) this new guest worker program had a number of important long-term effects. On the most fundamental level, the program not only reopened the southern border to Mexican labor, but also more significantly, reinstituted the use of large numbers of immigrant workers in the U.S. economy for the first time since the Depression. The scale of the program remained fairly modest through the war years, with an average of about 70,000 contract laborers working in the country each year during the war. Over time, however, the Bracero Program, which was extended by various means after the war, had the effect of priming the pump for the much more extensive use of such workers. By 1949, the number of imported contract workers had jumped to 113,000, and then averaged more than 200,000 per year between 1950 and 1954. During the peak years of the program between 1955 and 1960, an average of more than 400,000 laborers (predominantly from Mexico, but augmented by smaller numbers of Jamaicans, Bahamians, Barbadians, and Hondurans as well) were employed in the U.S. By the time the program was finally terminated in 1964, nearly 5 million contracts had been issued.[7]

The guest worker program instituted in the early 1940s also had the largely unanticipated effect of increasing both sanctioned and unsanctioned migration to the U.S. from Mexico. By reinforcing communication networks between contract workers and their friends and families in their places of origin in Mexico, increasing numbers of Mexicans were able to gain reliable knowledge about labor market conditions, employment opportunities, and migration routes north of the border. Consequently, the number of Mexicans who legally immigrated to the U.S. increased steadily in the 1950s and 1960s, rising from just 60,000 in the decade of the 1940s to 219,000 in the 1950s and 459,000 in the 1960s.[8]

More importantly over the long run, the Bracero Program helped to stimulate a sharp increase in unauthorized Mexican migration. Drawn to the prospect of improving their material conditions in the U.S. (where wages were anywhere from seven to ten times higher than those paid in Mexico), tens of thousands of Mexicans (almost all of them males of working age) chose to circumvent the formal labor contract process and instead crossed the border surreptitiously. This was seen in the sudden increase in the apprehension of unauthorized immigrants, which rose from a negligible number in 1940, to more than 91,000 in 1946, nearly 200,000 in 1947, and to more than 500,000 by 1951.[9]

The increasing circulation of unauthorized workers in this era suited employers, who sought to avoid the red tape and higher costs associated with participation in the formal labor importation program, and would-be Mexican braceros who were unable to secure contracts through official means. Indeed, the mutual economic incentives for unsanctioned entry (bolstered by ever more sophisticated and economically lucrative smuggling, communication, and document-forging networks) increased so much in this period that it is estimated that at different times, the ratio of unauthorized workers to legally contracted braceros was at least two-to-one, and in some cases, was even higher in specific local labor markets. That the use of unauthorized labor had become a systemic feature of the U.S. economy is further reflected in that fact that over the 24 years of the Bracero Program, the estimated number of unauthorized persons apprehended—nearly 5 million—was roughly equivalent to the total number of official contracts issued.[10]

Although the U.S. government has never achieved an accurate count of the number of unauthorized Mexican migrants circulating or settling in the U.S. at any one time, population movement of this magnitude inevitably contributed to a steady increase in the permanent resident ethnic Mexican population. According to U.S. Census data (which again, significantly undercounted undocumented residents in each census) and recent demographic analyses, the total ethnic Mexican population of both nationalities in the U.S. grew from about 1.6 million in 1940, to 2.5 million in 1950, and reached 4 million by 1960.[11] The historical significance of the Bracero Program as a precursor to neoliberal economic practices and a driver of demographic change has recently been recognized in a number of public history projects, including the Smithsonian's ongoing Bracero Archive project and the "Bittersweet Harvest" traveling exhibition.[12]

PUERTO RICANS

The growth of the Puerto Rican population in the continental U.S. has even more complicated origins. Almost exactly a half-century after the end of the Mexican War, the island of Puerto Rico became an "unincorporated territory" of the U.S. after Spain ceded the island and other colonial possessions at the end of the Spanish-American War of 1898. In the first years of American rule, Puerto Ricans were governed under the terms of the Foraker Act of 1900, which established the island as an unincorporated possession of the U.S. and provided a civil government consisting of a Governor appointed by the U.S. President, an Executive Council comprised of 6 Americans and 5 Puerto Ricans, and an integrated court system. In 1917, the U.S. Congress, responding to an increasingly aggressive Puerto Rican independence movement, passed the Jones Act. The Jones Act sought to quell local unrest by providing a number of political reforms including a bicameral legislature (although still under the ultimate authority of a U.S.-appointed Governor, the U.S. Congress, and President of the U.S.), and a Puerto Rican Bill of Rights. More importantly, the Jones Act granted U.S. citizenship to all Puerto Ricans except those who made a public choice to renounce this option, a momentous decision made by nearly 300 Puerto Ricans at the time.[13]

Although the authors of the Jones Act had not anticipated that their actions would open the door to Puerto Rican migration to the continental U.S., the extension of U.S. citizenship to island residents ended up having just this effect. Indeed, one of the lasting ironies of the U.S. government's action in 1917 was that even though congressional leaders had expected to continue to control Puerto Rico as a remote colonial possession, a Supreme Court ruling soon revealed the Pandora's Box Congress had opened by granting U.S. citizenship to the island's inhabitants. In the case *Balzac v. Porto Rico* (1922), the Court held that although Puerto Ricans on the island did not have the same constitutional standing as "ordinary" U.S. citizens (based on the logic that the Constitution's plenary power granted Congress almost unlimited authority to decide which specific rights people in unincorporated territory could enjoy), it also ruled that the conferral of citizenship allowed Puerto Ricans the unfettered right to migrate anywhere within U.S. jurisdiction. More important, the Court ruled further that once there, Puerto Ricans were by law "to enjoy every right of any other citizen of the U.S., civic, social, and political."[14]

Puerto Ricans soon took advantage of this oversight by exercising one of the most basic rights of U.S. citizenship—that of free movement within the territorial boundaries of the U.S. and its possessions. Beginning soon after the *Balzac* ruling, but increasingly after the Great Depression, growing numbers of Puerto Ricans began moving to the continent, and especially to New York City. Migration from the island was spurred by an evolving colonial economy that simply did not provide sufficient employment to keep up with population growth. Prior to the 1930s, the Puerto Rican economy was heavily oriented toward sugar production, which required intensive labor for only half the year and idled cane workers for the rest of the year. With unemployment now a structural feature of the island economy, the first wave of Puerto Ricans began to leave for the mainland, either searching for work or after having been recruited to work in the agricultural industry. Consequently, the mainland population began to grow. Between 1930 and the outbreak of the Second World War, the mainland Puerto Rican population grew modestly from 53,000 to nearly 70,000, though by now, the overwhelming majority of Puerto Ricans (nearly 88 percent) could be found in New York City where they became low-wage workers in the region's expanding clothing manufacturing and service sectors. In addition, Puerto Rican entrepreneurs also began to expand what would soon become a thriving ethnic economy servicing the needs of the region's rapidly expanding population.[15]

Puerto Rican emigration to the mainland accelerated after the war. Facing chronic unemployment on the island (which fluctuated between 10.4 percent and 20 percent for the entire period between 1949 and 1977), and the dislocations in both the rural and urban work forces caused in part by Operation Bootstrap, a massive government-sponsored plan to attract investment and light industry to the island, the Puerto Rican mainland population jumped from fewer than 70,000 in 1940 to more than 300,000 in 1950 and continued to climb to 887,000 by 1960. Although the systematic shift from agriculture to "export-platform industrialization" under Operation Bootstrap was intended to stimulate economic growth and lift workers out of poverty (which occurred for a minority of Puerto Rican workers) chronic unemployment and underemployment—and the economically driven migration that resulted—have been facts of Puerto Rican economic life since the 1950s.[16]

DEMOGRAPHIC DEVELOPMENTS SINCE 1960

The demographic landscape of Latino America began to change dramatically in the 1960s as a result of a confluence of economic and geopolitical trends. In 1959, a revolutionary insurgency in Cuba led by Fidel Castro and Ernesto "Ché" Guevara shocked the world by overthrowing the regime of dictator Fulgencio Batista. Although Castro's political intentions remained unclear in the first months of his rule, by 1960 the ruling junta made it plain that it intended to rule Cuba under Marxist principles. In quick succession, a series of political purges and trials, expropriations, the nationalization of key industries and institutions (including labor unions and private schools), and the aborted invasion attempt by Cuban exiles at the infamous Bay of Pigs in the spring of 1961, led to a mass exodus of disaffected Cubans. Although a significant Cuban population had existed in the U.S. since the 19th century (mainly concentrated in Florida and New York City), virtually overnight the exodus of Cubans after the revolution created a major new Latino American population. Numbering fewer than 71,000 nationwide in 1950, the Cuban immigrant population shot up to 163,000 by 1960.[17]

A second wave of Cuban immigration occurred between 1965 and the early 1970s when the Castro regime agreed to allow Cubans who wished to be reunited with family members already in the U.S. to do so. Although initially caught by surprise by the Cuban government's decision, U.S. immigration officials provided a mechanism for the orderly entry of nearly 300,000 additional Cuban refugees. As a result, the Cuban population of the U.S. reached 638,000 by 1970, which accounted for 7.2 percent of nation's Latino population at the time.[18] During the 1980s, a third wave of out-migration from Cuba occurred (the infamous "Mariel boatlift"), swelling the numbers of Cubans in the U.S. by another 125,000.[19] These three major waves of post-1960 immigration provided the foundation for the modern Cuban American population, which currently stands at nearly 1.786 million, or 3.5 percent of the pan-Latino population of the U.S.[20]

The majority of Cubans and their children have tended to congregate in South Florida (nearly 70 percent of all Cubans continue to reside in Florida) but over time, Cubans and Cuban Americans—like other Latino migrants—have become more geographically dispersed. Although the different socioeconomic profiles of the three distinct waves of Cuban migration created a heterogeneous population in class terms, in aggregate, the immigrants that established the Cuban American population have the highest levels of socioeconomic attainment of the three major Latino subpopulations in the U.S. For example, in 2008, 25 percent of Cubans and Cuban Americans over age 25 had obtained at least a college degree (compared to just 12.9 percent of the overall U.S. Latino population); median income for persons over 16 was $26,478 (compared to median earnings of $21,488 for all Latinos); and 13.2 percent of Cubans lived below the poverty line (compared to 20.7 percent of the Latino population and 12.7 percent of the general U.S. population at that time).[21]

Political turmoil elsewhere in Latin America during the 1970s and 1980s—particularly in the Central American nations of El Salvador, Guatemala, Honduras, and Nicaragua—also contributed to significant new Latin American immigration to the U.S. Again, although citizens of each of these nations had established small émigré populations in the U.S. well before the 1970s, the political turmoil of the 1970s and 1980s resulted in an unprecedented wave of migration as hundreds of thousands of Central Americans—many of them undocumented—fled the violence of their homelands to enter the U.S. Caught between authoritarian regimes (often overtly or covertly supported by elements of the U.S. government) and left-wing insurgencies, Central American migrants became a significant part of the U.S. Latino population by 1990, when they reached an aggregate population of nearly 1.324 million. Reflecting their diverse origins and experiences Central Americans have clustered in different areas of the country, with Salvadorans prominent in Los Angeles, Houston, San Francisco, New York, and Washington, D.C.; Guatemalans in California and Texas; Nicaraguans in Miami; and Hondurans in Florida, Texas, and elsewhere. Although most of the Central American nations have stabilized politically since the 1990s, the long-term economic disruption and displacement caused by protracted civil and guerrilla wars in the region have contributed to the continuing growth of this population (discussed further below).[22]

ECONOMIC FACTORS

As dramatic as the story of Cuban and Central American political migration has been, however, the most significant development in Latino migration to the U.S. in recent history is rooted in profound economic shifts occurring both in the U.S. and in countries in the Western Hemisphere since the late 1960s and early 1970s. The first signs of things to come were the end of the Bracero Program in 1964 and a major overhaul of U.S. immigration law in 1965. Although both events have been touted as part of the wave of liberal reforms (including the Civil Rights Act of 1964 and the Voting Rights Act of 1965) that characterized this tumultuous era, the end of the contract labor program and revamping of the U.S. immigration system helped hide from view some significant changes both in patterns of immigration and the utilization of immigrant labor in the U.S. These events also tended to obscure important structural changes in both the U.S. economy the economies of Latin America that continue to the present day.

One change that largely escaped public view at the time was the gradual replacement of braceros with unauthorized workers, the vast majority of them originating in Mexico. Although the use of braceros had steadily declined in the early 1960s until Congress allowed the program to lapse at the end of 1964, there is no indication that the steady demand for labor that had driven both authorized and unauthorized migration for the previous quarter-century had suddenly dropped appreciably. Given historical trends, it is much more likely that, as the program ran down, braceros were gradually replaced by unauthorized workers—or, after their contracts expired, simply became unauthorized workers themselves.

In any case, border apprehensions began to rise again almost immediately after the guest worker program's demise. Whereas the INS reported apprehending an average of about 57,000 unauthorized migrants per year in the nine years between Operation Wetback, a federal program that deported illegal Mexican immigrants from the southwestern U.S., and the end of the Bracero Program, apprehensions approached 100,000 again in 1965 and continued to rise sharply thereafter.[23] In that same year, the passage of the Immigration and Nationality Act (INA) Amendments (79 Stat. 911) almost certainly exacerbated this trend. Although the new law greatly liberalized extant policy by abolishing the national origins quota system and providing a first-come, first-served system for eligible immigrants, for the first time in history the INA imposed a ceiling of just 120,000 legal immigrants per year for the entire Western Hemisphere. Later adjustments in the law further lowered the number of visas available to Western Hemisphere countries.[24]

On the economic front, the 1973 Arab oil embargo further disrupted the American labor market and eventually helped lay the foundations for an even greater influx of both legal immigrants and unauthorized workers. The extended period of simultaneous contraction and inflation that followed the 1973 crisis—and a series of neoliberal economic reforms that were instituted in response—signaled a massive reorganization of work and production processes that in many ways continue to the present day. This ongoing restructuring was regionally and temporally uneven, but across the economy the general long-term trend was toward a contraction of comparatively secure high-wage, high-benefit (often union) jobs in the manufacturing and industrial sectors and a corresponding growth of increasingly precarious low-wage, low benefit, often non-union jobs in the expanding service and informal sectors of a transformed economy.

In the international arena, the deepening global debt crisis and austerity measures imposed on many Latin American countries over this same period by the World Bank and International Monetary Fund set the stage for even more drastic economic restructuring and displacement abroad.[25] These developments also dramatically altered the gendered composition of immigrant flows. Whereas prior to this time, migration from Latin America to the U.S. was heavily skewed toward males of working age, economic restructuring abroad eventually led to a growing number of women and children entering the migrant stream. The gender breakdown of immigrant populations varies from region to region (with Mexican migration, for example, remaining somewhat skewed toward males and Dominican migration heavily skewed toward females), but the general trend in Latin American immigration since the 1970s and 1980s has been a pronounced feminization of migratory flows. As a result, although men still outnumber women, the aggregate Latin American population of foreign birth in the U.S. is rapidly approaching gender equilibrium.[26]

The effects of the combination of these dramatic structural shifts have played out differently in different regions of Latin America. In Mexico, the nation that historically has sent the largest numbers of migrants to the U.S., the deepening debt crisis, periodic devaluations of the peso, and natural disasters like the great earthquake of 1985 helped to stimulate even more intense waves of out-migration by both males and females. As already noted, political turmoil and violence had similar effects on the nations of Central America. Moreover, in impoverished Caribbean nations like the Dominican Republic, the attraction of finding work in the U.S. (especially for Dominican women) has led to even more explosive growth in the émigré population. Whereas the Dominican population of the U.S. stood at fewer than 100,000 in 1970, by 1980 it had grown to more than 171,000 and, as will be seen below, has continued to grow dramatically since.[27]

At the other end of the economic spectrum, ongoing economic restructuring in South America has led to a situation in which highly educated and highly skilled individuals from countries including Argentina, Chile, Columbia, Peru, Ecuador, and others have emigrated to the U.S. seeking economic opportunities not available to them in their places of origin. For example, according to a recent analysis of 2000 U.S. Census data, whereas only 2.3 percent of all Mexican migrants arriving in the U.S. in the 1980s had bachelor's degrees, 30 percent of those arriving from Peru and Chile, 33 percent of Argentine immigrants, and 40 percent of all Venezuelan immigrants had at least a bachelor's degree. For different reasons, this kind of "brain drain" migration has increased significantly in recent years. For example, between 2000 and 2010, the U.S. population of Chilean and Colombian descent or origin nearly doubled, and the resident population of Argentinian, Bolivian, Ecuadorian, Peruvian, and Venezuelan origin or heritage more than doubled.[28]

As always, the economic dependence of the U.S. labor market on both "legal" and "illegal" immigrants has inevitably cemented and extended links of mutual dependence to immigrant-sending regions and thus has also contributed to the continuing cycle of licit and illicit movement into U.S. territory. Since the 1970s, the same kinds of social networks previously established by European, Asian, and Mexican immigrants have been expanded by more recent migrants, strengthening the bonds of interdependence that have tied some immigrant-source regions to the U.S. for more than a century. The

especially given the increasingly integral role unauthorized workers have come to play in the economy.[38]

One other note should be added to this discussion. Although for reasons discussed elsewhere in this essay the phenomenon of illegal immigration has commonly been associated almost exclusively with Mexicans, one should note that most migration scholars agree that somewhere between 40 and 50 percent of all persons not legally in the country are individuals who did not cross the border illegally but rather have overstayed valid tourist, student, or other visas. Thus, although illegal immigration has come to be perceived primarily as a "Mexican problem," Mexicans ultimately accounted for about 58 percent of the estimated total in 2010—the remaining 42 percent, many of them visa violators, came from virtually every other nation in the world.[39]

FUTURE TRENDS

It is impossible to predict the future, but the entwined questions of Latin America immigration and the status of the millions of unauthorized Latin American immigrants currently in the U.S. will almost certainly continue to be two of the most complex and vexing issues on the American political landscape. On the one hand, growing international market competition makes it likely that the U.S. economy will continue to depend heavily on the labor of foreigners—and if patterns of regional economic integration continue, it is almost certain that Latin American immigrants of all statuses will continue to play a major role in the economic development of the nation. Indeed, before the current economic contraction, patterns of immigrant labor insourcing had accelerated to the extent that immigrants of all legal statuses were filling jobs in the U.S. at a rate comparable to the one that existed in the great age of industrial migration more than a century ago. Although the ongoing recession has clearly suppressed the hiring of both native and foreign workers, recent data reveals just how much immigrant workers have become crucial components of American economic life.

According to U.S. Census data, as recently as 2007, highly-skilled "legal" immigrants had become essential in many key economic sectors, constituting fully 44 percent of all medical scientists, 37 percent of all physical scientists, 34 percent of all computer software engineers, 31 percent of all economists, 30 percent of all computer engineers, and 27 percent of all physicians and surgeons. With citizen members of the "baby boom" generation entering retirement in ever-increasing numbers, demographers predict that pressure to recruit highly educated and highly skilled immigrants will continue to rise.[40]

In the vast occupational landscape below such elite professions, immigrant workers of all legal statuses (the U.S. Census does not distinguish between "legal" and unsanctioned workers) have also become structurally embedded in virtually every job category in the economy. As would be expected, more than half of all agricultural workers, plasterers, tailors, dressmakers, sewing machine operators, and "personal appearance workers" are immigrants. Authorized and unauthorized immigrant workers are estimated to constitute another 40 to 50 percent of all drywall workers, packers and packaging workers, and maids and housekeepers. In the next tier, immigrants comprised 30 to 40 percent of all roofers, painters, meat and fish processors, cement workers, brick masons, cooks, groundskeepers, laundry workers, textile workers, and dishwashers. Beyond their expected presence in these labor-intensive occupations, however, immigrants of all statuses are estimated to hold 20 to 30 percent of at least 36 additional occupational categories.[41] But in addition to the numbers captured in official labor statistics, it is also important to keep in mind that untold numbers of other noncitizens toil in the vast and expanding reaches of the "informal" or unregulated "gray" and subterranean "black" market economies.[42] Indeed, the turn to licit and illicit immigrant labor at all levels of the economy has been so great that it is estimated that foreign workers accounted for *half* of all jobs created in the U.S. between 1996 and 2000 and comprised at least 16 percent of the total U.S. workforce at the turn of the 21st century.[43]

Of course, on the other hand, the increasingly visible use of immigrant workers and the growth and dispersal of the Latino population since the 1980s into areas such as the American South and the industrial Northeast—places where few Latinos have ever been seen in substantial numbers before—have fanned the flames of dissent and nativism among those who are infuriated not only with what they see as the unconscionable expansion of the nation's unauthorized population, but more generally, with the erosion of domestic living standards associated with the ongoing restructuring of the U.S. economy. Fears about the inexorable aging of the "white" citizen population and the rapid growth of a comparably youthful non-white Latino population have tended to heighten resentment against the foreign-born and their children—and especially against those without legal status. (In 2010, the median age of non-Hispanic white persons was 42, compared to a median age of 27 for all Latinos).[44] The widespread sense that the Federal Government—and lawmakers in both political parties—have not seriously enforced existing law obviously has also added to the frustration of those holding such views.

Consequently, in what is clearly the most dramatic recent development in the debate over immigration and border control policy, states and localities have entered the fray by enacting a range of measures designed to pressure unauthorized persons to leave their jurisdictions. Following precedents set by activists in California and elsewhere, localities such as Hazleton, Pennsylvania, in the East, Escondido, California, in the West, and at least 130 other American towns and cities in between have passed local ordinances that do everything from criminalizing the hiring of unauthorized day laborers, making it illegal to rent to unauthorized residents, suspending business licenses of firms employing unauthorized workers, and criminalizing the public use of languages other than English. In addition, a number of states—perhaps most notoriously Arizona, and more recently, Indiana, Georgia, Alabama, and others—have debated and/or enacted a variety of measures designed to pressure unauthorized persons to depart their jurisdictions. In 2010 alone, states passed more than 300 such laws, including measures requiring local law enforcement officials, teachers, social workers, health-care providers, private-sector employers, and others to verify the citizenship of any individual they encounter in their official duties or businesses—and make it a crime for non-citizens not to have documents verifying their legal status. Some have gone so far as to propose that unauthorized persons be prohibited from driving (or, for that matter, be barred from receiving any kind of state license), and that states not recognize the U.S. citizenship of infants born of unauthorized residents, regardless of the birthright citizenship provision of the Fourteenth Amendment to the U.S. Constitution. Federal courts have thus far tended to enjoin or strike down such statutes as violations of federal prerogative in immigration matters, but the future in this arena of immigration and citizenship politics and jurisprudence remains uncertain.[45]

Given the tremendously unstable state of the U.S. and global economies and the highly politicized debate over border enforcement and undocumented immigration in the second decade of the century, it is impossible to predict even partial resolution to these festering controversies. Although the continuing precariousness of the economy may well lay the groundwork for the projection of more force on U.S. borders and an even more hostile climate for Latinos and non-citizens already within U.S. territory, global economic trends will almost certainly continue to create incentives for the ongoing structural use and abuse of both officially authorized and unauthorized Latino immigrant workers. Under these circumstances, it is likely that the historical debate over border enforcement, the continuing growth of the pan-Latino population, and the status of unauthorized persons will persist into the foreseeable future.

NOTES

1. Susan B. Carter et al., eds., *Historical Statistics of the United States: Earliest Times to the Present*, vol. 1, part A-Population (New York: Cambridge University Press, 2006), 1–177, table Aa 2189–2215, "Hispanic Population Estimates, by Sex, Race, Hispanic Origin, Residence, Nativity: 1850–1990"; and Seth Motel and Eileen Patten, "Hispanic Origin Profiles" (Washington, DC: Pew Hispanic Center, June 27, 2012), 1.

2. For brief overviews of the U.S.-Mexican War and the Treaty of Guadalupe Hidalgo, see Richard Griswold del Castillo, *The Treaty of Guadalupe Hidalgo: A Legacy of Conflict* (Norman: University of Oklahoma Press, 1990); and Ernesto Chávez, *The U.S. War with Mexico: A Brief History with Documents* (Boston: Bedford/St. Martin's, 2008).

3. For detailed data on Mexican immigration during the 19th century, see Susan B. Carter et al., eds., *Historical Statistics of the United States: Earliest Times to the Present*, vol. 1, part A-Population (New York: Cambridge University Press, 2006), table Ad 162–172, "Immigration by Country of Last Residence—North America: 1820–1997," 1–571.

4. See Arnoldo De León and Richard Griswold del Castillo, *North to Aztlán; A History of Mexican Americans in the United States*, 2nd ed. (Wheeling, IN: Harlan Davidson, 2006), 87, table 5.1, and 90, table 5.2; and Brian Gratton and Myron P. Gutmann, "Hispanics in the United States, 1850–1990: Estimates of Population Size and National Origin," *Historical Methods* 33, no. 3 (Summer 2000): 137–153.

5. For details of the Mexican repatriation campaigns of the 1930s, see Francisco E. Balderrama and Raymond Rodríguez, *Decade of Betrayal: Mexican Repatriation in the 1930s*, rev. ed. (Albuquerque: University of New Mexico Press, 2006).

6. For trenchant analyses of the politics surrounding the development of the Emergency Farm Labor Program, see Manuel García y Griego, "The Importation of Mexican Contract Labors to the United States, 1942–1964," in *The Border That Joins: Mexican Migrants and U.S. Responsibility*, ed. Peter G. Brown and Henry Shue (Totowa, NJ: Rowman & Littlefield, 1983): 49–98; and Katherine M. Donato, "U.S. Policy and Mexican Migration to the United States, 1942–1992," *Social Science Quarterly* 75, no. 4 (1994): 705–29. For discussion of the Bracero Program in the global context of other "guest worker" programs, see Cindy Hahamovitch, *No Man's Land: Jamaican Guestworkers in America and the Global History of Deportable Labor* (Princeton, NJ: Princeton University Press, 2011).

7. See United States Congress, Senate, Committee on the Judiciary, *History of the Immigration and Naturalization Service*, 96th Cong. 2d Sess., Dec. 1980 (Washington, DC: U.S. Government Printing Office, 1980): 51, 57, 65.

8. U.S. Department of Justice, Immigration and Naturalization Service, *Statistical Yearbook of the Immigration and Naturalization Service, 1978* (Washington, DC: U.S. Government Printing Office, 1978), table 13, 36.

9. Ibid., table 23, 62.

10. Philip Martin, "There Is Nothing More Permanent Than Temporary Foreign Workers," in *Backgrounder* (Washington, DC: Center for Immigration Studies, April 2001).

11. Gratton and Gutmann, "Hispanics in the United States," 143, table 3.

12. For information on the Smithsonian's Bracero Archive, see http://braceroarchive .org/, accessed June 19, 2012. For the Bittersweet Harvest project, see www.sites.si.edu/ exhibitions/exhibits/bracero_project/main.htm, accessed June 19, 2012.

13. For analysis of the convoluted politics surrounding the annexation of Puerto Rico and the framing of the Jones Act of 1917, see *Foreign in a Domestic Sense: Puerto Rico, American Expansion, and the Constitution*, ed. Christina Duffy Burnett and Burke Marshall (Durham, NC: Duke University Press, 2001).

14. See *Balzac v. Porto Rico* 258 U.S. 298 (1922), 308. See also José A. Cabranes, *Citizenship and the American Empire: Notes on the Legislative History of the United States Citizenship of Puerto Ricans* (New Haven, CT: Yale University Press, 1979).

15. U.S. Bureau of the Census, *Census of the Population, 1970*, Subject Report PC (2)-1E, *Puerto Ricans in the United States* (Washington, D.C., 1973), table 1. For incisive analyses of the establishment and expansion of the Puerto Rican community of greater New York, see Kelvin A. Santiago-Valles and Gladys M. Jiménez-Muñoz, "Social Polarization and Colonized Labor: Puerto Ricans in the United States, 1945–2000," in *The Columbia History of Latinos Since 1960*, ed. David G. Gutiérrez (New York: Columbia University Press, 2004), 87–145; and Lorrin Thomas, *Puerto Rican Citizen: History and Political Identity in Twentieth-Century New York City* (Chicago: University of Chicago Press, 2010).

16. See James L. Dietz, *Economic History of Puerto Rico: Institutional Change and Capitalist Development* (Princeton, NJ: Princeton University Press, 1986); and Pedro A. Caban, "Industrial Transformation and Labor Relations in Puerto Rico: From 'Operation Bootstrap' to the 1970s," *Journal of Latin American Studies* 21, no. 3 (Aug. 1989): 559–91.

17. *Historical Statistics of the United States*, 1–177, table Aa 2189–215.

18. See María Cristina García, "Exiles, Immigrants, and Transnationals: The Cuban Communities of the United States," in *The Columbia History of Latinos in the United States Since 1960*: 146–86.

19. See ibid., 157–67; and Ruth Ellen Wasen, "Cuban Migration to the United States: Policy and Trends" (Washington, DC: Congressional Research Service, June 2, 2009) www.fas.org/sgp/crs/row/R40566.pdf, accessed March 25, 2012.

20. See Sharon R. Ennis, Merarys Ríos-Vargas, and Nora G. Albert, "The Hispanic Population: 2010," *2010 Census Briefs* (Washington, DC: U.S. Census Bureau, 2011), table 1.

21. See Pew Hispanic Center, "Hispanics of Cuban Origin in the United States, 2008— Fact Sheet," (Washington, DC: Pew Hispanic Center, April 22, 2010).

22. See Norma Stoltz Chinchilla and Nora Hamilton, "Central American Immigrants: Diverse Populations, Changing Communities," in *The Columbia History of Latinos Since 1960*: 186–228.

23. See INS, *Statistical Yearbook, 1978*, table 23, 62.

24. See Patricia Fernández Kelly and Douglas S. Massey, "Borders for Whom? The Role of NAFTA in Mexico-U.S. Migration," *Annals of the American Academy of Political and Social Science* 610, no. 1 (Mar. 2007): 98–118; Douglas S. Massey, Jorge Durand, and Nolan J. Malone, *Beyond Smoke and Mirrors: Mexican Immigration in an Era of Economic Integration* (New York: Russell Sage Foundation, 2002); and Raúl Delgado Wise and Humberto Márquez Covarrubias, "Capitalist Restructuring, Development and Labor Migration: The U.S.-Mexico Case," *Third World Quarterly* 29, no. 7 (Oct. 2008): 1359–74.

25. For discussion of the broad implications of these worldwide shifts in economic activity, see David Harvey, "Neoliberalism as Creative Destruction," *Annals of the American Academy of Political and Social Science* 610, no. 1 (Mar. 2007): 21–44; and Cheol-Sung Lee, "International Migration, Deindustrialization, and Union Decline in 16 Affluent OECD Countries, 1962–1997," *Social Forces* 84, no. 1 (Sept. 2005): 71–88.

26. For discussion of the changing gender balance of Latin American immigration, see Jacqueline M. Hagan, "Social Networks, Gender, and Immigrant Settlement: Resource and Constraint," *American Sociological Review* 63, no. 1 (1998): 55–67; Shawn M. Kanaiaupuni, "Reframing the Migration Question: Men, Women, and Gender in Mexico," *Social Forces* 78, no. 4: 1311–48; Pierrette Hondagneu-Sotelo, *Gender and U.S. Immigration: Contemporary Trends* (Berkeley: University of California Press, 2003); and Katherine M. Donato, "U.S. Migration from Latin America: Gendered Patterns and Shifts," *Annals of the American Academy of Political and Social Science* 630 (2010): 78–92. For a statistical breakdown of the gender balance for both foreign-born and U.S.-born Latinos see, Pew Hispanic Center, *Statistical Portrait of Hispanics in the United States: 2010* (Washington, DC: Pew Hispanic Center, 2012), Table 10a—Age and Gender Distribution for Race, Ethnicity, and Nativity Groups: 2010.

27. See Ramona Hernández and Francisco L. Rivera-Batiz, "Dominicans in the United States: A Socioeconomic Profile, 2000," *Dominican Research Monographs* (New York: City University of New York, Dominican Studies Institute, 2003), table 1.

28. See U.S. Census, "The Hispanic Population, 2010," table 1; and Çağlar Özden, "Brain Drain in Latin America," paper delivered at the Expert Group Meeting on International

Migration and Development in Latin America and the Caribbean, Population Division, Department of Economic and Social Affairs, United Nations Secretariat, Mexico City, Nov. 30–Dec. 2, 2005, UN/POP/EGM-MIG/2005/10 (Feb. 2006), www.un.org/esa/population/meetings/ltt MigLAC/P10_WB-DECRG.pdf.

29. See Roberto Suro, "Remittance Senders and Receivers: Tracking the Transnational Channels" (Washington, DC: Pew Hispanic Center, Nov. 23, 2003).

30. World Bank, Migration and Remittances Unit, *Migration and Remittances Factbook, 2011*, www.worldbank.org.prospects/migrantandremittances, accessed July 25, 2011.

31. See Fernández Kelly and Massey, "Borders for Whom?"; Wise and Covarrubias, "Capitalist Restructuring"; and Raúl Delgado Wise, "Migration and Imperialism: The Mexican Workforce in the Context of NAFTA," *Latin American Perspectives* 33, no. 2 (Mar. 2006): 33–45.

32. See Mary M. Kent, Kelvin J. Pollard, John Haaga, and Mark Mather, "First Glimpses from the 2000 U.S. Census," *Population Bulletin* 56, no. 2 (June 2001): 14; and Jeffrey S. Passel and D'Vera Cohn, "How Many Hispanics? Comparing New Census Counts with the Latest Census Estimates" (Washington, DC: Pew Hispanic Center, March 30, 2011).

33. See U.S. Census Bureau, "The Hispanic Population: 2010," table 1.

34. See Passel and Cohn, "How Many Hispanics?"; and Pew Hispanic Center, "Statistical Portrait of Hispanics in the United States, 2010," table 1.

35. See Jeffrey Passel and D'Vera Cohn, "The Unauthorized Immigrant Population: National and State Trends, 2010" (Washington, DC: Pew Hispanic Center, Feb. 1, 2011).

36. See Richard Marosi, "New Border Foe: Boredom," *Los Angeles Times*, April 21, 2011: A1.

37. See U.S. Immigration and Customs Enforcement, "ICE Total Removals through Feb. 20, 2012," www.ice.gov/doclib/about/offices/ero/pdf/eroremovals1.pdf, accessed June 15, 2012.

38. For a recent analysis of the downturn in both authorized and unauthorized migration from Mexico, see Jeffrey Passel, D'Vera Cohn, and Ana González-Barrera, "Net Migration from Mexico Falls to Zero—and Perhaps Less," (Washington, DC: Pew Hispanic Center, April 2012).

39. Passel and Cohn estimate that of the non-Mexican unauthorized population, 23 percent originated in Latin America, 11 percent in Asia, 4 percent in Canada and Europe, and another 3 percent, or about 400,000 persons, in Africa and elsewhere in the world. See Passel and Cohn, "The Unauthorized Immigrant Population: National and State Trends, 2010," 11.

40. See Teresa Watanabe, "Shortage of Skilled Workers Looms in U.S.," *Los Angeles Times*, April 21, 2008: A1; and Ricardo López, "Jobs for Skilled Workers Are Going Unfilled," *Los Angeles Times*, June 8, 2012: B1.

41. See Steven A. Camarota and Karen Jensenius, "Jobs Americans Won't Do? A Detailed Look at Immigrant Employment by Occupation" (Washington, DC: Center for Immigration Studies, Aug. 2009), especially table 1; American Immigration Law Foundation, "Mexican Immigrant Workers and the U.S. Economy: An Increasingly Vital Role," *Immigration Policy Focus* 1, no. 2 (Sept. 2002): 1–14; A.T. Mosisa, "The Role of Foreign-Born Workers in the U.S. Economy," *Monthly Labor Review* 125, no. 5 (2002): 3–14; Diane Lindquist "Undocumented Workers Toil in Many Fields," *San Diego Union-Tribune*, Sept. 4, 2006: A1; and

Gordon H. Hanson, "The Economic Logic of Illegal Immigration," *Council Special Report No. 26* (Washington, DC: Council on Foreign Relations, 2007). For an insightful case-study analysis of the structural replacement of domestic workers by the foreign-born in one key industry, see William Kandel and Emilio A. Parrado, "Restructuring the U.S. Meat Processing Industry and New Hispanic Migrant Destinations," *Population and Development Review* 31, no. 3 (Sept. 2005): 447–71.

42. See James DeFilippis, "On the Character and Organization of Unregulated Work in the Cities of the United States," *Urban Geography* 30, no. 1 (2009): 63–90.

43. See M. Tossi, "A Century of Change: The U.S. Labor Force, 1950–2050," *Monthly Labor Review* 125, no. 5 (2002): 15–28.

44. See Pew Hispanic Center, "Statistical Portrait of Hispanics in the United States," table 9.

45. See J. Esbenshade and B. Obzurt, "Local Immigration Regulation: A Problematic Trend in Public Policy," *Harvard Journal of Hispanic Policy* 20 (2008): 33–47; Kyle E. Walker and Helga Leitner, "The Variegated Landscape of Local Immigration Policies in the United States," *Urban Geography* 32, no. 2 (2011): 156–78; Monica W. Varsanyi, "Neoliberalism and Nativism: Local Anti-Immigrant Policy Activism and an Emerging Politics of Scale," *International Journal of Urban and Regional Research* 35, no. 2 (March 2011): 295–311; and Richard Fausset, "Alabama Enacts Strict Immigration Law," *Los Angeles Times*, June 10, 2011: A8.

6

LATE-TWENTIETH-CENTURY IMMIGRATION AND U.S. FOREIGN POLICY
Forging Latino Identity in the Minefields of Political Memory

Lillian Guerra

This essay illuminates the often dramatic differences in political perspective and general "visibility" in U.S. culture that characterize Cold War Latinos by exploring the ways in which U.S. policy toward Central American and Caribbean regimes shaped the economic and political possibilities open to these countries before and after the Cold War. It also reveals the hidden challenges that many survivors of Cold War violence faced upon arrival in the U.S. as they and their children struggled to make sense of their experiences and find their place in a society that frequently denied, confused, or ignored their reasons for being here. Although most Central American refugees arrived as undocumented refugees in the 1980s and subsequently spent years legalizing their status in order to improve their economic standing and gain greater political representation, Cubans who arrived in the 1960s and early 1970s became known for their unprecedented economic success compared with other Latinos and presumed unity behind unchanging U.S. foreign policy toward Castro's Cuba. However, even though Cubans have continuously benefitted from U.S. support for their immigration as part of a longstanding strategy to weaken the Communist regime in Cuba, Cuban communities have also become much more diverse than they are popularly perceived, especially since the 1980s and 1990s when tens of thousands of Cubans who experienced revolutionary Cuba brought more nuanced understandings of it and the Cold War with them to former enclaves founded by early wave "exiles" such as Miami.[1] Indeed, these exiles' success in South Florida has made it a haven for Cubans of all generations, transforming Miami from a city dominated by white Southerners (who constituted 79 percent of the population in 1970) to a cultural mecca for all Latinos and the city with the highest proportion of foreign-born residents nationwide, including thousands of Central Americans and Haitians.[2]

Differences in U.S. government support for Caribbean and Central American refugees undoubtedly affected their respective ability to consolidate a cultural and political presence on the public stage. Yet with or without this support, it is clear that refugees of the Cold War have successfully forged distinctive Latino identities based on historically meaningful memories of trauma, survival, and resilience that continue to transform political institutions, federal policies toward disadvantaged groups, urban landscapes, and cultural understandings of what it means to be "American" in countless ways.

Ironically, however, many foreign policies ultimately responsible for the creation of new Latino communities from Central America and the Caribbean in the U.S. were meant to have the opposite effect. One of the best illustrations of this can be found in President Ronald Reagan's famous nationally televised address on U.S. foreign policy toward the region, delivered on May 9, 1984. Portraying the emergence of revolutionary movements across Central America as the result of Cuban-Soviet machinations rather than any homegrown political or economic factors, Reagan warned that "Cuban-supported aggression" had already "forced more than 400,000 men, women, and children to flee their homes. And in all of Central America, more than 800,000 have fled . . ." Pinning the blame for Nicaragua's recent revolution against the U.S.-backed Somoza dictatorship on Cuba's Fidel Castro, Reagan predicted that the refugee crisis would only worsen if the U.S. once again allowed Castro to "deceive Western public opinion" by fooling citizens into believing that any revolution against the authoritarian regimes of Central America would *not* automatically lead to Communism. "Communist subversion," Reagan argued, "poses the threat that a hundred million people from Panama to the open border of our South could come under the control of pro-Soviet regimes," jeopardizing the U.S. way of life and hemisphere as a whole. In short, Reagan declared, "America *is* Central America."[3] The speech left little room to doubt either the logic or the merits of Reagan's primary goal: renewal of U.S. funding for military dictatorships in Central America with few, if any, conditions attached.

At that very moment, the U.S. Congress was seriously debating Reagan's demands with respect to El Salvador's military-dominated government.[4] In the wake of Reagan's speech and the well-timed appeal of visiting Salvadoran President José Napoleón Duarte, the U.S. Congress approved $196.6 million in funding for El Salvador in the fiscal year of 1984 alone, a sum two and a half times greater than the year before; moreover, U.S. aid was no longer contingent on democratic reforms.[5] Yet despite Reagan's promises that increasing aid would stem the flow of refugees, his policy of providing unconditional support to a military regime best known for ordering wide-scale massacres of unarmed civilians and selective assassinations of Catholic clergy had the opposite effect: not only did U.S. aid to El Salvador promote the state terror that led hundreds of thousands of civilians to flee across Mexican and U.S. borders, but U.S. aid also ensured that rampant corruption among Salvadoran officials continued to go unchecked.[6] By the late 1980s, the combination of war and graft had so crippled El Salvador's economy that President Duarte sent a personal appeal to President Reagan that he *stop deporting* thousands of undocumented Salvadoran refugees who found sanctuary in the U.S. Without the hundreds of millions of dollars in remittance payments that these refugees sent their families every year, Salvadoran society would have ceased to function.[7]

Today, it is clear that the consistency of U.S. support for military regimes and dictatorships across the region of Central America and the Caribbean played a major role in the creation of diaspora communities across the U.S. that can trace their origins to the Cold War, a period that spanned the end of World War II through the collapse of the Soviet Union in the early 1990s. According to the 2010 U.S. Census, Cubans and Salvadorans compete for the top spot in terms of sheer numbers of Cold War era communities, with each community hovering around 1.7 million nationwide. At slightly over 1.4 million members, Dominicans come in third place, with Guatemalans and Haitians close behind. Nicaraguans and Hondurans constitute the smallest of Latino communities who can trace their foundations to the effects of the Cold War in their home countries, numbering approximately 350,000 and 630,000 respectively. Although the vast majority of Cubans, Dominicans, and Haitians settled in only one city (Cubans and Haitians in Miami; Dominicans in New York), Salvadorans, the second-largest group of Cold War Latinos can be found in almost equal numbers in Los Angeles, New York, and our nation's capital, Washington, DC. (See table 6.1.)

Salvadorans, Cubans, Dominicans, Guatemalans, Haitians, Nicaraguans, and Hondurans send billions of dollars annually to relatives and friends in their homelands. Contrary to expectation, the amount sent per group does not necessarily correspond to its numeric size or relative wealth. Indeed, Cubans, whose population and capital far exceeds that of Dominicans, Guatemalans, and Haitians, send roughly the same amount home: about one billion dollars a year since the mid-1990s. In all cases, national governments of these countries now count remittances as an important part of their countries' GDP, or Gross Domestic Product; without it, their economic and political stability would inevitably suffer.

Nonetheless, most U.S. Americans, regardless of generation, remain profoundly unaware of how dramatically U.S. Cold War policy disrupted the lives and livelihood of these millions of Latinos from Central America and the Caribbean. As Juan Romagoza Arce, a former doctor who suffered torture and detention without charge at the hands of the Salvadoran military recalls of his arrival in the U.S., "I was surprised by how little people knew about what was happening outside their [borders]. People didn't know too much about the war in Central America—all they knew were 'communists.' . . . That was a shock. Because I suffered the consequences" of U.S. policies.[8]

Indeed, the rhetoric and logic of U.S. policies, as typified by Reagan's 1984 speech, still represents how much of the U.S. public continues to understand the violence that consumed the countries of Guatemala, Nicaragua, El Salvador, Haiti, and the Dominican

TABLE 6.1   2010 U.S. Census Bureau's American Community Survey Results

Group (Ranked by Size)	Total 2010 U.S. Population	Largest Concentrations
1. Cuban	1,785,547	1. Miami-Fort Lauderdale-Pompano Beach, FL (919,486)
		2. New York-Northern New Jersey-Long Island, NY-NJ-PA (134,519)
		3. Tampa-St. Petersburg-Clearwater, FL (77,366)
2. Salvadoran	1,648,968	1. Los Angeles-Long Beach-Santa Ana, CA (387,401)
		2. Washington-Arlington-Alexandria, DC-VA-MD-WV (211,844)
		3. New York-Northern New Jersey-Long Island, NY-NJ-PA (180,810)
3. Dominican	1,414,703	1. New York-Northern New Jersey-Long Island, NY-NJ-PA (796,166)
		2. Miami-Fort Lauderdale-Pompano Beach, FL (88,843)
		3. Boston-Cambridge-Quincy, MA-NH (87,167)
4. Guatemalan	1,044,209	1. Los Angeles-Long Beach-Santa Ana, CA (235,555)
		2. New York-Northern New Jersey-Long Island, NY-NJ-PA (90,818)
		3. Miami-Fort Lauderdale-Pompano Beach, FL (50,351)
5. Haitian	881,488	1. Miami-Fort Lauderdale-Pompano Beach, FL (267,958)
		2. New York-Northern New Jersey-Long Island, NY-NJ-PA (214,387)
		3. Boston-Cambridge-Quincy, MA-NH (56,709)
6. Honduran	633,401	1. New York-Northern New Jersey-Long Island, NY-NJ-PA (89,326)
		2. Miami-Fort Lauderdale-Pompano Beach, FL (77,503)
		3. Houston-Sugar Land-Baytown, TX (50,642)
7. Nicaraguan	348,202	1. Miami-Fort Lauderdale-Pompano Beach, FL (122,459)
		2. Los Angeles-Long Beach-Santa Ana, CA (40,741)
		3. San Francisco-Oakland-Fremont, CA (28,243)

Source: All figures from 2010 U.S. Census. The author gratefully thanks Christopher Woolley for his assistance in crafting this table.[9]

Republic from the 1950s to the mid-1990s. Fleeing "Communism" and *not* state terror or the generalized climate of repression created, in part, by U.S. policies in the region, also remains the way in which most Central American and Caribbean communities are arguably perceived by the average U.S. American. Seen as indirect victims of *Soviet* aggression rather than refugees of the U.S's alliance with *national* aggressors, Central Americans' and Caribbeans' complex, sometimes contentious views of their new adoptive home of the U.S. are often not only missed but also *dismissed* by journalists, politicians, teachers, and neighbors as confused, inaccurate, or worse, "un-American."

LIVING HISTORY: THE U.S.'S LONG COLD WAR IN CENTRAL AMERICA AND THE CARIBBEAN

For contemporary U.S. diasporas of Central America and the Caribbean, the most burdensome legacy of U.S. Cold War policy may be *living with the knowledge of that history itself and not knowing what to do with it*—how to fit one's country and one's personal experience into larger narratives about U.S. democracy, its commitment to human rights, the "American Dream," and the victorious outcome over the Soviet Union in the Cold War that saturate the popular culture and mainstream discourse of today's U.S. There are several reasons for this disparity. One is simply that most U.S. educators and public historians rely on history books that represent the Cold War as a triumphalist process that glosses the aim of U.S. foreign policy as simply containing Soviet designs.[10] The denial of the U.S.'s record in Latin America is particularly poignant for the children of Latinos from Central America and the Caribbean who frequently encounter total silence in schools, museums, and the media on the relationship between the U.S.'s role in stoking the violence that gripped their home countries and the conditions that provoked their families' flight to the U.S.

Thirsting for knowledge of their countries' past and a way of relating it to the democratic values and struggle for cultural dignity that define them as U.S. Latinos, students at Los Angeles' Belmont High School recently developed a popular (and free) on-line video game called Tropical America. Their goal was to teach themselves and others the lessons and legacies of surviving hundreds of years of Spanish colonialism as well as dozens of non-representative republican governments, many of which cooperated with foreign investors and U.S. corporations, before and after the Cold War, to prevent tangible democratization.[11] While these first-generation Latinos invented their own video game to explain the complexities of the U.S's Cold War in Latin America, most U.S. teenagers and young adults preferred the simpler story told by "Call of Duty: Black Ops", a widely marketed commercial video game in which players compete to reverse the U.S.'s Cold War "losses" in Cuba and elsewhere through missions such as assassinating Cuban leader Fidel Castro. As the game's popularity soared in 2011, many Cuban American parents were patently offended, pointing out that the game does not teach history but amnesia. Ironically, "Call of Duty" marked a rare case in which many Cubans in the U.S. and officials of the Cuban government could—and did—find total agreement.[12]

The "Kill Castro" scenario of "Call of Duty: Black Ops" as well as the game's now blockbuster status speaks volumes about the many factors that distort mainstream views of Central American and Caribbean history as well as the Cold War policies that produced unprecedented spikes in legal and illegal immigration from this region. These factors include the Castrocentric nature of public discourse regarding events in Latin America and the way in which early communities of Cuban exiles lined up their narratives of flight from Communism with the monolithic interpretations that U.S. officials derived from confrontations with revolutionary Cuba.

In part, the astounding ability of what has become known as the "Cuban exile lobby" to restrain changes in U.S. policy toward Cuba even as other barriers to normal relations with formal Cold War enemies like Vietnam collapsed can be traced to the Reagan era. Within a year of its organization, the exile-led Cuban American National Foundation became a primary advisor to the Reagan team on foreign policy toward Latin America, not just Cuba. Thus, Reagan's approach to El Salvador in the May 1984 speech cited above echoed a larger tendency to reduce popular revolutionary movements in Central America and the Caribbean to the influence of one man, Fidel Castro. However, all U.S. Presidents after World War II, with the exception of Jimmy Carter, shared much of this view: that is, they interpreted the nationalist goals of movements that defied the power of local oligarchs and called for reforming economic models of development that benefitted only elites and foreign investors as the first step toward Communism and Soviet control.[13] This was especially true after 1959, when Cuba's revolutionary state launched an unprecedented attack on U.S. investments and the legitimacy of a U.S. role in Cuban political affairs.[14]

Not only did a broadly popular movement force Fulgencio Batista, a U.S.-supported dictator, from power in 1959, but also within three years, the new government overturned the previous six decades of near constant U.S. military occupations, interventions, and U.S. ownership of the most lucrative parts of Cuba's national economy.[15] Standoffs between the U.S. and Cuba emerged almost immediately in January 1959 as the revolutionary government began to try, convict, and execute hundreds of officials and supporters of the Batista regime for "war crimes" associated with the disappearance and assassination of thousands of opponents over the course of the Batista dictatorship (1952–59).

When U.S. officials protested the clear bias of the trials and summary executions, their protests only lent greater validity to the process as millions of Cubans gathered in mass demonstrations to defend "revolutionary justice." Why, Fidel Castro repeatedly asked, had the same U.S. officials not issued similar protests when the tortured corpses of civilians still littered Cuba's streets only a few months earlier and Batista's air force was bombing peasant homes? Indeed, early popular support for repression of opponents facilitated the expansion of such methods and their reproduction over the course of the Revolution's first decade. Similar standoffs with the U.S., a rupture in diplomatic relations and U.S.-direction of the invasion at the Bay of Pigs created the pretext for the subsequent execution of hundreds of counterrevolutionaries and the jailing of tens of thousands more opponents and public critics, many of them former Castro supporters.[16]

In 1961, Cuba became the only society in Latin America where the U.S. was not present and not welcome. Except among former Batista supporters who had fled to Miami in 1959 and the once supportive Cuban middle class whose exodus to the U.S. reached its peak between 1965 and 1972, Cuba's consolidation of national sovereignty seemed to generate an incalculable degree of empowerment and national pride among the majority of islanders.[17] Even Fidel Castro's eventual embrace of socialism and the Soviet Union only hours before the disastrous CIA-directed invasion at the Bay of Pigs strengthened most Cubans' faith in the Revolution's moral righteousness vis à vis U.S. efforts at subversion.[18]

As historian Thomas Paterson has argued, U.S. officials' unflinching preoccupation with determining if Fidel was a Communist or not rendered them incapable of recognizing the critical role of anti-imperialist nationalism that Fidel tapped among the Cuban people and that he himself came to embody.[19] Subsequently, the primary lesson that U.S. officials drew from Cuba was *not* that dictators like Batista and repeated U.S. violations of national sovereignty promoted radical politics and anti-imperialist sentiment by repressing moderates and discrediting compromise; rather, it was that radical politics and "anti-American" sentiment provoked and justified the repression of moderates and the discrediting of compromise.

Thus, over the next three decades, stagnant and largely ineffective policies of isolating Cuba and attempting to assassinate Fidel Castro went hand-in-hand with unconditional support for "kleptocratic" dictatorships like that of the Duvaliers in Haiti, the Somoza family in Nicaragua, and the Balaguer regime in the Dominican Republic.[20] Periodically, these dictators' talent for embezzling foreign aid often exceeded their propensity to kill or intimidate opponents.[21] Nonetheless, these dictatorships produced just as many immigrants seeking political refuge as Castro's Cuba: indeed, because most opposition activists in countries like Haiti and the Dominican Republic hailed from the middle and educated classes, the first waves of immigrants to arrive in the 1960s coincided with Cuban exiles in terms of timing as well as social background. Where they differed was in their attitude toward the U.S. and the aid they received from federal agencies: Dominicans and Haitians were, after all, fleeing the violence of regimes that the U.S. supported while Cubans were fleeing the U.S's primary enemy, revolutionary Cuba. That most U.S. Americans might have inaccurately perceived Dominicans, Haitians, and other immigrants from Cold War hot spots in the region as "economic refugees" rather than political refugees on the order of Cuban exiles is not surprising. In many ways, such a view derived easily from U.S. officials' public statements and the belief that if the U.S. supported them, right-wing military regimes opposed to Communism could simply *not* produce political refugees.

At the same time, U.S. Cold War policies of preventing "other Cubas" by supporting authoritarian states—regardless of the means they employed—simply reinforced a deeply embedded pattern in the region that predated the Cold War. Until World War II, U.S. companies operated hand-in-hand with the U.S. government to thwart the possibility that national states might pass laws favoring local capitalists' interests and/or workers' rights to the detriment of foreign businesses. U.S. companies frequently achieved this by securing concessions that gave them monopolies on trade, production, infrastructure, and control over workers on massive estates.[22] Through such means, the United Fruit Company (popularly known as *El Pulpo*, "the Octopus") became a ubiquitous and infamous presence across Latin America as well as the largest landowner in Guatemala, Cuba, and other places.[23] In its efforts to prevent unionization, the United Fruit Company also recruited contract workers extensively across the Caribbean, creating racially and nationally mixed diasporas in plantations from Costa Rica, Panama, and Honduras to Cuba and Jamaica. Galvanized by a work experience that often made them proficient in multiple languages and radical proponents of labor rights, thousands of United Fruit workers made their way to cities such as New Orleans, Mobile, and New York as early as the 1910s. There, former United Fruit workers such as Marcus Garvey championed black pride and social justice, forever transforming the nature and direction of U.S. civil rights struggles in the 20th century.[24]

Often, U.S. investments in Latin America depended on the U.S.'s reliance on military interventions and occupations that protected those investments and, often, the local political status quo. Thus, the U.S. carried out military occupations of the Dominican Republic (1916–1924), Nicaragua (1926–1934), Haiti (1915–1934) as well as repeated interventions in Cuba, including two military occupations (1898–1902; 1906–1909) and support for at least two coups by sectors of Cuba's U.S.-trained national army (1933 and 1952). Despite officials' justifications of intervention in the name of fomenting democracy and generalized prosperity, U.S. military occupations did not lead to democratic regimes and more inclusionary national economies. On the contrary, in the countries that experienced them, U.S. military occupations led to some of the longest standing and bloodiest dictatorships in the world, including that of Anastasio Somoza whose family ruled Nicaragua from 1936–1979 and Rafael Trujillo who ruled the Dominican Republic from 1930–1961. Both were star pupils of U.S. Marine training schools and the first chiefs of the "National Guards" that replaced U.S. forces when they withdrew.[25] In Cuba, two-time dictator Fulgencio Batista began his political career in 1933 as the U.S.'s handpicked alternative to a revolutionary government that passed a slate of democratic reforms and repealed the Platt Amendment, a U.S.-imposed constitutional mandate that had allowed the U.S. to intervene militarily on behalf of U.S. interests since 1902.

Needless to say, ignorance about the history of U.S. interventions in the political and economic development of these countries *before and after* the start of the Cold War in 1948 can be astounding to those who live with the legacies of those interventions. Cases in point include that of Guatemala whose democratically elected government was toppled by the CIA five years *before* the Cuban Revolution for attempting to carry out a much needed agrarian reform because that reform targeted U.S. investments, especially the United Fruit Company. The Guatemalan government therefore constituted a "Communist menace," despite its unprecedented electoral validation and popularity in a country where universal suffrage and fair elections had been unknown less than a decade before.[26]

One legacy can be tallied in the number of human lives lost to the repressive policies of the dictatorships and military regimes that dominated five of these six countries from the 1950s through the 1990s; another lies in the vast waves of refugees that U.S.-financed policies of state terror and counterinsurgency warfare produced at the same time. Counting just the countries of Central America characterized by U.S.-backed military regimes and outright counterinsurgency wars targeting civilians, the totals are devastating: Nicaragua lost more than 80,000, of whom more than 30,000 died in the U.S.-sponsored Contra War against a revolutionary regime in the 1980s; in El Salvador and Guatemala respectively, 75,000 and 200,000 were killed or disappeared.[27] According to the United Nations' brokered truth commissions, which formed a key part of peace negotiations in all three cases, U.S.-trained armed forces were responsible for the vast majority of deaths and atrocities. In the case of El Salvador, state terror accounted for 85 percent of deaths and abuses.[28] In Guatemala, the commission found the state responsible for 93 percent of atrocities; it also qualified military strategies against Mayan Indians as genocidal because they accounted for 83 percent of all killed.[29] In addition, two million fled Central America.

In Haiti, where the Duvalier dynasty ruled from 1957 to 1986, state terror killed an estimated 30,000 to 50,000 civilians under Papa Doc's reign alone (1957–1971) with an additional 90,000 Haitians seeking refuge in the U.S. from the 1960s through the 1970s.[30] Tens of thousands more would die under Baby Doc as well as the multiple coups and counter-coups that followed his 1986 flight from power. The shattering of democratic hopes and ever-worsening economic conditions in the 1990s eventually produced a diaspora in the U.S. of Haitians that numbers just under one million today.[31]

Dominicans also fled the terror that followed the 1961 assassination of dictator Rafael Trujillo as Joaquín Balaguer, Trujillo's former vice president, and Trujillo's military struggled to contain the radical impulses of the country's long repressed citizenry. At first, the U.S. Embassy refused visas for Dominicans seeking asylum from the political terror that Balaguer unleashed because of their presumably radical political credentials; however, in 1965, it reversed course. By then, a U.S. military occupation had toppled a popularly installed revolutionary government from power and reasserted the authority of former Dominican military allies, including Joaquín Balaguer. Immigration visas thus became an additional weapon in the U.S.'s counterinsurgency arsenal because allowing political activists to escape "neo-trujillista" reprisals by Balaguer's death squads acted as a safety valve for radicalization. Ironically, escape to the country most Dominicans blamed for the thirty-year Trujillo dictatorship and the violence that followed helped to dissipate the possibilities for re-organizing revolutionary forces. U.S. officials assumed that any reorganization of nationalist activism would undermine U.S. power and embolden other societies to imitate their example.[32]

In all cases except the Dominican Republic and Cuba where the granting of visas complemented U.S. foreign policy until the early 1970s, most of those fleeing state terror and political violence for the U.S. were undocumented upon arrival. Subsequently, refugees who applied for a legalization of their status encountered pronounced discrimination on the part of U.S. Immigration and Naturalization Services [INS] based on the contention that they were economically motivated, exaggerating claims of individual repression or simply unable to "prove" that they would suffer persecution if returned to their homeland, however obvious the condition of generalized violence.[33] For certain groups at the height of conflict, such as Salvadorans and Guatemalans in the 1980s, the political reasoning behind INS denials of claims for asylum had everything to do with U.S. Cold War policy toward their homelands.

Since the late 1960s, the Salvadoran military had increasingly relied on U.S. training and diplomatic support to prevent any substantive reforms and thereby preserve a tiny elite's control over the national economy through a vast campaign of political violence.[34] By 1980, that campaign had expanded far beyond its original targeting of left-wing guerrillas and unarmed activists to attack thousands of civilians, including students, professors, doctors, international aid workers, a disproportionately high number of peasants as well as dozens of Catholic laypeople, nuns, and priests.[35] Most famously, in March 1980, the head of El Salvador's national security agency ordered the assassination of Archbishop Oscar Romero, a vociferous critic of U.S. aid; the military then fired on the 30,000 mourners who gathered for his funeral, killing dozens.[36] The military went as far as to threaten the entire Jesuit order with "extermination" and famously abducted, raped, and killed four U.S. church women, three of them nuns, on the presumption that their work with the poor made them allies of left-wing guerrillas.[37] In the first four years of Reagan's presidency alone, the military murdered between eight and nine thousand civilians per year; the Salvadoran government ordered not a single investigation of their deaths.[38]

Not surprisingly, as legal scholar Michael H. Posner noted at the time, it was extremely difficult for the U.S. to admit tens of thousands of refugees and "thus acknowledge political persecution by the government of El Salvador, and yet ask Congress to certify more military assistance to that country based on significant human rights improvements of the refugees' government."[39]

Indeed, from June 1983 to September 1990, only 2.6 percent of Salvadoran and 1.8 percent of Guatemalan asylum seekers succeeded.[40] In the case of Haitian refugees where a related, although highly racialized, logic applied, *only eleven* of 22,940 Haitians intercepted at sea were deemed qualified to apply for political asylum between 1981 and 1990. Three years later, after the Bush administration sanctioned another bloody coup, this time against the democratically elected government of Jean-Bertrande Aristide, only 11,000 Haitians of 38,000 who attempted to enter the U.S. were granted the right to apply for political asylum. The U.S. Coast Guard returned the rest to Haiti.[41] Surprisingly, refugees from Nicaragua did not necessarily benefit from INS largesse despite the fact that they were displaced by a civil war that pitted the country's revolutionary government troops against the Contras, an army organized by the CIA, led by former *somocista* National Guardsmen and financed by the U.S.[42] Only 9 to 11 percent of Nicaraguan refugees were granted asylum until 1985–1987 when Reagan's drive for massive aid to the Contras resulted in a spike in approvals as high as 84 percent. Once Congress cut off aid again, however, levels dropped to their previous rates.[43]

By contrast, Cubans or applicants from Eastern bloc countries enjoyed near automatic entrance to the U.S.[44] Cubans, who had benefitted from U.S. State Department visa waivers in the early years of the Revolution, subsequently enjoyed automatic permanent residency status and additional benefits such as food, cash allotments, Cubans-only educational programs, and other privileges never extended to other immigrants or minority groups based on the 1966 Cuban Adjustment Act and the two-billion-dollar Cuban Refugee Program that provided unprecedented federal support to individual refugees as well as schools, businesses, and state agencies attending them until 1980.[45] Although Cubans arriving by sea must make landfall to avoid deportation since 1994, U.S. law has continued to consider virtually anyone who wants to leave Cuba a "political refugee," no questions asked. As María de los Angeles Torres explains, "For the U.S. government, Cuban émigrés provided the rationale for continuing a foreign policy aimed at containing communism and expanding the forces needed for battle."[46] On this basis, nearly one million Cubans were admitted, with 20,000 more arriving every year through a U.S.-sponsored visa lottery and thousands of others by land and sea in the post-Cold War era.

Undoubtedly, Cuban exiles and those of more recent migrations struggle with unique traumas associated with living under the domain of a Communist state that has tolerated little if any dissent and an official political culture that, until recently, identified anyone who left or wanted to leave as a traitor, sell-out, *escoria* (scum), and even "*anti-cubano*." Many exiles of the 1960s lived with memories of having suffered public humiliation at the hands of proponents and agents of Castro's popular revolutionary regime. In the weeks before a family departed, government ministries carried out inventories of their home and forced them to pay for any goods that did not appear at the time of the final inspection: they were effectively charged with having "stolen" their own property from "the people." Those leaving after 1962 could no longer take anything with them except $5 and a small suitcase carrying the barest necessities. Years later, the strongest memory that some exiles carry with them is not of leaving their relatives behind but of being treated like common criminals at the Havana airport. Charged with inspecting departing "*gusanos*" for hidden cachés of diamonds or jewels, militia men and women inspected body orifices; for men, this meant the anal cavity and for women, the vagina.[47]

Caught up in a "class war" for which most exiles felt they were not responsible, Cuban exiles bonded with one another in the famously all-Cuban enclaves of Little Havana and Hialeah in Miami Dade County, re-establishing the newspapers and small businesses that they had lost in Cuba and refounding the many Catholic schools to which they had sent their children. While the wealthiest exile elite, including a majority of *batistianos* (former Batista supporters), recreated racially segregated institutions like the Havana Yacht Club (renamed the Havana Yacht Club in Exile) and exclusive lily-white neighborhoods like Miramar, working-class and middle-class Cubans killed and roasted whole pigs in their backyards, bought land to grow traditional Cuban foods for local markets, and opened up grocery stores and restaurants for other Cubans.

Yet for Cubans of all social classes, Miami was not necessarily a welcoming place in the 1960s and early 1970s when nearly half a million refugees first arrived. Indeed, the display of "For Rent" signs in Miami that also read "No Children, No Pets and No Cubans" became a legendary example of the hostility that greeted many early refugees.[48] Because Miami's schools, beaches, and public spaces were still racially segregated, thousands of Cubans—whom local whites perceived as non-white however the Cubans themselves may have identified—courageously defied racial and cultural barriers en masse. Indeed, African-Americans "watched in disbelief" as Cuban black and mulatto children attended formally all-white schools, together with their racially mixed and Hispanic Cuban compatriots.[49]

Forced to accommodate thousands of Spanish-speaking Cuban children and hundreds of highly qualified, if uncertified, Cuban teachers, Miami's public schools expanded wildly. Between 1960 and 1965, the U.S. Department of Health, Education and Welfare established teacher training programs to jumpstart the certification of Cuban teachers, created the country's first federally funded bilingual schools, opened vocational training courses for adults, launched Cuban-specific college loan programs, and found jobs for the hundreds of University of Havana professors who had settled in Miami Dade County.[50] Cubans also received cash relief at levels much higher than native residents and became the first beneficiaries of government-surplus food.[51] Perhaps most ingenious was the "Training for Independence" program, targeted specifically at Cuban single-mothers and unmarried women in Miami who depended on relief. Offering intensive English-language classes and job training, the mandatory program was so successful that it became a model for welfare assistance projects nationwide.[52]

Undoubtedly, the symbolic competition between the U.S. and the Soviet bloc during the Cold War inspired much of the creativity and generosity behind these federal programs. Yet their success in aiding Cubans adjust and succeed ultimately helped justify the claims of other minorities, not just other Latinos, for similar kinds of federal support as well as policies that would promote multi-culturalism, not simply assimilation. Indeed, while Cubans were the principal beneficiaries of the Cuban Refugee Program, the hundreds of millions of dollars it pumped into South Florida schools, infrastructure and economy indirectly benefitted the whole regional economy, increasing tourism and catalyzing a long-term real estate boom. Despite this, Miami's self-described "Anglos" led the U.S.'s first English-only movement in 1980 that eventually amended the Florida Constitution to specify English as the official language of the state in 1988. In response, Cubans mobilized to defeat the Democratic politicians responsible for the amendment by registering to vote. Overwhelming the electorate in sheer numbers, Cubans ultimately overturned the amendment in 1993 and permanently established the character of Florida as a place that values bilingualism and promotes pride in Spanish fluency.[53] As one Cuban writer has put it, "the Miami of today can hardly be compared to any city in the Cuba we remember. . . . [However, in Miami] an exile has a choice to be one, the other, or both [Latino and American], and to communicate using English, Spanish or both languages—this is a key point."[54]

Today, any Latino resident of Miami would likely agree with this sentiment and the reasons extend far beyond Cubans' struggle to preserve their language. While Cubans faced cultural and racial marginalization for the first twenty to thirty years of their settlement in Miami, the most Cuban-identified areas of Miami are now the most culturally integrated by other Latino refugees, especially those from Central America, despite the array of public monuments and markers designating these areas as historically and culturally Cuban. "Calle Ocho" (or Eighth Street) in Little Havana provides a case in point. There, restaurants such as "Fritanga Erika" promise Nicaraguan food with Cuban flare and "Café Latina" advertises Central American fusion alongside authentic Cuban espresso. Even iconic spaces, long ago declared Florida Heritage Sites, have broadened the cultural identities and histories that they celebrate, to include far more than Cubans. For example, a large, painted mural featuring the images of Latin American leaders gathered at a summit in Miami during the Clinton administration flanks one side of the Parque Máximo Gómez, a small park where elderly Cuban men and women have gathered to play dominoes and talk politics since 1976. Calle Ocho also features a Hollywood-style walk of fame on its sidewalk with virtually as many Latin American entertainment stars as Cubans. A few blocks away, Cafetería Guardabarranco's colorful mural also announces the unity of Cubans with other Latinos. One end features the faces of Afro-Cuban musician Celia Cruz, Puerto Rican bandleader Tito Puente, Mexican American Selena, and Argentina's Carlos Gardel; the other end highlights the visages of Latin America's most famous nationalists alongside a bustling scene of traditional village life and the phrase, *"¡Viva Nuestra Raza!"* [Long live our race!].

Still, despite these clear signs of solidarity and inclusion, Little Havana remains the symbolic heart of official exile narratives about their place in the U.S.'s Cold War past. Erected through local fundraising efforts and maintained by the combined efforts of city government and vigilant residents, historical monuments punctuate the area. A monument featuring the Virgin of Charity, Cuba's patron saint, announces Miami Cubans' commemoration of the one-hundred-year anniversary of Cuba's last war for independence against Spain with no mention of the U.S.'s fateful intervention of 1898 in the war and Cuban patriots' subsequent struggle to rid the island of a four-year-long U.S. military occupation: indeed, the monument gives the impression that none of these things ever happened. Similarly, Little Havana's monument to Cuban exile "martyrs" at the Bay of Pigs calls the event an "assault" rather than the more familiar U.S. term of "invasion" or "operation." Most bizarre of all is a monument to Manolo Fernández, "*El Caballero del Tango*" [The Knight of the Tango], which features a dedication by its chief funder, Gilberto Casanova, whom a plaque describes as the Secretary of Acción Cubana, or "Cuban Action." Founded in the early 1970s by Cuban exile extremists in protest of what they perceived as the softening of U.S. foreign policy toward Latin America and growing complacency among fellow exiles toward Castro, Acción Cubana claimed responsibility for the bombings of dozens of Cuban embassies and consulates throughout Latin America.[55]

These monuments speak to the minefield of memory in which Cubans of different generations have forged their identity in South Florida. The region's political culture developed in tandem with two, largely unique processes: first, the development of unprecedented programs of covert and overt subversion by national security agencies to topple and undermine the Cuban government led by Fidel Castro; and second, the development of equally unprecedented programs of direct legal, educational, and financial aid to Cuban refugees that no other immigrant or minority group has ever enjoyed. The former initially entailed easy employment in the world's largest CIA station at the University of Miami. Endowed with an annual budget of $50 million a year, the CIA hired a staff of 400 agents and over ten to fifteen thousand informants, saboteurs, and self-appointed political saviors drawn from the early ranks of Cuban exiles.[56] In addition, the CIA's funding of front businesses in Miami ensured that certain Cuban exiles enjoyed a "subsidized" and financially guaranteed version of the American Dream while Anglo-owned businesses and all others simply had to fend for themselves.[57] Until 1980 when the much darker, much more working-class *marielitos* arrived, Cubans also enjoyed a variety of advantages in their public image thanks to a sympathetic U.S. media that usually depicted them as white, educated, and affluent, all qualities that mattered in a still highly segregated U.S. culture, even though in most cases, Cubans did not necessarily fit the bill. Moreover, their access to public funds facilitated by agencies of the U.S. government ensured that, among other privileges, Cubans gained greater access to federally funded loans in comparison to Dominicans, Puerto Ricans, and African Americans.[58]

Cubans of subsequent generations who grew up in Miami continue to prosper from the historically accumulated advantages that their parents and grandparents' utility to U.S. foreign policy granted them. But Cubans were not just beneficiaries of U.S. policy, they were also its victims. From the 1960s through the early 1990s, paramilitary groups based in Miami not only launched raids on Cuba with the support of the CIA; they also attempted to silence those Cuban exiles who favored dialogue with and travel to the island. The paramilitary groups used selective assassinations, death threats, and bombings of post offices, banks, the airport, an exile-owned art gallery, Miami's FBI headquarters, and other institutions to intimidate their fellow exiles. Testifying to the deep connections that Cuban exiles enjoy at the centers of power, no group or individual was ever charged with these crimes.[59]

U.S. intelligence agencies' willingness to either sponsor or tolerate illegal and criminal methods employed by right-wing exile groups to police the attitudes, public speech, and political positions of other Cubans and Cuban-Americans has played a key role in maintaining U.S. policy toward Cuba on a wartime footing. It has also fomented a culture of political "intolerance" in South Florida, especially Miami.[60] As a result, individual Cubans and Cuban-Americans who disagree with exile points of view on U.S. policy toward Cuba or question key aspects of the exile narrative on the Cuban Revolution (most commonly portrayed as an event that never needed to have happened) often encounter hostility, name-calling, job discrimination, arguments with friends and relatives, as well as overt forms of intimidation.[61]

Importantly, Cubans who most disagree with the U.S. embargo and travel ban on Cuba today are not registered to vote.[62] Equally important is the overwhelming support for change in U.S. foreign policy toward Cubans among Florida's Cuban community, despite the public positions taken by Cuban exiles and Cuban American elected officials, both locally and nationally. According to a Florida International University Cuba Study Group poll, conducted regularly since 1991, the percentage of Cubans favoring the re-establishment of diplomatic relations between Cuba and the U.S. reached 58 percent in 2011.[63]

The contradiction in positions between elected representatives and the Cuban community that elects them on the issue of U.S.-Cuban relations remains difficult to explain. Fear of rejection by one's community as a Castro sympathizer and the apathy that over-politicization of life in *both* Cuba and among Cuban communities in the U.S. undoubtedly play a role. Yet despite the tensions with which Cubans live in the U.S., their numeric concentration in primarily one spot and their relatively high visibility in public consciousness gives Cubans an organizational advantage when it comes to representing their interests and identity at the local and national level.

By contrast, other Latinos who trace their community's origins to Cold War struggles in their home countries find themselves geographically fragmented across multiple cities in the U.S. and far less empowered at all levels, culturally, politically, and economically—in part, because they largely arrived as undocumented refugees. Ignored by the mainstream media or simply "generalized" into the panethnic category of Latino with little analysis of what makes each group's culture and politics different, other refugees from Central America and the Caribbean often feel frustrated by the invisibility of their culture and the Castro-centrism that tends to pervade public representations of the Cold War. Getting beyond this Castro-centrism involves understanding how stories of trauma, survival, and recovery have woven themselves into the process of identity building among these Latino communities and members' everyday lives.

GETTING BEYOND CASTRO-CENTRISM: LIVING THE LEGACY OF POLITICAL VIOLENCE AND TORTURE AMONG CENTRAL AMERICANS

How do Salvadorans or Guatemalans in the U.S. who suffered brutal forms of torture and mass terror at the hands of state security forces in the 1980s and 1990s *talk* about their society's ordeal in a cultural context that fails to recognize that it even happened? How do they explain to their friends and neighbors their fear of visiting their homelands where, for the most part, the military officers responsible for atrocities not only enjoy near-total impunity but have remained critical players in their current government's post-war "democratic" regimes? For years, Juan Romagoza Arce, a Salvadoran survivor of torture, asked himself such questions everyday. One way he responded to them was to courageously challenge the officials responsible for his torment, El Salvador's Minister of Defense and Chief of the National Guard, in U.S. federal courts. Awarded multiple honors by U.S. officials, the generals had retired to South Florida where they led normal lives until Romagoza and two other Salvadorans won their case against the men in 2002.[64] When the court's ruling was repeatedly upheld under appeal, Romagoza then joined new litigants in launching another successful case, this time in Memphis, Tennessee, against Colonel Nicolás Carranza, El Salvador's former Vice Minister of Defense and Public Security who oversaw the National Guard and National Police.[65] These cases represent enormous symbolic victories for survivors of torture everywhere, as their lawyers at the Center for Justice and Accountability based in San Francisco made clear.

Every case and investigation draws communities in Central America and the U.S. together in a process of survival and healing that helps younger generations share the historical witness that often mark their parents' and grandparents' perspectives. While the experience may unite and strengthen Central Americans' transnational identity, it is unclear what effect it may have on uninformed or disinterested mainstream Americans in the U.S. Judging from the testimony delivered at the time of the Salvadoran generals' landmark trial, not only did plaintiffs have to educate judge and jury as to the nature of their abuse, but they also had to battle the deeply ingrained discourse for which Reagan became so famous, that is, of equating Central American counterinsurgency methods with "freedom-fighting." Attesting to this in the 2002 case, the defense attorney, in his closing remarks, compared the Salvadoran generals responsible for the atrocities civilians suffered to Thomas Jefferson and John Adams.[66]

Romagoza and his fellow plaintiffs' victories represent one of many instances where victims of Salvadoran and Guatemalan government atrocities have sought redress transnationally, that is, either in U.S. courts or through the aid of international human rights activists and even historians based in the U.S. These instances, perhaps more than other examples, have helped make the presence and story of Central American migration more visible and relevant to the U.S. public. For Guatemalans who can afford it or have ties to U.S. institutions in the U.S., trying security agents responsible for individual deaths of relatives in U.S. courts has also become a means for contesting the impunity enjoyed by former military officers-turned-politicians, such as General Efraín Ríos Montt, Guatemala's dictator of the early 1980s whom the United Nations accused of genocide.[67] Addressing the Guatemalan military's strategies against largely rural Mayan communities has also entailed transnational cooperation in excavating bodies from massacre sites as well as unearthing critical documents. In 2005, historians discovered a secret police archive containing 30,000 files of citizens arrested and disappeared during the 1980s. In its analysis and preservation, Guatemalan historians and U.S. historians of Guatemala like Greg Grandin have played a vital role.[68]

Nonetheless, Central American refugees, like many Haitians, face the daily paradox of having sought refuge in the very society that many blame for the extent of the violence that they suffered in their homelands. Many also face the equally paradoxical reality of having fought deportation from the U.S. for years on the charge that they were not "real" political refugees but economic migrants, seeking jobs not sanctuary in the U.S. Incredibly, hundreds of former generals and other top security officers responsible for war crimes often found easy routes to permanent residency and eventual citizenship. For many, the INS's apparent preference for deporting illegal immigrants from Central America, even if they were victims of human rights abuses, was not only complemented by a willingness to aid and abet known abusers, but a policy of helping them cover up past crimes.[69] According to Amnesty International, about 400,000 survivors of politically orchestrated torture live in the U.S. and about 1,000 alleged torturers live among them, including many from Haiti, Nicaragua, and El Salvador.[70] During the course of conflict and afterward, solidarity networks linking Catholic-led organizations such as Witness for Peace as well as non-profit Latino organizations such as La Peña in Berkeley and the Esperanza Peace and Justice Center in San Antonio played pivotal roles in helping Cold War refugees find sanctuary, help, and advice in making the transition to life in the U.S.

Violence has nonetheless remained a permanent part of life for many Central Americans who live in poor neighborhoods, especially in Los Angeles where young Salvadoran gang members govern key aspects of the drug trade, just as they do in San Salvador. In explaining the emergence of the gangs, many analysts point to the role played by child soldiers in the Salvadoran war, particularly those forcibly recruited into the state military ranks where they witnessed and carried out torture and corporal mutilation. In order to solve a deficit in the number of recruits, military forces regularly kidnapped individual boys as they were walking to school, running errands, or playing; they also raided middle schools, abducting into their ranks whole classrooms or all the boys in particular grades.[71] Of the government's troops, 80 percent were under the age of eighteen, with most averaging 14–15 years old at the time of their incorporation. By contrast, 30 percent of guerrillas were minors.[72] Often orphaned by army offensives, they joined the guerrillas out a desire to avenge their dead family members or because they had no one to care for them and therefore no other choice.[73] Recently, Central American gangs have garnered increasing attention in the U.S. media, especially as former guerrilla commanders, Catholic Church authorities, and Homies Unidos, a Los Angeles-based gang intervention project, prepared to broker a truce among gang members from California to El Salvador in May 2012.[74]

Unfortunately, few would contend that knowledge of their wartime roots plays a role in how most young gang members are perceived. The scars that they carry are as invisible as those carried by older immigrants and migrants, despite the fact that in recent years, the U.S. Federal Government has taken remarkable steps to recognize and deal with the trauma that the legacies of torture can inflict on families and communities, often for years. Such steps include the funding of clinics meant to treat torture victims and the Healing Club, a support group in Los Angeles for torture victims and their families. The club forms part of two dozen little-known, federally funded torture rehabilitation programs in the U.S.[75]

The attention of Federal Government agencies and legal victories over human rights abusers clearly have made Central Americans know that they are not alone in burdening the costs and the knowledge of history that they bear. Such a shift forms part of a larger process of empowerment that has clearly emerged in the last fifteen years as the majority of first-wave Central American refugees legalized their status and thereby increased their political activism on behalf of community needs, fielded candidates for political office, and became key players in transnational efforts to subvert official silences in their homelands.[76] For example, María Teresa Tula, leader of the human rights group known as Co-Madres that Archbishop Romero founded in San Salvador shortly before he was assassinated, came to the U.S. as an undocumented refugee in 1987 despite the fact that Co-Madres had received the Robert F. Kennedy Human Rights Award three years earlier. However, Tula's long-standing ties to peace activists in the U.S. and U.S. academics who sponsored speaking tours in which Tula shared her story ultimately served to bring her and other Salvadorans' struggle to greater public consciousness. A transcript of María Teresa Tula's life history, published in 1999, quickly became and remains a bestselling textbook in U.S. colleges nationwide.[77] Moreover, from her home in the U.S., Tula and the Co-Madres successfully led an alliance of NGOs that pressured the Salvadoran government to create the country's principal war memorial in 2003. Modeled on the Vietnam War Memorial in Washington, "The Wall" in San Salvador's central Cuscatlán Park conmemorates the thousands of dead and disappeared at the hands of the Salvadoran military.

Although even the largest Salvadoran community in Los Angeles does not yet boast its own monuments, it has scored several recent victories in gaining official recognition and support for public sites honoring Salvadoran history and presence. In 2000, the Salvadoran American National Association partnered with Catholic parishes in Los Angeles to commission a replica of the nation's revered sacred image of Jesus Christ, Divine Savior, which normally resided in San Salvador's cathedral. Highly symbolic of so many refugees' own perilous journey, the statue left El Salvador on a pilgrimage through Guatemala and Mexico before finally arriving at the Dolores Mission Church.[78] In 2009, Cal State University, Northridge, the General Consulate of El Salvador in Los Angeles, and Museo de la Palabra y la Imagen in San Salvador sponsored a series of multimedia events at the Los Angeles Theatre Center called *"Preservación de la Memoria Histórica Salvadoreña"* (Salvadoran Preservation of Historic Memory). Meant to address "the civil war's haunting legacy while looking toward the future of Salvador's people, at home and abroad," the program included a photo exhibit, a symposium on historic memory, discussions of Salvadoran writers, and theatrical presentations celebrating indigenous heritage. In explaining his motivations for staging the festival William Flores, director of Olin Theater Presenters, noted, "Memory is something that mustn't be lost. . . . To kill memory is to kill the human being."[79]

Salvadorans in Los Angeles have also found new sites to anchor, cultivate, and restore their much ravaged memory and cultural knowledge in a section of Vermont Avenue known as the El Salvador Community Corridor. Although it already boasts twenty-five restaurants and eighty other Salvadoran-owned businesses, the area still lacks the murals, monuments, and museums that typify historic districts such as Little Havana's Calle Ocho. Moreover, while a plaza in the corridor was named for the Salvadoran patriot and spiritual hero Archbishop Oscar Romero, it might soon compete with another commemorative space also named for Romero if a group of Salvadoran leaders succeeds in renaming MacArthur Park in the fall of 2012.[80]

As this essay shows, the struggle for greater political representation and prosperity that arguably all immigrants face was notably complicated in the case of Cold War Latinos by the complex and contradictory history that led to their presence in the U.S. Their ability and willingness to forge a public identity and image for themselves has also been undercut by the ways in which memories of that history remain buried, distorted, or simply unknown to most U.S. Americans. Nonetheless, the political transformation that they have achieved and continue to achieve at the national and local levels is as important as the cultural transformation; one is inevitably linked to the other. Ironically, even as federal programs undoubtedly favored Cubans in important material ways, their ascent as a community undoubtedly served to further other Central American and Caribbean Latinos' self-representation in government, the media, and public space. While much of U.S. Cold War policy in their home countries might have backfired, the unexpected creation of new Latino communities in the U.S. that resulted from this policy clearly strengthened U.S. democracy at home and affirmed the right of all members of our society to pursue justice, freedom, and their own American dreams.

NOTES

1. Susan Eva Eckstein, *The Immigrant Divide: How Cubans Changed the U.S. and Their Homeland* (New York: Routledge, 2009), 23–39, 70–87.
2. Ibid., 46–47.

3. Ronald Reagan, "Address to the Nation on United States Policy on Central America," May 9, 1984. www.reagan.utexas.edu/archives/speeches/1984/50984h.htm. Accessed on April 2, 2012.

4. William M. LeoGrande, *Our Own Backyard: The United States in Central America, 1977–1992* (Chapel Hill, NC: University of North Carolina Press, 1998), 253.

5. LeoGrande, 256–258.

6. Mario Lungo Uclés, E*l Salvador in the Eighties,* translated by Amelia F. Shogan (Philadelphia: Temple University Press, 1996), 90–91, 101–102; Tommie Sue Montgomery, "El Salvador: Roots of Revolution" in *Central America: Crisis and Adaptation,* edited by Steve C. Ropp and James A. Morris (Albuquerque, NM: University of New Mexico Press, 1984), 79–80.

7. María Cristina García, *Seeking Refuge: Central American Migration to Mexico, the United States, and Canada* (Berkeley, CA: University of California Press, 2006), 110.

8. Joshua E. S. Phillips, "The Case Against the Generals," *The Washington Post* (17 August 2003), W-06.

9. Information on the concentration of these and other ethnic groups may be found on the U.S. Census Bureau's "American Factfinder" website at: http://factfinder2.census.gov/faces/nav/jsf/pages/index.xhtml. To replicate the data in the table found in this essay go to the American Factfinder website and follow the steps below:

- Click on Geographies-Metropolitan Statistical Area/select Microstatistical area 2010/select "All Metropolitan and Micropolitan Statistic Areas within the United States and Puerto Rico." [click "Add to your selection," Close]
- Click on Topics/select People/select Population Change/select Migration (Previous Residence) [Close]
- Click on People/Type in a race, ancestry, or tribe [e.g. Dominican, Salvadoran, Cuban, etc.] and click "Go"/Population Group Name [select group, click Add, Close]
- Select table BO7204 "Geographical Mobility Within the Past Year for Current Residence—State, County and Place Level in the United States"/select View Table

For the group selected, the above table gives the total population for the largest 90–180 U.S. cities to include information on migration. It should be noted that these numbers are derived from the U.S. Census Bureau's American Community Survey and are current estimates based on both the 10-year U.S. Census and the Bureau's annual surveys.

10. Gilbert Joseph, "What We Know and Should Know: Bringing Latin America More Meaningfully into Cold War Studies," in *In From the Cold: Latin America's New Encounter with the Cold War,* edited by Gilbert Joseph and Daniela Spenser (Durham, NC: Duke University Press, 2008), 11–15.

11. Susan Carpenter, "Latin America's Past Relived in Video Game," *Los Angeles Times* (11 December 2003), E30.

12. Paul Haven, "Cuba Denounces 'Virtual' Castro Plot in New Game," *The Washington Times* (10 November 2010), http://www.washingtontimes.com/news/2010/nov/10/cuba-denounces-virtual-castro-plot-in-new-game.

13. Stephen G. Rabe, *Eisenhower and Latin America: The Foreign Policy of Anticommunism* (Chapel Hill, NC: University of North Carolina Press, 1988) and *The Most Dangerous Area in the World: John F. Kennedy Confronts Communist Revolution in Latin America* (Chapel Hill, NC: University of North Carolina Press, 1999); John H. Coatsworth, *Central America and the United States: The Clients and the Colossus* (Boston, MA: Twayne Publishers, 1994); Walter LaFeber, *Inevitable Revolutions: The United States in Central America,* 2nd ed. (New York: W. W. Norton, 1993).

14. Morris H. Morley, *Imperial State and Revolution: The United States and Cuba, 1952–1986* (New York: Cambridge University Press, 1987); Lars Schoultz, *That Infernal Little Cuban Republic: The United States and the Cuban Revolution* (Chapel Hill, NC: University of North Carolina Press, 2009).

15. Louis A. Pérez, Jr., *Cuba: Between Reform and Revolution* (New York: Oxford University Press, 1995); Lillian Guerra, *The Myth of José Martí: Conflicting Nationalisms in Early Twentieth-Century Cuba* (Chapel Hill, NC: University of North Carolina Press, 2005).

16. Lillian Guerra, *Visions of Power in Cuba: Revolution, Redemption and Resistance, 1959–1971* (Chapel Hill, NC: University of North Carolina Press, 2012), 46–49, 90–92, 115–117, 130–131, 187–188, 219, 295, 409 n.3.

17. María Cristina García, *Havana USA: Cuban Exiles and Cuban Americans in South Florida, 1959–1994* (Berkeley, CA: University of California Press, 1996), 13–45.

18. Marifeli Pérez-Stable, *The Cuban Revolution: Origins, Course and Legacy,* 2nd ed. (New York: Oxford University Press, 1999); Guerra, *Visions of Power in Cuba.*

19. Thomas G. Paterson, *Contesting Castro: The United States and the Triumph of the Cuban Revolution* (New York: Oxford University Press, 1994).

20. Don Bohning, *The Castro Obsession: U.S. Covert Operations against Cuba, 1959–1965* (Washington, DC: Potomac Books, 2006); Morris Morley and Chris McGillion, eds. *Cuba, the United States, and the Post–Cold War World: The International Dimensions of the Washington-Havana Relationship* (Gainesville, FL: University Press of Florida, 2005).

21. Elizabeth Abbott, *Haiti: A Shattered Nation* (New York: Overlook, 2011); Frank Moya Pons, *The Dominican Republic: A National History,* 3rd ed. (New York: Marcus Weiner Publishing, 2011); Jonathan Hartlyn, *The Struggle for Democratic Politics in the Dominican Republic* (Chapel Hill, NC: University of North Carolina Press, 1998); John A. Booth, *The End and the Beginning: The Nicaraguan Revolution,* 2nd ed. (Boulder, CO: Westview, 1985).

22. Thomas O'Brien, *The Century of U.S. Capitalism in Latin America* (Albuquerque, NM: University of New Mexico Press, 1999); Paul J. Dosal, *Doing Business with the Dictators: A Political History of United Fruit in Guatemala, 1899–1944* (New York: Rowman & Littlefield Publishers, 1995); Lester D. Langley, *The Banana Men: American Mercenaries and Entrepreneurs in Central America, 1880–1930* (Lexington, KY: The University Press of Kentucky, 1995).

23. Jason M. Colby, *The Business of Empire: United Fruit, Race and U.S. Expansion in Central America* (Ithaca, NY: Cornell University Press, 2011); Stephen Striffler and Mark Mobert, eds., *Banana Wars: Power, Production and History in the Americas* (Durham, NC: Duke University Press, 2003).

24. Winston James, *Holding Aloft the Banner of Ethiopia: Caribbean Radicalism in Early Twentieth-Century America* (New York: Verso, 1999).

25. Knut Walter, *The Regime of Anastasio Somoza, 1936–1956* (Chapel Hill, NC: University of North Carolina Press, 1993); Eric Roorda, *The Dictator Next Door: The Good Neighbor Policy and the Trujillo Regime in the Dominican Republic, 1930–1945* (Durham, NC: Duke University Press, 1998).

26. Stephen Schlesinger and Stephen Kinzer, *Bitter Fruit: The Story of the American Coup in Guatemala* (Cambridge, MA: Harvard University Press, 1999); Piero Gleijeses, *Shattered Hope: The Guatemalan Revolution and the United States, 1944–1954* (Princeton, NJ: Princeton University Press, 1991).

27. Ilja A. Luciak, *After the Revolution: Gender and Democracy in El Salvador, Nicaragua and Guatemala* (Baltimore, MD: Johns Hopkins University Press, 2001), 32–33.

28. Wood, 8–9.

29. Commission for Historical Clarification, "Human Rights Violations, Acts of Violence and Assignment of Responsibility," *Guatemala: Memory of Silence* (1999), see http://shr.aaas.org/guatemala/ceh/report/english/conc2.html.

30. James Ferguson, *Papa Doc, Baby Doc: Haiti and the Duvaliers* (New York: Blackwell Publishers, 1988), 57–58; Christopher Mitchell, "U.S. Policy toward Haitian Boat People, 1972–93," *Annals of the American Academy of Political and Social Science* 534 (July 1994), 70.

31. See http://www.census.gov/prod/2010pubs/acsbr09-18.pdf.

32. Jesse Hoffnung-Garskof, *A Tale of Two Cities: Santo Domingo and New York after 1950* (Princeton, NJ: Princeton University Press, 2008), 70–80.

33. García, *Seeking Refuge,* 84–89.

34. As Elizabeth Jean Wood summarizes this process, "The Salvadoran civil war was, at the macro level, a struggle between classes. The long-standing oligarchic alliance of the economic elite and the military led to a highly unequal society in which the great majority of Salvadorans were excluded from all but the most meager life opportunities. The response of this oligarchic alliance to the social movements of the 1970s and their demands for economic reform and political inclusion was repression, not compromise." See Wood, *Insurgent Collective Action and Civil War in El Salvador* (New York: Cambridge University Press, 2003), 11.

35. Wood, 9; Garcia, *Seeking Refuge,* 22–26; LeoGrande, 49–50.

36. LeoGrande, 48–50.

37. Janet Schenck, *El Salvador: The Face of Revolution* (Boston: South End Press, 1981), 60–62; García, 23; LeoGrande, 61; 63–64.

38. Human Rights Watch, *El Salvador's Decade of Terror: Human Rights Since the Assassination of Archbishop Romero* (New York: October 1991).

39. Quoted in Malissia Lennox, "Refugees, Racism and Reparations: A Critique of the United States' Haitian Immigration Policy," *Stanford Law Review* 45: 3 (February 1993), 709.

40. García, *Seeking Refuge,* 113.

41. Lennox, 704.

42. LeoGrande, 89, 110–115, 121, 289, 298; LaFeber, 300–304; García, *Seeking Refuge,* 174 n.23.

43. García, *Seeking Refuge,* 113–115.

44. Ibid., 87–88.

45. Torres, 72, 80; García, *Havana USA*, 22–30, 36–37, 41–45, 84–86, 216 n.26, 216 n.28, 217–218 n.41.

46. Torres, 72.

47. These stories have yet to make their way into academic works. However, they are common to my personal and scholarly experience as the child of Cuban exiles with deep roots in Miami.

48. Miguel de la Torre, *La Lucha for Cuba: Religion and Politics on the Streets of Miami* (Berkeley, CA: University of California, 2003), 73.

49. García, *Havana USA*, 29.

50. Ibid., 26–30, 40–41.

51. Ibid., 29, 41.

52. Ibid., 42.

53. Eckstein, 49–51.

54. Hector R. Romero, "Life in Exile: My Perspective" in *ReMembering Cuba: Legacy of a Diaspora*, edited by Andrea O'Reilly Herrera (Austin: University of Texas Press, 2001), 19.

55. García, *Havana USA*, 140, 144.

56. Guerra, *Visions of Power*, 4.

57. Torres, 75–76.

58. Ramón Grosfoguel and Chloe S. Georas, "Latino Caribbean Diasporas in New York" in *Mambo Montage: The Latinization of New York* (New York: Columbia University Press, 2001), 97–118; Torres, 74, 77.

59. Robert Levine, *Secret Missions to Cuba: Fidel Castro, Bernardo Benes and Cuban Miami* (New York: Palgrave, 2001); María de los Angeles Torres, *In the Land of Mirrors: Cuban Exile Politics in the United States* (Ann Arbor: University of Michigan Press, 2001).

60. Lillian Guerra, "Elián González and the 'Real Cuba' of Miami: Visions of Identity, Exceptionality and Divinity," *Cuban Studies/Estudios Cubanos* (2007) 1–25.

61. Eckstein, 34–38.

62. Ibid., 96–97.

63. Cuban Research Institute, "2011 Cuba Poll," page 10. PDF available through http://cri.fiu.edu/research/cuba-poll/.

64. Joshua E. S. Phillips, *The Washington Post* (17 August 2003), W: 06.

65. "Memphian Carranza Found Guilty of Human Rights Abuses," *Memphis Daily News* 124: 54 (19 March 2009), 1.

66. David González, "Torture Victims in El Salvador Are Awarded $54 Million," *The New York Times* (24 July 2002), A8.

67. Juanita Darling, "Unsolved Murder Weakens Faith in Guatemalan Justice System," *Los Angeles Times* (30 May 1999), 3.

68. N. C. Aizenman, "Exhuming the Past in a Painful Quest: Guatemalan Victims' Families Seek Closure, Justice," *The Washington Post* (28 September 2006), A1.

69. In 1988, a federal district judge found the INS guilty of discriminating against Salvadorans and favoring automatic deportation in order to serve U.S. foreign policy. A year later, evidence also emerged of collaboration between the INS and Salvadoran security forces in covering up the military's assassination of six Jesuit priests, their cook, and her daughter. See "Judge Tells U.S. to Stop Coercion of Salvadorans Seeking Asylum," *The New York Times*

(1 May 1988) A1; "Why Apologize for El Salvador?" *The New York Times* (25 December 1989), 1: 30; "Asylum for the Abusers," *The Washington Post* (14 June 1999), A21.

70. Juliana Barbassa, "Torture Victims Find Justice in U.S. Court," *Los Angeles Times* (25 February 2007), B7.

71. Beth Verhey, "The Demobilization and Reintegration of Child Soldiers: El Salvador Case Study," *UCA/UNICEF Executive Summary* (Washington, DC: 2000), 7–9; the experience was dramatized in *Las Voces Inocentes,* directed by Luis Mandoki (Mexico, DF: 20th Century Fox and Altavista Films), 2004. The author is grateful to Jocelyn Courtney for bringing these sources to my attention. Courtney wrote a brilliant, unpublished thesis on child soldiers in El Salvador for Yale College under my advisement in 2007.

72. U.S. Department of State, *El Salvador, Country Reports on Human Rights Practices, 2004* (Washington, DC: Bureau of Democracy, Human Rights and Labor, 2005).

73. *If the Mango Could Speak: A Documentary about Children and War in Central America,* directed by Patricia Goudvis (New Jersey: New Day Films, 1993); Michael Wessells, *Child Soldiers: From Violence to Protection* (Cambridge, MA: Harvard University Press, 2006), 31–35.

74. Tom Hayden, "Peace Is Breaking Out Among Salvadoran Gang Members," *The Nation* (14 May 2012), http://www.thenation.com/print/article/167875/peace-breaking-out -among-salvadoran-gang-members.

75. Anne-Marie O'Connor, "Out of the Ashes: Helping Torture Survivors Heal Is Becoming a Public Health Specialty," *Los Angeles Times* (22 October 200), E1; Thomas H. Maugh, "Immigrants Suffer Legacy of Violence," *Los Angeles Times* (6 August 2003), B7.

76. Leslie Berestein, "Look Homeward, Angels: Salvadoran Refugees in LA Have Joined Forces to Help Rebuild Their War-Torn Homeland," *Los Angeles Times* (16 April 1995), 12.

77. Lynn Stephen and María Teresa Tula, *Hear My Testimony: María Teresa Tula, Human Rights Activist of El Salvador,* translated and edited by Lynn Stephen (Cambridge, MA: South End Press, 1999).

78. Margaret Ramírez, "Symbol of El Salvador Goes North," *Los Angeles Times* (28 July 2000), 1.

79. Reed Johnson, "Salvaging El Salvador: A Week of Multimedia Events in LA Brings the Country's Murky Past out of the Shadows," *Los Angeles Times* (23 October 2009), D1.

80. Frank Shyong, "LA Salvadoran Community Sees Hope Along a New Corridor," *Los Angeles Times* (9 September 2012), latimes.com/news/local/la-me-salvadorans20120910,0 ,7437736.story.

PART 3

THE CONUNDRUMS OF RACE

The principal categories used in the 2010 census to designate racial and ethnic groups in the United States were "White," "Black," "American Indian," "Alaska Native," "Asian," "Native Hawaiian," "Pacific Islander," and "Latino or Hispanic." When we think about racial matters in the United States, we often imagine terms that describe world geography or phenotypes (where skin color, hair, eyes, nose, mouth, and other somatic features serve as racial signifiers). White people are from Europe, American Indians and Alaska Natives are from the Americas, Asians are from the Far East, Native Hawaiians and Pacific Islanders are from the Pacific, and Latinos are from the Americas and Caribbean. Although we recognize that these designations are inherently problematic, we nonetheless assume that race is principally marked by the physical features of people from such regions. While there may have been some arguable basis for such a perception before European colonization in the late fifteenth century, such a view is untenable today. The colonization of Asia, Africa, the Pacific, and the Americas, and the widespread racial mixing and population movements that followed, profoundly undermined the possibility of discrete racial categories.

The processes of biological mixing and hybridization are brought into clear focus when we consider the racial designations applied to Latinos in the United States. Latino populations have a long history of racial classification that dates back to the Spanish colonial period. The continual racial mixing (*mestizaje*) of Spanish conquering troops, indigenous subjugated peoples, and imported African slaves, over time produced distinct color and class hierarchies. In those countries where the Spanish and indigenous populations forged that conjugation, gradated intermediate categories of racial differences and status proliferated. Terms such as *mestizo* and *moreno* gained currency in the sixteenth century, and still have resonance today among Mexicans and Central Americans. In the Spanish Caribbean, the biological mixing between Spaniards and African slaves (who replaced the indigenous populations) led to parallel hierarchies of race where intermediate terms such as *mulato* (in Cuba) and *trigueño* (in Puerto Rico) were prevalent. In Brazil the large brown intermediate group created through the mixing between Portuguese colonizers and African slaves was termed *pardo*.

Where indigenous populations predominated as the principal colonial labor force, as in Mexico, Peru, and Central America, it was indigenous ancestry that was devalued and its distinct phenotype most socially stigmatized. In areas where African slave labor replaced the indigenous population that quickly succumbed to diseases and exploitation, such as the Caribbean islands of Cuba, Hispaniola, and Puerto Rico, blackness and negritude became marks of shame and derision. In both settings, either white and black, or white and Indian, were at opposite ends of this racial hierarchy, and a large set of intermediate brown categories that complexly stratified the population were deemed to occupy the middle. Latino populations that have emigrated to the United States from different regions in Latin America bring elements of these racial logics with them. But these hierarchical racial classificatory regimes travel poorly and are easily assimilated in the America dominant binary system of racial reckoning.

U.S. Latinos and Hispanics are not specifically designated by the U.S. Census Bureau as a "racial group" but instead are considered an ethnic group who share a common ethnic culture unified by their Catholic religion and Spanish language. None of the five other racial groups identified by the census have any fundamental cultural cohesion that links them in this same way. As a result, the only major "ethnic" distinction made by the U.S. Census Bureau is between those who are culturally "Hispanic or Latino" and those who are "Not Hispanic or Latino." The primacy of this ethnic distinction is clearly evident when the U.S. Census Bureau defines a Hispanic or Latino as "a person of Cuban, Mexican, Puerto Rican, South or Central America, or other Spanish culture or origin *regardless of race*" (emphasis added). The multiracial nature of Latinos makes it impossible to define them in ways that parallel other population groups racialized as one distinct category. Unlike other "people of color," Latinos can be racially designated as being either white, black, American Indian and Alaska Native, Asian, Native Hawaiian and Pacific Islander, or combinations thereof.

How Latinos reconcile constructions of race fashioned in their countries of origin with those deployed by the U.S. Census Bureau, is carefully assessed in the first essay in part 3. Anthropologist Jorge Duany studies the racial classification of Puerto Rico's population in chapter 7, "Neither White nor Black: The Representation of Racial Identity among Puerto Ricans on the Island and in the U.S. Mainland." Relying on U.S. Census data and his own ethnographic research, Duany shows that Puerto Ricans have a very gradated and nuanced understanding of race, arguing that racialized images of both Indians and Africans have dominated the way Puerto Ricans think of themselves. They do so by systematically overvaluing the island's Spanish heritage, romanticizing their long-lost indigenous ancestry, and denigrating the African slave past.

Duany's ethnographic work documents that at least nineteen different racial categories are relied upon by Puerto Ricans on the island to classify themselves and others. Skin tones, hair types, facial features, and other somatic characteristics are all drawn upon to differentiate the population in a variety of intermediate categories between white and black. Among this large intermediate or "brown" category are designations for people who identify as *trigueño/a* (wheat colored), *moreno/a* (dark skinned), *indio/a* (brown skinned with straight hair), *café con leche* (tan or brown skinned), or *piel de canela* (cinnamon skinned). Those who claim to be white often rely on categories such as *blanco/a* (white), *colorado/a* (reddish white), *rubio/a* (blond), *jincho/a* (pale skinned), and *jabao/a* (fair skinned with curly hair). The few persons who identify as black do so by invoking terms such as *prieto/a* (dark skinned), *grifo/a* (dark skinned with curly hair), or *de color* (colored), and *negro/a* (black).

Despite these highly gradated racial classifications in thought and action, when the 2000 decennial census was taken on the island, 80.5 percent of the Puerto Rican population classified themselves as white, 8 percent declared themselves black, and another 11.5 percent said they belonged to other races. On the mainland, the same census reported that approximately half of all Puerto Ricans indicated that they are white, 6 percent identified as black and less than 1 percent claimed indigenous ancestry. Puerto Ricans thus seem to highly value their Spanish or Hispanic ancestry, embrace an indigenous past they deem brown, and distance themselves from the island's historic African slave population.

The devaluation of blackness by Caribbean Latinos is also explored by Ginetta E. B. Candelario in chapter 8, "Hair Race-ing: Dominican Beauty Culture and Identity Production." Like Puerto Ricans, Dominicans also have complex understandings of race as organized into three major groups: white, brown, and black. Dominicans likewise highly value their Hispanic origins, distance themselves from association with the country's black African slave past, and predominantly identify with a number of racial terms associated with indigenousness. According to Candelario, this middle ground is captured through terms like *indio, indio claro* (light Indian), *indio oscuro* (dark Indian), *trigueño* (wheat colored), and *moreno/a* (dark brown) that Dominicans invoke to racially identify themselves. Unlike in the United States, where ancestry and skin color are the key bases for ascribing race, Candelario shows that hair is an important racial signifier for Dominicans. Like Puerto Ricans, Dominicans take pains to avoid being categorized as black. The only persons referred to as black by Dominicans are Haitian immigrants. Even the darkest-complexioned Dominican of apparent African phenotype is elevated into the intermediate *indio* category, to avoid being deemed Haitian.

Candelario's ethnographic research in New York City Dominican beauty shops helps us understand how and why they have a stake in this middle group. Her work shows the particular importance of hair as a racial signifier among Dominicans in the United States. Dominican woman highly value and prefer a hair style that projects a "Latin look," one that signals their Indo-Hispanic ancestry. They invest considerable time and money to achieve *pelo bueno* (good hair), or hair that is soft, straight, wavy, or loosely curled, which they consciously equate with whiteness and with the melding of both *"lo indio"* and *"lo Hispano."* Consequently, they tame or process what they deem to be *pelo malo* (bad hair) and remove any association with the tightly curled, coarse, and kinky hair that signals African ancestry. According to Candelario, "Those with good hair are, by definition, not black, skin color notwithstanding." Dominicans on the island likewise embrace the *indio* racial category to affirm their Hispanic origins and to distance themselves from the negritude associated with Haitians.

Dominican women in New York City similarly differentiate and distance themselves from the African American women who occasionally make their way into Dominican beauty shops. Stylists in these shops often hold unflattering and disparaging views of African American women, describing their features as "rough" and "ordinary" as evident in their "black muzzle," "big mouth," and "flat nose." Needless to say, African American women were not always treated as welcome clients in New York City's Dominican-owned hair salons. There is some irony here. No matter how European their facial features or soft and silky their hair, Dominicans have a hundred-year-long tradition of acknowledging that ultimately they are all "black behind the ears." Yet this acknowledgment seems to be belied when they spend hours weekly in beauty shops transforming their hair into the "Hispanic look" that will cover those ears.

In the final essay in part 3, chapter 9, "Race, Racialization, and Latino Populations in the United States," sociologist Tomás Almaguer studies how Latinos racially identify and the specific cultural meaning of that identity. Almaguer reviews how Latinos have been enumerated on the decennial census, beginning in 1850, right after the U.S.-Mexico War, when Mexicans were counted as "white," then in 1930 they were listed as a distinct "Mexican" race, and finally between 1970 and 2000 the census tried to capture the diversity of Hispanics and Latinos in the United States, taking ethnicity more seriously. In the 1980 census "Spanish/Hispanic origin" first appeared, and in 2000 "Latino" was added. Since the 1850s the U.S. Census Bureau has used a number of categories to describe the country's Hispanic and Latino populations, such as "Spanish surname," "Spanish speakers," and place of birth.

This transformation of Latinos from a race to an ethnicity is most apparent in the 1977 directive issued by the U.S. Office of Management and Budget, "Race and Ethnic Standards for Federal Statistics and Administrative Reporting," known as Directive 15. By then, heightened levels of immigration from Latin America required a rethinking of the "Latino" category to account for the increasing African ancestry among Cubans, Puerto Ricans, and Dominicans. While Mexicans had had de jure claims to whiteness since the Treaty of Guadalupe Hidalgo in 1848, by 2000 the counting of Caribbean Latino immigrants and their children as white became increasingly problematic due to their African ancestry and personal identities. The solution became to define Hispanics and Latinos as an ethnicity that could be of any race.

Whatever the categories of the census, Almaguer next takes us to the granular level, to the often fractious relationship between Mexicans and Puerto Ricans in places where they live side by side in the United States. In Chicago, for example, Mexicans tend to view Puerto Ricans in essentially "black" terms, while Puerto Ricans deem Mexicans "Indian." While both populations have asserted claims to whiteness over the years, they both resort to racializing one another by drawing upon the most stigmatized racial categories in Mexico and Puerto Rico. Thus, racial categories and classification that originated under Spanish colonial rule often get transported to new places where they are infused with new meanings. One can see this same process in Los Angeles when Mexicans and Central Americans share similar neighborhoods, and in New York City when Dominicans, Puerto Ricans, and Haitians co-reside.

7

NEITHER WHITE NOR BLACK

The Representation of Racial Identity among Puerto Ricans on the Island and in the U.S. Mainland

Jorge Duany

How is racial identity represented in an Afro-Hispanic Caribbean nation like Puerto Rico? And how do racial and ethnic categories shift in the diaspora? In 1990 I directed an ethnographic study of the sociocultural causes of the census undercount in Barrio Gandul, a poor urban community in San Juan (Duany, Hernández Angueira, and Rey 1995). At the beginning of our fieldwork, my colleagues and I asked our informants, "What race do you consider yourself to belong to?" Responses to this seemingly innocuous question ranged from embarrassment and amazement to ambivalence and silence: many informants simply shrugged their shoulders and pointed to their arms, as if their skin color were so obvious that it did not need to be verbalized. When people referred to others' race, they often used ambiguous euphemisms (such as "he's a little darker than me"), without committing themselves to a specific racial label. Sometimes they would employ diminutive folk terms such as *morenito* or *trigueñita* (referring to dark-skinned persons), which are difficult to translate into U.S. categories. For the purposes of this research, it seemed culturally appropriate to collect our impressions of people's phenotypes as coded in Hispanic Caribbean societies such as Puerto Rico and the Dominican Republic. However, this procedure left open the question as to what extent the researchers' racial categories coincided with the subjects' own perceptions.

My field notes for that project are full of references to the intermediate physical types of many residents of Barrio Gandul, including *moreno* and *trigueño*. For statistical purposes, these terms are usually grouped under the generic label "mulatto," but Puerto Ricans make finer social distinctions in their daily lives. For instance, our informants used the terms *grifo, jabao,* and *colorao* to refer to various combinations of hair types and skin tones. At least nineteen different racial categories are commonly used in Puerto Rico (see table 7.1; see also Godreau 2000). Contrary to the collapsing of racially mixed persons in the United States into the nonwhite category, residents of Barrio Gandul recognized several intermediate groups. In American racial terminology, most of our subjects would probably classify themselves as "other," that is, neither white nor black.

As table 7.1 suggests, popular racial taxonomies in Puerto Rico cannot easily be reduced to the white/black antithesis prevalent in the United States. Puerto Ricans usually group people into three main racial groups—black, white, and brown—based primarily on skin pigmentation and other physical traits, such as facial features and hair texture, regardless of their ancestry. In the United States, the dominant system of racial classification emphasizes a two-tiered division between whites and nonwhites deriving from the principle of hypodescent—the assignment of the offspring of mixed races to the subordinate group (Davis 1998; Harris 1964). According to the "one-drop rule," anyone with a known African ancestor is defined as black, regardless of his or her physical appearance. This clear-cut opposition between Puerto Rican and American conceptions of racial identity has numerous repercussions for social analysis and public policy, among them the appropriate way to categorize, count, and report the number of people by race and ethnicity.

The problem of representing the racial identity of Puerto Ricans, both on the Island and in the U.S. mainland, has troubled American scholars, census enumerators, and policymakers since the end of the nineteenth century. Two key issues have pervaded academic and public debates on race in Puerto Rico. On the one hand, the proliferation and fluidity of racial terms have puzzled outside observers. On the other hand, census tallies report a growing proportion of whites in Puerto Rico between 1899 and 1950 and then again in the year 2000. Even though the census's racial categories changed several times during this period, the white category remained intact, and the number of persons counted as white increased from one census to another. I discuss both these issues later in the chapter.

In the United States, Puerto Rican migrants do not fit well in the conventional white/black dichotomy and therefore challenge the hegemonic discourse on race and ethnicity (C. Rodríguez 1994a, 2000). Recent research efforts by the U.S. Bureau of the Census have focused on determining why so many mainland Puerto Ricans, as well as other Hispanics, choose the "other" category when asked about their racial identity. In the 2000 census, 42.2 percent of all Hispanics in the United States declared that they belonged to "some other race" besides white, black or African American, American Indian and Alaska Native, Asian, or Native Hawaiian and other Pacific Islander (U.S. Bureau of the Census 2001). The existence of a large and growing segment of the U.S. population that perceives itself ethnically as Hispanic or Latino, while avoiding the major accepted racial designations, is a politically explosive phenomenon. It is no wonder that the federal government has so far resisted public pressures to include a separate

TABLE 7.1   Major Folk Racial Terms Used in Puerto Rico

Term	Approximate Meaning
Blanco(a)	White
Blanquito(a)	Literally, little white; figuratively, elitist, upper class
Colorao(a)	Redheaded, reddish skin
Rubio(a)	Blond
Cano(a)	Blond, fair skinned
Jincho(a)	Pale skinned; sometimes used pejoratively
Blanco(a) con raja	Literally, white with a crack; white with some visible black features
Jabao(a)	Fair skinned with curly hair
Trigueño(a)	Literally, wheat colored or brunette; usually light mulatto
Moreno(a)	Dark skinned; usually dark mulatto
Mulato(a)	Mixed race; rarely used in public
Indio(a)	Literally, Indian; brown skinned with straight hair
Café con leche	Literally, coffee with milk; tan or brown skinned
Piel canela	Literally, cinnamon skin; tan or brown skinned
Prieto(a)	Dark skinned; usually derogatory
Grifo(a)	Dark skinned with kinky hair; usually derogatory
De color	Euphemism for black; usually meaning black
Negro(a)	Black; rarely used as a direct term of reference
Negrito(a)	Literally, little black; often used as a term of endearment

multiracial category (as opposed to "more than one race") in the census and other official documents. So have many African American, Latino, and Asian American lobbying groups, which perceive a threat to their numbers by creating further divisions within racial minorities. For these groups, checking more than one race in the census questionnaire means reducing their influence on public policymaking (see Schemo 2000).

In this essay I examine how Americans have represented the racial identity of Puerto Ricans, as well as how Puerto Ricans have represented themselves racially, both at home and in the diaspora. First I review census data on the racial composition of the Island's population between 1899 and 1950 and then again in 2000. Next I analyze estimates of the racial composition of Puerto Rican migrants between 1940 and 1999. I show that U.S. racial categories have historically been at odds, and continue to be so, with prevailing self-concepts among Puerto Ricans. My premise is that the changing racial categories used by the census in Puerto Rico and in the diaspora articulate the hegemonic discourse on race in the United States. However, Puerto Ricans continue to represent themselves differently from official views on race and ethnicity, both on the Island and in the mainland. Whereas Americans tend to draw a rigid line between white and black people, Puerto Ricans prefer to use a fluid continuum of physical types. In essence, different and competing racial discourses have produced incompatible portraits of racial identity on the Island and in the U.S. mainland. On the Island, the vast majority of Puerto Ricans regard themselves as white. In the mainland, most consider themselves to be neither white nor black but members of some other race. To many Americans, Puerto Ricans occupy an ambiguous position between white people and people of color.

THE MYTH OF RACIAL DEMOCRACY IN PUERTO RICO AND THE DIASPORA

During the 1940s, anthropological and sociological interest in race relations boomed on the Island, especially on the part of U.S. academics.[1] This growing interest was related to the "American dilemma" centered on black-white tensions and persistent racial inequality in socioeconomic opportunities, despite the dominant creed of equality and justice for all (Myrdal 1944). For many scholars, Puerto Rico (along with Brazil) seemed to be a racial paradise, especially because of the prevalence and popular acceptance of racial mixture on the Island. Compared with the southern United States, Puerto Rico appeared to be a racial democracy where blacks, whites, and mulattoes lived in harmony. Racial prejudice and discrimination seemed less pervasive and destructive on the Island than in the mainland.

Racial questions were not purely intellectual but utterly political, as American legislators and policymakers who visited Puerto Rico during the 1950s recognized. Arkansas senator J. W. Fulbright declared that the Island was "an example of a racial solution" through education, while George William Culberson, director of Pittsburgh's Commission on Human Relations, reported that "there are no racial prejudices in the public life" of Puerto Rico (El Mundo 1958, 1959). Governor Muñoz Marín (1960) believed that racial tolerance was one of the greatest spiritual contributions of Puerto Rican migrants to New York City. The myth of racial democracy in Puerto Rico was often deployed as an alternative to the American apartheid under Jim Crow laws, which enforced the strict separation between whites and blacks in education, housing, transportation, recreation, and marriage.

During the 1940s, several scholars contrasted the social construction of race in Puerto Rico and the United States (see, for instance, T. Blanco 1985 [1942]; Rogler 1940; Siegel 1948). One of the recurrent themes of this early literature was that the Island's history and culture promoted racial integration rather than segregation, as in the United States and South Africa. Outsiders were surprised that Puerto Ricans of different colors mingled freely in public activities and that many married across color lines. In particular, light mulattoes (known locally as "trigueños") mixed with lower-class whites and were often accepted as white, even by the local elite (Rogler 1972b [1944]). Social distance between whites and blacks also seemed less marked on the Island than in the mainland.

According to these studies, the main difference between the Puerto Rican and American models of racial stratification was not the treatment of blacks—who were accorded a subordinate status in both societies—but rather the treatment of the mixed group. In Puerto Rico, trigueños could often pass for whites, whereas in the United States, an intermediate racial category (such as mulattoes) had not formally existed since the 1930 census. Although racial mixture also occurred in the mainland, the federal government did not officially recognize it, except as part of the black population (Davis 1998). The symbolic boundaries between whites and mulattoes were apparently more porous in Puerto Rico than in the United States.

An important subtheme of this literature was whether color distinctions in Puerto Rico were better interpreted as a racial or class hierarchy. The Puerto Rican writer Tomás Blanco (1985 [1942]: 128) represented the dominant view that prejudice was "more of a social than a racial character in Puerto Rico" (see also Mintz 1966; Sereno 1947). According to Blanco, whatever racial prejudice may have been present on the Island was primarily a recent importation from the United States. Others, however, recognized the long history of racial prejudice and discrimination in Puerto Rican society, as expressed through folklore, occupations, religion, courtship, marriage, and voluntary associations. Although different from the American system of racial classification, the Puerto Rican system still assigned blacks and mulattoes a lower rank than whites (see Gordon 1949, 1950; Rosario and Carrión 1951). A consensus emerged from these classic studies that Puerto Rican society is stratified in both class status and color gradations ranging from white to brown to black. Whether race or some other variable such as occupation, education, or residence determines one's life chances continues to be debated.

Researchers have long been concerned with how Puerto Ricans define "race" or "color"; much of the literature treats the two terms as synonyms. Color distinctions on the Island involve a complex inventory of such physical traits as skin pigmentation, hair texture, nose shape, and lip form (Ginorio 1971; C. Rodríguez 1996; Seda Bonilla 1968; Zenón Cruz 1975). More than descent, phenotype defines one's racial identity in Puerto Rico, as in much of the Caribbean and Latin America. Socioeconomic variables such as occupational prestige and family connections can also alter a person's "race." Contrary to the United States, ancestry is not the most significant variable in assessing race in Puerto Rico. Rather, as the American sociologist Charles Rogler (1972a [1946]) noted long ago, Puerto Ricans place most emphasis on visual evidence of race, such as an individual's anatomic feature.

The proliferation, elasticity, and ambiguity of Puerto Rican racial terms have fascinated American social scientists. Rogler (1972b [1944]) was one of the first to write about the "confusion" among race, color, and class in Puerto Rico. He was frustrated by the weak correlation between racial terms and social interaction on the Island. The anthropologist Morris Siegel also perceived widespread confusion about the racial constitution of the Island's population. Siegel (1948: 187) recognized that Puerto Ricans are "terribly color-conscious" and that they pay much attention to visual cues to determine if a person is white, black, or an in-between type such as trigueño or jabao. Furthermore, many scholars found that "money whitens" on the Island: the wealthier a person is, the more likely she will be classified as light skinned or simply as white, regardless of her physical appearance. Like Brazil and other Latin American societies, Puerto Rico developed a "mulatto escape hatch" that allowed some persons of mixed ancestry upward social mobility (Degler 1971; Wade 1997).

Based on fieldwork conducted during the late 1950s and 1960s, Eduardo Seda Bonilla (1968, 1973) confirmed that most Puerto Ricans use phenotype rather than hypodescent as the main criterion for racial identity. Like many Latin Americans, Puerto Ricans tend to distinguish three basic physical types—white, black, and brown—defined primarily by skin color, facial features, and hair texture. Furthermore, whereas Americans pay close attention to national and ethnic background in defining a person's identity, Puerto Ricans give a higher priority to birthplace and cultural orientation. Among other features of the Puerto Rican discourse on race, Seda Bonilla noted the public recognition of racially intermediate types, the reduced social distance among contiguous categories, and the frequency of racial mixture.

Another common practice on the Island is a strong desire to whiten oneself (mejorar la raza), a tendency also known as "bleaching" (blanqueamiento). For decades, local enumerators have classified the vast majority of the Puerto Rican population as white, despite the high incidence of mestizaje (racial mixture). As Maxine Gordon (1949) pointed out long ago, census statistics since the mid-nineteenth century show the continuous rise of the white sector of the Island's population, at the expense of the black and mulatto sectors. These statistics are open to debate because of the flexible boundaries between racial groups as well as the lack of fit between local and U.S. concepts of race. However, they suggest that most Puerto Ricans perceive themselves as white rather than as black or mulatto and that this trend is increasing.

The generalized view about the virtual absence of racial prejudice and discrimination has made race a difficult research topic in Puerto Rico. As José Colombán Rosario and Justina Carrión (1951: 88) put it, "The discussion of the problem of the black [has] been kept in a humid and unhygienic obscurity." Most authors agreed with Rogler's assessment (1972b [1944]: 55) that "race competition, tension, and conflict are not conspicuous processes in most Puerto Rican situations," as they are in the United States. In a famous turn of phrase, Blanco (1985 [1942]: 103) compared racial prejudice in Puerto Rico to "an innocent children's game." According to Siegel (1948: 3), "The island is one of the few places in the world where interracial harmony has been achieved in high degree . . . the more overt and vicious forms of racism are largely absent." More recent writers have continued to downplay racial prejudice and discrimination in Puerto Rico (see Arana-

Soto 1976; Davis 1998; Fitzpatrick 1987; Hoetink 1967; Mintz 1966; C. Rodríguez 1974; Wolfson 1972). It is still extremely difficult to break through the "conspiracy of silence" that surrounds racial politics in Puerto Rico—what one author called "the prejudice of having no prejudice" (Betances 1972, 1973).

One of the earliest critics of standard views of race relations in Puerto Rico was the American sociologist Maxine Gordon (1949, 1950). She argued that historical and cultural factors—such as the absence of racial violence and the prevalence of racial intermarriage over several generations—fostered the belief that no racial prejudice existed on the Island. However, she found instances of racism in various Puerto Rican institutions, such as college fraternities and upper-class private clubs. Unfortunately, her thesis was poorly documented, having been based largely on anecdotal evidence from secondary sources, not on systematic fieldwork. As a result, Gordon's work could not seriously undermine the established discourse on race in Puerto Rico.

In the mid-1960s, Puerto Rican social scientists began to question the conventional wisdom that racial prejudice was absent on the Island. Juan Rodríguez Cruz (1965: 385) cautiously acknowledged "the existence of [racial] discriminatory practices in certain spheres of Puerto Rican society," such as private schools, the University of Puerto Rico, private enterprises, voluntary associations, and residential neighborhoods. Seda Bonilla's cited work was part of an emerging academic consensus that racism did indeed persist on the Island. Reviewing the literature from the United States, Samuel Betances (1972, 1973) sharply criticized the myth of racial integration in Puerto Rico. But the most sustained attack on Puerto Rican racism came from the literary critic Isabelo Zenón Cruz, whose two-volume treatise denounced the "constant and systematic marginalization" (1975: 23) of black Puerto Ricans as second-class citizens in elite and folk poetry, as well as in other areas of national culture. Although his work provoked an intense polemic on the Island, it did not foster new ethnographic or sociological fieldwork on race relations. It did, however, spark a new wave of revisionist research on the history of Puerto Rican slavery (see Díaz Quiñones 1985; Kinsbruner 1996; Scarano 1984).

Although the empirical evidence on racial politics in contemporary Puerto Rico is still scanty, several studies have documented that blacks are a stigmatized minority on the Island; that they suffer from persistent prejudice and discrimination; that they concentrate in lower classes; and that they are subject to an ideology of whitening through intermarriage with lighter-skinned groups and a denial of their cultural heritage and physical characteristics (Kantrowitz 1971; Picó de Hernández et al. 1985; Seda Bonilla 1973, 1980; Zenón Cruz 1975). The latter ideology helps to explain why an increasing proportion of Puerto Ricans have reported their race to be white over time, despite the absence of massive immigration to the Island during the first decades of the twentieth century. Many authors have noted the unreliable nature of census data on the racial composition of the Puerto Rican population (T. Blanco 1985 [1942]; Cabranes 1979; Fitzpatrick 1987; Rodríguez Cruz 1965; Rogler 1940; Siegel 1948). No published studies have yet explored the congruence between popular representations of race in Puerto Rico and the official racial categories of the United States.[2] Recent ethnographic fieldwork on racial issues has concentrated on Afro–Puerto Rican coastal communities and their cultural contributions to national identity (Godreau-Santiago 1999; Moira Pérez 1998; Torres 1998).

In addition, scholars have questioned whether the dominant white/black dichotomy can capture the complex racial situation of the Puerto Rican diaspora. Since World War II, massive migration from Puerto Rico to the mainland has pitted two racial classification systems against each other: the Puerto Rican one, based largely on physical appearance, and the American one, based largely on ancestry. Thus, when Puerto Ricans move abroad, they confront a different construction of their racial identity (Fitzpatrick 1987; Ginorio 1979; Montero Seplowin 1971; C. Rodríguez 1974; Seda Bonilla 1980). In the 1940s, C. Wright Mills, Clarence Senior, and Rose Kohn Goldsen (1950) found that one of the main problems of Puerto Ricans in New York City was racial prejudice and discrimination. They noted that adaptation was particularly difficult for racially intermediate types (such as the so-called *indios*) and blacks, who were more prone to return to the Island than whites.

The dominant opposition between whites and nonwhites in the United States eludes many Puerto Rican migrants, who have African as well as European backgrounds and range phenotypically across the entire color spectrum from black to brown to white. As a result of their racial heterogeneity, mainland Puerto Ricans are often lumped together with blacks. Those with mixed racial ancestry lose their intermediate status in a white/nonwhite dichotomy. Light-skinned immigrants are sometimes called "white Puerto Ricans," whereas dark-skinned immigrants are often treated like African Americans. In New York City, many are simply classified as "Pororicans," as if this were a distinct racial category.[3] Like other ethnic minorities, Puerto Ricans have been thoroughly racialized in the United States (see V. Rodríguez 1997; Rodríguez-Morazzani 1996).

The work of New York–based Puerto Rican sociologist Clara Rodríguez has dominated academic discussions about race among Puerto Rican migrants. Based on the analysis of the Public Use Microdata Sample of the 1980 census as well as her own survey results, Rodríguez reports that many members of the Puerto Rican community in New York resist being classified as either black or white and prefer to identify themselves as "other." In the 1980 census, 48 percent of New York City's Puerto Ricans chose this category, sometimes adding terms such as Hispanic, Latino, Spanish, and Boricua (C. Rodríguez 1989, 1990, 1992; Rodríguez and Cordero-Guzmán 1992). In 1990 nearly 46 percent of all Puerto Ricans in the United States classified themselves as "other" (C. Rodríguez 2000). Hence, many Puerto Ricans and their descendants continue to employ a tripartite rather than a dual scheme of racial classification. Contrary to Seda Bonilla's (1980) prediction that they would split along color lines, most migrants reject their indiscriminate labeling as members of a single race (see also Ginorio 1979).

Rather than splintering themselves into white and black, Puerto Ricans recognize that they are a multiracial people.[4]

Rodríguez's work points to the need for further research and reflection on the conflicts and negotiations between popular and official representations of Puerto Rican identity. Víctor Rodríguez (1997) has argued that Puerto Ricans in the United States have been racialized through close association with African Americans. From a different perspective, Roberto Rodríguez-Morazzani (1996) suggests that mainland Puerto Ricans have avoided identification as black to escape their negative racialization. I would argue that a similar process took place on the Island, where the U.S. government has attempted to impose its bipolar view of race on the Puerto Rican population. This effort has mostly failed, as witnessed by the continued use of a folk system of racial classification that differs markedly from the one prevailing in the mainland (compare tables 7.1 and 7.2).[5] How does one translate the multiple and fluid racial labels popular on the Island into the smaller number of categories used by the U.S. census?

In sum, the Puerto Rican model of race relations has several distinguishing features. Unlike Americans, most Puerto Ricans do not consider race primarily a question of descent. Like other Caribbean and Latin American people, Puerto Ricans emphasize physical appearance in representing racial identity (Hoetink 1967; Seda Bonilla 1968). As a result, a person of mixed racial background is not automatically assigned to the black group in Puerto Rico. Rather, racial classification depends largely on skin color and other visible characteristics such as the shape of one's mouth and nose and hair texture. Social status (including income, occupation, and education) is also taken into consideration. Unfortunately, Puerto Ricans have developed an elaborate racist vocabulary to refer to racially stereotyped characteristics—especially the idea that kinky hair is "bad" (*pelo malo*). Furthermore, Puerto Ricans usually distinguish blacks from mulattoes, whereas Americans tend to view both groups as nonwhite. In contrast to the U.S. model, which tends to be dichotomous, the Puerto Rican racial model is based on a threefold scheme.

Finally, because of the proliferation of intermediate physical types, Puerto Rico has not established a two-tiered institutionalized system of racial discrimination such as that of the United States. For example, lower-class urban settlements in San Juan, such as Barrio Gandul, are not strictly segregated by color but primarily by class (Duany, Hernández Angueira, and Rey 1995). Nonetheless, racial prejudice on the Island is expressed in myriad forms—such as folk humor, beauty contests, media portrayals, and political leadership. In all these areas, whites are usually depicted as more intelligent, attractive, refined, and capable than are blacks. As Seda Bonilla (1968: 592) has underlined, both the Puerto Rican and U.S. models "commit the inhuman error of assigning intellectual, moral, or social superiority to some racial categories over others." In Puerto Rico, as well as in the United States, an ideology of white supremacy and black inferiority has prevailed since the days of colonial slavery.

"THE WHITEST OF THE ANTILLES": REPRESENTING RACE IN PUERTO RICO

One of the first official acts of the U.S. government in Puerto Rico after acquiring the Island in 1898 was to conduct a census of its population. The War Department assumed that task in 1899. Since 1910, the Department of Commerce has been in charge of the census in Puerto Rico as well as in the U.S. mainland. Until 1950, the Bureau of the Census attempted to quantify the racial composition of the Island's population, while experimenting with various racial taxonomies. In 1960 the census dropped the racial identification question for Puerto Rico but included it again in the year 2000 (see table 7.2). The only category that remained constant over time was white, even as other racial labels shifted greatly—from colored to black, mulatto, and other; back to colored and other races; then to nonwhite; again to Negro and other races; and finally to black or African American and other races. Regardless of the precise terminology, the census reported that the bulk of the Puerto Rican population was white from 1899 to 2000.

From the beginning of the twentieth century, American observers remarked on the "surprising preponderance of the white race" on the Island (*National Geographic Magazine* 1900: 328). One travel writer called Puerto Rico "the whitest of the Antilles" (White 1898). In a widely distributed piece, a geologist (Hill 1899c: 93) wrote that the Island was "notable among the West Indian group for the reason that its preponderant population is of the white race." In a more academic book, he reiterated that "Porto Rico, at least, has not become Africanized, as have all the other West Indies excepting Cuba" (Hill 1903: 165). Such authoritative reports helped to allay the common racist fear that the U.S. government had annexed a predominantly black population after the War of 1898. Such a view still surfaces in contemporary debates about the Island's political status, albeit indirectly.

Table 7.3 compiles the available census statistics on the proportion of whites and nonwhites in Puerto Rico between 1802 and 2000. The Spanish censuses show that Puerto Ricans were about evenly divided between whites and nonwhites until the mid-nineteenth century. Since 1860, the proportion of the Island's population classified as white has increased steadily, except for the year 1899, when the first U.S. census registered a small decrease. Correspondingly, the proportion of people reported as nonwhites (including blacks and mulattoes) has diminished, again except for 1899. In the 2000 census, 80.5 percent of the Island's residents classified themselves as white, with only 8 percent black and 11.5 other races. According to these statistics, the Puerto Rican population has become increasingly whiter, especially during the first half of the twentieth century.

What social factors account for this dramatic transformation in the official representation of Puerto Rico's racial composition? To some extent, the gradual lightening of the Island's population was due to European immigration, especially during the second half of the nineteenth century (Hoetink 1967). But the number of white immigrants was not

TABLE 7.2   Racial Categories Used in the Census of Puerto Rico,
1899–2000

Year	Category	Number of Persons	Percentage
1899	White	589,426	61.8
	Colored	363,817	38.2
1910	White	732,555	65.5
	Black	50,245	4.5
	Mulatto	335,192	30.0
	Other	20	0
1920	White	948,709	73.0
	Black	49,246	3.8
	Mulatto	301,816	23.2
	Other	38	0
1930	White	1,146,719	74.3
	Colored	397,156	25.7
	Other races	38	0
1935	White	1,313,496	76.2
	Colored	411,038	23.8
1940	White	1,430,744	76.5
	Nonwhite	438,511	23.5
1950	White	1,762,411	79.7
	Negro	446,948	20.2
	Other races	1,344	0.1
2000	White	3,064,862	80.5
	Black or African American	302,933	8.0
	Other	440,815	11.5

Sources: Administración de Reconstrucción de Puerto Rico 1938; Departamento de la Guerra 1900; U.S. Bureau of the Census 1913, 1921, 1932, 1943a, 1953a, 2001.

large enough to produce such a significant shift in racial groups during the first half of the twentieth century. Nor was there a massive outflow of blacks to the United States or other countries at this time. Barring major population movements into and out of the Island until the 1940s, scholars have proposed several additional hypotheses.

Rogler (1940: 16) put forth one of the most popular explanations: "The Census

TABLE 7.3 Racial Composition of the Puerto Rican Population, as Reported in the Census, 1802–2000 (in Percentages)

Year	White	Nonwhite[a]
1802	48.0	52.0
1812	46.8	53.2
1820	44.4	55.6
1827	49.7	50.3
1830	50.1	49.9
1836	52.9	47.1
1860	51.1	48.5
1877	56.3	43.7
1887	59.5	40.5
1897	64.3	35.7
1899	61.8	38.2
1910	65.5	34.5
1920	73.0	27.0
1930	74.3	25.7
1935	76.2	23.8
1940	76.5	23.5
1950	79.7	20.3
2000	80.5	19.5

Sources: Administración de Reconstrucción de Puerto Rico 1938; Departamento de la Guerra 1900; U.S. Bureau of the Census 1913, 1921, 1932 ,1943a, 1953a, 2001.

[a] Includes black, colored, mulatto, mixed-blood, and other races.

includes as colored both full-blooded and mixed. The census estimate is probably low because many who are known to have colored blood are counted as white. . . . Because of the absence of marked race prejudice, and also because of the tendency to deal with color as a class rather than a race phenomenon, the attitude of the community as a whole operates to reduce materially the percentage classified as colored and to classify many quadroons and octoroons as white." While Rogler points out that light mulattoes are often accepted as whites in Puerto Rico, he fails to acknowledge that "passing" also takes place in the United States, although it operates differently there and without official approval. Moreover, the whitening of the Puerto Rican population is hardly due to the absence of racial prejudice but rather to its very presence: many people prefer to iden-tify as white to avoid racial stigmatization. Nor is it a question of conflating color and class, although the two factors are closely linked. As elsewhere, Puerto Ricans clearly distinguish a person's physical appearance and socioeconomic status. Finally, racial categories such as quadroons and octoroons are meaningless in contemporary Puerto Rico, precisely because it is practically impossible to determine the degree of racial mixture in much of the population (see Fitzpatrick 1987).

Rogler (1972a [1946]: 62) provides a second explanation: "This apparent decline [in the nonwhite population] is probably the consequence of changing race conceptions or, more specifically, the social definition as to who is a person of color. In other words, these percentages would suggest that many persons of color are moving into the white race." I would accept the first premise of this proposition—that census categories reflect changing discourses on race—but would reject its second implication—that Puerto Ricans jumble together white and black people. On the contrary, the Puerto Rican scheme of racial classification is primarily concerned, perhaps even obsessed, with dis-tinguishing various shades of skin color. However, such definitions of race clash with the categories imposed by the U.S. Bureau of the Census. Hence, the problem is not, as Siegel (1948:189) believed, that "the reliability of Puerto Rican racial classifications is open to serious criticisms." *All* such classifications are historically contingent, culturally relative, politically contestable, ultimately arbitrary, and of dubious scientific value (see Omi and Winant 1994).[6]

The Bureau of the Census itself has offered a third explanation for the apparent increase in Puerto Rico's white population: "The percentage of the population which was colored, according to the census returns, declined from 38.2 percent in 1899 to 23.8 percent in 1935. A part of this nominal decline, however, was without doubt the result of the gradual change in the concept of the race classification as applied by the census enumerators" (Administración de Reconstrucción de Puerto Rico 1938: 17). I doubt that Puerto Rican census takers substantially altered their racial concepts dur-ing this period and therefore counted more people as white. Since 1899, enumerators have been recruited from the Island's population and have presumably applied local standards of racial classification. According to the *National Geographic Magazine* (1901: 80), "The facts presented in the reports were gathered in all cases by the [Puerto Rican] people themselves, as the most intelligent of the better classes were induced to compete for positions as census-takers by the relatively handsome salaries offered by the U.S. government." Until the 1960 census, enumerators in Puerto Rico as well as in the U.S. mainland usually judged their informants' physical appearance as a visual cue of racial identity (Ruggles et al. 1997; Torres Aguirre 2000). Only in the 2000 census was the racial question based on self-classification in Puerto Rico.

My own interpretation of the Island's changing racial statistics focuses on the trans-actions between state-supported and popular representations of race. From the begin-ning, the U.S. government attempted to divide the Puerto Rican population neatly into "two main classes, pure whites and those who are not" (Departamento de la Guerra 1900: 57). In turn, Puerto Ricans insisted on distinguishing blacks from mulattoes and blurring the boundaries between "pure whites" and "mixed blood." In 1930 the Bureau of the Census dropped mulattoes from its count of the Puerto Rican population and lumped them together with blacks under "colored." This change paralleled the collapsing of blacks and mulattoes into a single category in the mainland (Davis 1998; Domínguez 1998). Between 1900 and 1930, the U.S. census counted persons of mixed black and white ancestry as a separate group. But in 1940, such persons were considered Negro (see table 7.4). On the Island, census enumerators tended to avoid the "colored" and "black" labels altogether and to identify their informants as white. Thus, the official disappearance to racially intermediate types accelerated the movement from nonwhite to white categories on the Island.

In short, the U.S. government sought to apply a binary race model to a fluid multiracial situation in Puerto Rico. As an official report to the local House of Representatives noted, "The population is extremely mixed and there are not just two colors but rather an infinite number of hues" (*El Mundo* 1945). Although the census recognized that most "colored" people were mulattoes rather than "pure blacks" (the terms used by the census), the dominant discourse on race silenced that trend after 1930 (see table 7.5). From an American standpoint, only two distinct races existed in Puerto Rico—white and black (variously called Negro, colored, or nonwhite). Well into the 1940s, the Bureau of the Census claimed that racial terms "probably need no definition" (U.S. Bureau of the Census 1946: 2). However, it instructed local enumerators to classify persons of mixed ancestry as "colored" rather than white (U.S. Bureau of the Census 1943a: 100). As a Bureau of the Census (1963: ix) report understated, "It is likely that the commonly held conceptions of race among Puerto Ricans in Puerto Rico, among Puerto Ricans in the United States, and among other persons in the United States are somewhat different, and there was a considerable variation in the classification." For instance, the 1950 census categorized persons of mixed ancestry according to the race of the nonwhite parent, following the rule of hypodescent (U.S. Bureau of the Census 1953a: 53-V). In contrast, Puerto Ricans classified them primarily according to their physical appearance. Whereas the census insisted on distinguishing only two groups, white and nonwhite, Puerto Ricans continued to use three or more categories, including trigueño, moreno, indio, and other folk terms. Many people in Puerto Rico contested the racial practices articulated by the Bureau of the Census.

The racial politics of census enumeration in Puerto Rico reveal a sharp discrepancy between self-representations and representations by others. In 1899 nearly two-thirds of all Puerto Ricans were considered white. In 2000 more than four-fifths classified themselves as white. However, many Americans—including visiting scholars and public officials—mistrusted such statistics, believing instead that the Island's "colored" population was much larger than suggested by the census. Some Puerto Rican authors granted that the majority of the local population was composed of mulattoes (T. Blanco

TABLE 7.4   Major Racial Categories Used in the Census of the United States,
1900–2000

Year	Categories
1900	White, black, mulatto, Indian, Chinese, Japanese, Filipino, Hindu, Korean, Mexican
1910	White, black, mulatto, Chinese, Japanese, Indian
1920	White, black, mulatto, Indian, Chinese, Japanese, Filipino, Hindu, Korean
1930	White, black, mulatto, Indian, Chinese, Japanese, Filipino, Hindu, Korean, Mexican
1940	White, Negro, Indian, Chinese, Japanese, Filipino, Hindu, Korean
1950	White, Negro, Indian, Chinese, Japanese, Filipino
1960	White, Negro, American Indian, Japanese, Chinese, Filipino, Hawaiian, Part Hawaiian, Aleut, Eskimo
1970	White, Negro or black, Indian (Amer.), Japanese, Chinese, Filipino, Hawaiian
1980	White, Negro or black, Japanese, Chinese, Filipino, Korean, Vietnamese, Indian (Amer.), Asian Indian, Hawaiian, Guamanian, Samoan, Eskimo, Aleut
1990	White, black or Negro, Indian (Amer.), Eskimo, Aleut, Asian or Pacific Islander
2000	White, black or African American, American Indian or Alaskan Native, Asian, Native Hawaiian or other Pacific Islander

Sources: Office of Management and Budget 1997; Ruggles et al. 1997.

TABLE 7.5   Mulatto and Black Populations of Puerto Rico,
as Reported in the Census, 1899–1920 (in Percentages)

	1899	1910	1920
Mulattoes	83.6	86.9	85.9
Blacks	16.4	13.1	14.1
Total "colored"	100	100	100

Sources: Departamento de la Guerra 1900; U.S. Bureau of the Census 1913, 1921.

1985 [1942]; Rodríguez Cruz 1965). In 1960 the federal government eliminated any references to race or color from the census of Puerto Rico, apparently because it considered them to be unreliable and practically useless. A brief note in the 1950 census reads: "There is considerable evidence which indicates that color is misreported [in Puerto Rico]. The comparison of the 'white' and 'nonwhite' total from census to census reveals the tendency of the enumerator to report persons with varying amounts of Negro blood as 'white'" (U.S. Bureau of the Census 1952: viii). Racial statistics on the Island did not generate a portrait compatible with the dominant discourse on race in the United States.

For its own reasons, the Puerto Rican government attempted to eliminate references to race from most public documents on the Island. According to the director of the Office of the Census of the Puerto Rican Planning Board, Lillian Torres Aguirre (letter to the author, January 21, 2000), the race question was dropped because the Commonwealth's constitution prohibits discrimination by race or color and because the local government is not required by law to collect racial statistics in order to provide public services. In 1978 an attorney working for the Office of Legal Affairs of the Puerto Rican Planning Board recommended that "the most adequate and convenient solution for our economic, social, and cultural reality is not to include the question about racial determination in the 1980 census questionnaire" (Mercado Vega 1978: 3). Between 1960 and 1990, the census questionnaire in Puerto Rico did not ask about race or color. Racial categories therefore disappeared from the official discourse on the Puerto Rican nation.

However, the 2000 census included a racial self-identification question in Puerto Rico and, for the first time ever, allowed respondents to choose more than one racial category to indicate mixed ancestry. (Only 4.2 percent chose two or more races.) With few variations, the census of Puerto Rico used the same questionnaire as in the U.S. mainland. This decision was a response to intense lobbying by former governor Pedro Rosselló's administration to include Puerto Rico in federal census statistics, along with the fifty states (see Mulero 1999). According to census reports, most islanders responded to the new federally mandated categories on race and ethnicity by insisting on their "whiteness"; few declared themselves to be black or some other race (U.S. Bureau of the Census 2001). Clearly, many of the census's racial categories—such as American Indian, Alaska Native, Asian, Hawaiian, or Pacific Islander—are irrelevant to most of the Puerto Rican population.

WHITE, BLACK, OR OTHER?: THE RACIAL REPRESENTATION OF PUERTO RICAN MIGRANTS

If classifying the race of Puerto Ricans on the Island was complicated, the task became even more daunting to government authorities in the U.S. mainland. Since the beginning of the twentieth century, the Bureau of the Census has frequently altered its racial designation of Puerto Rican and other Hispanic immigrants. For instance, the census counted Mexicans as a separate (nonwhite) race in 1930, white between 1940 and 1970, and of any race between 1980 and 2000. Until 1970, most Puerto Ricans living in the United States were considered white, "unless they were definitely Negro, Indian, or some other race" (Domínguez 1998). In 1980, the census introduced two separate self-identification questions, one on Hispanic origin and one on race, based on the premise that Hispanics could be of any race. Consequently, the federal government encouraged

Puerto Ricans to classify themselves primarily as Hispanics rather than as white or black.

Table 7.6 presents census data on the racial composition of Puerto Ricans in the United States from 1940 to 1990.[7] First, the proportion of mainland Puerto Ricans who were reported to be white decreased drastically after 1970, largely as a result of the inclusion of the new Hispanic category. In 1990 the proportion of Puerto Ricans who classified themselves as white (nearly 46 percent) was slightly more than half the 1940 figure (87 percent). Second, the proportion of black Puerto Ricans has remained extremely low since 1950 (between 4 and 8 percent). Third, those reporting other races jumped from less than 2 percent in 1970 to more than 47 percent in 1990. Thus, over the past several decades, Puerto Ricans in the United States have changed their racial self-perception from a predominantly white population to a hybrid one. Contrary to the dominant trend among Puerto Ricans on the Island, fewer of those residing in the mainland reported that they were white between the 1970 and 1990 censuses.

Let me review some possible reasons for this change and then offer my own explanation. Several authors have argued that Puerto Ricans in the United States tend to reject their labeling as black, because that would mean accepting an inferior position within American society. From this perspective, the migrants assert a separate cultural identity to evade rampant prejudice and discrimination against African Americans (Fitzpatrick 1987; Montero Seplowin 1971; Rodríguez-Morazzani 1996; Seda Bonilla 1968; Wolfson 1972). Although this argument may help to explain why many dark-skinned Puerto Rican migrants do not align themselves with African Americans, it misses two basic points. First, about the same proportion of Puerto Ricans on the Island and in the mainland (8 percent, according to the census) classify themselves as black rather than white or other races. Second, proportionally fewer Puerto Ricans in the mainland than on the Island classify themselves as white when offered an opportunity to declare other races. The key question then becomes why so many U.S. Puerto Ricans chose the "other" category—neither white nor black—in the last two censuses.

Clara Rodríguez believes that Puerto Ricans in New York City continue to define their racial identity according to a color continuum from white to black. As in Puerto Rico, this continuum is based on phenotypic categories ranging in pigmentation, hair form, and facial features. Surprisingly, few of her Puerto Rican interviewees reported that they were "other" because of racial mixture as such. The majority stated that they had chosen the "other race" option because of their culture, family, birthplace, socialization, or political perspective. However, most respondents placed themselves in racially intermediate positions between black and white. They rarely used conventional U.S. terms to describe their racial identity and preferred to say that they were Spanish, Puerto Rican, Boricua, or trigueño (C. Rodríguez 1990, 1992, 2000; Rodríguez and Cordero-Guzmán 1992). From this perspective, the growing use of the term "other" among Puerto Rican and other Hispanic immigrants reflects their disapproval of the American racial classification system.[8]

TABLE 7.6   Racial Composition of Puerto Ricans in the
United States, as Reported in the Census, 1940–1990
(in Percentages)

Year	White	Nonwhite[a]	Other
1940	86.8	13.2	n/a
1950	92.0	8.0	n/a
1960	96.1	3.9	n/a
1970	92.9	5.3	1.8
1980	48.3	4.3	47.5
1990	45.8	7.1	47.2

Sources: Almaguer and Jung 1998; U.S. Bureau of the Census 1953b, 1963, 1973.

Note: For 1940, refers only to persons of Puerto Rican birth; for other years, includes persons of Puerto Rican birth or parentage. Until 1970, "race" was based on the census enumerators' judgment; since then, it has been based on the respondents' self-reports.

[a] Includes Negro or black, Native American or American Indian, and Asian and Pacific Islander.

Despite its eloquence, this thesis raises some unresolved issues. As Rodríguez (1997) recognizes, the meaning of census racial categories has shifted greatly for Puerto Ricans and other Latinos in the United States. Thus, it is difficult simply to juxtapose American and Latin American discourses of race and to suggest that the latter are more attuned to large-scale racial mixture and conceptual fuzziness. Both types of discourses may be converging: American black/white relations have been complicated by the growth of "brown" groups such as Asian Americans or Latinos, while Latin American race relations, at least in Brazil, are increasingly polarized between whites and nonwhites (Winant 1994).

Furthermore, the rise of new ethnic/racial labels, such as "Hispanics" and "Latinos," has affected the self-definition of Puerto Ricans and other Latin American immigrants in the United States (see *Latin American Perspectives* 1992; Oboler 1995). Among other repercussions, the official adoption of the Hispanic label by the Bureau of the Census and other federal government bureaucracies often treats Puerto Ricans as racially distinct from both non-Hispanic whites and blacks. The quasi-racial use of the term "Hispanic" has led Puerto Ricans to move away from the black/white dichotomy in the United States.

Finally, many Puerto Ricans choose the catchall "other" as a proxy for brown or tan—that is, as neither white nor black but an in-between color (Fitzpatrick 1987). As several researchers have found, migration to the mainland tends to produce a "brown-

TABLE 7.7 Racial Self-Identification of Puerto Ricans in the United States in the Current Population Survey, 1992–1999 (in Percentages)

Race	1992	1993	1994	1995	1996	1997	1998	1999
White	89.0	89.1	81.5	79.3	91.8	88.9	90.9	90.6
Black	6.4	4.4	6.1	4.8	7.0	10.7	7.4	7.9
American Indian[a]	0.1	0.5	0.2	0.2	0.3	0.1	0.7	0.3
Asian[b]	n/a	0.4	0.4	0.4	0.9	0.3	1.0	1.2
Other	4.5	5.6	11.8	15.3	n/a	n/a	n/a	n/a
Total	100	100	100	100	100	100	100	100

Source: U.S. Bureau of the Census 1999.

[a] Includes Eskimo or Aleut.

[b] Includes Pacific Islander.

ing effect" (Ginorio 1979; A. R. Martínez 1988; C. Rodríguez 1996), as opposed to the whitening of the Island's population. The contemporary self-representation of Puerto Ricans in the United States may therefore constitute a rupture, rather than a continuity, with the dominant racial discourse on the Island. However, most migrants have not adopted the U.S. racial model wholesale but have adapted it to their particular situation of racial mixture and heterogeneity.

Recent studies by the Bureau of the Census provide empirical support for this alternative conception of the othering trend among Puerto Rican migrants (Tucker et al. 1996). The 1995 Current Population Survey supplement included four versions of the race and Hispanic origin questions, with and without a multiracial category. More than 70 percent of Puerto Ricans in the United States identified as Hispanic in a combined race and ethnicity question. Only 7 percent chose the multiracial category in the separate race and Hispanic origin panel, while less than 3 percent did so in the combined panel. However, more than 32 percent of the respondents classified themselves as "all other" when they were asked separate race and ethnicity questions, as currently formulated in the decennial census. In short, "other" seems to be increasingly used as a racialized synonym for Hispanic.

The Current Population Survey, conducted annually in March by the Bureau of the Census, allows one to construct a brief time series on this issue (see table 7.7). Between 1992 and 1995, the proportion of U.S. Puerto Ricans who classified their race as "other" increased from less than 5 percent to more than 15 percent. However, when the Bureau of the Census eliminated the "other" category, the proportion of whites rose from less than 80 percent in 1995 to nearly 91 percent in 1999. The percentage of blacks rose from less than 5 percent to almost 8 percent during this period. Throughout the 1990s, only between 1 and 2 percent classified themselves as American Indian or Asian. These data confirm that an increasing number of Puerto Ricans prefer not to label themselves as either white or black when they have another option presumably indicating mixed descent.

In sum, census figures suggest two main trends in the racial self-identification of Puerto Ricans in the United States. On the one hand, mainland Puerto Ricans classify their "racial" identity primarily as Hispanic, regardless of federal government policy stating that Hispanics can be of any race. Most Puerto Ricans prefer to place themselves in an intermediate position between white and black, even when offered a multiracial option. On the other hand, if forced to separate their Hispanic origin from their racial identity, many Puerto Ricans choose to call themselves "other." This option seems to provide a third alternative, conceptually equivalent to brown, which eludes the white/black dichotomy altogether. Either as Hispanics or as others, Puerto Ricans in the United States are increasingly racialized. Rather than repudiating the dominant American scheme of group classification, as Rodríguez claims, mainland Puerto Ricans may be assigning new meanings to existing racial and ethnic categories.[9]

CONCLUSION

During the twentieth century, the problem of defining, classifying, and representing the racial identity of Puerto Ricans was officially addressed in two main ways. On the Island, the Bureau of the Census did not collect any racial statistics between 1950 and 2000, largely because they were incompatible with the dominant U.S. scheme of racial classification. Furthermore, Commonwealth officials were not interested in dividing the Puerto Rican population by race but in uniting it under a common nationality. In the mainland, the 1980 census asked people to identify themselves as either Hispanic or not Hispanic, and then as white, black, American Indian, Asian, or other. Whereas most islanders describe themselves as white, most mainland Puerto Ricans now consider themselves to be neither white nor black but other. Many use Hispanic, Latino, or Spanish origin as racial self-designators. The increasing racialization of such panethnic terms has numerous implications for American society, such as the possible broadening of a bipolar racial order into a tripartite color scheme including white, black, and brown (see Winant 1994).

The study of race relations in Puerto Rico (as in Brazil and other Latin American countries) traditionally counterposed the Island's racial discourses and practices to those of the United States. Whereas Puerto Ricans defined race phenotypically, Americans used the principle of hypodescent. While the Puerto Rican system recognized physically intermediate types, the American system dwelled on the dichotomy between white and black. In contrast to a high degree of racial mixture and integration in Puerto Rico, segregation and conflict characterized race relations in the United States. This binary opposition led many scholars to minimize racial prejudice and discrimination on the Island prior to the importation of the U.S. racial model (see T. Blanco 1985 [1942]; Mintz 1966; Rogler 1940; Sereno 1947; Siegel 1948). After an initial wave of studies celebrating Puerto Rico as a racial democracy in the 1940s, a critical perspective emerged in the late 1960s and early 1970s denouncing racial inequality and exclusion on the Island (Betances 1972, 1973; Picó de Hernández et al. 1985; Seda Bonilla 1968, 1973; Zenón Cruz 1975; see also Gordon 1949, 1950; Rosario and Carrión 1951). However, academic discourse on Puerto Ricans and race has been limited during the past two decades, both in the Island and on the mainland (C. Rodríguez 1997). The "conspiracy of silence" continues today as a result of the paucity of fieldwork and official data on racial distinctions among Puerto Ricans (Routté-Gómez 1995).

Between 1899 and 1950, the U.S. Bureau of the Census computed the number of white and nonwhite people in Puerto Rico. In spite of changing racial categories, as well as their popular contestation, the census reported that Puerto Ricans were becoming whiter over time. This trend continued with the 2000 count. The "bleaching" of the Island's population is partly due to the propensity to incorporate light mulattoes (trigueños) into the white category, as well as the common belief in "improving one's race" through intermarriage with lighter-skinned persons. But the main reason for the transformation of Puerto Rico's racial statistics was the growing polarization between whites and nonwhites in the census. The American scheme of racial classification diverged from local discourses and practices, which paid more careful attention to gradations in skin color and recognized multiple physical types between white and black, such as trigueño, indio, and jabao, as well as the more exotic *café con leche, piel canela,* and *blanco con raja.* A bipolar racial model could not capture such fine social distinctions.

Since 1940, the Bureau of the Census has faced the challenge of counting a growing number of Puerto Ricans in the continental United States. At first, the U.S. government considered most Puerto Ricans to be whites whose mother tongue happened to be Spanish. By 1980, the census had adopted "Hispanic" as a quasi-racial term and encouraged Puerto Ricans and other Latin American immigrants to identify with that category, rather than with non-Hispanic whites or blacks. In 1990 and 2000, an even larger proportion of Puerto Ricans, Mexicans, Dominicans, and other Hispanics reported that they belonged to other races (*Latin American Perspectives* 1992; C. Rodríguez 1992, 2000). For U.S. Puerto Ricans, "other" has multiple semantic connotations, including trigueño, tan, brown, Spanish, Hispanic, Latino, Boricua, or simply Puerto Rican. Contrary to the whitening of the Island's population during the first half of the twentieth century, mainland Puerto Ricans underwent a browning tendency during the second half of the century.

Throughout this essay, I have argued that the popular racial categories used by Puerto Ricans on the Island and in the diaspora depart from dominant American racial codes. Although the official racial terminology in the United States has changed over time, the two main categories—white and black—have remained relatively stable, distinct, and opposed to each other (Domínguez 1998). The presumed purity and homogeneity of the white and black races, however, clashed against the prevalence of racial mixture among Puerto Ricans. The multiplicity of physical types, produced by seemingly endless combinations of skin color, facial features, and hair texture, could not easily be accommodated within the U.S. hegemonic racial taxonomy. From the standpoint of the federal government, Puerto Ricans on the Island had to be labeled according to discrete racial groupings—or not at all. But most islanders insisted that they were white, even if they knew they had some African ancestry. In contrast, migrants to the mainland evaded the bipolar racial order by choosing a third alternative, "other," which increasingly mirrored their Hispanic identity.

The contested representation of the racial identity of Puerto Ricans has wider theoretical and practical implications. This case study confirms that all racial classification systems are scientifically invalid as representations of human biological diversity. They are even less appropriate as explanations for social and cultural differences. Although some group variations related to skin, hair, and eye pigmentation, stature, and body form are hereditary, such variations are difficult if not impossible to categorize in a reliable way. Phenotypically, Puerto Ricans display the full range of characteristics traditionally associated with both whites and blacks. According to American standards, they should be counted as people of color because of their mixed ancestry. According to Puerto Rican standards, they should be considered white if they have light skin color, thin lips, elongated noses, and straight hair. It is sterile to argue that one scheme is right and the other wrong, or that one is morally superior to the other. Instead, both systems are historically and culturally grounded in racist ideologies originating in colonialism and slavery (see Omi and Winant 1994).

The practical implications of this analysis are ominous, especially for racial counting efforts such as the census. Allowing respondents to choose more than one racial category did not change substantially the proportion of Puerto Ricans on the Island or in the mainland who classified themselves as whites or blacks. Instead, the racial self-identification question has opened a Pandora's box in Puerto Rico. Most islanders—more than 80 percent—checked the "white" box on the 2000 census questionnaire because local standards of race allow them to consider themselves white even though some of them might not be accepted as such according to American standards. Like Hispanics in the mainland, islanders could have chosen "other," or they might have opted for both "black" and "white." Then again, Puerto Ricans could have defined themselves according to multiple racial categories, but most did not. In the 1998 status plebiscite, Island residents had to choose among four alternatives: the current Common-wealth, free association, independence, or statehood. The largest proportion of voters supported "none of the above." Perhaps, to recycle that formula, the best response to the racial question in the 2000 census would also have been "none of the above."[10]

NOTES

1. This section draws on and expands an earlier review of the literature on race in Puerto Rico; see J. Duany, "Reconstructing Racial Identity: Ethnicity, Color, and Class among Dominicans in the United States and Puerto Rico," *Latin American Perspectives* 25, no. 3 (1998): 147–72.

2. Between July and October 2000, the Bureau of the Census commissioned an evaluation of the high nonresponse rate to the 2000 census of Puerto Rico. According to a personal conversation with one of the fieldworkers, Isar Godreau, the study found that many islanders were puzzled by the race and ethnicity questions on the census questionnaire. Unfortunately, the results of this research have not yet been made public.

3. In the 1950s an official New York City report made headlines in Puerto Rico because it distinguished Puerto Ricans as a racial type, separate from whites and nonwhites (*El Mundo* 1954).

4. The memoirs of Bernardo Vega document that Puerto Rican settlements in New York City at the turn of the twentieth century were not strictly segregated by color. The residents of today's barrios continue to be racially heterogeneous. See Vega, Bernardo. *Memorias de Bernardo Vega: Contribución a la historia de la comunidad puertorriqueña en Nueva York,* edited by César Andreu Iglesias. 5th ed. (Río Piedras, P.R.: Huracán, 1994 [1977]).

5. A current application form to the Teaching Practicum at the College of education of the University of Puerto Rico, Río Piedras, inquired about "ethnic origin" and included the following categories: "White," "Black," "Trigueño Claro," "Trigueño Oscuro," and "Other." I thank Isar Godreau for providing me a copy of this document.

6. Virginia Domínguez has reviewed changing racial taxonomies in the United States, as reflected in Hawaiian censuses during the twentieth century. She found much categorical flip-flopping in U.S. concepts of race since the first census of 1790. Since 1900 the census has used twenty-six different terms to identify the racial composition of the American population. See Domínguez, Virginia, "Exporting U.S. Concepts of Race: Are There Limits to the U.S. Model?" *Social Research* 65, no. 2 (1998): 369–400.

7. Before 1940 it is practically impossible to obtain separate cross-tabulations for Puerto Ricans and race in the United States. At the time of this writing, the U.S. Bureau of the Census had not yet released separate data for the race of mainland Puerto Ricans in 2000.

8. Similarly, Benjamin Bailey found that young Dominican Americans in Providence, Rhode Island, describe their race as Spanish, Hispanic, Dominican, or Latino, but never as black or white. See Bailey, Benjamin, "Language and Ethnic/Racial Identity of Dominican American High School Students in Providence, Rhode Island." Ph.D. diss., University of California, Los Angeles, 1999.

9. As Angela Ginorio argues, the recognition of a third racial group such as brown or other to designate Native Americans, Chicanos, Puerto Ricans, and other Latinos does not fundamentally challenge the American system of racial classification. Rather, it merely adds another discrete category based on ethnic background. See Ginorio, Angela Beatriz, "A Comparison of Puerto Ricans in New York with Native Puerto Ricans and Native Americans on Two Measures of Acculturation: Gender Role and Racial Identification." Ph.D. diss., Fordham University, 1979: 107.

10. The racial implications of the various status options for Puerto Rico lie beyond the scope of this chapter. However, many black Puerto Ricans have traditionally supported the Island's annexation to the United States, while the pro-independence movement has been predominantly white. The impact of racial distinctions on local elections remains unknown as a result of lack of research.

REFERENCES

Administración de Reconstrucción de Puerto Rico. 1938. *Censo de Puerto Rico: 1935. Población y agricultura.* Washington, D.C.: Government Printing Office.

Arana-Soto, S. 1976. *Puerto Rico: Sociedad sin razas y trabajos afines.* San Juan: Asociación Médica de Puerto Rico.

Bailey, Benjamin. 1999. Language and Ethnic/Racial Identity of Dominican American High School Students in Providence, Rhode Island. Ph.D. diss., University of California, Los Angeles.

Betances, Samuel. 1972. The Prejudice of Having No Prejudice in Puerto Rico. Part 1. *The Rican* 2:41–54.

———. 1973. The Prejudice of Having No Prejudice in Puerto Rico. Part 2. *The Rican* 3:22–37.

Blanco, Tomás. 1985 [1942]. *El prejuicio racial en Puerto Rico.* 3rd ed. Río Piedras, P.R.: Huracán.

Cabranes, José A. 1979. *Citizenship and the American Empire: Notes on the Legislative History of the United States Citizenship of Puerto Ricans.* New Haven: Yale University Press.

Davis, F. James. 1998. *Who Is Black? One Nation's Definition.* University Park: Pennsylvania State University Press.

Degler, Carl N. 1971. *Neither Black nor White: Slavery and Race Relations in Brazil and the United States.* New York: Macmillan.

Departamento de la Guerra, Dirección del Censo. 1900. *Informe sobre el censo de Puerto Rico, 1899.* Washington, D.C.: Imprenta del Gobierno.

Díaz Quiñones, Arcadio. 1985. Tomás Blanco: Racismo, historia, esclavitud. Introduction and preliminary study to *El prejuicio racial en Puerto Rico,* by Tomás Blanco, 13–91. Río Piedras, P.R.: Huracán

Domínguez, Virginia. 1998. Exporting U.S. Concepts of Race: Are There Limits to the U.S. Model? *Social Research* 65 (2): 369–400.

Duany, Jorge. 1998. Reconstructing Racial Identity: Ethnicity, Color, and Class among Dominicans in the United States and Puerto Rico. *Latin American Perspectives* 25 (3):147–72.

Duany, Jorge, Luisa Hernández Angueira, and César A. Rey. 1995. *El Barrio Gandul: Economía subterránean y migración indocumentada en Puerto Rico.* Caracas: Nueva Sociedad.

El Mundo. 1945. Comite Bell preocupado con gobierno insular. May 2, 5.

———. 1958. Senador J. W. Fulbright: Afirma la isla es ejemplo solución racial. April 15, 1.

———. 1959. George William Culberson: Impresionado por ausencía de prejuicios raciales aquí. October 19, 17.

Fitzpatrick, Joseph P. 1987. *Puerto Rican Americans: The Meaning of Migration to the Mainland*. 2nd ed. Englewood Cliffs, N.J.: Prentice-Hall.

Ginorio, Angela Beatriz. 1971. A Study in Racial Perception in Puerto Rico. Master's thesis, University of Puerto Rico.

———. 1979. A Comparison of Puerto Ricans in New York with Native Puerto Ricans and Native Americans on Two Measures of Acculturation: Gender Role and Racial Identification. Ph.D. diss., Fordham University.

Godreau, Isar P. 2000. La semántica fugitiva: "Raza," color y vida cotidiana en Puerto Rico. *Revista de Ciencias Sociales*, n.s., 9:52–71.

Godreau-Santiago, Isar Pilar. 1999. Missing the Mix: San Antón and the Racial Dynamics of "Nationalism" in Puerto Rico. Ph.D. diss., University of California, Santa Cruz.

Gordon, Maxine. 1949. Race Patterns and Prejudice in Puerto Rico. *American Sociological Review* 14 (2): 294–301.

———. 1950. Cultural Aspects of Puerto Rico's Race Problem. *American Sociological Review* 15 (3): 382–92.

Harris, Marvin. 1964. *Patterns of Race in the Americas*. New York: Norton.

Hill, Robert T. 1899. Mineral Resources of Porto Rico. *U.S. Geological Survey, Annual Report for 1898–99* (20): 771–78.

———. 1903. *Cuba and Porto Rico, with the Other Islands of the West Indies*. 2nd ed. New York: Century.

Hoetink, Harmannus. 1967. *Caribbean Race Relations: A Study of Two Variants*. London: Oxford University Press.

Kantrowitz, Nathan. 1971. Algunas consecuencias raciales: Diferencias educativas y ocupacionales entre los puertorriqueños blancos y no blancos en los Estados Unidos continentales, 1950. *Revista de Ciencias Sociales* 15 (3): 387–97.

Kinsbruner, Jay. 1996. *Not of Pure Blood: The Free People of Color and Racial Prejudice in Nineteenth-Century Puerto Rico*. Durham: Duke University Press.

Latin American Perspectives. 1992. The Politics of Ethnic Construction: Hispanic, Chicano, Latino. . . ? Thematic issue. 19 (4).

Martínez, Angel R. 1988. The Effects of Acculturation and Racial Identity on Self-Esteem and Psychological Well-Being among Young Puerto Ricans. Ph.D. diss., City University of New York.

Mercado Vega, César A. 1978. Memorandum to Rosendo Miranda Torres, November 13. Xeroxed copy. Junta de Planificación de Puerto Rico, San Juan.

Mills, C. Wright, Clarence Senior, and Rose Kohn Goldsen. 1950. *The Puerto Rican Journey: New York's Newest Migrants*. New York: Harper.

Mintz, Sidney W. 1966. Puerto Rico: An Essay in the Definition of a National Culture. In *Selected Background Studies Prepared for the U.S.-P.R. Commission on the Status of Puerto Rico*, ed. U.S.-P.R. Commission on the Status of Puerto Rico, 339–434. Washington, D.C.: Government Printing Office.

Montero Seplowin, Virginia. 1971. Análisis de la identificación racial de los puertorriqueños en Filadelfia. *Revista de Ciencias Sociales* 15 (1): 143–48.

Mulero, Leonor. Ingresa la Isla a las estadísticas del censo federal *El Nuevo Día*, January 9, 10.

Muñoz Marin, Luis. 1960. Discurso a los puertorriqueños en Nueva York pronunciado por el Gobernador Muñoz Marín el 10 de abril de 1960. Section V: Governor of Puerto Rico, 1949–1964; Series 9: Speeches; Box 16: Status; Folder 7. Fundación Luis Muñoz Marín, Trujillo Alto, P.R.

Myrdal, Gunnar. 1944. *An American Dilemma: The Negro Problem and Modern Democracy.* New York: Harper.

National Geographic Magazine. 1901. Cuba and Porto Rico. 12 (2): 80.

Oboler, Suzanne. 1995. *Ethnic Labels, Latino Lives: Identity and the Politics of (Re)Presentation in the United States.* Minneapolis: University of Minnesota Press.

Omi, Michael, and Howard Winant. 1994. *Racial Formation in the United States: From the 1960s to the 1990s.* 2nd ed. London: Routledge.

Pérez, Moira. 1998. From Mask Makers to Bell Boys: Tourism and the Politics of Community Organization in Puerto Rico. Ph.D. diss. proposal, University of California, Berkeley.

Picó de Hernández, Isabel, Marcia Rivera, Carmen Parrilla, Jeannette Ramos de Sánchez de Vilella, and Isabelo Zenón. 1985. *Discrimen por color, sexo y origen nacional en Puerto Rico.* Río Piedras, P.R.: Centro de Investigaciones Sociales, Universidad de Puerto Rico.

Rodríguez, Clara. 1974. *The Ethnic Queue in the United States: The Case of Puerto Ricans.* San Francisco: R & E Research Associates.

———. 1989. *Puerto Ricans: Born in the U.S.A.* Boston: Unwin Hyman.

———. 1990. Racial Identification among Puerto Rican Men and Women in New York. *Hispanic Journal of Behavioral Sciences* 12 (4): 366–79.

———. 1992. Race, Culture, and Latino "Otherness" in the 1980 Census. *Social Science Quarterly* 73 (4): 930–37.

———. 1994. Challenging Racial Hegemony: Puerto Ricans in the United States. In *Race,* ed. Steven Gregory and Roger Sanjek, 131–45. New Brunswick, N.J.: Rutgers University Press.

———. 1996. Puerto Ricans: Between Black and White. In *Historical Perspectives on Puerto Rican Survival in the United States,* ed. Clara E. Rodríguez and Virginia Sánchez Korrol, 23–36. Princeton: Markus Wiener.

———. 1997. Rejoinder to Roberto Rodríguez-Morazzani's "Beyond the Rainbow: Mapping the Discourse on Puerto Ricans and 'Race.'" *Centro* 9 (1): 115–17.

———. 2000. *Changing Race: Latinos, the Census, and the History of Ethnicity in the United States.* New York: New York University Press.

Rodríguez, Clara E., and Héctor Cordero-Guzmán. 1992. Placing Race in Context. *Ethnic and Racial Studies* 25 (4): 523–42.

Rodríguez Cruz, Juan. 1965. Las relaciones raciales en Puerto Rico. *Revista de Ciencias Sociales* 9 (4): 373–86.

Rodríguez, Víctor M. 1997. The Racialization of Puerto Rican Ethnicity in the United States. In *Ethnicity, Race, and Nationality in the Caribbean,* ed. Juan Manuel Carrión, 233–73. San Juan: Institute of Caribbean Studies, University of Puerto Rico.

Rodríguez-Morazzani, Roberto P. 1996. Beyond the Rainbow: Mapping the Discourse of Puerto Ricans and "Race." *Centro* 8 (1–2): 150–69.

Rogler, Charles C. 1940. *Comerío: A Study of a Puerto Rican Town.* Kansas: University of Kansas.

———. 1972 [1946]. The Morality of Race Mixing in Puerto Rico. In *Portrait of a Society: Readings on Puerto Rican Sociology*, ed. Eugenio Fernández Méndez, 57–64. Río Piedras, P.R.: University of Puerto Rico Press.

Rosario, José Colombán, and Justina Carrión. 1951. *El negro: Haití—Estados Unidos— Puerto Rico*. 2nd ed. Río Piedras, P.R.: División de Impresos, Universidad de Puerto Rico.

Routté-Gómez, Eneid. 1995. A Conspiracy of Silence: Racism in Puerto Rico. *San Juan City Magazine* 4 (8): 54–58.

Ruggles, Steven, et al. 1997. Integrated Public Use Microdata Series: Version 2.0. Enumerator Instructions. Electronic document. http://www.ipums.umn.edu.

Scarano, Francisco. 1984. *Sugar and Slavery in Puerto Rico: The Plantation Economy of Ponce, 1800–1850*. Madison: University of Wisconsin Press.

Schemo, Diana Jean. 2000. Despite Options on Census, Many to Check "Black" Only. *New York Times*, February 12. Electronic document, http://archives.nytimes.com.

Seda Bonilla, Eduardo. 1968. Dos modelos de relaciones raciales: Estados Unidos y América Latina. *Revista de Ciencias Sociales* 12 (4): 569–97.

———. 1973. Los *derechos civiles en la cultura puertorriqueña*. 2nd ed. Río Piedras, P.R.: Bayoán.

Segal, Aaron. 1996. Locating the Swallows: Caribbean Recycling Migration. Paper presented at the XXII Annual Conference of the Caribbean Studies Association, San Juan, May 27–31.

Sereno, Renzo. 1947. Cryptomelanism: A Study of Color Relations and Personal Insecurity in Puerto Rico. *Psychiatry* 10 (3): 253–69.

Siegel, Morris. 1948. A Puerto Rican Town. Unpublished manuscript. Río Piedras, P.R.: Social Science Research Center, University of Puerto Rico.

Torres, Arlene. 1998. La Gran Familia Puertorriqueña "Ej Prieta de Beldá." In *Blackness in Latin America and the Caribbean*, ed. Arlene Torres and Norman E. Whitten Jr., 2:285–306. Bloomington: Indiana University Press.

Tucker, Clyde, Ruth McKay, Brian Kojetin, Roderick Harrison, Manuel de la Puente, Linda Stinson, and Ed Robinson. 1996. *Testing Methods of Collecting Racial and Ethnic Information: Results of the Current Population Survey Supplement on Race and Ethnicity*. Bureau of Labor Statistical Notes no. 40.

U.S. Bureau of the Census. 1943. *Sixteenth Census of the United States: 1940. Puerto Rico: Population. Bulletin no. 2: Characteristics of the Population*. Washington, D.C.: Government Printing Office.

———. 1952. *United States Census of Population: 1950. General Characteristics: Puerto Rico*. Washington, D.C: Government Printing Office.

———. 1953a. *Census of Population: 1950*. Vol. 2, *Characteristics of the Population. Parts 51–54: Territories and Possessions*. Washington, D.C.: Government Printing Office.

———. 1963. *U.S. Census of Population: 1960. Subject Reports: Puerto Ricans in the United States*. Washington, D.C.: Government Printing Office.

———. 2001. American Factfinder: Census 2000 Data. Electronic document. <http:www.census.gov/main/www/cen2000.html>.

Vega, Bernardo. 1994 [1977]. *Memorias de Bernardo Vega: Contribución a la historia de la comunidad puertorriqueña en Nueva York*. Edited by César Andreu Iglesias. 5th ed. Río Piedras, P.R.: Huracán.

Wade, Peter. 1997. *Race and Ethnicity in Latin America*. London: Pluto.

White, Trumbull. 1898. *Our New Possessions*. Boston: Adams.

Winant, Howard. 1994. *Racial Conditions: Politics, Theory, Comparisons*. Minneapolis: University of Minnesota Press.

Wolfson, Alan R. 1972. Raza, conocimiento del inglés y aprovechamiento social entre los inmigrantes puertorriqueños de Nueva York: Una aplicación de la teoría de grupos de referencia. Master's thesis project, School of Social Work, University of Puerto Rico.

Zenón Cruz, Isabelo. 1975. *Narciso descubre su trasero: El negro en la cultura puertorriqueña*. 2nd ed. 2 vols. Humacao, P.R.: Furidi.

8

HAIR RACE-ING
Dominican Beauty Culture and Identity Production

Ginetta E. B. Candelario

Use to be
Ya could learn a whole lot of stuff
sitting in them
beauty shop chairs
Use to be
Ya could meet
a whole lot of other women
sittin there
along with hair frying
spit flying
and babies crying
Use to be
you could learn a whole lot about
how to catch up
with yourself
and some other folks
in your household.
Lots more got taken care of
than hair . . .

—WILLI COLEMAN,
"Among the Things
That Use to Be"

At the most banal level, a beauty shop is where women go for beauty. But as Willi Coleman evocatively notes, at beauty shops "lots more [gets] taken care of than hair." The degrees, types, and technologies of artifice and alteration required by beauty are mediated by racial, sexual, class, political, and geographic cultures and locations. Thus, beauty shops can be considered as sites of both cultural and identity production. Some have argued that if the female body generally has been subjected to "externalization of the gendered self" (Peiss 1994, 384), the explicitly racialized female body has been subjected to "exile from the self" (Shohat and Stam 1994, 322–33). With the rise of global colonialism, slavery, neocolonialism, and imperialism, African-origin bodies have been stigmatized as unsightly and ugly, yet, simultaneously and paradoxically as hypersexual (Hernton 1988). White female bodies are racialized as well, but this racialization is enacted via the assumption of de-racination, racial neutrality, and naturalized white invisibility (Frankenberg 1993). This white supremacist racial history interacts with masculinist imperatives of gender and sexual homogenization and normalization in particular ways (Young 1995). Moreover, bodily beautification requires material resources and aesthetic practices that are class bound. The beauty shop, then, can be analyzed as a site where hegemonic gender, class, sexuality, and race tropes simultaneously are produced and problematized.

In particular, hair—the subject and object of beauty shop work—epitomizes the mutual referentiality of race/sex/gender/class categories and identities. One can, as I found during a six-month participant observation at a Dominican beauty shop in New York City, "learn a whole lot of stuff sittin' in them beauty shop chairs." Here, the concern is to present both the representational and the production practices of hair culture as a window into the contextualized complexity of Dominican identity. The hair culture institutions, practices, and ideals of Dominican women in New York City during the late 1990s are presented as an instructive selection from a larger study (Candelario 2000).

DOMINICAN IDENTITY: ETHNICITY AND RACE IN CONTEXT

The importance of hair as a defining race marker highlights the centrality of beauty practices. Hair, after all, is an alterable sign. Hair that is racially compromising can be mitigated with care and styling. Skin color and facial features, conversely, are less pliant or not as easily altered. That Dominicans have equated whiteness both with *lo indio*, an ethno-racial identity based on identification with the decimated Taino natives of the island that now houses the Dominican Republic and *"lo Hispano"* or hispanicity, reflects the multiple semiotic systems of race they have historically negotiated. *La/o india/o* is invoked to erase the African past and Afro-diasporic present of Dominicans (Howard 1997). Hispanicity affirms the ethno-racial distance between Dominicans and Haitians, an organizing principle in Dominican national imaginaries since the rise of the state.

Operating in the context of both Latin American and United States' notions of race, transnational Dominicans engage in a sort of racial "code switching" in which both Latin American and U.S. race systems are engaged, subverted, and sustained in various historical and biographical and spatial contexts and moments. For example, for a variety of reasons I explore at length elsewhere (Candelario 2000), Dominicans in Washington, D.C., identify as black nearly twice as often as Dominicans in New York (see also Dore-

Cabral and Itzigsohn 1997; Levitt and Gomez 1997; Duany 1994). Confronted in New York City with the U.S. model of pure whiteness that valorizes lank, light hair, white skin, light eyes, thin and narrow-hipped bodies, the Dominican staff and clients at Salon Lamadas continue to prefer a whiteness that indicates mixture. The identity category labeled "Hispanic" is deployed as the signifier of somatic, linguistic, and cultural alterity in relation to both Anglo whiteness and African American blackness. That *Hispanic* looks are preferred over both the Anglo and African American somatic norm images (Hoetink 1985) of the host society attests to resistance to acculturation and insistence on an alternative, or "other" space.

Dominicans, who might have been considered black by European and U.S. observers were it not for their own colonial antipathy toward Haiti and later, toward Haitians, historically have been endowed with a sort of literary and political honorary whiteness in the service of both the domestic elite and the military and political-economic interests of the United States. It is an ethno-racial identity formulation predicated on the physical disappearance of Taino natives, coupled with their literary (Sommer 1983), iconographic, and bodily re-inscription, and a concomitant textual and ideological erasure of blackness (Torres-Saillant 1999). Rather than use the language of Negritude—*negro*, *mulatto*, and so forth—to describe themselves, Dominicans use language that limits their racial ancestry to Europeans and Taino "Indians"—*indio, indio oscuro, indio claro, trigueño, moreno/a*. The result is an ethno-racial Hispanicized Indian, or an Indo-Hispanic identity.

A series of regionally anomalous events in the political economic history of Santo Domingo accounts for this distinctive formulation of whiteness. Chief among those anomalies are the relatively short duration and limited importance of plantation slavery, the massive depopulations caused by white emigration, the impoverishment of the remaining white and creole colonials during the seventeenth-century devastation, and the concomitantly heavy reliance upon blacks and mulattos in the armed forces and religious infrastructure (Moya Pons 1995; Torres-Saillant 1996). At the same time, Spanish colonial norms of whiteness, what Hoetink (1967) has called the "Iberian variant" of a white "somatic norm image," were darker than the contemporary Anglo-European version.

French travel writers of the nineteenth century, when visiting the Spanish part of the island then called Saint Domingue, noted that people who seemed obviously of mixed African and Spanish descent considered themselves, not mulattos or colored, but *los blancos de la tierra*, literally, "the whites of the land." According to Moya Pons, "This meant that despite their color, [the whites of the land] were different from the slaves whom they saw as the only blacks of the island" (1996, 16). In other words, in Dominican history, whiteness—whatever its bodily parameters—is an explicitly achieved (and achievable) status with connotations of social, political, and economic privilege. It is, moreover, understood to be a matter of context.

The representation of Dominican women in the beauty shop occupations reflects both the importance of beauty culture to Dominican women, and the shifting opportunities available in the New York economy. When Dominican women first began to arrive in New York in the 1960s and 1970s, they generally frequented shops owned by other Latina/os, especially Cubans and Puerto Ricans, who were already established in Upper Manhattan (Masud-Piloto 1996; Rodriguez 1991; Sánchez-Korrol 1983). Although Dominicans had been migrating to New York City since the early nineteenth century, the Dominican community began to establish itself more permanently after the 1965 revolution and the 1965 U.S. Immigration Act (Martin 1966). The post-1980 flow of Dominican women into beauty shop occupations—whether as owners, hairdressers, manicurists, shampoo girls, estheticians, or masseurs—reflects simultaneously changes in the New York economy from manufacturing to service industries, changes in the demographics of the Washington Heights area, and changes in Dominican beauty culture in the Dominican Republic as well (see New York City Department of City Planning 1995). While Dominican women continue to be overrepresented in the nondurable goods manufacturing sector (Hernández 1989; Hernández et al. 1997), particularly in the apparel industry (Pessar 1987a, 1987b; Waldinger 1986), the volatility of that sector, together with the regimentation, occupational hazards, low pay, and low status of manufacturing and much service-sector employment, make beauty shop ownership and employment appealing by comparison.

In addition, in the Dominican Republic beauty culture has come to be seen as a respectable and professional field. Although commercial beauty shops have existed in the Dominican Republic since at least the 1930s, they generally serviced the elite. The majority of Dominican beauty culturalists operated out of their homes until the 1980s. Typically these shops were located in a converted front room, patio, or garage space and consisted of an owner-operator and a young neighborhood assistant. Shop owner-operators and assistants alike were considered nearly at par with domestic workers, and thus were of low socio-economic status. Additionally, beauty culturalists were reputed to be women of loose sexual morals. In the early 1980s, however, beauty culturalists began to professionalize, via the establishment of a professional organization, Asociación de Estilistas Dominicanas (Dominican Hair Stylists Association), the proliferation of beauty schools and certification programs, and a shift from the use of domestic and home-manufactured products to an increasing reliance upon hair-care products and technologies imported from the United States. Beauty shop work, in other words, has come to be viewed as a skilled profession one trains for and pursues.

Work in the New York Dominican beauty shop, while not entirely autonomous or especially well-paying, makes possible greater autonomy and flexibility and higher earnings and community status. Job quality and job satisfaction are often higher than in manufacturing or other service-sector employment. In addition, the Dominican beauty shop represents a female-dominated entrepreneurial sector, somewhat parallel to the male-dominated Dominican *bodega* (grocery store). In his study of Dominican entrepreneurs in New York City, Guarnizo (1993) found that entrepreneurial Dominican women frequently chose beauty shops as their niche. He reported, "One out of every five respondents is a woman. Unlike male [business] owners, however, women are clustered in a single sector: 60 percent of women own service firms (especially beauty salons and other personal service establishments) while only 25 and 15 percent of them own commercial or manufacturing firms, respectively" (121).

The appeal of this sector for Dominican women in New York City is manyfold. In economic terms, beauty shop start-up costs are substantially lower than commercial or manufacturing firms, and therefore are more accessible to low-earning, poorly capitalized, or less-educated women. Further, barriers to entry are fewer, both in terms of fixed capital and human capital (Schroder 1978; Willet 1996). In cultural terms, beauty shop work is considered women's purview, while commercial or manufacturing ventures are generally considered male domains. *Bodegüeras* (female grocery shop owners), for example, while not uncommon, often have male kin *representandolas* (representing them) at the store counter. Similarly, while Dominican men do own beauty shops, they are less likely to be owner-operators, preferring instead to hire women managers.

Currently there is a thriving Dominican beauty culture industry in New York City, supported primarily by Dominican, and increasingly by African American women (Williams 2000). In Washington Heights/Inwood alone, that is, in the vicinity of northwestern Manhattan from 155th street to the 190s, from the Harlem River on the east to the Hudson River on the west, where 40 percent of the Dominican population in New York resides, there are 146 salons (1992 Economic Census, Service Industries, Firms Subject to Federal Income Tax, Zip Code Statistics, *Manhattan Yellow Pages, April 1999—April 2000*). On average, these salons are two-tenths of a mile (or one-and-one-half blocks) apart from one another. There is, in other words, a salon on nearly every single block in Washington Heights.[1]

By comparison, there are only 103 (or 40 percent fewer) beauty shops in the far wealthier Upper East Side, which is the district from East 61st to East 94th Streets, from Fifth Avenue to the East River. These salons are eight-tenths of a mile apart on average. In Harlem, where average per capita income is nearly identical to that in Washington Heights/Inwood, there are 112 shops. Shops in this district, which ranges from 114th to 138th Streets, and from Fifth Avenue to the Hudson River, are four-tenths of a mile apart on average. Washington Heights/Inwood is only slightly more densely populated than Harlem, but has 30 percent more shops. These numbers are all the more impressive given the exceedingly high poverty rate (36 percent) and low per-capita income level ($6,336) among Dominicans in New York City. It is quite clear that hair and beauty shops are important to Dominicans.

Today, the Dominican salon in New York City is a neighborhood institution that indicates community actualization. If, as the old sociological maxim holds, for most immigrant communities the establishment of ethnically specific funeral homes indicates community salience (e.g., Park et al. 1925; Gans 1962), for Dominicans, the beauty shop holds a similar role in the community. The Dominican beauty shop, with the physical space it plots out and the social relationships it contains, is a site that not only reflects transnational community development and cohesion, but helps sustain it.

SALON LAMADAS

Salon Lamadas, where I spent six months as a participant-observer, is in many ways a typical Dominican salon.[2] It is located in the heart of Washington Heights, on St. Nicholas Avenue several blocks south of the 181st Street shopping district. Surrounding the salon are a telephone station, a pharmacy, a Pronto Envio (remittances center), and a family restaurant. This is a typically busy commercial and residential street, trafficked primarily by Dominicans, Puerto Ricans, Cubans, and, increasingly, Mexicans.

Founded in 1992 by an owner operator, Salon Lamadas is an average-sized shop with four stylists, including the owner, and a shampooer, a manicurist, and a facialist/ masseuse. Music is always playing at the salon, sometimes quite loudly. Generally it is merengue and salsa, although one or two ballads surface. Often in the afternoon the television is turned on, as well, and is usually tuned to *Cristina*, a popular Miami-based, Spanish-language talk show. In addition to the music and the television, the blow dryers are constantly going. Despite all this noise, the women hear each other quite well, and carry on conversations across the room. The atmosphere is one of conviviality and easy familiarity.

The salon is open seven days a week. Although many salons in the United States close on Mondays, Dominican salons do not. This is true for several reasons. First, Dominican women use salons for regular weekly hair care, not for intermittent haircuts and hair treatments. Therefore, there is steady demand throughout the week, although Fridays and Saturdays are still the busiest days. Second, the staff needs to work six days a week in order to earn enough money to survive in New York and to remit dollars to their families in the Dominican Republic (Hernández and Torres-Saillant 1998; Grasmuck and Pessar 1991). Third, because Dominican women are heavily represented in blue- and pink-collar work (Hernández 1989; Hernández, Rivera-Bátiz, and Agodini 1995), the salon must accommodate to their varied and long working hours.

Salon Lamadas, like most neighborhood salons, has a core of clients who frequent the shop regularly, usually once a week. Thirty of those "regulars" were approached for interviews. Fifteen agreed. Although this is not a statistically representative sample, neither in size nor in selection, they are a diverse group in terms of current age, age at migration, generation of migration, residency status, labor-force participation rates, professional status, educational attainment levels, Spanish- and English-language proficiency, marital status, household composition, and physical appearance.

The interviews consisted of two or three separate three-hour interviews. The first was a life-history interview, in which the respondent's migration, labor markets and educational experience, family life, and personal history were explored. The second interview inquired into the respondent's experience of Dominican beauty culture, both at Salon Lamadas and more generally. In addition, a third interview consisting of a photo elicitation component was conducted, following Furman (1997) and Kottak (in Harris 1964: 57). Using color photocopies of images copied from hairstyle books utilized at Salon Lamadas, respondents were asked to select and describe the women they found "most attractive" and "least attractive."

The explicit work of the salon, the transformation of a Dominican woman's hair into a culturally acceptable sign of beauty, hinges the customer's sense of self and beauty on certain racialized norms and models. The Dominican salon acts as a socializing agent. Hair care and salon use are rites of passage into Dominican women's community. At the salon, girls and women learn to transform their bodies—through hair care, waxing, manicuring, pedicuring, facials, and so forth—into socially valued, culturally specific, and race-determining displays of femininity.

Many of my respondents recalled visiting beauty shops as children with their mothers. Chastity, for example, said, "I used to always go with my mother to this shop in Flushing, where I grew up. She would go all the time and I'd go with her. I must have been real little because I remember being like "Wow" and "Ooo" about everything. They all looked glamorous to me. (Laughs) She still goes there, and it was the first shop I used myself. I still go there sometimes just to catch up on the neighborhood gossip."[3] As Chastity explains, for young girls with their mothers, the shop seems "glamorous" and adult, and therefore awe-inspiring.

These shops act as community centers; the exchange of information and women's insights is as much a part of their function as the production of beauty. Further, as in Chastity's case, it was often the mother's shop that young women first visited. Generally speaking, however, they themselves did not become beauty shop clients until they were about fifteen years old. That fifteen is the age when Latin American girls of means are introduced into society, and when Latin American girls generally are socially considered "women," is not coincidental (King 1998). Kathy recalled her first salon visit: "Aha, the first time I went to a shop I was already like fifteen years old. And it was to have my hair trimmed a little. But I already wanted to get out of the ponytails and buns already. And so I went to a neighbor who had a shop in her house and I had my hair washed, trimmed, and set. Oh, I looked so pretty." The repeated refrain of how "pretty" they looked after their first beauty shop visit also marks the transition from "innocent" childhood to "sexual" young womanhood. All of the respondents raised in the Dominican Republic, and several who were raised here, recalled that the transition from childhood to young womanhood was marked by the loosening of their hair from ponytails and *moños* (buns).

Others recalled first visiting a beauty shop in preparation for their migration to the United States, a moment which also might mark the transition from girlhood to adolescence. Nurka, for example, recalled that before migrating, when she was fourteen, her mother took her sisters and her to a beauty shop in town:

> Look, it was to come here. Exactly. Yes. (Chuckles) I had never gone to a salon. I always, I had two pony tails like this, and that was it. But I went. When we were coming here, mommy went to pick us up. And she took the three of us to the salon. I think my brother also had a haircut. And it was, we were in the country, and mommy took us to the east, to Bayaguana, the place was called. She took us there to have us all have our hair cut. They trimmed our hair, they washed our hair and it was, "Oh!" Everyone, "Oh! What pretty hair! Oh, how pretty!" (Laughs) And that was true, yes of course. I remember it as if it were today, yes.

For Nurka, the transition from childhood to adulthood was marked as much by the change from pigtails to hair done at the shop, as by the move to New York. Her transformation into young womanhood is socially recognized by people who acclaim her "pretty hair," now loose and womanish.

Like Nurka, Chastity remembers her grandmother styling her hair into pigtails and later *moños* for neatness and ease of care. So long as mother and grandmothers were responsible for their children's hair, these were the preferred styles. As Nana explained,

> Look, I hated those buns. It was three buns, one here, one here, and one here. My grandmother used to make them with a piece of string. And the other children used to make fun of them saying like "*Tin mari de dos pingó, cucara macara titire fué*" [a nonsensical children's rhyme]. I used to tear them [the buns] apart when I was walking to school. So then, when I became a little bigger, my grandmother told me that I was already old enough to take care of my hair myself. And that was such a joy for me! Oh! I started wearing curlers and styling my hair well.

The transition of hair care from one's caretaker's hands into one's own, thus, paralleled the increasing responsibility for one's own body and self.

RACIALIZED REPRODUCTION AND HAIR CULTURE

. . . Cause in our mutual obvious dislike
for nappiness
we came together
under the hot comb
to share
and share
and share

> —WILLI COLEMAN,
> "Among the Things That Use to Be"

A central aspect of Dominican hair culture has been the twin notions of *pelo malo* (bad hair) and *pelo bueno* (good hair). Bad hair is hair that is perceived to be tightly curled, coarse, and kinky. Good hair is hair that is soft and silky, straight, wavy, or loosely curled. There are clearly racial connotations to each category: the notion of bad hair implies an outright denigration of African-origin hair textures, while good hair exalts European, Asian, and indigenous-origin hair textures. Moreover, those with good hair are, by definition, not black, skin color notwithstanding. Thus, hair becomes an emblem of the everyday engagement of *blanqueamiento*, or whitening.

The Dominican salon, in being the preeminent site of Dominican hair culture practices and technologies, provides insight into the relative saliency of *blanqueamiento*, which is fundamentally about physical relations, sexual and otherwise, between people. This is not to say that *blanqueamiento* does not operate in nonmaterial culture realms as well, as Piedra's (1991) work on literary whiteness has aptly illustrated it does. However, there is an explicit physicality to *blanqueamiento*, particularly as it implicates racialized gender. It is there that beauty culture practices comes into play. *Blanqueamiento* is a long-term process of encoding whiteness bodily. Hair culture is a much more immediate, if more ephemeral, solution.

In the United States, non-African American women rarely have the opportunity to interact with African American women around beauty regimes. Consequently, they do not experience first-hand the variety of hair textures in the African diaspora through touching, washing, or styling "black hair," through seeing media depictions of black hair care, or through seeing African American women themselves caring for their hair. African American women, on the other hand, constantly are exposed to white women's hair care and hair textures through a variety of hegemonic media: dolls, television, cinematic and print media representations, and through observing first hand white women's hair ministrations throughout the day. Currently, women with non-African-diaspora hair textures spend a great deal of time throughout the day grooming their hair—brushing it, tying it up, loosening it, washing it, drying it, or otherwise fussing with it. By contrast, African-diaspora hair once styled retains its set and is typically washed every third or fourth day at home or in the salon. Thus, many non-African Americans simply do not know what "black hair" feels like, how it is maintained, what products are used on it, and what beauty practices are employed.

The first time that many white women are exposed to black women's hair in close quarters is when they are put into a communal living situation, such as a school dormitory or armed services barracks. A commonly cited experience of black women is that of the white housemate who asks to touch her hair, thus exposing the white woman's segregated upbringing, the novelty (specifically, the racialized exoticism) of African-diaspora hair textures, and, ultimately, her own white aesthetic privilege. Black women often recount the strong impact and significance of these encounters, while white women seem surprised at the hostility with which their seemingly innocent desire to touch is met (Cary 1991; Frankenberg 1993).

Beauty shops in the United States originated as, and continue to be, socially segregated spaces, in practice if not by law (Willet 1996). Schroder, for example, relates the story of the disruptive effect of a new hire's "ethnic clientele" in the implicitly (if not explicitly) white racialized "atmosphere existing in the salon" (1978, 193). African Americans and Anglo Americans alike hesitate to frequent each other's shops, although from the mid-1980s a series of individual and legal challenges to those social norms have occurred (C. Coleman 1995; Goodnough 1995; Willet 1996).

Dominican women, conversely, do not experience this brand of racial segregation. Simply stated, Dominican families are comprised of people with a variety of hair textures, facial features, and skin tones. Girls and young women are allowed "hands-on" exposure to a range of hair textures throughout their lives. Fannie, for example, utilized one hair care regime at home suited to her mother's and her own fine, lank hair. As she came of age, however, and began to socialize with her cousins, whose hair care regimes included roller sets, relaxers, and *doobies* (hair wraps), she became versed in those methods as well. Responding to the question of how she came to work in a beauty shop, she notes that her first experiences with Dominican beauty culture occurred in the context of her family, which is "very large" and very diverse. As she recalls:

> We would all go to the beach together; in Barahona, there are a lot of beaches. And when we would come back from the beach, I would return with my hair dry and straight, you know? And then, they would come with their hair, you know, curly. You know, bad hair that is relaxed? That when it comes into contact with sea waters it becomes, you know, Dominican hair, black women's hair? And they would say to me, "Oh! You're all set to go dancing, but not me. Come on then, and get to work fixing my hair too." And so I, in order to hurry up and for us to all get ready at the same time, I wanted to help. And that's how I started practicing. "Let me set your hair." "Here, fix my hair." You know? Between ourselves, girls to the end, getting together.

Fannie's story highlights several themes that will be explored in this section. It was in participating in her cousins' hair care regimes that she learned and began to practice setting hair. Further, her cousins marshaled her assistance in caring for their hair, evidently undaunted by her personal unfamiliarity with their hair texture. In helping to care for each other's hair, a spirit of feminine intimacy across racial boundaries marked by hair care practices—"between ourselves, girls to the end"—was developed and sustained. Finally, although she herself is Dominican and has fine, lank hair, light eyes, and freckled white skin, Fannie equates "Dominican hair" with "black women's hair" and "bad hair that is relaxed." It is her cousins' beauty culture practices, in other words, that "typify" Dominican women's hair culture.

Similarly, Dominican mothers and daughters often have dissimilar hair textures, yet mothers have to care for and style their daughter's hair. Doris, for example, never used curlers herself, nor did her sisters, but she had to set her daughters' hair, which is thick and curly. "I myself haven't used them yet," she said. "It was out of necessity, out of necessity that I learned. I'd put them and they'd come out, more or less, with lots of pins and things like that. . . . I saw at the salon how they did it and I, more or less, in my mind I had an idea of how they were done, and I did them and they didn't come out too badly. Because you know, it's very difficult to get them to come out as nice as they do." This passage indicates that the salons Doris frequented catered to clients with hair like hers, as well as to clients who used roller sets. In other words, unlike U.S. shops, the typical Dominican beauty shop caters to women of various hair textures. Further, the work done in the shops, as Doris points out, is "very difficult" and requires a degree of skill. Finally, as with Fannie and her cousins at home, the beauty shop helped to socialize Doris, and later her children, into Dominican beauty culture.

"A RICE-AND-BEANS FACE":
LOOKING DOMINICAN, SEEING HISPANIC

For Dominicans, hair is the principal bodily signifier of race, followed by facial features, skin color, and, last, ancestry. Juan Antonio Alix's nineteenth-century *décima*, or ten-line poem, *"El negro tras las orejas"* ("Black Behind the Ears") illustrates this phenomenon well:

De la parienta Fulana	Such and such relative's
El pelo siempre se mienta;	Hair is always mentioned;
Pero nunca la pimienta	But never the black pepper
De la tía siña Sutana.	Of aunt so and so.
Por ser muy blanco se afana,	One strives to be very white,
Y del negro hasta se aljea	Even distances oneself from the black man
Nublando siempre una ceja	Always arching an eyebrow
Cuando aquél a hablarle viene	When he comes to speak with one
Porque se cree que no tiene	Because one thinks that one does not have
"El negro tras de la oreja."	"The black behind the ears."

[Alix 1996, 8, trans. by author]

Although Alix's *décima* was written in 1883, the role of hair as race-signifier among Dominicans dates back to at least the late eighteenth century (Moureau de Saint-Méry 1944, 95).

Given that Dominicans are endowed with many of the physical signs to which they attribute blackness, and that they draw a distinction between blackness and hispanicity, how do they discern who is "Hispanic" and who is not?[4] Hairstyle books offer an invaluable window into how Dominicans read bodies racially. I elicited formal responses to pictures in these books during interviews with salon clients. In addition, on several occasions when the shop was quiet and there were no clients, I opened the books and asked the staff, individually and collectively, for their opinions of the hairstyles and models depicted.

The core questions guiding the elicitation were: Who do Dominican women consider beautiful? Is the norm closer to, or further from, whiteness or blackness? How are "Hispanic looks" conceptualized? What is the relationship between aesthetic preferences and social status? While a sample of eighteen respondents is not a statistically valid one, the results resonate with larger, historical indications of Dominican notions of beauty and race, as well as with my ethnographic findings in the beauty shop.

At Lamadas, of the thirteen books customers use when selecting a hairstyle, ten are of white models and hairstyles. Three of the books feature African American women. One afternoon I approached owner-operator Chucha with one of the three African American hairstyle books and asked her about the styles it contained.

CHUCHA: I just bought that book. I bought it because my clients have to locate themselves in the hair they have.

ME: How so?

CHUCHA: Why, Dominican women don't want to see that book. They ask for the white women's book; they want their manes long and soft like yours.

ME: Why?

CHUCHA: It's because of racism. It's just that we don't even know what race we are. That if we're white, that if we're black, *indio*, or what. . . . I don't want to know about blacks, so I don't have to be fucking around with kinks. Look, I came out like one of my aunts, and that was suffering in my house in order to lower my kinks. The Dominican woman wants her soft mane, long hair. I bought that book now so they can start to locate themselves well. They don't want to see that book. They ask for the white women's book, the one for good hair like yours. Look, I have a client who brings me a three-year-old girl so I can blow dry her hair. You know what that is? Three years old. And in the end, when she gets home and starts playing, her hair stands on end again. (Laughs.) The latest was that she wanted her to have her hair set. That little girl sat under the dryer better than some big ones, reading her magazine. Do you think that's right? That's suffering. It's not fair. I tell her, "Leave her with her curly hair, put a ribbon in it and leave it!" But no, they want their soft manes.

Chucha wants to help her clients "locate themselves," and the selves she is pointing Dominican women to are black. But this is a self-image rejected by her clients, who "don't want to see that book." Instead, they "ask for the white women's book." Attributing the desire for long and soft hair to racism and to racial confusion, Chucha reiterates the equation of blackness with kinky, difficult hair, a result of failed *blanqueamiento*. As she indicates by tracing her own *"greñas"* (kinks) to her aunt, blackness is errant, and betrays. It leads to "suffering."

Interestingly, Chucha depersonalizes her own suffering, referring instead to "Dominican women," to her clients, or to her family's suffering. The ambivalence Chucha expresses, as a woman whose own hair was treated as a cause of sorrow in her childhood and as a stylist who actively participates in the very system she condemns, typifies the paradox of Dominican beauty culture. She is critical of her clients for choosing the white book, for subjecting their three-year-olds to suffering under the dryer, and for preferring "long manes." She relishes the resiliency and unruliness of a child's kinky hair that refuses to relax. Yet, she is an active agent of the very system she criticizes. Further, she is subjected to it herself, even as an adult.

The texture of Chucha's hair was variously presented as *"pelo macho"* (macho hair), *"pelo durito"* (slightly hard hair), and *"pelo fuerte"* (strong hair) by her staff, and as *"greñas"* (kinks) and *"pasas que hay que bajarlas"* (these raisins that have to be tamed) by herself. Much like the customers who pretend not to notice the waiter's gaffe in order to support his role (Goffman 1959), Lamadas' staff politely overlook and accommodate Chucha's hair texture, both through their grooming of her hair and through their softened descriptions of it. Yet Chucha herself is ambivalent about her hair, as the following selection from my field notes indicates:

Chucha and Leticia attended a Sebastian hair product seminar in New Jersey today. The topic was how to use a new color product. Chucha sat down and recounted the details of her experience to Maria: "They don't work on bad heads there. It's all for good hair, like hers (pointing to me) and yours (Maria)." I asked why not, and whether they had ever asked for a different kind of hair on the dummies. Again Chucha responded: "There it is! Our job is to adapt straight hair, good hair products, to ours. I was dying laughing, thinking about the surprise they'd experience if my hair got wet!" she laughed. "If my hair got wet!"

The "they" Chucha refers to are the Anglo-American producers, marketers, and beauty culturalists at Sebastian. Chucha's laughter and pleasure in relating the story indicate to me her awareness of her corporate host's reliance on superficial appearances. Water would return her hair to its natural, tightly curled state. Her looks, she recognizes with relish, are deceiving. So, it seems that on some level Chucha is well aware that she is transforming herself racially when she does her hair. The question is, what is she transforming into? I argue that it is not a desire for whiteness that guides Dominican hair culture. Instead, it is an ideal notion of what it means to "look Hispanic."

Again, situating Dominican identity in the appropriate spatial and political context is necessary. The use of the term *Hispanic* in Spanish by Dominicans in New York is an engagement with both the historic hispanophile identity institutionalized by the Dominican state and elite, and with the white supremacist foundations of the United States racial state (Omi and Winant 1994). For Dominicans, to say in Spanish that they are "Hispanic" is at once a connection to a European linguistic and cultural legacy and also a recognition of subordinate ethno-racial status in the United States (Oboler 1995). In this tense negotiation of multiple historical contexts and codes, the usual United States notions of both whiteness and blackness are subverted.

However, merely subverting whiteness and blackness is not liberating, for the concept of race as an organizing principle remains intact. The bounds of the categories are altered, but their hierarchical systematization is not. Blackness continues unabashedly to be equated with ugliness. When asked for their opinions of the appearance of women depicted in an African American braiding book, Salon Lamadas' staff was vehemently derogatory in their commentary. At one point a debate ensued over whether the woman who Chucha had previously described as having *"una cara de arroz con habichuelas"* (a rice-and-beans face) was Latina or African American. Nilda, Maria, and Flor felt that she was Latina. Nené, Alma, and Leonora disagreed, particularly Nené, who felt that she was definitively black.

NENÉ: Her features are rough, ordinary—black muzzle, big mouth, fat nose.

NILDA: Blacks are dirty and they smell. Hispanics are easy to spot! (Turning to me.) You have something Hispanic.

ME: What?

NILDA: Your nose. Fannie is white, with good hair, but her features are rough black ones.

LEONORA: It's just that black shows.

HILDA: Black is not the color of the skin. Really pretty, really fine. The white person has black behind the ears.

In this exchange, several things become apparent. First, those who "look" Latina/o could easily be African American, and vice versa. Second, "blackness" is discerned through a sometimes contradictory, but cohesive, system of bodily signs: hair, skin, nose, and mouth. When these features are "black" they are perceived to be animalistic and crude, as the terms "rough" and "muzzle" and the attribution of filth and odor indicate. Yet, they are also common, if base, among Dominicans as the term "ordinary" implies. At the same time, an intermediate category, "Hispanic," is deployed to contain the fluid middle between black and white. Ancestry, even if not discernible through skin color and facial features, is immutable. Thus, my nose indicates my African ancestry. But, as the repeated references to my "good" hair as signifier of whiteness indicate, ancestry does not determine current identity. Finally, the continuing currency of the one-hundred-year-old expression "black behind the ears" is striking.

"BLACK WOMEN ARE CONFUSING, BUT THE HAIR LETS YOU KNOW"

But now we walk
heads high
naps full of pride
with not a backward glance
at some of the beauty which
use to be.

—WILLI COLEMAN,
"Among the Things That
Use to Be"

Dominican women are lay anthropologists, employing the sort of reading of the racialized body utilized by, for example, Franz Boas. Boas was often called as an expert witness in legal cases in which the determination of a person's "race" was required. In one instance, he was asked to determine whether a "golden-haired blonde with beautiful gray eyes and regular features" married to a prominent Detroit doctor was passing for white. (Her husband was suing her for divorce based on his belief that she was.) Boas concluded that the woman was not black, explaining, "If this woman has any of the characteristics of the Negro race it would be easy to find them. . . . One characteristic that is regarded as reliable is the hair. You can tell by a microscopic examination of a cross section of hair to what race that person belongs" (Boas, in Rooks 1996, 14). Microscopic examinations, it seems, can also be made without benefit of a microscope.

Bodies are racially coded in distinct, referential, and ultimately arbitrary ways in any given historical and cultural context (Gilman 1998; Gould 1996; Montague 1974). Race is a biological fiction that nonetheless has been institutionalized into a social fact through particular cultural practices. In a community that strives for *blanqueamiento*, race for Dominican women assumes immediate importance as a personal bodily, social, and cultural attribute.

Simply stated, Dominican women consider women they perceive to be Hispanic, and specifically Dominican, as most beautiful. *Hispanic* (or Latina) is often synonomous with *Dominican*. Both terms are taken to mean "a middle term," "a mixture of black and white," an intermediate category. Latin looks, accordingly, are those that contain elements from each constitutive "race." As the illustrations below indicate women selected most often as looking Hispanic are also the ones most often selected as prettiest. The top three "prettiest" women were all thought to look Latina. The top eight of the nine women selected as prettiest were thought to look Latina by 20 percent of the respondents. Only the ninth woman of those selected as prettiest was a blonde-haired, white-skinned woman who was universally declared to "not look Latina." At the same time, there were no "white" women among the women perceived as "least pretty." Instead, as the Looks Hispanic Ratio indicates, the women considered "least pretty" were those African diaspora women furthest away from standard Hispanic-looking woman (fig. 8.1).

	1st Choice	2nd Choice	3rd Choice
Prettiest			
Looks Latina Ratio	13:13	7:13	6:13
Least Pretty			
Looks Latina Ratio	4:13	4:13	1:13

FIGURE 8.1

Perceived Prettiness with Looks Hispanic Ratio   The images in figures 8.1–8.4 are taken from these sources: *Before and After: American Beauté*, vol. 2 (Freehold, N.J.: Dennis Bernard); *Family Album III*, (Auburn, Mass.: Worcester Reading Co.); *Family Images*, vol. 2 (Auburn, Mass.: Worcester Reading Co.); and *Ultra World of Hair Fashion* (Auburn, Mass.: Worcester Reading Co.).

Since the Looks Hispanic category included women in nearly equal proportion from the white and black hairstyle books, there does not seem to be a preference for "pure" or "European" whiteness. Rather, each of the women selected as looking Latina was selected because her face and/or hair were perceived to indicate some degree of both African and European ancestry (fig. 8.2). Those thought not to evidence any degree of mixed ancestry were also those thought to Not Look Hispanic. (fig. 8.3) It is the lack of "naturalness" in sculpted and obviously processed hairstyles that Dominican women point to as disconcerting, and as distinguishing African American hair culture from Dominican hair culture.

Dominican women place great emphasis on hair that appears "healthy, natural, and loose." As Nuris put it, "The difference between here and there, black women here, they use a lot of grease, their hair looks, it doesn't look as loose as Dominican women's. Dominican women don't use it that way, they wear their hair processed, but the hair

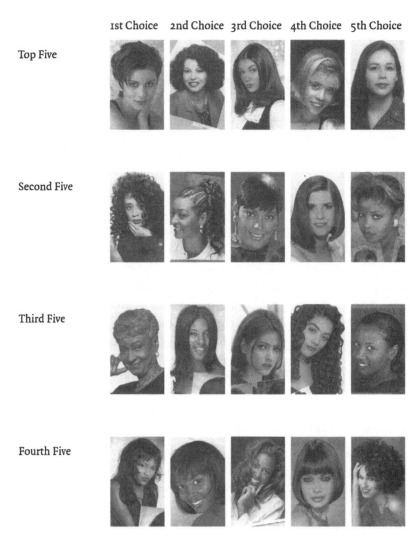

FIGURE 8.2
Looks Hispanic, in Order of Frequency Selected

FIGURE 8.3
Does Not Look Hispanic

looks healthy, it stays well, very pretty, the hair, the hair always looks healthy. . . . I think the difference is like to look more natural. To look more, like, for the hair to look looser. That's it." In other words, the extensive technology, time, and effort employed to make the hair "loose and manageable" must not show. Indeed, it is precisely the emphasis on naturalness that signifies the racial iconography of Dominican hair culture. In this way, Dominican whiteness both subverts U.S. white supremacy based on the "one drop of blood rule" (where "one drop" of African "blood" makes one black [Davis 1991; Harris 1964]) and sustains the *blanqueamiento*-based white supremacy of Dominican hispanicity.

Similarly, while light skin is generally valorized, white skin in and of itself is insufficient, and skin that is too white is considered unsightly. As Chucha put it: "There are blacks who have pretty faces. And there are whites who have ugly faces." Nonetheless, the fact that each of these possibilities is constructed as exceptional points to the standard equation of whiteness and blackness with beauty and ugliness, respectively. Consider the following exchange between Doris, a white-skinned, straight-haired Dominican woman married to a brown-skinned, curly-haired Dominican man, and me, a similarly white-skinned, straight-haired Dominican woman. Recall that Doris is the woman who learned to set her daughters' hair by observing stylists at her salon.

ME: Tell me something. You've just told me that we value hair a lot and color less, in the sense that if hair is "good" you are placed in the white category. What happens in the case of someone who is very light but has "bad hair"?

DORIS: No, that one is on the black side because it's just that the *jabao* in Santo Domingo is white with bad hair, really tight hair. Well, that one is on the black side because I myself say, "If my daughters had turned out *jabá*, it's better that they would have turned out brown, with their hair like that, *trigueño*." Because I didn't want my daughters to come out white with tight hair. No. For me, better *trigueña*. They're prettier. I've always said that. All three of my children are *trigueños*.

ME: Why? What makes them prettier?

DORIS: Well, their color. Because for me, someone white, an ugly, ordinary white person, looks worse than a brown one, a black one who doesn't, who really is black. If they're white like that, the way there are some white, those white people, white, white, fine, they look exaggeratedly white like that. They don't look good. To me, they're not attractive. I prefer someone of color.

Of color, but not black. The aesthetic model is the body that is a "middle term" as my respondents named it, neither too white nor too black. In other words, the mestiza/mulatta, the embodiment of the Taina/o icon displayed at the Dominican museum,

TABLE 8.1   Binding of "Most Attractive" and "Least Attractive" Images

Descriptors	Number	Percent
"Most Attractive"	60	100
Selected from "white" hairstyle book	39	65
Selected from "black" hairstyle book	21	35
"Least Attractive"	59	100
Selected from "white" hairstyle book	17	29
Selected from "black" hairstyle book	42	71

in the Dominican beauty pageant, in the Dominican media, and in Dominican history books.

The question remains, however: How do contemporary Dominican women and girls look at pictures of African American women who look like them and yet distance themselves from this similarity? What is taking place when women at the salon identify with the women in the white hairstyles book, and distance themselves adamantly from those in the African American hairstyles book? Are they doing psychic violence to themselves? I argue that they are not, to the extent that Dominicans identify as "Hispanic" and consider those who evidence a degree of mixture to "look Hispanic." Thus, if one were to be guided simply by the fact that Dominican women at Salon Lamadas preferred to look at the white hairstyles book, it could easily be concluded that Dominican women prefer "white" looks. See table 8.1, which records the preference for images selected from the "white" book, and the concomitant rejection of images from the "black" book.

However, the symbolic and literal binding of the images into one of two choices—black or white—reflects the U.S. dichotomization of race. There are no "Latina" or "Hispanic" hairstyle books. Once the images are considered outside of the context of their bindings, however, as they were by Salon Lamadas' clients during the photo elicitation interviews, it becomes clear once again that the preference is not for U.S. whiteness, but for "Hispanic" or mixed looks. In other words, it is neither the white book nor the black book *per se* that Salon Lamadas' clients prefer or reject. It is the images contained in each book that they consider to approximate or not approximate a "Hispanic" ideal, an ideal dually defined as containing elements from both blackness and whiteness where Dominicans are concerned, and, more generally, as indicating *mestizaje* (see table 8.2). Thus, nearly all of the women selected as attractive from the "white" book, and 100 percent of the women selected as attractive from the "black" book were also thought to look Hispanic. And while neither of the two women from the "black" book who were considered to be unequivocally black were considered among the prettiest, only one of the two

TABLE 8.2 Perceived Ethnicity/Race and Perceived Prettiness

| Attributes | Described as Hispanic | | Described as Non-Hispanic White | Described as Non-Hispanic Black |
	White Book	Black Book		
Prettiest	92%	100%	8%	—
Least Pretty	71%	83%	29%	17%

FIGURE 8.4
Looks Dominican

white women considered unequivocally non-Hispanic was among the prettiest. None of the top three choices as the prettiest of the women was perceived to be a white Anglo (see fig. 8.1). The top choice was considered unequivocally Latina, while the second and third choices were "probably" Latina and "possibly Latina, possibly black" respectively.

Again, although Anglo white women were not considered prettiest, they were also less likely to be categorized as "least pretty." The top three choices for "least pretty" all were perceived as closer to blackness and further from Latina-ness (fig. 8.2). What's more, those perceived to be whiter Latinas were more heavily represented among the top nine prettiest women. Most interesting, however, was the assessment of the appearance of the woman selected both as most Latina-looking and prettiest.

The top choice in both the "Looks Hispanic" and "Prettiest" categories is almost stereotypically Latina. Clara Rodriguez has noted the media representation of "Latin looks" in the United States consists of skin that is "slightly tan, with dark hair and eyes" (1997, 1), a reasonable description of the top choice in this study. That said, it is important to note that half of the twenty women my respondents perceived to look Hispanic were drawn from the African American hairstyles book and had features that the respondents considered to connote a degree of ancestral blackness. Further, it was also those women that my respondents selected as looking "typically" Dominican (fig. 8.4).

"Looking Dominican" as noted above, evidently means having visible African features. Thus, one discerns who is simply "black" and who is "Dominican" not only by signs of mixture—lighter skin, looser hair, thinner features—but by reference to hair culture, because, as Lamadas client Paulina explained, "Black women are confusing, but the hair lets you know."

CONCLUSION

Cause with a natural
there is no natural place
for us to congregate
to mull over
our mutual discontent
Beauty shops
could have been
a hell-of-a-place
to ferment
a . . . . revolution.

—WILLI COLEMAN,
"Among the Things
That Use to Be"

In stretching the bounds of whiteness in the United States to accommodate their own definition and understanding of it, Dominican women's hair culture stands in sharp contrast to African American hair culture. When Chucha notes that the job of the Dominican hair stylist is to "adopt white products to our hair," she is pointing to precisely that alternative understanding of whiteness. African Americans, by contrast, have developed their own unique system of hair care and hair care products—at times in opposition to, at times parallel to, and at times simply oblivious of the Anglo somatic norm image. For Hoetink (1967) it is "illogical" that African Americans "despite [their] adoption of the whole [white] preference pattern, nevertheless place [themselves] at the top of the [aesthetic] preferences list" as a study of African Americans' aesthetic preferences in St. Louis found (160). What Hoetink overlooks, and what therefore makes African Americans' self-valuation logical in the context of white supremacy, is that segregation forced African Americans to create their own social, economic, and aesthetic spaces. Straightening their hair, for example, is not necessarily a "white wish" on the part of African Americans. Rather, as Mercer (1994) points out, it is often a means to an explicitly "black" hairstyle. Certain sculpted hairstyles require chemically processed hair for their construction. The explicit artificiality of hair sculpting stands in sharp contrast to naturalness in the European model, indicated not only by "hair that moves," but by "natural" styles such as Afros and dreadlocks.

In a recent video documentary featuring the African American millionaire and beauty products entrepreneur Madam C.J. Walker, several former Walker agents and customers emphasized that black women cared for their hair with Walker products and methods, not in order to look white, but "to be beautiful" (Nelson 1987). They repeatedly stressed African American women's desire to be pretty in their own right, noting that Walker didn't sell "straighteners" or "relaxers," and that she emphatically disallowed the use of those words in her advertisements and sales pitches (Rooks 1996). The question for Dominican women is whether it is possible similarly to engage in beauty practice outside of the patriarchal imperatives of *blanqueamiento*.

Given that contemporary Dominican beauty practices require alteration, consumption, and production of ephemeral capitalist goods and services; expenditure of limited financial and temporal resources; and denigration of blackness, can beauty be empowering? Individual women do empower themselves through beauty. In the context of white supremacist and heteronormative patriarchy, beauty is a form of cultural capital that can be exchanged for symbolic and economic capital (Bourdieau 1984). But can Dominican women as a political group, as a social category, be empowered by beauty regimes? In a word, the answer is no. For beauty regimes require ugliness to reside somewhere, and that somewhere is in other women, usually women defined as black. Who is black in the Dominican context of New York City is mediated by the historic relationship between Haiti and the Dominican Republic, the current relationship between Dominicans and African Americans, and the continually mutual constituitiveness of beauty and race semiotic systems. Racial identity is enacted through racialized reproduction practices and beauty practices. Beauty is a scale, a continuum of some kind, whether hierarchical or linear. The absence of beauty, culminating in ugliness, carries the threat of derision, expulsion, and even violence.

And yet, while beauty regimes are not empowering, the community that is developed around beauty practices often is. Small revolutions ferment in the beauty shop daily when Dominican women confront oppressive conditions generated by government offices, hospitals, schools, employers, husbands, and lovers, with the support and assistance of their beauty shop community and kin. This is the paradox of Dominican women's beauty culture.

NOTES

The research for this article was funded by a Rockefeller Fellowship at the Dominican Studies Institute of the City College of New York and by a Latino Studies Predoctoral Fellowship at the Smithsonian Institute.

1. Dominican population data are taken from Duany 1994. Information on number of salons is taken from the 1992 Economic Census, and geographic dispersal of salons is derived from the yahoo.maps website.

2. Proper names of businesses and of individuals interviewed have been changed in the interests of confidentiality.

3. All interview excerpts have been translated from Spanish by the author.

4. The term *hispano* (Hispanic) almost universally was used interchangeably with *Latino*. It was the more prevalent term, however, and will be used here when paraphrasing or quoting others. *Latina/o* will be used as the author's descriptive.

REFERENCES

Alix, Juan Antonio. 1966. *Décimas inéditas*. With a prologue by Emilio Rodriguez Demorizi. Santo Domingo: Impresora Moreno.

Bourdieu, Pierre. 1984. *Distinction: A Social Critique of the Judgement of Taste*. Cambridge, Mass.: Harvard University Press.

Candelario, Ginetta E. B. 2000. "Translating Race: Dominican Ethno-Racial Identity in the United States." Ph.D. Diss., City University of New York Graduate Center.

Cary, Lorene. 1991. *Black Ice*. New York: Alfred A. Knopf.

Coleman, Calmetta Y. 1995. "Style Over Substance: Power of a Good Perm Brings Us Together." *Wall Street Journal*. 22 September.

Coleman, Willi. 1983. "Among the Things That Use to Be." In *Home Girls: A Black Feminist Anthology*. Edited by Barbara Smith. New York: Kitchen Table: Women of Color Press.

Davis, F. James. 1991. *Who Is Black? One Nation's Definition*. University Park, Pa.: Pennsylvania University Press.

Dore-Cabral, Carlos, and José Itzigsohn. 1997. "La formación de la identidad hispana entre los immigrantes dominicanos en Nueva York." Paper presented at Congreso Internacional: La República Dominicana en el Umbral del Siglo 21. 24–26 July. Pontíficia Universidad Católica Madre y Maestra, Santo Domingo, Dominican Republic.

Duany, Jorge. 1994. "Quisqueya on the Hudson: The Transnational Identity of Dominicans in Washington Heights." New York: Dominican Studies Institute, City College, City University of New York.

Frankenberg, Ruth. 1993. *White Women, Race Matters: The Social Construction of Whiteness*. Minneapolis: University of Minnesota Press.

Furman, Frida Kerner. 1997. *Facing the Mirror: Older Women and Beauty Shop Culture*. New York: Routledge.

Georges, Eugenia. 1987. "New Immigrants and Political Process: Dominicans in New York." Occasional Papers. New York University.

———. 1992. *The Making of a Transnational Community: Migration, Development and Cultural Change in the Dominican Republic*. New York: Columbia University Press.

Gilman, Sander L. 1998. *Creating Beauty to Cure the Soul: Race and Psychology in the Shaping of Aesthetic Surgery*. Durham: Duke University Press.

Goffman, Erving. 1959. *The Presentation of Self in Everyday Life*. Garden City, N.Y.: Doubleday.

Goodnough, Abby. 1995. "Refused a Haircut, an Official in Stamford Closes a Salon." *New York Times*. 20 March.

Gould, Stephen J. 1996. *The Mismeasure of Man*. New York: Norton.

Grasmuck, Sherri, and Patricia Pessar. 1991. *Between Two Islands: Dominican International Migration*. Berkeley: University of California Press.

Guarnizo, Luis. 1993. "One Country in Two: Dominican-Owned Firms in New York and in the Dominican Republic," Ph.D. diss. Johns Hopkins University.

Harris, Marvin. 1964. *Patterns of Race in the Americas*. New York: Walker.

Hernández, Ramona. 1989. "Notes on the Incorporation of Dominican Workers into the Labor Market of New York." *Punto 7 Review* 2, no. 1.

Hernández, Ramona, Francisco Rivera-Bátiz, and Roberto Agodini. 1995. *Dominican New Yorkers: A Socioeconomic Profile, 1990*. New York: Dominican Studies Institute, City College, City University of New York.

Hernández, Ramona, and Silvio Torres-Saillant. 1998. *The Dominican Americans*. Westport, Conn.: Greenwood Press.

Hernton, Calvin C. 1988 [1965]. *Sex and Racism in America*. New York: Grove.

Hoetink, Harry. 1967. *The Variants in Caribbean Race Relations: A Contribution to the Sociology of Segmented Societies*. London: Oxford University Press.

———. 1985. "'Race' and Color in the Caribbean." In *Caribbean Contours*. Edited by Sidney Mintz and Sally Price. Baltimore: Johns Hopkins University Press.

Howard, David. 1997. "Colouring the Nation: Race and Ethnicity in the Dominican Republic." Ph.D. diss. Jesus College, Oxford University.

King, Elizabeth. 1998. *Quinceañera: Celebrating Fifteen*. New York: Dutton.

Levitt, Peggy, and Christina Gomez. 1997. "The Intersection of Race and Gender among Dominicans in the U.S." Paper presented at the ASA Conference, Toronto, Canada, 8–13 August.

Martin, John Bartlow. 1966. *Overtaken by Events*. New York: Doubleday.

Masud-Piloto, Felix. 1996. *From Welcomed Exiles to Illegal Immigrants: Cuban Migration to the United States, 1959–1995*. Lanham, Md.: Rowman & Littlefield.

Meisenheimer, Joseph R. II. 1998. "The Services Industry in the 'Good' versus 'Bad' Jobs Debate." *Monthly Labor Review* (February).

Mercer, Kobena. 1994. *Welcome to the Jungle: New Positions in Black Cultural Studies*. New York: Routledge.

Montague, Ashley. 1974. *Man's Most Dangerous Myth: The Fallacy of Race*. New York: Oxford University Press.

Moreau de Saint-Méry, M. L. 1944. *A Topographical and Political Description of the Spanish Part of Santo Domingo*. Translated by C. Armando Rodríguez. Ciudad Trujillo: Editora Montalvo.

Moya Pons, Frank. 1995. *The Dominican Republic: A National History*. New York: Hispaniola.

———. 1996. "Dominican National Identity: A Historical Perspective." *Punto 7 Review* 3, no. 1.

Nelson, Stanley, director. 1987. *Two Dollars and A Dream*, N.Y.: Filmakers Library.

New York City Department of City Planning. 1995. *The Newest New Yorkers, 1990–1994*. New York: New York City Department of City Planning.

Oboler, Suzanne. 1995. *Ethnic Labels, Latino Lives: Identity and the Politics of (Re)Presentation in the United States*. Minneapolis: University of Minnesota Press.

Omi, Michael, and Howard Winant. 1994. *Racial Formation in the United States: From the 1960s to the 1980s*. N.Y.: Routledge.

Peiss, Kathy. 1994. "Making Faces: The Cosmetics Industry and the Cultural Construction of Gender, 1890–1930." In *Unequal Sisters: A Multicultural Reader in U.S. Women's History*, 2nd ed. Edited by Vicki Ruiz and Ellen Carol DuBois. New York: Routledge.

Pessar, Patricia. 1987a. "The Dominicans: Women in the Household and the Garment Industry." In *New Immigrants in New York*. Edited by Nancy Foner. New York: Columbia University Press.

———. 1987b. "The Constraints Upon and Release of Female Labor Power: The Case of Dominican Migration to the United States." In *Women, Income, and Poverty*. Edited by D. Dwyer and J. Bruce. Stanford, CA: Stanford University Press.

Piedra, José. 1991. "Literary Whiteness and the Afro-Hispanic Difference." In *The Bounds of Race: Perspectives in Hegemony and Resistance*. Edited by Dominick LaCapra. Ithaca: Cornell University Press.

Rodriguez, Clara E. 1991. *Puerto Ricans: Born in the U.S.A.* Boulder, Colo.: Westview.

———, ed. 1997. *Latin Looks: Images of Latinas and Latinos in the U.S. Media*. Boulder, Colo.: Westview.

Rooks, Noliwe M. 1996. *Hair Raising: Beauty, Culture, and African American Women*. New Brunswick, N.J.: Rutgers University Press.

Sánchez Korrol, Virginia. 1983. *From Colonia to Community: The History of Puerto Ricans in New York City, 1917–1948*. Westport, Conn.: Greenwood.

Schroder, David. 1978. *Engagement in the Mirror: Hairdressers and Their Work*. San Francisco: R & E Research Associates.

Shohat, Ella, and Robert Starn. 1994. *Unthinking Eurocentrisim: Multiculturalism and the Media*. New York: Routledge.

Sommer, Doris. 1983. *One Master for Another: Populism and Patriarchial Rhetoric in Dominican Novels*. Lanham, Md.: University Press of America.

Torres-Saillant, Silvio. 1989. "Dominicans as a New York Community: A Social Appraisal." *Punto 7 Review* 2, no. 1.

———. 1996. "The Tribulations of Blackness: Stages in Dominican Racial Identity." Unpublished manuscript.

———. 1999. "Introduction to Dominican Blackness." Dominican Studies Working Paper Series 1. Dominican Studies Institute, City College of New York.

Waldinger, Roger. 1986. *Through the Eye of the Needle*. New York: New York University Press.

Willet, Julie A. 1996. "Making Waves: Race, Gender, and the Hairdressing Industry in the Twentieth Century." Ph.D. diss. University of Missouri-Columbia.

Williams, Monte. 1999. "Flak in the Great Hair War; African-Americans vs. Dominicans, Rollers at the Ready." *New York Times*, 13 October.

Young, Robert J. C. 1995. *Colonial Desire: Hybridity in Theory, Culture and Race*. New York: Routledge.

9

RACE, RACIALIZATION, AND LATINO POPULATIONS IN THE UNITED STATES

Tomás Almaguer

The racial and ethnic landscape of the United States has been rapidly transformed in the twenty-five years since the initial publication in 1986 of Michael Omi and Howard Winant's *Racial Formation in the United States*.[1] Since that time scholars have built upon Omi and Winant's powerful theoretical approach in order to perceptively remap how the long-standing "black-white" binary in this country has been rapidly transformed. Some have argued that this framework has morphed into a "nonwhite-white" binary, while others have argued that our racial and ethnic landscape has taken a decidedly "Latin Americanization" form in recent years.[2] In both cases, overpowering demographic trends and formidable structural factors have moved the United States away from a two-tiered racial hierarchy to a more complex and variegated, multi-tiered structure.

   This essay explores some of these recent demographic and structural changes, with a specific focus on the Latino population. My goal is to assess the impact that the precipitous increase in the Latino population in the United States has had on this racial topography in two specific ways. First, I explore the vexing conundrums that Latinos have posed for how we think about race and ethnicity in this country. The accelerated growth of an increasingly diverse Latino population has profoundly complicated Latinos' placement in both the evolving racial hierarchy and the popular imagination in the United States. Second, I assess the troubling ways that Latinos have increasingly come to racialize one another and that could not have predicted twenty-five years ago. Briefly stated, Latinos have taken the way that racial lines were drawn and given meaning both in the Spanish colonial world and in the United States to reracialize one another in disturbing ways. Recent ethnographic studies have perceptively documented this process and provide valuable insights into this unexplored aspect of the racial formation process. I explore both of these nettlesome issues in turn and, in so doing, draw on a variety of primary and secondary sources to support the analysis.

THE RACIALIZATION OF LATINOS IN THE UNITED STATES

The Latino population has historically occupied a unique position in the racial and ethnic hierarchy of the United States. It is important to assess how Latinos have been racialized over time and the various ways that they have complicated how we think about race. Between 1970 and 2000, the U.S. Census Bureau increasingly attempted to define and count the diverse ethnic origins of residents with ancestral roots in Spain and Latin America, and did so by slowly introducing identity categories in popular everyday use. In 1970, a long-form census questionnaire sent to a small sample asked, "Is this person's origin or descent: Mexican; Puerto Rican; Cuban; Central or South American; Other Spanish; or None of these." A shorter census form sent to all households in 1980 queried, "Is this person of Spanish/Hispanic origin or descent?" The response options were, "Mexican, Mexican-American or Chicano," "Puerto Rican," "Cuban," or "other Spanish/Hispanic." This was the first use of "Hispanic" as a U.S. census category; "Spanish" had long been employed to enumerate persons born in Spain. Finally, in the 2000 census, the addition of "Latino" to "Spanish/Hispanic," further expanded the country's official understanding of the unity and diversity of these ethnic groups.

When *Racial Formation in the United States* was published in 1986, the federal government's standards for defining racial and ethnic groups had recently been reformulated. In 1977 the Office of Management and Budget's Statistical Policy Division and Office of Information and Regulatory Affairs issued "Directive 15: Race and Ethnic Standards for Federal Statistics and Administrative Reporting." That decree standardized the governmental collection and use of "racial" and "ethnic" statistics in the United States. It provided new operational definitions for the OMB's racial/ethnic cartography of the United States. Directive 15 clearly specified the codification of four major "races"—"American Indian or Alaska Native," "Asian or Pacific Islander," "Black," and "White"—and the delineation of two "ethnic" groups—"Hispanic origin" and "not of Hispanic origin." According to Ruben Rumbaut, "Since that time, in keeping with the logic of this classification system, census data on Hispanics have been officially reported with a footnote indicating that 'Hispanics may be of any race'" (Rumbaut 2009, 24).

These race and ethnic standards were revised in 1977 in response to mounting criticisms of the way these categories were deployed in implementing Directive 15. In that year, the federal government adopted a new set of standards for defining racial/ethnic categories, which led to the formalization of five "racial" groups rather than four. In essence, the "Pacific Islander" population was disaggregated from the "Asian American" population and placed in a separate racial category. Census 2000 offered respondents for the first time the option of selecting more than one racial designation and reworded the two existing "ethnic" categories as "Hispanic or Latino" and "not Hispanic or Latino." In so doing, the census formally defined an individual of "Hispanic or Latino" background as "a person of Cuban, Mexican, Puerto Rican, South or Central American, or other Spanish culture or origins, regardless of race."

The revisions to Directive 15 in 1977 were the product of intense political contestations and vociferous criticisms from various quarters. In this regard, as Rumbaut discovered, the announcement reporting these changes in the *Federal Register* candidly noted: "The categories in this classification are social-political constructs and should not be interpreted as being scientific or anthropological in nature. . . . The standards have been developed to provide a common language for uniformity and comparability in the collection and use of data on race and ethnicity by Federal agencies" (Rumbaut 2009, 25). In his perceptive assessment of these OMB changes, Rumbaut concludes: "The classification of 'Hispanic' or 'Latino' itself is new, an instance of a panethnic category created by law decades ago. But the groups subsumed under that label—Mexicans, Puerto Ricans, Cubans, Dominicans, Salvadorans, Guatemalans, Colombians, Peruvians, Ecuadorians, and the other dozen nationalities from Latin American and even Spain itself—were not 'Hispanics' or 'Latinos' in their countries of origin; rather, they only became so in the United States. That catchall label has a particular meaning only in the U.S. context in which it was constructed and is applied, and where its meaning continues to evolve" (16–17).

Yet many Latinos continue to base their racial identities on the way that the various nationalities were racialized in their country of origin when it was part of the Spanish colonial empire.[3] However, this highly variegated and nuanced racial system clashes with the way racial categories are more starkly drawn and defined in the United States. It appears that Latino immigrants are racialized in one particular way in the Spanish colonial context and then reracialized under the cultural logic of another racial order when they come to this country.

This difficulty in unambiguously racializing the Latino population has a long and complex history in this country that dates back to at least the middle of the nineteenth century when the United States seized control of the American Southwest through the U.S.-Mexico War of 1846–48. For example, it was principally as a result of the annexation of the Southwest that the Mexican population was formally granted U.S. citizenship and, in effect, deemed an "honorary white" population. The nearly 110,000 Mexicanos who remained in the territory ceded by Mexico one year after the ratification of the Treaty of Guadalupe Hidalgo (1848) became U.S. citizens with formally recognized claims to the prerogatives and privileges of whiteness. (Whether they were ever fully or meaningfully extended in the various territories and eventual states is quite another matter altogether.)[4]

Clear codification of the racial status of the Mexican population can be seen in the 1850 decennial U.S. census; when the newly conquered Mexican population in the American Southwest was enumerated as "White," as it remained until 1930. In that year, they were summarily removed from the white category and placed in a separate racial designation as "Mexican." By the Great Depression, the number of Mexican people in the United States had grown to more than 1.5 million and had become the source of intense anti-immigrant xenophobia.

By 1940, however, the Mexican population was once again redefined as part of the "white" population and marked as speaking the "Spanish mother tongue." In that year, the federal census classified "persons of Mexican birth or ancestry who were not defined as Indian or some other nonwhite race . . . as white." The federal censuses of 1950 and 1960 continued to enumerate Mexicans as "white persons of Spanish surname."[5]

When one spoke of the Latino/Hispanic population in the late 1960s, before the publication of *Racial Formation in the United States*, one still referred primarily to Mexicans. This was at a time before widespread and sustained Puerto Rican, Cuban, or Central American immigration to the United States. After 1960, however, things changed dramatically and quickly. The explosive rise in Latino immigration after 1965 led to the exponential increase in the pan-Latino population in the United States, one not only far larger but also more racially diverse than it had been in prior years.

In 1970 the federal census relied on the category "Hispanic" to capture the tremendous internal diversity of the various Latino nationalities in the United States. It underscored their common "Hispanic" (i.e., Spanish) ethnicity and former status as part of the Spanish colonial world. Having a "common culture" rooted in the Spanish language and Catholic religion was the key ethnic signifier that bound these diverse nationalities into one category.[6] This shared ethnic background is something that none of the other racialized populations have in common that are placed in the discrete racial categories deployed in the United States. None of the groups racialized as "White," "Black," "Asian," "Hawaiian/Pacific Islander," or "American Indian" share a common culture solidly anchored in one particular language or religious background. Latinos are thus a unique population in this regard.

By 1970 there were more than 10 million "Hispanics" in the United States. Mexicans were still the largest Latino population, numbering 4.5 million and accounting for nearly 45 percent of Hispanics in the United States at the time. In that year there were also 1.5 million Puerto Ricans; 550,000 Cubans; 1.5 million Central and South Americans; and another million designated as some "Other Spanish" population.

By 1990, a mere twenty years later, the Hispanic population had more than doubled to nearly 22 million. By the time Census 2000 was taken, the Hispanic/Latino population had dramatically risen to 35.2 million and accounted for nearly 12.5 percent of the total U.S. population. Mexicans still remained the largest Latino nationality, comprising 60 percent of the Latino population in that year. They were followed by Puerto Ricans (9.7%), Central Americans (3.5%), South Americans (4.0%), Dominicans (2.3%), and the "Other Hispanic" category (15.7%).

By the time Census 2000 was taken, Latinos had actually surpassed African Americans as the largest racial-ethnic group in the United States. Each accounted for 35 million individuals that year, or approximately 12.5 percent of the total U.S. population. However, by 2007 the number of Latinos in the United States had dramatically swelled to nearly 45 million, or 15 percent of the total population. In the fifty-year period from 1950 to 2000, the Latino population had dramatically increased from approximately 4 million to over 35 million individuals. Census 2010 data has documented that the Latino population grew from 35.3 million in 2000 to over 50 million in 2010 (U.S. Bureau of the Census 2010). Current population trends suggest that by the year 2050 Latinos will have increased in number to an estimated 128 million people, or 29 percent of the total U.S. population. Demographers predict that they will significantly exceed the total number of all other racial/ethnic groups combined. African Americans, for example, are projected to continue to account for only 13 percent of the national total; while Asian Americas will account for another 9 percent of the U.S. population in 2050 (Rumbaut 2009, 17).

This monumental population increase has been accompanied by a number of profound structural changes that have powerfully impacted our perceptions of race and race relations in the United States. Among these changes worth noting here have been the momentous change in U.S. immigration policy in 1965 (which shifted the focus away from Western Europe and toward Latin America and Asia), the hard-won victories of the Civil Rights Movement (which arguably extended meaningful, first-class citizenship rights to African Americans and other people of color), and the overturning of anti-miscegenation laws, through *Loving v. Commonwealth of Virginia*. That 1967 Supreme Court decision put an end to more than three hundred years of legal prohibitions on interracial marriages in the United States and directly contributed to the recent rise of a growing "multiracial" population. This mixed-race population grew by nearly 30 percent from 2000 to 2010 and now comprises approximately 3 percent of the total U.S. population (U.S. Bureau of the Census 2010). If one were to combine this "multiracial" population with the Latino population, approximately 18 percent of the total U.S. population is arguably mixed-race. This is clearly a very recent historical development that has had profound implications for how we understand the meaning of race and for the changing nature of race relations in the contemporary United States.

THE CONUNDRUMS OF RACIAL IDENTITY AMONG THE LATINO POPULATION

We know from the way that Latinos responded to both the race and ethnic questions in Census 2010 that many had difficulty placing themselves in the discrete racial categories used in the federal census. It appears that many Latinos resorted to constructions of racial categories and identities drawn from the Spanish colonial world or simply used their nationality as the basis of their racial identity. In 2010, more than half (53 %) of the pan-Latino population racially defined themselves as "White." Despite the central role that the Indigenous and African populations played in the Spanish racial regime, it is surprising that so very few Latinos actually identify as either Indian or black. Less than

2 percent (1.4%) defined themselves in Census 2010 as "American Indian" or "Alaska Native, Asian, or Native Hawaiian or other Pacific Islander." Only 2.5 percent of Latinos racially defined themselves as "Black," while only 0.1 percent claimed to be "Native Hawaiian or Pacific Island." More than one-third of the total population, or 36.7 percent of those enumerated, indicated that they were of "Some Other Race." Most of the individuals who indicated they were of "Some Other Race" listed their specific nationality as their answer to the race question and were summarily placed in that category. Another 6 percent claimed to be of "two or more races" in 2010.

There are, of course, significant differences among the pan-Latino population in how the different nationalities racially identify themselves. Cubans had by far the highest percentage of Latinos that identified as White (85.4%). They were followed by South Americans (65.9%) which included those reported as being Argentinean, Bolivian, Chilean, Colombian, Ecuadorian, Paraguayan, Peruvian, Uruguayan, Venezuelan, South American Indian groups, or simply as "South American." Among other Caribbean Latinos the numbers varied from 53.1 percent of Puerto Ricans and only 29.6 percent of Dominicans who indicated their race as "White." Among Central Americans: 52.8 percent of Mexicans, 38.5 percent of Guatemalans, 40.2 percent of Salvadorans, and 48.5 percent of Other Central Americans identified in the same way. (The latter category included those reported as being Costa Rican, Honduran, Nicaraguan, Panamanian, Central American Indian groups, from the Canal Zone, or simply as "Central American".)

Given the prerogatives and entitlements of whiteness extended to both Mexicans and Puerto Ricans as a result of U.S. colonial conquest (the Treaty of Guadalupe Hidalgo in 1848 and the Jones Act in 1917), it is not surprising that both of the two largest Latino groups generally see themselves as a White population.[7] In 2010, approximately 53 percent of both Mexicans and Puerto Ricans racially defined themselves as White.

"Some Other Race" was the second-largest category enumerated by Mexicans (39.5%) and Puerto Ricans (27.8%) when they were asked to racially identify themselves in Census 2010. Less than one percent of Mexicans defined themselves as being racially "Black" (0.9%). Despite the growing number of indigenous people from Mexico now in the United States, only 1.4 percent of Mexicans racially self-define as "Indian." A small number of Puerto Ricans identified themselves as "Indian" (0.9%), while a more significant number (8.7%) racially defined themselves as "Black." Both groups made significant use of the "two or more races" category. However, given their mixed-raced ancestry, it is surprising that only 5 percent of Mexicans and 8.7 percent of Puerto Ricans claimed more than one racial background.[8]

THE RERACIALIZATION OF LATINO POPULATIONS IN THE UNITED STATES

While this ambiguity in how Latinos racially identify themselves is understandable given that they have straddled two very different racial regimes, they apparently have far less trouble racializing one another. Nowhere is this more apparent than in the ways that the two largest Latino populations have increasingly come into conflict in ways that can be traced to how each group racializes the other. In other words, Mexicans and Puerto Ricans have increasingly come to racially define each other through the lens and logic of the Spanish racial regime that previously ensnared them. They apparently rely on this cultural logic after immigrating to the United States.

Growing evidence of this pattern can be seen in a number of recent ethnographic studies that have explored the often contentious relationship between the two Latino populations. Let us now explore the curious way that this reracialization unfolds and how it complicates the forging of a pan-Latino identity among the various Latino nationalities in the United States.

Some of the most interesting, and troubling, research in Latino studies has produced superb ethnographic studies of multiple Latino populations in areas where they have converged in recent years. Nicholas de Genova and Ana Ramos-Zayas' *Latino Crossings* (2003), de Genova's *Working the Boundaries* (2005), Gina Perez's *The Near Northwest Side Story* (2004), Arlene Davila's *Barrio Dreams* (2004), and Robert Smith's *Mexican New York* (2006) are a few examples of this sophisticated ethnographic research. While each of these scholars addresses a distinct set of issues, all have in the process also documented the increasing tensions between recent Mexican immigrants and Puerto Rican migrants in Chicago and New York City.

De Genova and Ramos-Zayas's powerful book *Latino Crossings* offers the following troubling summary of this contentious intergroup conflict:

> What emerge are competing visions of each groups "civilized" or "modern" qualities in juxtaposition to the other's purported "rudeness" or "backwardness." . . . Mexican immigrants often generalized from the allegation that Puerto Ricans were "lazy" to posit variously they were like-wise untrustworthy, deceptive, willing to cheat, disagreeable, nervous, rude, aggressive, violent, dangerous, and criminal. In constructing these racialized images of the character of Puerto Ricans as a group, Mexicans were implicitly celebrating themselves as educated, well-mannered, and civilized. In contrast, Puerto Ricans frequently elaborated further upon their perceptions of Mexicans as uninitiated into the workings of the sociopolitical system in the United States and inclined to sacrifice their dignity in a desperate quest for work. Puerto Ricans commonly coupled these judgments with allegations that Mexicans, as a group, were submissive, obliging, gullible, naïve, rustic, out-moded, folksy, backward, and predominantly "cultural," in contrast to a vision of themselves as political, principled, sophisticated, stylish, dynamic, urban, and modern. Remarkably, these parallel discourses on the parts of both groups served to sustain their own divergent claims of civility or modernity, in ways that implied their differential worthiness for the entitlements of citizenship. (de Genova and Ramos-Zayas 2003, 83)

While there is considerable merit in de Genova and Ramos-Zayas's characterization of this ethnic tension, I suspect that there is something far more fundamental taking place here than a cultural conflict between two Latino populations. At the core of these tensions are the different ways that each group constructs the meaning of race in its country of origin and how each group reracializes the other in the United States. It is the distinct constructions of race in the Spanish and U.S. colonial contexts that leads to each group viewing the other through the eyes of the two colonial regimes that have largely structured their historical experiences. In other words, Mexicans appear to view Puerto Ricans principally through the lens of how "blackness" is constructed in both Mexico and in the United States. Puerto Ricans, on the other hand, essentially come to view Mexicans through the lens of how "Indianness" is given meaning in Puerto Rico and in the United States. While notions of "civilization" and "modernity" undeniably play a role in these racialized constructions, they do so through the way that blackness and Indianness have been infused with racialized cultural meaning in their distinct historical experiences.

These racialized constructions are the product of the ways that each group has internalized its Spanish colonial world's view of the African and Indigenous populations subjugated in Mexico and Puerto Rico. Added to that foundation, these groups then reracialize each other under the discursive logic that structures the meaning of race in the United States. Mexicans take what they learned from their Spanish colonizers and fuse that with what they quickly learn about the meaning of race in the white supremacist United States. The negative constructions of blackness that Mexican immigrants bring with them from Mexico are exacerbated by the way in which African Americans and black Latinos are racially constructed by the white population in the United States. Puerto Ricans, and also many African Americans, tend to immediately mark and position Mexicans as a largely backward population that they view as fundamentally "Indian."

MEXICAN VIEWS OF RACE IN MEXICO AND THE UNITED STATES

Racial categorization and self-identity among ethnic Mexicans in the United States generally crystallizes along lines of racial difference that position them within a skin-color hierarchy, or pigmentocracy. Those at the very top are usually the most fair-complexioned and light-skinned Mexicans who can claim some Spanish ancestry. This status is generally marked by use of terms such as *güero* and *güera* (light-skinned) or *blanco* and *blanca* (white). This has been, and remains, a privileged racial status with a profound impact on the life chances and mobility opportunities of the Mexican population.

Mexicans have had long and deep investments in claiming whiteness in the United States. From the mid-nineteenth century, when they were first granted an "honorary white" status after the U.S.-Mexico War, through the mid-twentieth century, Mexicans struggled for equal rights by vigilantly claiming the rights and entitlements of whiteness. It was not until the late 1960s, at the height of the Chicano Movement, that Mexicans began to redefine themselves as a "brown" population and, in the process, explicitly claim and celebrate their Indian ancestry. In so doing, they systematically devalued any claims to European ancestry and completely denied any African ancestry.[9]

The superordinate status of "whiteness" among ethnic Mexicans is generally followed by the large intermediate racial category that the vast majority of the population occupies. The most commonly used term designating this status is *mestizo* (mixed-race; typically of Spanish and Indian ancestry) or the skin-color referent *moreno* (medium brown). It is generally acknowledged that most ethnic Mexicans have a mixed-race ancestry and are largely *mestizo* in origins.

Recent ethnographic research in Mexico has documented that in areas where Mexicans with palpable African ancestry reside, individuals often invoke skin color distinctions to distinguish them from the *blanco/a* and *moreno* populations. These shades of difference are made with reference to individuals seen as either *moreno claro/a* (light brown) or *moreno oscuro/a* (dark brown) (Sue 2009, 115). This strikingly parallels the way that Dominicans designate those mixed-race individuals of African ancestry into *Indio claro* or *Indio oscuro* categories.

There are, however, other racial categories and skin color referents invoked among ethnic Mexicans to mark other phenotypical distinctions made among them. Racial categories such as *negro* (black), *Chino* (Chinese, or Asian more generally), and *indio* (Indian) are widely used by ethnic Mexicans to designate individuals with African, Asian, or Indian phenotypical features. It was very common in the Southern California world in which I was raised to find individuals with strong African, Asian, or Indian features who were referred to in these terms. They were generally ranked below *mestizos* (because they were less white) and placed near the bottom of the racial hierarchy. But it is very clear that the most derisive term and devalued racial category invoked was the term *indio*. It signified the very bottom tier of the Mexican gradational racial hierarchy or pigmentocracy.

In its most common usage throughout Mexico (and much of Latin America) *indio* is not just a neutral term for being "Indian" or "*indígena*." Instead, it is most often used as a derogatory epithet synonymous with being "rude," "uncouth," or generally "backward." Other anthropologists suggest that the term *indio* went hand in hand with the notion of Indians as lazy, idle, or shiftless, as in the phrase laboring "*como indio*" (Stephen 2007).

The way in which Spanish-Indian relations in Mexico clearly elevated the white Spanish population and summarily subordinated the Indigenous population to the bottom of that racial regime has a long and sordid history. To call a fellow Mexican an *indio* was to invoke a derisive racial epithet that connoted being ugly, dumb, and primitive. The term *indio* was a derisive racial slur that conveyed an image of a dark-complexioned, low-class, and ill-bred person.

It comes as no surprise, therefore, that other Latino groups (such as Puerto Ricans) would paint the Mexican population—especially recent undocumented individuals with indigenous ancestry from Oaxaca or Chiapas—as essentially Indians. This is probably the most offensive thing one could possibly say to a Mexican *mestizo*. It captures and reflects the negative status of the Indian population under the Spanish colonial dominion of Mexico and in the American Southwest prior to U.S. annexation.

Blackness, however, is also marked in a derisive way by recent Mexican immigrants as well as by second- and third-generation Mexican Americans and Chicanos. While it may be true that *negrito* is often used as a diminutive term of endearment, it is nonetheless an inherently problematic construction. This is clearly seen when the base term *negro* is used to describe an adult black person: *"un negrote"* (a huge, menacing black person). The diminutive construction of blackness is marked as unthreatening, while the latter construction is unambiguously marked as threatening with troubling sexual connotations.[10]

There can be little doubt that ethnic Mexicans have systematically devalued and denied the full extent of their African ancestry, while simultaneously valorizing either their Spanish or Indian ancestry. The full extent of this negrophobia is clearly seen when one considers that the Mexican national census in 1646 documented that there were slightly more people of African descent than Spaniards enumerated in that year (Menchaca 2001, 61). From this fact, it seems clear that ethnic Mexicans actually have far more African ancestry than they have been willing to acknowledge. This troubling denial and negrophobia has curiously affected the way blackness has been constructed by both native-born Mexican Americans and the recent immigrant population.

In the case of Chicago, for instance, de Genova has discussed how blackness carries racial significance in the Mexican immigrant's description of the African American population in that city. The most common and benign constructions were made with reference to their being dark-complexioned, such as references to them as *"negros"* (blacks), *"morenos"* (dark brown or dark-skinned), or *"prietos"* (dark or swarthy). However, the most common of these terms used by Mexicans to refer to African Americans was *"morenos,"* which de Genova maintains was often used as a way of avoiding the use of the term *negroes* or the n-word. According to him:

> What is remarkable in the ubiquitous usage of the term moreno in place of negro, however, is that many Mexicans (perhaps the majority) would have been most commonly inclined to describe themselves in Mexico (before migrating) as morenos, and—excluding diminutive uses that are always relative and highly contextual—would have tended to reserve the category negro for Mexicans considered to be of recognizable African ancestry. In the course of reracialization in the United States, however, the two were conflated as markers of Blackness, and the term moreno was displaced onto African Americans as a generic and collective (racial) category. . . . Thus, the fairly ambiguous, highly contextual, sweeping middle term moreno—the color category that brushes the broad mass of "brown" Mexicans within Mexico's distinct and relatively fluid racial order—is deflected altogether from Mexicans as a group in the United States and tends to be fixed unequivocally upon African Americans as a rigid generic racial category. (de Genova 2005, 196–197)

However, both recent Mexican immigrants and Chicanos or Mexican Americans find common ground in making widespread use of the same racialized term in referring to African Americans. In this regard, *El Libro de Caló: The Dictionary of Chicano Slang* offers an insightful confirmation of this convergence in the way that both groups racialize African Americans (Polkinhorn, Velasco, and Lambert 2005). This dictionary affirms that the most commonly used term to designate blackness among ethnic Mexicans is *mayate* or *piñacate*. Both terms refer to a black beetle (a Mexican dung beetle in the first case and, in the second, a smaller black beetle commonly found in the Southwest). The term *mayuco*, which is also widely used, appears to be a variant of *mayate*. These designations foreground the blackness of these insects while also providing a sweeping, dehumanizing move in the racialization process. Other zoomorphic terms such as *changos* or *chanates* (monkeys) are also used and share disturbing commonalities with the way African Americans have been historically racialized in the United States.

Interestingly, the majority of the other terms Chicanos use to designate blackness are less inflected by these zoomorphic referents and, instead, foreground dark complexion. For example, disparaging references to African Americans as *prietos* (blackish, dark), *tintos* (dyed, stained), *oscuros* (dark), *tostados* (toasted, dark brown), *quemados* (burned, very dark), or simply *negros* (black, swarthy) all focus on their dark complexion as the key signifier in this racialization.

But the term *mayate* is clearly the most commonly used racial epithet invoked by ethnic Mexicans and is always used in a disparaging way. The term appears to have taken on particular significance in various subcultural worlds among ethnic Mexicans. It was often used in the 1940s to describe a hip African American zoot-suiter who donned the same stylized garb that the Mexican *pachuco* wore. Despite their shared sense of style and affinities in music and dance, it was always used as a disparaging racial slur.

Alternatively, it was also used in a more sexually explicit way by queer Latino men to describe virile, heterosexual African American men who anally penetrate sexually passive homosexual men. These black men were never stigmatized as being homosexual because they assume the active, inserter role (i.e., "*activo*" as opposed to "*pasivo*"). In this particular usage of *mayate*, the association between homosexuality and anal sex—and its simultaneous use to refer to a big black beetle that feasts on dung—does not require too much imagination to see the racialized sexualization of African Americans.[11]

PUERTO RICAN VIEWS OF RACE IN PUERTO RICO AND THE UNITED STATES

Like ethnic Mexicans, Puerto Ricans in both the United States and the island also invoke a gradational racial hierarchy to mark lines of racial difference among themselves. In his interesting analysis of racial identity among Puerto Ricans, anthropologist Jorge Duany has documented at least nineteen different ways in which Puerto Ricans have racially defined themselves on the island. Among these racial categories and skin-color referents are *blanco* (white), *trigueño* (wheat-colored or brunette; usually light mulatto), *moreno* (dark-skinned; usually dark mulatto), *mulato* (mixed-race; rarely used in public); *indio* (literally, Indian; brown skin with straight hair); *prieto* (dark-skinned; usually derogatory); *negro* (black; rarely used as a direct term of reference); and *negrito* (literally, little black) (Duany 2002b).

Duany maintains that "racialized images of Indians and Africans have dominated how Puerto Ricans imagined their ethnic background" (Duany 2002b, 276). "Puerto Rican identity," he contends, "reveals the systematic overvaluation of the Hispanic element, the romanticization of Taino Indians, and the underestimation of the African-derived ingredients" (280). Like Mexicans, Puerto Ricans also have long and deep investments in their claims to whiteness. For example, in response to the Census 2000 question on race, approximately 48 percent of Puerto Ricans in the United States claimed to be "White," while another 38 percent gave responses that led to their being categorized as belonging to "Some Other Race" (Jung and Almaguer 2004, 72). Despite the widespread racial mixing in their Spanish colonial history, very few Puerto Ricans actually claim to be either "Black" or "Indian" in any significant numbers. Only 5.8 percent of Puerto Ricans identified as "Black," and less than 1 percent as "Indian" in Census 2000 (Jung and Almaguer 2004, 72). Curiously, Duany has shown that the actual number of Puerto Ricans on the island—known as "the whitest of the Antilles"—who identify as "White" has actually grown over the years and was calibrated at over 80 percent in Census 2000 (Duany 2002b, 248).

What is so interesting about the racial classifications deployed among Puerto Ricans is the particular way in which Indianness is socially marked. The preconquest indigenous Taino population has taken on importance in the way that Puerto Ricans have come to racialize Mexicans. Being of Taino ancestry assumes certain social associations that capture the way in which Indianness is infused with racial meaning in Puerto Rico. The dominant characterizations of the Taino, according to Duany, constitute the prototype of Rousseau's "noble savage" (in which these indigenous people are seen as "docile, sedentary, indolent, tranquil, and chaste") (Duany 2002b, 268).

In terms of skin color, the most relied-upon racial descriptions of the Taino is "neither white nor black but brown or 'copper like' and that their intermediate phenotype placed them between Europeans and Africans in moral and ascetic terms" (Duany 2002b, 270). Duany contends that few "standard descriptions of the Taino Indians fail to mention their skin color, physical stature, bodily constitution, hair texture, and facial features. . . . For example, one third-grade textbook widely used in Puerto Rico today lists the following 'characteristics of the Taino race': medium build, copper-tone skin, black and straight hair, prominent cheekbones, slightly slanted eyes, long nose, and relatively thick lips. These features are sharply contrasted with the phenotypes of both Spaniards and Africans" (270).

In Chicago, Puerto Ricans are quick to acknowledge that Mexicans have a much closer and deeper association with Indianness than do Puerto Ricans. As one informant told de Genova and Ramos-Zayas: "Mexicans have real Indians. We (Puerto Ricans) have Indian blood in our heritage, be we are not *Indian* Indian" (2003, 192). According to sociologist Robert Smith, the racial mapping of Mexican bodies in Indian terms also occurs in New York City (R. Smith 2006).

Arlene Davila also underscores this point in her book *Barrio Dreams*. Therein she acknowledges that Herman Badillo, the Puerto Rican chairman of the board of trustees at the City University of New York and unsuccessful candidate for mayor in 2001, articulated the commonly held view among Puerto Ricans that Mexicans "'came from the hills,' from countries with little tradition of education, and were mostly short and straight haired Indians. These racist comments exposed stereotypes of Mexicans as less educated or unsophisticated 'newcomers,' as opposed the 'urban savviness' of Puerto Ricans" (Davila 2004, 173).

This perception that Mexicans are racially "more Indian" than Puerto Ricans occasionally finds expression in how these Latino groups explicitly racialize one another's gendered bodies. A conversation among young Puerto Rican informants in *Latino Crossings* offers an insightful example of this racialization: "You can tell if someone is Mexican or Puerto Rican by looking at their asses. . . . Yeah, you see, Puerto Ricans have an ass and Mexicans are flat-assed—they have an Indian ass. . . . Yeah, Selena was real pretty. She looked Puerto Rican, you know. She had an ass. . . . Women who have big tits have flat asses. If you really want to know if a woman has a flat ass, you look at her chest. That's why you have a lot of Mexican women who are big on top and have no ass" (quoted in Davila 2004, 193).

This ethnographic data documents the troubling way that Latino populations previously ensnared by the Spanish colonial empire have come to view one another in the United States. This brings us back to how Puerto Ricans view the Mexican immigrant population in Chicago as essentially "Indians." It is their construction of the Taino that provides a window on how they have come to construct recent Mexican immigrants. This is, in one respect, just the other side of the way Puerto Ricans have been constructed as "black" by the Mexican population in Chicago.

CONCLUSION

This essay has explored the unique way in which the Latino population has been racialized in the United States and situated within its racial and ethnic landscape. I have shown that Latinos stand alone among communities of color in the United States in that they are principally defined in ethnic—rather than racial—terms. It is fundamentally on the basis of their common culture (based on the Spanish language and Catholic religion) that they are placed in the "Spanish/Hispanic/Latino" category rather than one discrete racial category. In other words, it is the cultural logic of ethnicity, rather than that of race per se, that leads to placing the multiracial Latino populations in the "Spanish/Hispanic/Latino" ethnic category.

In addition to the unique way that Latinos are located within the racial and ethnic landscape of the United States, I have attempted to make sense of the equally curious and troubling way that Latinos have come to racialize one another in areas where they have increasingly settled in the United States. There is mounting ethnographic evidence that Latinos have resorted to stigmatizing one another by using the ways in which racial categories were infused with meaning in the Spanish colonial world. It is in the disparaging ways that Indianness and blackness are given cultural meaning in the countries of origin that we are able to better understand the documented tensions between the two largest Latino populations in the United States. Mexicans and Puerto Ricans, both of whom have valorized and made direct claims to the privileges and entitlements of "whiteness," resort to racializing each another by drawing on the most stigmatizing ways that race is defined in Mexico and Puerto Rico. Mexicans largely denigrate Puerto Ricans on the basis of their African ancestry, while Puerto Ricans denigrate Mexicans based on their putative Indianness.

The complex meaning of race and the particular way that racialization unfolds in the United States is an ever changing sociohistorical process. Nowhere are the ambiguities and vagaries of racial formation in this country more starkly evident than in the case of the Latino population. Making sense of the unique way that race and racialization has been given cultural meaning among Latinos provides yet another window on a process that has been most eloquently articulated in Michael Omi and Howard Winant's seminal work. *Racial Formation in the United States* has enabled us to clearly see that race is fundamentally a sociohistorical category at once fictional and yet also profoundly real in its sociological implications.

One of these implications is the particular way that the United States has given cultural meaning to racial designations and attempts to locate various populations within the logic of the racial categories deployed in the United States. It is here that the Latino populations continue to complicate the very logic of the racial formation process in this country. As I show here, there is also mounting ethnographic evidence that Latinos often resort to the way that race was given specific meaning in the Spanish colonial context to racialize one another. It is here, in the troubling convergence of two distinct racial regimes in the lives of the Latino population, that we may illuminate the conundrums and contestations inherent in the racial formation process in the United States.

NOTES

1. The second edition of the book was published in 1994 under the slightly revised title *Racial Formation in the United States: From the 1960s to the 1990s.*

2. See, for example, O'Brien 2008; Bonilla-Silva 2003a; Murguia and Forman 2003; and Forman, Goar, and Lewis (2002).

3. In this regard, see the canonical study by Ramón Gutiérrez on the way these racial

lines were initially drawn in Spanish colonial New Mexico (Gutiérrez 1991). Also see his classic essay "Hispanic Identities in the Southwestern United States" (Gutiérrez 2009).

4. A number of scholars have explored the racialization of the Mexican population after the U.S.-Mexico War. See, for example, Menchaca 2001, 2007; Haas 1995; Almaguer 1994; Foley 1997, 2007; Montejano 1987; Guglielmo 2006; Ruiz 2004; Gómez 2007, 2009.

5. A number of scholars have written about the historical and contemporary ambiguities in the placement of Latinos in the decennial census. See, for example, C. Rodríguez 2000, 2009; and Tienda and Ortiz 1986.

6. See, for example, Portes 2007.

7. The scholarly literature on the claims to whiteness by both Mexicans and Puerto Ricans continues to increase over time. On the Mexican population, for example, see Almaguer 1994; Foley 1997, 2007; Guglielmo 2006; and Menchaca 2007. On Puerto Ricans, see Duany 2002a, 2003, and 2007; Loveman and Muniz 2007; Landale and Oropesa 2002; and Vidal-Ortiz 2004.

8. These figures are based on the use of U.S. Census Public Use Microdata Samples (PUMSs) for 2000 that are gathered in Jung and Almaguer 2004, 72.

9. See, for example, the compelling book on this topic by Haney-Lopez (2004).

10. See, for example, Vaughn 2005 and Lewis 2000.

11. See, for example, the discussion of the politics of active and passive sexual roles among Latino gay men in Vidal-Ortiz et al. 2010. See also the use of the term *bugarron* among Dominicans as a parallel term for *mayate* in Padilla 2007 and among Puerto Ricans in Guzman 2005.

REFERENCES

Almaguer, Tomás. 1994. *Racial Fault Lines: The Historical Origins of White Supremacy in California*. Berkeley: University of California Press.

Bonilla-Silva, Eduardo. 2003. "New Racism," Color-Blind Racism, and the Future of Whiteness in America. In *White Out: The Continuing Significance of Race*, ed. Eduardo Bonilla-Silva and Ashley "Woody" Doane. New York: Routledge.

Candelario, Ginetta E. B. 2007. *Black behind the Ears: Dominican Racial Identity from Museums to Beauty Shops*. Durham, NC: Duke University Press.

Davila, Arlene. 2004. *Barrio Dreams: Puerto Ricans, Latinos, and the Neoliberal City*. Berkeley: University of California Press.

de Genova, Nicholas. 2005. *Working the Boundaries: Race, Space, and "Illegality" in Mexican Chicago*. Durham, NC: Duke University Press.

de Genova, Nicholas, and Ana Y. Ramos-Zayas. 2003. *Latino Crossings: Mexicans, Puerto Ricans, and the Politics of Race and Citizenship*. New York: Routledge.

Duany, Jorge. 2002a. Neither Black nor White: The Representation of Racial Identity among Puerto Ricans on the Island and in the U.S. Mainland. In *The Puerto Rican Nation on the Move: Identities on the Island and in the United States*. Chapel Hill: University of North Carolina Press.

———. 2002b. *The Puerto Rican Nation on the Move: Identities on the Island and in the United States*. Chapel Hill: University of North Carolina Press.

———. 2007. Nation and Migration: Rethinking Puerto Rican Identity in a Transnational Context. In *None of the Above: Puerto Ricans in the Global Era*, ed. Frances Negrón-Muntaner. New York: Palgrave MacMillan.

Foley, Neil. 1997. *The White Scourge: Mexicans, Blacks, and Poor Whites in Texas Cotton Culture*. Berkeley: University of California Press.

———. 2007. "God Bless the Law, He Is White": Legal, Local, and International Politics of Latina/o and Black Desegregation Cases in Post–World War II California and Texas. In *A Companion to Latino Studies*, ed. Juan Flores and Renato Rosaldo. Malden, MA: Blackwell Publishing.

Forman, Tyrone A., Carla Goar, and Amanda E. Lewis. 2002. Neither Black nor White? An Empirical Test of the Latin Americanization Thesis. *Race and Society* 5: 65–84.

Gómez, Laura E. 2007. *Manifest Destinies: The Making of the Mexican American Race*. New York: New York University Press.

Guglielmo, Thomas A. 2003. *White on Arrival: Italians, Race, Color, and Power in Chicago, 1890–1945*. New York: Oxford University Press.

———. 2006. Fighting for Caucasian Rights: Mexicans, Mexican Americans, and the Transnational Struggle for Civil Rights in World War II Texas. *Journal of American History* 92 (4): 1212–1237.

Gutiérrez, Ramón A. 1991. *When Jesus Came, the Corn Mothers Went Away: Marriage, Sexuality, and Power in New Mexico, 1500–1846*. Stanford: Stanford University Press.

———. 2009. Hispanic Identities in the Southwestern United States. In *Race and Classification: The Case of Mexican Americans*, ed. Ilona Katzew and Susan Deans-Smith. Stanford: Stanford University Press.

Guzman, Manolo. 2005. *Gay Hegemony/Latino Homosexualities*. New York: Routledge.

Haas, Lisbeth. 1995. *Conquests and Historical Identities in California, 1769–1936*. Berkeley: University of California Press.

Haney-López, Ian. 2004. *Racism on Trial: The Chicano Fight for Justice*. Cambridge, MA: Harvard University Press.

Jung, Moon-Kie, and Tomás Almaguer. 2004. The State and the Production of Racial Categories. In *Race and Ethnicity: Across Time, Space, and Discipline*, ed. Rodney D. Coates. Leiden, The Netherlands: Brill.

Landale, Nancy S., and Ralph Salvatore Oropesa. 2002. White, Black, or Puerto Rican?: Racial Self-Identification among Mainland and Island Puerto Ricans. *Social Forces* 81 (1): 231–254.

Lewis, Laura. 2000. Blacks, Black Indians, Afromexicans: The Dynamics of Race, Nation, and Identity in a Mexican *Moreno* Community (Guerrero). *American Ethnologist* 27 (4): 898–926.

Loveman, Mara, and Jeronimo O. Muniz. 2007. How Puerto Ricans Became White: Boundary Dynamics and Inter-census Racial Reclassification. *American Sociological Review* 72 (6): 915–939.

Menchaca, Martha. 2001. *Recovering History, Constructing Race: The Indian, Black, and White Roots of Mexican Americans*. Austin: University of Texas Press.

———. 2007. Latinos/as and the *Mestizo* Racial Heritage of Mexican Americans. In *A Companion to Latino Studies*, ed. Juan Flores and Renato Rosaldo. Malden, MA: Blackwell.

Montejano, David. 1987. *Anglos and Mexicans in the Making of Texas, 1836–1986*. Austin: University of Texas Press.

Murguia, Edward, and Tyrone Forman. 2003. Shades of Whiteness: The Mexican American Experience in Relation to Anglos and Blacks. In *White Out: The Continuing Significance of Race*, ed. Eduardo Bonilla-Silva and Ashley "Woody" Doane. New York: Routledge.

O'Brien, Eileen. 2008. *The Racial Middle: Latinos and Asian Americans Living beyond the Racial Divide*. New York: New York University Press.

Padilla, Mark. 2007. *Caribbean Pleasure Industry: Tourism, Sexuality, and AIDS in the Dominican Republic*. Chicago: University of Chicago Press.

Pérez, Gina M. 2004. *The Near Northwest Side Story: Migration, Displacement, and Puerto Rican Families*. Berkeley: University of California Press.

Polkinhorn, Harry, Alfredo Velasco, and Malcom Lambert. 2005. *El Libro de Caló: The Dictionary of Chicano Slang*. Revised Edition. San Francisco: Floricanto Press.

Portes, Alejandro. 2007. The New Latin Nation: Immigration and Hispanic Population in the United States. In *A Companion to Latino Studies*, ed. Juan Flores and Renato Rosaldo. Malden, MA: Blackwell.

Rodríguez, Clara E. 2000. *Changing Race: Latinos, the Census, and the History of Ethnicity in the United States*. New York: New York University Press.

———. 2009. Counting Latinos in the U.S. Census. In *Race and Classification: The Case of Mexican Americans*, ed. Ilona Katzew and Susan Deans-Smith. Stanford: Stanford University Press.

Ruiz, Vicki L. 2004. *Morena/o, blanca/o y café con leche:* Racial Constructions in Chicana/o Historiography. *Mexican Studies/Estudios Mexicanos* 20 (2): 343–359.

Rumbaut, Ruben G. 2009. Pigments of Our Imagination: On the Racialization and Racial Identity of "Hispanics" and "Latinos." In *How the United States*. Racializes Latinos: White Hegemony and Its Consequences. Boulder: Paradigm Publishers, 228–44.

Smith, Robert Courtney. 2006. *Mexican New York: Transnational Lives of New Immigrants*. Berkeley: University of California Press.

Stephen, Lynn. 2007. *Transborder Lives: Indigenous Oaxacans in Mexico, California, and Oregon*. Durham, NC: Duke University Press.

Sue, Christina A. 2009. The Dynamics of Color: *Mestizaje*, Racism, and Blackness in Vera Cruz, Mexico. In *Shades of Difference: Why Skin Color Matters*, ed. Evelyn Nakano Glenn. Stanford: Stanford University Press.

Tienda, Marta, and Vilma Ortiz. 1986. "Hispanicity" and the 1980 Census. *Social Science Quarterly* 67 (1): 3–20.

Torres-Saillant, Silvio. 1998. The Tribulations of Blackness: Stages in Dominican Racial Identity. *Latin American Perspectives* 25 (3): 126–146.

U.S. Bureau of the Census. 2010. *Overview of Race and Hispanic Origin: 2010*. Issued March 2011 http://www.census.gov/prod/cen2010/briefs/c2010br-02.pdf. Accessed January 8, 2012.

Vaughn, Bobby. 2005. Afro-Mexico: Blacks, *Indigenas*, Politics, and the Greater Diaspora. In *Neither Enemies nor Friends: Latinos, Blacks, and Afro-Latinos*, ed. Anani Dzidzienyo and Suzanne Oboler. New York: Palgrave MacMillan.

Vidal-Ortiz, Salvador, Carlos Decena, Hector Carrillo, and Tomás Almaguer. 2010. Revisiting *Activos* and *Pasivos*: Toward New Cartographies of Latino/Latin American Male Same-Sex Desire. In *Latina/o Sexualities: Probing, Powers, Passions, Practices, and Policies,* ed. Marysol Asencio. New Brunswick, NJ: Rutgers University Press.

PART 4

WORK AND LIFE CHANCES

The majority of Latinos now living in the United States came here looking for work, seeking better opportunities, higher wages, and safer labor conditions, hoping that through their toil they would accumulate wealth and eventually realize the American dream, or if not that, at least gain skills to improve their lot in life. Who works and why is deeply enmeshed in antique moral arguments about the differential worth of persons. Does work purify or demean? Does it bring salvation or perdition? In the moral discourses about the work Latinas and Latinos have performed in the United States during the past 150 years, that labor often has been stigmatized and reviled as the product of chronically lazy persons who have never learned English or Americanized, and who are here illegally. If only they worked harder, if only they were more compliant, if only they limited their reproduction, they might realize the American dream. These are old rants, repeated over and over again as each generation of native-born Americans judges the fitness of immigrants for membership in society. The readings on work gathered here by Patricia Zavella, Nicholas de Genova and Ana Y. Ramos-Zayas, and Manuel Pastor Jr. all explore the paradoxical evaluations of the human labor of the most powerless in society. Latinos have long been desired as workers and recruited specifically to work, but they are then reviled because they perform the dirtiest, low-wage, backbreaking work that few Americans will accept. Latinos come to the United States brimming with immigrant industriousness and hope, taking whatever jobs they can find, which they soon discover are dangerous and only lead to dead ends, both figuratively and literally. Whether in the United States legally or not, they live lives of poverty that often get perpetuated generation after generation.

In chapter 10, "Mexicans' Quotidian Struggles with Migration and Poverty: The Working Poor," Zavella takes us to Santa Cruz County in northern California, to explore at a granular level the texture of the lives of Mexican immigrant workers employed in this relatively prosperous region. Here both immigrants and citizens toil largely on farms producing broccoli, spinach, brussels sprouts, carrots, and cauliflower, picking apples for juice and cider, and gathering raspberries, blackberries, and strawberries. Smaller numbers are employed in construction and in garment production, but most also enter the service sector when in need of temporary work or in search of a second job.

When the dominant food-packing industry in Santa Cruz County was unionized, its workers had job security, living wages, and enviable benefits. In the 1990s that began to change as large multinational food corporations such as Birds Eye shifted their production from California to Mexico, where wages were much lower and unions did not constrain corporate profits. The move resulted in massive unemployment and underemployment, intense competition between older workers and younger recent immigrants and between men and women over what constituted "men's work" and "women's work," and between English-speaking Mexican Americans and monolingual Mexicans competing with one another for the remaining poorly paid service sector jobs already dominated by unauthorized immigrants. These workers, like their citizen co-ethnics, quickly entered the ranks of the working poor, an indignity that was only compounded by discrimination, racist insults, and daily acts of humiliation that only exacerbated their sense of being outcasts.

In de Genova and Ramos-Zayas's chapter 11, "Economies of Dignity: Ideologies of Work and Worth among Mexicans and Puerto Ricans in Chicago," we explore the stereotypes Puerto Ricans and Mexicans have of one another about the meaning of work in Chicago's Humboldt Park neighborhood, where, side by side, they live, love, and die. Both groups are racialized as inferior by Chicago's dominant white population; the racism gets compounded when they couch their caricatures of their neighbors in a moral rhetoric that is used to demean. Mexicans deem Puerto Ricans morally undisciplined and lazy, with the women living as welfare queens who keep having babies to avoid work and to collect government assistance. Puerto Ricans are thus viewed as just another group of undeserving poor akin to African Americans, who are national liabilities and lack a strong work ethic.

Most Mexicans in Chicago's Latino neighborhoods work without authorization, and this fact stigmatizes them in the eyes of Puerto Ricans, who see them all as "illegal aliens" unworthy of membership in the community of citizens. Though Puerto Ricans admit that ethnic Mexicans in Chicago as a group work hard, they nevertheless berate them as being needlessly subservient, unfairly competing for work by accepting the low wages others will not, rarely standing up for their rights, and never actively contesting their plight. The behavioral types that generate these stereotypes are certainly rooted in facts, but the deprecating caricatures they hurl at one another simply blame the poor for their own plight.

Pastor's chapter 12, "Not So Golden? Latino Fortunes and Futures in California's Changing Economy," returns our focus to California's ethnic Mexicans in the present, showing that their fortunes are meager and their prospects grim, even in this state known for its obscene fortunes and historic promises of gold. While xenophobes often moralistically argue that Latino poverty is rooted in Latinos' lack of labor force participation, the opposite is true for both women and men, as Pastor empirically shows. Latinos have long had the highest rates of labor force participation in California, but they remain at the bottom of the social structure because more than half of them are immigrant workers who lack a high school education and are thus forced into segregated occupations that pay poorly and offer no employment security or benefits.

The majority of Latinos live lives of bare existence and working poverty. Many individuals are employed at two and three jobs simultaneously. One out of every ten of these workers have full-time jobs, but their earning are so low that they struggle to exist. This was true in California as early as 1980. It was true before the Great Recession of 2008. It is true even more so now, contributing to one of the greatest levels of income inequality the country has ever known. In 2012, 39 percent of California's Latinos lived in working poverty, more than twice the rate of non-Hispanic whites, and even higher than the rate of 33 percent of African Americans. Latinos in California, particularly the immigrants, are stuck. They are structurally relegated to unskilled, low-wage work, with few imaginable avenues out. For these bleak realities to change, Pastor urges Latinos to get better educated and more extensively trained, to militate for a higher minimum wage, and to join unions to better their working conditions and employment benefits, particularly access to health care.

10

MEXICANS' QUOTIDIAN STRUGGLES WITH MIGRATION AND POVERTY

The Working Poor

Patricia Zavella

Se me hizo muy gaucho regresar sin dinero y sin hilacho.
(It seemed uncouth to return without money or deed.)

—ERNESTO PESQUEDA,
"El Bracero Fracasado" (The Failed Bracero)

Recent scholarship on labor shows that the interconnected macro processes of global-ization, the restructuring of regional economies, and increased migration are related as the poor are displaced from underdeveloped regions and move in search of work in other labor markets. In the context of globalization, capitalist logic pushes employers to restructure in ways that provide regionally specific options for work that then affect remuneration for local and migrant workers. Global cities are often seen as the product of these political-economic and social forces.[1] However, increasingly rural areas and suburbs in the United States are globalized as regions undergo transformations that attract those who migrate transnationally and from within the nation. In Santa Cruz County, the two largest cities—Watsonville in the south and Santa Cruz in the north—are shaped by globalization, restructuring, and migration in different ways and both provide few jobs that would allow pathways out of poverty. Watsonville, a city of 51,000 surrounded by agricultural production, is where many agricultural laborers live. Santa Cruz, with 58,000 residents, is at the water's edge with a tourism-based economy and is the site of one of the branches of the University of California. These cities are only about fifteen miles apart, linked by a scenic highway, yet economically, demographically, and socially they are very different. Both are suburbs of Silicon Valley, whose highly paid professionals increasingly live and work in Santa Cruz County, contributing to high local housing costs and traffic congestion.

Christian Zlolniski argues that the restructuring of local labor markets along with increased unauthorized migration from Latin America, especially from Mexico, in the wake of immigration reform proposals leads to the recomposition of local labor forces and reduction of costs by intensifying the labor process and creating flexible uses of labor. Management attempts to create labor flexibility by reorganizing the work process, replacing workers, or responding to fluctuations in the regional economy, which labor contests. Labor flexibility also leads to labor subcontracting in numerous industries where employers rely on Mexican migrant labor and expands the informal labor market where the undocumented generate income outside of formal employment. Both mechanisms engender lower pay and frequent periods of unemployment and workers become part of the working poor. Migrant workers supplement their wages by small-scale vending, often within their own neighborhoods, utilizing their social networks and establishing dense mechanisms of social exchange. Zlolniski suggests that, rather than taking migrants' labor flexibility for granted, we should examine how labor is continuously negotiated and contested in regional labor markets.[2]

The availability of undocumented migrant workers has profound implications in relation to labor flexibility. Ever since the Immigration Reform and Control Act of 1986 (IRCA) set penalties for employers who knowingly hire unauthorized migrant workers, all potential employees must submit identification documents to their employers. This requirement established a thriving underground economy in false documents so migrants can be hired legally. To get around this provision, employers have been known to provide false documents or the unauthorized are paid "under the counter" in cash.[3] Further, undocumented workers experience formidable barriers to the privileges of paid employment and are unlikely to receive benefits such as medical insurance or unemployment insurance.[4] More telling, the unauthorized are well aware they are subject to outright abuse and the continual risk of deportation, so often they do not complain about workplace abuses that result in occupational injuries. In a survey with 4,387 workers in Los Angeles, Chicago, and New York, of whom 70 percent were migrants and 39 percent undocumented, researchers found widespread abuses such as ignoring the minimum wage, denial of overtime or breaks, illegal deductions, unpaid hours, or serious injuries.[5] In the post-IRCA era, the unauthorized work longer hours than those who are authorized.[6] Many undocumented workers pay into Social Security and Medicare yet do not file tax returns or use their Medicare benefits (or in California, renters' credit) out of fear of deportation. Economists estimate that about 10 percent of the Social Security surplus, the difference between what the system receives in payroll taxes and what it pays out in pension benefits, can be attributed to undocumented workers.[7] Except for certain federal jobs, authorized migrants may work without hindrance and are eligible for the same protections (or lack thereof) as their citizen counterparts. In the contemporary period, scholars estimate that the undocumented make up 5 percent of the civilian labor force of the United States. Mexican migrants who had arrived in the United States between 1980 and 1990 and were not U.S. citizens had a labor force participation rate of 88 percent, 18 percent higher that that of the total population.[8]

Migration also often includes racialization processes as those who migrate, especially the unauthorized, find themselves in regions where their racial status matters. There is a rich literature on how racialization is constructed in relation to migrants in local labor markets and is evident in labor processes and the racial divides that overlay the class divisions between workers and managers at work sites.[9] Migrants make up high proportions of particular unskilled occupations notorious for poor wages, dangerous working conditions, and few benefits: these are what Lisa Catanzarite calls "brown collar jobs" because they are predominantly performed by Latino migrant workers.[10] According to de Genova, racialization at work sites goes hand in hand with the social space of illegality, "an erasure of legal personhood—a space of forced invisibility, exclusion, subjugation, and repression."[11] In Santa Cruz County, despite the marginalization engendered by illegality, migrant workers can find jobs with fellow Spanish speakers and supervisors, which makes work accessible despite their unauthorized legal status.

In addition, gendered differences in local labor markets profoundly influence how migrants adapt since female migrants often have an easier time finding paid employment. Within labor markets and work sites segregated by race and gender in the United States, Mexican women are concentrated within "women's jobs," with migrants at the bottom of the occupational structure in the secondary labor market.[12] Like "brown collar jobs," "women's jobs" often are nonunion, have few benefits, are seasonal, or are subject to displacement (such as the garment industry), and they often require relatively low training or educational levels (although the work itself may be quite skilled) and pay the minimum wage, which is still no higher after inflation than it was in the early 1980s. Those working in the informal sector performing reproductive labor (e.g., as house cleaners, live-in nannies, or maids) are subject to irregular work hours, little oversight over work conditions, and few recourses if their employers do not pay them or underpay them. According to Rhacel Parreñas, such reproductive labor is "needed to sustain the productive labor force. Such work includes household chores, the care of elders, adults, and youth, the socialization of children, and the maintenance of social ties in the family."[13] The new domestic labor positions human care on one side of the desirability scale and independent housekeeping work at the other end.[14] Both are forms of socially necessary labor that increasingly Mexican migrant women engage in and redefine to assert boundaries and better working conditions.[15] This often puts them at odds with employers who seek greater flexibility in the definition of the job, the working conditions, and the pay. Even workers who are located in unionized sectors (e.g., electronics, food processing, or garments) find that unions are often unresponsive to migrants or women's particular needs, and union democracy struggles have been waged over translating contracts and union meetings into Spanish and electing representatives who understand the needs of the Mexican workers.[16]

Here I explore the following questions: What are the labor market options in this region and how do workers maximize income-generating activities? How do local labor options contribute to poverty? And how do workers respond to racial or gender segregation in the labor market? I illustrate how subjects struggle to find work in a region where the labor market is dominated by agriculture and tourism.

My analysis has four layers. As I charted the work histories of the research participants, I was impressed by the large number of job moves as workers strategically tried to maximize their wages, benefits, hours, schedules or work seasons, or to find jobs less demanding on their bodies or with less onerous tasks. Despite their efforts, the better jobs do not provide the means for moving out of poverty. For example, in a ten-year period, thirty-four-year-old Angélica López worked at five different jobs—as a farmworker, dishwasher, nursing home aide, drycleaners presser, and janitor. Once her husband got a job in a nonunion factory, Angélica left the labor market to take care of their four children full time, a strategy that saved on day-care expenses yet left the couple dependent on her spouse's low income. I argue that in this region, there are several restructuring processes occurring in the labor market that lead to the formation of the working poor (those who fall below the poverty line but are still involved in full-time or significant work). Second, work is fundamental to masculine and feminine identities as well as ethno-racial identities where finding and keeping stable work has high stakes. Men and women attempt to find jobs that will provide the best resources for themselves and their families. Whether they are migrants or Mexican Americans, workers can find employment prospects within local economies, which have profound implications for seasonal or long-term employment and wage rates as well as the experience of work itself. Third, I focus on the commonalities and tensions between recent migrants and Mexican Americans. Once they become integrated into work sites, migrants share a sense of injustice with Mexican Americans about exploitation and racial discrimination. In other work sites, tensions between migrants and Mexican Americans come to the fore with competing notions of cultural authenticity around language use—English for Mexican Americans and Spanish for migrants from Mexico. Finally, peripheral vision also comes into play when migrants and Mexican Americans think about the prospect of struggling in the United States or returning to Mexico or evaluate their work in relation to options on "the other side."

THE INFORMAL ECONOMY

Feminist scholars have challenged the dichotomy of labor into public and private spheres and suggest instead that we examine the interdependence that exists between productive and reproductive labor.[17] Work in the informal economy in private homes, "under the table" as it is often called, often generates significant household income. It is attractive to employers since they do not pay taxes or benefits yet unauthorized workers have little leverage for negotiating tasks or wages. Informal work allows women to combine domestic and wage labor by keeping an eye on children or the infirm, or organize their tasks so they can perform household chores in between work for wages. However, when women take on these dual work roles at one time, they are forced to accept poor working conditions, low wages, and variable hours, and their families must continually adjust to employers' needs.[18]

Mexicans participate in a variety of formal, informal, and underground economies precisely because of their legal status. If men's social networks cannot provide access to jobs, they often resort to labor shape-ups (*la parada*), informal markets on street corners where daily labor is contracted on the spot. In driving around town I often go by lumberyards or large retail stores that have shape-ups. In Santa Cruz, these shape-ups shifted from being overwhelmingly Latino in the late 1980s to include a number of whites during the recession in the early 1990s; they became predominantly Latino again after that and during the 2009 recession there were white men again. In South County, there are several shape-ups for farmworkers looking for jobs, with some groups as large as about eighty, all Latino men. I never saw any women in local shape-ups like there are in New York City.[19] Labor shape-ups provide the public face to migrant work experiences, where men face possible deportation if they are undocumented yet they are so desperate for a day's work that they risk apprehension. However, their experiences are not well known to the public, which often sees them as dangerous nuisances or as emblems of the failure of immigration policies.[20]

Day laborers are usually paid in cash, often are provided a meal, and perform the most distasteful and hazardous work. Surveys from different day-labor sites across the nation show that participants tend to be recently arrived unauthorized Latino migrant men with little formal education and limited English proficiency. They tend to perform construction, janitorial, gardening, or warehouse work or occasionally labor in factories.[21] Informal, anonymous work can include pressure to perform distasteful tasks. A study of 450 male day laborers in different locales around the country found that 38 percent had been solicited for sex work while seeking day work and 10 percent of them accepted the offer since they needed the money and had no other offers.[22] This pressure is well known to migrants, male and female; as one man said: "They say there is a lot of prostitution." None of the women I interviewed or who participated in focus groups disclosed any experience with sex work; however, they knew of local bars, labor camps, or streets that sex workers would frequent, especially on paydays. One woman hinted during an interview that she might have been forced to exchange sex for money: "The things one has to do to survive . . . " her voice trailed off and she changed the subject. Those who work with young migrant men have heard of some who exchange sex for money after they arrive in the United States but the prevalence of these exchanges is hard to gauge.

My interviews with day laborers or their partners confirmed that they are vulnerable to abuses that many day laborers face, such as not being paid, and they are among the most exploited, working without protection from dangerous work practices or unscrupulous employers.[23] The most poignant stories are from those who rely on day-labor wages to support their families. If the men are unsuccessful in finding work, there is no money for food or rent, often pushing women into finding informal jobs themselves.

Melissa García, for example, started taking care of children in her home without a license to generate cash for basic living expenses after her spouse was unable to find consistent work at the shape-up. The income she gained from fellow migrant women workers was very low but the benefit was that she did not have to arrange for the care of her own young children while working. Without any permits or licenses, Isabella Morales ran an informal café out of her kitchen, charging $7 for a meal (mainly to single men), as well as providing day care to a child and selling tamales by the dozen to her neighbors and friends. Yet participating in the informal economy has its drawbacks. Isabella was forced to move her family of seven because her landlord found out about the tamales. As long as she makes the rent, her current landlord does not mind that she works out of her home.

   Finding work in the informal economy, then, left men and women scrambling to make ends meet, subject to labor violations and abuse, and with minimal, unsteady income.

RESTRUCTURING OF AGRICULTURE

If men cannot find work at local shape-ups, they can usually find at least temporary employment in the fields during the harvest season. Historically, farmers grew wheat, sugar, and cotton in South County's agricultural fields surrounded by verdant hills. After the Second World War, Watsonville became an agricultural hub, providing the system of coolers and distributors mainly for apples and later strawberries established by grower cooperatives. Jobs in agriculture were plentiful by the late 1960s as local growers produced vegetables such as broccoli, spinach, brussels sprouts, carrots, and cauliflower for freezing and apples for juice and cider; indeed, according to interviewees Watsonville was called La Cuidad Manzanera (Apple City). More recently, lettuce, straw-berries, and cane berries (e.g., raspberries and blackberries) are the largest crops and South County accounts for nearly half of the strawberry-growing acreage in California, which supplies approximately 85 percent of the nation. Often families would have some members working in the fields and some in the canneries. During the harvest season, one can see fields with farmworkers toiling under the hot sun.

   The canneries, packing sheds, and frozen-food plants provided highly valued union-ized jobs. According to life histories, Watsonville growers and processors, who wanted a more stable workforce, actively recruited women, both migrants and Mexican Ameri-cans, and even sent recruiters to South Texas in the 1960s. The International Brother-hood of Teamsters unionized the industry so wages were relatively good and the benefits package included medical insurance.[24] With the availability of unemployment benefits during the off-season, workers could provide support to their families even when they were not actually on the job, making these jobs particularly attractive to women who could combine seasonal cannery work with family responsibilities, so women returned to the canneries season after season. By 1982, there were 11,500 full-time food-process-ing jobs in California.[25] By the mid-1990s, according to Joe Fahey, then the Teamsters

Union International President of the Watsonville Local, there were 8,000 peak season food-processing jobs in Watsonville. The overwhelming majority of workers were Mexicanas and Mexican American women.[26] Until the mid-1990s, Watsonville called itself the "Frozen Food Capital of the World" and had eleven food-processing plants. At that time one out of four Watsonville residents were Teamsters and more Mexicans voted in union elections at the canneries, which required only union membership, than in city elections. Until 1989, the structural impediments of citywide elections made it virtually impossible to elect Latino city council members by the predominantly white electorate.[27]

As agricultural industries were expanding acreage and moving into new crops, the food-processing industry began restructuring globally and downsizing locally beginning in the 1980s.[28] The restructuring of agriculture began with the attempt to cut wages for unionized cannery workers, which provoked a strike in Watsonville in 1985–87. The strike was initiated by rank-and-file Mexican workers and then supported by the Teamsters. The conflict polarized Watsonville around race as managers, their staff and sympathizers, and the local power structure were offended by the militancy of the predominantly Mexican strikers. The strikers critiqued the racialization inherent in police enforcement and court rulings preventing the congregation of striking workers, in unsympathetic press coverage, and in the willingness of a local bank to bail out the cannery, which allowed management to hold out longer. Eventually the strike became a national cause célèbre as labor leaders and political organizers, including César Chávez, Dolores Huerta, and Jesse Jackson, came to support the strikers. The strike was remarkable since none of the strikers crossed the picket line and women in particular took on leadership roles.[29] Despite eventually having to accept pay cuts, the workers were able to retain their jobs and benefits. The success of the Watsonville cannery strike was based on solidarity between Mexican American and migrant workers from Mexico as well as other racial groups and the support of labor unions and community-based organizations.

Even before the strike, some firms such as Green Giant and Birds Eye as well as locally owned firms began opening plants in Mexico and began a series of cannery closures. From 1979 to 1991, 2,000 food-processing jobs were lost to outsourcing to Mexico or other lower-cost production centers in the United States.[30] Between 1990 and 2005 the food-processing sector dropped from 6,300 to 3,100 jobs.[31] With the phased closure of Birds Eye in 2006, another 800 jobs were lost.[32] By 2000, only one frozen-food plant remained and the firm employed about 400 workers.[33] This firm developed a specialized market niche, processing products such as peaches from throughout California or broccoli trucked in from Mexico for processing instead of only locally grown products. The marketing of Watsonville as the frozen-food capital of the world was abandoned.

When the factories began closing down, workers mobilized their political contacts and informal social networks to form El Comité de Trabajadores Desplazados (the Committee of Displaced Workers). During the NAFTA hearings in 1993, members of

El Comité joined the Teamsters' anti-NAFTA demonstrations around the state. The Teamsters also organized several trips to Irapuato, a regional food-processing center in Mexico, to meet with El Frente Auténtico del Trabajo, an opposition labor organization. The purpose of this meeting was to explore whether there was a basis for common struggle between food-processing workers in Irapuato and Watsonville, to engage in dialogue, and to impart the message that globalization under NAFTA could hurt workers in Irapuato as well. As Joe Fahey recalled, "We had a broader message, which was, these companies are not your salvation. They left us for a particular set of reasons and they will leave you for other reasons, but they will leave when they are good and ready to." While in Irapuato, the groups protested the low wages and poor working conditions in food-processing factories. Rosario Cabañas, who was a member of El Comité, noted: "We confronted that we needed to unite ourselves and struggle for justice, not only personally but locally and internationally. Because what affects them there [in Mexico] affects us here too." These workers took peripheral vision to a political stance, well aware that globalization affected working-class Mexicans on both sides of the border.

The effects of plant closures in Watsonville have been devastating. In 1994 after the first cannery layoffs, local unemployment rates were high at 16 percent, compared to 8 percent for the county as a whole, the second highest in the region from Oregon to southern Monterey County.[34] Food-processing workers either moved into the expanding service sector or left town.[35] The minimum hourly wage in California in 1994 was $4.25. For those displaced in 2006 from an average of $10 to $22 an hour they had to take minimum wage jobs at $6.75 an hour.[36] Clearly, displaced cannery workers experienced increased poverty and instability.

In this subregional economy where agriculture is so central, the unemployment rate in Watsonville consistently remains about twice the rate in the county and is higher than that for California and the United States, as seen in figure 10.1.[37] Long-term unemployment became increasingly common as the recession lingered. By July 2009, the number of nonfarm jobs was the same in California as in January 2000 when there were 3.3 million *fewer* working-age individuals.[38] By June 2009 when unemployment reached 9.7 percent nationally and 11.6 percent in California, unemployment reached 10.6 percent in Santa Cruz County, 8.8 percent in the City of Santa Cruz, and 22.2 percent in Watsonville.[39] These figures would increase through November 2009.

Displaced workers, who were often middle-aged, competed with younger, more recent migrants and bilingual Mexican Americans for the jobs available locally. Further, those who lost the unionized cannery jobs experienced a "mismatch in skills": their limited fluency in English, job experiences, and education levels meant that many could not make the transition to other jobs easily and many experienced long-term unemployment and stress, or retired early.[40] Most of the displaced Birds Eye workers surveyed wanted English instruction.[41] The workers who went through training programs after the plant closures (funded through the county) found no direct links to new jobs. Further, they could not afford to go to school full time since they had to find jobs to support

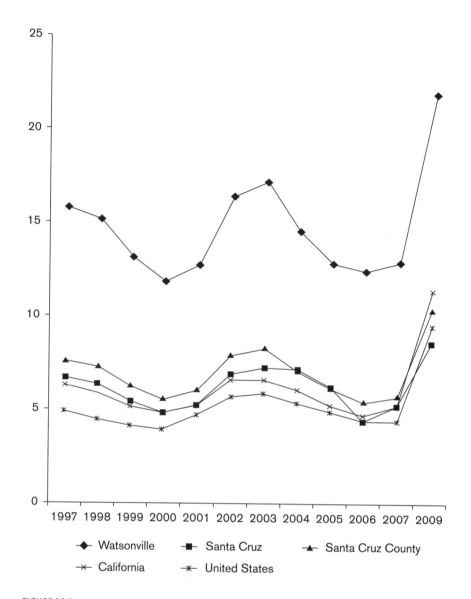

FIGURE 10.1

Comparative Unemployment Rates, 1997–2009

their families. Pedro Muñoz, for example, had worked in food processing for twenty-four years after share-cropping strawberries so he and his wife could purchase a house for their eight children. When the cannery laid off most of the workforce, Pedro retired and received a modest pension. He took bilingual training for mechanics but his English was not good enough so he did not finish the entire course. Pedro then began working part time at a lower pay scale, sorting at the local recycling center. He and his wife struggled to make payments for their mortgage and for a loan taken out after a 1989 earthquake damaged their home. Gonzalo Rivas also experienced a significant drop in income after the Green Giant plant closed. He found employment at another cannery, but it was only part time with no fixed hours: "One never knows. Sometimes it can be many hours and sometimes just a few." He gave me a copy of his Social Security Administration report that documented his wages dropped to those of his wife, Maria, who also worked part time at the cannery (see figure 10.2). Gonzalo seemed sad as he reflected on his options: "Life is hard. I want to return to Mexico but I can't because now that both my kids are in high school, I have to be here; they are depending on me for another four or five years."

Displaced workers were well aware that migrants from Mexico make it difficult to find noncannery jobs. Lucio, who had migrated at fifteen, was forceful in comparing job prospects in California and Mexico: "There should be good jobs in Mexico so that so many Mexicans would not come here. And if the good jobs did not go to Mexico they wouldn't leave us here unemployed." Knowing that she and her spouse had close relatives living in Mexico, Rosario had considered then discarded the possibility of moving back. With five children, some of whom were teenagers and one entering college, it would be difficult to move the family. She also had a binational view on what should be done: "If companies go there [Mexico] they should not take all their production because we need jobs here too. And they should pay well." She concluded, "I think the government should bring about more equality, both in Mexico and here [in the United States]." Pedro, who was offered a job in a new factory in Mexico, considered his options on either side of the border: "I told my supervisor, 'Well, if I go to Mexico to work will you give me a job?' And he said, 'Yes, but we are going to pay you what they pay over there.' I told him, 'No thanks, I'm not going; I'll stay here.' With that money over there, well, I'm not going to do anything because it's so little. At least here it is possible to gain money by doing other things. Anyway, my family is already situated here." Those who had worked in canneries usually had positive memories of unionized jobs with benefits, relatively higher wages compared to their current jobs, as well as a sense of camaraderie with fellow workers. Perhaps more than many others, displaced cannery workers evaluated their work options in relation to possibilities in Mexico.

Those who were forced to make the transition to other jobs had a difficult time. Lucio, for example, was job hunting and taking classes in construction along with English classes: "I spent about six months looking for a job, anything." He attempted to return to farm work and found that he just could not take the strain on his thirty-eight-year old body so he signed on as a union organizer. The couple's five children were all born in Watsonville. His wife, Rosario, admitted, "When we worked at Green Giant we never thought that we would lose our job. . . . Afterwards, there were days when we didn't have milk and it tore at my soul to tell my children when we had never lacked food. . . . And we didn't qualify for welfare because we were receiving unemployment benefits and had a relatively new car. That was a very difficult crisis." With her English skills, Gloria Betancourt, a former strike leader during the fifteen-month cannery strike of 1985–87, was able to land a job as a retail clerk at much lower wages.[42]

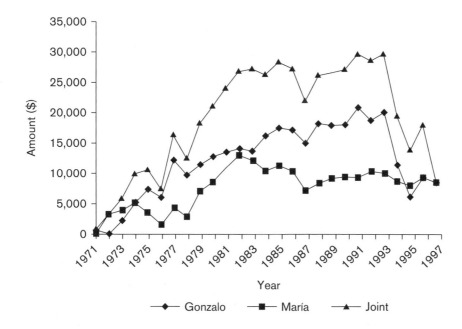

FIGURE 10.2

Wage History for Gonzalo Rivas and María Rivas, 1971–97

After the cannery closures, the City of Watsonville began a redevelopment program that attracted large retail outlets, which hired bilingual workers as clerks but few displaced cannery workers except as janitors or laborers. Watsonville was declared an "enterprise zone" by the state, which provides tax breaks for companies that move to the city or hire laid-off employees. A local retail development was supposed to provide opportunities for starting small businesses to displaced cannery workers, but according to an interview with one manager, Malena Bueno, she was the only displaced cannery worker when the development opened. Watsonville has embarked upon a development strategy based on attracting large stores in an attempt to increase sales taxes and stop the leakage of about $150 million in retail sales to surrounding areas. The projected job growth is in food services, retail sales, hospitality, the general service industry, and accounting. All these jobs require educational levels and bilingual skills that many cannery workers did not have.

In South County, agribusiness continues to be a major employer despite the contraction in food processing. The continuing restructuring of agriculture means that other crops are now prominent. The total production value of crops in Santa Cruz County increased from $289 million in 1997 to $414 million in 2006 with significant growth in certain crops as seen in table 10.1. Yet despite the growth in agricultural production, intensification of the labor process by mechanization meant total employment in Santa Cruz County agriculture dropped 27 percent between 1998 and 2007.[43]

TABLE 10.1   Production Value of Top Agricultural Crops,
Santa Cruz County, 1998–2007 (in Millions of Dollars)

Crops	1998	2007	% Increase
Strawberries	$72	$197	174
Raspberries	$24	$71	196
Landscape Plants	$14	$34	143

Source: Applied Survey Research 2008, 25.

Those who found jobs in agriculture became ensconced in the increasingly longer work season that included long-term workers and temporary migrants who work for the season.[44] Strawberry production has a relatively long season that requires higher maintenance than other crops, providing work in preparing the fields (see Table 10.1), planting, weeding, and during the harvest season, picking, recording the amount picked, loading, and truck driving. The long season also exposes workers to the pesticides used on strawberries.[45] Those who have jobs as quality inspectors, supervisors, or directors of harvest or production often settle permanently and there is some socioeconomic mobility by local farmworkers. All of these work possibilities contribute to workers' longer duration in the region and affect daily life.[46] During the winter months—normally November through February— seasonal workers migrate to other regions in search of work or they return to Mexico to celebrate the Christmas holidays with their families.

Seasonal unemployment contributes to poverty and is very hard on workers and their families. Rosario recalled when she and her spouse were both working as farmworkers: "It was really hard because we both worked in the fields and during the winter we didn't have anything. Everything we earned went for the rent and food for our kids. That was a very difficult time for us."

Strawberries require relatively little capital to start a commercial enterprise and they produce higher yields on fewer acres than most crops. Thus a sizable number of former farmworkers and cannery workers have been able to become part of a force of small growers by leasing or sharecropping the land. Lucio worked as a sharecropper in the late 1970s and found it extremely difficult. "I did it only for a season because, well, it doesn't allow you to get ahead because the owner takes all the profits. And you are left paying unemployment, with huge bills, and you have to pay for the pesticides, a bunch of things and it doesn't work out. So I left and went to work in the cannery." Pedro and his wife had worked for many years in the 1970s for entire weeks with no days off, which caused family tensions so they stopped sharecropping. Others had better luck and especially the sharecroppers can tap their own families for labor, cutting costs. By 1997, there were five hundred Latino strawberry growers in the Pájaro Valley and they were about a third of the operators in Santa Cruz County.[47] The sizeable number of Latino growers led a local journalist to observe: "In Watsonville, perhaps more than anywhere else in the state, the Latino growers' success is historically significant. Latino pickers, who toil long hours for low wages, have been the backbone to the strawberry industry for decades."[48]

Some of these Latino growers, especially those running the smaller farms, exploit migrant workers. For example, there are reports that one strawberry farmer had his workers living in caves and he calls Immigration and Customs Enforcement (ICE) when he owes the workers a lot of money.[49]Yet small growers also may include positive relations: "Unlike most of California's agriculture industry, strawberry production is still dominated by local farmers managing small landholdings . . . [which] engenders an unusually high level of contact between owners and pickers."[50] This contact, which often includes other social ties such as kinship or mutual communities of origin, facilitates communication between workers and employers and the development of familiarity and trust.[51] Strawberry workers are often allowed to bring boxes of strawberries home or to go pick them on weekends, as I witnessed firsthand, which also contributes to a sense of belonging to the firm.

One of the most well-known and liked employers was Señor Navarro. Prior to his death in 1997, Navarro was known as a compatriot who would provide work to those from his village of origin in San Pedro Tesitán in Jalisco. He was appreciated for his custom of loaning money, up to $500, to newly arrived migrants from San Pedro Tesitán who were in dire circumstances. Señor Navarro had sponsored the annual barbecue in Watsonville for residents from San Pedro Tesitán, as well as quinceañeras (coming-of-age-ceremonies for young women when they turn fifteen). Navarro was also seen as a kindly employer, someone who does not yell at his workers. Israel Mata said, "I think that here in Watsonville there is no other boss like him. He is a person who, I don't know how to say this, he shares everything." This patron-client relationship, rooted in kinship networks and a community of origin, established expectations for reciprocity between workers and growers.

Some believe that these social relations undercut the efforts by the United Farm Workers Union (UFW) to unionize strawberry workers in a one-million-dollar campaign funded by the AFL-CIO. Farmworker advocates, including the UFW, have waged a battle for unionization of the predominantly Latino workers. The UFW staged a demonstration in 1997 that attracted between 15,000 and 20,000 supporters, mostly from out of town, and national political luminaries like Jesse Jackson and Dolores Huerta.[52] Growers fought back with accusations and lawsuits, and 3,000 to 4,000 local strawberry workers marched against the UFW.[53] According to the workers I interviewed, the anti-UFW organizing occurred with the aid of Latino growers, some of whom used their kin and village networks to recruit seasonal workers from Mexico, who were then reluctant to join an organization of "outsiders."

Regarding the prospect of a unionizing drive by the UFW in 1997, for example, José Castañeda opined: "I think that it will be very hard to have a union there with Navarro because he never has treated his people badly. His supervisors have never treated people badly. Everything was well organized. He has a good way of managing, so much so that all the Navarro workers care for him very much." Apparently Navarro even helped some of his workers secure their permanent residence through the Special Agricultural Workers program, traveling back to San Pedro Tesitán to deliver letters to migrants stranded there so they could arrange their paperwork. Thus because of his largess and ties to so many Watsonville residents, Navarro's death in 1997 was mourned in a large community event. Meanwhile, unionized farmworkers are very much in the minority—the UFW won a contract at Coastal Berry in 2003 and renegotiated it in 2006 and with Swanton Berries in 2008.[54] Gilbert Mireles suggests that the high social solidarity between Mexican growers and workers (many of whom were ambivalent toward the UFW), intra-ethnic differences between Chicano UFW organizers (some of whom did not speak Spanish well) and Mexican migrant workers, and the hierarchical UFW's organizational culture and structure contributed to the failure of the UFW campaign and the popularity of the anti-UFW Comité.[55] Lucio, who worked temporarily as a UFW organizer, also believed that the union paid more attention to organizing than to providing services to union members, a view shared by many.[56] Some scholars believe that structural differences between Mexican Americans and migrants are impeding unionization. For migrants, there was the need to generate dollars to send home, which made labor struggles less urgent, and migrant workers are often politically vulnerable if they are unauthorized.[57]

It is estimated that one million undocumented workers make up about 90 percent of the agricultural laborers in California's 76,500 farms and over 90 percent are Mexican, predominantly male; these findings are replicated in a local survey with 688 farmworkers and 81 farmworker employees.[58] Increasingly, more farmworkers in this region are indigenous; 17 percent indicated on my survey, a significant increase from the mid-1990s when local scholar-activist Gaspar Rivera estimated there were about thirty indigenous families in all Santa Cruz County. Some predict that indigenous migrants will make up 20 percent of California's farmworkers by 2010.[59]

With the decline of membership in the UFW, agricultural wages for some jobs remain low. In 1993, a strawberry picker earned $3.70 an hour plus 60–65 cents per box. By picking between twenty-five and twenty-six boxes a day (considered to be a slow pace), one earned about $200 a week. In 2006, farmworkers who participated in my survey indicated they made piece rates starting at $2.25 an hour plus 85 cents per box. Their average weekly wages of $308 shows how fast they worked. Sixty-one percent of survey respondents worked seasonally, so like other farmworkers they must get by on unemployment insurance or move in search of other jobs.[60] With these types of wages, farmworkers, not surprisingly, have very low annual salaries. Of course, most of them did not work the entire year as farmworkers. In their survey of 971 farmworkers, Villarejo and his colleagues found that the median annual earnings from all sources were between $7,500 and $9,999, placing the workers well below the federal poverty level.[61]

Within farm work there is a hierarchy of jobs from lettuce pickers, who are paid the highest wages, to those who pick apples, to the lowest-paid strawberry workers. Some farmworkers are able to work on a part-time basis. Israel Mata, for example, continued to work in the fields despite his age (fifty-eight) and his work-related permanent injury. On good weeks he made about $200. Rosario Lemus (who was sixty-three when I interviewed her) and her spouse worked part time in the fields picking apples to supplement her Social Security stipend and pension from her job after thirty years at the cannery. Farm work is often a point of entry for the newly arrived or undocumented or it is a job some turn to when there are few other options.

In addition to low wages and health risks, the threat of being detained by the ICE (formerly the Immigration and Naturalization Service) while working in the fields is ever present. Lucio worked picking strawberries beginning in 1971 and he recalled his struggle with illegality and exploitation in the fields: "The INS would come every once in a while. And you have to struggle with the work, the pain of working and making sure that your boxes [of strawberries] are well arranged. The whole time you are worried that the INS might get you. It was tough." Ester Moreno, who was undocumented at the time, recalled a workplace raid that had frightened her: "I told my sister-in-law, 'I have to learn to pick.' My husband gave me permission to go to work with his sister so I went to harvest. A week later after we were working, someone made a report and *la migra* arrived at the field. My sister-in-law told me, 'Don't you move from here. Keep working. If they come to ask questions, I'll go with you so you won't be alone.' But everyone ran; only those with papers remained. There were only four of us left and they [*la migra*] didn't question us. My husband got scared and he wouldn't let me return to work." Not surprisingly, workers were bitter when they believed their own employers had called *la migra*. One man said: "It seems like they are two-faced because it is in their interest that we are here. I think that we are something they [employers] want but that they don't want to treat us like they should."

In 2007, growers claimed there were labor shortages and they supported a congressional bill that would allow an undocumented worker with 150 days of work over the past two years to become a temporary legal resident with a "blue card" that would replace the permanent resident card, or green card.[62] By May 2008 the Senate Appropriations Committee approved the Agjobs legislation, which was negotiated with growers and farmworkers and supported by the American Farm Bureau, the United Farm Workers, and other organizations across the nation.[63] Whether there were actual shortages is unclear since locally the labor shape-ups indicated there was a pool of workers looking for jobs although they were probably unauthorized. Employers are articulating that they feel besieged, circumstances that could be alleviated if policies authorized more migrants to work in the United States.

Clearly, the displacement of unionized cannery workers, the failure to unionize farmworkers, and the presence of so many undocumented workers in agriculture contribute to the low wages and the formation of the working poor in the local agricultural sector.

Located between San Francisco and Los Angeles, with a spectacular coastline, accessible beaches with strong surf, abutting redwood-forested mountains and open space protected by a local ordinance, Santa Cruz County has long been an important area for recreation, vacation, and retirement. The tourist infrastructure—hotels, the over one-hundred-year-old Boardwalk and roller coaster, and beachside cottages—is all designed for luring visitors. Tourism continues to be a major source of revenue for Santa Cruz. Even the nightlife is interesting, with first-rate musicians who perform locally in between gigs in the big cities. As with other coastal cities in the state, local developers continue to advertise Santa Cruz County as a paradise—a place to have fun, retire, or raise a family. When the University of California opened in 1965, Santa Cruz County was predominantly white, a sleepy retirement and agricultural region, with conservatives at the helm.[64] The pressing political issues centered on zoning and congestion in neighborhoods near the beaches and there was a decidedly pro-growth sentiment in the political arena.

Since then, the City of Santa Cruz (the county seat) became known for its alternative lifestyle, which is evident by its downtown stores that sell "world" trinkets; by its population of local musicians, hippies, "Deadheads," and costumed street people; and by several large farmers' markets and spontaneous drummers' circles that form at sundown along the beaches. A local bookstore owner started a successful campaign called "Keep Santa Cruz Weird," which activists converted to "Keep Santa Cruz Queer," proudly displayed on bumper stickers and in local parlance. Known as "Surf City" since Hawaiian royalty introduced surfing there in 1885, Santa Cruz attracts major surf tournaments and regional day-trippers who come to enjoy the beach and the Boardwalk with its rides, games, and fast food.[65] Activists consistently elect empathetic City Council members in Santa Cruz and Watsonville and on the County Board of Supervisors, as evident in the services the city provides to the homeless.

Tourist businesses—restaurants, hotels, bike or surfboard rentals, and so forth—have a seasonal spike in employment during holidays and the summers. Yet, overall, employment related to tourism decreased by 6 percent between 1998 and 2007.[66] Businesses based on tourism typically employ Mexican migrants at the bottom of the job ladder as dishwashers, busboys, janitors, and gardeners for men, and housekeepers and janitors for women, while waiters and managers in the big hotels or restaurants are usually white men or women. There is also a slight mismatch between work experience by migrants and the jobs they take in Santa Cruz County. According to the Mexican Consulate, in the region in which Santa Cruz County is located, 82 percent of migrants had been agricultural workers in Mexico yet 95 percent of these former campesinos were working in service occupations locally.[67] There is anecdotal evidence from my students and interviewees that in some restaurants and nightclubs that cater to tourists, those who are blond and blue-eyed, that is, those who look like stereotypical "beach bunnies" or "surfers," are hired first as waiters and waitresses. Celia Tejada remarked, "There are a lot of women that can't get a job. If you're not pretty or [do not] have a good shape you can't find a job here."

Working in a restaurant can be very difficult work. Besides the long hours, low pay, and physical exertion of standing all day, sometimes workers have to deal with English-speaking customers who are openly rude. Ana Acuña, who had a degree in accounting from Mexico, began working at a fast-food chain after she overstayed her visa. She found adjusting to the work very frustrating. She recalled one day in particular when a customer shouted at her and made racist comments; "I thought, 'I cannot believe that this is happening to me.'" She tried to complain to her manager who was not sympathetic: "He said, 'You have to stand there [and take it] or else the door is wide open.'" One employer provides alcohol to his employees, presumably because it gets hot inside the kitchen, which increases the risk of occupational injuries and also makes workers more vulnerable to alcoholism. Joel García, who worked as a cook's helper and had an employer who supplied beer while he worked, explained, "Sometimes when I leave work late at night I feel a little dizzy, well, tipsy. When you're working fast you don't notice how much you drink until you leave." One male restaurant worker was bitter over the low wages for busboys: "You go to the north and work a shitload [un chingo] to earn very little."

Women who worked in local motels often had additional chores added on, for example, having to clean the manager's apartment in addition to the hotel rooms. Melissa was dismissed after she informed her manager that she would no longer make beds since it hurt her back. The manager sent her away with a check of $6.00, informing her it was because she was undocumented: "He told me I couldn't complain or he would call la migra."

In my neighborhood, service work by migrants is widespread; virtually all crews performing house cleaning, yard care, or home maintenance have Latino workers and in conversations one can glean information on their states of origin. Once I advised some tree trimmers that their employer was supposed to provide goggles to protect their eyes from flying debris but they did not feel comfortable requesting them. Often these workers are overly deferential, suggesting their legal vulnerability—work crews will ask permission to sit on the grass to eat their lunches, for example, and if the owner is not there, they will sit on the curb. Individual house cleaners or gardeners will advertise their services through flyers left in driveways or on doors. One Latina left a photocopy of her work authorization card with her flyer advertising house-cleaning services at my house, presumably to dispel any concerns that she is undocumented.

Others work taking care of children, with licenses in their own homes or in day-care centers. Elder care was another source of employment, although the pay was very low with long hours. Angélica, for example, left a nursing home after one year because they expected thirteen-hour shifts (6 a.m. to 7 p.m.), gave employees only one hour off during the entire day, and gave one day off a month. These labor violations went unreported because most of the employees were undocumented. Service sector employees typically receive few benefits and must endure the social affronts or paternalism of those with higher status.[68]

The working conditions that many recent Mexican migrants must endure are exploitative, demeaning, and occasionally truly traumatic. Farm work is notoriously dangerous, and workers typically are not offered health insurance unless unionized.[69] Seventeen percent of those surveyed by the Mexican Consulate indicated that they had been injured on the job. Most of them said that the lack of safety training contributed to their injuries. Only 38 percent had received safety training.[70] Perhaps the most poignant story of workplace injuries was that of Juan Gómez. His job was to tar roofs and he received minimal safety training. One summer day he had a horrible accident. The container of hot tar spilled and as he tried to prevent it from tipping over he fell into it, severely burning his hands: "I was swimming in it, trying to get out." Three months after an operation his doctor claimed he was ready to return to work, despite two tendons that were fused, which limited his ability to use the hand. He seemed traumatized and depressed over his decreased income and few options. Juan did not know the source of his disability checks, why he was seeing a psychologist, and the long-term effects, saying, "That is what makes me nervous, because I don't know anything. Now they tell me, 'You have an appointment tomorrow,' and in a little while, I forget. I don't know anymore, after a while." Like so many migrant workers, those who have occupational injuries often are unaware of possible legal remedies.

MIGRANTS AND MEXICAN AMERICANS

I always asked research participants if they had experienced any form of prejudice or discrimination and occasionally some individuals did not. However, the overwhelming majority had, either in finding housing or on the job. Their descriptions of racialization were quite graphic. Ana had a supervisor who was outright racist and exacerbated her job dissatisfaction: "She is always saying that we Latinos are nothing but trash." However, despite discrimination or maltreatment based on undocumented status or gender, the research subjects, particularly migrants, perceive these as forms of racialization. This finding counters the notion that "race and racism were of far more concern among U.S.-born Latinos than among recent arrivals, reminding us that immigration and length of stay in the United States are central variables affecting an individual's experience, awareness, or expression of U.S. race and racism."[71] On the contrary, migrants voiced their critiques of racialization processes and racism as well. Mexican Americans were also keenly aware of the liabilities related to class and race, as Larry Gonzales pointed out in response to my question about discrimination: "That's a really complicated question because I don't think I have ever been told to my face anything derogatory but just in subtle ways: Like when I first moved here, Santa Cruz was more white than it is now. When you go into a store and you buy something the reaction of people if you're using credit cards then they ask you for lot of IDs but yet the previous customer who is white isn't asked. And I remember once at a cocktail party this woman asked me where I lived and [after] I told her she says in a real condescending way, 'But I thought just rich people

lived there.' So I told her 'That's why I live there' [we laughed], even though I was poor."
Mirella Fernández also felt her supervisor was subtle by picking on the quality of her
work even though her work was praised by those above the supervisor.

In addition to racial prejudice or discriminatory treatment by employers who were
predominantly though not exclusively white, there was sometimes also marked tension
between migrants and Mexican Americans on the job. In a national survey, 50 percent
of Latinos believe that the growing number of undocumented migrants has had a positive impact on Latinos living in the United States. Only 20 percent believe unauthorized
migrants have had a negative impact, and the rest either say there has been no impact
or they don't have an opinion.[72]

Even though a minority perceives tensions between migrants and Mexican Americans, participants in my study were vocal about their meanings. According to María
Pérez, these tensions centered on language use and her negative perception about Mexican Americans: "There's tensions with Chicanas, a lot, around their lack of self-esteem
and feeling threatened by your intelligence. Language has a lot to do with it because
they feel threatened that I speak so beautiful of a Spanish. Besides I'm a poet and I have
been a public speaker and I have been so many things in my life. I have a leadership
role so that's one of the dynamics in their subconscious and I have faced that kind of
discrimination." María also had a critique of Mexican American women in workplaces
that have a largely migrant clientele as she illustrates in the following dialogue:

MARÍA: I don't think that Chicanas can try to provide cultural sensitive [sic]
         services to Mexicanas; I'm sorry [but] you can't.
PZ: So, do you think Chicanas can provide culturally sensitive services to
         Chicanas?
MARÍA: To Chicanas but not to Mexicanas.
PZ: Do you think that culturally sensitive services for Mexicanas should be
         provided by Mexicanas?
MARÍA: [she nodded]: By Mexicanas.
PZ: So there is such a huge gulf between Mexicanas and Chicanas that it's
         almost like a different culture?
MARÍA: [nodding]: There are huge differences.

In response to my question, "Have you ever experienced discrimination or prejudice?" Frida, María's partner at the time, replied: "For my accent. Many times they
would tell me that they don't understand me and once my evaluation said I should try
and not speak Spanish at work. And I was hired to be a bilingual staff person! So I kept
speaking Spanish at work. . . . I've also felt homophobia. . . . For me, it was the Chicanas
who discriminated more. They seemed threatened by someone at their same intellectual level who was out of the closet." In the moral economy of authentic Mexicanness

related to facility in Spanish and knowledge of Mexican culture, Mexican Americans come up short.

By the same token, some Mexican Americans felt as if migrants looked down on them. One Mexican American woman said, "The only discrimination I've ever had has been from Mexicans. They make fun of my accent when I try to say something in Spanish and they call me *pocha* [figuratively inauthentic]. They shouldn't be so rude." In response to a question about whether she had ever experienced discrimination, Dirana Lazer said no, then reconsidered and told a story about her treatment in Mexico while traveling and camping in a Volkswagen bus: "I didn't get treated very nicely at all. When we got to downtown Puerto Vallarta we went for groceries and we hadn't cleaned up. We were treated rudely and looked at in a funny way and I felt badly. . . . And I got called a *pocha* while I was there. I've been called that all my life by my own family members but still I felt bad." Mexican Americans believed their differences from Mexicans were often obvious and painful.

Migrants could be just as insensitive to the plight of their fellow migrants, voicing criticisms of their antisocial behavior. Isabella, for example, had harsh words about women who received welfare: "I know women who only have children so they can get welfare and they don't work anymore. And they are the ones who will feel it if they return to Mexico because here they are like a fat pig." Even though she spoke very little English when she arrived in Watsonville, Celia Tejada referred to migrants from Mexico as "nationals" with some tinge of deprecation. Another woman believed that in the Beach Flats neighborhood, Salvadorans received advantages in finding rentals or jobs over Mexicans.

The fault lines between Mexican migrants and Mexican Americans were mitigated by several structural similarities. A number of Mexican Americans recalled being placed in noncollege preparation courses, for example, primarily because of their Spanish surname, mobility as farmworkers, or teachers' expectations they would not do well. Paul Weller, for example, a native English speaker who was half white with very fair complexion and hair, said, "I was called in for an English-language exam by the ESL [English as a Second Language] director who said, 'Oh, we were reviewing your file. We found out you're Mexican and we just want to make sure you speak English properly.' [Chuckles.] It was amusing at the time but ultimately, looking back, it was something that indicated I had a certain kind of outsider status to the whole system." Further, several Mexican Americans began their work histories in the fields or sweatshops where their fellow workers were migrants from Latin America and they experienced firsthand the dangerous, distasteful, exploitative jobs. This often engendered a sense of solidarity between migrants and Mexican Americans. Paul's first job, for example, was performing manual labor in a factory during summers, and he recalled, "It was a horrible experience. The health conditions were, of course, deplorable." Danny Ramírez recalled his childhood in South County: "I've worked in the fields; I worked in construction. And I didn't like it. I felt bad for the Mexican [migrant] kids that couldn't go to school. They were really smart. They were my friends too."

Mexican Americans also compared work options in Mexico in relation to local jobs. One of the most demoralizing processes is when migrants cannot use their advanced degrees or technical training for jobs in the United States. Celia reflected on the vulnerability of migrants from Mexico: "I know people right now that have a diploma, they have qualifications, and they are working here in the strawberries. For instance, the guys that own that little restaurant [she names it]? They are both doctors. He's a heart doctor and his partner is a heart surgeon and look at what they are doing right here, because they can't get a good job over there [in Mexico] with insurance and social security. It's just one example. Of course, it's better than in Mexico." From her point of view, their struggles to develop their human capital had no payoffs in the United States.

Enrico Marcelli and Wayne Cornelius demonstrate that more recent cohorts of migrants are different than previous ones, which often came from rural areas in west-central Mexico. In the post-IRCA era, migrants from Mexico are younger with higher educational levels, and increasingly they are likely to originate in southern Mexico and the Mexico City metropolitan area or other urban areas in Mexico.[73] However, higher education does not always lead to better jobs in the United States. Regardless of their work experiences in Mexico, every one of the migrant research participants who had advanced degrees began their work histories in the United States at the bottom of the labor market, as farmworkers, flyer distributors, hotel cleaners, or day laborers. María, who had a master's degree from a Mexico City university, began her work trajectory in Watsonville as a farmworker. Iliana had four years of training in accounting yet she worked as a dishwasher because she did not speak English. Ana, who also had a degree in accounting, worked at an electronics factory and was frustrated with her few options: "Here they don't accept the degree for which one has studied. And if one is not documented they won't admit you to college. Then you are obliged to accept jobs that are below that of a professional." However, since her job had medical insurance, she put up with this treatment: "But I tell you, the first opportunity I get where I find work that does not ask for my legal status, I will leave." Given that IRCA requires all employers to ask new employees for documentation such as a Social Security card, the only employers who would not ask for her legal status would be in the informal economy. After working their way up, the highly educated or professionals still find themselves working at jobs for which they are overqualified.

The Mexican Americans I interviewed were in similar straits. Every one of the eleven had completed high school and two had additional vocational training while six had some college education. They too were working in jobs that paid low wages, placing them among the working poor, or they were unemployed.

Finally, I would be remiss if I did not point out the social affiliations between migrants and Mexican Americans. Mexicans in this county belong to a wide variety of organizations, including El Comité; Horizontes, a prevention-based support and social group for Spanish-speaking men who have sex with men; an organization that set up a community garden in the Beach Flats; and hometown associations that collect funds to develop projects in Mexico. Migrants and Mexican Americans volunteer at elementary schools to provide unpaid bilingual assistance to teachers, as unpaid shop stewards at the canneries, and within a number of community-based organizations. Some men are fervent sports participants, spending their evenings and weekends on the soccer fields or taking their children to play on local soccer teams. Some of these volunteers seek to work mainly with migrants; others such as El Comité include participants based on common class interests regardless of national or ethnic origins. A mix of Latino migrants, Mexican Americans, whites, and an African American worked on Binational Health Week. Whether they work on behalf of displaced workers, schools, health, recreation, or hometowns, migrant workers labor to create their lives among obstacles, often in collaboration with Mexican Americans and others.

CONCLUSION

As we have seen, migrants are segregated in low-wage jobs and subject to exploitation and discrimination, including by Mexican Americans and fellow migrants, and they experience occupational hazards or racial tensions. In South County, restructuring of agriculture led to a series of plant closures that displaced the predominantly Mexican workforce and expanded fresh production. Increased undocumented migration from Mexico in the wake of immigration reforms led to labor subcontracting. In agriculture, employers rely on Mexican migrant labor by using contractors to verify the documentation of farmworkers, creating a labor niche for low-wage migrant labor even as agriculture provides some avenues for stable jobs among the working poor. In North County, the predominantly tourism-based economy provides service sector and retail jobs subject to seasonal downturns. In both locations, the informal labor market, where the undocumented generate income outside of formal employment, expands during economic downturns as workers strategize to generate income through day labor or small-scale vending, often within their own neighborhoods, yet they earn lower pay, have no benefits, and have more frequent periods of unemployment.

Christian Zlolniski characterizes migrant workers, especially the unauthorized, as constituting a subproletarian class since they are denied most of the rights that the rest of the working population takes for granted. His conclusions apply equally to Santa Cruz County: "Located at the bottom of the hierarchy of the region's working-class, subproletarian immigrants often receive casual rather than protected wages, do not benefit from a stable contractual relationship with employers, receive few if any working benefits, have limited access to state and welfare benefits, and are denied most of the political rights of legal citizens."[74]

By living in a region with one of the highest costs of renting or purchasing a house in the country, Santa Cruz County workers struggle to make ends meet. In this regard migrants and Mexican Americans alike pursue options by leaving work sites in search of better jobs and by maximizing their pay and benefits in relation to their needs for day care, transportation, a better work climate, or a sense of dignity. Occasionally they find common cause against employers who take advantage or out of sympathy for those whose plight is most dire. Yet the tensions between Mexican Americans and migrants at work can be high as they assert particular notions of cultural authenticity. Members of each group had very unkind things to say about one another as they judged each other for improper language use and indicated clear social distance from each other.

For migrants, the "journey of the self" continues as they negotiate workplaces gendered differently than in Mexico and fulfill expectations about masculinity or femininity by providing for their families. Opportunities for work, possible benefits, or career prospects in the United States are carefully weighed in relation to those left behind or waiting if they were to return to Mexico. And even Mexican Americans reflect on local work options in relation to those in Mexico.

NOTES

1. Sassen 1991.

2. Zlolniski (2005) is specifying how the domestic social structures of accumulation (Cleaver 1979) take into account the "Latinization" of labor pools.

3. Massey, Durand, and Malone 2002, 123. For example, the U.S. Department of Labor reached a $1.9 million settlement with Global Building Services, a contractor for the Target Corporation, after finding the firm had not paid overtime to hundreds of migrant janitors who often worked seven nights a week cleaning Target stores. Some of the workers had been paid in cash without having payroll taxes or workers' compensation deducted from their pay, and workers had no vacation time despite years on the job (Greenhouse 2004, A14).

4. In contrast, refugees may work and are eligible for federally funded job training and placement assistance, while asylum seekers cannot legally work for at least six months (longer if the government has detained them) and must then apply to the government for permission (Luibhéid 2005, xxvi).

5. Bernhardt, Milkman, Theordore, Heckathorn, Auer, DeFilippis, González, Narro, Perelshteyn, Poison, and Spiller 2009; Brown 2002.

6. Massey, Durand, and Malone 2002, 125.

7. In 2002, the Social Security Administration had nine million W-2 forms with incorrect Social Security numbers, accounting for $56 billion in earnings or about 1.5 percent of total reported wages. An audit found that 17 percent of businesses with inaccurate W-2 forms were restaurants, 10 percent were construction companies, and 7 percent were farm operations, exactly the types of employers offering jobs that migrants are likely to take (Porter 2005).

8. De Genova and Ramos-Zayas 2003, 61. Compared to other ethno-racial groups, Latino men have had the highest labor force participation rates between 1940 and 2000 (Hayes-Bautista 2004).

9. Barrera 1979; de Genova 2005; Zavella 1987; Zlolniski 2005.

10. Catanzarite 2000. According to the Pew Hispanic Center, migrants are 36 percent of insulation workers, 29 percent of miscellaneous agricultural workers, 29 percent of roofers; 28 percent of drywall and ceiling tile installers; 27 percent of construction helpers; 27

percent of poultry and fish processing workers; 26 percent of pressers of textile, garment, and related materials; 25 percent of grounds maintenance workers; 25 percent of construction laborers; and 25 percent of brick masons, block masons, and stonemasons (Pear 2007a). Migrants from Latin America overwhelmingly perform farm labor in California (Griffith, Kissam, Camposeco, García, Pfeffer, Runsten, and Valdés Pizzini 1995, 243).

11. de Genova 2002, 427.

12. For analyses of occupational segregation by race and gender in the labor market, see Catanzarite 2000; Lamphere, Zavella, Gonzales, and Evans 1993; V. Ruiz 1987a, 1987b; Segura 1989, 1992; Zavella 1987; and Zlolniski 2005.

13. Parreñas 2001, 61.

14. Ibarra 2000, 2002, 2003a, 2003b.

15. The scholarship illustrates the dynamics of exploitation as well as how migrant women disrupt hegemonic gendered and racialized attempts at labor flexibility in which women organize and network with one another as well as with community-based organizations, professionalize the work, and demand higher wages. See Coyle, Hershatter, and Honig 1984; Cranford 2007; Hondagneu-Sotelo 1994, 2001; Parreñas 2001; Romero 1992; V. Ruiz 1987a; Salzinger 1991; Soldatenko 2000; and Zavella 1987, 1988.

16. W. Flores 1997; Friaz 2000; Lamphere and Zavella 1997; and Zavella 1987, 1988.

17. Lamphere 1987; Stephen 2005; Zavella 1987.

18. Torres Sarmiento 2002, 147.

19. N. Bernstein 2005.

20. See the documentary film *Farmingville* (2004), directed by Carlos Sandoval and Catherine Tambini, which covered the hate-based attempted murder of two Mexican day laborers and antimigrant organizing that took place in a town on Long Island.

21. Abel Valenzuela (2003; 2006; 2009) has conducted research on day labor throughout the United States and in Japan. Drawing on a survey and qualitative research, he suggests that even though day labor is unregulated, unstable, and prone to workplace abuses, day laborers' development of social networks allows a sizable number to negotiate fair wages with their employers. According to Valenzuela, Kawachi, and Marr (2002), day labor also includes work contracted through temporary staffing agencies.

22. Abram 2006.

23. For research on the occupational health risks faced by migrants, see Brown 2002; X. Castañeda 2007.

24. In the 1970s, the Teamsters and the United Farm Workers Union signed an agreement specifying the Teamsters would have jurisdiction over canneries and packing sheds and the United Farm Workers Union would cover farmworkers (Zavella 1987, 64–67).

25. Segal 1988, 120.

26. Bardacke 1987. This race and gender occupational structure in food-processing plants replicates what I found in the late 1970s in the Santa Clara Valley: predominantly Mexican women (Zavella 1987).

27. Takash 1990.

28. Borrego 2000; Zavella 2002.

29. Bardacke 1987; Flores 1997. This strike was immortalized in the award-winning documentary *Watsonville on Strike*, directed by Jon Silver.

30. Barnett 1996a; Beebe 1993; Hohmann 2006a, 2006b. Wrigley's, the gum maker, also shut down in 1997, laying off 170 employees.

31. Interview with Joe Fahey, Teamsters Union International, President of Watsonville Local, 25 October 1995; Jones 2006. Segal (1988, 120) found there were approximately 11,500 workers in the frozen fruits and vegetables industry in California in 1982; however, those were full-time jobs.

32. Hohmann 2006a.

33. Hohmann 2006b.

34. *Register Pajaronian* 1994.

35. Interview with Watsonville City Council member, August 20, 1996.

36. The minimum wage was raised to $8.00 on January 1, 2008. http://www.dir.ca.gov/Iwc/MinimumWageHistory.htm, accessed on July 27, 2009.

37. State of California Employment Development Department, Labor Market Information Division, 2008; and U.S. Department of Labor, Bureau of Labor Statistics, 2008, cited by Applied Survey Research 2007, 29; 2008, 29.

38. Anderson, Macías, and Sandler 2009, 3.

39. Applied Survey Research 2009, 33.

40. Castro, Romero, and Cervantes 1987 document the stress related to job loss.

41. Hohmann 2006a.

42. Jones 2006.

43. Applied Survey Research 2008, 27.

44. Santa Cruz County Farmworker Housing Committee 1993, 10.

45. Even though methyl bromide is not supposed to be applied near schools, tests at local schools found unacceptably high levels. Teachers claimed the chemical induced allergies, rashes, instances of breast cancer, miscarriages, and babies with birth defects among their colleagues (Kleist 2001). The chemical is being replaced by methyl iodide that has similar toxicities. See the Pesticide Action Network of North America, http://www.panna.org/resources/specific-pesticides/methyl-iodide, accessed on October 15, 2010.

46. Mireles 2005, 149. For similar shifts in the class structure by farmworkers in other California agricultural valleys, see Palerm 1991.

47. Between 1982 and 1992, all California farm operators declined by 6 percent, Asian/Pacific Islander farm operators declined by 1 percent, and black operators declined by 29 percent, while Latinos increased by 28 percent (Cha 1997). For an analysis of the strawberry industry in the Pájaro Valley in the 1990s, see Wells 1996.

48. Cha 1997, 1A.

49. Mireles 2005, 158.

50. Ibid., 15, 80; Wells 1996.

51. In a survey of 555 migrant seasonal farmworkers in Idaho, Chávez, Wampler, and Burkhart (2006) found that they have equally low levels of trust toward whites and Mexican Americans, suggesting a considerable difference exists between migrant seasonal farmworkers and other Latinos unless the former are incorporated into community activities.

52. Woolfolk 1997; Barnett 1997. This demonstration undoubtedly gave strength to the UFW, which won a historic contract with grower Bruce Church to cover lettuce workers, mainly affecting workers in the nearby Salinas Valley (Rodebaugh 1996).

53. Barnett 1996b. For a fuller discussion, see Mireles 2005.

54. The number of unionized workers affiliated with the UFW is subject to debate. Mireles (2005, 19) estimates the UFW had about five thousand members in 1993 at the time of César Chávez's death.

55. Mireles 2005.

56. Ibid.

57. Durand 1998, 213.

58. Kissam 2000; Santa Cruz County Farmworker Housing Committee 1993; Villarejo, Lighthall, Williams, Souter, Mines, Bade, Sarnules, and McCurdy 2000; Wells 1996. For a discussion of poverty among the farmworker population, see Griffith, Kissam, Camposeco, García, Pfeffer, Runsten, and Valdés Pizzini 1995. Kissam and Jacobs (2004, 311) estimate that less than half of California farmworkers were identified in the decennial census precisely because they were undocumented migrants. For research on Latina farmworkers, including women's efforts at human agency, see Buss 1993; Castañeda and Zavella 2003; Harthorn 2003.

59. Rufino Domínguez Santos (2004), a former General Coordinator of the Frente Indígena de Organizaciones Binacionales.

60. For discussions of the low pay and efforts to unionize the more than ten thousand strawberry workers in the fields of the Pájaro Valley in Santa Cruz County, see Mireles 2005 and the documentary film Nada Más lo Justo (Only What's Just, 1997), directed by Francisco Nieto, Rafael Chávez Hernández, and Carlos Bazúa Morales.

61. Villarejo, Lighthall, Williams, Souter, Mines, Bade, Sarnules, and McCurdy 2000.

62. Gaouette 2007a.

63. See Press Releases, May 15, 2008, on Senator Feinstein's Web site, http://feinstein .senate.gov/public (search: "Passing Agjobs"), accessed on June 27, 2008.

64. Rotkin 1991.

65. Community Chautauqua 1994. The city of Huntington Beach (south of Los Angeles) sued successfully for exclusive use of the term "Surf City."

66. Applied Survey Research 2008, 27.

67. This region includes Santa Clara, Santa Cruz, and Monterey counties (Mexican Consulate 2006, 2).

68. Glenn 1992; Hondagneu-Sotelo 2001; Ibarra 2000, 2002, 2003a, 2003b; Romero 1992.

69. Farmworkers have some of this nation's most severe social problems and are at greater risk for infectious diseases and chronic health conditions than the general population due to poverty, malnutrition, exposure to pesticides, and hazardous working conditions. A farmworker's life expectancy is estimated to be only forty-nine years. Some health concerns include toxic chemical injuries, dermatitis, respiratory problems, dehydration, heat stroke, sexually transmitted infections, substance abuse, or urinary tract infections. Other problems, such as depression, diabetes, or tuberculosis, stem from social isolation, stress, and poor living conditions. There are allegations that the fumigant methyl bromide, which is injected into soil before planting strawberries and other crops, depletes the ozone and creates health risks. See Castañeda and Zavella 2003; Harthorn 2003; Villarejo, Lighthall, Williams, Souter, Mines, Bade, Sarnules, and McCurdy 2000.

70. Mexican Consulate 2006, 4.

71. Dávila 2001, 201.

72. Pew Hispanic Center 2007, 4.

73. Marcelli and Cornelius 2001.

74. Zlolniski 2005, 174.

REFERENCES

Abram, Susan. "Day Laborers Targeted for Sex." *San Jose Mercury News*, July 10, 2006, 4B.

Anderson, Alissa, Raúl Macías, and Ryan Sandler. "In the Midst of the Great Recession: The State of Working California 2009." Sacramento: California Budget Project, 2009.

Applied Survey Research. "Life in Santa Cruz County, Year 13, 2007: Community Assessment Project Comprehensive Report." Watsonville, Calif.: Applied Survey Research, 2007.

———. "Life in Santa Cruz County, Year 14, 2008: Community Assessment Project Comprehensive Report." Watsonville, Calif.: Applied Survey Research, 2008.

———. "Santa Cruz County Community Assessment Project Comprehensive Report: Year 15, 2009." Watsonville, Calif.: Applied Survey Research, 2009.

Bardacke, Frank. "Watsonville: How the Strikers Won." *Against the Current* May/June (1987): 15–20.

Barnett, Tracy L. "Food Workers Protest Plant Closing: 700 Workers Will Lose Jobs." *Santa Cruz Sentinel*, February 6, 1996a.

Barnett, Tracy L. "Thousands Rally for UFW." *Santa Cruz Sentinel*, April 15, 1997, 1A.

Barrera, Mario. *Race and Class in the Southwest: A Theory of Racial Inequality*. Notre Dame: University of Notre Dame Press, 1979.

Beebe, Greg. "Green Giant to Close Watsonville Plant." *Santa Cruz Sentinel*, September 28, 1993.

Bernhardt, Annette, Ruth Milkman, Nik Theordore, Douglas Heckathorn, Mirabai Auer, James DeFilippis, Ana Luz González, Victor Narro, Jason Perelshteyn, Diana Polson, and Michael Spiller. "Broken Laws, Unprotected Workers: Violations of Employment and Labor Laws in America's Cities." Los Angeles: Center for Urban Economic Development, National Employment Law Project, UCLA Institute for Research on Labor and Employment, 2009.

Bernstein, Nina. "Hungry for Work, Immigrant Women Gather on Corners and Hope for the Best." *New York Times*, August 15, 2005, A1, A17.

Borrego, John. "The Restructuring of Frozen Food Production in North America and Its Impact on Daily Life in Two Communities: Watsonville, California and Irapuato, Guanajuato." In *New Frontiers of the 21st Century*, edited by Norma Klahn, Pedro Castillo, Alejandro Álvarez, and Federico Manchón, 491–544. Mexico City: La Jornada Ediciones y Centro de Investigaciones Colección, 2000.

Brown, Marianne P. "Voices from the Margins: Immigrant Workers' Perceptions of Health and Safety in the Workplace." Los Angeles: UCLA Labor Occupational Safety and Health Program, 2002.

Buss, Fran Leeper. *Forged under the Sun/Forjado bajo el sol: The Life of María Elena Lucas*. Ann Arbor: University of Michigan Press, 1993.

Castañeda, Jorge G. *Ex Mex: From Migrants to Immigrants*. New York: New Press, 2007.

Catanzarite, Lisa. "'Brown Collar Jobs': Occupational Segregation and Earnings of Recent-Immigrant Latinos." *Sociological Perspectives* 43, no. 1 (2000): 45–75.

"Central Coast Unemployment Rate Holds Steady." *Register Pajaronian*, November 29, 1994, B1.

Cha, Ariana E. "Immigrants Alter Face of State's Farms, Minorities Reap Success in a Field Long Dominated by Whites." *San Jose Mercury News*, August 25, 1997, 1A.

Chávez, Maria, Brian Wampler, and Ross E. Burkhart. "Left Out: Trust and Social Capital among Migrant Seasonal Farmworkers." *Social Science Quarterly* 87, no. 5 (2006): 1012–29.

Cleaver, Harry. *Reading Capital Politically*. Austin: University of Texas Press, 1979.

Community Chautaugua. "Focus Group Report: Tourism." Santa Cruz, Calif.: Beach Area Outlook Conference, 1994.

Coyle, Laurie, Gail Hershatter, and Emily Honig. "Women at Farah: An Unfinished Story." In *A Needle, a Bobbin, a Strike: Women Needleworkers in America*, edited by Joan M. Jensen and Sue Davidson, 227–77. Philadelphia: Temple University Press, 1984.

Cranford, Cynthia. "'¡Aquí Estamos y No Nos Vamos!' Justice for Janitors in Los Angeles and New Citizenship Claims." In *Women and Migration in the U.S.-Mexico Borderlands: A Reader*, edited by Denise A. Segura and Patricia Zavella, 306–24. Durham: Duke University Press, 2007.

Dávila, Arlene. *Latinos, Inc.: The Marketing and Making of a People*. Berkeley: University of California, 2001.

de Genova, Nicholas P. Migrant 'Illegality' and Deportability in Everyday Life." *Annual Review of Anthropology*, no. 31 (2002): 419–67.

de Genova, Nicholas P. *Working the Boundaries: Race, Space, and "Illegality" in Mexican Chicago*. Durham: Duke University Press, 2005.

de Genova, Nicholas, and Ana Y. Ramos-Zayas. *Latino Crossings: Mexicans, Puerto Ricans, and the Politics of Race and Citizenship*. New York: Routledge, 2003.

Domínguez Santos, Rufino. "The FIOB Experience: Internal Crisis and Future Challenges." In *Indigenous Mexican Migrants in the United States*, edited by Jonathan Fox and Gaspar Rivera-Salgado, 69–80. La Jolla: Center for U.S.-Mexican Studies, Center for Comparative Immigration Studies, University of California, San Diego, 2004.

Durand, Jorge. "Migration and Integration: Intermarriages among Mexicans and Non-Mexicans in the United States." In *Crossings: Mexican Immigration in Interdisciplinary Perspectives*, edited by Marcelo M. Suárez-Orozco, 209–21. Cambridge: Harvard University Press, 1998.

Flores, William V. "Mujeres en Huelga: Cultural Citizenship and Gender Empowerment in a Cannery Strike." In *Latino Cultural Citizenship: Claiming Identity, Space, and Rights*, edited by William V. Flores and Rina Benmayor, 210–54. Boston: Beacon, 1997.

Flores, William V., and Rina Benmayor, eds. *Latino Cultural Citizenship: Claiming Identity, Space, and Rights*. Boston: Beacon, 1997.

Friaz, Guadalupe M. "'I Want to Be Treated as an Equal': Testimony from a Latina Union Activist." *Aztlán* 20, no. 1–2 (2000): 195–202.

Gaouette, Nicole. "Bill Aims to Fix Farmworker Shortage: California Senators Push Path to Citizenship." *San Jose Mercury News*, January 11, 2007a, 5B.

Glenn, Evelyn Nakano. "From Servitude to Service Work: The Historical Continuities of Women's Paid and Unpaid Reproductive Labor." *SIGNS: Journal of Women in Culture and Society* 18, no. 1 (1992): 1–44.

Greenhouse, Linda. "Justices Rules Drunken Driving Cannot Mean Automatic Deportation of Immigrants." *New York Times*, November 10, 2004, A15.

Griffith, David, Ed Kissam, Jeronimo Camposeco, Anna García, Max Pfeffer, David Runsten, and Manuel Valdés Pizzini, eds. *Working Poor: Farmworkers in the United States*. Philadelphia: Temple University Press, 1995.

Harthorn, Barbara Herr. "Safe Exposure? Perceptions of Health Risks from Agricultural Chemicals among California Farmworkers." In *Risk, Culture, and Health Inequality*, edited by Barbara Herr Harthorn and Laury Oaks, 143–62. Westport, Conn.: Praeger, 2003.

Hayes-Bautista, David E. *La Nueva California: Latinos in the Golden State*. Berkeley: University of California, 2004.

Hohmann, James. "Chill Descends as Jobs Vanish." *San Jose Mercury News*, August 10, 2006a, 1A, 15A.

———. "Third Wave of Layoffs Hits Birds Eye." *San Jose Mercury News*, December 22, 2006b, 1B, 10B.

Hondagneu-Sotelo, Pierrette. *Gendered Transitions: Mexican Experiences of Immigration*. Berkeley: University of California Press, 1994.

———. *Doméstica: Immigrant Workers Cleaning and Caring in the Shadows of Affluence*. Berkeley: University of California, 2001.

Ibarra, María. "Mexican Immigrant Women and the New Domestic Labor." *Human Organization* 59, no. 4 (2000): 452–64.

———. "Emotional Proletarians in a Global Economy: Mexican Immigrant Women and Elder Care Work." *Urban Anthropology* 31, no. 3–4 (2002): 317–51.

———. "*Buscando la Vida*: Mexican Immigrant Women's Memories of Home, Yearning, and Border Crossings." *Frontiers* 24, no. 2 and 3 (2003a): 261–81.

———. "The Tender Trap: Mexican Immigrant Women and the Ethics of Elder Care Work." *Aztlán* 28, no. 2 (2003b): 87–113.

Jones, Donna. "Birds Eye Workers Face Challenging Transition." *Santa Cruz Sentinel*, July 29, 2006, A1.

Kissam, Edward. "No Longer Children: Case Studies of the Living and Working Conditions of the Youth Who Harvest America's Crops." San Mateo, Calif.: Aguirre International, 2000.

Kissam, Edward, and Ilene J. Jacobs. "Practical Research Strategies for Mexican Indigenous Communities in California Seeking to Assert Their Own Identity." In *Indigenous Mexican Migrants in the United States*, edited by Jonathan Fox and Gaspar Rivera-Salgado, 303–40. La Jolla: Center for U.S.-Mexican Studies, Center for Comparative Immigration Studies, University of California, San Diego, 2004.

Kleist, Trina. "Pesticide Fears Fanned: School Tests Find Unacceptable Levels of Methyl Bromide." *Santa Cruz Sentinel*, February 16, 2001, 1A.

Lamphere, Louise. *From Working Daughters to Working Mothers: Immigrant Women in a New England Industrial Community*. Ithaca: Cornell University Press, 1987.

Lamphere, Louise, Patricia Zavella, Felipe Gonzales, and Peter B. Evans. *Sunbelt Working Mothers: Reconciling Family and Factory*. Ithaca: Cornell University Press, 1993.

Lamphere, Louise, and Patricia Zavella. "Women's Resistance in the Sunbelt: Anglos and Hispanas Respond to Managerial Control." In *Women and Work: Exploring Race, Ethnic-*

ity, and Class, edited by Elizabeth Higginbotham and Mary Romero, 76–100. Thousand Oaks, Calif.: Sage, 1997.

Luibhéid, Eithne. "Introduction: Queering Migration and Citizenship." In *Queer Migrations: Sexuality, U.S. Citizenship, and Border Crossings*, edited by Eithne Luibhéid and Lionel Cantú Jr., ix–xlv. Minneapolis: University of Minnesota Press, 2005.

Marcelli, Enrico A., and Wayne A. Cornelius. "The Changing Profile of Mexican Migrants to the United States: New Evidence from California and Mexico." *Latin American Research Review* 36, no. 3 (2001): 105–31.

Massey, Douglas S., Jorge Durand, and Nolan J. Malone. *Beyond Smoke and Mirrors: Mexican Immigration in an Era of Economic Integration*. New York: Russell Sage Foundation, 2002.

Mexican Consulate. "Ventanilla de Salud." San Jose, Calif.: Mexican Consulate, 2006.

Mireles, Gilbert Felipe. "Picking a Living: Farm Workers and Organized Labor in California's Strawberry Industry." PhD diss., Yale University, 2005.

Palerm, Juan Vicente. "Farm Labor Needs and Farm Workers in California, 1970–1989." Sacramento: California Agricultural Studies, Employment Development Department, 1991.

Parreñas, Rhacel Salazar. *Servants of Globalization: Women, Migration, and Domestic Work*. Stanford: Stanford University Press, 2001.

Pear, Robert. "Many Employers See Flaws as Immigration Bill Evolves." *New York Times*, May 27, 2007a, 15.

Pew Hispanic Center. "National Survey of Latinos: As Illegal Immigration Issue Heats Up, Hispanics Feel a Chill." Washington: Pew Hispanic Center, 2007.

Porter, Eduardo. "Illegal Immigrants Are Bolstering Social Security with Billions." *New York Times*, April 5, 2005, A1, C6.

Rodebaugh, Dale. "UFW, Lettuce Grower to End 17-Year Battle." *San Jose Mercury News*, April 29, 1996, 1A.

Romero, Mary. *Maid in the U.S.A.* New York: Routledge, 1992.

Rotkin, Michael E. "Class, Populism, and Progressive Politics: Santa Cruz, California, 1970–1982." PhD diss., University of California, Santa Cruz, 1991.

Ruiz, Vicki L. *Cannery Women, Cannery Lives: Mexican Women, Unionization, and the California Food Processing Industry, 1930–1950*. Albuquerque: University of New Mexico Press, 1987a.

———. "By the Day or the Week: Mexicana Domestic Workers in El Paso." In *Women on the U.S.-Mexico Border: Responses to Change*, edited by Vicki L. Ruiz and Susan Tiano, 61–76. Boston: Allen and Unwin, 1987b.

Salzinger, Leslie. "A Maid by Any Other Name: The Transformation of 'Dirty Work' by Central American Immigrants." In *Ethnography Unbound: Power and Resistance in the Modern Metropolis*, edited by Michael Burawoy, Alice Burton, Ann Arnett Ferguson, Kathryn J. Fox, Joshua Gamson, Nadine Gartrell, Leslie Hurst, Charles Kurzman, Leslie Salzinger, Josepha Schiffman, and Shiori Ui, 139–60. Berkeley: University of California Press, 1991.

Santa Cruz County Farmworker Housing Committee. "Santa Cruz County Farm Worker Housing Needs." Santa Cruz, Calif., 1993.

Sassen, Saskia. *The Global City: New York, London, Tokyo*. Princeton: Princeton University Press, 1991.

Segal, Sven William. "Economic Dualism and Collective Bargaining Structure in Food Manufacturing Industries." PhD diss., University of California, Berkeley, 1988.

Segura, Denise A. "Chicana and the Mexican Immigrant Women at Work: The Impact of Class, Race, and Gender on Occupational Mobility." *Gender and Society* 3, no. 1 (1989): 37–52.

———. "Walking on Eggshells: Chicanas in the Labor Force." In *Hispanics in the Workplace*, edited by Stephen B. Krause, Paul Rosenfeld, and Amy L. Culberston, 173–93. Beverly Hills, Calif.: Sage, 1992.

Soldatenko, María Angelina. "Organizing Latina Garment Workers in Los Angeles." *Aztlán* 20, no. 1–2 (2000): 73–96.

Stephen, Lynn. *Zapotec Women.* Second ed. Durham: Duke University Press, 2005.

Takash, Paule Cruz. "A Crisis of Democracy: Community Responses to the Latinization of a California Town Dependent on Immigrant Labor." PhD diss., University of California, Berkeley, Department of Anthropology, 1990.

Torres Sarmiento, Socorro. *Making Ends Meet: Income-Generating Strategies among Mexican Immigrants.* New York: LFB Scholarly Publishing, 2002.

Valenzuela Jr., Abel, Janette A. Kawachi, and Matthew D. Marr. "Seeking Work Daily: Supply, Demand, and Spatial Dimensions of Day Labor in Two Global Cities." *International Journal of Comparative Sociology* 43, no. 2 (2002): 192–219.

Valenzuela Jr., Abel. "Day Labor Work." *Annual Review of Sociology* 29 (2003): 307–32.

———. "New Immigrants and Day Labor: The Potential for Violence." In *Immigration and Crime: Race, Ethnicity, and Violence*, edited by Ramiro Martinez Jr. and Abel Valenzuela Jr., 189–211. New York: New York University Press, 2006.

———. "Working Day Labor: Informal and Contingent Employment." In *Mexicans in California: Transformations and Challenges*, edited by Ramón Gutiérrez and Patricia Zavella. Urbana: University of Illinois Press, 2009.

Villarejo, Don, David Lighthall, Daniel Williams, Ann Souter, Richard Mines, Bonnie Bade, Steve Sarnules, and Stephan A. McCurdy. "Suffering in Silence: A Report on the Health of California's Agricultural Workers." Davis: California Institute for Rural Studies, 2000.

Wells, Miriam J. *Strawberry Fields: Politics, Class, and Work in California Agriculture.* Ithaca: Cornell University Press, 1996.

Woolfolk, John. "Thousands Take Part in UFW March." *San Jose Mercury News*, April 14, 1997, 1A.

Zavella, Patricia. *Women's Work and Chicano Families: Cannery Workers of the Santa Clara Valley.* Ithaca: Cornell University Press, 1987.

———. "The Politics of Race and Gender: Organizing Chicana Cannery Workers in Northern California." In *Women and the Politics of Empowerment: Perspectives from the Workplace and the Community*, edited by Ann Bookman and Sandra Morgen, 202–24. Philadelphia: Temple University Press, 1988.

———. "Engendering Transnationalism in Food Processing: Peripheral Vision on Both Sides of the U.S.-Mexico Border." In *Transnational Latina/o Communities: Politics, Processes, and Cultures*, edited by Carlos G. Vélez-Ibáñez and Anna Sampaio, 225–45. Lanham, Md.: Rowman & Littlefield, 2002.

Zavella, Patricia, and Xóchitl Castañeda. "Sexuality and Risks: Young Mexican Women Negotiate Gendered Discourse about Virginity and Disease." *Latino Studies* 3, no. 2 (2005): 226–45.

Zlolniski, Christian. *Janitors, Street Vendors, and Activists: The Lives of Mexican Immigrants in Silicon Valley.* Berkeley: University of California Press, 2005.

11

ECONOMIES OF DIGNITY

Ideologies of Work and Worth among Mexicans and Puerto Ricans in Chicago

Nicholas de Genova and Ana Y. Ramos-Zayas

"Mexicans see Puerto Ricans as U.S. citizens who come to this country with a lot of privileges and we don't take advantage of those privileges," explained Adriana Cruz, an eighteen-year-old Puerto Rican high school student. "That we are lazy. That we like living off welfare, that we have this welfare mentality." Discourses of "welfare," which signal differential relations to the substantive entitlements of U.S. citizenship, were variously elaborated in terms of competing ideologies of work and competence, as well as respectability and dignity. Through a stigmatization of "welfare dependency," the U.S. citizenship of Puerto Ricans invariably came to be conflated with their racialized denigration as "lazy," lacking a good "work ethic," and, in effect, being the kind of "undeserving" poor who were ultimately a liability to the U.S. nation. In this sense, many Mexican migrants commonly constructed themselves in contradistinction to precisely these images—as being "hardworking," and capable of making do without having to ask for "handouts"—and so, implicitly subscribed to hegemonic stereotypes about the virtues of "good immigrant values." These same postures, however, were intended to deflect the pervasive and likewise racialized allegations that Mexicans were merely opportunistic "illegal aliens" subverting the "rule of law" and thus corroding the moral fabric of U.S. society.

The presumption of "welfare dependency" as a self-evident indicator of "laziness" was embedded in notions of "respectability" constituted through "hard work" that enabled Mexican migrants to racialize Puerto Ricans in ways that approached or approximated the racial Blackness of African Americans. By contrast, without celebrating the stigma of "welfare," Puerto Ricans nevertheless posited their own political sophistication and their capabilities in maneuvering through the social inequalities orchestrated by U.S. political institutions, in ways that constructed Mexicans as "illegal," helpless, and submissive newcomers from a "Third World" (and by implication, premodern) social background, lacking a sense of dignity and allowing themselves to be easily subjected to exploitation. Thus, around elementary but substantial differences founded upon the unequal politics of citizenship, Mexicans and Puerto Ricans elaborated competing moral economies through which to render meaningful their own locations in the social order of the U.S. nation-state. In so doing, they also commonly produced the grounds for producing and upholding differences that could demarcate a more or less durable divide between their distinct groups—a defining division that tended to be readily racialized.

CITIZENSHIP AND "ILLEGALITY"

Most Puerto Ricans, both on the Island and the U.S. mainland alike, do not tend to see a contradiction between being U.S. citizens and belonging to the Puerto Rican nation (Duany, 2000; Morris, 1995). Rather than expressing nationalism at the level of electoral politics by demanding Puerto Rico's national sovereignty, Puerto Ricans on the Island commonly negotiate the contradictory demands of nationalism in the realm of popular culture (Díaz-Quiñones, 1993; Duany, 2000). Hence, while Puerto Ricans on the Island have consistently voted against both independence from the U.S. and permanent annexation as the fifty-first state of the union, neither these political options nor the prolongation of the status quo are perceived as in any way negating the existence and vitality of a Puerto Rican "nation" defined in cultural and linguistic terms on the Island.

Among Puerto Ricans in the U.S., a U.S. citizenship identity has become not only compatible with nationalist activism, but actually plays a critical (and largely neglected) role in the creation of a Puerto Rican national identity within broader racialization processes concerning *Latinidad*. Alma Juncos, a Puerto Rican parent-volunteer at Roberto Clemente High School, articulated this emphasis on a citizenship identity. When asked to describe the area where she was living, Alma replied:

> Where I live, some Puerto Ricans and some Mexicans moved in. There's a building that is mostly Mexican, Guatemalan. Puerto Ricans don't live there. Where I live I feel fine. As Puerto Ricans, we help each other, we motivate each other. And I've also helped Mexican people, a guy who is mute, who lives on the ground floor of my building. I took him here to the West Town clinic and they gave him good attention, they recommended a school to him. I think that many of them are jealous of Puerto Ricans. My [Puerto Rican] neighbor told me: "The thing with Mexicans is that they know they are wetbacks." And, since we [Puerto Ricans] are [U.S.] citizens, they hate us because of that.

During a historical period when anti-immigrant nativism and broader racialization discourses around *Latinidad* persistently located groups of Latin American and Caribbean ancestry outside of the juridical and ideological borders of the United States, Puerto Ricans found themselves having to straddle the fraught divide between the increasingly counterpoised categories of "Latino" and "Puerto Rican" by embracing and reaffirming their (non-immigrant) citizenship identity.

A U.S. citizenship identity allowed even the most vulnerable Puerto Rican barrio residents to articulate their legal rights and make claims for entitlements and resources while simultaneously endorsing community-building projects grounded on popular nationalist discourses. The emphasis on a citizenship identity in relation to other Latinos repeatedly emerged in Ramos-Zayas's life history interviews and informal conversations with a group of Puerto Rican parent-volunteers at the barrio high school where Alma Juncos volunteered, among individuals who routinely interacted with Mexican parents, students, and administrators. This discourse of citizenship identity tended to automatically assume that Mexicans and other Latinos were not U.S. citizens. Nevertheless, Puerto Ricans still upheld the critical distinction between their status as colonial subjects and what they perceived to be "real" "American"-ness, which most associated with racial whiteness.

While a U.S. citizenship identity was evoked to emphasize a specifically Puerto Rican nationality in contradistinction to a more diffuse Latino identification, theirs was a citizenship identity that remained indelibly marked by its nonwhiteness and subordinate (or "second-class") character. The invocation of a citizenship identity among Puerto Ricans was, in general, unequivocally *not* an assertion of their "American"-ness. For their part, Mexican migrants tended to have little or no historical knowledge about the colonial condition of Puerto Rico. Most commonly, they knew only that here was another Latino group, but one who enjoyed what appeared to them to be a privileged relationship to the U.S. state. Although Mexican migrants did not tend to comment explicitly upon Puerto Ricans' U.S. citizenship, they commonly identified some of the substantive features of that citizenship (such as eligibility for various social welfare programs), which they could conceive of only as a tremendous advantage. Especially during the mid-1990s, with a dominant political climate of distrust and disdain of both "immigrants" and "welfare" in all its forms, the discourse surrounding "welfare" was one that skillfully manipulated the intrinsic ambiguities embedded in the category. Precisely when the aim has been to insinuate that undocumented migrants represent an overall drain on public revenues, the stigmatized charge of the term "welfare" has been deployed very broadly, if also crudely, by fiscal conservative nativists to refer even to such public entitlements as access to emergency medical care or public schooling (cf. Calavita, 1996). Nevertheless, the frontal assault against "welfare" as such during the 1990s, which culminated in the so-called Welfare Reform legislation of 1996, was primarily directed against programs such as Aid to Families with Dependent Children (AFDC), Supplemental Security Income (SSI), General Assistance, or the Special

Supplemental Food Program for Women, Infants and Children (WIC), more conventionally known as "food stamps." The typical beneficiaries of these programs were the U.S.-citizen poor, with racialized "minorities" such as African Americans and Puerto Ricans very prominently targeted as "undeserving" abusers of the state's presumed beneficence.

Mexican migrants, especially the undocumented as well as many who had been previously undocumented, were most often legally ineligible, or even when they may have been eligible, most often presumed themselves to be forbidden from these entitlements. Thus, it is crucial to identify the way that discourses of "welfare" among Mexican migrants were always inherently concerned with the unequal politics of citizenship, and that such substantive entitlements of U.S. citizenship as access to these "welfare" programs were a preeminent material manifestation of the palpable difference between what it meant to be an "immigrant" and what it meant for Puerto Ricans to be U.S. citizens. In 1990, Mexican migrants who had arrived in the U.S. between 1980 and 1990, and were not U.S. citizens, had a labor-force participation rate (87.5%) that was 17.6% higher than that of the total U.S. population (74.4%). A preeminent exemplar of the working poor, however, their poverty rate (36.6%) was almost three times that of the total U.S. population (13.1%), and roughly comparable to that of Puerto Ricans as a group.[1] Nevertheless, this Mexican/migrant population in poverty received 82.1% less in public assistance payments per capita than the U.S. total poverty population.[2] These dramatic disparities reflect several decisive determinants: the exclusion of undocumented migrants from welfare programs (Supplemental Security Income [SSI], Aid to Families with Dependent Children [AFDC], and General Assistance), the five-year prohibition on receipt of welfare for most migrants whose immigration statuses were adjusted (or "legalized") through the "Amnesty" of the Immigration Reform and Control Act (IRCA) of 1986, as well as standard Immigration and Naturalization restrictions against applicants or their relatives becoming "a public charge." Although Mexican migrants' poverty had been deployed against them by recourse to the allegation of their "liability to become a public charge" throughout much of the twentieth century, it was seldom substantiated.[3]

Whereas Puerto Rican poverty in the U.S. has been abundantly documented, considerably less research has focused upon Puerto Rican labor-force participation. The percentage of Puerto Ricans in "managerial/professional" occupations, though low (15.5% for men and 18.5% for women), is almost twice as large as the percentage of Mexicans in such occupations and comparable to percentages for other Latino groups, which of course continues to be significantly lower than that of whites (IPRP, 1993). In 1993, Puerto Ricans had higher median earnings than Mexicans, and Puerto Rican female median earnings were almost equal to those of non-Latino white females. Nevertheless, as we have already discussed, the poverty rate for Puerto Ricans was simultaneously the highest among all Latino groups. Furthermore, as a characteristic and implicitly pathologizing indicator of "welfare dependency," twice as many Puerto

Ricans as Mexicans were likely to be "females heading households." Based on data from the 1990 Census, an Urban Institute study prepared for the U.S. Department of Health and Human Services determined that 23.9% of Mainland-born Puerto Rican teen mothers, 34.5% of Island-born Puerto Rican teen mothers, 30.9% of Mainland-born Puerto Rican young mothers (ages 20–24), and 35.3% of Island-born Puerto Rican young mothers received transfer income from Aid to Families with Dependent Children (AFDC), Supplemental Security Income (SSI), or other forms of public assistance. In contrast, only 3.7% of "foreign-born" Mexican/migrant teen mothers and 6.4% of "foreign-born" Mexican/migrant young mothers received any of these forms of welfare benefits (Kahn and Berkowitz, 1995, tables A.6, B.5).[4] One of the inferences that we can draw from these admittedly oversimplified statistical portraits is that there is a starkly pronounced bifurcation among Puerto Ricans in the U.S. labor market; at one end are those Puerto Ricans who are in the labor force and doing reasonably well, and at the other end are Puerto Ricans who are unemployed or are among the working poor. Both of these significant differences between Puerto Ricans and Mexican migrants, however, had everything to do with the inequalities systematically generated and sustained by the politics of citizenship.

When their U.S. citizenship identity comes to be conflated with claims about Puerto Rican "culture," however, or, worse, more plainly racializing claims about the inherent traits of Puerto Ricans as a group, discourses of Puerto Rican "welfare dependency" predictably and almost invariably invoke various insinuations about a "culture of poverty" soon thereafter (e.g., Lewis, 1970).[5] An important and bitter irony of Puerto Ricans' U.S. citizenship, therefore, is that it extended welfare benefits to them and thereby apparently corroborated the racist equation of Puerto Ricanness with laziness, "underclass" pathologies, and anything considered "un-American." These stereotypes effectively conceal the fact that, historically, the predominant labor-market trajectory of Puerto Rican migrants to the Mainland, as colonial subjects, was largely restricted to serving U.S. industries that soon thereafter closed down or were relocated abroad before the Puerto Rican newcomers had had any chance to make any substantial occupational gains that might have supplied a foothold for subsequent U.S.-born generations (History Task Force, 1979). As unionized manufacturing jobs came increasingly to be substituted with low-wage and widely ridiculed low-status service sector employment with few or no benefits, many Puerto Ricans entered the growing ranks of the permanently poor for whom welfare frequently became little more than an insufficient complement to other odd jobs for subsistence (cf. Newman, 1999).

Ramos-Zayas met Carmen Rivera through her son Juan, who was a student at the local high school and a member of a youth salsa band that played at neighborhood festivities. The widowed mother of three sons, Carmen had lived in Chicago for ten years. Like most of the parents of the high school students with whom Ramos-Zayas worked, Carmen had experienced frequent and recurrent cycles of underemployment in which she combined part-time "off the books" employment and one or another form of public assistance. Although she could have easily qualified for maximum public aid benefits, Carmen tenaciously held on to her tenuous labor-force connections and drew great pride from the work she did. When asked to describe how she managed to raise three sons on such a tight budget, Carmen did not mention receiving public assistance, but rather focused instead on the clever and skillful ways in which she was able to make ends meet. She emphasized her hard work and budgeting skills, how she had learned to make do with the little that she earned from odd jobs as a part-time caterer, and how her sons helped her with the little they made in after-school jobs (which for Carmen was a meaningful proof of the "good work ethic" she had instilled in them). Although Carmen was receiving welfare in the form of Medicaid and food stamps, she considered herself "hardworking"—she excelled at her part-time job as a caterer—and, furthermore, a kind of role model of civic responsibility, as she sometimes served as a parent-volunteer at Roberto Clemente High School, where many students regularly came to her for advice.

In contrast to her self-image as, in effect, a "good citizen," despite her poverty, Carmen recognized that Mexicans often worked multiple low-wage jobs simultaneously for inordinately long hours, but perceived the jobs that Mexicans were presumably "willing to take" as clear examples of an extraordinary exploitation that was degrading. In these respects, Carmen focused on what she perceived to be the desperation that was rooted in Mexicans' poverty, rather than on their "hard work." Referring explicitly to the spatialized underpinnings of the racialized distinction between Puerto Ricans and Mexicans, she compared the North Side and the South Side of Chicago:

> The South Side is much poorer, lots of vacant buildings. The Mexican part is like a bit of Central America in the city. The Mexicans try to live as if they were in Mexico. All you see is their culture, people in the streets, selling on the streets. They work very hard. Yes, they do any kind of work. You see them on the bus going to work, from here to there—they're always on their way to work or from work. You can tell because you hear them talking among themselves. Many of them are very poor, because they come here with nothing. And their relatives . . . Let me tell you something, one thing I've noticed is that they are a little into themselves, they don't help each other very much . . . not all of them, but some of them. Where I live there's a lot of problems among the Mexicans. They bicker with each other [se tiran unos a otros]. At least where I live there's a lot of Mexicans, a lot! The ground floor is always packed with Mexican families, packed, packed! Mexicans live their own lives. One thing I've noticed is that they are rude [groseros]—they don't help each other out, not even among themselves.

Carmen associated "the South Side" with Mexico, as epitomized by Mexican/migrant street vendors who reenacted a kind of impoverished "Third World" informal economy. Carmen seemed to suggest, furthermore, that as a consequence of the desperate scramble to accept any job, under any circumstance, Mexicans tended to live in competition with one another. The direct contrast that she drew between Mexicans and Puerto Ricans was underscored on one occasion in November of 1994, when Ramos-Zayas visited Rivera to talk about her son's college plans. Carmen was concerned because her son wanted to become a chef and she did not know how much culinary school would cost. Carmen praised her son's cooking:

> Sonia, you know her, right? [Ramos-Zayas nodded] She lives right here, in the building right here. Well, Sonia is always on the lookout to see when Juan is going to cook. She tells me: "Let me know when he cooks, so that I can come over!" [laughed] Because Juan has always been a good cook. Since he was little. He'd tell me, "Mami, how do you prepare this [food]? What [ingredients] do you put in?" Always. So when he cooks, I send Sonia a plate. And also when she cooks, she sends me a plate. That's a custom that we keep as Puerto Ricans. We always care for each other and we're there for each other.

Carmen Rivera claimed a higher moral ground for Puerto Ricans by constructing Mexicans' eagerness to "work at anything" as an ultimate shortcoming that undermined their solidarity as compatriots.

Like many other Puerto Rican barrio residents, Carmen also believed that Mexicans saw Puerto Ricans as U.S. citizens who had enjoyed legal privileges for many generations yet had not had the wherewithal to achieve the "American Dream." Citizenship, along with all that it implies in the U.S. nationalist imaginary (e.g., extended residence, high levels of English-language proficiency, institutional access, and ultimately, "assimilation"), could be presumed to be an automatic predictor of Puerto Ricans' upward social mobility. When Puerto Ricans' citizenship was instead associated with poverty, "welfare dependency," social stagnation, and marginality, therefore, the perceived failure appeared to be that of the Puerto Ricans themselves. As a consequence, those who have glorified their own U.S. citizenship but still live in poverty come to be suspect as culturally "deficient" and culpable as socially "deviant."

THE MORAL ECONOMY OF "WELFARE"

Puerto Ricans, regardless of social class, overwhelmingly endorsed a "work ethic" that was indeed very conventional, and largely recapitulated the hegemonic litanies of U.S. society concerning the moral value of "hard work" and economic "independence." "Welfare" tended to be stigmatized not only by those who did not receive these benefits, but also by those who had relatives who were receiving or had previously received public assistance, and even those who themselves were collecting one or another form of welfare payment (cf. Newman, 1999). However, most Puerto Ricans recognized meaningful distinctions among various kinds of "welfare," and deployed diverse contextual considerations alternately to condemn or sanction welfare use. The differentiation of welfare into distinct components—such as disability, Aid to Families with Dependent Children (AFDC), Medicaid, food stamps, Section 8—served to categorize specific types of welfare as "good" or "bad." Popular discourses of "welfare abuse," "cheating," "taking advantage," and "laziness"—which resonated with hegemonic scripts—abounded among Puerto Ricans in Chicago.

For many barrio residents, however, there were also particular circumstances demanding that welfare use be scrutinized in light of the recipients' specific predicaments, employment patterns, and even parenting skills or community involvement. Given the complexities of public assistance, as a social institution, and the particularities of any given person's conceivably multiple social identities, not all forms or instances of welfare use were perceived to be incompatible with being a productive member of society. Among Puerto Ricans in the Humboldt Park barrio, popular perceptions and judgment concerning welfare often depended on a textured understanding of a particular individual's entire life history and public identity, not merely her generic status as a welfare recipient. Hence, those who admitted to being "on welfare" also were commonly inclined to accentuate their own alternative "productive" citizenship identities; some familiar examples included serving as a part-time volunteer at a community organization, former military service, or even gainful "off-the-books" employment on the part of workers for whom public aid was a necessary supplement to low wages and limited opportunities. Sometimes "going on welfare" was perceived to be a rather noble public act of humility, signally a personal recognition of the limited possibilities or inability of any given individual to pull him- or herself up "by the bootstraps," single-handedly support his/her family, and secure basic needs. In contrast, collecting welfare for "no good reason"—for instance, when an individual had a not-so-obvious disability but received workers' compensation—was roundly derided. The recognition of welfare's complexity, therefore, still did not preclude the moral dilemmas entangled in the perceived contradiction between being a properly "productive" U.S. citizen and the commonplace construction of receiving public assistance as being a public liability. The case of Adriana Cruz was illustrative of these tensions.

In August of 1994, Ramos-Zayas was teaching at a Puerto Rican–identified alternative high school in West Town when she met Adriana Cruz, a young Puerto Rican woman who was enrolled as a student there. Adriana had grown up in a predominantly Mexican neighborhood on the South Side, but she, her mother, and her brother had decided to relocate to the Humboldt Park area on the North Side to be closer to Adriana's maternal aunt and cousins. Adriana participated in Ramos-Zayas's "Latino Literature" class, and was one of the students most interested in receiving college counseling and pursuing her higher education. Most of the journal entries Adriana wrote for the class stressed her efforts to get into college; one typical entry read: "Today I started filling out my college applications. I thought it was going to be easy, but it was not and I got mad after a while. I got confused with some of the parts. I got so frustrated I started crying" (10/2/94).

The long college and financial aid application process led Ramos-Zayas to spend many hours with Adriana, as well as some of Adriana's friends. The one theme that continuously came up during those conversations, as well as in the journal entries that

Cruz shared with Ramos-Zayas, involved Adriana's frustrations with and low opinion of women her age who were getting pregnant. Interestingly, Adriana repeatedly emphasized that her friends who wanted to get pregnant lived on the South Side:

> Today a friend from the South Side [. . .] was telling me about one of our close friends. Her name is Delana and she is Mexican. She is going to take a pregnancy test over the weekend. I think Delana is stupid because she wants to get pregnant. She has her whole life ahead of her and she is throwing it down the drain. Well, one thing is for sure, her mother will be happy because she always told me she wanted Delana to get pregnant at the age of eighteen. I guess her wish is becoming true (9/27/94).

Much of Adriana's frustration with her Mexican friends' pregnancies was certainly inspired by her own educational and career goals and her sense that she and all of her peers confronted formidable obstacles in their shared plight as working-class Latinas. However, the marking of the space of the South Side as "Mexican" became entangled in Adriana's negative appraisal of teen pregnancy. Notably, since Adriana's Mexican friends were largely born in the U.S. and thus U.S. citizens like herself, Adriana's criticisms were implicitly directed against the presumed "backwardness" of a "cultural" environment that she identified as "Mexican," which seemed to subvert higher educational and career ambitions and life goals for the young women she knew. On another occasion, she wrote:

> Maria is one of my friends from the South Side. She is two months pregnant. She told her parents and her father doesn't want her to live at home anymore. Her mother wants her to drop out of school. Lizette was telling me about all the girls we went to school with on the South Side; half are pregnant and the other half dropped out (10/4/94).

This distinction between Adriana's aspirations and the tragic example of her South Side (Mexican) friends, largely inseparable from the equation of teen pregnancy and hopelessness, was a recurrent theme. Teen pregnancy seemed synonymous with dropping out of school, and thus symbolized an abrupt "dead end" for a young woman's life trajectory.

Adriana's concern with pregnancy and dropping out of school, moreover, always also implied a certain probability of becoming a welfare recipient. Like many other young Puerto Ricans in Humboldt Park, Adriana remembered the humiliation she had felt as a child when she would accompany her mother to welfare offices or to grocery stores where they had to use food stamps. Not uncommonly these personal experiences with welfare translated for young Puerto Ricans like Adriana into insensitive criticisms of neighbors and relatives receiving public aid. Thus, teen pregnancy was not stigmatized on moralistic grounds or developmental concerns related to the immaturity of the mother-to-be. Rather, the figure of unwed teen mothers signaled a young woman's inability to provide financially for her baby and the seeming inevitability of becoming trapped in a cycle of poverty with no prospects for escape. Rather than because of considerations of age, in other words, Puerto Ricans like Adriana stigmatized teen pregnancy because of its presumed connection to welfare.

Significantly, Adriana Cruz took great pride in her job. On one occasion in November of 1994, Ramos-Zayas noticed that Cruz (and other young women in the class) looked extremely tired. She teasingly asked them if they had been out late, partying, but was not surprised by their replies. They were simply juggling very strenuous, thirty-hour ("part-time") work schedules in addition to being full-time students. Adriana also wrote about these strains in her journal: "As you know, I got the job at Target. I was hired to fix up the department. I work in the Green World. Target goes by worlds, not departments. I started at $5.00 per hour and I just got a raise of 50 cents. In a month and a half I will get another raise. I work during the week right after school and on the weekends I work from 10 a.m. through 6:30 p.m." (11/30/94). Although Adriana valued school and had a clearly defined identity as a student (e.g., participating in school-sponsored activities, getting good grades), this school identity was integrated into a more complex sense of herself as a worker as well, with significant responsibilities at her job.

By the end of her senior year, Adriana had been accepted into some quite competitive colleges in the Midwest, with very good financial aid packages. She started at one of the schools, but dropped out after a semester. Even with financial aid, the college expenses were beyond Adriana's reach, and the academic demands limited her ability to work full-time, as she had done during high school. The rural location of the college was also an unwelcome change for Adriana, who was used to living in the city and close to her family. Adriana returned to Chicago and went back to working in retail, this time at a shoe store in the middle-class Lakeview neighborhood. There she met Ricardo, a Mexican raised in the U.S. who had moved from Los Angeles to Chicago a few years prior, and worked as a manager. After a year, Adriana and Ricardo moved in together, and a few months later, in November of 1997, Adriana became pregnant. The unexpected pregnancy put a great deal of strain on the relationship, despite the fact that Ricardo was financially and emotionally supportive of Adriana's decision to have the baby. Eventually, Adriana's family became enthusiastic about the pregnancy and her mother began buying various things for the baby. Adriana continued working at the shoe store, even though she found herself enduring a difficult pregnancy and Ricardo was urging her to stay home. Finally, at Ricardo's insistence, Adriana quit her job during her seventh month.

At this point, Adriana decided to seek public assistance. A highly motivated young woman, who had worked an average of thirty hours a week throughout all of her high school education, and who had always associated welfare with laziness, Adriana agonized during the weeks prior to deciding to seek public assistance. She called Ramos-Zayas several times and Ramos-Zayas tried to assure her that, contrary to her own perceptions, receiving public assistance would not make her a lazy or bad person, as she seemed to imply.

In March of 1999, Ramos-Zayas went to visit Adriana and her then seven-month-old baby girl. Adriana was living close to O'Hare Airport, a twenty- to thirty-minute subway ride outside of "the Puerto Rican neighborhood." Adriana called David and Mike, two former classmates whom she had not seen since college, to tell them that Ramos-Zayas was in town and to invite them for lunch. When Adriana met the two former high school classmates, she explained to them that she had had to stop working because of the pregnancy. She quickly added, however, that she planned to go back as soon as the baby got older. Whenever Adriana mentioned being "on welfare," she quickly explained that she had decided to pursue Medicaid because of her "bad pregnancy" [*mala barriga*] and, once the baby was born, to cover regular medical checkups. Adriana's insistence on specifying that she was receiving "Medicaid," a less stigmatized form of public assistance, was revealing of her concern that other components of welfare, such as disability and food stamps, tended to be more highly criticized and perceived as more frequently subject to "cheating" and "abuse." Furthermore, although Ricardo and Adriana had intended to marry, their plans had been postponed so that Adriana could continue to receive public assistance, since Ricardo's salary was not enough to make ends meet for the struggling young family.

As a first-time mother, Adriana could be "on welfare" in a manner that others, such as her former classmates David and Mike, could perceive as unequivocally related to the well-being of her child, and thus as more socially acceptable. David and Mike, who themselves had previously been harsh critics of people receiving welfare, were supportive of Adriana because they were well acquainted with her work history and because she was a first-time mother in a "stable" relationship. Implicit in such justifications, however, was the recognition that Adriana did not fit the pathologized stereotype of a woman "abusing" welfare by "having a bunch of kids by different fathers"—something that would be morally chastised. Rather, in spite of her financial difficulties, she remained within the purview of a presumed moral "mainstream." Welfare was perceived to be a minimal and temporary condition in Adriana's life, and thus its stigma was mitigated. At the same time, such affirmations of the fine line between "good" and "bad" welfare served nonetheless to rationalize the more diffuse forms of patriarchal control that monitored and regulated poor women's sexuality and general autonomy.

THE MORAL ECONOMY OF "WORK"

In April of 1995, on the occasion of visiting the home of Angélica Sandoval (who had participated in a math course he had taught at the Imperial Enterprises factory) and her husband, Leobardo (whom he was meeting for the first time), with the purpose of tutoring their daughter in math, de Genova conducted an informal interview during which Angélica spoke minimally while her husband presided. Leobardo Sandoval was immediately curious to know where de Genova was from, and upon discovering that he had been born in the U.S. and was not of Latino parentage, Leobardo was even more intrigued at how it happened that de Genova spoke Spanish and lived in the Pilsen barrio. When de Genova explained a bit about his research and mentioned the subject of discrimination against Mexicans as a concern of his study, Sandoval immediately replied:

You know why? It's because we're taking over, and they're afraid of what we can do—not like the Blacks, they don't want to work—the Americans don't want to work, neither the Blacks [negros] nor the whites [blancos]—even my own kids! I tell my daughter, who is sixteen, "You have to work hard and make something of yourself." But the Americans don't understand this, they don't understand that you can't just sit around and expect something to come to you—you have to take advantage of your situation and make something out of life. But that's why they're afraid, because we're going to control everything! I'm not saying in five years, but in twenty years, or fifty years—from Canada to the Panama Canal—just like the Aztecs who were a very good people and knew how to dominate other people and places, the Mexicans are going to take over. I was reading that this new House Speaker Newt Gingrich, he wants to help Mexico with a lot of money—not to help the people, but he's afraid there are going to be 50 million Mexicans coming to the U.S.! They think that they can control Mexico that way, but they'll see—we're going to turn it back on them. Because where would the U.S. be without the Spanish-speaking countries? Nobody else in the world wants the U.S., so where would they be if we turned our back on them?!? And Mexico is the head of all of Latin America—if we turn our back on the U.S., everyone else will follow us, and then they will have nobody.

But I have to admit—I have never been discriminated against; everyone has always treated me nice, with respect. I never had any problem. The only ones that have a lot of problems are the ones who get into trouble, and drink a lot, and make a mess of things, like over there on 26th Street [Little Village] and 18th Street [Pilsen]. I go over there and I feel embarrassed. I say to the people, "Why do you throw garbage on the street? You should make it so people come here and say, 'Wow, they keep it nice over here!'" But me, I never drank a lot or got into trouble, like a lot of the ones that come over nowadays. And why do they stay there, living that way? Why don't they work to change their situation and move out of those neighborhoods? I bought this house when I was illegal, because I worked hard and wanted to have something in this. My dream now is to get a single-family home in the suburbs, but also keep this apartment building. [. . .] I have always lived around here, since I was a boy. In the '80s, it was becoming almost all Mexican, but now it's mainly doctors and lawyers and other people with money. My daughter has had many friends who had to move out because the rents went up, but I own this building. Most of the people who live here now don't have children [. . .] they're buying it as an investment, and that means that they want to maintain it in good condition and keep it clean.

But I bought this building and fixed it up when I was still illegal. And nobody gave me any problem; I was never discriminated against. But it's because I work—not like the Puerto Ricans or the Blacks who just go on welfare and don't do anything for themselves. They're very conformist, very resigned, but Mexicans are not. Mexicans work two jobs, sometimes three. I would work for $400 a month if I had to, just to make something for myself. I would sleep only two or three hours a night, if I had to. And that's why we're going to take over everything.

During the course of the interview, Leobardo also emphasized that when he had first come, "there were almost no Mexicans in Chicago—the only place was Pilsen, and you had to go there to buy Mexican foods or find services in Spanish, but they used to say that Immigration would sit outside of Casa del Pueblo [a grocery store] and grab people when they came out." He criticized Mexicans, however, for not learning English, and complained, "Everywhere you go, everything is in Spanish—look at me, I never finished fifth grade, but I picked up little bits of English everywhere I went, all the time."

In this context, but also cognizant of the fact that de Genova's grandparents had migrated from Italy, Sandoval went on to declare that his greatest admiration was for "Polish and Italians, because they come to work and make something for themselves and don't waste time, don't go on welfare, learn English." At this juncture, Sandoval asked de Genova's opinion of whether or not he and his wife looked like "typical Mexicans," adding that many people took him to be Italian. With recourse to a somewhat tentative whiteness (modified as "Italian"), Leobardo seemed to be making a rather direct appeal (albeit implicit) to the white anthropologist to confirm and thus, in some sense, validate his own desire for the racialized status of whiteness. At this moment, Angélica, who was indeed quite light-skinned (and much lighter than her husband), complicated the already complexly racialized scenario by adding that people usually tended to think that she was Puerto Rican. Expected to supply a response, however, de Genova evaded a direct reply to the question and suggested, "Many whites have a stereotype of what Mexicans look like, but it's harder for me to say because I already know the great variety that exists among Mexican people—but there is a common stereotype of what Mexicans look like because they are always put between white and Black in this country." Leobardo replied, "That's right," and Angélica added, "There are lots of white people in Mexico." Leobardo went on to affirm, "You see people with blond hair and green eyes and blue eyes," and Angélica continued, "You could mistake them for Polish." Interested in complicating this turn in the conversation, de Genova added, "There are Black people in Mexico, too." Angélica quickly agreed, "Yes, Blacks too." De Genova then suggested, "But it seems to me that all of those differences are understood differently there, in Mexico." With this, however, Leobardo was able to resume some of the momentum of his earlier remarks, "Yes," he declared, "because in reality there is no racism in Mexico—it's not like here. If they don't like Americans, it's not because of the color of their skin, it's because of the place that they're from. Because all of this land was ours, and the English came and took it all away from us. So now we're taking it back. You go to Miami, it's all Cubans. Texas, it's all Mexicans; California, all Mexicans; Chicago, all Mexicans."

Despite some of his more favorable pronouncements with regard to Mexico, such as its purported leadership of Latin America and the denial of any racism, and his elision of the virtues of Mexico and Mexicans notwithstanding, Leobardo also was fairly critical of Mexico. Due to the undocumented status of both Leobardo and Angélica until they became eligible for the "Amnesty" after the 1986 legislation (IRCA), the Sandoval family had not visited Mexico until 1987. Leobardo had not returned in twenty years. He recounted driving into Mexico with their two young daughters. He said it was shocking to him to be in Mexico again, once he had stopped at the restaurants on the road, seen the conditions, used the bathrooms. At first, he explained, he had been excited when he drove across the border and saw the countryside open up in front of him, but then he was shocked and had a hard time getting used to it, because he had gotten so used to life in the U.S. Leobardo also declared that he never once dreamed of going back to live in Mexico ever since he came, explaining, "because in Mexico they have everything we have here, except it's all on the top shelf and only the tall [high] people [*la gente alta*] can have it, but in the U.S. all you have to do is work hard and you can have whatever you want—the rich people might have five VCRs, but so can you if that's what you want."

Leobardo Sandoval's faith in the ideology that, in the U.S., "all you have to do is work hard and you can have whatever you want" was in striking contrast to most Mexican migrants' experiences of exploitation and the critical perspectives often elaborated by many concerning how thoroughly disillusioning their work experiences had been. Indeed, Leobardo's account of his own work history was rather less sanguine. Leobardo had previously been employed at Imperial Enterprises, where his wife was still working, but as he explained, "they didn't want to pay very much." At the time of the interview, he worked in a foundry. He added meaningfully that this workplace had previously employed 120 people, but now had only 35 workers remaining. When asked why, Leobardo stated plainly, "New machines." When asked, "Are you working harder now than before?" Sandoval replied unequivocally, "Yes, much harder." "So the new machines only meant that each person who's still working is doing two or three people's jobs," de Genova posited. "You can say that, yes," he agreed soberly.

Leobardo had migrated from the Mexican city of San Luis Potosí with his father at the age of twelve, in 1967, and immediately went to work, first as a busboy in a Chicago restaurant. He had never attended school in the U.S. In these ways, while his overall experience was not at all exceptional, Leobardo had nonetheless begun his working life as a Mexican migrant in Chicago at an exceptionally young age.[6] The overwhelming majority of Mexicans who had migrated to Chicago had done so as young adults, even if still in their teens, had immediately gone to work, and had never attended school in the U.S. Even if a considerable proportion might have already been working to help support their families in Mexico at the age of twelve, few had actually migrated to begin working at that age; most tended to have been in the range of at least fifteen to seventeen years of age, or older. (Indeed, Angélica herself, who had migrated at the age of eighteen, in 1973, from a small town in the Mexican state of Zacatecas, had a migration trajectory that was more typical, and confided later that she disagreed with her husband about many issues.) When de Genova suggested that Leobardo Sandoval's lack of interest in returning to Mexico probably had to do with how young he was when he came to the U.S., that this seemed to be quite unlike most people who come from Mexico, who typically migrate with the intention of returning, Leobardo said, "That's true, almost all of them, but 90% probably never do, because they also get used to what they can have here and the conveniences of life here; like me, they have their home and their kids here, and eventually they decide to stay." Notably, it is relevant to add that there was a small U.S. flag displayed at the top of a decorative china cabinet in the Sandoval dining room where the interview took place—something not at all common in most Mexican/migrant homes in Chicago, where it would be infinitely more likely to see a Mexican flag instead.

This extended discussion of Leobardo Sandoval is not at all intended to be "representative" of Mexican migrants in Chicago; neither the defining aspects of his experience nor many of his most forceful opinions are typical. Indeed, he is truly exceptional, precisely inasmuch as he more readily resembles the iconic figure of "the immigrant" whose devotion to an ideal of leaving behind his native country and remaking himself through hard work in a chosen land of opportunity is central to the sustenance of U.S. nationalism (de Genova, 1999: 19–104, in press; cf. Chock, 1991, 1996; Honig, 1998). There are, however, quite remarkable ambivalences evident in Leobardo's discourse. Although he acknowledged the fact of racism in the U.S. while extolling Mexico's virtues, he nonetheless more than once disavowed the significance of racist oppression and racialized exploitation in the U.S. by, in effect, blaming the victims. In the case of Blacks and Puerto Ricans—"they don't want to work," "just go on welfare and don't do anything for themselves," "they're very conformist, very resigned"—the predominant allegation was laziness and an aversion to work. In the case of Mexicans—"the only ones that have a lot of problems are the ones who get into trouble, and drink a lot, and make a mess of things"—the apparent failure to take advantage of opportunities in the U.S. was cast in terms of the moral deficiencies of individuals (cf. R. T. Smith, 1996). Although he was triumphalist about the prospect of Mexican industriousness poised to "take over" and "control everything" and expressed a certain suspicion about U.S. political machinations toward Mexico, he also produced a critique of Mexican social inequalities and celebrated the U.S. as a bastion of opportunity, such that migration to the U.S. emerged tacitly as a necessary precondition for Mexican "hard work" to prevail. Although he embraced crucial dimensions of U.S. nationalism, he nevertheless characterized himself always as Mexican and was critical of all "Americans"—whites and Blacks, and even his own U.S.-born children. And yet, despite this inclusive construction of who exactly might be "Americans," he also referred to Mexican attitudes toward "Americans" as having to do not with "the color of their skin" but rather with a history of conquest by "the English"—implicitly treating "American"-ness as a name for racialized whiteness in much the same manner as other Mexican migrants (as well as Puerto Ricans). Despite this pronouncedly Mexican self-identification, he revealed a considerable investment in whether he appeared (phenotypically) to be Mexican or Italian, and was eager to recuperate a certain fact of whiteness within Mexicanness. Coupled with his praise for the Polish and Italians (migrant groups who have come to be racialized as white in the U.S.) and his frank derision toward African Americans and Puerto Ricans, his generationally inflected and moralistic ambivalence about barrio Mexicans—specifically, "a lot of the ones who come over nowadays"—revealed the tormenting question that seemed to be Leobardo's central dilemma: What will Mexicans prove themselves to be?

This quandary of Leobardo's helps to situate the more general social predicament of Mexican migrants in the U.S.—that of a group racialized as neither white nor Black within the hegemonic bipolarity of white supremacy within the space of U.S. nation-state. In these respects, Leobardo's discourse did indeed exhibit certain key features in common with perspectives that were rather ubiquitous among Mexican migrants in Chicago: the identification of "American"-ness with racialized whiteness; the denigra-tion of racialized Blackness; the reformulation of Mexicanness as a transnationality, racialized in relation to both whiteness and Blackness within the U.S. but simultane-ously posited in relation to Mexico as well; the unequivocal equation of welfare with laziness and an aversion to work; and the demotion of Puerto Ricans to a degraded racialized status, approaching or approximating Blackness (de Genova, 1999: 287–356, in press). Indeed, all of these characteristics of the historically specific racialization of Mexican migrants, we would propose, reveal something definitive, not really so much about "Mexicans" as such, but rather about the racialized character of citizenship within the U.S. nation-state and, likewise, about U.S. nationalism as a racial formation.

THE RACIAL ECONOMY OF WELFARE AND WORK

Most Mexican migrants in the U.S., unlike Leobardo Sandoval, would not endorse the view that "all you have to do is work hard and you can have whatever you want"—know-ing very well that they have never done anything in the U.S. if not work hard, but without any spectacular rewards. But they were virtually unanimous in their sense that Mexicans as a group are extraordinarily distinguished for "wanting to work," for "know-ing how to work," for "not being afraid to work," and for "being ready to work hard" (de Genova, 1999: 261–65). It was hardly surprising, then, when one of the countless industrial day-labor services in Chicago, which specialize in extracting a profit from the recruitment and placement of undocumented workers for local factories, circulated fly-ers in Pilsen in the summer of 2000 that read: "Seeking people who truly want to work and are not afraid of work! [¡Se busca gente que en verdad quiera trabajar y no le tenga miedo al trabajo!]." These specific qualifications, of course, are the ubiquitous conditions of possibility for undocumented workers in particular to serve as an exceptionally vulner-able workforce, presumed by employers to be "cheap" and tractable, and thus, honored as a labor pool of choice. These same virtues, likewise, were commonly marshaled by Mexican migrants as the qualities that rendered as competitive and prized the commod-ity that was their labor-power, in opposition to that of their most proximate competitors in the labor market, who could be denigrated as "lazy."

The topic of welfare was inseparable, among Mexican migrant workers, from allega-tions of "laziness." At a factory called Czarnina and Sons, in March of 1994, a worker named Evangelina put it concisely: "Mexicans don't go on welfare; welfare is for Blacks, Americans, and Puerto Ricans, because they're lazy; a Mexican might have ten kids, but the kids go to work; ten years, twelve years old, the kids help pay, no problem . . ." She chuckled, but then after a moment's pause, added somewhat more seriously, "Well, it depends on the father, because the mother doesn't want to make the kids work." Evangelina's endorsement of this severe and laborious ideal of "Mexican"-ness was first enthusiastic and then more ambivalent, and overtly gendered. There was certainly an element of hyperbole in this defense of the pronouncedly working-class status honor of Mexicans against "Blacks, Americans, and Puerto Ricans," and Evangelina's mirth acknowledged her own exaggeration. But then, perhaps because she was embarrassed to have depicted her community to a white "American" in terms that could make Mexicans seem extreme and even heartless, she abruptly began to qualify her own claim and convey her own reservations about the harsh image she had just portrayed. Clearly, it is significant that Evangelina did so in gendered terms that suggested a critique of men's patriarchal authority within the family, thereby also implying a direct link between male power and this quite masculinist construction of "Mexican"-ness in terms of "hard work."[7]

It is illuminating here to consider a joke that was circulating among Mexican migrants in Chicago in the spring of 1997. Jokes, of course, operate within a certain moral economy of pervasive assumptions, at the same time as they are really interventions in their own right that reaffirm and help to reproduce those same assumptions. Reduced to its basic elements, the joke can be summarized as follows: It is the time of the Mexican Revolution, and Pancho Villa's army has just captured an invading U.S. regiment; addressing his lieutenants, Pancho Villa gives the order: "Take all the Americans [americanos]—shoot them, kill them; the Blacks [morenos] and Puerto Ricans—just let them go." The lieutenants are confused and dismayed: "What?! What are you saying?!? But why??" Coolly, Pancho Villa replies, "Don't waste the bullets—they'll all just die of hunger—because here, there's no welfare." Clearly, in order to be apprehended as "funny," a punch line such as this—which imputes that Black people and Puerto Ricans would be literally incapable of sustaining themselves without welfare, indeed that their laziness is so intractable that they would starve to death—must correspond to the presumed assumptions of an intended audience. Indeed, this joke reiterates the hegemonic racial script that has already been seen to have infused many Mexican migrants' commonplace production of their difference from both African Americans and Puerto Ricans. The joke is clearly reminiscent of both Leobardo's and Evangelina's remarks.[8] The expected reception of the joke's irony resides in a collective sentiment that counterpoises the industriousness (and also thrift) of Mexican workers to the "laziness" of their most proximate competitors in the U.S./Chicago labor market—so that what at first appears to be startlingly counterintuitive, even nonsensical, in Pancho Villa's order, is revealed as shrewd wisdom that flatters the commonsense.[9]

The racialized categories of social differentiation to be discerned in the joke's language, moreover, deserve further examination. The joke produces a reductive representation of the U.S. racial economy—one that is specifically resonant for Mexicans in Chicago—but reterritorialized onto Mexican terrain. Within the joke's refracted space, Mexican migrants contend with the U.S. racial economy as Pancho Villa's soldiers (which is to say, as "Mexicans") battling the arrayed forces of the U.S., which in no simple sense comprise only "Americans," but rather, include "Americans" as well as "Blacks" and "Puerto Ricans." Notably, Evangelina had used precisely the same categories, and the opposition in both instances implicitly posited "Mexicans" (as migrants) against an array of U.S. citizens. Three of these four operative categories could be mistaken for "nationality," but what is decisive is precisely the remaining term—"Blacks"—which reveals that it would be erroneous to simply read the other categories according to their explicit "national" surface. That these categories all stand alongside of one another as formal equivalences in the structure of the joke, requires that the apparently "national" skins of three of these terms ("Mexican," "American," and "Puerto Rican") be brought into alignment with the purely and plainly racialized identity of the fourth ("Black"). The lines of adversity are drawn around the axis of citizenship, but this division becomes apprehensible only when it is further fractured by racialized distinctions.

Notably, African Americans are perceived to be separate, distinct, and, indeed, excluded from the category "Americans"—exposing the fact that "American" comes to connote whiteness.[10] As such, "American"-ness is unavailable to Blacks *or* Latinos (whether they be noncitizen Mexican migrants or Puerto Ricans who are born into U.S. citizenship). Neither for African Americans nor for Puerto Ricans does birthright U.S. citizenship secure the status of "American"-ness, which constitutes a national identity that is understood, in itself, to be intrinsically racialized—as white. The nationally or "culturally" inflected differences between Mexicans and Puerto Ricans, furthermore, do not suffice to account for the racialized distinctions introduced by the joke, because the differences between Mexicans and Puerto Ricans are posited in the joke as analogous to those between Mexicans and whites and Blacks. Both Mexicans and Puerto Ricans— together as Latinos—occupy racialized locations in an intermediate space between white and Black, but the more palpable form of their respective differences here is most likely that, rather than being racialized together more generically as "Hispanics" or "Latinos," Mexicans tend to be racialized simply as "Mexicans" (cf. Barrera, 1979; D. Gutiérrez, 1995: 24; Mirandé, 1985: 76, 1987: 3–9; Montejano, 1987: 5, 82–85; Paredes, 1978 [1993: 38]; Vélez-Ibáñez, 1996: 19, 70–87), and Puerto Ricans, likewise, tend to be racialized simply as "Puerto Ricans" (Grosfoguel and Georas, 1996: 195; Urciuoli, 1996: 41–72).

Puerto Ricans, moreover, are specifically coupled here with Blacks. Within the terms of the joke, "Mexican"-ness is doubly constituted. First, there is a frank recognition of "American" power as a distinctly white power. Against the invasive (colonizing) power of "Americans"—that is, whites—the joke, in a way reminiscent of Leobardo's remarks, constitutes a heroic "Mexican"-ness as a physical and moreover intellectual force to be reckoned with, truly capable of vanquishing the genuine threat of this opponent, which is so thoroughly fearsome and resilient that it must be completely obliterated ("shoot them, kill them"). Simultaneously, "Mexican"-ness—as a muscular, masculinist, indeed militaristic kind of diligence and self-sufficiency—is constituted not only against African Americans but also Puerto Ricans, both of whom are constructed to be so lazy as to be helpless, and ultimately negligible. Their mutual fate is formulated in relation to "welfare," an institution of the U.S. state to which both groups have access as a substantive entitlement of their shared citizenship status. The allegation of welfare dependency becomes inseparable, however, from the racialized insinuation of laziness (otherwise equated with Blackness). Within the terms of the joke, then, Mexicans must relegate Puerto Ricans to a racialized status that approximates (or at least approaches) Blackness. Such acts of demotion serve the purposes of a kind of racialized self-promotion among those who are corralled in that agonistic and contradictory space between white and Black and must vie with one another for position. What is revealed about that space, moreover, is that these intermediate racialized conditions—those racialized as neither white nor Black—consistently seem to be already entrenched in the hegemonic denigration of Blackness.

NOTES

1. These statistics for "foreign-born" Mexican migrants as a whole are less extreme but still rather high. In 1990, 18.4% of all Mexican migrants in Illinois were living below the poverty level, and for noncitizen Mexicans the poverty rate was 19.2% (Paral, 1997: table 21).

2. These statistics, based upon U.S. Census Bureau data, U.S. Immigration and Naturalization Service surveys, and research by the National Immigration Law Center, were compiled by the Legal Center of the Hermandad Mexicana Nacional (1994).

3. For instance, although the Illinois Legislative Investigating Commission's report on the "The Illegal Mexican Alien Problem" (1971) was explicitly interested in establishing that undocumented Mexican migrants represented a fiscal burden to the state, the Commission's random survey to determine the scope of unemployment benefits and public aid payments made to undocumented Mexicans was able to identify only two migrants (representing only 1.05% of the sample) who had received any form of public assistance payment whatsoever (Illinois Legislative Investigating Commission, 1971: 36–37).

4. While comparable figures for U.S.-born Mexican women were considerably higher—13.9% of teen mothers and 16.6% of young mothers receiving welfare payments, respectively—their participation in these public assistance programs was nevertheless significantly lower than that of their Puerto Rican counterparts (Kahn and Berkowitz, 1995; tables A.6, B.5).

5. It is ironic for our purposes that Oscar Lewis's "culture of poverty" thesis (1959; cf. 1970) was originally formulated on the basis of his research among both Mexicans (in Mexico) and Puerto Ricans (in both Puerto Rico and New York City). Lewis posited that "poverty . . . creates a subculture of its own," and that "one can speak of the culture of the poor, for it has its own modalities and distinctive social and psychological consequences . . . [that

cut] across regional, rural-urban, and even national boundaries" (1959: 2); furthermore, he contended that "once [the culture of poverty] comes into existence, it tends to perpetuate itself from generation to generation [such that] by the time the slum children are age six or seven they have usually absorbed the basic values and attitudes of their subculture and are not psychologically geared to take full advantage of changing conditions or increased opportunities which may occur in their lifetime" (1966: xlv). Thus, Lewis pathologizes the behaviors and values of poor people, regardless of their particular cultural milieus, but by culturalizing these pathologies, his position encourages the view that poor people become trapped in endemic poverty because of their "culture." Such concepts have continued to be remarkably influential in much of contemporary hegemonic social science research, as evidenced by the "underclass" theories of the 1980s and '90s.

6. It may be useful to emphasize here that it is not at all unusual for Mexican migrants to begin working at such a young age (and younger) in U.S. agriculture.

7. For a more extended treatment of the gendered dimensions of Mexican migrants' racialized constructions of "laziness," see de Genova (1999: 287–356, in press).

8. This joke is also gendered in a manner that parallels Evangelina's remarks, inasmuch as the figure of Pancho Villa is a premier symbol, not merely of a romanticized nationalist Mexicanness, but more accurately, of a heroic, popular-nationalist, Mexican masculinity (cf. Paredes, 1971 [1993: 234]).

9. For a discussion of Pancho Villa jokes as a distinct genre, see Reyna (1984). For a more extended discussion of this joke, especially in relation to Blackness, see de Genova (1999: 287–356, in press).

10. It is possible to identify the same distinctions, deployed fairly consistently, in the transcripts of ethnographic interviews with Mexican migrants compiled by Jorge Durand and his collaborators, and published in Spanish (1996). One encounters the phrase "*americanos o negros*" (p. 217), as well as an operative mutually exclusive juxtaposition of "*gringos*" and "*negros*" (pp. 92–93, 106), or "*gabachos*" and "*negros*" (p. 57).

REFERENCES

Barrera, Mario
1979   *Race and Class in the Southwest: A Theory of Racial Inequality.* Notre Dame: University of Notre Dame Press.

Calavita, Kitty.
1996   "The New Politics of Immigration: 'Balanced Budget Conservatism' and the Symbolism of Proposition 187." *Social Problems* 43(3): 284–299.

Chock, Phyllis Pease
1991   "Illegal Aliens" and "Opportunity": Myth-Making in Congressional Testimony. *American Ethnologist* 18(2): 279–294.

de Genova, Nicholas
1999   Working the Boundaries, Making the Difference: Race and Space in Mexican Chicago. Ph.D. dissertation, Department of Anthropology, University of Chicago.

Díaz-Quiñones, Arcadio

1993   *La memoria rota.* Río Piedras, Puerto Rico: Ediciones Huracán.

Duany, Jorge

2000   Nation on the Move: The Construction of Cultural Identities in Puerto Rico and the Diaspora. *American Ethnologist* 27(1): 1–26.

Durand, Jorge, ed.

1996   *El Norte es como el mar: Entrevistas a trabajadores migrantes en Estados Unidos.* Guadalajara, México: Universidad de Guadalajara.

Grosfoguel, Ramón, and Chloé S. Georas

1996   The Racialization of Latino Caribbean Migrants in the New York Metropolitan Area. *CENTRO: Journal of the Center for Puerto Rican Studies* 8(1&2): 191–201.

Gutiérrez, David G.

1995   *Walls and Mirrors: Mexican Americans, Mexican Immigrants, and the Politics of Ethnicity.* Berkeley, CA: University of California Press.

History Task Force

1979   *Labor Migration Under Capitalism: The Puerto Rican Experience.* New York: Centro de Estudios Puertorriqueños.

Honig, Bonnie

1998   Immigrant America? How Foreignness "Solves" Democracy's Problems. *Social Text* 56: 1–27.

Illinois Legislative Investigating Committee

1971   *The Illegal Mexican Alien Problem.* Springfield, IL: State of Illinois Printing Office.

Kahn, Joan, and Rosalind Berkowitz

1995   "Sources of Support for Young Latina Mothers." Washington, DC: The Urban Institute.

Mirandé, Alfredo

1985   *The Chicano Experience: An Alternative Perspective.* South Bend, IN: University of Notre Dame Press.

1987   *Gringo Justice.* Notre Dame, IN: University of Notre Dame Press.

Montejano, David

1987   *Anglos and Mexicans in the Making of Texas, 1836–1986.* Austin, TX: University of Texas Press.

Morris, Nancy

1995   *Puerto Rico: Culture, Politics, and Identity.* New York: Praeger Publishers.

Newman, Katherine

1999   *No Shame in My Game: The Working Poor in the Inner City.* New York: Russell Sage Foundation.

Paral, Rob

1993   NAFTA and Chicago's Latinos. *Latino: A Publication of the Latino Institute* 6 (1 [August 1993]): 1,6.

Paredes, Américo

1978   The Problem of Identity in a Changing Culture: Popular Expressions of Culture Conflict Along the Lower Rio Grande Border. Chapter 2 (pp. 19–47) in Paredes, *Folklore and Culture of the Texas-Mexican Border*. Austin, TX: Center for Mexican American Studies, University of Texas Press.

Reyna, José R.

1984   Pancho Villa: The Lighter Side. *New Mexico Humanities Review* 7(1): 57–62.

Smith, Raymond T.

1996   *The Matrifocal Family: Power, Pluralism, and Politics*. New York: Routledge.

Urciuoli, Bonnie

1996   *Exposing Prejudice: Puerto Rican Experiences of Language, Race, and Class*. Boulder, CO: Westview Press.

Vélez-Ibáñez, Carlos G.

1996   *Border Visions: Mexican Cultures of the Southwest United States*. Tucson: University of Arizona Press.

12

NOT SO GOLDEN?
Latino Fortunes and Futures in California's Changing Economy

Manuel Pastor Jr.

INTRODUCTION

The Great Recession changed the economic landscape of California. As dramatic as the earlier 2001 recession might have been—it certainly had a more colorful name, having been dubbed the "dot bomb" due to its roots in a tech sector meltdown—it was merely a sharp adjustment in comparison to the number of layoffs, foreclosures, and government interventions that followed the financial crash of late 2008. The state and nation are finding their footing again, but there are fundamental questions about how we are reimagining our economies to be responsive to the everyday realities of our changing nation.

Part of that change is demographic: by 2043 the nation is predicted to be majority-minority, a mark California passed in 1999. According to official statistics, by mid-2014, California's Latino population exceeded that of whites, constituting 39.0 percent of the total compared to 38.8 percent for non-Hispanic whites, nearly 6 percent for African Americans, 13 percent for Asian Americans, and 3 percent for multiracial residents (Office of the Governor—California 2014: 151). Perhaps most significant for the Golden State, Latino population growth is slated to continue, and Latino political influence has been on the rise. In 2014, for example, Kevin de León became the president pro tempore of the State Senate, the first Latino to hold that post in more than a century. But that just builds on a recent history in which Latino Speakers of the Assembly have included John Pérez (2010–2014), Fabian Núñez (2004–2008), Antonio Villaraigosa (1998–2000), and Cruz Bustamante (1996–1998).

However much the demographic share has expanded, Latinos have yet to hit the economic mainstream, and remain in the center of the state's working-poor population as they have been before, during, and after the 2008 Great Recession. Indeed, while the economic slump affected all Californians, Latinos experienced the brunt of these shifts (Taylor et al. 2012): the collapse of employment and wages (affecting incomes), foreclosures (affecting wealth), and fiscal shortfalls for the state (affecting the ability of younger Latinos to be educated and prepared for the future). This was not a one-off but reflects a longer-term vulnerability and inequality baked into the very structure of the California economy. Perhaps as important: given the state's demographics, whether the Latino community recovers or not will determine the future not just of Latinos but of the state overall.

Accordingly, this chapter seeks to offer a longer-run look at the situation of Latinos in the California economy. I begin with a brief review of employment and distributional trends of the last decade and a half. I then profile key economic characteristics of California's Latinos, especially the striking contradiction between high rates of labor force participation and high rates of poverty, and suggest that a significant portion of this gap has to do with lower levels of job quality and educational attainment. I note that Latinos are a disproportionate share of the state's working poor and stress that strategies geared to the working poor should be of special interest to Latinos. I conclude with a brief discussion of both the policies and the political changes that will be necessary to make this happen and a discussion of the immigrant integration policies that may be a sign of changing times in the state.

A few caveats are in order. First, I do not focus on Latino small business; in Pastor (2003) I offer a more-detailed account of that sector and stress the importance of such businesses in hiring other co-ethnics and thus enhancing employment. I also note there the potential contribution of small business to community and economic development, emphasizing how the flowering of a middle class with sufficient assets and political power can help a general Latino agenda, particularly when that middle class is only one generation and modest amounts of income away from its working-class origins. The good news is that the number of Latino businesses has grown dramatically: between 2002 and 2007, there was an increase of more than 100,000 Latino-owned businesses in California, and total receipts for those businesses grew by more than $20 billion. At the same time, Latino-owned businesses are not the biggest or most impactful in the economy: they make up about 17 percent of all businesses but only about 8 percent of firms with paid employees (i.e., they are disproportionately sole proprietorships), and they receive only about 2 percent of total business receipts in the state.[1] So the major driver for Latino economic outcomes remains the experience in labor markets.

Second, I do not offer a detailed analysis of the stock of wealth by ethnicity in the state. This is an important issue since generational advantage is often passed on through wealth, and enhanced private wealth, including home equity, can make it easier for communities to borrow, start businesses, and further economic development. Lopez and

Moller (2003) cover this dimension in some detail, including an analysis that suggests that in the early 2000s, the average non-Hispanic white household in California had around four times the level of wealth of the average Latino household, with the wealth disparity even larger if one does not include home equity but instead focuses in on financial assets. As bad as that might sound, those authors may have been analyzing a high-water mark: the recession has disproportionately affected assets in communities of color, with one estimate suggesting that between 2005 and 2009 median household wealth fell by 16 percent for non-Hispanic white households and by 66 percent for Latino households nationwide (Kochhar, Fry, and Taylor 2011). While I do touch a bit on the asset issue by considering changes in home ownership (an important part of the recession experience), that is not the primary focus of this chapter.

Finally, while I note what the literature has told us about the relative importance of immigrant status, education, and other factors, I do not offer any independent regression analysis of the determinants of Latino economic performance in the state (for that, see Pastor Jr. 2003). In general, the bottom line from such statistical studies squares with common sense: while discrimination, networks, and other factors also play a role, immigration, education, and job quality are among the most important variables in explaining Latino well-being in the state (see Pastor, Scoggins, and Tran 2010, for example). This suggests that a Latino economic agenda may wish to focus on those measures, as well as to accept that the very nature of the "new economy" requires improvements in basic labor standards, especially for Latino economic advancement. To begin to lay out and understand that central message, I start below by analyzing the broad economic background that helps explain Latino fortunes (or lack thereof) in California.

THE GENERAL ECONOMIC PICTURE AND LATINOS

The California economy has been on a bumpy ride for the past several decades. The 1990s began with a sharp recession, which, given its origins in cutbacks in national spending on defense and aerospace, had the sharpest impact on Southern California, particularly the Los Angeles metropolitan area. The 2000s began with another recession, this time spurred by a flurry of speculation in high-tech and Internet stocks that resulted in a meltdown of the NASDAQ stock market and a sharp slowdown in the Silicon Valley and the Bay Area. While both were important and damaging experiences for the California economy, neither compares to the startling economic shock of the late aughts.

One metric that shows why this was a "Great Recession": from a peak in 2007, by 2009 the state had lost more than 1 million jobs, which is the greatest drop-off for any state, causing some to argue that California was the epicenter of the crash (Bardhan and Walker 2010). Unemployment was a staggering 12 percent by December 2009—higher than the national average of 10 percent (Bardhan and Walker 2010). By August 2010, 702,000 homes throughout the state of California were in foreclosure, and the state was

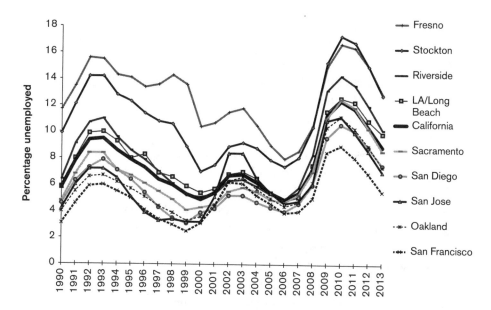

FIGURE 12.1

Unemployment Rates in California and Its Regions, 1990–2013

fourth in the nation in terms of the share of mortgages that were seriously delinquent, meaning those in foreclosure or 90 days behind in payments (Bocian et al. 2010).

Figure 12.1 shows the annual unemployment experience in the state as a whole from 1990 to 2013, along with the pattern in several key metro areas: San Francisco (which includes Marin and San Mateo Counties), Fresno, Stockton, Sacramento, Oakland (which includes Alameda and Contra Costa Counties), Los Angeles/Long Beach, Riverside, San Jose, and San Diego metro areas, all of which, except as noted, include only the county in which the city is located.[2] Fresno and Stockton exhibited the highest unemployment rates from 2008 to 2010, but Los Angeles had the highest rates among urbanized areas. As recovery has proceeded since 2010, the San Jose and San Francisco metro areas—that is, the Silicon Valley—have led California's economy out of the wilderness with unemployment rates well below the state average.

Latinos were particularly affected because the Great Recession was largely triggered by a housing bubble collapse with residual effects on other sectors of the economy, especially construction and then retail trade and manufacturing when consumer spending collapsed. In 2007, on the eve of the recession, 14.3 percent of the immigrant Latino workforce was in the construction industry, 15.1 percent in manufacturing, and 18.6 percent in retail trade (U.S.-born Latinos are an even higher share in this final sector). By contrast, 7.5 percent of the non-Hispanic white workforce was employed in construction, 9 percent in manufacturing, and 15.2 percent in retail trade.[3] Latinos, particularly immigrants, were on the front lines of the slowdown.

What did this long-term pattern of ups and downs mean for distributional outcomes over time? To get at this and other indicators, I combined data from the decennial censuses for 1980, 1990, and 2000 and the American Community Survey (ACS) from 2005 to 2012. This results in a three-decade estimate for any particular variable (1980, 1990, and 2000), followed by yearly outcomes that illustrate what happened just before, during, and after the Great Recession. (It should be noted that income from the decennial census is for the year before, while income from the ACS is more or less for the year of the survey itself.)[4] Such an approach is unique and allows us to look at patterns in much more detail, but it also requires careful interpretation of the graphs as we jump from decadal observation to mid-decade (2005) and then yearly.

What do the data suggest? Adjusting income to 2012 dollars to account for inflation, we see that California's income distribution started off being quite unequal: for 1990 (remember, this is actually 1989 data), the income for those at the 20th percentile of the income distribution was just below $29,000, the income level for the median household was at $66,000, and the income for those at the 90th percentile was about $160,000. Inequality of distribution worsened over the next 20-odd years: by 2012, those at the 20th percentile had slipped by almost $6,000 in real inflation-adjusted income, those at the median had lost about $8,000, and those at the 90th percentile had gained nearly $8,000. This is exactly the "widening divide" that has worried so many analysts, policy makers, and average residents of the state. Depending on how inequality was measured, California clocked in with the second- or third-highest levels of inequality among all states in the years 2008–2010 (McNichol et al. 2012).

Charting income by dollar amount can obscure change because the top income-earning households are so far above the others. Figure 12.2 makes the pattern more apparent by normalizing the income levels at 100 for the initial starting point for our data in 1980 (again, actually 1979), and then tracking the various income distribution points discussed above. Remember that despite the fact that all the series start at 100, they represent very different levels of initial income. The chart highlights that while the 2008 recession clearly had a much larger impact on the middle and bottom of the income distribution, those groups were already doing relatively poorly before 2008.[5] Over the whole period charted, between 1980 and 2012, incomes for those at the 90th percentile of the income distribution went up by 19 percent, while incomes for those in the middle of the income distribution fell by nearly 4 percent and for those at the 20th percentile of the income distribution declined by 13 percent.[6]

The overall pattern does suggest the importance of a strong or weak economy to those in the lower half of the distribution, but it also shows the long-run trend toward inequality despite particular ups and downs.[7] These distributional trends are especially salient for Latinos. In figure 12.3, for example, I look at the ethnic composition of households by income deciles in California for 2012. As might be expected, the non-Hispanic white share of households steadily rises in the higher deciles, peaking at 68 percent of households in the top decile; African Americans have their highest representation

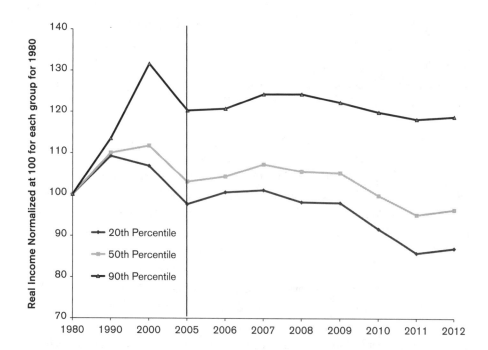

FIGURE 12.2

Income Shifts at Various Percentile Breaks for California Households, 1980–2012

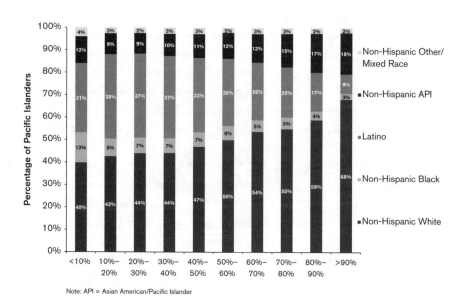

Note: API = Asian American/Pacific Islander

FIGURE 12.3

Ethnic Composition of Households by Household Income Deciles in California, 2012

in the lowest decile (13 percent); the Asian American/Pacific Islander community is bifurcated, with significant representation at the lowest and highest deciles at 12 and 18 percent, respectively; and Latino households peak in the second, third, and fourth deciles for households ranked by income (a pattern consistent with working poverty, a topic I explore below).

Another way to look at the differences by ethnicity is to chart household income by race over time. Two patterns stand out in figure 12.4. First, Latinos and African Americans are both at the bottom, substantially below non-Hispanic white households and Asian American/Pacific Islanders (AAPI but shortened to API in the figures)—reflecting a sort of tale of two economies.[8] Second, while all groups were affected by the Great Recession, the 2012 data hint at an upturn for whites and Asians even as Black household income was stagnating and Latino household income was continuing to fall. Finally, any income analysis fails to highlight the tremendous loss in assets that also occurred as a result of the recession: Partly because Latinos were often given risky subprime loans and subject to predatory practices by banks (Rokosa 2012), nearly 50 percent of all foreclosures from 2006 to 2009 were on Latino borrowers (Bocian et al. 2010). As a result, according to our data, home ownership rates in California fell from 65 percent to 63 percent for non-Hispanic whites but from 48 percent to 42 percent for Latinos over a similar period (between 2007 and 2012).

When we look at the experience of Latinos, it may be useful to look not just at household income but also at persons in poverty. After all, many Latino households, particularly those with foreign-born household heads, have a larger number of workers per household (in 2012, about 20 percent more workers in households headed by immigrant Latinos than in households headed by U.S.-born whites and about 30 percent more than in households headed by U.S.-born blacks). This makes it possible, depending on the number of earners *and* dependents, to both fall below a specified poverty level (which controls for the number of people in a household) and still be doing better in terms of the household income distribution (which does not control for the number of people or earners in a household).[9]

In looking at poverty, I use as a benchmark 150 percent of the poverty rate—that is, persons are designated as poor if the households in which they live have incomes that, if adjusted for household size, would place them below 150 percent of the federally determined poverty level. This poverty level is becoming more common in economic analysis, partly because the calculation of the federal poverty level has not been adjusted for years and seems absurdly low in the context of California's high housing prices; for example, the 150 percent poverty threshold was around $36,000 in 2014 for a family of four, a level most observers would associate with hardship in high-cost California.

As can be seen in figure 12.5, Latino poverty rates in 2012 were the highest in the state, well above those of non-Hispanic whites but also exceeding the poverty rates for African Americans. The chart also shows that poverty rates for Asian Americans exceeded those for non-Hispanic whites. This may surprise some readers since a previous chart rightly

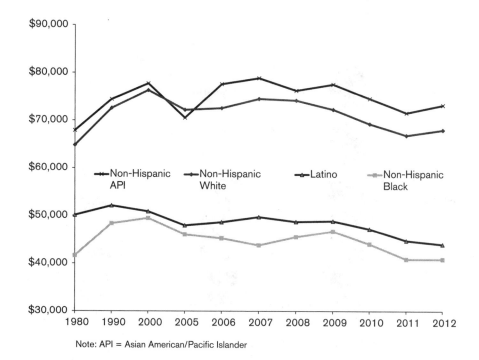

Note: API = Asian American/Pacific Islander

FIGURE 12.4

Median Household Income by Ethnicity in California in 2012, 1980–2012

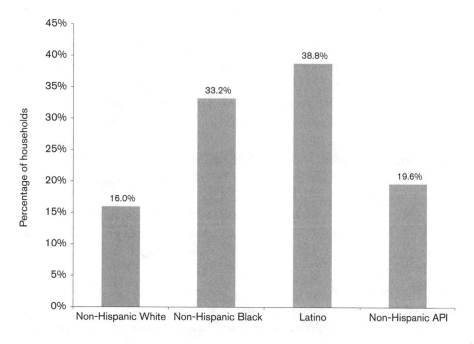

FIGURE 12.5

Percentage of Households below 150% of Poverty Level by Race for California, 2012

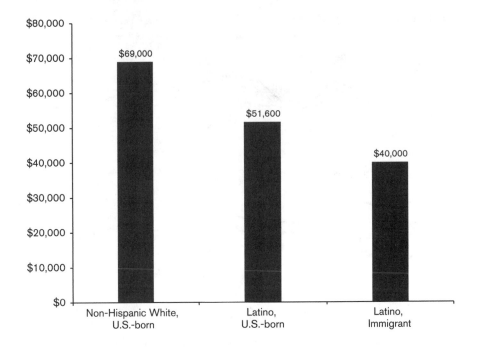

FIGURE 12.6

Household Income of U.S.-Born Non-Hispanic Whites, U.S.-Born Latinos, and immigrant Latinos in California, 2012

depicted Asian Americans as enjoying relatively high household incomes. However, some subgroups like Southeast Asian immigrants and Filipinos fare less well than others, and Asian households are often larger as well, meaning that household incomes need to stretch farther. Still, the most striking fact for this analysis is that nearly 40 percent of the California's Latinos fell below 150 percent of the poverty level, a condition most observers would term quite challenging.

While some may assume that these high poverty outcomes are largely due to the presence of low-earning immigrants, this is not a full explanation. Figure 12.6 turns back to the household income data. The figure shows that immigrant Latino households are certainly low earners, but even households headed by U.S.-born Latinos earn only about three-quarters of the income of their non-Hispanic white counterparts. Something besides the generational immigrant experience is factoring in here—and that other key variable is education.

Over the past few decades, the returns to education—the additional income yielded from an additional year of schooling—have been on the rise. Data from the Economic Policy Institute, for example, indicate that real wages for those with less than a high school education declined by more than 20 percent between 1979 and 2011, while wages for those with a college degree rose by 12 percent over the same period and wages for

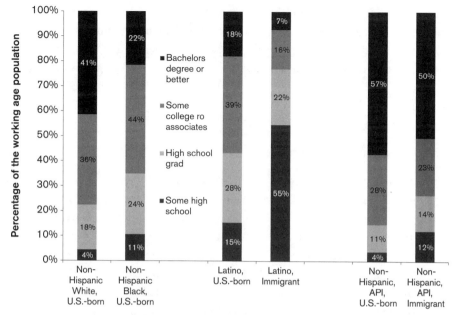

FIGURE 12.7

Educational Attainment for the Working-Age Population (ages 25 to 64) by Ethnicity and Nativity, California, 2012

those with an advanced degree rose by 20 percent over the same period. In short, the earnings gap between the more educated and less educated grew wider.[10] This has negative implications given the generally low educational attainment of Latinos.

Figure 12.7 illustrates this by depicting the educational levels for those who are working-age adults in California (ages 25–64) by race and nativity. The figure shows that education levels are higher for all groups if we focus our attention on those in the civilian labor force, but that important comparison can miss how those who are less educated may simply drop out of the labor force altogether. As can be seen, more than half of Latino immigrants who are of working age lack a high school education, clearly a factor in the earnings disparity for immigrants. What is perhaps more striking is the low rates of college graduates in the workforce for the US-born Latino workforce, even when compared to African Americans, as well as the relatively high percentage of those who have not completed high school.[11]

An early analysis by Stephen Trejo (1997) suggests that the big educational differences evidenced in figure 12.7 account for virtually all of the difference in economic outcomes between non-Hispanic whites and second- and third-generation Mexican Americans, in particular. I have argued that for a variety of reasons this likely overstates the contributing role of education and diminishes the impact of both social networks and ongoing discrimination in labor markets (Pastor and Marcelli 2003). At the same time, it is clear that raising the educational profile of U.S.-born Latinos is a must if one hopes to see any decline in the poverty and income gaps depicted in the various figures above. The other must-do, however, is to tackle the basic nature of the jobs being generated in the California economy, and for this I turn to a deeper analysis of poverty and job creation.

WORKING POVERTY AND LATINOS

The traditional story with regard to poverty suggests that it stems from low levels of attachment to the labor force. That is, individuals become poor when they are not able to obtain employment, perhaps because they have inadequate skills, live far from available jobs, or are saddled with significant childcare responsibilities (Wilson 1997). Yet Latinos do not fit this mold, with males in the state exhibiting the highest rates of labor force attachment of any ethnic group and females parallel with other groups, with the latter particularly impressive since Latinas are far more likely to have children and therefore have various reasons to stay out of the workforce.[12] Instead, the key issue for Latinos is working poverty: having a job but being unable to garner sufficient earnings from that job to support a family.

The nature of poverty matters. First, the remedies are quite different depending on its cause. If the problem is nonworking poverty, connecting people with a job is crucial; if it is working poverty, connecting workers with career advancement is more significant. If the challenge is nonworking poverty, unions could be an impediment, as they often limit entrance to a field; if it is working poverty, unions are crucial, since they can lift the wages of organized workers as has happened in Los Angeles for Latino immigrant workers (for example, see Milkman 2006). If the problem is nonworking poverty, daytime classes that build hard skills and soft skills for employment are essential (as may be programs to help the formerly incarcerated reconnect to jobs); if it is working poverty, classes had better be scheduled at night and had better be focused on hard skills (since presumably those already employed have already acquired a working base of soft skills such as showing up on time, behaving appropriately in the workplace, etc.).

The nature of poverty also matters politically. The U.S. public is generally negatively disposed toward those who do not labor and receive public welfare. On the other hand, polls and focus groups suggest a deep sympathy to those who labor but still fall below the poverty line.[13] Many policy measures that have proved popular in California—such as increases in the state minimum wage, living wage ordinances, and now local minimum wage campaigns—have appealed to the public by lifting up the image of hardworking residents who, due to the vagaries of the economy, were not able to see their efforts translate into more-productive outcomes. Not only does this imagery square with values deeply held by many in the society, it also tends to connect with the insecurities of middle-class Californians who feel as though they are one paycheck away from destitution

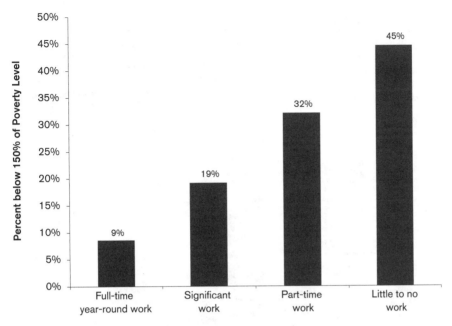

Full-time year-round work = 50+ weeks a year and 40+ hours a week
Significant work = 40–50 weeks a year and 25+ hours a week
Part-time work = 14–40 weeks a year and 10+ hours a week
Little to no work = <10 weeks a year or <10 hours a week

FIGURE 12.8

Percentage of Household Poverty Rate by Work Status of Householder (Ages 25 to 64), California, 2012

themselves—a message that is especially resonant post-2008 recession. For all these reasons, working poverty has surfaced as a major focus for both analysts and advocates.

As can be seen in figure 12.8, work is certainly a major antidote for poverty. For this exercise, I slightly modify the usual census definitions and define full-time work as having worked at least 50 weeks a year and at least 40 hours a week. I also offer a definition for significant work as having worked less than full-time but at least 40 weeks a year and more than 25 hours a week. Part-time work is defined as having worked less than a significant worker but at least 14 weeks a year and more than 10 hours a week; those in the little-to-no-work category have worked less than 10 weeks a year or less than 10 hours a week.[14] I limit my attention to those between the ages of 25 and 64 and focus here on the work experience of the householder, although I take the poverty level from the household as a whole; while there are some potential problems with this strategy (particularly if others in the household are actually the primary earner), it is a useful way to identify ethnicity, poverty, and work experience all at the same time, and more complicated analyses yield similar patterns by ethnicity and other variables (Pastor and Scoggins 2006).

In any case, the figure looks at data from 2012 and illustrates that those who work are far less likely to fall into the poverty trap—45 percent of those ages 25 to 64 who head house-

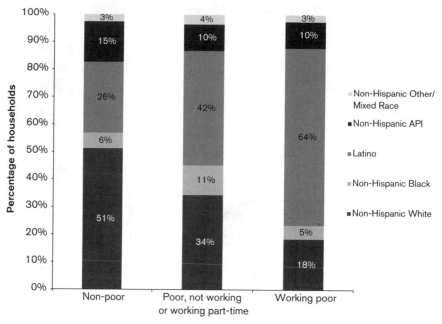

Non-poor   Poor, not working   Working poor
or working part-time

- Non-Hispanic Other/Mixed Race
- Non-Hispanic API
- Latino
- Non-Hispanic Black
- Non-Hispanic White

Note: API = Asian American/Pacific Islander

FIGURE 12.9

Percentage of Non-Poor, Poor but Not Working or Working Part-Time, and Working-Poor
Households Headed by Working-Age Persons (Ages 25 to 64) in California, 2012

holds and are mostly disengaged from the labor market find themselves living below 150 percent of the poverty level. But the chart also shows that nearly one-tenth of full-time, year-round workers and almost 20 percent of those who are engaged in significant work head households that fall below the 150 percent of the poverty level. Who are those individuals who are falling below the poverty level but are still involved in full-time or significant work?

Figure 12.9 helps us understand the demographics by contrasting the ethnic composition of those householders who are non-poor, those who are poor and are not working or are working part-time, and the working poor (those who are poor but have either full-time or significant work); again, the data are from 2012 and are for householders between the ages of 25 and 64. The pattern is striking: Latinos rise from 26 percent of the non-poor households to 42 percent of those who are poor but not working or working part-time (recall the definition above), and then rise again to nearly 64 percent of what we might term "working-poor households." This trend of overrepresentation in the working poor outpaces that of all other groups and is a striking difference from the pattern for African Americans: in California, African Americans are about 6 percent of the non-poor and 5 percent of the working poor, but are 11 percent of the poor who have little or no work.

Another way to look at the same phenomenon is to ask how important the experience of working poverty is to each ethnic group. For this view the focus is on what share of

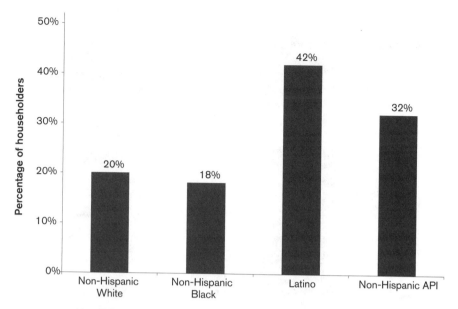

Note: Full-time year-round work = 50+ weeks a year and 40+ hours a week; significant work = 40–50 weeks a year and 25+ hours a week; API = Asian American/Pacific Islander.

FIGURE 12.10

Percentage of Poor Who Are Working Full-Time or Doing Significant Work by Ethnic Group (Ages 25 to 64), 2012

the poor households in each ethnic group falls into the category of working poor. The results are depicted in figure 12.10. As can be seen, 42 percent of the Latino poor fall into the working category (that is, poor but working full-time or a significant amount, as defined above), higher than all other groups. And, as shown in figure 12.9, Latinos compose nearly two-thirds of all the working poor. So improving the quality of employment for Latinos is key to their economic well-being.

This is not to say that unemployment is unimportant—both Latinos and African Americans (especially the latter) have higher rates of unemployment than do non-Hispanic whites. Simultaneously, Latinos, particularly immigrants, have become "embedded" into the structural demand for low-wage labor in the California economy (Cornelius and Marcelli 2000; Cornelius 1998). One way to see this is to decompose the working poor in terms of the immigrant status, particularly recency of arrival. This is done in figure 12.11: note that immigrants overall are about 40 percent of those who are poor but not working or are working part-time, but they are more than 60 percent of those who are poor but have full-time or significant work. In that latter group, the largest overrepresentation comes from the immigrant waves of 10 to 30 years ago, the period of most-intense migration from Mexico and Central America.

All this speaks to a precarious situation in the labor market, another aspect of which

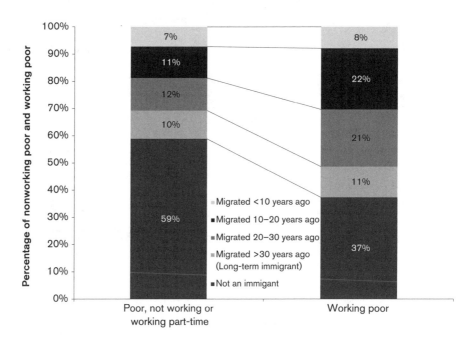

FIGURE 12.11

Immigrant Status of Nonworking Poor and Working Poor in California, 2012

is seen in health insurance coverage. Figure 12.12 shows the situation for working-age adults, breaking out both Latinos and Asians by whether they are U.S.-born or immigrants. Shockingly, nearly 50 percent of Latino immigrants lack health insurance. While the 2014 implementation of the Affordable Care Act (ACA; also known as "Obamacare") has likely improved the situation for the U.S.-born, a significant share of Latino immigrants are undocumented and thus unable to either purchase insurance on the new health exchanges or receive benefits from any expansion of Medicaid. Poor but working, motivated but uninsured, Latino immigrants are certainly facing a perfect recipe for insecurity. The flip side is that select interventions could significantly improve outcomes for Latinos and, by extension, for California as a whole.

ECONOMIC FUTURES AND LATINOS

The economic future of Latinos in California is uncertain. On the one hand, the current economic outlook is problematic, and indicators like educational attainment are not promising. On the other hand, many of the needed policy interventions are known—and we highlight them in this section. These programs and policies are being held back mostly by a lack of public will. There is a ray of hope: in 2013 California adopted a series of immigrant integration policies to support the immigrant community. This and other political realignments may signal a brighter future for Latino Californians.

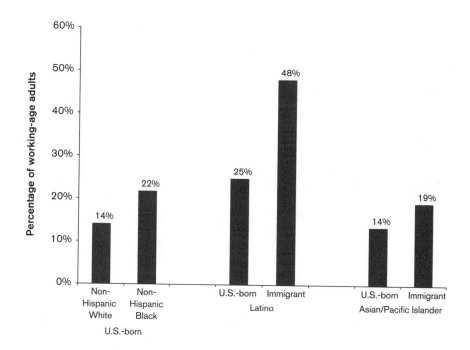

FIGURE 12.12

Percentage of Working-Age Adults (Ages 25 to 65) Who Have Health Insurance Coverage, by Ethnicity and Nativity, in California, 2012

The first step to addressing the economic future of Latinos is to acknowledge that low-wage work seems to have become a permanent part of the economy. This may, at first glance, seem surprising. California is usually depicted as the center of the new economy, complete with its high-tech industries and highly trained populations, certainly factors that have contributed to the resurgence of the state economy. But low-wage jobs in the local-serving sector have often been the flip side of high-tech growth: computer programmers and web designers working 16-hour days wind up needing restaurant, laundry, and childcare services, and those are jobs are filled by large numbers of Latino, immigrant, and other minority workers.

Indeed, such relatively low-wage jobs seem to be an important part of the state's future. Table 12.1 highlights the 20 occupations projected to have the most growth in job openings between 2012 and 2022 according to the California Employment Development Department. While a few might be indirectly in the high-tech industry (for example, general and operations managers as well as accountants and auditors), eight of the top ten require no more than short-term on-the-job training and are exactly the low-quality employment that has contributed to poor outcomes for Latinos in California.[15]

Given this economic backdrop, there are three general matters to better labor market outcomes for Latinos in the state: strong economic growth to expand the pie; targeted

TABLE 12.1   Top Twenty Occupations with the Greatest Number of Job Openings in
the California Economy, 2012–2022

Occupation	Number of Openings	Educational/Training Requirements
Personal Care Aides	228,000	Short-term on-the-job training
Retail Salespersons	220,000	Short-term on-the-job training
Cashiers	189,500	Short-term on-the-job training
Combined Food Preparation and Serving Workers, Including Fast Food	185,700	Short-term on-the-job training
Waiters and Waitresses	162,600	Short-term on-the-job training
Laborers and Freight, Stock, and Material Movers, Hand	135,600	Short-term on-the-job training
Farmworkers and Laborers, Crop, Nursery, and Greenhouse	109,400	Short-term on-the-job training
Office Clerks, General	99,500	Short-term on-the-job training
Registered Nurses	92,300	A.A. degree
General and Operations Managers	89,400	B.A. degree
Customer Service Representatives	85,200	Short-term on-the-job training
Janitors and Cleaners, Except Maids and Housekeeping Cleaners	76,100	Short-term on-the-job training
Stock Clerks and Order Fillers	73,500	Short-term on-the-job training
Accountants and Auditors	70,600	B.A. degree
First-Line Supervisors of Office and Administrative Support Workers	64,900	H.S. diploma or equivalent
Secretaries and Administrative Assistants, Except Legal, Medical, and Executive	62,900	Short-term on-the-job training
Cooks, Restaurant	56,800	Moderate-term on-the-job training
Construction Laborers	55,100	Short-term on-the-job training
Landscaping and Groundskeeping Workers	53,600	Short-term on-the-job training
Maids and Housekeeping Cleaners	50,200	Short-term on-the-job training

Source: CA Employment Development Department, Labor Market Information Division, 9/19/14

education, training, and placement to ensure mobility; and improved labor standards to lift the bottom. Taking these up in turn, the first matter is that we must acknowledge that growth is a sine qua non, although it is an issue often overlooked by progressive thinkers and advocates. It is hard to generate the resources for investment in training and job opportunities if the economy is stalled: the largesse is not there, and neither is the political will. In this light, it is good to know that unemployment rates have been on the decline; from 2011 to 2014 California has been among the top 10 states with the highest rates of employment growth (Kirkham and Hsu 2014).

At the same time, California is increasingly a bifurcated "new economy" that is marked by thriving high-tech industries located in the San Francisco and San Jose area, a slowly recovering inland California, and a sizable low-skilled occupational workforce marked by unemployment and underemployment that is concentrated primarily in communities of color (Weller, Ajinkya, and Farrel 2012). Addressing these disparities is important for growth, particularly since recent research suggests that income inequality, racial segregation, and social separation actually have a deleterious impact on the sustainability of economic growth (Benner and Pastor 2014; Eberts, Erickcek, and Kleinhenz 2006). Still, Latino leaders will have to think hard about the levers of economic growth: what sectors of the economy to support and where public investment could have the most positive impact.

The second matter is to recognize that education and training are an important part of mobility. Educational attainment must be improved, particularly in the public schools that train the lion's share of Latino youth. Indeed, more than 50 percent of all students in California's K–12 are Latino, and this share will only increase (California Budget Project 2013). Passed by California voters in 2012, Proposition 30 has increased state revenues and boosted school spending throughout the state (California Budget Project 2013), but the state still lingers near the bottom in terms of per-student education expenditures. While California's high school graduation rate has increased, Latinos still make up the largest share of all high school dropouts (CDEDRC 2013).

Part of addressing the education challenge will involve encouraging stronger parent and community engagement at the local level. In Los Angeles, Service Employees International Union (SEIU) Local 1877—the so-called Justice for Janitors union—has worked in conjunction with the University of California, Los Angeles (UCLA) to create a "Parent University" program to support the children of union members through educational success and parental involvement workshops (Terriquez et al. 2009). Programs like Parent University cannot fully solve the problem of Latino high school dropout rates, but they do provide a vehicle for Latino working families to advocate for their educational concerns.

As noted earlier, econometric and other evidence suggests that there is a high payoff from a college education: outreach programs for the University of California (UC) and the California State University systems are therefore especially important for Latino economic advancement. Unfortunately, these sorts of programs and public education in general have been very much threatened by the state's current fiscal problems. From 2008 to 2012, the California state government made nearly $1 billion in cuts to the UC system, and, more recently, the UC Regents voted to increase UC tuition by 30 percent over the next five years (Murphy 2014). Tellingly, these cuts come at a time when frustrations have increased about the low enrollment of Black (especially) and Latino students.

The community college system is critically important, as it provides practical training activities for both job seekers and incumbent employees. This is an especially important entry point for those who lack a college degree, including the immigrant population and U.S.-born Latinos. Latino high school graduates are actually more likely to enroll in California community colleges than are non-Hispanic whites or African Americans (Malcolm-Piqueux 2013). Yet California community college budget cuts have totaled more than $1.5 billion from 2007/2008 to 2011/2012 (Bohn, Reyes, and Johnson 2013). At the same time, there was a decrease in enrollment on the order of almost 500,000 students from 2008/2009 to 2011/2012, similar to the declines during the recession in the early 2000s (Bohn et al. 2013).

Adult education and specific job training made available by community colleges, Workforce Investment Boards, and others is critical for supporting the working poor as they move into more-sustainable careers—and must be regeared to suit the population. This should involve mundane matters like the timing of classes, the desirability of on-site training, and the need to couple vocational English training with worker education about basic labor rights. English skills are especially important: they can boost wages for full-time workers by more than 15 percent, even controlling for education, immigrant status, and other factors that usually affect wage outcomes (Pastor Jr. and Marcelli 2000). It would also be useful to consider incentives for employer provision of on-the-job training, something that would be particularly helpful to incumbent workers.

The third matter is to address labor standards—measures that range from minimum wage laws to enhancements in the capacity to join a union to strategies to expand health insurance. The state minimum wage was increased in 2014, and on New Year's Day of 2016 it rose to $10 per hour.[16] In some places in the state, that amount will be even higher: in San Francisco, the city's minimum wage will be $15.00 by 2018 (Office of Labor Standards Enforcement 2014), and in Los Angeles Mayor Eric Garcetti is proposing $13.25 by 2017 (Reich et al. 2014). While a higher minimum wage is helpful, the government could also encourage Latinos to improve their own situations by facilitating worker representation through unions. Ensconced among the working poor, Latinos have been quite receptive to new organizing efforts; in fact, labor's most dramatic organizing successes in recent years—including janitors and home health care workers—have been achieved with largely Latino immigrant workforces (Milkman 2006). The government could help this along through modest changes in labor law that would make it easier for workers to seek union representation. For example, government could adopt regulations that would call a union election quickly after cards are signed rather than allowing companies a lengthy period to convince workers to either vote for the company or face quiet harassment and/or firing.

Wages are only one part of job quality, and the security that comes with health insurance is also critical. The aforementioned Affordable Care Act expanded health insurance to ensure that more people—especially those with irregular work like temp positions—can have access to medical services. According to a summer 2013 survey and subsequent report, 62 percent of the total uninsured in California are Latinos (Kaiser Family Foundation 2014). Our own calculations from the ACS suggest that 56 percent of the working-age uninsured population in 2012 was Latino, and, indeed, 41 percent were immigrant Latinos. This is critical because the Kaiser study also concluded that 29 percent of those who were uninsured could not participate in ACA expansions because of their immigration status. And this goes beyond those individuals: although the U.S.-born children of the undocumented have access to health coverage and access to medical services, their rates lag behind their peers, often because their parents fear that accessing services will get them tangled up in a system more likely to deport than to support immigrants and their families (Marcelli, Pastor, and Wallace 2014).

All this suggests why another critical part of improving the future for Latinos in California involves a commitment to both immigration reform and immigrant integration. There are an estimated 11 million undocumented immigrants nationwide, and roughly one-quarter of them reside in California (Pastor and Marcelli 2013). While that population does exhibit demographic diversity, a full 84 percent of the undocumented are from Mexico and Central America. And this is not a temporary population: it is likely that well over half have been in the country longer than 10 years, and our estimates suggest that fully one-sixth of California's children have at least one undocumented parent, with about 80 percent of those children being U.S.-born citizens. They and their parents are not going anywhere: they are undocumented, but they are Californians, and their well-being is critical to the state's welfare.

Recent years have seen significant advances on immigrant integration issues. California passed legislation to grant driver's licenses for undocumented immigrants; to allow undocumented immigrants to apply for professional state licenses to work as doctors, dentists, nurses, and in other professions; to create the State Dream Loan Program, which will provide $9.2 million for state public universities to administer loans to undocumented students; and to create the California Trust Act, limiting the state's cooperation in handing over undocumented residents detained for minor crimes to Immigrant and Customs Enforcement for potential deportation (Burrell 2014). Much of this has been done with modest political blowback—but that is not really that surprising given that 83 percent of California's adults favor a path to citizenship for undocumented immigrants who meet certain characteristics, such as paying fines and back taxes and learning English (Baldassare et al. 2014).

Of all the policy prescriptions above, only one—immigration reform—is "Latino" in the traditional sense of an ethnic agenda, and that one is broadly popular. Indeed, issues more typical of an ethnic agenda are important: dual language learning programs can help many transition to English, affirmative action has proven quite helpful to the creation of a middle class, and civil rights enforcement is necessary to prevent the sort of bank redlining that impedes Latino businesses and Latino homeownership. But the sort of strategies targeted to lift up this group—better wages, better education, better employment growth, better health insurance, and a fuller engagement in civic and economic life—are both multiethnic in nature and economically effective.

While Latinos may now be the largest ethnic group in the state, they need not and should not go it alone. A sustainable California is one where civic engagement is robust, and economic growth is equitable for all. Pursuing a Latino economic agenda will mean working with others, especially other disadvantaged communities of color, to help realize the community's economic potential. As Latinos continue to grow, working in coalition will ensure a better future for all Californians.

NOTES

1. US Census Bureau, 2002 and 2007 Survey of Business Owners, http://www.census.gov /econ/sbo/; and IOTD Hispanic Research Center and World Demographic Research (2011).

2. Employment data are from California's Employment Development Department, Labor Market Information Division (see www.edd.ca.gov). Note that the Central Valley has very high and persistent rates of unemployment. The experience of Latinos in agriculture and rural areas is important and unique, and deserving of treatment separate from what is offered here.

3. All data are from the specially pooled sample of the decennial census and American Community Surveys as explained below.

4. The decennial census is administered once a decade and always asks about household income for the year before; the ACS asks about income in the last year, but it is a rolling survey done every month, so by the December wave, it is actually collecting information about the year of the ACS.

5. The peak for the 90th percentile in 2000 likely reflects the high-tech boom occurring in that period (that is, in 1999).

6. Some might suggest that this shifting income distribution is simply the result of immigrants entering the labor force at the bottom and thus dragging down certain percentiles simply by their low-earning presence. While this analysis does not completely disentangle that impact, we also looked at the income distribution for just U.S.-born Californians from 1980 to 2012. For that group, the downward shift for those at the 20th percentile was a bit smaller; the median fell by only 1 percent, but the gains at the 90th percentile were even larger. In short, the inclusion of immigrants in the data presented does not seem to distort the underlying distributional shifts in the economy.

7. In Pastor and Zabin (2002), we use state-provided data from the Occupational Employment Statistics Survey to show the changes in wages at various points on a wage distribution—for the worker at the 25th percentile, one at the 50th percentile, and one at the 75th percentile—and find that the latter part of the boom in the 1990s brought great gains

for those on the bottom. By contrast, the weakness of the economy in the latter part of the 2000–2009 decade brought a large hit to those in the middle, and especially to those with the lowest incomes.

8. In 2005, AAPI household income was below that of non-Hispanic whites. This may be due to an anomaly or smaller sample (2005 was the first year of the ACS, so it may have not been as stable as it later became). With the exception of that data point, AAPI household income consistently exceeds that of non-Hispanic whites.

9. This realization does not prevent Rodriguez (1996) from making what I think is a misleading analytical decision—using median household income as a cutoff point for determining whether a household is middle class. This winds up counting many large households with multiple earners of low-wage earners as part of a growing Latino "middle class" in Southern California. In fact, household income may be moderate, but resources per person can be low.

10. "Hourly Wages by Education, 1973–2011 (2011 dollars)," *The State of Working America* (Washington, DC: Economic Policy Institute, 2012), http://www.stateofworkingamerica .org/chart/swa-wages-table-4-14-hourly-wages-education/.

11. See Pastor, Scoggins, and Tran (2010) for a discussion of the difference in labor market signals sent by immigrant and U.S.-born Latinos with or without a high school diploma. In brief, lacking a diploma as an immigrant from Latin America is much less damaging than for the U.S.-born in terms of indicating a job candidate's basic job readiness; lacking a diploma or GED for a U.S.-born Latino is interpreted very negatively by employers.

12. The data are more complicated, but the picture is more complete when we take nativity into account. For males, U.S.-born whites and U.S.-born Latinos have about the same rate of labor force attachment (defined as someone between the ages of 25 and 64 who is either working or looking for work) at around 83 percent, while immigrant Latino men have a labor force participation rate of 90 percent and African-American men have a rate of only about 68 percent (part of the reason why the jobless story has been so prevalent in the discussion of urban poverty is those high rates of disconnection for Black men). As for females, the labor force participation rate for U.S.-born Latinas actually exceeds that of whites, but the rate for immigrant Latinas is much lower; the rate for African-American women is just shy of the figure for U.S.-born whites. All calculations are from the ACS for 2012.

13. For more information on polls, see Center for American Progress, "New Poll on the Legacy of the War on Poverty and American Attitudes about Work, Economic Opportunity, and the Safety Net," news release, January 7, 2014, https://www.americanprogress.org/ press/release/2014/01/07/81657/release-new-poll-on-the-legacy-of-the-war-on-poverty-and -american-attitudes-about-work-economic-opportunity-and-the-safety-net/.

14. A similar work breakdown is developed and utilized in Pastor Jr. and Marcelli (2000). The breaks for weeks may be a bit odd—why 14 hours for part-time work?—but they are dictated by the breaks that have become part of the new ACS variable for weeks worked per year (which used to be continuous but is now categorical).

15. The data come from California Employment Development Department, "Labor Market Information," http://www.labormarketinfo.edd.ca.gov/.

16. California Department of Industrial Relations, "Minimum Wage," http://www.dir.ca .gov/dlse/faq_minimumwage.htm.

REFERENCES

Baldassare, Mark, Dean Bonner, Sonja Petek, and Jui Shrestha. 2014. *Californians and Their Government*. Public Policy Institute of California. http://www.ppic.org/content/pubs/survey/S_114MBS.pdf.

Bardhan, Ashok, and Richard A. Walker. 2010. "California, Pivot of the Great Recession." Institute for Research on Labor and Employment. Retrieved November 17, 2014. http://escholarship.org/uc/item/0qn3z3td.

Benner, Chris, and Manuel Pastor. 2014. "Brother, Can You Spare Some Time? Sustaining Prosperity and Social Inclusion in America's Metropolitan Regions." *Urban Studies* 52 (7): 1339–56.

Bocian, Debbie, Peter Smith, Ginna Green, and Paul Leonard. 2010. *Dreams Deferred: Impacts and Characteristics of the California Foreclosure Crisis*. Center for Responsible Lending. http://responsiblelending.org/california/ca-mortgage/research-analysis/dreams-deferred-CA-foreclosure-report-August-2010.pdf.

Bohn, Sarah, Belinda Reyes, and Hans Johnson. 2013. *The Impact of Budget Cuts on California's Community Colleges*. Public Policy Institute of California. http://www.ppic.org/content/pubs/report/R_313SBR.pdf.

Burrell, Julian. 2014. "Immigration Reform 2014 News: CA Governor." *Latin One*, October 1. http://www.latinopost.com/articles/8905/20141001/immigration-reform-2014-news-ca-governor-signs-reform-bills-makes-them-law.htm.

California Budget Project. 2013. *Rising to the Challenge: Why Greater Investment in K–12 Education Matters for California's Students*. California Budget Project.

CDEDRC. 2013. *Dropouts by Ethnic Designation 2012–13 State of California*. California Department of Education Data Reporting Office. http://dq.cde.ca.gov/dataquest/DropoutReporting/DrpByEth.aspx?cDistrictName=State&CDSCode=00000000000000000&Level=State&TheReport=dEthnic&ProgramName=All&cYear=2012–13&cAggSum=StTotGrade&cGender=B.

Cornelius, Wayne. 1998. "The Structural Embeddedness of Demand for Immigrant Labor in California and Japan." Paper presented at the Winter 1998 Workshop of the Comparative Immigration and Integration Program at the University of California, San Diego. February 20.

Cornelius, Wayne, and Enrico A. Marcelli. 2000. "The Changing Profile of Mexican Migrants to the United States: New Evidence from California and Mexico." Discussion Paper No. 220. Bonn, Germany: Institute for the Study of Labor, 2000, 45. http://repec.iza.org/dp220.pdf.

Eberts, Randall, George Erickcek, and Jack Kleinhenz. 2006. *Dashboard Indicators for the Northeast Ohio Economy: Prepared for the Fund for Our Economic Future*. Cleveland, OH: Federal Reserve Bank of Cleveland. http://www.clevelandfed.org/Research/Workpaper/2006/wp06–05.pdf.

IOTD Hispanic Research Center and World Demographic Research. 2011. *Hispanic Business Report: California, 2011—Documenting the Economic Impact of Hispanics in California and in Los Angeles County*. Stockton, CA: IOTD Hispanic Research Center and World Demographic Research. http://www.lbausa.com/wp-content/uploads/Hispanic-Business-Report-California.pdf.

Kaiser Family Foundation. 2014. "Where Are California's Uninsured Now? Wave 2 of the Kaiser Family Foundation California Longitudinal Panel Survey." Kaiser Family Foundation. Retrieved November 25, 2014. http://kff.org/health-reform/report/where-are-cali fornias-uninsured-now-wave-2-of-the-kaiser-family-foundation-california-longitudinal -panel-survey/.

Kirkham, Chris, and Tiffany Hsu. 2014. "California's Unemployment Rate Falls to 7.4%." *Los Angeles Times.* http://www.latimes.com/business/la-fi-california-jobs-20140719-story .html.

Kochhar, Rakesh, Richard Fry, and Paul Taylor. 2011. *Wealth Gaps Rise to Record Highs Between Whites, Blacks and Hispanics.* Washington, D.C.: Pew Hispanic Center. Retrieved December 24, 2014. http://www.pewsocialtrends.org/files/2011/07/SDT-Wealth-Report_7–26 –11_FINAL.pdf.

Lopez, Elias, and Rosa Maria Moller. 2003. *The Distribution of Wealth in California, 2000.* Sacramento: California Research Bureau. http://www.library.ca.gov/crb/03/10/03–010.pdf.

Malcolm-Piqueux, Lindsey. 2013. "Latina and Latino High School Graduates Are Disproportionately Enrolled in Community Colleges." Tomás Rivera Policy Institute. Retrieved November 26, 2014. http://trpi.uscmediacurator.com/cc-enrollment/.

Marcelli, Enrico, Manuel Pastor, and Steve Wallace. 2014. *Ensuring California's Future by Insuring California's Undocumented: Why Excluding Undocumented Californians from the Affordable Care Act Hurts All of Us.* http://dornsife.usc.edu/assets/sites/731/docs/Ensur ing-CA-Future-Health4All-web.pdf.

McNichol, Elizabeth, Douglas Hall, David Cooper, and Vincent Palacios. 2012. "Pulling Apart: A State by State Analysis of Income Trends." Center on Budget and Policy Priorities. http://www.cbpp.org/research/poverty-and-inequality/pulling-apart-a-state-by-state -analysis-of-income-trends.

Milkman, Ruth. 2006. *L.A. Story: Immigrant Workers and the Future of the U.S. Labor Movement.* New York: Russell Sage Foundation.

Murphy, Katy. 2014. "University of California: The Hidden Cost of Tuition Hikes." *San Jose Mercury News,* November 23. Retrieved November 26, 2014. http://www.mercurynews .com/education/ci_26998525/hidden-cost-ucs-tuition-hike.

Office of Labor Standards Enforcement. 2014. *Minimum Wage Ordinance.* City and County of San Francisco. http://sfgsa.org/index.aspx?page=411.

Office of the Governor—California. 2014. *Governor's Budget Summary, 2014–15.* Sacramento, CA: Office of the Governor. http://www.ebudget.ca.gov/2014–15/pdf/BudgetSummary/ FullBudgetSummary.pdf.

Pastor, Manuel, Jr. 2003. "Rising Tides and Sinking Boats: The Economic Challenge for California's Latinos." In *Latinos and Public Policy in California: An Agenda for Opportunity,* edited by David Lopez and Andres Jimenez. Berkeley, CA: Berkeley Public Policy Press.

Pastor, Manuel, Jr., Peter Dreier, J. Eugene Grigsby III, and Marta Lopez-Garza. 2000. *Regions That Work: How Cities and Suburbs Can Grow Together.* Minneapolis: University of Minnesota Press.

Pastor, Manuel, Jr., and Enrico A. Marcelli. 2000. "Men N the Hood: Skill, Spatial, and Social Mismatch among Male Workers in Los Angeles County." *Urban Geography* 21(6): 474–96.

———. 2003. "Somewhere over the Rainbow?: African Americans, Unauthorized Mexican Immigration, and Coalition Building." *The Review of Black Political Economy* 31(1–2): 125–55.

———. 2013. *What's at Stake for the State: Undocumented Californians, Immigration Reform, and Our Future Together.* Los Angeles: USC Program for Environmental and Regional Equity. Retrieved October 29, 2013. http://csii.usc.edu/undocumentedCA.html.

Pastor, Manuel, Jr., and Justin Scoggins. 2006. *Working Poor in the Golden State.* Santa Cruz: University of California, Santa Cruz. http://cjtc.ucsc.edu/docs/r_golden_state.pdf.

Pastor, Manuel, Jr., Justin Scoggins, and Jennifer Tran. 2010. *A State Resilient: Immigrant Integration and California's Future.* Los Angeles: USC Center for the Study of Immigrant Integration. Retrieved November 25, 2014. http://dornsife.usc.edu/assets/sites/731/docs/state_resilient_reduced.pdf.

Pastor, Manuel, Jr., and Carol Zabin. 2002. "Recession and Reaction: The Impact of the Economic Downturn on California Labor." University of California Institute for Labor and Employment. Retrieved November 25, 2014. http://escholarship.org/uc/item/79j2w7q0.

Reich, Michael, Ken Jacobs, Annette Bernhardt, and Ian Perry. 2014. *The Mayor of Los Angeles' Proposed City Minimum Wage Policy: A Prospective Impact Study.* Center on Wage and Employment Dynamics. http://www.irle.berkeley.edu/cwed/briefs/2014–05.pdf.

Rodriguez, Gregory. 1996. *The Emerging Latino Middle Class.* Malibu, CA: Davenport Institute, School of Public Policy, Pepperdine University. http://publicpolicy.pepperdine.edu/davenportinstitute/reports/latino/latino1.html.

Rokosa, Jennifer. 2012. "Latinos Bearing the Brunt of the Foreclosure Crisis." Center for American Progress. Retrieved November 19, 2014. https://www.americanprogress.org/issues/housing/news/2012/04/19/11416/latinos-bearing-the-brunt-of-the-foreclosure-crisis/.

Taylor, Paul, Mark Hugo Lopez, Gabriel Velasco, and Seth Motel. 2012. "Latinos and Homeownership." Pew Research Center's Hispanic Trends Project. Retrieved November 24, 2014 http://www.pewhispanic.org/2012/01/26/iii-latinos-and-homeownership/.

Terriquez, Veronica, John Rodgers, Gary Blasi, Janna Hernandez, and Lauren Applebaum. 2009. *Unions and Education Justice: The Case of SEIU Local 1877 Janitors and the "Parent University."* UCLA Institute for Research and Labor Employment. http://www.irle.ucla.edu/publications/documents/ResearchBrief3.pdf.

Trejo, Stephen J. 1997. "Why Do Mexican Americans Earn Low Wages?" *Journal of Political Economy* 105(6): 1235–68.

Weller, Christian, Julie Ajinkya, and Jane Farrel. 2012. "The State of Communities of Color in the U.S. Economy." Center for American Progress. http://www.nanworld.org/pdf/comm_of_color.pdf.

Wilson, William J. 1997. *When Work Disappears: The World of the New Urban Poor.* New York: Random House.

PART 5

CLASS, GENERATION, AND ASSIMILATION

The United States has been long hailed as the land of opportunity, where immigrants of humble origins are given the chance to improve the quality of their lives and achieve the proverbial American dream. That dream was often successfully attained by the first generation of immigrants who came to this country during the long and storied history of ethnic group migration in the nineteenth and twentieth centuries. More often, however, it has been their children who benefitted from the sacrifices that immigrant parents made in the United States. Yet the unsettling reality has been that not every immigrant group that came to the United States has successfully experienced upward mobility in their members' lifetimes (intragenerational mobility), nor have their children always attained socioeconomic success (intergenerational mobility) in anticipated ways. This upward movement in socioeconomic status and cultural assimilation have been concerns of American sociologists since the early twentieth century. Robert E. Park, a sociologist at the University of Chicago, was among the first to explore this process, in the 1920s and 1930s. He famously proposed that U.S. racial and ethnic groups have followed a systematic integrative process through various cycles of group interaction. Park posited that this "race relations cycle" comprises four stages: contact, conflict, accommodation, and assimilation. The first stage is one of group contact, followed by group competition, then group accommodation, and culminating in group assimilation.

Sociologist Milton Gordon expanded on this pattern of racial and ethnic group integration in his book *Assimilation in American Life*.[1] Gordon's contribution centered on devising a more complex and nuanced pattern of race and ethnic relations that comprises seven stages: acculturation (adopting to the language, customs, values, and norms of the host society), structural assimilation (widespread participation in the dominant institutions of the host society), marital assimilation (intermarriage between dominant and subordinate groups), identification assimilation (minorities' embrace of the identity of the dominant culture), attitude reception assimilation (the absence of group prejudice), behavior reception assimilation (the absence of discrimination), and civic assimilation (the absence of conflict in values and power struggles). While there have been various critiques of this process, the value of sociologists' attention on these patterns and processes continues to have relevance to this day.

But not every social scientist has been as optimistic about the contemporary assimilative potential of Latinos in the United States, especially the large Mexican immigrant population that has been the lightning rod of nativist hostility in recent years. For instance, Samuel P. Huntington, the eminent political scientist who spent most of his academic career as a professor at Harvard University, became particularly shrill about the presence of Latinos in the United States, progressively escalating his xenophobic call to arms in a number of publications. In "The Hispanic Challenge," Huntington argued that America was being invaded by Mexicans and Cubans who were forming ethnic enclaves, refusing to learn English, and failing to assimilate—in short, refusing to embrace America's "core Anglo-Protestant culture" that had been dominant since the republic's foundation. As the Hispanic population in the United States became numerically dominant, would, for example, the use of English and Spanish be considered appropriate in congressional debates and in the conduct of government? Would English speakers feel disadvantaged and grow resentful when they competed with Spanish-English bilinguals for jobs in regions of the country where Latinos predominated? Would America become "MexAmerica" or "Amexica"? Unless white American patriots organized themselves, they would soon see "the end of the America we have known for more than three centuries." "Americans should not let that change happen," Huntington implored, rehearsing these same arguments in far greater detail in his 2004 book, *Who Are We? The Challenges to America's National Identity.*[2]

Huntington's closing assertion was that "There is no *Americano* dream. There is only the American dream created by an Anglo-Protestant society. Mexican Americans will share in that dream and in that society only if they dream in English." Chapter 13 by Luis Fraga and a group of his colleagues, "Latino Lives: Trying for the *Americano* Dream: Barriers to Making the United States 'Home,'" forcefully retorts Huntington's rant. Relying on extensive survey research, the authors show that the American dream has been a powerful aspiration for Latinos, just as it has been for immigrants from all parts of the world, promising success and upward mobility for those willing to uproot and work hard in America. The 2004 and 2007 attitude surveys they drew on mainly equated the *Americano* dream with financial security. Latinos wanted good, secure, well-paying jobs, with older respondents hoping for good health and access to medical care, and younger ones aspiring to home ownership, good schools, and the ability to move to better neighborhoods. When respondents were asked to identify the most significant barriers to the realization of their dreams, they pointed to discrimination and poor-quality schools. Without education and English-language mastery, upward mobility was often beyond their reach; without English-language fluency, they experienced unfair and discriminatory treatment in public. Unless they could overcome these barriers, their dreams would surely be stalled, postponed for many generations, if not completely dashed. Foreign-born Latinos understood that to make it in America they had to adapt, and incorporate into their communities, which they indeed do, frequently socializing with neighbors and fellow churchgoers, enlisting in the military, in many cases marrying non-Latinos, and eventually thinking of themselves as Americans.

Numerous studies exist on the ways Latino populations have integrated into the fabric of American society in broad generational terms. Much of this literature's focus has been on the Mexican-origin population because of their longstanding presence in the southwestern United States and their long history of immigration from Mexico for more than one hundred years. The opportunities and life chances extended or denied to generations of Mexican immigrants was foundationally studied by Leo Grebler, Joan W.

Moore, and Ralph C. Guzman in their book *The Mexican-American People: The Nation's Second Largest Minority.*[3] They documented the various dilemmas and obstacles that Mexicans experienced in attempting to move up the socioeconomic ladder and culturally assimilate into American life. Based on household survey data collected in Los Angeles, California, and San Antonio, Texas, in 1965 and 1966, *The Mexican-American People* documents that some sectors of the Mexican population in these cities were indeed entering the middle class and making notable inroads into American society. Yet they also confirmed that others were not as successful in this assimilation process, even if they had lived here for several generations. As a result, they came to the sobering conclusion that "astonishingly little" collective assimilation and group integration existed in these two large cities or elsewhere where Mexican-origin immigrants had settled for generations.

In 2008 sociologists Edward Telles and Vilma Ortiz updated and extended the data used in the Grebler, Moore, and Guzman study by thirty-five years in their follow-up study *Generations of Exclusion: Mexican Americans, Assimilation and Race.*[4] Chapter 14, the "Conclusions" of their book, provides a long view of the mobility process for four generations of Mexican-origin people in the United States. While this process cannot be mechanically extended to other Latino immigrant populations of more recent vintage, it does provide a comprehensive, multigenerational assessment of the structural and cultural assimilation of Latinos. Telles and Ortiz's book compellingly argues that the ongoing denial of educational opportunity in the United States has been the "linchpin" of the failure of Mexicans to rapidly move up the socioeconomic ladder. Their meaningful realization of the American dream has been largely denied because of this structural factor, and it has subsequently led to "generations of exclusion." They compellingly show that each succeeding generation of Mexicans settling in Los Angeles and San Antonio has not fully assimilated or been structurally integrated as classic assimilation theory has predicted.

While Mexican Americans of the second generation do experience a significant rise in their overall status compared to that of their immigrant parents, subsequent generations do not continue this steady rise in socioeconomic status and rapid acculturation. Instead, most third- and fourth-generation Mexican Americans do not experience widespread loss of their ethnic identity, accelerated intermarriage rates, the absence of residential segregation, or a significant decline in labor market discrimination. To the contrary, these ethnic boundaries have stubbornly persisted over time and are more than merely symbolic obstacles to their attaining the American dream. For example, meaningful educational opportunities are often interrupted by the second generation and continue to stagnate thereafter for the third and fourth generations. This accounts for the Mexican-origin population having the worst educational attainment profile of any racial-ethnic population in the country. Although a small segment of the Mexican population has fared well, the vast majority of Mexican Americans continue to languish and be denied the promises of socioeconomic mobility that classic assimilation theory predicted. To redress this situation Telles and Ortiz call for a new Marshall Plan that would invest heavily in improving the quality of public school education and address the structural obstacles that have systematically impeded the educational attainment of Mexican-origin students and the meaningful improvement of the contemporary life chances of Latino populations.

Part 5 closes with chapter 15, Richard L. Zweigenhaft and G. William Domhoff's study "Latinos in the Power Elite" and chapter 16, their updated "Postscript" to that essay. These chapters move our attention away from the daunting challenges that generations of Mexican immigrants have faced attempting to improve the quality of their lives. Instead, they focus our attention on that segment of the Latino population that has successfully reached the highest rungs of the socioeconomic hierarchy in the United States. Drawn from their book *Diversity in the Power Elite: How It Happened, Why It Matters*,[5] the chapter offers an eye-opening and sobering view of those individuals who have made inroads into what they term the "power elite." These are not the middle-class individuals who have successfully attained privileged educational and employment opportunities that sociologists have perceptively documented. Rather, they are Latinos of different nationalities from privileged backgrounds who have successfully found a place among the corporate elite, in presidential cabinets, among the military elite, in the U.S. Senate and House of Representatives, and on the Supreme Court. In terms of income, wealth, power, and influence, these individuals constitute the most successful Latinos in the country.

Who are these individuals? How did they become so successful and powerful? What does their success indicate about the opportunity open to others to also reach these vaunted heights? Is their extraordinary socioeconomic success a sign that the proverbial "glass ceiling" can be smashed and that meaningful opportunities can be extended to previously denied groups? Are Latino populations now being granted access to the most privileged echelons of society that were once only open to and dominated by white, Christian, Ivy League–educated, heterosexual men?

Zweigenhaft and Domhoff document that Latinos have indeed made inroads into these privileged sectors but that success has been granted to only a small segment of the population, and that segment has not been significantly expanded in recent years. Chapter 15 shows that it does include some individual rags-to-riches stories. But the majority are individuals who began their ascent from already privileged social locations, and those inroads have been limited to those with the ability to work within, rather than transform, the opportunity structure that is denied to the vast majority of the Latino population. For example, in 1995 the list of the seventy-five richest Latinos included twenty-seven Cuban Americans, twenty-five Mexican Americans, and eight others from Chile, Colombia, Costa Rica, the Dominican Republic, Ecuador, Uruguay, Venezuela, and Puerto Rico. Most of the Cubans who made that list had come from privileged families prior to migrating to the United States, while the majority of Mexican Americans, on the other hand, followed the rag-to-riches pathway.

Vilma S. Martínez is a rare example of the latter, a working-class Latina who climbed into the power elite. She came from a humble but proud Mexican American family of modest means from San Antonio, Texas. After experiencing bitter discrimination as a child, she attended the University of Texas as an undergraduate student and later earned a law degree from Columbia University. Martinez would then serve as a staff attorney for the NAACP Legal Defense Fund and as staff attorney for the New York State Division of Human Rights, and then she helped establish the Mexican American Legal Defense Fund. In 1973 she became the organization's general counsel and president. After a stint as a regent for the University of California system at the age of thirty-two, Martinez joined the prestigious Los Angeles law firm of Munger, Tolles & Olson in 1982, and by 2005 she was serving on the boards of three *Fortune* 500 corporations: Anheuser-Busch, Burlington Northern Railroad, and Fluor Corporation.

The late Roberto Goizueta, who is of Basque and Spanish ancestry, left his native Cuba in 1949 to attend Yale University. He represents the move into this power elite by way of a privileged family background. By the 1960s he had become assistant to the senior vice president of Coca-Cola in the Bahamas and then assistant to the vice president for research and development at the company's Atlanta headquarters. From this auspicious start, he eventually became the corporation's vice president for engineering, senior vice president, and then executive vice president. In 1980 Goizueta was named president and chief operating officer and in 1981, chairman of the board and CEO. When he passed away in 1997, he was one of the most powerful members of the corporate elite in the United States.

Zweigenhaft and Domhoff convincingly show that despite these divergent pathways into the power elite, Latinos who have gained access share a number of characteristics that have facilitated their precipitous climb and full acceptance. These two major factors include their religious background (they are largely Christian and most often from Catholic families) and their skin color and facial features (they are decidedly European in appearance and light complexioned). Of the latter factor, they argue that most of these individuals overwhelmingly appear "Anglo." They further contend that a place among the power elite has been primarily granted to fair complexioned, high-status Latinos who are racially and culturally similar to other European immigrants already ensconced in the power elite. These characteristics have made it possible for these individuals to secure a privileged education at elite Ivy League schools and develop the "cultural capital" to comfortably rub elbows and gain acceptance from the straight, white, Christian males who have traditionally dominated elite circles in the United States.

NOTES

1. Milton Gordon, *Assimilation in American Life* (New York: Oxford University Press, 1964).
2. Samuel P. Huntington, *Who Are We? The Challenges to America's National Identity* (New York: Simon & Schuster, 2004).

3. Leo Grebler, Joan W. Moore, and Ralph C. Guzman, *The Mexican-American People: The Nation's Second Largest Minority* (New York: The Free Press, 1970).

4. Edward E. Telles and Vilma Ortiz, *Generations of Exclusion: Mexican Americans, Assimilation and Race* (New York: Russell Sage Foundation, 2008).

5. Richard L. Zweigenhaft and G. William Domhoff, *Diversity in the Power Elite: How It Happened, Why It Matters* (Lanham, MD: Rowman & Littlefield, 2006).

13

LATINO LIVES:
TRYING FOR THE *AMERICANO* DREAM
Barriers to Making the United States "Home"

Luis Ricardo Fraga, John A. Garcia,
Rodney E. Hero, Michael Jones-Correa,
Valerie Martinez-Ebers, Gary M. Segura

In a focus group in Los Angeles, the moderator asked our participants, "Can you ever imagine immigrating to Mexico and becoming a citizen?" The immediate response from multiple people was an emphatic NO! "Why not?" asked the moderator. One man explained: "It's the freedom here, the economy. There's no pay there." Another man simply stated: "It's the American dream." The "American dream" is a term that has been in usage for a long time by persons throughout the United States. It is a subjective expression that means different things to different people but usually implies achieving a successful and satisfying life as a result of hard work (Adams 1934; Cullen 2003). While many people measure their achievements in life in material terms, such as earning a high income or owning a house, others' perceptions of living the American dream are more abstract, typically described in terms of having personal freedom, enjoying equal rights, and ensuring safety or security for self and family (Hochschild 1995). The allure of the American dream has been pointed to as the motivation of countless generations of immigrants who came to the United States to escape the lack of opportunity and poor quality of life in their home countries. Yet, critics of Latino immigration, especially immigration from Mexico, warn that unless Latinos better assimilate into mainstream society, they will not be sharing in the *"Americano* dream" (Huntington 2004a).

What does "living the dream" mean to Latinos? What are they willing to do to achieve that life? What role does assimilation play in their efforts to achieve their life goals? In this essay, we endeavor to answer these questions. Before we examine what the dream means for our focus group participants, we first examine more systematically how most people in this country think about the American dream. Then we briefly review the conceptual development and controversy of assimilation and consider whether Latinos view "assimilation"—or at least some sense of assimilation—as their path to the American dream. Finally, we look at the extent to which Latinos are integrating into majority society—becoming part of the American fabric—by focusing on select aspects of cultural, structural, and marital assimilation as evidenced in the attitudes and behaviors of our focus group participants and some of the aggregate indicators from the Latino National Survey and other studies.

DEFINITIONS, BARRIERS, AND ATTAINING THE AMERICAN DREAM

As points of comparison, before we discuss what "living the American dream" means to Latinos, we should have some idea of what the dream means for most Americans. Besides their definitions, we should know what they feel are barriers to obtaining it and to what extent they believe the dream is attainable, both personally and for other people. Two national surveys, conducted independently in 2004[1] and 2007,[2] focus on each of these topics.

The targeted populations of the two surveys were distinctly different. The 2004 survey was designed to ensure a broad representation of the total U.S. adult population. Demographic comparisons of the surveyed respondents with U.S. census data suggest the 2004 survey was highly successful in capturing the views of the general population. The 2007 survey was intended to measure the attitudes of workers in nonsupervisory positions. The demographic profile of 2007 respondents was obviously less representative of the general adult population, but these comparatively younger, less educated, less affluent, and primarily blue-collar and service industry employees more closely match the aggregate characteristics of the U.S. Latino population (Ramirez and de la Cruz 2002).

In the first survey, 1,002 respondents were asked: "How do you personally define the American dream?" and were allowed to provide up to three definitions. Financial security/stability was the most frequently provided response (24%). Good jobs/careers and personal freedom tied for the second most commonly provided answer; both were cited by 14%. Having a family (13%) and living comfortably (12%) rounded out the five most mentioned definitions (National League of Cities [NLC] 2004). However, significant racial/ethnic, generational, and social class differences were apparent in the collection of definitions.

"Having choices" or "freedom" was significantly more likely to be mentioned by non-Hispanic whites, 18- to 29-year-olds, college graduates, and those with household incomes over $75,000. "Financial stability" was the top definition voiced by nonwhites, blue-collar workers, and those making less than $30,000. "Good health" was the dominant factor in older respondents' version of the dream (NLC 2004: 6).

When given a predetermined list of definitions and asked to select only two, respondents' priorities changed somewhat but components of the dream remained essentially the same. "Living in freedom" became the top definition (33%), followed by "being financially secure" (26%), "a quality education for my children" (17%), "having a family" (17%), and "enjoying good health" (16%). Having "a good job" (9%) dropped out of the top five, placing a somewhat distant sixth among the offered definitions, which also included "owning a home" (8%), "living in a good community" (6%), and "a secure retirement" (6%). One quarter of the respondents volunteered that everything on this list was part of their American dream (NLC 2004: 28).

When respondents were asked to select two of the most serious barriers or obstacles to achieving the dream from a list of ten items, "poor quality public education" was the most frequently chosen answer (27%). The remaining top five selections were "not being financially secure" (22%), "inability to find a good-paying job" (19%), "limited access to health care or health insurance" (17%), and "racial or ethnic discrimination" (14%). Interestingly, in a separate question, respondents were asked whether they agreed with the statement "Where I live (community, city, or town) has limited my ability to achieve the American dream" and 31% agreed (NLC 2004: 29, 31).

According to this survey, however, Americans remain optimistic about their personal situation: Two thirds of the respondents said they were currently living the American dream. Among those who reported they were *not* living the dream, a majority were still somewhat confident (33%) or very confident (19%) that they eventually would. They had considerably less confidence in others' abilities; 67% agreed with the statement "The American dream is becoming more difficult for average people to obtain," and 70% also agreed that "It is becoming much harder for young families to achieve" (NLC 2004: 30).

In the second comparison survey, a national sample of 800 nonsupervisory workers[3] was asked an open-ended question of what the American dream meant to them; 37% provided answers that focused on the basics of personal economic security, saying that it meant "having a good job," "being able to make a comfortable living," and the more general answer of "financial security." Having a good place to live or raise a family was also cited by 29% of the respondents. Other less frequently offered definitions included personal freedom (15%), owning a home (14%), and having opportunity/choice in life (9%) (Lake Research Partners [LRP] 2007: 6–7).

When asked to assess the importance of American dream-related or life goals identified by others, 80% ranked "having a job that pays enough to support a family" as extremely important, 75% ranked "having affordable quality health care on a dependable basis" as extremely important, and 74% said "having the means to ensure his/her children have the opportunity to succeed" was also extremely important. After these three economic concerns, "being treated with respect" was the next most important component of the American dream for these workers (71% ranked extremely important) (LRP 2007: 8).

When asked to name the number one reason the American dream was becoming

TABLE 13.1   Comparison of the Representativeness of Survey Respondents and
Answers to American Dream Questions, among 2004 NCL and
2007 LRP Survey Respondents

Comparison	2004 Respondents	2007 Respondents
Representativeness of survey respondents	General population including more white collar	Exclusively blue collar, working class
Most frequently cited definition of American dream	Living in freedom	Economic security
Most frequently cited barrier to American dream	Poor quality of education	Income/employment concerns
Percentage who believe they have achieved the American dream	66%	18%

NCL = National League of Cities; LRP = Lake Research Partners

more difficult to reach, 49% gave income-related reasons (for example, low wages, high cost of living, lack of good jobs). Tied for second place, about 10% said the primary obstacle was politics or was the government's fault, while an equal percentage cited changes in Americans' morals or work ethic. In third place, 8% cited problems in education.

Although a majority believed the dream was still obtainable, three quarters of those surveyed felt it was becoming harder to achieve. In sharp contrast to the 2004 survey, in which two thirds reported they had already obtained the American dream, only 18% of these working-class respondents felt they were currently living the dream (see table 13.1). Nearly 70% felt that policies of the government would determine the future for the American dream.

A closer inspection of the results of both surveys suggests one obvious divergent pattern in respondents' answers. Social class (education, job type, and income) significantly constrains individuals' definitions of the American dream as well as perceptions of its attainability. The answers of college-educated, white-collar workers with more affluent incomes suggest that the sense of individual freedom, having options, and making choices, are key ingredients of the American dream. Most believe they will or already have attained the dream. In sharp contrast, for those without college degrees, in blue-collar jobs making considerably less money, the goal of being able to financially provide for their family and their future is foremost in their minds when they describe what it means to be "living the dream." Many believe this goal is attainable, but very few feel like they have achieved it. How do these two distinct visions of the American dream compare with those held by Latinos?

Unlike the surveys, in which respondents were asked direct questions, the focus groups were not specifically solicited for their thoughts on the American dream. However, the notion of wanting the dream and the process or actions required for achieving it emerged *independently* as a theme in focus group conversations across the country. At least four participants made specific reference to the concept, and there were numerous comments—regarding participants' life goals or ambitions, barriers that impeded their efforts, and the progress (or lack thereof) that they thought they had made in attaining those goals—that can be used to depict what living the *Americano* dream means to Latinos.

In major ways, the dream seems to have the same meaning for Latinos as it does for other working-class Americans. With a few exceptions, most notably the English-language focus groups in Washington, DC, the demographics of our focus group participants closely mirror the demographic profile of respondents in the 2007 survey. And, like the workers surveyed in 2007, our participants' comments also focused most on the comforts that come from having good-paying, steady jobs. They want to own homes in safe neighborhoods with high-quality schools for their children. They also want to be respected and treated fairly. Freedoms associated with the First Amendment were important to only a few.

The central focus of the dream for Latinos is the financial security that comes with regular employment. Foremost, they want *good jobs*. Every focus group assessed particulars of their personal employment status and the general climate of jobs available to Latinos. With the exception of a few who originally came to this country to further their education or to flee dangers of political instability at home, most participants acknowledged that Latinos came to the United States primarily to find work. This is certainly not a surprise (Alba and Nee 2003). Recently arrived immigrants reveled at the fact that they were able to find "many good-paying jobs." Later generations, and some of the immigrants who had spent significant portions of their lives in the United States, prized finding jobs that paid well too, but they also were more likely to wish for (and if they had it, to express satisfaction with) a positive working environment (that is, providing "benefits," "good relations with co-workers," "respect and trust from supervisors," and having jobs that they preferred over "jobs that no one else would do"). In Dalton, GA, for example, respondents noted their preference, not just for any work, but for what they perceive as *good* work:

> *Pablo, immigrant (Dalton, GA, S):*[4] I have not seen any difficulties. I like it here, jobs are well paid and because they are not out on the fields.
>
> *Valdemar, U.S. born (Dalton, GA, S):* I like it because the majority of jobs offer good benefits, like medical insurance.

Another component of the *Americano* dream, a part that is greatly dependent on getting good-paying jobs, is being able to move *away from rough parts of town* or to move *out of the barrios.* A conversation thread found in groups held in all the major cities was the desire to avoid or escape the "noise" (from too many "people crowded together," "bottles breaking," and "gunshots"), the "drugs," the "gangs," and other bad elements. Contrary to recent commentary that recent Latino arrivals choose to remain in ethnic enclaves separated from the Anglo population (cf. Huntington 2004b), a majority of those in our focus groups wanted away from the places that had "too many" of their co-ethnics. We see examples in the Miami and New York City focus groups:

> *Multiple respondents (Miami, S):* "Little Havana is a bad neighborhood." "It's really bad. . . . Now there are gangs and thieves." "There's so many [Latinos]." "You can't leave your house. People just sit in their house." "The houses they depreciate there." "The culture is depreciated; there's criminals and drugs." "I want away from there." *(Collective agreement):* "Yeah."

> *Ivan (New York, E):* What I like is that there are not many Latinos. It is very quiet, I feel that there is peace. I don't hear the noise . . . so it is peaceful.

> *Victor (New York, E):* I like the neighborhood where I live now because it is quiet, it's clean. Everyone is working people. It is quiet most of the time. I lived in Harlem for 28 years and the reason I left is because I had two big bullet holes on my wall, and I said I better get out of here before I get killed because of these guys out there selling drugs. I said I had to work hard. Back then I used to do things foolishly, but now I save my money and use it wisely. I LIKE where I live now.

A third component of the *Americano* dream is the goal of *home ownership* in a community that is good for raising a family. With very few exceptions, participants indicated how much they valued being able to purchase a home in a quiet neighborhood that had safe streets and good schools for their children. Every focus group had people mention their goal (either desired or realized) to live in a place that was "quiet," "tranquil," and "safe" enough for "children [to] play outside" or where they could "walk the street at night" without fear.

> *Eric (New York, E):* Where I live now is day and night from where I grew up. Even now when I go to visit my mom, who still lives in the projects, it is LOUD, there are people all over the place, music, throwing bottles. . . . I don't want to go back. I am working very hard to buy a house.

> *Nicholas (Houston, E):* Now I got it GOOD . . . I moved out [of Alief, TX] and over by I-464. Just bought a brand-new house. It's quiet. . . . We got a three-bedroom home and it's quiet. I love it! I don't hear sirens. I love it! . . . I know I don't have children yet . . . but I always wanted something where I knew my kids would grow up safely and in a good area.

> *Roberto (Miami, S):* The tranquility in the streets. My kid can play ball in the street . . . : The unity of family is important where I live, neighbors with families. It is safe and you get a sense of security.

Quality education for their children or themselves is another integral part of the *Americano* dream. Contrary to some popular opinion that Latinos have low expectations and low priorities for education (Badillo 2006), participants in all of our groups referred to the importance of education, especially "having good schools for their children" and "more education" for Latinos in general.

> *Elsa (Muscatine, IA, S):* I am proud to see Hispanic students on honor rolls and to see more Hispanic young adults attending college.

> *Francisca, immigrant (Houston, S):* [S]ome Hispanics are better prepared than others, right? At least for me. I studied nursing, and for 10 years I worked to support myself as a voluntary [nurse], over there [in Mexico]. . . . When I came here I felt comfortable when I saw a Hispanic, but I have seen that because they are better prepared with English and all, is like they treat us with inferiority. Now that I have my kids I want them to study and prepare themselves to go farther than me.

The final part of the dream for Latinos is to *be treated fairly and respectfully by others*. In every focus group there was discussion about perceived discourteous behavior or discrimination from Anglos and other Latinos. However, these discussions were often balanced by comments regarding positive interactions and how much they appreciated it when these occurred. The following experience provided by a naturalized Latino in Houston conveys both the sting felt by discriminatory treatment and the sincere appreciation for a salesman who treated him well:

> *Fernando (Houston, S):* Once, I was helping one of my cousins to buy a car. . . . When we got there we saw a Hispanic guy. We said to ourselves, "We are lucky; he is going to give us a hand." We felt supported. We came close, he saw us and ignored us; he didn't help us. I think because of the way we were dressed and maybe because he thought we were Hispanics and we might not have money, or he thought we didn't have enough to put down about $500, or who knows, but he did not want to help us. Then, an African American came and asked, "How may I help you?" So, we told him that we would like to buy a car. He said, "Okay," he helped us very well, much better than we expected, and on top of that he gave us a discount on the car. My cousin gave the money to pay for the car in full and, in cash, as appreciation for his help my cousin gave him $500. He went in front of the Hispanic that was working there and told him, "For not wanting to help him, see what he gave me?" Just because of [our] appearance he [Hispanic salesperson] didn't want to give us a hand.

BARRIERS TO ACHIEVING THE DREAM FOR LATINOS

Barriers to achieving the American dream as identified in our focus groups overlap somewhat with those cited by the survey respondents in the previous studies, specifically problems with both the quality of schools and discrimination. However, other noted obstacles were more likely to be immigrant-specific concerns. The most frequently cited barrier is a problem for many immigrants from non-English-speaking countries, English proficiency. Another widely acknowledged barrier, sometimes expressed as an individual concern but more commonly identified as a barrier for Latino immigrants in general, was legal status, either their lack of citizenship or lack of documentation.

With respect to the top obstacle, there was universal agreement across the focus groups that limited English proficiency decreased the likelihood of achieving success with respect to jobs and equal treatment. The following examples directly illustrate how participants tied job advancement and upward mobility with having good English speaking skills:

> *Mario (Washington, DC, S):* Language is the most difficult barrier. Moving up and making more money depends on speaking good English.
>
> *Cubia (Washington, DC, S):* If you don't know English, you work in jobs that nobody wants with low pay and sometimes no pay.
>
> *Nicholas (Houston, E):* The guy that's been there the longest is Mexican. . . . The fact that he hasn't moved up, like the other guys that are equal to him at that time is because of the fact that he doesn't speak English well. . . . That's what's holding him back.
>
> *Ivan (New York, E):* I think they [immigrants] would have to speak English. If you don't speak English you will not get a good job. I studied [in] high school and it was different when I came here because of the accents, but English is the key.

Legal status or, more specifically, the lack of documentation to regularize their status, was a topic of personal concern for only a few participants. However, multiple people in every focus group said that they personally knew Latinos who were undocumented and described the difficulties faced by these individuals regarding matters of employment, education, and place of residence due to their illegal status. Others also lamented the fact that they, or their spouse, were not U.S. citizens, and that this put them at a disadvantage in the workplace and in going to college:

> *Arturo (Washington, DC, S):* When you don't have papers it is harder to find work and people who know or think you don't have papers will treat you bad.
>
> *Randy (New York, E):* If you don't have a green card you can't get into a university.
>
> *Man (Los Angeles, E):* They take advantage of the Latino workers. They don't pay them the salaries they are supposed to get paid. I know a girl working three different jobs. She doesn't get the pay she deserves. She is illegal and they take advantage of it.
>
> *Marie (Houston, S):* I know my husband would have kept his job if he were a citizen.

Concern for the poor quality of education noted by survey respondents was echoed in the comments of focus group participants, especially those who had direct experience with the secondary schools in large urban areas such as Houston, New York City, and Miami. However, it is also important to note that participants in these same cities were very satisfied and appreciative of the opportunities provided by higher education in their areas. For example, a common theme in their comments was the acknowledgment that both participants and their children were "doing better financially because [they were] now able to go to college" and "achieved greater success in their careers because they went to college."

LATINO OPTIMISM FOR THE ATTAINABILITY OF THE *AMERICANO* DREAM

Like most of the surveyed Americans, Latinos think the American dream is becoming harder to achieve, but overall they are optimistic about the prospect of attaining it, for themselves and for Latinos collectively. For example, in a New York focus group, the moderator asked participants, "What is the future of the Latino here in the United States?" The replies were:

> *Multiple respondents (New York, E):* "Whatever you make it." "Good, if you know how to defend yourself and know what you are doing." "Good, there are lots of opportunities with education, so anyone who comes can do it." "The opportunities are there, but you have to look for them. They will not find you. You have to be willing to do whatever it takes." *(Collective agreement):* "Yeah."

One comment from an immigrant in Los Angeles is especially illustrative of the optimism shared among many of the foreign-born respondents:

> *Immigrant man (Los Angeles, E):* As time goes by, they [Latinos] can elevate their position. I started in warehouse sales and moved up making more money. Dreams don't die: they only die if you don't pursue them.

Perhaps the best indicator of the continuing appeal of the American dream for foreign-born and U.S.-born Latinos alike is found in their commonly expressed preferences to remain in the United States when asked whether they (focus group participants) could see themselves returning or moving to home/ancestral countries on a permanent basis. The response of an immigrant from Chile captures the sentiment expressed by many foreign-born:

> *Graciela, immigrant (Washington, DC, S):* This place is everything I dream for and more. I like very much living here. It is beautiful, tranquil. My son has a good job, he is happy. . . . My son's children will go to the university. . . . I am staying here.

Second-generation and higher respondents generations were even more direct in expressing their commitment to remaining in the United States to attain their long-term goals. As reported in the introductory remarks of this essay, whenever the moderator asked second- and third-generation Latinos whether they could ever imagine themselves immigrating to their family's home country, their immediate and unanimous response was an emphatic "NO!" Moreover, the follow-up conversations clearly supported the conclusion of one participant, who reported: "The quality of life I want is only found in the United States."

IS ASSIMILATION PART OF THE AMERICAN DREAM?

Given these understandings of Latinos' aspirations about the American dream, especially their focus on economic success and security, do their views on related topics suggest that assimilation is seen as (implicitly or explicitly) part of, essential, or instrumental to their realization of "living the dream"? Is the extent of assimilation itself suggestive of some movement toward the American dream? To explore these possibilities, let us begin with a brief discussion of the complex concept of assimilation. We can then consider Latinos' understanding(s) of the concept as well as the extent to which Latinos appear to be thinking, acting, and experiencing social outcomes that seem compatible with movement toward assimilation and, in turn, toward something approaching the American dream.

THE COMPLEXITY OF ASSIMILATION

There is no simple or widely agreed upon definition of "assimilation" except to say that it refers to a multigenerational process by which the "characteristics of members of immigrant groups and host societies come to resemble one another" (Brown and Bean 2006). Early articulations of the concept (still in vogue among Huntington and others who believe in a single Anglo-Saxon Protestant culture) were normative and prescriptive. Assimilation was characterized as a "straight-line" progression whereby all immigrants eventually conform, abandoning their original cultural attributes and adopting the behaviors and customs of the Anglo-Saxon majority as they advance both socially and economically (Park 1950; Warner and Srole 1945). Milton Gordon's *Assimilation in American Life* (1964) more accurately described a process that was considerably more complex, involving numerous dimensions besides culture and the possibility of different outcomes besides Anglo-Saxon conformity. Later scholars of assimilation no longer claim that conformity is even necessarily a desirable outcome (Portes and Rumbaut 2001).

Today, the classic model of assimilation ("straight-line") has essentially been eclipsed by a variety of alternative theories of how the process occurs (for example, "bumpy-line," "segmented," "two-way"), with differing opinions on which dimensions of assimilation are most important for immigrants and minorities to survive and thrive within

TABLE 13.2   Importance of Learning English/Retaining Spanish across Generations (in Percentages) among LNS Respondents

	Learn English		Retain Spanish	
Generation	Somewhat Important	Very Important	Somewhat Important	Very Important
First	5.5	94.5	9.9	90.0
Second	9.5	90.3	12.5	87.4
Third	12.9	86.8	18.9	80.7
Fourth	13.7	85.7	25.5	73.9

LNS = Latino National Survey

the larger society (Alba and Nee 2003; Gans 1996; Portes and Zhou 1993). Still, most scholars agree that certain factors can delay or even block assimilation. Two of these factors include racial/ethnic discrimination and governmental policies that limit social and economic mobility (Brown and Bean 2006).

CULTURAL ASSIMILATION

According to Gordon (1964), *cultural* assimilation, or alternatively "acculturation," is likely to be the first adaptation to occur when immigrants come into contact with the majority population. Acculturation refers to the *two-way* process whereby both immigrants and majority citizens adjust their values and behaviors, as opposed to the classical view of assimilation that the direction of change is only one way, whereby immigrants change their appearance, diet, language, religion, social customs, and core values to comply with those of the majority. Some cultural practices (for example, attire, eating habits, and social customs) are considered more easily surrendered than others (for example, core values or religious identity), but "changing" is not necessarily a subtractive process. Gibson (1988) argues that assimilation/acculturation is *selective* and should be viewed as additive in purpose; that is, minority individuals make deliberate decisions to adopt certain practices of the majority that they think are useful to their future success. They also work to retain salient ethnic cultural traits. In turn, the majority often adopts from the minority culture whatever they find appealing.

English proficiency is widely considered to be the most important aspect of cultural adaptation if immigrants are to be successful outside of their ethnic enclaves, but immigrants may also value the retention of their native languages (Alba and Nee 2003). We can see evidence of this longing to "have it both ways" in LNS respondents' answers to contrasting questions on learning English and maintaining Spanish (table 13.2).

Especially among the foreign born (first generation), overwhelming majorities think it is very important to learn English while also thinking Spanish maintenance is very important: 94.5% and 90%, respectively.

The goal of being equally proficient in both English and Spanish was also very evident in the comments of the focus group participants. Immigrant participants were keenly aware that they had problems communicating effectively in English, and many expressed the desire for their children, if not for themselves, that they would "get better" or "good at" speaking English. However, most of the Spanish speakers also wanted their children and grandchildren to be bilingual. U.S.-born participants were especially mindful of the economic advantages of being bilingual:

> *Della (Miami, E):* Every time you look in the paper you have to be bilingual.
>
> *Jose Luis (Muscatine, IA, S):* It is important to be bilingual. My brother lost his Spanish. He went to school and became a lawyer [but] he had to change jobs because of his location and Spanish was the language most used and he didn't know it.

Participants in the English-language focus groups frequently expressed regret at not having made more of an effort to learn or maintain their Spanish and also to pass it along to their children. An exchange in one of the focus groups in New York is illustrative of this sentiment:

> *Christopher (New York, E):* We want them to think like all the other races. . . . We want them to learn English. As long as there are grandmothers around, you are going to learn Spanish. It will be heard. That is what would happen to me. I wanted to shy away from Spanish, but I couldn't. . . . I am glad now for it.
>
> *Eric (New York, E):* That's the thing, while we are American, born here, we can't forget our heritage. My daughters, I try to teach them Spanish; I bought DVDs to teach them Spanish. They only speak English, and I am trying to tell their mother as well because you can never forget your heritage. We are American, and we do have to speak English well, but don't forget where you came from.
>
> *Shirley (New York, E):* I think with every generation you lose more and more. I read and write Spanish, but growing up, my mother—born and raised in Puerto Rico—taught us Spanish and we learned our English in school, which to me was an advantage because here in New York, they know how to speak it but not write it, and it is good to know it all. . . . I do get disappointed with myself for not teaching my daughters.

Interestingly, the level of English proficiency and Spanish retention among the U.S. Latino population is something about which there is a great deal of information. A great deal of longitudinal data is available on the topic from the U.S. Census Bureau and from other national studies. Basically, the data are consistent across these sources. Roberto

Suro, former Director of the Pew Hispanic Center, aptly summarizes the findings from these data:

> [A]bout three-quarters of foreign-born Latinos, the first generation, speaks only Spanish and the rest of the immigrants are bilingual to some extent. The second generation—the children of immigrants—are about evenly divided between English speakers and bilinguals, with almost none reaching adulthood speaking only Spanish. And, among Hispanics of longer tenure in the U.S.—those born here, of American-born parents—more than three-quarters speak only English and the rest are bilingual to some extent, though often their Spanish is weak. So we know for certain that a transition to English is taking place across generations with a lot of bilingualism along the way. (Suro 2006: 3)

We also know something about another indicator of cultural assimilation that, according to Gordon (1964), is significantly less subject to change: religious affiliation and practices. Religious identity was characterized by Gordon as an intrinsic trait that is "essential and vital to a groups' cultural heritage" (Gordon 1964: 72). Change in their traditional affiliation (which is Catholicism for Latinos) to Protestantism, the predominant religious identity of American society, could be viewed as a convincing measure of cultural adaptation. We find evidence of this type of assimilation from a national telephone survey of 2,310 Latinos conducted in 2000 on religious life in the United States. According to the survey:

- The first generation of Latino immigrants is 74% Catholic and 15% Protestant.
- The second generation is 72% Catholic and 20% Protestant.
- The third generation is 62% Catholic and 29% Protestant (Espinosa, Elizondo, and Miranda 2005).

We also see evidence of religious adaptation when we look at the levels of Catholicism across generations among respondents in the 2006 LNS. Looking at the first row of table 13.3, we can see a modest but steady decline in the numbers of Catholics with each generation. The biggest drop in Catholics [or Catholicism] occurs between the third and fourth generations.

As hypothesized by Gordon, the change in Latino religious affiliation is occurring more slowly relative to other aspects of cultural assimilation. The difficulty or reluctance in changing religious practices was discussed by immigrant participants in the Washington, DC, focus group who were fully bilingual and participated in our English-speaking session:

> *Man (Washington, DC, E):* There is a church here in Alexandria in Spanish, but sometimes I go to the one in English even though the one in Spanish is easier to understand. The Americans that go to church still seem cold, while the Mexicans show they care.

TABLE 13.3 Selected Markers of Assimilation across Generations (in Percentages) among LNS Respondents

	First	Second	Third	Fourth
Roman Catholic	73.6	70.6	65.0	58.0
Participation in civic groups	14.1	23.4	29.3	31.7
Has mostly Latino friends	44.6	28.0	22.0	16.7
Military service	15.9	46.3	66.3	68.5
Education less than high school	48.7	23.1	18.4	17.3
Household income less than $35,000	53.3	35.6	28.5	34.2
Married to non-Latinos	13.5	28.9	38.9	49.1

LNS = Latino National Survey

Woman (Washington, DC, E): I still can't learn the prayers in English.

Man (Washington, DC, E): I had the same experience. I made my communion over there when I was 17, and all prayers were in Spanish. Then I came here and I had to learn them in English, and I can't relate to them. I know them though.

Woman (Washington, DC, E): I learned them in Spanish, and I came here when I was 24, and I have found it very difficult to learn them or say anything in English. I can't follow the Mass in English.

Changing religious affiliation is seemingly one critical indicator of assimilation, but it could be argued that it may be more important for Latinos to be attending churches with significant numbers of non-Latinos. Participation in integrated mainstream organizations is an important component of *structural* assimilation, the entrance into or participation of minority individuals in primary groups and institutions of the majority society (Brown and Bean 2006; Gordon 1964). Whenever church or religion was discussed in the focus groups, there were always some participants who said the membership of the church they attended was mixed, including some that said their church was mostly Anglo. However, there were always other participants who said they felt "more comfortable" attending services that were conducted in Spanish or with their co-ethnics.

STRUCTURAL ASSIMILATION

Gordon deemed that once structural assimilation begins, it stimulates all other dimensions of assimilation. Activities as varied as participation in integrated social/civic/work organizations, friendships with persons outside of one's ethnic group, and U.S. military service are all indicators of structural assimilation. Increasing levels of education and home ownership are also proxy measures of structural assimilation (Brown and Bean 2006). We see evidence of increasing structural assimilation among the LNS respondents across generations along most of these indicators when we examine rows two through five in table 13.3. The biggest change in each of these measures occurs between the first (foreign-born) and second (U.S.-born) generations.

The sharp decline in the percentage of those with less than high school education somewhat overstates the improvement in educational status of Latinos (primarily because the Latino dropout rate continues to be a serious problem), but the only indicator on this table that does not show steady improvement across generations is household income. There is substantial improvement between the first and second generations, reflected by the big drop in the percentage making less than $35,000, but the decline is small between the second and third generations and actually increases between the third and fourth generations.

Further evidence of structural assimilation was revealed when focus group participants discussed the race/ethnicity of their co-workers and friends and their degree of interaction with them. Many referenced in a very positive light the racial/ethnic diversity of their workplaces and neighborhoods. Many said that they socialized regularly with non-Latino co-workers and friends. Interestingly, however, those they considered "close friends" were more likely to be fellow Latinos. Participants in New York, Miami, and Los Angeles also noted that they felt "more comfortable doing different things" with their non-Latino friends, such as going to the gym, and had "more fun partying" or simply "hanging out" with their Latino friends. This suggests that their structural assimilation is selective. They are comfortable in integrated work and social settings, but at times they prefer to be with people from their own culture. On the other hand, recent immigrants and participants who had recently relocated to rural towns were more likely to live almost segregated lives, reporting that their co-workers, friends, and neighbors were all mostly Latino and that the attitudes of long-term residents were "not friendly."

MARITAL ASSIMILATION

The incorporation of Latinos into the American fabric may be occurring primarily through marital or family integration. Over the past 30 years the number of Latinos marrying non-Latino spouses has more than doubled, from 600,000 in 1970 to 1.8 million in 2000. This is a significant trend since the same data show that many Latino immigrants arrive already married. Even with the surge in Latino immigration between 1990 and 2000, the percentage of Latino intermarriages remained fairly stable: between 23% and 25%. As the proportion of U.S.-born Latinos increases relative to the proportion of foreign-born, the percentage of intermarriages is predicted to climb even higher (Lee and Edmonston 2005).

The reported pattern of increasing marital assimilation is clearly shown across the generations of LNS respondents (see the bottom row of table 13.3). Again, as with previously discussed indicators, the biggest change occurs between the first and second generation, but there is at least a 10% increase with each subsequent generation. By the fourth generation, nearly half of the respondents are married to non-Latinos.

These aggregate indicators are reflected in the marital circumstances of our focus group participants. Although approximately one third of the participants were single or divorced, many of these reported having parents or siblings who were married to non-Latinos. Having non-Latino spouses was very common among the U.S.-born married participants; about half reported they were married to non-Latinos. Out-group marriages were far less common among immigrant participants, with several reporting that they immigrated to the United States with their wives/husbands.

The significance of having a non-Latino American spouse for facilitating the process of becoming a part of the majority society is best illustrated by the comments of a Miami participant who immigrated to this country as an adult from Majorca, Spain:

> *Rosa (Miami, E):* I came here when I was 21 years old. . . . I am an outsider. My husband is American. He is from upstate New York. A little town in upstate New York and also has family in Pennsylvania. They never make me feel like an outsider. They try to talk to me slowly when I first came to this country and be friendly and give me all that food. I was like "Oh, my God. What is that? Give me some snails to eat." But they were friendly and everything. . . . They don't make me feel outsider.

It is equally significant to note that marriage to a non-Latino does not necessarily result in the loss of Latino cultural ties. Participants' comments seem to suggest that acculturation is the more common effect as families learned to appreciate, or at least accept, the customs and practices of the different cultures. The following, somewhat lengthy, Miami focus group discussion regarding the differences in holiday practices provides several acculturation examples.

> *Omar (Miami, E):* My wife is American. They're very relaxed like most people but when I say "party," I want to go to a Latin people party. Let's say for Christmas, celebrating Christmas with a Latin family is very different than an American family. I like it better with the Latin family, even though I spend most of the time with my wife's family because my parents are not here.
>
> *Toni (Miami, E):* The customs are different. Like for Christmas, Christmas Eve for Hispanics is a big thing, whereas for Americans they celebrate more on Christmas day than Christmas Eve.
>
> *Joni (Miami, E):* I have been here long enough to celebrate both ways but we keep our traditions. We do the *Noche Buena*, the Christmas Eve. We invite a lot of people.
>
> *Marisol (Miami, E):* When it's work related, I will go with anybody. I work as a realtor and there are a lot of nationalities where I work. . . . But when it comes

to something personal, I would rather stick with what I know and like, which is the Latin side of my life. When it comes to me and my family . . . the weird part is growing up here and being from another country is really sometimes you are like this: "Christmas Eve, Christmas day, what do I do?" Sometimes you end up doing both, which is a lot of fun. Because I love Thanksgiving, and I was raised in New York where Thanksgiving is Thanksgiving. But then I get down here [Miami], and they are having Cuban food at 11:00 at night. It's weird. When I was in New York, we knew we had to eat turkey, got dressed, the table was totally beautiful. Down here it's different.

Joni (Miami, E): I think it's because they like food and they like partying, because Thanksgiving is not part of Cuban tradition. And yet, Cubans and Hispanics in general celebrate Thanksgiving as if they have been celebrating it their whole life. They take advantage of both, their heritage and what they've learned in this country. Because there is no such thing as Thanksgiving over there. Take advantage of both.

Maria (Miami, E): My mother came to the U.S., my [American] father brought her to the U.S., and she was raised most of her life in Majorca. You celebrate Thanksgiving and you have a turkey and you stuff it with bread and it was so foreign to her. So she had to transition. She always put her spin on it. She always put chorizo in the sauces. . . . She had to incorporate in her Latin experience to celebrate American tradition.

SELF-RECOGNIZED IMPORTANCE OF ADAPTING TO "AMERICAN" WAYS

The self-reported characteristics of participants suggest there is great variation in the level or extent of assimilation represented among the focus groups. Some participants who were in this country for less than one year and spoke only Spanish appeared to be just beginning the process, while others, primarily second- and third-generation participants who spoke only English, were clearly further along in the process of fitting into American society. However, recognition of the importance of assimilation or at least "accommodating American ways" was evident in similar comments made in practically every focus group we held. For example:

Woman (Los Angeles, E): If you come from Mexico with attitude, you are going to have lots of problems. If you come willing to adapt, you won't have problems. . . . Pride is a big killer. Sometimes you will have to go down to go up. You might be the most educated person and start out as a housekeeper with a company, just to get your foot in the door.

Immigrant woman (Washington, DC, S): When you come to the U.S., you have to accustom yourself or nothing. . . . Do whatever it takes.

Marisol, immigrant in U.S. 10 years (Miami, E): I really believe that everybody should learn English personally. If you're here, you should speak English. If some people want the schools in Spanish, I think that's wrong. . . . You have to change.

Nicholas (Houston, E): There ain't no leaders in the Hispanic [community] that you can talk to. So anytime you want to move ahead you have to talk to some other races. We ain't got no presidents. . . . There is nobody in office for us, you know what I mean? For us to even get there we would have to go through another race. You have to be able to adapt, you got to learn other things.

CONCLUSIONS

It seems that Latinos share the same vision as other working-class Americans of what it means to be successful and satisfied in life. Their focus is primarily on material success and economic opportunities and not on political freedoms or the more abstract ideas identified with those in the middle class. While some of our focus group participants appear to be very satisfied with where they currently live and work, most are still striving to reach their life goals. For the most part, participants' attitudes about the future for themselves and for Latinos in general are upbeat and confident.

Interestingly, in most cases, immigrant participants were generally more satisfied and optimistic than the U.S.-born we talked with. Perhaps because the U.S.-born were significantly more aware of the barriers to upward mobility, they were less optimistic and more cynical about the prospects of achieving their dreams as they defined them. They also seemed to be more aware that many of the obstacles were out of their control, such as the quality of schools and the attitudes of elected officials or residents (including other Latinos) in new receiving communities.

As previously stated, Latinos know they must adapt—at least in some ways—if they want to improve their status. They clearly recognize that they must learn to speak English (and to speak it well) if they are to have continued success in moving up the socioeconomic ladder. However, judging from the other information presented here, from a variety of credible aggregate sources, and from the individual comments from those in our focus groups, there are other signs besides English acquisition that Latinos are integrating into American society—through marriage, friendships, churches, and military service, for example. The ways that Latinos are becoming a part of the American fabric are similar to the behaviors followed by previous waves of immigrants (Sassler 2006); from this perspective Latinos' behavior reflects more continuity than change.

Yet, the decision to adapt (assimilate) is complicated by the fact that Latinos also want to maintain their cultural traditions, such as their Spanish proficiency (as we saw in their answers presented in table 13.2). Further evidence of the complexity or contradictions in Latinos' feelings about assimilation can be seen in table 13.4, which provides LNS respondents' answers to questions regarding how important they think it is for Latinos to attempt to "blend into the larger American society" and also to "main-

TABLE 13.4   Preference for Cultural Assimilation and Distinctness (in Percentages)
among LNS Respondents

Generation	Blend into Larger Society		Maintain Distinct Culture	
	Somewhat Important	Very Important	Somewhat Important	Very Important
First	27.2	60.4	16.8	78.3
Second	33.4	42.1	18.0	75.7
Third	36.9	37.7	20.3	74.2
Fourth	37.5	34.0	26.0	66.0

LNS = Latino National Survey

tain their distinct cultures." Large majorities in each generation say *both behaviors* are somewhat or very important. Moreover, support for blending into the larger culture and for maintaining a distinct culture is positively related ($r = .1415$); they are not viewed as either/or propositions.

The likelihood of Latinos fully incorporating into American society is obviously complicated. The pursuit of the American dream and subsequent Latino incorporation faces potential roadblocks—some mentioned by focus group participants, such as poor schools, legal status, and discrimination.

NOTES

1. Conducted by the National League of Cities (NLC).
2. Conducted by Lake Research Partners (LRP).
3. More specifically, the respondents were *not* full-time students, retirees, business owners or CEOs, company executives, managers/supervisors, or professionals but they *were* employed at least 20 hours per week or actively looking for work.
4. The use of "S" and "E" denote the language of the focus group participants: English (E) and Spanish (S).

REFERENCE

Gibson, Margaret. 1988. *Accommodation without Assimilation: Sikh Immigrants in an American High School.* Ithaca, NY: Cornell University Press.

14

GENERATIONS OF EXCLUSION
Mexican Americans, Assimilation, and Race

Edward Telles and Vilma Ortiz

The Mexican American experience requires that we look beyond the traditional assimilation versus race theories that have been based almost entirely on the European American and African American experiences. The well-known assimilation story, in its classic and modern forms, has been the dominant theory for explaining immigrant integration and was derived from the experiences of European immigrants to the United States and their descendants. Even though many of them occupied the bottom rungs of the American class structure when they arrived, their children and grandchildren successfully rode the mobility escalator to middle class status, stopped speaking their native languages, and thoroughly mixed with the general white population, including the descendants of other recent European immigrants. Overall, they would no longer be differentiated from other Americans, and were hardly ethnic by the third generation. We find that is not at all the story for Mexican Americans, whose ancestors immigrated during the same period as the Europeans and in some cases were natives of what was then Mexico but is now the United States.

For third- and fourth-generation Mexican Americans, we find that ethnic boundaries are much more than merely symbolic, which they are for later-generation European Americans. Mexican American ethnicity continues to influence their language, who they choose as friends and marriage partners, where they live, how they see themselves, and how they vote. Unfortunately, it also shapes their class position. However, the slow acculturation and persistent low status of Mexican Americans is also clearly not the rigid caste-like type predicted by the internal colonial model or by theories predicated on the African American example. Mexican Americans intermarry much more than do blacks, live in less segregated areas, and face less labor market discrimination, which suggests a path also different from that of African Americans. In this sense, racial boundaries for Mexican Americans are clearly less rigid than for African Americans, despite even worse schooling.

Using state-of-the-art social science methods, we have followed the intergenerational experience of Mexican origin adults in 1965 to their children as adults in 2000. As far as we know, this research design is unique and for many reasons it is the most appropriate for addressing the actual intergenerational integration of immigrants and their descendants. Among its advantages, it permits the investigation of real intergenerational change by seeing how events occurring during childhood or a generation ago are related to adult outcomes and by matching parents to their actual children rather than relying on proxies.

We have shown that the experience of assimilation, where it occurred, was far slower than it was for European Americans. The erosion of ethnic boundaries over generations between Mexicans and Anglos, the defining feature of assimilation in our view, is most apparent in the linguistic realm. Although English proficiency is virtually universal for the U.S.-born today, Spanish fluency is not. There is a gradual weaning away from Spanish so that by the fourth generation (or more), only one-third of the child sample is able to speak Spanish and fully 94 percent speak mostly or only English to their fifth-generation children at home.

However, there is a surprising amount of ethnic persistence into the fourth generation regarding identities, voting behaviors, and some cultural practices. Among fourth-generation Mexican Americans, most live in majority Hispanic neighborhoods, most marry other Hispanics, most frequently think of themselves as Mexican, and most agree that the United States should allow Mexicans to immigrate to the United States if they want to. Although intermarriage with other groups tends to grow with each generation, it is so slow so that even by the fourth generation, nearly two-thirds are still married to other Hispanics. Their identity change is far from complete in the third or even fourth generation and their politics continue to be on the left of the spectrum and to strongly support ethnic issues. All of these sharpen racial and cultural boundaries between Mexican Americans and Anglos, which in turn further restricts their assimilation. Although they may have lost some ethnic cultural attributes like language, most fourth-generation Mexican Americans in our study experience a world largely shaped by their race and ethnicity.

In education, which best determines life chances in the United States, assimilation is interrupted by the second generation and stagnates thereafter. Considering the education of parents, it can even be characterized as backward. Mexican Americans, three or four generations removed from their immigrant ancestors, are less likely than the Mexican American second generation of similar characteristics to have completed either high school or college. Mexican Americans also have lower levels of schooling than any other major racial-ethnic group. Because education helps propel individuals toward assimilation on most other dimensions, a lack of educational progress thus limits Mexican American assimilation overall. In terms of adult socioeconomic status, there are no differences by generation-since-immigration. While the children of U.S.-born parents (third generation-since-immigration or more) benefit from having parents with higher levels of schooling than Mexican-born parents, the children of Mexican immigrants (second generation-since-immigration) seem to benefit from greater optimism about life in the United States and seem to have higher human and social capital for the same years of schooling.

We extended the scope of previous investigations by introducing a long dureé, multigenerational perspective that covers much of the twentieth century, by examining variation within Mexicans, and by investigating a fuller range of dimensions in which integration may occur. Moreover, we disentangle the generally intertwined dimensions of generation-since-immigration from historical or family generation, which has confounded previous studies of immigrant integration. For example, we find backward assimilation in education from the perspective of generation-since-immigration, but from the perspective of historical or family generation, we find gradual educational assimilation over the course of the twentieth century. The former supports the ideas of segmented assimilation theory[1] while the latter suggests a slow but constant assimilation over the course of the twentieth century though one that is far from complete even after four or five generations.

GENERATION-SINCE-IMMIGRATION

From the perspective of generation-since-immigration, we find slow assimilation on most dimensions but stalled or reversed on education. Linguistic assimilation toward English monolingualism is constant and occurs more rapidly than on any other dimension though it was clearly slower than for other ethnic groups.[2] Despite linguistic assimilation, though, other behaviors and ethnic identities suggest strong attachment to the ethnic group and they often remain even for those who are four generations removed from immigration. Marriage within the group, residential segregation, ethnic identity, and support for pro-ethnic group social policies persisted well into the fourth generation, though their strength tends to slightly erode with each generation-since-immigration. This is in marked contrast to European Americans, whose assimilation on most dimensions was rapid and complete by the third generation. Most notably, though, levels of education peak among the children of immigrants and worsen for the third and fourth generation. Education, the most important variable determining adult socioeconomic status, bucks the path expected by assimilation theory. It is affected by generation-since-immigration but in a way that runs contrary to traditional assimilation theory and to the experiences of long-settled European immigrant groups in the United States.

Generation-since-immigration simulates the "intergenerational experience" of an ethnic group at one point in time, though this experience actually occurs over time, by definition. One advantage of such a simulation is that data are more easily available cross-sectionally. A more important one, however, is that it allows one to keep the historical context constant. Thus, the second-generation respondents are not the children of the immigrant respondents, at least not those who are of comparable ages. Rather, they are children of immigrants a historical generation earlier and may have had characteristics that were quite different from the immigrant generation at the same timepoint.

The multivariate statistical analyses we present throughout this chapter permits us to simulate the independent effects of generation-since-immigration on Mexican Americans of similar backgrounds—including parents' education, urban background, age, gender, and skin color. After we statistically controlled for other variables thought to affect the assimilation outcomes of interest, only education and language were independently related to generation-since-immigration, which we present in figure 14.1. Other variables—including occupation, income, wealth, homeownership, segregation, intermarriage, racial identification as white, and experience with discrimination—were not, though there may have been indications of a relationship in the bivariate analysis. Figure 14.1 shows that third and fourth generations did statistically worse in schooling than immigrants who came as children or the children of immigrants. The collective second generation (generations 1.5 and two) completed decidedly more education than their parents, while further educational gains were aborted for the third and fourth generations. Second-generation Mexicans, compared to their immigrant parents, seemed to assimilate at least as rapidly as second-generation Italians and other European groups.[3] For the third generation, however, educational assimilation abruptly halted and even slightly reversed. Unlike European ethnics, whose status continued to rise into the third generation, low levels of schooling kept Mexican Americans concentrated in working-class or low-level white-collar occupations well into the third and fourth generation.

Why then did education fall for Mexican Americans from the second to the third generation? We controlled for all hypothesized nonracial causes but the negative trajectory of generation-since-immigration only sharpened. The leading explanation for why the second generation did better is that a more optimistic disposition among immigrants and their families cushioned them from the full effects of racialization. Immigrant parents and their immigrant children, often believing in the American dream, probably perceive the advantages of a better life in the United States, whereas U.S.-born parents do not have that reference but instead an Americanized image of their proper place.[4] Their acculturation is not only one of losing ethnic cultural traits but probably also of acquiring a strong sense of the American racial hierarchy. Our analysis shows that the low levels of education of later generations are unlikely to be attributable to the alleged cultural deficiencies sometimes used to explain low education for immigrant children, such as poor ability in English or the lack of discipline or knowledge of American schools.

Figure 14.1 also shows a quite different pattern for language. Specifically, it reveals a

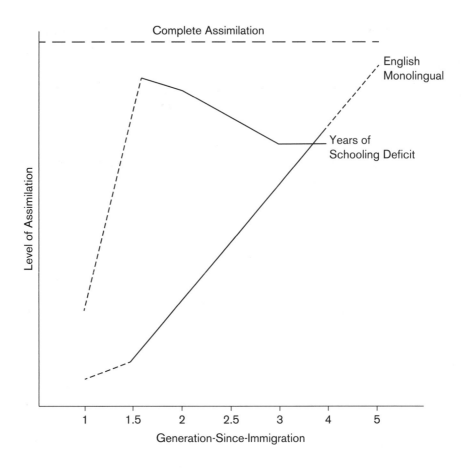

FIGURE 14.1

Educational and Linguistic Incorporation by Generation-Since-Immigration, 2000 (from multivariate analysis among children)·

Source: Mexican American Study Project.

slow but certain linear trend toward universal English monolingualism, which is consistent with reaching full assimilation on the linguistic dimension. Mexican Americans retain Spanish more than other groups but do not keep it indefinitely. In the American context, the eventual loss of the ethnic language of immigrant ancestors is considered normal and even desirable, though bilingualism is common and often perceived as indispensable in other societies. Virtually all other groups in the United States lost their ethnic-origin languages within two or three generations. Even though bilingual education is favored by most Mexican Americans of all generations, Spanish fluency is close to extinct by the fifth generation. More than any other dimension, language can be expected to exhibit a linear assimilatory path because of a ratcheting effect. Because ethnic languages are learned mostly at home, once the previous generation is no longer fluent, the children miss the best opportunity to learn the language. Thus, the percentage of those who can speak an ethnic language can only get smaller from generation to generation, unless a compelling reason drives large numbers to learn it later in life.

THE HISTORICAL PERSPECTIVE

Our study demonstrates the importance of separating two very different generational processes of immigrant and ethnic group integration previously seen as a single process or, at best, consistent processes. A historical or family generation perspective yields distinct results from those based on generation-since-immigration. Specifically, our analysis of changes from the original respondents in 1965 to their children in 2000 suggests considerable assimilation over that period. From 1965 to 2000, assimilation for Mexican Americans was probably faster that it has ever been, on many dimensions. We find a slow but constant assimilation of Mexican Americans in education over historical time as the gap between levels of schooling between Mexican Americans and Anglos slowly decreased over the course of the twentieth century. Various other types of ethnic boundaries also softened. For example, English monolingualism and intermarriage rapidly increased, probably the results of overall changes in American society, such as the spread of English-language media, the growing participation of women in the labor market, and greater universalism in education. This is broadly consistent with predictions of assimilation[5] but the slowness of change suggests that optimism regarding improvements in the group's status is unwarranted.

We present the findings for some of our key indicators in figure 14.2. The figure mostly suggests a slow historical trajectory from 1965 to 2000 toward assimilation and the erosion of ethnic boundaries. Specifically, the bold lines in figure 14.2 show the real intergenerational changes from the second generation in 1965 to their third-generation children in 2000. Given that one may expect signs of assimilation for subsequent generations despite the historical context, we also plotted a dotted line to show the difference between the third generation in 1965 and in 2000. Although the trends may be sharper when comparing second- to third-generation changes, the dotted lines connecting third generations reveal that these trends are nonetheless affected by the historical context.

Figure 14.2 (panel a) shows that the college completion gap with white Americans gradually decreased, though it remained substantial. Based on the college completion rates we calculated, we show that by 2000, third-generation Mexican Americans in our child sample were about 30 percent as likely as non-Hispanics to have completed college. This compares to just over 10 percent for their second-generation parents (original respondents) and less than 25 percent among the third-generation original respondents. Given the affirmative action policies of universities to accept more Mexican Americans, their intentions seem to have helped but nonetheless fallen short. Although the proportion of Mexican Americans graduating from college increased, they continued to lag far behind the also large increases in college completion among the general population. Critics might argue that downward assimilation from the second to the third generation

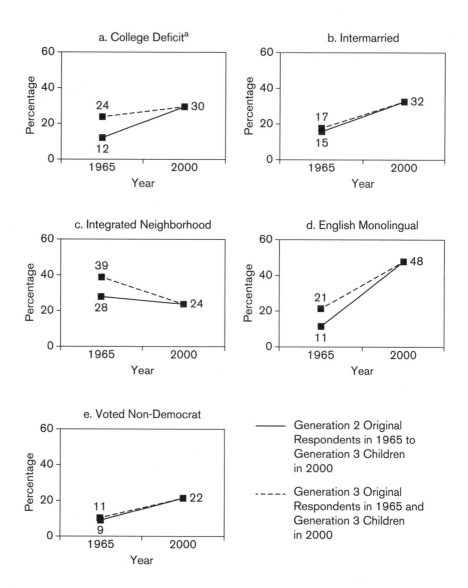

FIGURE 14.2

Intergenerational Patterns of Incorporation for Mexican Americans, 1965 to 2000

Source: Mexican American Study Project. [a]Odds of completing college for Mexican Americans compared to non-Hispanic whites.

in the cross-sectional analysis might be explained by relatively high selectivity of pre-1965 immigrants. The historical data, however, show that real educational progress among the descendants of an even earlier immigration moved forward only at a crawl.

Most Mexican Americans age thirty-five to fifty-four in 2000 were high school graduates with no or some college, a large improvement over the previous generation's high school completion. Nevertheless, the persistence of high school dropout rates of 15 to

25 percent over generations-since-immigration is a cause for concern. Such high rates appear to persist for recent graduates in very recent cohorts.[6] The persistence of gang membership among many later-generation Mexican Americans also raises concerns about the formation of a multiple generation Mexican American underclass. States like California and Texas have class systems with bottoms already occupied mostly by those of Mexican origin, including many U.S.-born. Given that the white working class is more likely to move up and that it is increasingly moving to states away from those where Hispanics and blacks are concentrated,[7] the danger of a largely Hispanic working class becoming an underclass is real if not for robust labor markets.

Figure 14.2 (panel d) also shows decline in Spanish language ability, or linguistic assimilation. A shift to English monolingualism was particularly strong from 1965 to 2000. Whereas only a little over 10 percent of the second generation in 1965 were English monolinguals, nearly 50 percent of their third generation children were. The dotted lines for language show that there have been sharp declines in Spanish language fluency among later-generation Mexican Americans. Whereas 80 percent of third-generation Mexican Americans spoke some Spanish in 1965, only about half of the third generation children did so in 2000.

Similarly, intermarriage increased substantially from about 15 percent for both the second- and third-generation original respondents to 30 percent for the third-generation children (panel b of figure 14.2). The percentage not voting for the Democratic candidate for president increased from about 10 percent for both generations in the 1964 election to about 20 percent in 1996 (panel e of figure 14.2). Also, though not shown, the increase in the number of non-Catholics from 10 percent in 1965 to about 40 percent in 2000 demonstrates sharp religious assimilation to the mostly working-class fundamentalist and evangelical religions.

Contrary to the assimilation direction of other dimensions, levels of residential isolation for Mexican Americans increased from 1965 to 2000. Almost a quarter of second-generation original respondents lived in a neighborhood in which Hispanics were a small minority in 1965, and about the same percentage of their third-generation children did so in 2000. This contrasts with the 32 percent of third-generation respondents who lived in such neighborhoods in 1965. This was largely due to the resurgence of immigration from Latin America, which increased the percentage of Hispanics in neighborhoods throughout the Southwest. Therefore, even though some of our respondents may have moved to more integrated and higher status neighborhoods in, say, 1980, the neighborhoods were likely to become increasingly Hispanic because of immigration after that time. These changes in the ethnic composition of the neighborhood are thus likely to have altered the ethnic experience of Mexican Americans and their children in 2000 with respect to the average experiences of Mexican Americans in the 1960s. We expect that rates of intermarriage for later-generation Mexican Americans will remain stable or even decrease for the next generation, because childhood segregation shapes the extent of intermarriage, as our results showed.

There was no information on race in the 1965 survey. However, we can speculate that identification as white declined between 1965 and 2000, even though racial boundaries became more fluid. Many of Mexican origin, especially in Texas, sought to avoid a Mexican identity in the 1940s and 1950s because of its extreme racial stigma. Years later, though, being Mexican, Mexican American, or even Chicano came to be proudly accepted with the social justice and often nationalist social movements of the 1960s.[8] Although the original respondents were not asked their race in the 1965 survey, the sample was selected from the 1960 census population of "white persons of Spanish surname," a proxy for Mexican Americans in the Southwest. Certainly, Mexican Americans were generally not considered white, as historic evidence shows,[9] but were usually labeled as such in official documents by 1965. Most of our respondents did not identify as white in our 2000 survey and nearly half of Mexican Americans also did not in the 2000 U.S. Census. Moreover, we found a smaller number of the children sample identifying as white compared to their parents, which also suggests that Mexican Americans are increasingly likely to see themselves as nonwhite.

However, most boundaries between later-generation Mexican Americans and whites seem to soften from 1965 to 2000. The 1960s marked a period of major legislation and policy changes in favor of civil rights and the end of egregious racism and segregation in the American Southwest, which was largely directed at Mexican Americans. Up to that time, racial boundaries in such areas as housing, employment, and even romance were often cast in law or policy, sometimes heavily policed, formally and informally, and generally accepted as natural. A slowly declining educational gap over time may be partly attributable to civil rights gains for minorities, including affirmative action in universities, policies to improve equity in public spending for schools, and the end of de jure segregation, though a persistent gap, in light of these changes, remains worrisome. Assimilation over time is also probably related to growing universalism through structural and political change, which largely resulted from the earlier civil rights struggles of Mexican Americans and other minorities. However, a surge in immigration helped increase residential isolation, which may lead to lower intermarriage rates for Mexican Americans in the future. Additionally, and contrary to the assimilation thesis, the Chicano nationalist movement helped shape more racialized and nonwhite identities.

In sum, historical change for equivalent generations-since-immigration among Mexican Americans shows assimilation but one much slower than for European Americans. The assimilation of European Americans involved a historical and political process of their becoming or being accepted as white in the first half of the twentieth century,[10] rather than merely a process of integration thought to naturally occur over generations-since-immigration. That magic historical moment of incorporation did not happen for Mexican Americans. Widespread participation in international wars[11] and unionization in Los Angeles did not help them like it helped European Americans. Indeed, they were mostly excluded from this process as they were perceived as insufficiently American or white, and historically, they were subject to a comprehensive system of racial domination, unlike any experienced by European Americans.[12] By the 1960s, when third-generation European Americans had become nearly fully incorporated, third-generation Mexican Americans had not. By 2000, they still had not. Although ethnic boundaries with whites became more fluid and their situation improved from 1965 to 2000, Mexican Americans were still far from assimilated and definitely had not become accepted as white. For a process of assimilation to occur for them, a new and more inclusive historical context must emerge. Without such a change, assimilation is not likely.

VARIATION AMONG MEXICAN AMERICANS

We have sought to overcome a general tendency in the literature to emphasize differences between ethnic groups and downplay the substantial diversity within groups. Certainly some Mexican Americans have been able to penetrate racial or ethnic boundaries and move into the mainstream more easily than others. A few may even assimilate to a point where their ethnicity makes little or no difference. Richard Alba and Victor Nee and Portes and Rumbaut note that particular variables may hasten or impede assimilation, but tend to assign such variables wholesale to one or another ethnic group.[13] Instead, we found wide variation in the extent of assimilation among the Mexican American population, despite their generation. For example, those who attained relatively high levels of education, those growing up in more integrated neighborhoods, especially in Los Angeles, and those with parents of mixed ethnic origin assimilate more easily. Although group-level experiences largely predict individual experiences of integration, individuals within the group may also be subject to a wide range of contextual and social forces.

Some U.S.-born Mexican Americans become solidly middle class and occasionally even very successful in their field. Such persons tend to have grown up in households where parents had relatively high levels of schooling and greater economic and social resources. Those who attended Catholic schools also tend to be better educated and thus have greater life chances than those who attended public schools. At the same time, these more economically successful individuals are especially likely to have integrated into the American mainstream and have cultural or linguistic attributes that are decidedly mainstream American. A disproportionate number, though, continue to occupy the lower ranks of the American class structure. Certainly, later-generation Mexican Americans and European Americans overlap in their class distributions. The difference is that the bulk of Mexican Americans are in lower class sectors, but only a relatively small part of the European American population is similarly positioned.

EDUCATION AS THE LINCHPIN OF SLOW ASSIMILATION

More than any other variable, education accounts for the slow assimilation of Mexican Americans on most social dimensions. Our statistical models have shown that the low education levels of Mexican Americans have impeded most other types of assimilation,

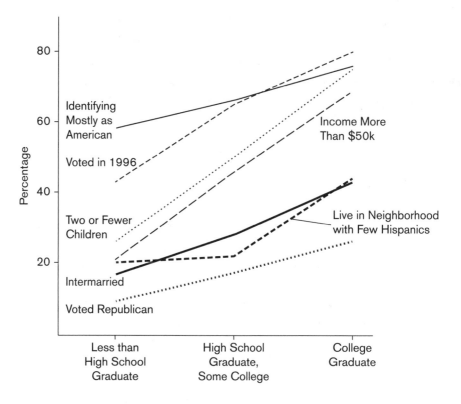

FIGURE 14.3

Assimilation and Education among Children, 2000.

Source: Mexican American Study Project.

thus reinforcing a range of ethnic boundaries between them and white Americans. Mexican Americans with low levels of schooling tend to have lower income, wealth, and occupational status, which limit their ability to move out of the barrio. Their limited schooling locks many of them into a future of low socioe-conomic status. A disproportionate segment of the Mexican American population is thus subordinated in the youthful process of educational and human capital formation.[14] Low levels of education also predict lower rates of intermarriage, a weaker American identity, and lower likelihood of registering to vote and voting. Just as segregation has been described as the linchpin of the African American experience,[15] low education is the linchpin of the ethnic persistence of Mexican Americans.

We illustrate the difference that one's level of schooling makes on these and other indicators for the children sample in figure 14.3. We present differences in the extent of integration along seven indicators by three levels of schooling: less than high school, high school graduates with no or some college, and college graduates. Figure 14.3 demonstrates that assimilation on each dimension increased with the level of schooling.[16] It shows, for example, that Mexican Americans with higher levels of education are more

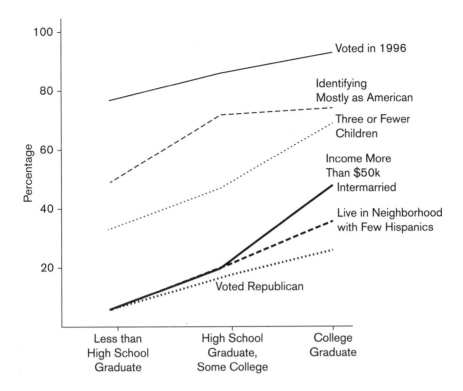

FIGURE 14.4

Assimilation and Education among Original Respondents, 2000

Source: Mexican American Study Project.

likely to have an American than an ethnic identity and are more likely to vote, suggesting greater integration in the American polity. Relatedly, they are also more likely to vote Republican, suggesting that they are less committed to the usual party of the ethnic group. Their level of education makes a notable difference in socioeconomic status (percentage with incomes greater than $50,000)[17] and exposure to other groups (percentage living in a neighborhood with 25 percent or fewer Hispanics and percentage intermarried). Finally, they also have lower fertility (percentage with two or fewer children), itself an important determinant of the educational level of the next generation.

These patterns are similar for the original respondent generation, though the rates are often lower. We show these results in figure 14.4. For example, only about 5 percent of high school dropouts among the original respondents intermarried, versus more than 40 percent of college graduates. This compares with their children's generation, in which about 15 percent of high school dropouts intermarried and nearly 40 percent of college graduates did. Thus, at the less-educated end, rates of intermarriage increased about three times. At the other, though, intermarriage rates have surprisingly remained stable from 1965 to 2000. To take two more examples, less-educated people in 1964 were much less likely to vote than in 1996 but were also much more likely to live in integrated neighborhoods in 1964 than in 1996.[18] The most important point of figures 14.3 and 14.4, though, is to show that assimilation is consistently related to education for two distinct generations of Mexican Americans and the persistence of educational disadvantage largely predicts the group's slow or halted assimilation.

Race, ethnicity, and class are thus deeply intertwined for Mexican Americans. Low levels of education puts them largely in working-class sectors (including low-level white-collar jobs) and the ethnic boundaries of later generations are especially strong for the working class. Since low education tends to be transmitted across generations, this segment of the Mexican American population is likely to remain working class and especially immersed in ethnic culture for several generations. For the middle class, however, ethnic boundaries are relatively light. Thus, class defines race and ethnic experiences to a large extent.

OTHER FACTORS AFFECTING MEXICAN AMERICAN INTEGRATION

We also discuss how urban context, parental status, gender, intermarriage, and skin color also help shape Mexican American integration. These variables influence individual prospects for assimilation and the way Mexican Americans experience race and ethnicity. We begin with an analysis of urban context at the metropolitan and at the neighborhood level.

THE URBAN CONTEXT

Our sample consists of Mexican Americans growing up in Los Angeles County and San Antonio City in the 1960s. These two areas represented the largest concentrations of Mexican Americans at the time and often represented quite distinct socioeconomic, political, and cultural experiences. Based on select indicators such as education and income, the average outcome for Mexican Americans in general seems to lie between the two. More important, these two areas illustrate how urban contexts can shape the experience of ethnicity in the United States. Local political and economic histories have varied substantially and left their mark on how race and ethnicity have been experienced.

The specific differences in our study between Los Angeles and San Antonio continue to be quite striking even after controlling for many other respondent characteristics, including the extent of residential segregation and human capital. The context of much of the Southwest is bicultural but this is especially true in San Antonio. More third- and fourth-generation Mexican Americans raised in San Antonio are proficient in Spanish than in Los Angeles, revealing the importance of the particular local context in which ethnicity is sustained. Spanish language dies earlier in Los Angeles but such acculturation does not affect socioeconomic assimilation. Mexican Americans are similarly disadvantaged in both cities, though San Antonians were clearly worse off at the time of the original study (1960s). Despite this, they became similar socioeconomically to their counterparts in Los Angeles by 2000.

Mexican Americans are more Mexican in lifestyle and behaviors in San Antonio but are more Democratic and politically liberal in Los Angeles. Besides being more likely to speak Spanish, San Antonians are more likely than Angelenos both to marry and live near other Mexican-origin persons and to remain in the area they grew up in. On the other hand, despite a history of greater racialized oppression, Mexican Americans growing up in San Antonio are much more likely to identify as white. They are also more likely to identify as Hispanic and to vote Republican, reflecting the more conservative and assimilationist political strategies that Mexican American leaders pursued in Texas.

Such differences between the two places may also be related to more traditional Anglo-Mexican relations in San Antonio. Such relations probably derive from Mexican San Antonio's recent emergence from a deeply racialized system. Racialization for Mexican Americans in San Antonio until well into the 1960s included widespread segregation, poverty, and social isolation as well as a related tradition of patronage in politics and paternalism. Thus, when our child respondents were growing up, racial boundaries between Anglos and Mexicans were much more rigid in San Antonio than in Los Angeles. These boundaries sealed off much of the Mexican American community, thus promoting ethnic culture and possibly traditional ways of thinking and deference in an especially hierarchical society. At the same time, Mexican American San Antonians were more likely to identify as white, in that nearly Southern city, where clear distinctions from blacks were socially and politically valued. In contrast, racial boundaries and relations were more fluid in the more cosmopolitan and integrated Los Angeles of the 1960s, where legal segregation and explicit racism had become less common. Assertions of an explicitly nonwhite racial identity also emerged by the late 1960s, especially in Los Angeles, which provided fertile ground for progressive political activism.

A changing industrial structure and the opportunities for mobility that it affords have been commonly used to explain why European immigrants succeeded and why the descendants of immigrants today will have a harder time moving into the middle class.[19] Under the pre-1970s industrial structure, manual jobs paid well, were unionized, had long-term security, and provided opportunities for career mobility. Because of this, we would expect that the children of Mexican American Angelenos would do better than those of San Antonians, given that Los Angeles had a large industrial base much like East Coast American cities[20] and San Antonio did not. Mexican Americans in Los Angeles in the original sample had better economic opportunities, indicated by their concentration in manufacturing jobs and their higher incomes. In addition, the profitable industrial composition of Los Angeles likely contributed to better schools in the region overall. However, we found no evidence that Mexican American children growing up in Los Angeles did better socioeconomically than in San Antonio, nor did we find that children of parents working in industrial manufacturing did better educationally. Apparently, the advantages of a traditional manufacturing economy did not extend to the Mexican American population. Relatedly, the availability of manufacturing jobs also did not help the next generation of Mexican Americans in Los Angeles to secure more professional and high status occupations than their San Antonio counterparts.

A major point of the industrial restructuring argument is that the less educated had better labor market opportunities under the old industrial structure and that by the third generation, schooling had often become high enough for such individuals to enter secure professional occupations. That favorable economic structure is often used to argue how immigrants were able to move up the occupational ladder in two or three generations-since-immigration. However, the educational and socioeconomic status of the original respondents and their children were similar in Los Angeles and San Antonio, despite the greater economic opportunities in the "most industrialized city west of the Mississippi."[21] Moreover, the pattern of third-generation decline or maintenance of status was also similar in both cities. Apparently, the more robust Los Angeles economy seemed to make little difference, probably because Mexican Americans were generally excluded from many industrial occupations and neighborhoods. Moreover, educational opportunities were far from evenly distributed. European immigrants and their descendants, by contrast, seemed to benefit from industrialization because they could be fully integrated in industrial employment. This is not to deny that even relatively poor manufacturing jobs could have provided greater mobility and wages but that these apparently lower middle class jobs cited by Grebler, Moore, and Guzman as evidence of an emerging Mexican American middle class could also be found in San Antonio's large government and military sector.

Neighborhood segregation also affected the assimilation prospects of some Mexican Americans. Our sample in Los Angeles had neighborhood experiences varying from nearly complete segregation to those where they were a small minority whereas the San Antonio sample tended to grow up in more segregated areas. Those in more segregated neighborhoods clearly have lower educational outcomes than those in more integrated neighborhoods, but educational levels for those in integrated schools and neighborhoods also fell below those of whites. However, controls for parental socioeconomic status reveal that segregation itself had almost no independent effect on schooling. Rather, it was the lower parental education and their consequently low financial resources that often limited Mexican-origin persons to segregated neighborhoods and schools.[22]

Growing up in a segregated or ethnically concentrated neighborhood heightens other dimensions of the ethnic boundary. Mexican Americans raised in barrios were more likely to marry Hispanics and more likely to live in segregated neighborhoods themselves, even after controlling for socioeconomic and other factors. Ethnic culture and identity are shaped by the extent to which one lives in an ethnic context. Thus the slow assimilation of Mexican Americans was partly attributable to their uniquely large size and demographic concentration, both in 1965 and 2000. However, greater spatial isolation was also attributable to their low levels of education, which is a better predictor of the lack of assimilation overall.

PARENTAL SOCIOECONOMIC STATUS

As the large sociological literature on status attainment repeatedly confirms, a primary determinant of one's status in American society is the status of parents. Our findings show that this is no different for the Mexican American population. The most educated and the most successful Mexican Americans tended to have parents with relatively high levels of schooling. Similarly, parental income and whether parents were homeowners also affected the education of children. In turn, such parent resources may facilitate assimilation and reduce the negative effects of racialization. However, the ability of subsequent generations to convert or improve on the education of their parents seems to be worse for Mexican Americans than for other major racial-ethnic groups. Compared to African Americans, Mexican Americans certainly have higher returns to human capital in the labor market, but they also have lower educational returns to the education of their parents.

The assimilation literature takes status attainment a step further and predicts upward economic mobility from low status immigrant to U.S.-born generations, at least until ethnic groups reach the overall status of the mainstream. For the descendants of European immigrants, human capital deficits were generally overcome by the third generation. Their returns to parental human capital are relatively high and thus they are especially likely to overcome the educational deficiencies of earlier generations. The Mexican American case, however, differs because there were only modest gains, at best, after the second generation. The lack of educational and economic mobility across generations reinforces other ethnic boundaries. Given an intergenerational transfer of lower status, less educated parents also tend to have children who are less likely to culturally, residentially, and maritally assimilate. The disproportionately low education of the children further limits their societal integration as adults.

GENDER

Gender is not a central factor in assimilation theory, yet we find that it matters for some dimensions we studied. As has been well documented previously, we found lower earnings for women. This was, however, not coupled with disadvantages along other economic indicators. For example, women had similar occupational status to that of men. This suggests that Mexican American women were in jobs that might be considered women's work—jobs of a similar status to those of men but that tended to pay less. Moreover, we found that women did not have lower family income or net worth. This was attributable to their being married and being part of a two-earner household. Women also had somewhat less education than men. Our respondents were in their late thirties or older and thus educated by the late 1980s—a period during which men continued to do better educationally.[23] These results for socioeconomic status, though, tend to hold for the general population in the United States and Mexico and thus say little about how integration varies by gender.

Our findings on how women differed from men in their ethnic behaviors, attitudes, and culture are more revealing. For instance, Mexican American women had significantly higher Spanish proficiency than men, indicating slower linguistic assimilation. This might be attributable to women having closer relationships with family and therefore learning Spanish within the home context. We also found that Mexican American women reported less discrimination. This might be indicative of the experiences of nonwhite men in society today—where they are more likely to be penalized in the educational, labor market, and criminal justice system.[24] Compared to other ethnic groups, Mexican American women had especially high fertility even among the third and fourth generation. Mexican immigrants generally held traditional gender attitudes but became more egalitarian as generations further removed from the immigration generation. On the other hand, Mexican American men and women did not differ on most ethnic behaviors and attitudes. Women were not more likely to intermarry and did not differ in ethnic or racial identification.

INTERMARRIAGE

Intermarriage itself is an indicator of assimilation, particularly at the aggregate group level. Greater intermarriage implies that ethnic boundaries are relatively fluid or more easily crossed. Moderate rates of intermarriage for Mexican Americans suggest that they were accepted well enough by at least some of the white population. However, intermarriage often has limited effects on the individuals who intermarry, because factors such as language, identities, and politics are often consolidated by the time of marriage. More than likely, intermarriage is selective of those who are already more assimilated. We found, though, that intermarriage was particularly powerful for Mexican Americans in its effect on the children of intermarried couples. The 9 percent of children with a non-Hispanic parent were less likely to know Spanish, were more likely to intermarry themselves, identified less with their Mexican origin, and were more likely to call themselves Americans. Such children were often perceived as and understood themselves as less Mexican. In some cases they do not identify as Mexican origin at all, although we found very few such cases. We should note that the proportion of this group has roughly doubled in the past decade[25] compared to our children cohort, which was born from 1946 to 1966.

For our study, we generated a representative sample of all the children of the original respondents, regardless of whether or not they identified as Mexican origin, Hispanic, or the like. Official surveys like the Census are unable to identify such cases as part of the Mexican origin population and thus studies on Mexican Americans that use this data miss such individuals. However, such cases should be included to more accurately examine the nature or extent of intergenerational change. One might argue that we might miss such cases if persons in the 1965 sample screening did not similarly identify as Mexican or Spanish origin in 1965, but we consider this a relatively minor problem in a study such as ours. We have no doubt that the progeny of one or two generations of intermarriage sometimes may not identify as or be seen as a Mexican American, especially if they no longer live in places like San Antonio or Los Angeles or do not bear markers such as a Spanish surname. There simply is nothing like the unusual hypodescent (one-drop) rule for Mexican Americans, as there is for African Americans. Persons with small amounts of Mexican ancestry, unless they tend to identify as Mexican American, simply are not Mexican American. Why should they be if they don't consider themselves as such and society doesn't either? Such amalgamation may mean full assimilation but that is of little consequence or consolation to those who remain Mexican American. Once enough markers of Mexicanness or nonwhiteness have been removed through mixture with whites, complete assimilation might become possible, though some children of mixed unions will surely continue to identify and be identified as Mexican American, to varying degrees.[26]

SKIN COLOR

Given that skin color seems to be the primary marker of race in the United States, and that the Mexican-origin population runs the gamut from light and seemingly European to dark and seemingly indigenous, we expected that it would predict differences in many of our outcomes. One might, for example, expect that persons that physically appear as nonwhite or closer to the Mexican stereotype would be most discriminated and therefore suffer greater disadvantage. However, aside from reported discrimination and the extent to which one thinks of oneself as Mexican, we found no differences by color among the children of the original respondents, even though color affected education and income among a national sample for an earlier period.[27] We speculate that the lack of a skin color effect on variables such as occupation and education might be due to more generalized Mexican-origin stigma based on a variety of markers in Los Angeles and San Antonio, in contrast to less ethnic places, where it is easier to pass into the white category if one is light enough. That many or most Mexican Americans are perceived as nonwhite could negatively affect the entire group by further racializing them. Individual Mexican Americans who do not meet the physical stereotypes, though, may also be identified as such through other characteristics such as names, language or accent, friendships, or where they reside. While first impressions based on physical appearance may be especially important in other social arenas like racial profiling by police or in getting a job, other criteria may be as important in education, where social categorization is likely to be better, though perhaps not well, informed.

Skin color may also be more important nationally because Mexicans are less visible in many places other than in San Antonio or Los Angeles, and thus may be less threatening to whites. It is also possible that color today is less important than in the past. A study of African Americans found that younger cohorts raised in the post-civil rights era are unaffected by skin tone variation, unlike older African Americans.[28] The same may be true for Mexican Americans. In the future, though, as Mexican immigration increasingly involves indigenous and indigenous looking persons, skin tone may come to have a more prominent role in Mexican American integration, although it is far from being the only determinant in racialization.

REVISITING ASSIMILATION AND RACIALIZATION

There are two broad theories that have been used to explain the integration trajectories of particular ethnic groups in the United States. These are, generally, theories of assimilation and those of race. Specifically, the leading contenders today seeking to explain immigrant and ethnic incorporation are modern assimilation theory as espoused by Alba and Nee and segmented assimilation theory as developed by Portes and his colleagues. To be sure, these theories are much closer to each other than the older assimilation versus race (e.g. internal colonialism) theories that existed before them, thanks largely to increasing empirical evidence indicating that integration may be affected by assimilation, race, and a host of other factors. Both modern assimilation and segmented assimilation theories consider assimilation and race explanations though in different ways and to different degrees. We hope to have provided more evidence to further refine our understanding of ethnic integration, especially for the large Mexican origin population.

We have mentioned our contributions throughout the text, confirming and contesting previous theories including those of standard assimilation and segmented assimilation. We summarize eight of them here. First, we show the important effects of social barriers based on race for Mexican Americans that previous scholars often underestimated (Alba and Nee) or completely disregarded (Huntington). Second, we believe that most theories of integration including those by Portes and his colleagues and by Alba and Nee tend to confuse the effects of historical period with generation-since-immigration, generally slighting the former. We have shown the importance of disentangling these two types of generational comparisons. Third, we have shown that there is wide variation within the group that has been nearly ignored by both schools of thought, probably a consequence of the methodological tack of comparing several groups. Relatedly and fourthly, we demonstrated the sizeable effects of local context in shaping integration outcomes. Fifth, both schools of thought have exaggerated the consistency and uniformity in direction to which assimilation occurs across a wide range of social dimensions. We showed how assimilation, and the lack of it, can occur at quite distinct paces and even in an opposite direction. Sixth, we have also demonstrated how one factor—namely, the absence of educational assimilation—shapes most other types of assimilation, specifically by slowing it and thus fostering ethnic distinctions. Seventh, Portes and his colleagues blame status and linguistic dissonance between immigrant parents and their children as largely responsible for poor educational assimilation but we find that low education persists into the third and fourth generation when such dissonance no longer exists. Finally, we also find problematic any theoretical time frame where assimilation takes more than three generations, which would be needed to explain the Mexican American trajectory. Even if Mexican Americans were to fully assimilate within six or seven generations, how can assimilation theory be the principal explanation of ethnicity? How do we explain ethnic phenomenon, racialization, and periods of ethnic resurgence in the intervening 150 to 200 years?

Our study is designed to directly assess the direction and extent of assimilation as well as the effects of factors like education, urban and demographic context, parental resources, and home culture. While we find assimilation in social exposure, politics, identity, and especially cultural aspects, such assimilation is slower than has been shown for other groups. However, our evidence does not similarly support assimilation in educational and economic status for Mexican Americans, and there is little support for other theories like those based on culture, language, or industrialization. Instead, we find corroborating evidence suggesting racialization, which is not surprising give their history as victims of outright racial coercion, segregation, and discrimination. Racialization includes the societal practice of assigning others to a "race," which is generally ranked by characteristics such as intelligence and worth, or placing them in a racial hierarchy even if they are not referred to as a race. Direct proof of racialization and especially discrimination requires different study design from this one, which shows integration trajectories and the measurable factors that influence it.[29]

We have demonstrated that Mexican Americans are disproportionately sorted into the low socioeconomic strata, mostly via the educational system and while they are young. That suggests racialization. Moreover, the failure or insufficiency of other perspectives to account for the low education of Mexican Americans as well as the findings from other studies leads us to support a racialization hypothesis. Certainly, many of our respondents experienced discrimination and were aware of common stereotypes based on popular ideas that Mexican origin persons possess an inferior culture and an inherent unworthiness that keeps them from becoming fully American even when they may no longer bear the cultural characteristics attributed to the group.

Studies find that a range of institutional and interpersonal discrimination and racialization practices limit the educational attainment of Mexican Americans.[30] Institutional discrimination includes the underfinancing of public schools that mostly Mexican origin students attend and their avoidance by more experienced teachers as well as tracking these children into low level curriculum in the case of integrated schools. Interpersonal discrimination includes the racially distinct expectations of students by teachers and counselors and the stigmatizing of Mexican Americans as inferior, lazy, or less worthy students by society in general. Racialized ideas guide individual interactions, including those between student and teacher/counselor. These interactions may involve direct advice to students about which classes to take or avoid or they may send signals to students that shape personal identities, sense of adequacy, and more specifically, may limit self-investment and effort in school.[31] These adverse effects, though, do not deny that some of these students achieve academic success, especially under more favorable learning conditions[32] or when they possess an advantaged self-concept.[33]

TOWARD A HISTORICAL-STRUCTURAL THEORY OF MEXICAN IMMIGRATION AND MEXICAN AMERICAN INTEGRATION

We have described general patterns for the group as well as intra-group variation and we have suggested how various factors account for the peculiar integration of Mexican Americans. In particular, educational disadvantage persists for several generations-since-immigration and this partly accounts for their slow or uneven assimilation on various dimensions. We have also shown that other crucial determinants explain the low status and ethnic persistence of Mexican Americans, including demographic size and concentration, for which we have direct evidence, and racism and nativism, for which we have indirect evidence. Rather than review the list of causes, in this section we propose a heuristic model based on an ultimate single cause to account for the peculiar nature of Mexican American integration into the United States.

We argue that American capitalists' desire to quench its persistent thirst for cheap Mexican labor for a century, which is supported by the American state and enabled by Mexico's proximity and its large labor supply, can largely account for the persistent low status and ethnic retention of Mexican Americans. For an entire century, inexpensive and easily disposable Mexican labor has filled the labor needs of Southwest agriculture as well as those of Southwest urban employers. More recently, the reliance on Mexican labor beyond the Southwest and throughout the United States has grown.[34] Throughout the twentieth century and into the twenty-first, capitalist labor demands have been facilitated by United States immigration policy, which has often treated Mexicans as a special case.[35] This has led to an especially adverse context of reception in comparison to other immigrant groups.[36] The resultant nature of immigration perpetuates the racialization of Mexican American children in school, which slows or halts Mexican American economic, social, identificational, and civic assimilation. That historical process has also created a large and concentrated Mexican American population, which is fed by continuing immigration, all of which foster ethnic retention.

In many ways, the integration pattern of Mexican immigrants is thus the consequence of the witting and unwitting actions of the American state coupled with Mexico's own social condition and development needs. Largely through several amnesty programs, Mexicans continue to be the largest legal immigrant group but they have also comprised the majority of undocumented immigrants. By granting the right to live and work in the United States, legal status becomes the ultimate criteria of belonging to the American nation.[37] In contrast, the lack of legal status for many immigrants represents complete national exclusion but permits a cheaper and more disposable labor force to better satisfy employer demands. The fact that the citizens of one country are disproportionately illegal may create ethnic stereotypes and send signals to co-ethnics that they are not fully American, especially since the usual racial-categorical thinking of American society often fails to distinguish between natives and immigrants. Such nativism and stereotyping harms the image of Mexican Americans as Americans by denying them equal education, among other things, and this ultimately heightens racial and ethnic identities.[38]

Perceptions of Mexicans as low status persons and often illegal entrants and Mexico as perpetually impoverished, crime-ridden, and dependent on the United States has led to stereotyping of Mexican origin persons generally. With a century of continuous immigration, Mexican Americans of all generations often share residential, marriage, and labor markets, which further promotes the stereotypes and racialization of Mexican Americans irrespective of generations-since-immigration. Perceived as foreigners, even Mexican Americans with deep roots in the United States are excluded from enjoying a full American identity. Mexico and its non-emigrant citizens are also perceived as and treated as inferior neighbors. This is as true in public opinion as in economic and political relations. Although Mexico arguably benefits from immigration to the United States, it has, in the words of Mexico's former ambassador to the United Nations Adolfo Aguilar Zinser, simply become Washington's backyard as American interests have often been imposed, especially though a unilateral immigration policy.[39] American nativism is especially aimed against Mexicans, whether they are immigrant or non-immigrant citizens of Mexico. Whether or not it is also directed at U.S.-born Mexican Americans, nevertheless has the effect of limiting the identities of later generation Mexican Americans. It shapes their perceived role in American society and especially affects their educational experience. This persistent foreignness makes the Mexican Americans case different from that of African or European Americans.

The American reliance on Mexican labor has also led to a demographic predominance of Mexicans in the Southwest, especially in cities like Los Angeles and San Antonio. A century of immigration has produced a very large, though multigenerational, population. This is quite unlike the experience of European immigration before, which was nationally and linguistically diverse, and in which migration stopped after one generation, or Asian immigration today, in which no single national or linguistic group has predominated. The large presence of Mexican origin persons, immigrants and U.S.-born, in particular areas may create institutional incentives for mobility into jobs that serve the ethnic population and thus may also lower incentives to move away from these areas. Large numbers of Mexicans have also created both a large demand for Spanish-language media and a wide array of ethnic institutions, as well as allowed for large ethnic neighborhoods where there is often little contact with other groups and much contact between various generations of Mexicans. The moderate segregation and large size of the group means that residence and thus educational and other institutions are often demographically dominated by Mexican origin persons, which may include those of the fourth generation. This allows the top-down policies of state institutions to target particular communities or schools on the basis of Mexican ethnicity. Also, such residential segregation may regenerate ethnic identity for later-generation Mexican Americans and foster endogamous marriages and in-group social relationships.

The geographical concentration and the large size of the group also makes Mexican Americans especially visible, which itself evokes attention to the group and thus the tendency to categorize. The demographic predominance of this single low status and perceptibly foreign group reinforces xenophobic fears among non-Mexicans of labor market substitution, demographic inundation, and racial and cultural hybridization[40] Such fears are often directed at U.S.-born Mexican Americans as well. Immigration restrictionists generally believe that immigrants, most notably Mexicans, take jobs away from U.S.-born workers, even though the evidence shows that immigration, legal and illegal, benefit the vast majority of American workers and consumers.[41]

Furthermore, the low status of the immigrant generation throughout the twentieth century was produced originally by the selective needs of American employers. Since then, a system of cumulative causation and social networks expanded the sources of Mexican immigration and further decreased its selectivity.[42] As a result, immigration from the Mexican middle class is relatively rare, quite unlike immigration from other countries to the United States today.[43] Along with its large size and largely illegal status, the lack of Mexican immigrant selectivity, especially when contrasted to so much middle class immigration among many other national groups that comprise the new immigration population, continues to make the Mexicans case exceptional.[44] This low status contributes to their stigmatization in the educational system and on the American social totem pole generally.

This seems to contrast with the example of Asians today, in which changes in immigration policy since 1965 have been selective of persons with high education and professional occupations. As a result, the success of the Asian second generation today is largely due to their parents' high levels of education and other resources, as the status attainment model predicts. However, not all Asian immigration is of high status. Even though some Asians do not have the high levels of human and social capital associated with many of the immigrants, even those identified as Asian with relatively low human capital benefit from belonging or being ascribed to a successful group. Such benefits include high expectations by educators, employers, and other societal members. The obverse would thus seem to hold true for Mexican Americans, in that ascription to a group with little capital or status impedes the progress of even those individuals with relatively high status.

Finally, the century-long reliance on Mexican labor prolonged a nineteenth century racial order in which Mexicans were considered inferior and perceived as outsiders and even enemies of American nationhood.[45] These ideas continue to resonate in the public mind. Although it was nineteenth century or traditional views of Mexicans, driven in part by a legacy of war and conquest, that originally racialized Mexican Americans, stigmatization of Mexican origin persons persists largely because of the enduring American labor need and Mexico's large low-skilled labor supply. The American racial order has changed throughout that time, most notably for Southern and Central European groups,[46] but it has not for Mexican origin persons. Their position in the racial order continues to be near the bottom, which continues to be self-evident, commonsense, and natural in many American minds, despite the passing of time and the end of explicit racial policies or laws.

Racial discrimination against Mexicans no longer occurs in the classical sense but by way of a social stigmatization that is entwined in a series of economic, political, and social processes and practices. The idea of race continues to be an important concept among Americans, one in which particular racial categories carry meanings about one's capabilities and worthiness. They also create stereotypes that are used to rank ethnic groups in the American social hierarchy. National opinion research, for example, shows that the American public ranks Hispanics as the second lowest among racial-ethnic groups overall after blacks. A national survey also shows that Hispanics earn the lowest ranking of all groups when they are rated on the basis of poverty, intelligence, and patriotism.[47] These findings extend early findings by Bogardus in which Americans consistently ranked Mexican Americans near the bottom of the social scale from 1936 to 1966.

WHAT WOULD HAPPEN WITHOUT IMMIGRATION?

Mexican immigration and Mexican American ethnicity and racialization are intimately intertwined. An important theoretical question becomes "what would happen to Mexican Americans if there had not been the surge of post-1970 immigration?"[48] Can we assume there would have been rapid assimilation instead? Indeed, the assimilation of Italians and other groups is often argued to have been the result of an immigration hiatus soon after the larger waves of immigration.[49] In the case of Mexicans, though, things are not likely to be so simple. This question forces us to think about the processes of both assimilation and racialization. This question, though, is not as straightforward as it seems because immigration is not a static feature of society but rather both a consequence and cause of changes in the economy and politics. An end to immigration would affect assimilation prospects not only directly but also indirectly by causing changes in the structure of the economy and economic opportunity.

One might expect that Mexican Americans would probably assimilate to a greater extent without immigration because opportunities for speaking Spanish, living in barrios, and marrying other persons of Mexican origin would diminish because there would be fewer Mexican immigrants among the population. Moreover, growth in residential segregation in past decades for Mexican Americans has been driven by immigration.[50] Without immigration, Mexican American residential segregation would thus likely decrease, which would in turn trigger other assimilative processes, such as intermarriage and perhaps social and geographic mobility. Also, Mexican American politics and identity, which have jelled largely on issues of immigration, would probably not have formed as strongly as they have. A post–civil rights context, in which segregation and the most egregious of racism have ended, would further stimulate assimilation.

However, the absence of immigration, though it is unlikely to happen anytime soon, does not guarantee assimilation. The example of San Antonio today shows the persistence of racial boundaries despite little immigration to that city since 1929. The state of New Mexico is an even better case in that it has seen even less Mexican immigration since about the same time. There, Mexican Americans continue to be racialized, even with little immigration. An entrenched racialized way of thinking that places Mexicans in the lower rungs of society seems to be at least partly responsible for their persistently low status, though the stigmatized nature of Mexican immigration has maintained or lowered their status.

An end to immigration would require a new source of cheap labor if the American economy is to continue growing as it has. Given American history, that source is unlikely to be shouldered evenly by all Americans. Mexican Americans would be a ready source, especially because they tend to have low levels of education and they populate those regions where low-wage industries are concentrated to benefit from Mexican immigration. The end to immigration could even harden social boundaries for Mexican Americans, because labor market segmentation could increase where the dividing line would be less on immigration status and more on race or ethnicity. This possibility is enhanced given the growing income polarization of urban labor markets. On the other hand, assimilation for Mexican Americans might be especially likely if a large substitute source of cheap labor other than Mexican immigrants could be found or if the American demand for cheap labor could somehow be eliminated.

POLICY AND THE FUTURE

Most of the sociological literature about Mexican Americans focuses on what will happen to the children of the current wave of immigrants.[51] Our study has examined what did happen to the descendants of past waves of Mexican immigrants. This approach has allowed us to examine long-term integration. We believe, however, that the past is critical to informing the future as well. Although there has been a very gradual breaking down of Mexican American ethnic boundaries over the last 100 years, three disturbing trends in recent years might slow or even reverse the prospects for further integration. These are labor market polarization, worsening public education, and the growing size of the undocumented population. The course of labor market polarization is difficult to control, though public policy has shown it is capable of making major changes in education and immigration.

The potential policy levers for improving the integration prospects of Mexican Americans must, then, address education and immigration. Overall, we agree with Portes and Rumbaut that the dominant ideologies that propose either to stop immigration (intransigent nativism) or to force assimilation are short-sighted and unlikely to ever work.[52] Rather, we need to focus on investing in the education of the descendants of Mexican immigrants and on a fair and welcoming immigration policy with respect to Mexico that recognizes American needs for its labor. Not doing so will likely lead to continuously poor economic outcomes for Mexican Americans and their poor integration into American society. Such policies to improve their lot are likely to improve the lives of Americans in general, because Mexican Americans will soon represent most of the lower end work forces in vital states such as Texas and California. The retiring and mostly white baby boomers will also largely depend on the contributions of these mostly Mexican American youth, and their low education will translate into lower earnings to support these senior citizens.[53]

Public education is the greatest source of Mexican American exclusion, in that low education impedes their economic prospects. In California, a voter-led initiative in 1979 (Proposition 13) undermined its primary funding source and its quality has deteriorated at the same time that Hispanics have become the largest ethnic population among all public school students.[54] The future of Mexican Americans for at least the next twenty to thirty years depends largely on education today. About half of Mexican origin youth do not complete high school on time, apparently reversing improving trends in recent decades.[55] Although the lack of such an education could be overcome by manual labor jobs that ensured decent pay, stability, and mobility, such jobs are increasingly difficult to find as the divide between bad and good jobs widens. The choice for many U.S.-born Mexican Americans may be restricted to jobs that are not much better than those of their immigrant ancestors. Indeed, even with affirmative action, the large majority of even later-generation Mexican Americans still do not have a college education. This means they will continue to be concentrated in the lower rungs of a widening class divide. We found that the educational situation is as bad if not worse for later-generation Mexican Americans and more recent evidence shows that this pattern continues.[56]

Public schools are the single greatest institutional culprit for the persistent low status of U.S.-born Mexican Americans, although a few do well. Mexican Americans continue to have the lowest levels of education in the country. The public schools that serve Mexican American communities, which are largely in the central cities and in rural areas, are increasingly segregated and have been among this country's worst.[57] For those in integrated schools, schools are often better but educational scholars have found that Mexican-origin students are disproportionately tracked into lower level curricula and made to feel unwanted or uncomfortable in school.[58] Many of these are segregated schools but the problem is not limited to segregated schools. Most of our sample attended integrated schools.

For Mexican Americans to become successful, we need, above all, a Marshall Plan that invests heavily in public school education, addressing the issues that disadvantage students. We need to emphasize educational opportunities, rather than adoption of American values, since Mexican Americans already have these.[59] Sociologist Mary

Waters of Harvard University,[60] studying the integration experiences of the old classic wave of European immigrants and their descendants, found that the Americanization programs were not nearly as important as the enormous economic payoff to immigration that the descendants of European immigration enjoyed. For Mexican Americans, the payoff can only come by giving them the same quality and quantity of education as whites receive. The problem is not the unwillingness of Mexican Americans to adopt American values and culture but the failure of societal institutions, particularly public schools, to successfully integrate them as they did the descendants of European immigrants. Since the 1970s, schooling has become an ever more important predictor of success. A restructured economy has led to increased demand for the college educated and decreased demand for those with a high school education, making this a worrisome fact for the future of most Mexican Americans.

The growing population of undocumented immigrants in recent years, as in previous periods, has again brought the Mexican problem into the center of public debate. Nativists often make Mexicans the scapegoat for many social problems, which further stigmatizes the entire population of Mexican origin. Immigration proposals that seek to criminalize illegal immigration rather than offer paths to legal residency and citizenship also bode ill for the future of Mexican Americans. The illegality of many of today's immigrants is also likely to slow mobility for their children. Moreover, such policies not only harm Mexican Americans but American society in general because they increase the potential for creating a large number of persons without rights and further stigmatize the large population of Mexican Americans.

U.S. immigration policies have largely sought to control the flows of immigrants, particularly those coming from Mexico. The large size of the undocumented population reflects failed immigration policies and America's contradictory need for low-wage labor at the same time that nativist impulses feel that the border and immigration is out of control. Any attempt to seal off the U.S.-Mexico border, as some have suggested, represents an anachronism in a globalizing world, especially in a liberal democracy such as the United States. Moreover, this would be a slap at Mexico and the global community as well as a blow to human rights, which the United States claims to fiercely defend. Such an initiative may likely reinforce, rather than improve, the racialized status of Mexican-origin persons in the United States. American dependence on Mexican and Mexican American labor needs to be acknowledged without the common scapegoating of Mexicans as criminal trespassers and Mexican Americans as their unassimilable progeny.

NOTES

1. Portes and Zhou (1993); Portes and Rumbaut (2001).
2. Rumbaut, Massey and Bean (2006).
3. Alba (1985); Perlmann (2005).

4. Matute-Bianchi (1986); Kao and Tienda (1995).

5. Alba and Nee (2003).

6. Portes and Rumbaut (2001); Duncan, Hotz, and Trejo (2006).

7. Frey (1999).

8. Haney López (2003).

9. Foley (1997); Menchaca (1993); Montejano (1987).

10. Jacobsen (1998); Roediger (2005).

11. Rivas Rodriguez (2005). We also found that 54 percent of men among original respondents and 21 percent of men among the children were military veterans.

12. Roediger (2005); Ngai (2004); Foley (1997).

13. Alba and Nee (2003); Portes and Rumbaut (2001).

14. The lower rates of education for Mexican Americans than African Americans may be due to the fact that employability in low-skilled work is poorer for blacks, making staying in school a more attractive option.

15. Pettigrew (1979); Massey and Denton (1993).

16. Interestingly, Spanish fluency is an exception. Multivariate analysis shows a significant positive relationship between Spanish proficiency and education. This relationship becomes significant after we control for the negative relationship between parent's education and Spanish proficiency. In other words, children with less-educated parents are more likely to speak Spanish, but once we control for this, children with more education have greater Spanish proficiency.

17. Other indicators of socioeconomic status that are not shown—including wealth, occupational status, and rates of homeownership—are also clearly related to education.

18. This probably reflects a likely marriage market for Mexican Americans who finished college before 1965.

19. See, for example, Perlmann and Waldinger (1997); Perlmann (2005).

20. Soja (1989).

21. Ibid.

22. Quality of schooling may be another matter.

23. In 1976, 46 percent of Hispanics enrolling in college were women. By 2004, 59 percent of Hispanics enrolling in college were women (National Center for Education Statistics 2005).

24. We found that women were significantly less likely to be involved in gangs than men were.

25. Tafoya (2002) found that children born to Hispanic mothers and non-Hispanic fathers peaked at about 25 percent of all children born to Hispanic mothers in 1990 but had declined to nearly 20 percent in 2000. This seems to reflect the growing size of the first and second generation young adult population compared to later generations as well as the increasing residential isolation of all generations.

26. Jiménez (2004).

27. Telles and Murguía (1990); Murguía and Telles (1996).

28. Gullickson (2005).

29. See Pager (forthcoming) regarding the difficulty in measuring discrimination and for the few examples of direct measurement.

30. Valencia (2002); Conchas (2006); Vigil (1997).
31. Matute-Bianchi (1996); Valenzuela (1999); Bonilla-Silva (2003).
32. Conchas (2006); Gándara (1995); Valenzuela (1999).
33. Oyserman et al. (2003).
34. Zúñiga and Hernández (2005).
35. Massey, Durand, and Malone (2003).
36. Portes and Rumbaut (2001).
37. Waldinger (2007a).
38. Jiménez (2005).
39. Economic News and Analysis on Mexico (2003).
40. Huntington (2004b); Buchanan (2006).
41. Smith and Edmonston (1998).
42. Massey, Durand, and Malone (2003).
43. Feliciano (2005).
44. Perlmann and Waldinger (1997); Feliciano (2005).
45. Horsman (1981); Montejano (1987).
46. Roediger (1999); Jacobsen (1998); Bogardus (1967).
47. Tom Smith (1990).
48. This section was inspired by the comments of Rodolfo de la Garza, who questioned its absence.
49. Alba (1985).
50. Massey and Denton (1987).
51. Perlmann and Waldinger (1997); Portes and Rumbaut (2001); Zhou and Bankston (1998).
52. Portes and Rumbaut (2001).
53. Myers (2007).
54. Many, but not all, of our sample completed their K–12 education before this initiative (Proposition 13) went into effect.
55. Orfield and Yun (1999).
56. Portes and Rumbaut (2001); Duncan, Hotz, and Trejo (2006).
57. Orfield (1993, 2004).
58. Allen, Solórzano, and Carroll (2002); Oakes (2005); Valencia (2002).
59. De la Garza, Falcón, and García (1996).
60. Mary Waters (1999).

REFERENCES

Alba, Richard. 1985. *Italian Americans: Into the Twilight of Ethnicity.* Englewood Cliffs, N.J.: Prentice-Hall.

Alba, Richard, and Victor Nee. 2003. *Remaking the American Mainstream: Assimilation and Contemporary Immigration.* Cambridge, Mass.: Harvard University Press.

Allen, Walter, Daniel Solorzano, and Grace Carroll. 2002. "Keeping Race in Place: Racial Microaggressions and Campus Racial Climate at the University of California, Berkeley." *Chicano Latino Law Review* 23(Spring): 15–112.

Bogardus, Emory. 1967. *A Forty Year Racial Distance Study*. Los Angeles, Calif.: University of Southern California.

Bonilla-Silva, Eduardo. 2003. *Racism without Racists: Color-Blind Racism and the Persistence of Racial Inequality in the United States*. Lanham, Md.: Rowman & Littlefield.

Buchanan, Patrick J. 2006. *State of Emergency: The Third World Invasion and Conquest of America*. New York: Thomas Dunne Books.

Conchas, Gilberto Q. 2006. *The Color of Success: Race and High-Achieving Urban Youth*. New York: Teachers College Press.

De la Garza, Rodolfo, Angelo Falcon, and Chris Garcia. 1996. "Will the Real Americans Please Stand Up: Anglo and Mexican-American Support of Core American Political Values." *American Journal of Political Science* 40(2): 335–51.

Duncan, Brian, Joseph V. Hotz, and Stephen J. Trejo. 2006. "Hispanics in the U.S. Labor Market." In *Hispanics and the Future of America*, edited by Marta Tienda and Faith Mitchell. Washington: The National Academies Press.

Economic News & Analysis on Mexico. 2003. "President Vicente Fox Removes Mexico's U.N. Ambassador Adolfo Aguilar Zinser Over Comments on U.S." November 19,2003. Accessed at http://www.accessmylibrary.com/coms2/summary_0286-32434092_ITM.

Feliciano, Cynthia. 2005. "Educational Selectivity in U.S. Immigration: How Do Immigrants Compare to Those Left Behind?" *Demography* 42(1): 131–52.

Foley, Neil. 1997. *The White Scourge: Mexicans, Blacks and Poor Whites in Texas Cotton Culture*. Berkeley, Calif.: University of California Press.

Frey, William, 1999. *Immigration and Demographic Balkanization: Toward One America or Two? America's Demographic Tapestry*. New Brunswick, N.J.: Rutgers University Press.

Gullickson, Aaron. 2005. "The Significance of Color Declines: A Re-Analysis of Skin Tone Differentials in Post Civil Rights America." *Social Forces* 84(1): 157–80.

Haney Lopez, Ian. 2003. *Racism on Trial: The Chicano Fight for Justice*. Cambridge, Mass.: Belknap Press of Harvard University Press.

Horsman, Reginald. 1981. *Race and Manifest Destiny: The Origins of American Racial Anglo-Saxonism*. Cambridge, Mass.: Harvard University Press.

Huntington, Samuel P. 2004b. *Who Are We?: The Challenges to America's National Identity*. New York: Simon & Schuster.

Jacobsen, Matthew Frye. 1998. *Whiteness of a Different Color. European Immigrants and the Alchemy of Race*. Cambridge, Mass.: Harvard University Press.

Jimenez, Tomas. 2004. "Negotiating Ethnic Boundaries: Multiethnic Mexican Americans and Ethnic Identity in the United States." *Ethnicities* 4(1): 75–97.

Kao, Grace, and Marta Tienda. 1995. "Optimism and Achievement: The Educational Performance of Immigrant Youth." *Social Science Quarterly* 76(1): 1–19.

Massey, Douglas S., and Nancy A. Denton. 1987. "Trends in the Residential Segregation of Blacks, Hispanics and Asians: 1970–1980." *American Sociological Review* 52(6): 802–25.

Massey, Douglas S., Jorge Durand, and Nolan J. Malone. 2003. *Beyond Smoke and Mirrors: Mexican Immigration in an Era of Economic Integration*. New York: Russell Sage Foundation.

Matute-Bianchi, Maria Eugenia. 1986. "Ethnic Identities and Patterns of School Success and Failure among Mexican Descent and Japanese-American Students in a California High School: An Ethnographic Analysis." *American Journal of Education* 95(1): 233–55.

Menchaca, Marta. 1993. "Chicano Indianism: A Historical Account of Racial Repression in the United States." *American Ethnologist* 20(3): 583–603.

Montejano, David. 1987. *Anglos and Mexicans in the Making of Texas: 1836–1986.* Austin, Tex.: University of Texas Press.

Murguia, Edward, and Edward E. Telles. 1996. "Phenotype and Schooling among Mexican Americans." *Sociology of Education* 69 (October): 276–89.

Myers, Dowell. 2007. *Immigrants and Boomers: Forging a New Social Contract for the Future of America.* New York: Russell Sage Foundation.

Ngai, Mae E. 2004. *Impossible Subjects: Illegal Aliens and the Making of Modern America.* Princeton, N.J.: Princeton University Press.

Oakes, Jeannie. 2005. *Keeping Track: How Schools Structure Inequality.* New Haven, Conn.: Yale University Press.

Orfield, Gary. 1993. *The Growth of Segregation in American Schools: Changing Patterns of Separation and Poverty since 1968.* Alexandria, Va.: National School Boards Association.

———. ed. 2004. *Dropouts in America: Confronting the Graduation Rate Crisis.* Cambridge, Mass.: Harvard Educational Press.

Orfield, Gary, and John Yun. 1999. *Resegregation in American Schools.* Cambridge, Mass.: The Civil Rights Project, Harvard University.

Oyserman, Daphna, Markus Kemmelmeier, Stephanie Frybers, Hezi Brosh, and Tamera Hart-Johnson. 2003. "Racial-Ethnic Self Schemas." *Social Psychology Quarterly* 66(4): 333–47.

Perlmann, Joel. 2005. *Italians Then, Mexicans Now: Immigrant Origins and Second Generation Progress, 1890 to 2000.* New York: Russell Sage Foundation.

Perlmann, Joel, and Roger Waldinger. 1997. "Second Generation Decline? Children of Immigrants, Past and Present—A Reconsideration." *International Migration Review* 31(4): 893–922.

Pettigrew, Thomas. 1979. "Racial Change and Social Policy." *Annals of the American Academy of Political and Social Science* 441(1): 114–31.

Portes, Alejandro, and Ruben Rumbaut. 2001. *Legacies: The Story of the Immigrant Second Generation.* Berkeley, Calif.: University of California Press.

Portes, Alejandro, and Min Zhou. 1993. "The New Second Generation: Segmented Assimilation and Its Variants." *Annals of the American Academy of Political and Social Science* 530(1): 74–96.

Rivas-Rodriguez, Maggie, ed. 2005. *Mexican Americans and World War II.* Austin, Tex.: University of Texas Press.

Roediger, David R. 1999. *The Wages of Whiteness: Race and the Making of the American Working Class.* London: Verso.

———. 2005. *Working Toward Whiteness: How America's Immigrants Became White.* New York: Basic Books.

Rumbaut, Ruben G., Douglas S. Massey, and Frank D. Bean. 2006. "Linguistic Life Expectancies: Immigrant Language Retention in Southern California." *Population and Development Review* 32(3): 447–60.

Smith, James P., and Barry Edmonston. 1998. *The Immigration Debate: Studies on the Eco-*

nomic, Demographic and Fiscal Effects of Immigration. Washington: National Academy Press.

Smith, Tom. 1990. *Ethnic Images*. General Social Survey, Technical Report 19. Chicago, Ill.: National Opinion Research Center, University of Chicago.

Soja, Edward W. 1989. *Postmodern Geographies: The Reassertion of Space in Critical Social Theory*. London: Verso.

Tafoya, Sonya. 2002. "Mixed Race and Ethnicity in California." In *The New Race Question: How the Census Counts Multiracial Individuals,* edited by Joel Perlmann and Mary Waters. New York: Russell Sage Foundation.

Telles, Edward, and Edward Murguia. 1990. "Phenotypic Discrimination and Income Differences Among Mexican Americans." *Social Science Quarterly* 71(4): 682–96.

Valencia, Richard R. 2002. "The Plight of Chicano Students: An Overview Schooling Conditions and Outcomes." In *Chicano School Failure and Success: Past, Present, and Future,* edited by Richard R. Valencia. London: Routledge/Falmer.

Valenzuela, Angela. 1999. *Subtractive Schooling: U.S. Mexican Youth and the Politics of Caring*. Albany, N.Y.: State University of New York Press.

Vigil, James. 1997. Personas Mexicanas: *Chicano High Schoolers in a Changing Los Angeles* Fort Worth, Tex.: Harcourt Brace College Publishers.

Waters, Mary C. 1999. *Black Identities: West Indian Immigrant Dreams and American Realities*. New York: Russell Sage Foundation.

Zhou, Min, and Carl Bankston III. 1998. *Growing up American: How Vietnamese Children Adapt to Life in the United States*. New York: Russell Sage Foundation.

Zuniga, Victor, and Ruben Hernandez-Leon, eds. 2006. *New Destinations: Mexican Immigration to the United States*. New York: Russell Sage Foundation.

15

LATINOS IN THE POWER ELITE

Richard L. Zweigenhaft and G. William Domhoff

When Roberto Goizueta left his native Havana, Cuba, in 1949 to begin his freshman year at Yale University, he had no idea that by the 1980s he would be running one of the largest corporations in the United States. Basque and Spanish in racial and cultural heritage and a member of the wealthy upper class in Cuba, he returned home to Havana after he had earned a degree in engineering, and from 1954 to 1960, he worked for the Coca-Cola subsidiary.

But Goizueta and other wealthy young Cubans did not count on the actions of another Cuban-born son of a successful Spanish immigrant, Fidel Castro, who turned his back on his father's large ranch and his own elite education to create the revolutionary army that overthrew Cuban dictator Fulgencio Batista in January 1959. By the early 1960s, Castro was threatening major capitalist enterprises, leading Goizueta and more than 380,000 other Cubans to emigrate to the United States by 1980.[1] In 1960, Goizueta became assistant to the senior vice president of Coca-Cola in the Bahamas, and by 1964, he was assistant to the vice president for research and development at the company's headquarters in Atlanta.

It took only a few years before Goizueta became a vice president for engineering; shortly thereafter, he was a senior vice president, then an executive vice president. He

Authors' Note: Little or nothing has changed for Latinos in the power elite in the decade since we wrote this chapter in 2005. If anything, things have gone slightly backward. So what you are about to read reflects the situation in 2016 as well as in 2005. We explain why in the new postscript written for this anthology.

was named president and chief operating officer in 1980 and became chairman of the board and CEO in 1981. When he died in October 1997, he was one of the most powerful corporate chieftains in the United States, atypical though he may be of most of the 41.3 million people identified as of July 2004 as Hispanic Americans.[2]

Vilma S. Martínez, born to Mexican American parents in 1943 in San Antonio, Texas, had a very different experience. As a young girl, she was bitter about the discrimination she experienced. She recalls that her junior high school counselor recommended that she go to a vocational or technical high school, her high school counselor would not advise her about applying to college, and her father, a construction worker, was skeptical about the usefulness of college for a woman, saying that she "would not complete school, that she would get married and have children." But she insisted on an academic high school, graduated from the University of Texas in two and a half years, and did not have the first of her two children until 1976, nine years after she had earned a law degree from Columbia University.[3]

Martínez practiced civil rights law as a staff attorney for the NAACP Legal Defense Fund from 1967 to 1970 and for the New York State Division of Human Rights after that. After two years as a labor lawyer with the Wall Street firm of Cahill, Gordon & Reindel, she became one of the prime movers in establishing the Mexican American Legal Defense and Education Fund (MALDEF). In 1973, she became MALDEF's general counsel and president. Three years later, the liberal Democratic governor of California, Jerry Brown, surprised everyone by appointing Martínez, only thirty-two years old, regent of the University of California, where she rubbed elbows with a cross-section of the California corporate rich and lobbied for greater diversity in the faculty and student body. In May 1982, she joined the Los Angeles law firm of Munger, Tolles & Olson, where her clients have included Pacific Telephone, Blue Cross, and Allstate Insurance.[4] As of 2005, she sat on the boards of three *Fortune* 500 corporations: Anheuser-Busch (#139 in 2005), Burlington Northern Santa Fe (#200), and Fluor (#241).

But not all Latinas from the Southwest are liberal enough to work for the NAACP or MALDEF. Those from New Mexico, whose ancestors were sometimes landholders before the American conquest of the territory, are often quite conservative. Patricia Díaz, born in Santa Rita, New Mexico, in 1946, was the daughter of an army sergeant who was transferred frequently. She spent her teenage years in Japan, graduated from a high school in Santiago, Chile, and received her BA in 1970 from UCLA and a law degree in 1973 from Loyola University in Los Angeles. After three years with a large corporate firm in Los Angeles, she became a management attorney specializing in labor disputes, first with Pacific Lighting and then with ABC in Hollywood. She was working for ABC in 1983 when Ronald Reagan unexpectedly named her as a "Democratic" appointee to the National Labor Relations Board, the second female and first Latina member in its forty-seven-year history. There she joined the majority in a wide range of decisions that were extremely damaging to labor organizing.[5] In 1986, she became a member of the Federal Communications Commission (FCC). After an equally conservative three-year tenure as an FCC commissioner, she returned to the private sector as a corporate lawyer for U.S. Sprint. In 1992, George H. W. Bush tried to improve his appeal to Mexican Americans in the Southwest by appointing Díaz as assistant secretary of state for human rights and humanitarian affairs. When Bush lost his bid for reelection, Díaz joined the Washington, D.C., office of the venerable Wall Street law firm of Sullivan & Cromwell and became a director of Telemundo, the second-largest Hispanic radio and television corporation in the United States. Married to Michael Dennis, a lawyer, and going by the name of Patricia Díaz Dennis, she left Sullivan & Cromwell to become senior vice president and general counsel for SBC Pacific Bell/SBC Nevada Bell. Her being a conservative Democrat has served Díaz Dennis—and the Republicans—extremely well.

Goizueta, Martínez, and Díaz Dennis are prime examples of why social scientists stress that it is very risky to generalize about the Hispanic or Latino experience in the United States. The 1.4 million Cuban Americans, many of whom were quite well off in Cuba, have one story, while the 3 million immigrants from Puerto Rico usually have another. (Actually, a few of the Puerto Rican immigrants are also wealthy, but most arrived poor.) Similarly, people of Mexican descent in New Mexico, many of whom have ancestors who have lived in the area for more than one hundred years and who sometimes call themselves "Spanish Americans," are different from the Mexican American immigrants to Texas and California. Moreover, the Mexican Americans of the Southwest range from middle-class entrepreneurs to migrant farm workers, and they vary greatly in color and appearance as well because of a history of inter-marriage with the indigenous Indian populations of Mexico. The Latino population in the United States also includes some immigrants from Spain and various Latin American countries. On a 1995 list of the seventy-five richest Hispanics, which was dominated by twenty-seven Cuban Americans and twenty-five Mexican Americans, there were also eight people identified as Spanish and one person each from Chile, Colombia, Costa Rica, the Dominican Republic, Ecuador, Uruguay, and Venezuela. Five Puerto Rican immigrants and three residents of Puerto Rico rounded out the list. At the top was Roberto Goizueta of Coca-Cola, whose net worth was estimated at $574 million.[6]

There is even disagreement among scholars and political activists about what general name, if any, should be used to characterize a group whose main common heritage is the Spanish conquest and the Spanish language. The term *Hispanic* is favored by some, especially on the East Coast; others prefer *Latino*, especially on the West Coast. In a 1990 survey, however, it was found that neither term was liked by most Americans of Cuban, Mexican, or Puerto Rican extraction. Most preferred labels that reflected their specific backgrounds. Moreover, the three groups have "little interaction with each other, most do not recognize that they have much in common culturally, and they do not profess any strong affection for each other." The authors of the survey wrote that "it is particularly noteworthy that more respondents prefer to be called 'American' than 'Latino,' the label that many members of the Latino intelligentsia, including ourselves, have insisted is both the 'correct' and the preferred label."[7]

Given these disagreements, we will continue to use the terms *Latino/Latina, Hispanic American,* and *Hispanic* interchangeably when a general term is needed. When possible, we will use specific ethnic identifications.

Underlying this diversity of national origins and the tendency to identify primarily with one's own subgroup, there are nonetheless two factors that powerfully shape the degree of acceptance and assimilation of all Latino immigrants. The first is their religion. The 70 percent who are Catholics can blend in easily with the largest single church in the United States (67.3 million strong, making up 23 percent of the U.S. population). Their Catholic heritage is an important piece of cultural capital because it provides entrée into new social circles as they attain education or a higher-status occupation. True, local parishes are sometimes differentiated by status and income levels, but new social connections can be made through new parishes if a person is climbing the social ladder.[8]

The second major factor influencing the fate of Hispanic Americans is skin color and facial features. As two sociological studies note, there is great variation in the appearance of Latinos, ranging from a pure "European" look to a Native American look.[9] In most Latin American countries, the lighter-skinned and more European-looking people tend to be in the higher social classes, and the darker-skinned and more Indian-looking people in the lower classes.[10]

Several journalists and social critics have concluded that darker-skinned Hispanics are also at a disadvantage in the United States. To test this claim, Edward Telles and Edward Murguia used information from a nationwide survey of Hispanics in 1979 to see whether those rated as light skinned by the interviewer had higher average earnings than those who were darker. Since the lightest-skinned group was too small for sound statistical comparisons, it was merged with a group judged to be of medium skin color, and a comparison was then made with the darkest group. The researchers found that there was a strong tendency for the lighter group to earn more than the darker one, and they argue that this cannot be explained in terms of educational differences because the two groups had very similar educational backgrounds.[11] A more recent study, based on the 2000 Census, showed that Latinos who identified themselves as white had higher levels of education and income than those who selected the "some other race" category.[12] As we shall show, our own study of the skin color of Hispanics in the corporate elite leads to the same conclusion: it is advantageous to be light skinned.

LATINOS IN THE CORPORATE ELITE

From 1990 through 2002 in its January issue, *Hispanic Business* published an annual list of "the boardroom elite." The list included Hispanics who served on "the boards of *Fortune* 1000 corporations, divisions, and subsidiaries." The inclusion of "divisions and subsidiaries" made these lists less exclusive than the ones we have used previously. In 2004, after skipping 2003, *Hispanic Business* published a list that only included directors on *Fortune* 500 companies.[13] We have gone back to the 1998 and 2001 lists and eliminated those seats on divisions and subsidiaries of *Fortune* 500 boards and those seats on boards that were ranked between #501 and #1000. The results reveal that the number of Hispanic directors on *Fortune* 500 boards increased from forty-seven in 1998 (these forty-seven held sixty-two seats), to fifty in 2001 (they held fifty-eight seats), and to sixty-nine in 2005 (they held ninety-five seats). Thus, although Hispanics now make up about 13.5 percent of the U.S. population, even with the gains made during this six-year period, only 1.6 percent of the approximately fifty-nine hundred *Fortune* 500 directors are Hispanic. Almost all are outside directors (only five were inside directors in 2001, and only three were in 2005).[14]

Although we have considerable confidence in these findings, it is important to stress that they are not perfect. Deciding who is and who is not Hispanic is not an exact science. As with Jews, names can be misleading. When a reader of *Hispanic Business* wrote to complain that John Castro, the CEO of Merrill Corporation, had been omitted from a list of corporate executives published in the January 1995 issue (along with the list of the "boardroom elite"), the editors replied that "company officials tell us he is not Hispanic."[15] Similarly, Arthur Martinez, the seemingly Latino CEO of Sears, Roebuck from 1992 to 2000, is mostly Irish. As a company spokesperson explained to us when we inquired, "He is mostly of Irish descent. A family member married someone from Spain generations ago, and that is where the name comes from."[16] There are also Hispanics whose names do not reveal that they are Hispanic: in 1994, H. B. Fuller Company selected Walter Kissling, born and raised in Costa Rica, as its CEO.[17]

We analyzed the social, educational, and career backgrounds of the 103 Latinos and Latinas who sat on *Fortune* 500 boards in 1998, 2001, 2004, and 2005. The gender difference was large: 81 percent were men, and 19 percent were women. Still, the 19 percent is considerably higher than the comparable percentage for non-Hispanic white women on boards (less than 14 percent in 2003), but lower than the figure for African American women (25 percent). As is the case for African Americans, the Hispanic women were more likely to sit on multiple boards than are the men (on average, the women held 1.53 seats, and the men 1.35).[18]

Although the available biographical information is not complete in all cases, a majority of the men and women on our list seem to have been raised in at least middle-class circumstances. Many others had an elite education at the undergraduate or graduate levels that gave them the social connections and educational credentials to move quickly into responsible positions in the corporate community. Only a few people on the list of directors could be considered genuine bootstrappers, making their way to the top of corporations without the benefit of family backing or an elite education.

As might be expected from our account of Roberto Goizueta's appointment as CEO at Coca-Cola and the large number of Cuban Americans among the wealthiest Hispanics, many of the successful entrepreneurs and executives on our list come from Cuban American backgrounds. Most had the advantage of being born to parents who were wealthy, well educated, or both. This was true, for example, for Roberto Mendoza, who, like Roberto Goizueta, was born in Cuba and educated at Yale and who became the head of mergers and acquisitions at Morgan Guaranty Trust in 1987, earning him a seat on the board.

And it was also true for Alfonso Fanjul. He and his brother José manage a fifth-generation, privately held family business, Flo-Sun, with cane fields in Florida and Puerto Rico, that is a leading sugar producer in the United States and the Dominican Republic. Forced to relocate to the United States when Castro came to power, the Fanjuls have by far the worst labor record of any sugar-producing company in the country, frequently violating minimum wage and labor laws with their predominantly Latino migrant labor force. In brushing off criticism of the Fanjuls, a New York friend of theirs said, "They are completely accepted by society [in Palm Beach]—they hang out with all the best people."[19] As of 2004, the family was estimated to be worth more than $500 million, with an estimated $65 million of its income each year due to government subsidies (and "untold hundreds of millions" from price supports).[20]

In 1996, the New York Times reported that, despite his permanent residency in the United States, Alfonso Fanjul (known as "Alfy") had Spanish citizenship. Some critics suggested that he preferred having Spanish citizenship to avoid U.S. estate taxes, but a flap over his large campaign finance donations—Alfy is a major donor to the Democratic Party—led him to claim that he was applying for American citizenship. His brother José (known as "Pepe") contributes to the Republicans (according to the Center for Responsive Politics, the Fanjuls gave $2.6 million to politicians and political committees between 1979 and 2004). Though they describe themselves as having political differences, political analysts attribute their donations to both parties simply as a calculated strategy to make sure that, no matter who is elected, they will have political clout.[21]

With the death of Roberto Goizueta, the most prominent Cuban American in corporate America is now Armando Codina. He, too, was born to privilege in Cuba—his father was the president of the Senate prior to the revolution—but Codina's route to the corporate elite was more difficult than Goizueta's. Codina's parents, who had divorced when he was young, were able to arrange for him to leave the island in the early 1960s as part of a program run by the Catholic Church called "Operation Peter Pan" (fourteen thousand youngsters participated in this program). He was sent to an orphanage in New Jersey, where he reports that he had a difficult time mixing with children from troubled backgrounds (when he arrived, he recalls, with "fine English flannel suits" that had been made specially for him by a tailor his mother had taken him to in Cuba, many of the other kids gave him a very hard time).[22]

He spent a few years in a foster home in New Jersey and then began college at Jacksonville University in Florida. His mother, who spoke no English and had never worked, was able to leave Cuba, and she came to live with him in Florida. In order to support the two of them, he dropped out of school, worked two jobs, and, with $18,000 that he borrowed from the Small Business Administration, he started a small business, a computer company that handled billing and processed forms for doctors. The business did well; he sold it in 1978 for $4 million and started the Codina Group, a real estate development company that was to be his ticket to the big time.[23]

Active in Republican politics, he became the chairman of the 1980 Bush campaign in Florida. After Bush lost that campaign and became Reagan's vice president, he asked Codina to hire his son, Jeb, as president of his company, which Codina did. Subsequently, as Jeb Bush ran for various offices in Florida—successfully for secretary of commerce and unsuccessfully for governor—he worked intermittently for the firm. While he worked for Codina, however, he made a lot of money. As William Finnegan wrote in the *New Yorker*, "people in Miami say, 'Codina made Jeb a rich man.'"[24] When Jeb Bush won the governorship in 1998, Codina paid him a bonus of $630,000.[25]

Codina has continued to support the Bush family—a fund-raiser at his house for George W. Bush as he geared up for the 2004 campaign netted $2 million—and he has served on numerous *Fortune*-level boards, including Winn-Dixie, BellSouth Corp, American Airlines, Florida Power and Light, and, as of 2002, General Motors (#3 on the 2005 *Fortune* list).[26]

Several directors are Spanish Americans from New Mexico. These include Katherine Ortega, whose paternal grandparents settled in New Mexico in the late 1880s. Her father owned a café, then a furniture business. Because he was a lifelong Republican, Ortega likes to say she was "born a Republican."[27] After graduating from Eastern New Mexico State University in 1957 with a degree in business, she started an accounting firm with her sister, which the family turned into the Otero Savings and Loan Association in 1974.

Ortega moved to California in the late 1960s, working first as a tax supervisor for the accounting firm of Peat, Marwick, Mitchell & Company and then as a vice president for Pan American Bank, where her bilingualism was valuable in working with the local Latino community. In 1975, she gained visibility as the first woman president of a California bank, the Latino-owned Santa Ana State Bank. Four years later, she returned to New Mexico as a consultant to her family's saving and loan association, and in 1982, Reagan named her to his Advisory Committee on Small and Minority Business Ownership.[28] From 1983 to 1989, she served in the Reagan administration in the largely ceremonial position of treasurer of the United States. That office gave her the public stature to give one of the keynote speeches at the 1984 Republican presidential convention. In 1989, she left her government position and marketed herself as a corporate director who could provide both Hispanic and female perspectives. By 1995, she sat on no fewer than six boards: Diamond Shamrock, ITT Raynier, Kroger Company, Long Island Lighting, Paul Revere Insurance Group, and Ralston Purina (by 2005, she was only on one *Fortune* 500 board: Kroger).

There are some rags-to-riches stories among the Latino directors. Most of them concern Mexican Americans. Edward Zapanta, for example, was told by his high school counselor that he should become a mechanic like his father, but he went on to earn a BA from UCLA and an MD from USC. He founded a medical clinic in a predominantly

Mexican American neighborhood near where he grew up, and he has been on the boards of Southern California Edison and the Times Mirror Company. William S. Davila provides another example. Neither he nor his parents graduated from college. Davila started as a stock boy at Von's Markets in 1948 and ended up CEO of the company in 1987 at the age of fifty-six. He retired from the position in 1992 but continued to serve as a director at various companies. As of 2004, he sat on the boards of three *Fortune* 500 companies (Home Depot, Hormel Foods, and Pacific Gas and Electric); as of 2005, he was only on the board of Home Depot.

Luís Nogales provides another example of a Mexican American rags-to-riches story. Nogales was born in 1943 in the central valley of California where his parents were farm workers, albeit farm workers who bought books on literature and history, in both English and Spanish, and "traveled with their own small library."[29] Nogales attended San Diego State University on a scholarship and graduated from Stanford Law School in 1969. After working for three years as Stanford's liaison to Mexican American students, he went to Washington, D.C., as a White House fellow and then became assistant to the secretary of the interior. He returned to the West Coast in 1973 to work for Golden West Broadcasting, owner of the California Angels baseball team, as well as radio and television stations. In 1983, he became executive vice president and in 1985 president of United Press International (UPI). When UPI was sold in 1986, he went to work in Spanish-language television for Univision. After negotiating the sale of Univision to Hallmark in 1988, he formed his own investment and consulting company, Nogales Partners. As of 2005, he was on the boards of two *Fortune* 500 companies: KB Home, Inc., and Edison International.

But not all of the Mexican Americans in the sample started at the bottom. Shortly after his graduation from Notre Dame in 1947, Ignacio E. Lozano Jr. became the assistant publisher of *La Opinión*, the highly successful newspaper his father founded in 1926. Now retired, he has served as a director of Bank of America, Walt Disney Company, Pacific Mutual Life, and Pacific Enterprises. His son, José, became the publisher of the paper, and his daughter, Monica, became first the managing editor of the paper (in 1987) and then the president and chief operating officer. In late 2003, the Los Angeles–based *La Opinión* merged with the New York–based *El Diario/La Prensa*, bringing the country's two largest Spanish-language newspapers under one umbrella company called ImpreMedia. At the time of the merger, José became vice chairman and executive vice president of ImpreMedia, and Monica became senior vice president. At that time, she also became the publisher and CEO of *La Opinión*. She has served on the boards of Disney, First Interstate Bank of California, Fannie Mae, and Tenet Healthcare.

Similarly, Enrique Hernández Jr. and Roland Hernández are Mexican Americans who had the advantage of being raised in a well-to-do family. Enrique Hernández Sr., a former police officer, created Inter-Con Security Systems, a company with offices in twenty-five countries that employs more than twenty-five thousand workers. As of 2005, Enrique Jr., a graduate of Harvard, sat on the boards of four *Fortune* 500 companies:

McDonald's, Nordstrom, Tribune Company (of Chicago), and Wells Fargo. Roland, also a Harvard alumnus, was a director at Wal-Mart and MGM Mirage in 2004.

LATINO CEOS AND THE CORPORATE PIPELINE

As of July 2005, there have been six Latino CEOs of *Fortune* 500 companies, all of them men.[30] The first, Roberto Goizueta, the Cuban-born immigrant who served as president and CEO of Coca-Cola from 1981 to 1997, we have already discussed earlier in this chapter. Carlos Gutierrez, also born in Cuba to a wealthy family, became CEO of Kellogg Corporation in April 1999. As we will see later in this chapter, early in 2005, Gutierrez left his position at Kellogg to become the secretary of commerce after George W. Bush was re-elected in 2004.[31]

Two of the Latino CEOs are from South American countries. Claudio Osorio, CEO of CHS Electronics, was born in Venezuela, where he studied law and business. Alain Belda, the son of a Spanish Republican father who fled Spain in the late 1930s and a Portuguese mother, has been the CEO of Alcoa since 2001, when he succeeded Paul O'Neill (who left to become George W. Bush's secretary of the treasury). Belda was born in French Morocco but moved to Brazil when he was three. The family then moved to Canada when he was thirteen and back to Brazil when he was seventeen (he is a Brazilian citizen).[32]

Two are Mexican Americans, and both seem to have authentic rags-to-riches stories. Carlos Cantu, the CEO of Servicemaster from 1993 until he retired in 1999, is the son of Mexican immigrants. He worked his way through Texas A&M, in part as a custodian (in 1999 he gave a million dollars to his alma mater for a study of the root causes of Hispanic high-school dropouts). Some considered Solomon Trujillo, who became the CEO of U.S. West in 1998, to be the most powerful Hispanic in America after the company merged with Qwest, but by February 2000, after citing "differences with the new owners," he announced that he was leaving the company. In June 2005, Trujillo became the CEO of Telstra, the dominant telecommunications provider in Australia. Trujillo is the son of a railway laborer (he earned both an undergraduate and business degree from the University of Wyoming).[33]

If we expand our list of Latino CEOs to include those who have been CEOs of companies that ranked between #501 and #1000 on the annual *Fortune* list, we add another six men. In 1991, Richard Carrion became the CEO of Popular, Inc., the holding company for Puerto Rico's largest bank chain, Banco Popular. Carrion is from one of the richest families in Puerto Rico (both his father and his grandfather served as presidents of the same bank). Benjamin Montoya, a Mexican American from Indio, California, who attended the Naval Academy and served in the navy for thirty-one years, rising to the rank of admiral, upon leaving the military became CEO of the Public Service Company of New Mexico in 1993 and served in that capacity until 2000. During his military career, he earned bachelor's degrees from the Naval Academy and Rensselaer Polytechnic Institute, a master's degree from Georgia Tech, and a law degree from Georgetown. Walter Kissling, CEO of H. B. Fuller from 1994 to 1998, grew up in Costa Rica, the son of German immigrants. Although he "attended" a class at the Harvard Business School at one point and spoke four languages, he did not have a college degree (he died in 2002). J. Philip Samper, whose father was Colombian and whose mother was Anglo and who grew up in Salt Lake City, became the CEO of Cray Research in 1995. He is a graduate of the University of California, Berkeley, and of MIT. Tony White, whose mother was from a wealthy Cuban family and whose father was from a working-class family in western North Carolina, has been the CEO of a company now called Applera (it was formerly called Perkin-Elmer) since 1995. Hector Ortino, who became CEO of Ferro in 1999, is from Venezuela.[34]

These twelve CEOs reflect familiar patterns. All are men. They are mostly well educated, though only two went to elite schools in the United States (Goizueta to Yale and Samper to Berkeley and MIT). The most noteworthy pattern that emerges with this group is their international makeup and the extent to which these international men of business grew up in economically and socially privileged circumstances in Venezuela, Brazil, Puerto Rico, and, of course, Cuba. Because of their worldly backgrounds and their fluency in languages other than English, they seem to be ideal corporate leaders in the current global economy. Consider, for example, these comments from Alain Belda, Alcoa's CEO: "Our board today is 50% American-born and 50% foreign-born. Our top management is 40% foreign-born and over 50% international, if we consider Americans that have lived long periods abroad. We have shared business systems and a common infrastructure applied across a globally connected workforce."[35]

A few, especially the Mexican Americans, grew up poor, but most, especially the Cubans, are from wealthy families (though the Cubans, of course, left after the revolution and often, though not always, left with very little money).[36]

Below the CEO level, the number of Latino executives remains small. Recent studies by the Hispanic Association on Corporate Responsibility (HACR), a coalition of eleven Hispanic community-based organizations, show that "the pipeline is thin." As the CEO of HACR put it in describing the findings of a study of *Fortune* 1000–level companies in 2003, "We also see the pipeline as a concern. If the pipeline extends beyond the CEO ranks to the ranks of Executive Officers—the future growth remains constrained knowing that only 1 percent of total Executive Officers are Hispanic." A year later, the organization found that Hispanics held only 1.8 percent of the board seats of *Fortune* 1000 companies and constituted "an even smaller percentage of executive officers (1.1 percent)."[37]

To develop a more general and long-term picture of Latino involvement in the corporate community, we drew on the Distinctive Hispanic Names technique developed by sociologist Abraham Lavender.[38] We used fifteen distinctive Hispanic names to estimate the number of Latinos listed in *Standard & Poor's Register of Executives and Direc-*

tors, the most comprehensive and readily accessible list of top managers and directors at more than fifty thousand public companies. We first determined that these fifteen names (Alvarez, Díaz, Fernández, Flores, García, González, Hernández, López, Martínez, Pérez, Ramírez, Rivera, Rodríguez, Sánchez, and Torres) accounted for 23 percent of the names appearing on lists of corporate directors and executives in *Hispanic Business* for 1993, 1994, and 1995, which gave us a factor of 4.35 (4.35 x 23 percent equals 100 percent) for estimating the total number of Latinos listed in *Poor's* at the midpoint in each decade since the 1960s.

According to this analysis, the total number of Latinos listed in *Poor's* rose from 78 in 1965, to 131 in 1975, to 235 in 1985, to 374 in 1995, and to 726 in 2004. Although these raw estimates provide a generally accurate picture of the rising rate of Hispanic participation in the business community from 1965 to 2004, one that indicates that there are almost ten times as many Latinos in *Poor's* as there were forty years ago, they in fact slightly underestimate the overall increase in the rate of participation because there were approximately 4,800 fewer names in *Poor's* in 2004 (70,823) than there were in 1965 (75,639). This notable increase reflects not only that there has been greater Latino involvement in non-Hispanic companies but that there are more Latino-owned businesses. Still, our estimates indicate that Latinos represented only 1.2 percent of executives and directors at publicly owned companies large enough to be listed in *Poor's* in 2004.

It is clear that Latinos have come a long way in forty years: some are in the corporate elite, and the number is increasing; some are or have been CEOs of non-Hispanic *Fortune*-level companies; and there are more and more Hispanics moving through the pipeline. Given the many Hispanics in America, though, a percentage of the population that is increasing substantially, they remain very much underrepresented in the higher levels of the corporate world.

SKIN COLOR AMONG HISPANICS

Taking our cue from the findings on skin color and income presented earlier in this chapter, we examined the skin color of 188 magazine-quality photographs of people who were selected as "top influentials" by *Hispanic Business* for 1993 and 1994. First, we wanted to see whether those identified as influential Hispanics in general were light skinned, and second, we wanted to see whether those who were *Fortune*-level directors were even lighter skinned than the other "influentials." We used the same nine color cards and the same two raters that we had previously used to assess photographs of African Americans.[39]

We used the average score based on the two raters' responses to each photograph. As was true for the African American sample, the two had a high level of agreement (89 percent of their ratings were within one point of one another on the nine-point color scale). As expected, the influentials as a group were light skinned. The overall mean score was 3.5 (on a 10-point scale), and less than 5 percent had ratings higher than 5; in contrast, the overall mean score for the African Americans was 5.9. In order to compare the scores of these Hispanic influentials with a group of whites, the photographs that accompanied the biographical sketches of those on the 1994 and 1995 *Forbes* "400 Richest Americans" lists were rated. Not every sketch included a photograph, and we omitted the one African American on the list for whom there was a photograph (Oprah Winfrey), but we were still left with 170 photographs to rate (96 in 1994, and 74 in 1995). The range of scores was from 1 to 6, and the mean score was 2.9. Thus, the skin-color ratings of Hispanic influentials were much closer to those of non-Hispanic rich whites than to those of prominent African Americans.

We also looked to see whether there were differences based on gender and whether those Hispanic influentials who sat on *Fortune*-level boards were rated as lighter skinned than the other influentials. Both variables were significant: the Latinas were rated as lighter (with a mean score of 2.82) than the Latinos (3.58), and the nine men and three women who sat on *Fortune*-level boards were rated as lighter (2.92) than the other Hispanic influentials (3.42).[40]

We were struck not only by the light skin color of the Hispanic corporate directors but by how overwhelmingly "Anglo" they appeared. We were sure we would have a hard time identifying some of them as Hispanics if we did not have other clues, like Hispanic-sounding names or inclusion of their photos in a magazine called *Hispanic Business*. In order to test this more systematically, we constructed a booklet with twenty-eight photographs of CEOs, chairpersons, or directors of large corporations, all of which we cut out of issues of *Fortune, Ebony*, or *Hispanic Business*. We collected seventeen photos of white men and women, three of black men, three of black women, three of Hispanic men, and two of Hispanic women. One of the Latinos was Cuban, and the other two were Mexican American; both Latinas were from New Mexico. We showed these to ten current or recent students at Guilford College in Greensboro, North Carolina, and asked them to tell us which of the twenty-eight people were white, which were black, and which were Hispanic. As expected, the accuracy rate was quite high for whites (87 percent); the relatively few errors were made because some students thought certain of the darker-skinned men or women were Hispanic. The accuracy rate was also quite high for black men (90 percent) and fairly high for black women (60 percent); the blacks who were misidentified were thought to be Hispanic, especially one of the three black women. In sharp contrast, and confirming our own less systematic observations, the accuracy rate for identifying Hispanics was only 40 percent for the men and 30 percent for the women; in every case but one, when errors were made, the Hispanics were thought to be white. (In the one exception, a Hispanic male was perceived by one of the raters as black.) We replicated this little study on the campus of the University of California, Santa Cruz (UCSC), and found that the students were a bit more accurate in identifying Hispanics but still thought they were white about half the time.[41]

It was not until 1988 that there was a Hispanic member of the cabinet, and he was an unexpected and unlikely one at that. On the eve of the Republican convention that year, as his eight years as president were about to end, Ronald Reagan's sudden announcement of Lauro Cavazos, a Democrat and college president, as the new secretary of education may have seemed a bit unusual to the casual eye. But his friend George Bush, who was then vice president, was struggling in his campaign for president at the time, especially in Texas. Because the Democratic nominee for vice president, Lloyd Bentsen, was a popular senator from Texas, the Republicans feared that Bush would lose the state and its many electoral votes. Since Bush had already proclaimed that he would become "the education president" and that he would appoint a Latino to his cabinet, Reagan decided to help matters along with a person who just happened to be a registered Democrat from Texas. In the words of Alicia Sandoval, a spokeswoman for the National Education Association, the appointment of Cavazos was "just a ploy to help get Bush elected and carry Texas . . . a classic case of tokenism."[42] Bush did carry Texas on his way to victory, and he reappointed Cavazos, who served until December of 1990, when he was forced to resign because Bush's advisers considered him ineffectual.[43]

Cavazos grew up on an eight-hundred-thousand-acre ranch, where his father worked for forty-three years as a foreman in the cattle division. He was educated in a one-room schoolhouse for the children of the ranch's Mexican laborers until, when he was eight years old, his father persuaded reluctant officials in a nearby town to let his children attend what had been up to that time an all-Anglo school. After graduating from high school in 1945, Cavazos served for a year in the army, then began what was to become a lengthy and conventional climb through the ranks of academe. First, he received a BA and an MA in zoology from Texas Technological College (now Texas Tech University) and a PhD from Iowa State. After teaching at the Medical College of Virginia for ten years, he left to become professor and chairman of the anatomy department at the Tufts University School of Medicine. He rose through the administrative ranks over the next sixteen years, becoming the dean in 1975. He left in 1980 to return to Texas Tech as president, the position he held when Ronald Reagan came calling.

Not content with one Latino cabinet member, Bush appointed Republican congressman Manuel Lujan of New Mexico as his secretary of the interior. Born in 1928, Lujan first won election in 1968. He is another example of a conservative Spanish American from New Mexico. In spite of twenty years as a member of the House Committee on Interior and Insular Affairs, where he usually sided with developers in their battles with environmentalists, Lujan showed little understanding of any important land, water, or environmental issues when he assumed his cabinet post. *Time* declared that his record was "dismal" and that he was "clueless on environmental issues and often embarrassed himself making policy statements on matters of which he was ignorant." The conservative British magazine the *Economist* said he had a "blank interior." An article in the

Audubon spoke of his "incompetence," and the *New Republic* called him "the dregs of the Bush cabinet."[44]

Lujan was raised near Santa Fe in privileged circumstances. His father ran a successful insurance agency and served three terms as mayor of Santa Fe, although he did fail in his bids for Congress and the governorship. Lujan joined his father's business in 1948 after graduating from the College of Santa Fe and worked there for twenty years, eventually moving the business to Albuquerque. He won a seat in Congress in the 1968 elections by making an ethnic appeal to the traditionally Democratic Mexican American voters in his district. By 1995, he was a *Fortune* 1000 director for the Public Service Company of New Mexico, a gas and electric utility.[45]

In January 1993, two Latino men, Henry Cisneros and Federico Peña, became members of Bill Clinton's cabinet. There are some striking similarities between the two. Both were born in Texas in the spring of 1947 into stable middle-class families (Cisneros's father was a civilian administrator for the army, and Peña's father was a broker for a cotton manufacturer). Both attended Catholic schools, received BAs from universities in Texas, went on to earn postgraduate degrees (a doctorate for Cisneros, a law degree for Peña), became the first Latino mayors of the cities in which they lived in the early 1980s (Cisneros of San Antonio in 1981, Peña of Denver in 1983), were reelected throughout the 1980s, and, by the early 1990s, were partners in private investment companies (Cisneros in Asset Management, Peña in Investment Advisors, Inc.). By spring 1995, both were out of the investment business and were being investigated by the Justice Department, Cisneros for allegations that he misled federal investigators during his prenomination interviews about payments he made to a former mistress and Peña in connection with a contract awarded in 1993 to an investment firm he had just left.[46]

In 1996, Janet Reno appointed an independent counsel to look into the accusations against Cisneros. After the election, he resigned from the cabinet and became president of Univision, the largest Spanish television broadcaster in the United States. Although he initially faced eighteen felony counts for having lied to the FBI about the payments he made to his former mistress, in September 1999 the case was settled when he pleaded guilty to one misdemeanor count of lying to the FBI about the payments; he was fined $10,000 (Clinton pardoned him as he was leaving office). In August 2000, he left Univision to run a newly formed housing company, American-City Vista, that would build affordable housing in downtown urban areas.[47] He is one of the directors included on the *Hispanic Business* "Boardroom Elite" list: in 2005, he sat on the board of Countrywide Financial (#150 on the 2005 *Fortune*-500 list), one of the largest mortgage lenders in the United States.

Peña continued as secretary of transportation throughout Clinton's first term and became the secretary of energy at the beginning of Clinton's second term. He resigned from that position after eighteen months, joining Vestar Capital Partners, a New York– and Denver-based investment firm. He became a managing director with Vestar in 2000 and, as of June 2005, was still working with them. He, too, is among the "Boardroom Elite"; as of June 2005, he was on the board of Principal Financial Group (#253 on the *Fortune* list in 2005).

In 1998, after Peña resigned as secretary of energy, Clinton replaced him with another Mexican American. William Blaine Richardson, known as Bill, was quite an atypical Mexican American. Richardson's father, an Anglo, was a well-to-do banker, and his mother was a Mexican citizen. Richardson, born in Pasadena, California, grew up in Mexico City, where his father was an executive for Citibank, the only foreign-based bank in the city at the time. He went to Middlesex, an exclusive New England prep school, then to Tufts for a BA in 1970 and an MA in international relations in 1971. After graduation, he spent three years in the State Department as a liaison with Congress, followed by three more years as a staff member for the Senate Foreign Relations Committee. Obviously looking for a place to settle where he could win a seat in Congress, Richardson moved to Santa Fe in 1979 to become executive director of the Democratic State Committee. In 1980, despite charges that he was a classic carpetbagger, he almost unseated the Republican incumbent, Manuel Lujan, outspending the affluent Lujan by more than $200,000. In 1982, he won a seat in a newly created district, carefully crafted by his Democratic friends in Congress to give him a strong Latino base, and in 1985, he was elected to a term as chair of the Congressional Hispanic Caucus. In 1997, Clinton appointed Richardson chief delegate to the United Nations, replacing Madeleine Albright. In 2002, Richardson became governor of New Mexico, winning by the largest margin of any candidate for that office since 1964. Many thought John Kerry would choose him as his vice presidential running mate in 2004.[48]

As of July 2005, George W. Bush had appointed three Latinos to his cabinets: Melquiades ("Mel") Martinez as secretary of housing and urban development, Carlos M. Gutierrez as secretary of commerce, and Alberto Gonzales as attorney general. Martinez, who was born in Cuba a few years before the revolution, is described on the HUD website as "a leader in implementing President Bush's faith-based initiatives." In December 2003, at the urging of White House strategists, Martinez resigned from his cabinet position so that he could run for the open Senate seat in Florida (created when Bob Graham sought the Democratic nomination). Martinez ran a senatorial campaign that was so negative about his Republican primary challenger that Jeb Bush asked him to take one of his television ads off the air, and the *St. Petersburg Times* rescinded its previous endorsement, accusing him of "hateful and dishonest attacks."[49] Still, he won the primary and then won a close race against Betty Castor, the Democratic nominee.

Shortly after the 2004 election, when Bush's secretary of commerce, Donald Evans, announced his resignation, the president named Carlos M. Gutierrez, one of the Latino CEOs discussed earlier in this chapter, as his replacement. As we have noted, Gutierrez was from a wealthy family in Cuba: his father was an exporter of pineapples, and his family was part of what he refers to as "Cuba's high society." When Bush named him, he had been president and CEO at Kellogg since 1999.[50] Ileana Ros-Lehtinen, a Republican member of Congress from Florida, was quick to claim that Gutierrez's appointment "says a great deal about the president's commitment to the Hispanic community and to the Cuban exile community in particular."[51]

Bush's third Latino cabinet appointment, Alberto Gonzales as attorney general (to replace John Ashcroft), was his most controversial. Gonzales is a genuine rags-to-riches story. The son of a migrant worker, he received his undergraduate degree from Rice and a law degree from Harvard. He became a partner at what the *New York Times* calls "one of the premier law firms in Texas" before he became general counsel to Bush when he was governor of Texas, and he was counsel to him when he became president in 2001. The controversy that surrounded his nomination was based especially on some of the legal advice he provided the president about the treatment of prisoners and about torture: in one memo, he advised the president that the Geneva Conventions did not apply to Al Qaeda or Taliban soldiers in Afghanistan or to the prisoners at Guantanamo; along the same lines, he solicited and participated in the preparation of another memo that redefined torture in such a narrow way that it only included physical abuse that produced the kind of pain that accompanies "serious physical injury, such as organ failure" or death. Despite editorial opposition, the Senate confirmed Gonzales.[52]

Thus, there have been eight Latinos in cabinets, three Democrats (Cisneros, Peña, and Richardson) and five Republicans (Cavazos, Lujan, Martinez, Gutierrez, and Gonzales).

LATINOS IN THE MILITARY ELITE

There have been few Latinos of general officer rank in the armed forces of the United States. Of the 1,067 people who held that rank in 1985, only two were Latinos (one in the navy, the other in the air force). Over the next decade, the number of Latinos with general officer rank increased steadily, but only to ten; the corresponding percentage increase was from 0.2 percent to 1.1 percent. None of the Latino general officers during that decade was a marine, and none of the ten in 1995 was a woman. (From 1986 through 1988, there was one Latina in the air force with general officer rank.) By September 2004, the number of Hispanics with general officer rank had increased to 15, which represented 1.7 percent of the 898 men and women at that level in the military hierarchy.[53]

In the spring of 2004, it appeared that Lt. Gen. Ricardo S. Sanchez, a three-star general and the commander of 160,000 American and allied troops in Iraq, would be promoted to four-star rank and thus become the army's highest ranking Hispanic officer. Sanchez rose from the bottom. He grew up in Rio Grande City, a southern Texas town a few miles from the Mexican border. His father, a welder, had abandoned the family when he was in elementary school, and his mother worked in a hospital to support Sanchez and his four siblings. To augment his mother's salary and the family's welfare payments, young Ricardo worked various odd jobs. The first in his family to graduate from high school, he won an ROTC scholarship to Texas A&I, and upon graduation, he joined the army. Over the years, he rose steadily through the ranks, though not without difficulty, for there was still, especially in his early years, "a lot of racial stuff within the ranks." His promotion, however, was derailed when the Abu Ghraib prison scandal broke. Sanchez had issued an order in November 2003 that officially gave tactical control over the prison to the 205th Military Intelligence Brigade (an order criticized by Maj. Gen. Antonio M. Taguba, who wrote a devastating report on the conditions at the prison); he had also authorized the presence of attack dogs during interrogation sessions. On May 25, 2004, it was announced that he was being replaced as U.S. commander, and he handed over command in early July. Two subsequent reports on the prison scandal, one by three army generals and the other by an independent panel headed by former secretary of defense James Schlesinger, were highly critical of Sanchez. Although he was cleared of wrongdoing in an army inspector general's report that came out in April 2005, it appeared that his promotion to four-star general had been permanently derailed.[54]

In late June 2005, however, the *New York Times* reported that Donald Rumsfeld, confident (as always) that the military had put the Abu Ghraib prison scandal behind it, was considering nominating Sanchez for a promotion to four-star. This appealed to many in the military because Sanchez, it was assumed, would serve as a valuable role model for potential Mexican American recruits. The army was having great difficulty persuading young people to enlist, and the percentage of Hispanic Americans among new recruits had increased over the previous decade from about 8 percent to about 13 percent. Many, including some in the military and some Republicans, were against such a promotion. The *New York Times* editorialized against promoting Sanchez: "He set aside American notions of decency and the Geneva Conventions, authorizing harsh interrogations—including forcing prisoners into painful positions for long periods, isolating them, depriving them of sleep and using guard dogs to, as he put it, 'exploit Arab fears.'"[55]

An examination of the next few levels of the officer ranks for the same years (1985 to 1995) suggests that Latino generals and admirals will remain rare. The percentage of Latinos at those levels increased from a meager 1.6 percent to only 2.5 percent. Because there are high attrition rates for all ethnic groups between colonel and general, there is very little chance of a substantial increase in Latinos at the elite level of the military in the near future.

As we had done previously with African Americans, we considered the longer-term prospects for an increasing Latino presence in the top levels of the military by looking at the makeup of current classes at the three major service academies. At West Point, approximately 6.4 percent of the members of the entering class of 2008 were Hispanic; at the Naval Academy, approximately 9 percent of the members of the entering class of 2007 were Hispanic; and at the Air Force Academy, 6.3 percent of the entering classes of 2005 to 2009 were Hispanic.[56] Although the number of Hispanics in the military has increased dramatically in recent years, this increase has not been matched by corresponding increases in their enrollment at the three major service academies.

Due to a concentrated population base in the state of New Mexico and in some congressional districts, Latinos have gradually developed a small amount of political representation in Congress. The story could begin with those few who were elected from the territories of Florida and New Mexico in the nineteenth century or with those elected to the House from Louisiana or New Mexico after 1912, but we will restrict ourselves to the four senators elected since 1935 and the twenty-two members of the House first elected after 1960.

THE SENATE

Until the 2004 elections, there had been two Latino senators, Dennis Chávez and Joseph Montoya, both Democrats from New Mexico whose families had lived in the area for several generations. Chávez, first appointed to the Senate in 1935, was born in 1888 on a family-owned ranch in New Mexico that traced back to a land grant from the king of Spain in 1769. Still, his parents were poor; he was one of eight children, and he was forced to drop out of school in the eighth grade to go to work. He drove a grocery wagon and then was hired to work in the Albuquerque Engineering Department. In the 1916 election, he worked as a Spanish interpreter for Democratic senator A. A. Jones. When Jones won the election, he took Chávez to Washington, D.C., where he became a Senate clerk. He studied law at Georgetown University (which required that he pass a special examination because he held no high school diploma) and received his LLB in 1920.

Chávez then returned to Albuquerque, set up a law practice, and was elected to the New Mexico House of Representatives and then the U.S. House of Representatives as a Democrat. In 1934, he ran for the U.S. Senate and lost a bitterly contested election to Bronson F. Cutting. While he was in the process of challenging the election, Cutting was killed in a plane crash, and Chávez was appointed to replace him. He went on to win a special election and was reelected to serve four more terms in the Senate. Although he had been ill with cancer for more than a year, he ran again for the Senate in 1962, was reelected, returned to the hospital the day after the election, and died a few weeks later.[57]

Montoya's parents were descended from Spanish immigrants who settled in New Mexico in the eighteenth century. His father was a sheriff. Montoya won election to the Senate in 1964. Like Chávez, he studied law at Georgetown Law School. While still a student there, he was elected to the New Mexico House of Representatives on the Democratic ticket. He moved from the state house to the state senate, became lieutenant governor, and, in 1957, was elected to the U.S. House of Representatives. After serving four terms in the House, he was elected to the Senate in 1964. Montoya was defeated in 1976 after a series of newspaper articles detailed alleged improprieties involving a shopping center he owned in Santa Fe, claiming that he had received "special treatment" from the IRS, whose budget was reviewed by a committee he headed. In addition, Montoya's name was one of those mentioned when South Korean businessman Tongsun Park was accused of attempting to buy influence in the United States by making contributions to the election campaigns of politicians. When Montoya died in 1978, he was "said to be a millionaire," according to the *New York Times*.[58]

There were no Hispanics in the Senate from Montoya's death until 2004, when two Hispanic men were elected. One, Mel Martinez, we have already mentioned: after being appointed George W. Bush's secretary of housing and urban development, he left that position to run for the Senate in Florida, where he won a close race against the Democratic nominee, Betty Castor, a politically moderate former state education commissioner. The other was Ken Salazar, a Democratic lawyer from a ranching family that has been in the Southwest for four centuries—thus, like Joseph Montoya, he is of Spanish heritage—who beat Republican beer executive (and heir) Peter Coors to become Colorado's first Hispanic senator.

THE HOUSE

Since 1960, thirty-seven Latinos have been elected to the House, thirty-two as Democrats and five as Republicans. In 1985, there were eleven Hispanics in the House; the number increased to seventeen in 1995, and to twenty-three in 2005 (thus, the percentage of Hispanics has risen from 2.5 to 5.3).[59] Typically, the Democrats have been Mexican Americans from Texas or California and Puerto Ricans from New York, although a Mexican American from Arizona was elected to the House in 1990 and a Puerto Rican from Illinois was elected in 1992. Until 1996, none of the Mexican Americans had been from a well-to-do background. The five Latino Republicans have tended to come from solidly middle-class or higher backgrounds. As we have indicated, Manuel Lujan who served as Reagan's secretary of the interior, was a member of Congress before he served in the cabinet; his father ran an insurance agency and served three terms as mayor of Santa Fe. Three of the other four have been Cuban Americans, an unsurprising finding given the prominence of Cuban Americans in the corporate elite.

There are some exceptions to these generalizations, but they turn out to be very atypical. Robert Menéndez, elected in 1992 as the first Hispanic American from New Jersey to serve in the House, is an unusual Cuban American Democrat. But Menéndez was born in New York City in 1954, before Castro came to power, and he did not have to leave his parents' native land under pressure. He grew up in New Jersey (his father was a carpenter, his mother a seamstress) and was elected to the school board in Union City in 1974 while he was working on his BA at St. Peter's College. After receiving his law degree from Rutgers in 1976, he became mayor of Union City in 1986 and a member of the state legislature in 1987, moving from the assembly to the senate in 1991. He is married to a non-Hispanic white, the former Jane Jacobsen. About 22 percent of the voters in his district are Latinos.[60] And, as we have noted above, former congressman

Bill Richardson, the son of a Citibank executive and a graduate of an elite prep school, is even more atypical.

The second Republican Hispanic elected to the House since 1960, Ileana Ros-Lehtinen, a Cuban American from Miami who had served in the state legislature since 1982, was seated in 1989 just as Lujan was leaving to become secretary of the interior. A 1975 graduate of Florida International University, she owned a private school in Miami. She was joined on the Republican side of the aisle in 1992 by a second Cuban American from southern Florida, Lincoln Díaz-Balart. Díaz-Balart's father, Rafael, was considered one of the founding fathers of Florida's anti-Castro, pro-embargo Republicans. His animus was personal as well as political. His sister, Mirta, was married to Fidel Castro and bore Castro's first son, Fidelito. Thus, Lincoln Díaz-Balart is Fidel's nephew and Fidelito's first cousin.[61]

Lujan, Ros-Lehtinen, and Díaz-Balart are prototypical Republicans, but another Republican Hispanic, Henry Bonilla of Texas, most decidedly is not. His victory over an incumbent Latino Democrat, however, was an unlikely one based on very unusual circumstances. Born in 1954 in San Antonio into a low-income Mexican American family, Bonilla graduated from the University of Texas in 1976, started as a radio announcer in Austin, and worked his way up in the television industry, including jobs in New York and Philadelphia, before returning to San Antonio in 1986 as an executive producer of the news and later a public relations officer for a network affiliate. His wife, Deborah Knapp, a non-Hispanic white, was well known as the station's nightly newscaster.

Bonilla jumped into the 1992 election as a rare Mexican American Republican because the four-term Democratic incumbent, Mexican American Alberto Busta-mante, had been caught in a House banking scandal. He also was exposed for building a $600,000 home just outside his district in a wealthy neighborhood, and he was convicted of taking $340,000 in bribes. Under these circumstances, Bonilla attracted the votes of angry Mexican American Democrats (who overwhelmingly supported the Clinton-Gore ticket), even though he was an extremely conservative candidate. Sensing Bustamante's vulnerability, leading Republicans from around the country came to the area to boost Bonilla's candidacy.[62]

The three Mexican Americans first elected to Congress in 1996 follow the patterns described so far in some ways, but they are distinctive in others. Like most Mexican Americans, all three were elected as Democrats. Silvestre Reyes started as a farm worker as a youngster but was regional chief of the Border Patrol in El Paso when he retired to run for office. He won his spurs with Mexican Americans and Anglos alike in 1993 when he stationed his staff one hundred yards apart, twenty-four hours a day, along the border to halt illegal immigration.

The second Mexican American elected in 1996, Ruben Hinojosa, is also a Democrat, but he came from more fortunate economic circumstances than any of the Mexican Americans previously elected to Congress. Hinojosa's family had owned and operated a successful family meatpacking company, H & H Meats of Mercedes, Texas. In the mid-

1990s, with Hinojosa as its president, it was the thirty-ninth-largest Hispanic business, with $52 million in sales and 320 employees. Hinojosa was the first Hispanic business leader of major stature to be elected to Congress.

The third Mexican American elected in 1996 was Laura Sánchez, who, like Reyes, was the child of immigrant parents (she was one of seven children). But Sánchez had married Stephen Brixey III, a bond salesman, earned an MBA, and become a Republican. In 1996, she switched her registration to Democratic, dropped her Anglo married name, and defeated an extreme right-wing incumbent in the Republican stronghold of Orange County, California, with the help of donations from women's groups, environmentalists, and gays and lesbians, all of whom found her opponent, "B-1 Bob" Dornan, to be one of their worst enemies in Congress. Sánchez got into some trouble with her Democratic colleagues during the 2000 Gore campaign when she scheduled a Democratic fund-raiser at the Playboy mansion in southern California. After considerable bad press, the event was cancelled.[63]

In 2002, Linda Sánchez, Laura Sánchez's younger sister, a lifelong Democrat, who did her undergraduate work at the University of California, Berkeley, and who has a law degree from UCLA, was elected to the House from a nearby district, making them the first sister team in the history of the House of Representatives. Unlike her middle-of-the-road, Republican-turned-Democrat sister, Linda is an authentic liberal who has been a union lawyer and handled civil rights cases.

In that same 2002 election, the arrival of a liberal Democratic Sánchez sister was matched by the arrival of a conservative Republican Díaz-Balart brother. Mario Díaz-Balart, the younger brother of Lincoln Díaz-Balart, having served in both the Florida House and Senate, was elected to a newly created seat in Florida. Mario, one of the few members of the House without a college degree (he attended the University of South Florida, but did not graduate) is, like his older brother, a Cuban American Republican and (as noted above) Fidel Castro's nephew.

Laura Sánchez and Mario Díaz-Balart are but two of ten Hispanics elected to the House since the 1996 elections, Díaz-Balart is the only Republican, though one of the Democrats, Henry Cuellar, who won a seat in Texas in 2004, endorsed Bush in 2000 and served in the administration of Bush's Republican successor as governor. After Cuellar almost defeated GOP incumbent Henry Bonilla in 2002, the Republicans redrew the district lines to protect Bonilla from a rematch, Cuellar then barely defeated the Democratic incumbent, Ciro Rodriguez, in the primary (Cuellar won by fifty-eight votes) and went on to win the November election.

THE SUPREME COURT

As of July 2005, there had been no Latino members of the Supreme Court. Among the many concerns raised about Alberto Gonzales's nomination to be attorney general was that George W. Bush had him in mind for a Supreme Court nomination. Ironically, although moderates and liberals opposed Gonzales's appointment as attorney general, when Sandra Day O'Connor announced her resignation and many people mentioned Gonzales's name as a possible replacement for her on the Supreme Court, it was the conservatives who reacted negatively, saying he was not conservative enough.

CONCLUSION

Hispanic Americans are part of the corporate community and will continue to be included, especially those with light skin, high-status social backgrounds in their ancestral countries, or both. Such people are racially and culturally similar to the Europeans who came directly to the United States. However, due to their origins in several different Latin American countries, they add an international flavor to the American power elite in an age of increasing corporate globalization. In the case of Cuban Americans, they build on a strong immigrant business community in southern Florida that will continue to generate a disproportionate number of new members in the corporate elite. This point is underscored by the fact that only eleven of the seventy-five wealthiest Latinos for 1995 sat on a *Fortune* 1000 board, so there is a large pool of likely directors ready to be tapped.

The acceptance of light-skinned Hispanic Americans into American society in general and the corporate elite in particular can be seen most clearly in the marriage partners of the three women corporate directors we have highlighted in this chapter. Vilma Martínez married Stuart Singer, a fellow lawyer, in 1968. Patricia Díaz married Michael Dennis, also a lawyer, also in 1968, and she goes by the surname of Díaz Dennis. Katherine Ortega also married a lawyer, Lloyd Derrickson, in 1989.

The military has not been as important an avenue of upward mobility for Latinos and Latinas as it has for African Americans, but it has not been notable for discrimination against Latinos in the past either. As for participation in the political arena, our conclusions are more tentative because there are too few cabinet appointees and elected officials to study. As with the other groups, though, appointed officials tend to come from higher socioeconomic backgrounds and to be present in both Republican and Democratic administrations. Elected officials, on the other hand, with the important exception of Cuban Americans, tend to come from the middle and lower levels of the society and to be Democrats. It is likely that Mexican Americans from the labor movement will play an increasing role in the Democratic Party, forcing the Republicans to redouble their efforts to recruit well-to-do Hispanics of all ethnic backgrounds to maintain their claims to diversity and inclusiveness.

NOTES

1. *Statistical Abstract of the United States* (Washington, D.C.: U.S. Government Printing Office, 1985), 86; see, also, www.census.gov/prod/www/abs/statab l951–1994.htm.

2. Pauline Jelinek, "Hispanics One-seventh of U.S. Population," *Greensboro News & Record*, June 9, 2005, A1. When he died, Goizueta was eulogized as representing the American dream, with little or no attention paid to his privileged background in Cuba before the revolution. See Richard Zweigenhaft, "Making Rags out of Riches: Horatio Alger and the Tycoon's Obituary," *Extra!* January–February 2004, 27–28.

3. Janet Morey and Wendy Dunn, *Famous Mexican Americans* (New York: Dutton, 1989), 65–67.

4. Morey and Dunn, *Famous Mexican Americans*, 70.

5. James A. Gross, *Broken Promise: The Subversion of U.S. Labor Relations Policy, 1947–1994* (Philadelphia: Temple University Press, 1995), 250–63.

6. "Emerging Wealth: The Hispanic Business Rich List," *Hispanic Business* (March 1996): 18. We recognize, of course, that Puerto Ricans are U.S. citizens and, thus, those who settle in the United States cannot technically be termed immigrants, but we adopt that term in order to avoid the repeated syntactical gymnastics that would otherwise be necessary. See, also, Roberto R. Ramirez and Patricia de la Cruz, "The Hispanic Population in the United States: March 2002," *Current Population Reports*, issued June 2003, U.S. Census Bureau.

7. Rodolfo de la Garza, Louis De Sipio, F. Chris Garcia, John Garcia, and Angelo Falcon, *Latino Voices: Mexican, Puerto Rican, and Cuban Perspectives on American Politics* (Boulder, CO: Westview, 1992), 13–14. See, also, Suzanne Oboler, *Ethnic Labels, Latino Lives* (Minneapolis: University of Minnesota Press, 1995).

8. See www.ncccusa.org/news/050330yearbook.html.

9. Carlos H. Arce, Edward Murguia, and W. Parker Frisbie, "Phenotype and Life Chances among Chicanos," *Hispanic Journal of Behavioral Sciences* 9, no. 1 (1987): 19–32; E. Telles and Edward Murguia, "Phenotypic Discrimination and Income Differences among Mexican Americans," *Social Science Quarterly* 71 (1990): 682–96; Aida Hurtado, "Does Similarity Breed Respect? Interviewer Evaluations of Mexican-Descent Respondents in a Bilingual Survey," *Public Opinion Quarterly* 58 (1994): 77–95.

10. For excellent accounts of the association of color and racial exclusion in Latin America, see Laura A. Lewis, "Spanish Ideology and the Practice of Inequality in the New World," in *Racism and Anti-Racism in World Perspective*, ed. Benjamin Bowser, 46–66 (Thousand Oaks, CA: Sage, 1995); Vânia Penha-Lopes, "What Next? On Race and Assimilation in the United States and Brazil," *Journal of Black Studies* 26, no. 6 (1996): 809–26.

11. Telles and Murguia, "Phenotypic Discrimination and Income Differences."

12. Sonya Tafoya, "Shades of Belonging," Pew Hispanic Center, Washington, D.C., December 2004.

13. As Mike Caplinger, research supervisor for *Hispanic Business* magazine, explained to us in an e-mail on August 31, 2004, they "narrowed down the listing from *Fortune* 1000 companies to *Fortune* 500 companies in an effort to further focus on the 'elite' Hispanics at the very top of the game."

14. Juan Solana, J. Tabin Cosio, Michael Caplinger, and Cynthia Marquez, "The Honored Few," *Hispanic Business*, January–February 2004, 48; "Ready for Progress," *Hispanic Business*, January–February 2005, 44–48. The *Hispanic Business* estimate of 1.6 percent is similar to that based on the data that we received from the Investor Responsibility Research

Center, which found that 154, or 1.1 percent, of the seats on the S&P 1500 were held by Hispanics in 2004.

In a study of the directors of twenty-seven of the top hundred companies on the 2004 *Fortune* list, the Hispanic Association on Corporate Responsibility (HACR) found that 3.85 percent of the total available seats were held by Hispanics, compared to 1.97 percent of the total available seats on the top thousand companies. As is the case with African Americans, the larger companies are more likely to include members of previously excluded groups than the smaller companies. None of the 27 companies had a Hispanic woman as one of its ten highest-paid executives, and most did not have a Hispanic woman as one of its top hundred executives. Alfonso E. Martinez, "HACR Corporate Index 2004," *HACR* (online), at www .hacr.org/mediacenter/pubID.86/pub_detail.asp.

15. Reply to letter to the editor, *Hispanic Business*, April 1995, 8.

16. Personal communication from director of community affairs, Sears, July 29, 1996. Despite this, in 1998, *Hispanic Business* included Martinez on its list of five Latinos who were CEOs of *Fortune* 1000 companies. See Maria Zate, "The Big Jump," *Hispanic Business*, January–February 1998, 32. Similarly, *Hispanic Business* included David Fuente, the CEO of Office Depot, as one of the five Latino CEOs in 1998, but the Office Depot public relations officer informed us that Fuente was born and raised in Chicago and is a Sephardic Jew. In all likelihood, his ancestors were expelled from Spain or Portugal in the fifteenth century, which stretches the meaning of "Hispanic" beyond the usual boundaries. Although *Hispanic Business* continues to include him on its "boardroom elite" list, he is listed as Caucasian, but not Hispanic, on the IRRC's S&P 1500 list.

17. "Who's News," *Wall Street Journal*, June 8, 1995.

18. The IRRC data for the directors who sit on the boards of the S&P 1500 yield comparable results. Hispanic men hold 83 percent of the 154 seats held by Hispanics, but, on average, Hispanic women directors sit on 2.0 seats, and Hispanic men sit on 1.4.

19. Jane Mayer, "Sweet Life: First Family of Sugar Is Tough on Workers, Generous to Politicians," *Wall Street Journal*, July 29, 1991.

20. Phyllis Berman, "The Set-Aside Charade," *Forbes*, March 13, 1995, 78–80, 82, 86; Phyllis Berman, "The Fanjuls of Palm Beach," *Forbes*, May 14, 1990, 56–57, 60, 64, 68–69; Eric Alan Barton, "From Bitter to Sweet: Forget the Awful Past, Say Alfonso and Pepe Fanjul, Florida's Sugar Barons," *Miami New Times* (online), August 26, 2004, at www.miami newtimes.com/issues/2004-08-26/feature.html.

21. Leslie Wayne, "Foreign G.O.P. Donor Raised Dole Funds," *New York Times*, October 21, 1996; Barton, "From Bitter to Sweet"; Timothy L. O'Brien, "The Castro Collection," *New York Times*, November 21, 2004, section 3, 1; Alexei Barrionuevo and Elizabeth Becker, "Mighty Lobby Is Losing Some Luster," *New York Times*, June 2, 2005, C1, C4.

22. J. P. Faber, "Chairman of the Board: Armando Codina," *South Florida CEO*, January 2004, 44–51.

23. Faber, "Chairman of the Board," 44–51.

24. William Finnegan, "Castro's Shadow," *New Yorker*, October 14, 2002, 101ff.

25. David Pedreira, "Strait-out Country; Bush Pals Vie for Charters," *Tampa Tribune*, March 28, 1999, 1.

26. Dusko Doder, "Our Tropical Terrorist Tourist Trap; As Fidel and His Critics Creak

toward Irrelevance, the Push for Normalized U.S.-Cuban Relations Grows Stronger," *The American Prospect*, October 7, 2002, 26.

27. Susan Rasky, "A 'Born' Republican: Katherine Davalos Ortega," *New York Times*, August 21, 1984.

28. Morey and Dunn, *Famous Mexican Americans*, 100–101.

29. Morey and Dunn, *Famous Mexican Americans*, 76.

30. We are not including David Fuente or Arthur Martinez. See n. 16 above.

31. Elizabeth Llorente, "The Breakfast Champ," *Hispanic Magazine* (online), January–February 2004, at www.hispaniconline.com/magazine/2004/jan_feb/Cover-Story. See Carlos M. Gutierrez, "The Boss: My Many Citizenship Quests," *New York Times*, August 22, 2001, C6.

32. Shailaja Neelakantan, "Picking His Targets," *Forbes* (online), August 11, 1997, at www.forbes.com/forbes/1997/0811/6003122a.html. In April 2000, CHS filed for bankruptcy. See Simon Robinson, "CHS Files for Bankruptcy Protection," *Hoovers* (online), April 5, 2000, at www.vnunet.com/crn/news/2006410/chs-files-bankruptcy-protection. Phyllis Berman, "The Cosmopolitan Touch," *Forbes* (online), June 21, 2004, at www.forbes.com/business/global/2004/0621/024.html.

33. Wayne Arnold, "Ex-Chief of US West to Lead Australian Telephone Giant," *New York Times*, June 10, 2005, C4; "Hispanics at the Top," *Hispanic Magazine* (online), September 1999, at www.hispanicmagazine.com/1999/sep/CoverStory. Henry Cisneros also called Trujillo "the most important Hispanic in corporate America today." See "U.S. West Elects New Chairman," *New York Times*, May 12, 1999, C8. According to *Hispanic Business*, Robert D. Glynn Jr., CEO at PG&E from 1997 until the end of 2004, is Hispanic. Glynn was born in Orange, New Jersey, and received a BA from Manhattan College and an MA from Long Island University. Although he was listed as one of five Hispanic CEOs of *Fortune*-level companies by *Hispanic Business* magazine in 1998 and included in a September 1999 cover story in *Hispanic Magazine* titled "Hispanics at the Top," we were unable to find any evidence of his Hispanic background. His biographical sketch on the PG&E website makes no mention of either Hispanic background or Hispanic affiliations, and the public relations people at PG&E did not respond to our queries. He is included in the IRRC's list of S&P 1500 directors as Caucasian.

34. "Hispanics at the Top"; www.incae.ac.cr/EN/40anios/walter_kissling_gam.shtml; Andrew Pollack, "The Genome Is Mapped. Now He Wants Profit," *New York Times*, February 24, 2002, section 3, 1.

35. Tonya Vinas, "Three Quick Questions with Alcoa CEO Alain Belda: Prepare for a Hard Landing," *IndustryWeek* (online), May 1, 2005, at www.industryweek.com/ReadArticle.aspx?ArticleID=10180.

36. Gutierrez's family, for example, was able to leave Cuba with more than the clothes on their back. According to Llorente in "The Breakfast Champ," "While many Cubans speak of coming to the United States with little more than pocket change and the clothes on their back, Pedro and Olga Gutierrez and their two sons were able to leave with $2,000 and 22 suitcases in 1960."

37. See the annual reports of the Hispanic Association on Corporate Responsibility, 2003 and 2004.

38. Abraham D. Lavender, "The Distinctive Hispanic Names (DHN) Technique: A Method for Selecting a Sample or Estimating Population Size," *Names* 40, no. 1 (1992): 1–16.

39. The use of color cards to assess skin color is described in Selena Bond and Thomas F. Cash, "Black Beauty: Skin Color and Body Images among African-American College Women," *Journal of Applied Social Psychology* 22, no. 11 (1992): 874–88.

40. These differences were statistically significant. When we ran a regression analysis in which skin color was the dependent variable and both gender and presence or absence on *Fortune* boards were predictive variables, the resulting F was 9.83 ($p < 0.0001$). As was the case with African Americans, sex was a stronger predictor (beta = 0.29, $p < 0.0001$) than presence on *Fortune* boards (beta = 0.11, $p < 0.12$).

41. The accuracy scores of the UCSC students were quite similar to those of the Guilford College students for whites (89 and 90 percent, respectively), black men (97 and 90 percent), and black women (54 and 60 percent). The UCSC students were more accurate than the Guilford College students in identifying both Hispanic men (57 and 40 percent) and Hispanic women (40 and 30 percent). Unable to contain our curiosity, we showed the photographs to six Latino students at UCSC. They were somewhat less accurate than the other UCSC students in identifying the Hispanic men (44 percent) but more accurate in identifying the Hispanic women (67 percent). Their combined accuracy rate for the Hispanics was 53 percent, virtually the same as that of the non-Hispanic UCSC students.

When a Latino reader in Texas chastised *Hispanic Business* in November 1996 because the 1995 and 1996 stories on the top influentials, top executives, and multimillionaires "failed to include a single dark face," the magazine replied that each of the three lists contained Hispanics with "African ancestry" and claimed that "basing your conclusions on visual evidence alone makes for a faulty argument." But as the reader was saying, and as our evidence shows, there are few "dark faces" at the top, whatever their ancestry. See Gustavo E. Gonzales, "Are Black Hispanics Being Ignored?" *Hispanic Business*, November 1996, 6.

42. "Lauro F. Cavazos, Jr.," *Current Biography* (1989): 97.

43. Maureen Dowd, "Cavazos Quits as Education Chief amid Pressure from White House," *New York Times*, September 13, 1990.

44. Ted Gup, "The Stealth Secretary," *Time*, May 25, 1992, 57; "The Blank Interior of Manuel Lujan," *Economist*, September 22, 1990, 34; "Talk of the Trail," *Audubon*, July 1989, 20; Bruce Reed, "Half Watt: The Dregs of the Bush Cabinet," *New Republic*, October 16, 1989, 20.

45. "Manuel Lujan," *Current Biography* (1989): 354–58.

46. "Henry G. Cisneros," *Current Biography* (1987): 87–96; "Federico F. Peña," *Current Biography* (1993): 460–64.

47. David Johnston, "Concluding That Cisneros Lied, Reno Urges a Special Prosecutor," *New York Times*, March 15, 1995; Steven A. Holmes, "Housing Secretary Resigns, Citing Financial Pressures," *New York Times*, November 22, 1996; Mireya Navarro, "Cisneros Leaving Univision to Run Housing Company," *New York Times*, August 8, 2000, C8.

48. See "Bill Richardson," *Current Biography* (1996): 37–40; James Brooke, "Traveling Troubleshooter Is Ready to Settle Down at the U.N.," *New York Times*, December 14, 1996; Rick Lyman, "An Activist Leader at Home and Nationally," *New York Times*, July 20, 2004, A14.

49. Abby Goodnough, "Ex-Cabinet Member Struggles in Florida Senate Primary," *New York Times*, August 31, 2004, A10.

50. See Gutierrez, "The Boss," C6.

51. Richard W. Stevenson, "Bush Nominates Kellogg Executive for Commerce Secretary," *New York Times*, November 30, 2004, A15. Ros-Lehtinen was less accurate when, in a typical effort to create an Horatio Alger story where there was none, she added, "We're ecstatic because he's a symbol of the Cuban success stories, coming here without a penny to his name and rising up the corporate ladder to become a CEO of a major company." The article notes that the family was allowed to leave Cuba with $8,000 and thirty-one bags of clothing.

52. David Johnston and Richard W. Stevenson, "Riding an Ideological Divide: Alberto R. Gonzales," *New York Times*, November 11, 2004, A28; "The Wrong Attorney General," *New York Times*, January 26, 2005, A20; Mark Danner, "Torture and Gonzales: An Exchange," *New York Review of Books*, February 10, 2005, 44–46; Jonathan Schell, "What Is Wrong with Torture," *The Nation*, February 7, 2005, 8; David Cole, "Gonzales: Wrong Choice," *The Nation*, December 6, 2004, 5–6.

53. See "Distribution of Active Duty Forces by Service, Rank, Sex and Race, 09/30/04," Department of Defense, DMDC-3035EO.

54. John F. Burns, "In the General's Black Hawk, Flying over a Divided Iraq," *New York Times*, January 11, 2004, A1, A4; "The Abu Ghraib Spin," *New York Times*, May 12, 2004, A22; Seymour M. Hersh, "Chain of Command," *The New Yorker*, May 17, 2004, 37–43; Eric Schmitt and Thom Shanker, "Pentagon Is Replacing Sanchez As the U.S. Commander in Iraq," *New York Times*, May 25, 2004, A1, A11; John F. Burns, "The General Departs, with a Scandal to Ponder," *New York Times*, July 22, 2004, A10; Douglas Jehl and Eric Schmitt, "Army's Report Faults General in Prison Abuse," *New York Times*, August 27, 2004, A1, A10; Josh White, "Top Army Officers Are Cleared in Abuse Cases," *Washington Post*, April 23, 2005, A1.

55. Eric Schmitt and Thom Shanker, "Posts Considered for Commanders after Abuse Case," *New York Times*, June 20, 2005, A1, A9; "Abu Ghraib, Rewarded," *New York Times*, June 22, 2005, A26. A study by the Pew Hispanic Center indicates that while about 10 percent of all enlisted personnel are Latinos, close to 18 percent find themselves on the front lines. See www.pewhispanic.org. Another study, based on the frequency of Hispanic surnames among the casualties, estimates that, as of late 2003, 20 percent of the casualties were Latinos. See Carol Amoruso, "The Military: What's in It for Latinos/as?" *IMDiversity.com*, at www.imdiversity.com/villages/hispanic/careers_workplace_employment/amoruso_latino_military.asp.

56. The figures for the Naval Academy and West Point are taken from their websites; the figures for the Air Force Academy were provided by the school's public affairs office. For some slightly older data on graduation rates, see "Hispanic-American Graduates of the Military Academies, 1966–1989," in *Hispanics in America's Defense* (Washington, D.C.: Department of Defense, U.S. Government Printing Office, 1990), 181.

57. "Dennis Chávez," *Current Biography* (1946): 109–12; "Senator Chávez, 74, Is Dead in Capital," *New York Times*, November 11, 1962.

58. "Joseph M. Montoya Is Dead at 62; Was Senator in Watergate Inquiry," *New York Times*, June 6, 1978.

59. *Congressional Quarterly*, January 31, 2005, 243.

60. In December 2005, Jon Corzine, who gave up his Senate seat to run for governor of New Jersey, appointed Menéndez to replace him in the Senate. Menéndez thus became the third Latino senator currently serving, along with Mel Martinez (R-FL) and Ken Salazar (D-CO). David W. Chen, "New Jersey's Newest Governor Basks, but only Briefly," *New York Times*, December 10, 2005, A14.

61. Roberto Lovato, "Rocking the Cuban Vote," *The Nation*, November 1, 2004, 24.

62. *Congressional Quarterly*, January 16, 1993, 136.

63. Lizette Alvarez, "Freshman Democrat Is Dogged by Relentless Foe," *New York Times*, October 5, 1997; Leslie Wayne, "The Democrats: The Money; Hefners' Record of Donations Reflects Their Liberal Ideology," *New York Times*, August 14, 2000, A16.

16

POSTSCRIPT
Latinos in the Power Elite, 2016

Richard L. Zweigenhaft and G. William Domhoff

Almost a decade has passed since we completed the research for the essay in chapter 15. Additional Latinos have joined the power elite, and some Latinos have left it, but little has changed in terms of the broader patterns that we depicted.

THE CORPORATE ELITE

The most striking change in the corporate elite in the last decade has been a dramatic increase in the number of those we call the "new CEOs"—that is, CEOs of *Fortune* 500 companies who are not white men. When we completed the research for the chapter on Latinos in the power elite, we identified and provided brief profiles of six Latinos who had headed *Fortune* 500 companies for a year or more since 1981, when Cuban American Roberto Goizueta became the head of Coca-Cola, the fifty-sixth largest company in the United States at the time. His appointment came several years before the appointment of the first Asian American CEO (1986), the first woman CEO whose parents did not own the corporation (1986), and the first African American CEO (1999).

By 2011, when the hardcover edition of our most recent book, *The New CEOs,* came out, the number of past and present Latino CEOs had increased to fifteen (Zweigenhaft and Domhoff, 2011, p. 54); by the time we updated that research for a 2014 paperback edition of the book, the number was up to twenty-six. This apparently steady increase in the total number of Latinos who have ever served as CEOs of *Fortune* 500 companies, however, masks a relatively recent downward trend that is apparent when one looks at the number of Latino CEOs in any given year. Looking at the appointments in this way, rather than cumulatively, reveals that the number of Latino CEOs peaked in 2008 at thirteen, and had dropped back to eleven in 2013 (as we write this postscript, late in 2015, the number is twelve). There was a similar decline in the number of African American CEOs (since 2007) and Asian American CEOs (since 2011). But there was a different trend for white women CEOs, who held twenty-two CEO positions in 2013, and as of late 2015, twenty-four CEO positions, which underscores a continuing climb from six in 2000 and thirteen in 2006 (Zweigenhaft and Domhoff, 2014, p. xii). Even at the peak, when there were thirteen Latino CEOs in 2008, they made up only 2.6 percent of the 500 CEOs of *Fortune* 500 companies. The eleven Latino CEOs in 2013 made up 2.2 percent. Strikingly, there has yet to be a Latina *Fortune* 500 CEO (there have been three Asian American women, one African American woman, and 41 white women *Fortune* 500 CEOs).

And, of course, the percentage of Latinos in the national population has increased dramatically in recent years, faster than any other ethnic or racial group. According to the U.S. Census Bureau, more than 17 percent of the population now are Latinos, making them the largest ethnic or racial minority group. Therefore, as the Latino population has been growing, the number of Latino CEOs has been decreasing. At the same time, however, the percentage of whites in the working age population will begin to decline within the next two decades, and native-born Latinos are increasing their share of good jobs, defined as the top one-quarter of all jobs (Alba, 2013).

When we conducted a study of the skin color of the new CEOs, a study similar to the one that we did on Latino corporate directors that is described in chapter 15, we found that the Latino CEOs were quite light-skinned. In fact, based solely on their photographs (but not their names), raters were unable to identify some of them as Latino (Zweigenhaft and Domhoff, 2014, pp. 62–63, and 165–176). This is not news to the Latino CEOs themselves. As Enrique Salem, the CEO of Symantec from 2009 through 2012, told a reporter for *Financial Times*, "To be honest, most people can't tell I'm Hispanic" (Jacobs, 2010).

Also noteworthy is the fact that most of the twenty-six Latino CEOs were born outside the United States (four were born in Cuba, two in Mexico, two in Spain, and the others in a range of Spanish-speaking countries). In this respect, they reflect the effects of globalization on the corporate elite, and they are not alone among CEOs in being foreign born (a number of *Fortune* CEOs were born in India, and others were born in Turkey, England, Germany, Morocco, Egypt, and elsewhere).

Nor has there been a significant increase in the percentage of Latinos on corporate boards. Our detailed look at the 4,324 men and women who sat on the boards of *Fortune* 500 companies revealed that the proportion of Latinos increased only from 1.6 percent in 2006 to 3.1 percent in 2011. Table 16.1 compares our findings on Latinos with those for other groups, and shows that there were far more male than female directors in all groups.

TABLE 16.1   *Fortune* 500 Directors by Race, Ethnicity, and Gender, 2011

	% of directors	% male directors	% female directors	M/F ratio
Whites (n=3791)	87.7%	74.4%	13.3%	5.6 to 1
African Americans (n=293)	6.8%	5.3%	1.5%	3.5 to 1
Latinos (n=136)	3.1%	2.4%	0.7%	3.4 to 1
Asian Americans (n=104)	2.4%	2.0%	0.4%	5 to 1
TOTAL (n=4324)	100.0%	84.1%	15.9%	5.3 to 1

These findings reveal that there was little change in Latino representation on *Fortune* 500 corporate boards from 2006 to 2011, a conclusion that is in line with the findings of a large-scale study published in 2013 by the Alliance for Board Diversity, an organization that includes four important advocacy groups for corporate diversity, one for women (Catalyst), one for African Americans (the Executive Leadership Council), one for Latinos (the Hispanic Association for Corporate Responsibility, or HACR), and one for Asian Americans (the Leadership Education for Asian Pacifics, or LEAP) (Alliance for Board Diversity, 2013). That study looked at directors from the *Fortune* 500 and the *Fortune* 1000, and compared representation in 2012 with previous data from 2004 and 2010. The researchers, too, concluded that "African Americans, Hispanics/Latinos and Asian Pacific Islanders have made only small gains or experienced losses in corporate boardroom representation" (p. 9).

Although the figures on college-educated Latinos and the growing percentage of native-born Latinos in the top one-quarter of the job ladder may portend a different future, a topic we return to later in this postscript, as of early 2014 there had been little or no increase in the past decade in the percentage of Latinos at the top of the corporate hierarchy. More generally, and as we already noted, corporate diversity has not increased for African Americans or Asian Americans either. After decades of efforts to diversify, corporate CEOs are 93.6 percent white and 94.8 percent male, and corporate boards are 87.7 percent white and 84.1 percent male. This stasis may signal the twilight of diversity, especially in light of the legislative and legal setbacks for affirmative action in higher education (Zweigenhaft and Domhoff, 2014, xi–xxvi).

THE POLITICAL ELITE: THE CABINET, THE SENATE AND THE HOUSE

THE CABINET

During the first term of his presidency, President Obama appointed two Latinos to his cabinet. One was Ken Salazar, who was secretary of the interior from 2009 through

2013. Born in Colorado and raised on the ranch his father, Enrique, had inherited from his father, Salazar attended St. Francis Seminary in Ohio, did his undergraduate work at Colorado College, and then went to law school at the University of Michigan. Salazar's ancestors in the southwestern United States date from the sixteenth century, and thus his heritage is Spanish, but he identifies as a Mexican American. The other Latino in Obama's cabinet during his first term was Hilda Solis, secretary of labor from 2009 through 2013. Solis's father, who worked in a battery recycling plant, was from Mexico, and her mother, who was an assembly-line worker, was from Nicaragua. Prior to serving in the cabinet (as the first Hispanic woman ever), she had served five terms in the House of Representatives as a Democrat from California.

When both Salazar and Solis left their positions, there was a period in 2013 when there were no Latinos in the cabinet. Under considerable pressure to diversify his cabinet, Obama then appointed Tom Perez, the son of Dominican parents, to replace Hilda Solis as secretary of labor. Perez, a graduate of Brown and Harvard Law School, was born in Buffalo, New York, where his father was a doctor (his mother's father had been the Dominican ambassador to the United States).

Obama then appointed Maria Contreras-Sweet as administrator of small business administration, which Obama had elevated to a cabinet-level position in early 2012. Born in Guadalajara, Mexico, she was five years old when she and her five siblings came to California with her mother, who worked at a chicken-packaging plant.

Obama's third Latino appointment was Julian Castro, a Mexican American, who became secretary of housing and urban development (HUD) in July 2014. Castro, a three-term mayor of San Antonio, was born in Texas to Mexican American parents. His father was a math teacher, and his mother a political activist who helped establish the political party La Raza Unida. He is the identical twin of Joaquin Castro, a member of the U.S. House of Representatives.

In March 2013, Obama nominated Ernest Moniz, an MIT professor, as secretary of energy. Although some acknowledged that Moniz's appointment added diversity to Obama's cabinet, those who thought he was Latino were mistaken. Moniz is the grandson of Portuguese immigrants, who are not traditionally considered Hispanic or Latino, and Moniz does not consider himself Latino. When the president of the National Council of La Raza was asked to comment on Moniz's appointment, she replied, "I'd like to think we are a big-tent community and would welcome anyone who wants to work with our community, but I think it's a stretch to call secretary-designate Moniz a major Hispanic announcement. He doesn't classify himself as Hispanic" (Eilperin, 2013).

Thus, as of August 2014, three of Obama's fifteen cabinet members were Latinos.

THE SENATE

In 2005, there were two Latinos in the Senate. Now there are three, all of whom were born to Cuban refugees, two in the United States and one in Canada. Bob Menéndez

(D-NJ) was appointed to the Senate in January 2006, when Jon Corzine, the previous senator, was elected governor of New Jersey and appointed Menéndez (at the time, Menéndez was in the U.S. House of Representatives). At the end of his one-year appointment, Menéndez then ran for the office in November 2006, and won reelection. He has a working-class background (his father was a carpenter and his mother a seamstress). Both parents left Cuba in 1953, moving first to New York City and then to New Jersey. Menéndez is the first in his family to attend college. Marco Rubio (R-FL) was elected to the Senate in November 2011. He, too, had previously served in the House of Representatives. His parents left Cuba in 1956, during Batista's regime, for better economic opportunities. His father worked for many years as a bartender, and his mother worked at various jobs in retail and in the service industry. After he graduated from high school in Miami, Rubio attended Tarkio College in Missouri for a year on a football scholarship. He then attended a community college in Santa Fe, transferred to and graduated from the University of Florida, and earned a law degree from the University of Miami. He has been called "the crown Prince" of the Tea Party movement (*Daily Telegraph* [London], 2010). The third Cuban American is Ted Cruz (R-TX), who was elected in November 2012. Cruz was born in Canada, where his Cuban American father and American-born mother had settled after leaving Cuba in 1957, two years before Castro came to power (his father had fought for Castro at the age of fourteen, and later became a staunch opponent). In Canada Cruz's parents owned a seismic data processing firm for oil drillers (his father graduated from the University of Texas; his mother graduated from Rice University with a degree in mathematics). Cruz himself is a graduate of Princeton and Harvard Law School, and Cruz, like Rubio, is a Tea Party favorite.

THE HOUSE

In 2005, there were twenty-three Latinos in the House. As a result of the November 2014 election, the number rose to 29, an increase from 5.3 percent to 6.7 percent; the large majority (83 percent) are male, and most are Democrats (76 percent). Of the twenty-two who have been elected since 2006, eighteen are male, and fourteen are Democrats. Four were born outside the United States (one in Cuba, one in Guatemala, one in Mexico, and one in Puerto Rico). Fourteen are Mexican Americans, five are Cuban Americans, and of the other three, one describes herself as "Hispanic American," and the other two were born in Guatemala and Puerto Rico. Most went to public schools, and the few who didn't went to private Catholic schools. All attended college, and thirteen of the twenty-two earned advanced degrees (mostly in law, but one has an MBA and one has an MD). Six went to elite schools either as undergraduates or for graduate work (one has a BA from Stanford, one from Harvard, and one from Dartmouth, two went to Harvard Law School, and the physician went to Harvard Medical School), but most attended state or local colleges and universities. Three come from privileged backgrounds in which their parents were professionals (for example, the father of one was a dentist, and the father of another was a judge), but most are from middle- or working-class families.

THE SUPREME COURT

The most striking Latino addition to the power elite in the past decade was the appointment in 2009 of Sonia Sotomayor to the Supreme Court. (Although C. Wright Mills, the author of the 1956 classic *The Power Elite*, did not include the Supreme Court as part of what he defined as the power elite, we have included it in our work.) Sotomayor, born in the Bronx to Puerto Rican parents, is the first person of Latino origin to sit on the Supreme Court, and the third woman. Her father, who had only a third grade education, died when she was nine, and she was raised by her mother, who worked as a telephone operator and as a practical nurse. After graduating from Cardinal Spellman High School as valedictorian, she attended Princeton on a full scholarship and graduated summa cum laude; she then graduated from Yale Law School, where she was the editor of the law review. (Eight of the nine members of the Court in 2014 were graduates of either the Yale or Harvard Law Schools; the ninth is a graduate of Columbia Law School.)

Sotomayor worked in the district attorney's office in New York for four years after her graduation, and then joined a corporate law firm, becoming a partner in 1988. She left the firm in 1992 after her appointment to the U.S. District Court for the Southern District in New York by Republican president George H. W. Bush. She gained the enduring gratitude of baseball fans across the United States in 1995 by ending a lengthy Major League Baseball strike with an injunction against the team owners, which stopped them from unilaterally instituting a new collective bargaining agreement and using replacement players. When Democratic president Bill Clinton nominated her to the United States Court of Appeals in 1998, Senate Republicans tried to block her appointment. She was eventually confirmed, and President Obama appointed her to the Supreme Court in 2009.

Sotomayor is one of six Catholics on the court, but she votes with the three Jewish members, two of whom are women, especially when there is a liberal-conservative split on social issues. However, along with most other members of the court, five of whom (like Sotomayor) worked as corporate lawyers early in their careers, she usually supports the U.S. Chamber of Commerce position when issues concerning corporations are brought before the court (Yeomans, 2012).

THE MILITARY ELITE

About 11.4 percent of all active-duty military forces were Latino in 2014, and that number is likely to increase (in 2011, almost 17 percent of all new recruits were Latino). In the last thirteen years, there has also been an increase in the percentage of Latinos holding general officer rank. In 2001, 2.5 percent of the 82,151 men and women who held general officer rank were Latinos, and 0.4 percent were Latinas. As of 2014, 4.5 percent of the 88,306 men and women holding general officer rank were Latinos, and 0.8 percent were Latinas. Therefore, both the number and the percentage of Latinos and Latinas holding general officer rank had increased (almost doubled), but the percentages remain far lower than the percentage of Latinos and Latinas in the military or in the larger population. Moreover, the ratio of Latinos to Latinas in 2001 was 5.94 to 1, and in 2014 it was almost exactly the same: 5.95 to 1.

WHAT'S NEXT FOR LATINOS IN THE POWER ELITE?

The growing number of Latinos, and the likely increase in the number of Latino college graduates, when coupled with the declining percentage of whites, suggests that there will be a higher percentage of Latinos in the power elite in the future. As Richard Alba, a leading expert on immigration points out, "There will be opportunities in the coming quarter century for the children of disadvantaged groups to move up without appearing to threaten the position of children of advantaged ones" (Alba, 2013, p. 165).

This might be the case especially among the political elite, and it may be the case in the military elite as well, because our research and that of others suggests that there are fewer barriers to advancement than in the business world (Moskos and Butler, 1996; and Zweigenhaft and Domhoff, 2006, pp. 118–121, 160–161, and 191–193). However, traditionally exclusionary barriers will continue to matter at the pinnacles of power in the business community, especially if the decline in affirmative action limits the number of Latinos who graduate from prestigious colleges and universities. If that proves to be the case, the elite-educated white males from the upper one-third of the socioeconomic class ladder who are in the power elite may prefer to help similarly elite-educated white women to advance, even more so in the future than at present. Nor are traditional affirmative action programs within corporations likely to be of any use because most of them do not work, and the few that have been shown to have any impact are used in less than 10–15 percent of corporations (Dobbin, Kim, and Kalev, 2011, 386–388 and 392; DiTomaso, 2013, p. xxi).

We have found that, consistent with the rise in white women as CEOs and the inadequacy of affirmative action programs within corporations, well-educated people of color, whatever their gender, are much more likely to be hired into entry-level management positions in the corporate world than they are to rise through the corporate hierarchy. Thus, the higher the position, the fewer the people of color. Still, gender comes into play as well, in an apparently exclusionary way, in terms of the advancement of people of color into higher-level positions. Despite the seeming openness to white women as high-level colleagues, this acceptance only rarely extends to black women and Latinas. Black women, for example, are more likely than black men to graduate from college and to earn MBAs, but black men are much more likely than black women to earn

$100,000 or more a year, or to hold the most senior corporate positions, including that of CEO (Zweigenhaft and Domhoff, 2014, 133–137). Moreover, as we noted earlier in this postscript, twenty Latinos have served as CEOs of *Fortune* 500 companies at one time or another since 1981, but there has yet to be a Latina CEO.

Class, education, and gender aside, skin color may be the characteristic that matters most of all for those Latinos who graduate from college and enter the corporate world. In addition to the fact that recent census data indicate that slightly more than one-third of Latinos now identify themselves as white, many studies show that colorism is pervasive in the Latino community as well as in the black and white communities, which may disadvantage darker-skinned Latinos even before they encounter a predominantly white (and Asian American) student body at the university level (see, for example, Chavez-Duenas, Adames, and Organista, 2014; Murguia and Forman, 2003; and Prado, 2012).

CONCLUSION: TWILIGHT OF DIVERSITY, A NEW DEMOGRAPHIC DAWNING, OR A LULL BEFORE THE STORM?

Much of what we have said in this postscript concerning the prospects for Latinos becoming a larger presence in the power elite applies to African Americans and Asian Americans as well, although Latinos are distinctive from the other two groups in that a significant percentage of them are indistinguishable from whites of European ancestry, especially if their parents and grandparents were from the upper socioeconomic levels in Cuba, Mexico, or South American countries.

However, as we have frequently learned to our chagrin, it is difficult to predict what combination of class, gender, education, and color will be ascendant at any given point for any specific previously excluded group. For example, we first thought that white males in the corporate world would prefer men of color to white women as colleagues, based upon the strong gender segregation on playgrounds, in teenage social groups, and in most occupations (Maccoby, 1998; Jacobs, 2003). Instead, as we have shown, there has been a much greater increase in the number of white women CEOs than men of color.

The trends that we have observed could signal the twilight of diversity, they could portend the last hurrah of an overwhelmingly white power elite, or they could antici-pate a lull before the storm if white elites reach lower into their talent pool to hang on to most top-level corporate positions. It is impossible to know which, if any, of these scenarios will occur for many reasons. It is, of course, generally impossible to predict the future, but, in this case, it is even more difficult because of the complex crosscur-rents created by the growing roadblocks to affirmative action, the increasing percentage of women graduating from universities and professional schools, and the pressures of a demographic transition to a more diversified American population. Perhaps the effects of these complex crosscurrents will be more apparent by the time you read this postscript.

REFERENCES

Alba, Richard. 2013. "Schools and the Diversity Transition." *Daedelus, the Journal of the American Academy of Arts and Sciences,* 142 (3), 155–69.

Alliance for Board Diversity. 2013. "Missing Pieces: Women and Minorities on *Fortune* 500 Boards—2012 Alliance for Board Diversity Census." Alliance for Board Diversity, August 15.

Chavez-Duenas, Nayeli Y., Hector Y. Adames, and Kurt C. Organista. 2014. "Skin-Color Prejudice and Within-Group Racial Discrimination: Historical and Current Impact on Latino/a Populations." *Hispanic Journal of Behavioral Sciences* 36 (1), 3–26. http://hjb.sage pub.com/content/early/2013/11/08/0739986313511306.

Daily Telegraph (London). 2010. "Midterms 2010: Tea Party 'Crown Prince' Marco Rubio Wins." November 3.

DiTomaso, Nancy. 2013. *The American Non-dilemma: Racial Inequality without Racism.* New York: Russell Sage.

Dobbin, Frank, Soohan Kim, and Alexandra Kalev. 2011. "You Can't Always Get What You Need: Organizational Determinants of Diversity Programs." *American Sociological Review* 76, 383–411.

Eilperin, Juliet. 2013. "Obama Cabinet Picks Add Diversity, but Still Frustrate White House Allies." *Washington Post,* March 4.

Jacobs, Emma. 2010. "20 Questions: Enrique Salem." *Financial Times,* April 15.

Jacobs, Jerry. 2003. "Detours on the Road to Equality: Women, Work, and Higher Education." *Contexts* 1 (2), 32–41.

Maccoby, Eleanor E. 1998. *The Two Sexes: Growing Up Apart, Coming Together.* Cambridge, MA: Harvard University Press.

Moskos, Charles C., and John Sibley Butler. *All That We Can Be: Black Leadership and Racial Integration the Army Way.* New York: Basic Books, 1966.

Murguia, Edward, and Tyrone Forman. 2003. "Shades of Whiteness: The Mexican American Experience in Relation to Anglos and Blacks." In *White Out: The Continuing Significance of Race,* edited by Ashley Doane and Eduardo Bonilla-Silva, 63–79. New York: Routledge.

Prado, S. R. 2012. "Colorism: The Relationship between Latino/a Self-Perceived Skin Color and Assimilation." Unpublished M.A. thesis, California State University at San Marcos, San Marcos, CA.

Yeomans, W. 2012. "How the Right Packed the Court." *The Nation,* October 8, 14–17.

Zweigenhaft, Richard L., and G. William Domhoff. 2006. *Diversity in the Power Elite: How It Happened, Why It Matters.* Lanham, MD: Rowman & Littlefield.

———. 2011. *The New CEOs: Women, African American, Latino, and Asian American Leaders of Fortune 500 Companies.* Lanham, MD: Rowman & Littlefield.

———. 2014. *The New CEOs: Women, African American, Latino, and Asian American Leaders of Fortune 500 Companies.* Paperback ed. with new introduction. Lanham, MD: Rowman & Littlefield.

PART 6

GENDER AND SEXUALITIES

In contemporary American society, most of us probably assume that we know what sex is. Do we? Back in 1998 the country was utterly riveted and significantly perplexed when then president William Jefferson Clinton emphatically declared, "I did not have sexual relations with that woman, Miss Lewinsky." In the revelations that emerged during the impeachment proceedings against the president, we learned that Monica Lewinsky did indeed engage in fellatio with the president, leaving undeniable genetic evidence on her dress. Was such behavior really sex? Most Americans agreed that it was not. In our times only intercourse counts as sex.

In chapter 17, "A History of Latina/o Sexualities," Ramón A. Gutiérrez explores the changing understandings and definitions of erotic activities over the course of several centuries, charting the evolution from notions of sin, honor, and respect to the invention of sex at the beginning of the nineteenth century. The invention of sex may seem counterintuitive. Haven't men and women, women and women, men and men been engaging in sex since the beginning of time? Of course they have. But such carnal relations were described with other nouns and were understood in more complicated ways. The actual word "sex" only entered the Latin American lexicon in the early 1800s. Before that there was a rich vocabulary that defined acts of self-pleasuring, moments of conjugation that could result in pregnancy, matings that produced considerable passion and pleasure but that were not always procreative. Since the founding of the Catholic Church, such acts had been known and defined mostly as transgressions and sins against the laws of God as interpreted by the Catholic Church.

Juxtaposed with the Church's value system was an equally antique culture of honor and respect that originated in the Mediterranean as an idiom for the competition over scarce resources. This alternative moral system of human behavior was secular in origin and equally complex, and it often conflicted with the meanings the Catholic Church ascribed to particular bodily acts. Rooted in the household economy and organized around patriarchal power and authority, this system also divided humans into males and females—bodies that were distinct, marked by different genitals that were believed to be the physiological basis of masculinity and femininity—and fashioned a set of ideals, normative expectations, and actual behaviors that were deemed intrinsic to men and women.

"Honor" was a word with two distinct but interrelated meanings: honor as social status (*honor*) and honor as virtue (*honra*). When communities assessed the social standing of their resident men, each head of household was judged as either having much honor, as having less honor, or, at the bottom of the social hierarchy, as having no honor. The latter were considered defamed, of ill repute, and thus infamous in the public world of men. Honor-status was a social judgment of a man's reputation achieved and maintained through brute force. Thus arose the legal maxim "death before dishonor," which still prevails as a military code in many places around the globe.

The honor-status of a patriarch was dependent on the honor-virtue, or the comportment (usually sexual) of the women and children under his control, who were prescribed a complex set of gender-based behavioral ideals and norms. Men possess honor-virtue as *honra* when they protect the shame (*vergüenza*), or sexual modesty, of their womenfolk, guarding the virginity of their unwed daughters and the marital fidelity of their wives while protecting their women against sexual assault and guarding their reputations as women of honor. A man's *honra* could also be simultaneously enhanced if he violated the integrity and reputation of women not his own. The conquest of Latin America's indigenous peoples is thus often described as the conquest of their women. The victorious Spanish conquistadors saw these females as the natural spoils of war, prizes that served as testaments to their virility. Indian men had been defeated, rendered effeminates in battle, and thus dishonored and defamed. It was out of these Janus-faced notions of masculine honor-virtue that Latin American *machismo*, or hypermasculinity, was born.

As Gutiérrez makes clear, both the Catholic Church and honor codes coexisted and persisted even after the invention of sex and the medicalization of identities in the second half of the nineteenth century. In part 6 we delve into the persistence of notions of honor and respect Latin American immigrants bring to the United States to understand their social status, their ideals of appropriate sexual comportment, and concern for their reputations. In chapter 18, "Gender Strategies, Settlement, and Transnational Life in the First Generation," Robert Courtney Smith introduces us to a group of Mexicans who migrated to New York City in the 1990s from their small Mixtec village of Ticuani in the Mexican state of Puebla. When they arrived in the United States they had a rather conservative set of ideas about the proper spaces men and women should inhabit and control, how men and women should relate to one another in public and private, and what was permissible and not in New York City. Transnational migration, the logic of work, and the range of obligations men and women had in their new habitat forced them to adapt, to change their ideas, and to become more pragmatic in defining gender ideals and their social reproduction, while nevertheless judging themselves and their peers by the standards of their *ranchero* ideals of honor and respect.

In Ticuani men were expected to impose their authority over their women and to have women acquiesce, even through force when necessary. Women passively accepted such domination, even if grudgingly. Men inhabited the public world of work and male sociality, while women controlled the private world of home, children, and domestic chores. When men reproduced their culture's gender ideals, they were deemed honorable and due respect, and it followed that their wives and daughters were judged *honradas*, because they properly displayed their *vergüenza*. In New York City, Ticuani men were limited by their skills to service sector jobs, which in Mexico were considered women's work. To exist and to advance economically, they creatively adapted their behavior, selectively choosing elements from Mexican and American models of masculinity and femininity to guide their daily comportment and to be judged worthy of honor and respect by their fellow compatriots, even in New York.

In Lorena García's essay in chapter 19, "Latina Girls and Sexual Identity: 'She's Old School Like That': Mother and Daughter Sex Talks," we move from New York to Chicago and to the conversations Mexican and Puerto Rican mothers have with their daughters when they discover that they have become sexually active. How do these adolescent women assert their subjectivity, negotiate their sexual pleasure, and navigate its dangers while maintaining their reputations as "good" respectable girls who do not act like licentious white girls?

Mexicans and Puerto Ricans left behind rural agrarian cultures but still carried with them conservative gender and sexual ideologies that were rigidly patriarchal, controlling women's bodies through violence, and expecting mothers to regulate the virginity of their daughters until marriage. If the honor and reputation of the family was to remain intact, mothers had to guard the *vergüenza* (sexual modesty) of their daughters, driving away and keeping at bay predatory males and females who had no real intention of marriage and stable family life.

Daughters were technically in the domestic domain that mothers controlled, and it was usually through surveillance that they discovered their daughters' sexual activity, quickly ascribing it to male trickery that left little possibility of female sexual agency. Mothers confronted the facts by imploring their daughters to respect themselves, emphasizing the riskiness of pregnancy and sexually transmitted diseases, and the importance of self-care. Daughters listened to their mothers' injunctions, to the stories of what had happened to them in their natal places when they were young. Daughters countered that they were no longer in Mexico or Puerto Rico and were negotiating their sexual lives through different power dynamics and transformed gender ideologies and norms that did not routinely privilege males and penalize females. "Old school" mothers thus struggled to explain the love affairs of their lesbian and heterosexual daughters, keeping them as discreet as possible, and most certainly keeping the facts from their husbands. What is particularly interesting about this essay, as we saw earlier in this volume in part 4 about work, are the caricatures Puerto Ricans and Mexicans living in Chicago had of one another regarding the sexual ethics of their daughters.

Tomás Almaguer's essay in chapter 20, "Longing and Same-Sex Desire among Mexican Men," explores the construction of homosexuality in present-day California. These men live in a world largely scripted by the same gender and sexual ideals prescribed for Latino heterosexual relationships. Masculinity is ascribed to the sexually insertive partner, or the *activo*, while the orally and anally receptive partner, the *pasivo*, is feminized by this posture. There is very little that is egalitarian about the way these sexual relationships are scripted and transacted. While some of these men are openly gay, others are bisexual men and only occasionally have sex with other men. Regardless of how they define their sexual identities, here too we see how the Spanish colonial idiom of male honor and female shame is inflected in both the homosexual world of Latino men and its heterosexual analogue. Through the sexual life histories of three men, Almaguer illustrates how masculinity and virility are valorized while simultaneously devaluing femininity, equating it with oral and anal receptive sexuality. The very terms that are used to describe these later acts reflect their association with effeminacy and "passivity": *puto, joto,* and *maricón.* These *pasivo* men, in turn, eroticize their sexual partner's masculinity: his musculature, height, ruggedness, chest, buttocks, and genitals. It is a world where idealizations of manhood, sexual potency, and size matter as they signal the power and dominance that ignites and scripts their same-sex desire. These hegemonic constructions of Mexican manhood do not subvert or even contest heteronormativity, rather they affirm and reinforce it.

17

A HISTORY OF LATINA/O SEXUALITIES

Ramón A. Gutiérrez

A history of Latina and Latino sexualities in the United States is not easy to write. The *Oxford English Dictionary* notes that the word "Latino" comes from the Spanish *latino-americano*, which means Latin American. Most of those who now call themselves Latinas or Latinos in the United States either migrated from one of Latin America's many nations or are descended from such immigrants and here putatively were transformed in some profound ways.[1] If we were simply dealing with one set of national values, ideals, and norms about sexuality coming into contact with another, that in itself would be terrain complex and difficult to map. What complicates the story are the immense social, cultural, and historical differences that developed in Latin America over time. The differential impact of Spanish colonialism on the hemisphere's indigenous peoples compounds the task, as does the massive importation of African slaves into the area; roughly 2 million between 1500 and 1821. (The total number of slaves imported to all the American colonies—British, French, Spanish, Portuguese—was 14 million, of which 10 million went to Brazil, with 2 million more going to British and French colonies.) Today Latin American nations have mostly erased this brutal history of oppression and extermination of indigenous and African peoples from their memories by proclaiming a history of *mestizaje*, a word that in the English language translates poorly as "miscegenation." The mythology of mestizaje cheerfully celebrates the extensive biological mixing that transpired in Latin America among Spaniards, Native Americans, and Africans, producing a hybrid race—a race of mestizos and mulattoes—through sometimes legal but most often illegal and violent conjugation.[2]

The Spanish conquistadores repeatedly said that they came to the Americas primarily to convert to Christianity the many pagans they encountered. But except for some of the Spanish crown's lofty but clearly delusional pronouncements on this point, conversion of the native peoples was quite a secondary goal. What really made the passions of the enterprising conquerors boil, what made them pant and slobber, what made them engage in death-defying feats, were gold and silver. When most of them failed to find such instant wealth, they turned to the next best thing: lordship over others and the accumulation of land.

The Spaniards who came to America were largely young and single men. From the start of the conquest, they exercised their sexual dominion over native women and men. The conquest of the Americas was a sexual conquest of Indian peoples. Indians were made objects both of desire and of derision, vessels that would reproduce a new people and that would provide the domestic labor to reproduce households, and ultimately, the profitability of a massive mercantile empire. The history of Latino and Latina sexuality thus necessarily begins with the conquest and proceeds by exploring the nexus among bodies, gender, and power. I draw most of my examples from colonial Mexico and Peru, which were the hubs of the Spanish Empire from 1500 to 1800, and from the experiences of *mexicanos* and *mexicanas* who set up residence in what became the United States or who in more recent times migrated there. Where the Mexican and Peruvian evidence is sketchy or incomplete, I draw on studies from other areas of Latin America, mainly from Argentina and Brazil. The general patterns of sexual ideology and behavior are really quite uniform across Latin America in colonial and early national times. As distinct nation-states were born in the hemisphere, different inflections were given to longer historical patterns of sexual ideology and behavior. At the end of this essay, I delve into these changes.

We moderns, living in the secularized, industrialized countries of the West, have very definite ideas about what we regard the "sexual" to be. Whether it be in defining the sexual and the asexual; what is heterosexual, homosexual, and bisexual; or pathologies that are thought of as having a sexual component, those categories come to us largely through the discourses of illness, crime, and depravity first articulated in late-nineteenth-century science. Today we deem the scientific ideas about sexuality to be "true" and "natural," or as the French philosopher Michel Foucault put it, "the truth of our being." Just how much we are still products of our historical moment is readily apparent on consulting the oldest known dictionary of the Spanish language, Sebastián de Covarrubias's 1611 *Tesoro de la lengua castellana o española*. The dictionary has no entry for the word *sexo* (sex) or *sexual* (sexual). Nor do these words appear in the 1732 *Diccionario de la lengua castellana*, prepared by the Spanish Royal Academy for King Philip V. *Sexo* first entered the Spanish language as a neologism in 1809, notes Joan Corminas in his *Diccionario crítico etimológico castellano e hispánico*. The etymology of *sexo* is the Latin *sexus*, which means "cut, divided," as into male and female organisms of the species. In colonial Spanish America, the very concepts that we now take for granted to describe the realm of the sexual simply did not exist then.[3]

Please do not misunderstand my point that the modern categories of the sexual did not come into existence until the end of the nineteenth century in Spanish America. My argument here is that the discourses that are used to define the body at any historical moment, to order the body into two genders, to articulate how, where, and for what end its parts could be used—be it for procreation, pleasure, or pain—are always the product of distinct warps in the distribution of power and are unique to specific historical moments. My goal here is to explore the dominant discourses that have been used in Latin America to describe the body as an erotic and reproductive site and to examine conflicting and contestatory discourses, particularly in moments of change.

DISCOURSES OF THE CATHOLIC CHURCH

For the inhabitants of Spanish America—natives, Africans, and Europeans—the religious discourses of the Roman Catholic Church, then Spain's official state religion, provided the basic categories for the regulation of the human body and its social life. These ideas were expressed by priests and theologians in biblical exegesis and juridical pronouncements, in rituals that marked every phase of the life cycle, in confessional manuals, and in guides for the administration of the sacraments. From this vantage point, the body was imagined dualistically as composed of spirit and substance, of soul and flesh. From the very moment of its conception, the body was endowed with an eternal soul that bore the stain of Original Sin, born of human sinfulness in the Garden of Eden. At the beginning of time, or so the book of Genesis explained, Eve, the first woman whom God created by taking a rib from Adam's side, ate of the forbidden fruit and thereby transgressed the commandment of God. As a result of this Original Sin, Eve and her husband, Adam, were expelled from Paradise and forced to endure privations of every sort, to feel hunger and cold, to experience shame over the nakedness of their bodies, and for women, to suffer great pain giving birth.

Daily in teaching from pulpits and in confessional boxes, clerics articulated the Church's vision of a properly ordered body politic, which was to be manifested through bodily behavior. To transform its ideology into action, the Church relied on penances imposed by its disciplinary agents: local priests, judges in ecclesiastical courts, officers of the Holy Office of the Inquisition. Through coercion and through fear, the Church imposed on physical bodies the social order envisaged in the Pater Noster, "on earth as it is in heaven."

Despite the Church's enormous power to impose its vision of a proper bodily regime, other models for the body politic constantly challenged, subverted, and threatened to undermine it. Among Spanish colonists there was a secular theory of power, power that did not derive from God but that emanated from physical mastery and sheer force. This discourse of the body had its own notion of a properly ordered polity, which likewise was writ large on the human body, proscribing its own ideals about the physical body, about procreation, and about its pleasures, desires, and pains. We know of these ideas and how they were displayed in behavior primarily through the repressive apparatus of the Church, through the workings of the Inquisition, and through the ruminations of clerics who often lambasted as pagan and sinful these alternative notions. As the power of religious discourses waned with the secularization of colonial society at the end of the eighteenth century, these secular ideas were increasingly embraced by state functionaries with the goal of subordinating the Catholic Church in society and undermining the authority of the clergy. The native peoples in the Americas whom the Spaniards called Indians had their own religious discourses about the place of the body in a harmonious cosmos, as well as ideas about the sources of chaos and destruction that could wreak havoc.

Since antique times the fathers of the Catholic Church had defined humans as constituted of body and soul. To engender a child, a man and woman united in intercourse, sharing physical substance, mixing semen and ovum. Once the child was conceived and born into the world, through the sacrament of Baptism a person was reborn into Christ, began a spiritual life, and had the stain of Original Sin cleansed from its soul. As Saint Thomas Aquinas noted in the *Summa Theologica*, when a priest christened a child, it was "born again a son of God as Father, and of the Church as mother."[4] According to the Church, this act of spiritual regeneration rivaled, if not surpassed, the act of physical generation itself.

The body, though base and vile, was but a transitory vessel for the eternal soul, whose spiritual journey to God was assured only through a virtuous life sanctified by the sacraments. Clerics maintained that because of the sinful quality of the flesh, the persons whom God most favored were prepubescent children and those who had completely forsaken the flesh and the vainglories of the world for a life of virginity and chastity. Mystical marriage to Christ and a union with God was the highest state of spiritual perfection to which one could aspire. The first marriage canon of the 1563 Council of Trent made this point clear: "Whoever shall affirm that the conjugal state is to be preferred to a life of virginity or celibacy, and that it is not better or more conducive to happiness to remain in virginity or celibacy than to be married, let them be excommunicated."[5]

Theologians viewed human marriage as a less desirable state that had only been elevated to a sacrament by Christ as a *remedium peccati*, a remedy for humanity's inherently sinful state. The function of marriage was primarily the reproduction of the species and only secondarily to provide for the peaceful containment of lust and desire. Most of the prescriptive literature produced by theologians and moral philosophers during Spain's colonial period thus did not focus squarely on what we now consider sexuality. The topic surfaced only tangentially as part of larger discussions of marriage as related to the Ten Commandments. "Thou shalt not commit adultery" and "Thou shalt not covet thy neighbor's wife," or glosses on these the sixth and ninth commandments, were the points at which extensive discussion of lust, conjugal intercourse, and physical desire most often appeared.

The Church maintained that marriage was the normative institution that assured the regeneration of the species, the peaceful continuation of society, and the orderly satisfaction of bodily desires. When couples channeled their sexual desires toward the explicit aim of procreation, they fulfilled God's natural design. The two most important objectives of marriage, explained Father Clemente de Ledesma in his 1695 *Confesionario del despertador de notícias de los Santos Sacramentos*, a confessional guide for the administration of the sacraments, were procreation and the satisfaction of the *débito conjugal*, the conjugal debt that required reciprocal service between husband and wife. Intercourse was imagined as a contractual exchange. Married couples could, so to speak, request a regular servicing of the debt by their partner and were duty bound to pay it. Intercourse could be withheld only if it was requested too frequently, during periods of illness or menstruation, or during religiously motivated temporary vows of chastity. Confessional manuals contained counsel for men to avoid excessive conjugal demands and injunctions for women to be charitable and understanding in giving what was requested of them.[6]

For clerics and theologians, the line between duty and sin was a very fine one. Couples were constantly advised not to be overwhelmed by lust, thereby losing control of their rational faculties. In his *Espejo de la perfecta casada* (1693), a manual for the Christian education of married women, Fray Alonso de Herrera cautioned that an excessive display of lust in marriage was tantamount to the sin of adultery. "Engaging one's wife like an animal, inflamed by the libidinous fire of desire, is a very grave sin," he warned.[7]

Churchmen often frenzied themselves with the minutiae of marriage, prescribing precisely where and in exactly what position the conjugal act should occur. "The natural manner for intercourse as far as position is concerned," advised the seventeenth-century Spanish theologian Tomás Sánchez in his *De sancto matrimonii sacramento* (1607), is for "the man [to] lie on top and the woman on her back beneath. Because this manner is the most appropriate for the effusion of the male seed, for its reception into the female vessel." Railing in condemnation about the *mulier supra virum* (woman atop man) coital position, Sánchez continued: "This method [of intercourse] is absolutely contrary to the order of nature. . . . It is natural for the man to act and for the woman to be passive; and if the man is beneath, he becomes submissive by the very fact of his position, and the woman being above is active." Sánchez added: "Who cannot see how much nature herself abhors this mutation? Because in scholastic history it is said that the cause of the flood was that women, carried away by madness, used men improperly, the latter being beneath and the former above." Needless to say, that a man might copulate with his spouse from behind, in *more canino* (the way of dogs), was clearly sinful and way beyond what could be tolerated among humans.[8]

Engaging in sex in places other than the conjugal bed also was frowned on by priests but apparently with only modest success. It was not uncommon for spouses and even for consorts to report that they had consummated their affections "in the woods," "by the river," or in some isolated natural setting. Since most couples lived with parents, other relatives, and children in close quarters, it was usually only outside, in nature, that lovemaking (*amores*) could escape the attentive eyes of others. Santa Fe, New Mexico, resident Juana Carrillo's 1712 admission that she had enjoyed the affections of a man while "out in the fields" during the spring planting aptly characterizes the type of spaces that proved to be expedient for such consummation.[9] Provided that churches, chapels, and shrines were not desecrated by such acts, priests had little ability to do much about it, though that did not keep them from constantly fulminating against it.

The "natural" function of marital intercourse was procreation. All sexual uses of the body's organs and orifices that did not have this as their ultimate goal were "unnatural" and punishable as violations of natural law, whatever one's marital state. Masturbation, or the sin of Onan (onanism), was said to pollute the body. In the parlance of the sixteenth and seventeenth centuries such self-pleasuring caused one a sinful pollution (*polución*). Masturbation was particularly evil for men because it wasted their seed in ways incapable of reproducing human life. From studies on the erotic behavior of nuns in convents and from Inquisition cases involving ordinary women we know that this solitary pleasure was not uncommon among women.[10]

Fray Bartolomé de Alva's 1634 *Confesionario mayor* urged confessors to interrogate women penitents about masturbation: "Did you repeatedly feel your body, thinking of a man, and wanting him to sin with you? Did you do it to yourself with your hands, bringing to a conclusion your lust?" While Alva did not urge confessors to ask their women penitents if they had used objects to reach a *polución*, other clerics did. Twenty-year-old Agustina Ruiz was interrogated by representatives of the Inquisition in Mexico in 1621 because of the autoerotic fantasies that constantly caused her pollutions whenever she looked at pictures of Jesus, the Virgin Mary, and a number of other saints in church. She would become so excited, she said, when Christ would expose his genitals to her that she would immediately pleasure herself right there in the sanctuary. Ruiz admitted that she frequently masturbated "more or less three times a day for the last nine years." She told the representatives of the Inquisition that from the age of eleven she had also carnally communicated with Jesus, Mary, and a number of saints in various positions, "with her underneath them, and from the side, and her on top of them, and also with her lying facing down while they conjoin themselves with both of her dishonest parts, both vaginally and anally."[11]

Sodomy (*sodomía*), which in colonial times was defined as anal copulation with a partner of either sex, was called the "abominable crime" (*abominable delito*) and the "nefarious sin against nature" (*pecado nefando contra natura*). Father Alva in 1634 again asked confessors to query not only male penitents, but females as well. "When your husband was drunk," Alva's manual asked, "did he have sex with you where you are a woman, or sometimes did he do the disgusting sin to you? Did you restrain him?" While sodomy between a man and a woman was deemed sinful, as Alva's confessional manual attests, it was primarily among members of the same sex that it provoked the most concern and punishment. Historian Mary Elizabeth Perry has argued that the revulsion over male same-sex sodomy was "not in ejaculating nonprocreatively, nor in the use of the anus, but in requiring a male to play the passive 'female' role and in violating the physical integrity of the male recipient body."[12]

Male same-sex sodomy is fairly well documented throughout colonial Spanish America. We know of its occurrence before the Conquest among indigenous men of the nobility, among priests and warriors, and among members of lower castes. During the colonial period male same-sex sodomy is copiously recorded in civil and ecclesiastical court cases between indigenous men, between Spaniards and African slaves, between Spaniards and Indians, between and among Spaniards of every class, and particularly among priests. From this documentation we know that there was a rather lively sodomitical subculture in monasteries, in the large cities of Mexico and Brazil, and undoubtedly in other places that we have still to learn about. These men had networks of erotic partners who regularly frequented certain parks, certain streets, certain taverns, knowing that they would surely find partners to partake of the nefarious vice. Often the status differences between partners were particularly marked, as when members of the nobility and of the clergy cavorted with their African and Indian male servants. But Spanish men of the same class mingled as well, mounting each other in the manner in which husbands bedded their wives. Indeed, judicial authorities were always particularly eager to know which person had played the *hombre* (male), or insertive, role in anal intercourse, and which the *mujer* (female), or receptive, role. Religious authorities in colonial Spanish America found it particularly repugnant that men were copulating as if they were husband and wife, using the anus as the feminine part. But sodomites, or *putos* (faggots) as they were then called, engaged in a great variety of other lascivious behaviors. The 1595 Inquisition case against André de Freitas Lessa documents such variety. Admitting that he had engaged in hundreds of acts of sodomy with male partners over the course of years, de Freitas Lessa said that he had "meetings of nefarious alternatives," "nefarious assaults from the back," "union of virile members from the front," "the spilling of seed between the legs," "*punhetas*" (*punho*: hand or self-masturbation in front of others), "pollution in the hands of others," "*coxetas*" (intercuripal sex, or rubbing the penis between a partner's legs), as well as phallic exposure. It seems likely that the only thing that kept de Freitas Lessa from engaging in oral copulation, what the Church called "viperous intercourse," were the low standards of bodily hygiene at the time.[13]

Both from confessional manuals and from litigation against women for sodomy, we know that women also shared intimacies with members of their own sex. Fray Bartolomé de Alva's confession manual instructed priests to question women about such behavior: "Were you responsible for dirty words with which you provoked and excited women? When you cohabited with some woman: did you show and reveal what was bad in front of those who had not yet seen the sin?"[14] From the 1598 case against Mariana de San Miguel, who was pursued by the Mexican Inquisition for heresy, claiming she had been personally illuminated by the Holy Spirit without clerical instruction, we learn that she too had religiously inspired erotic fantasies that frequently caused her pollutions. Mariana confessed that she and another *beata* (pious woman) would often meet and when they did, "ordinarily they kissed and hugged and put her hands on the breasts and . . . she came to pollution ten or twelve times, twice in the church." Similar erotic behaviors were reported among Mexico City's *beatas* in the colonial period in a number of other instances. These pious women wore clerical garb, lived cloistered lives, and refrained from public activities. And while no one to my knowledge has yet documented the erotic dimensions of the lives of nuns in colonial Spanish America, it would be naive to surmise that women's close, intimate friendships within the convent were always of a chaste sort.[15]

Sodomy, stated the 1585 *Tercero cathecismo y exposición de la doctrina Cristiana, por sermones*, was "for man to sin with man, or with woman not in the natural way, and even above all these, to sin with beasts, such as ewes, bitches, or mares, which is the greatest abomination." Incidents of bestiality, though infrequently reported, do occasionally appear in court cases. In 1801 José Antonio Rosas, an eighteen-year-old soldier stationed at Santa Barbara, California, was found guilty of mounting his mule for other than transportation. Both he and the mule were executed and publicly incinerated, the flames believed necessary to purify their wicked flesh. In a 1770s New Mexican case involving a young Indian boy from Isleta Pueblo and a cow, charges against the boy were dismissed because the lad had not yet reached the age of reason. He did not understand the gravity of his sin, the judge opined. Repeatedly the ecclesiastical judge queried the boy about whether the cow had been standing up or lying down. The boy, having never apparently understood the question the interpreter posed, failed to answer satisfactorily. Whether being in one position or the other would have spared the cow's life will never be known, as the court docket does not detail what happened to the beast.[16]

Both the prosecution and the punishment for sodomy varied considerably in colonial Spanish America by gender, by class, and by one's erotic posture in the act. Women were usually discovered in such nefarious deeds by accident, when they were accused of other profanations, such as heresy, as in the case cited above. It is hard to know whether such tales of erotic behaviors were introduced into testimony to win convictions, as a way of underscoring the severity of the sin committed and the depravity of the person involved. Few clerical women were accused of sodomy with other women, and many fewer were punished for the sin in any way. When a man shared his posterior part with another, there too the judicial outcome varied considerably by social class. Men of the nobility, landed aristocracy, and military, because of their status and connections, routinely made the accusations and concrete evidence against them disappear, particularly if they had sinned with their servants and subordinates, as so often was the case. So too was the case with priests. Ecclesiastical authorities preferred to keep their own sins hushed up and corrected by exile and simple penances, thus retaining intact the Church's rhetorical power to denounce society's sinfulness and to correct the popular classes without being seen as having a double standard.

The *Siete partidas*, the medieval legal code that ultimately became the law of Castile and of the Spanish colonies in the New World, prescribed that the "male," or insertive, partner in sodomy would be castrated and stoned to death. In the late fifteenth century, under the rule of King Ferdinand and Queen Isabella, the punishment was changed to burning. Who actually suffered this punishment? Men of the lower classes were the ones who most often endured the brunt of sodomy laws. Their bodies were whipped and tortured, publicly shamed and derided, and ultimately burned at the stake. From the perspective of the Catholic Church the integrity of the male who had played the receptive, or "female," role had been violated. This person was thus not guilty of sin. Indeed, he had been dishonored and used for the commission of a grievous sin. If the receptive partner had only allowed himself to be mounted once—say, while intoxicated, by a man of higher status and who was much stronger—such an individual was usually dispatched with a penance and the injunction never to so sin again. But when the evidence clearly existed, as it did in Mexico City and Puebla in 1657, when 123 men were discovered to be frequently engaging in sodomy—the receptive partners even sporting such nicknames as "La Estampa" (the Print), "La Morossa" (the Slow One), and "Las Rosas" (the Roses)—the Church had to confront the fact that this was habitual and deeply entrenched sin. It was punished fully according to the letter of the law.[17]

Perhaps because clerics considered women the weaker sex in need of male supervision, or perhaps because of their own sense of priestly modesty, cases of heterosexual sodomy seemed to have provoked less sustained anxiety, as is evident from the sketchy legal archives on the matter. Women appear to have routinely engaged in *amores secos*, as sodomy was sometimes called (literally "dry loves"; i.e., "dry" in comparison to "wet" vaginal sex), as a way of maintaining their virginity while still consenting to the sexual desires of their suitors and as a common form of birth control. Juana Rodríguez of Santa Fe, New Mexico, explained in 1705 that she had been coaxed and consented to amores secos with Calletano Fajardo because he had promised her marriage, saying that she would soon enough be his wife. Unfortunately for Rodríguez, Fajardo developed amnesia soon after their lovemaking. The onset of such a memory lapse was a common strategy men employed to avoid prosecution for such seductive acts. Since they had not deflowered a maiden, which was the actionable offense before the law, this strategy usually proved successful as a way for men to avoid punishment for their behavior.[18]

According to the sixth and ninth commandments, adultery and lust were the two sins that most threatened the social order based on marriage. Adultery violated the sexual exclusivity of the sacramental bond of matrimony, created the possibility of illegitimate children, occasioned the spread of disease, and potentially could disrupt the peaceful order of life. As for the unfettered expression of lust (*lujuría*; literally, luxury or excessive desire), the first bishop of Mexico, the Franciscan friar Juan de Zumárraga, railed in his 1543 catechism, *Doctrina breve muy provechosa*, that "nothing fouls or destroys the heart of men as much as the desires and fantasy of carnality." The Jesuit priest Fray Gabino Carta explicated the topic of lust thoroughly in his *Práctica de confessores: Práctica de administrar los sacramentos, en especial el de la penitancia* (1653), a manual for the administration of the sacrament of confession. He explained that lust was the most evil emotion because it occasioned such heinous mortal sins as fornication, adultery, incest, rape (*estupro*), abduction (*rapto*), sins against nature, and sacrilege. Carta defined fornication as any sexual act outside the sacrament of marriage. He differentiated rape from abduction—the former as forced intercourse, the latter a violation compounded by the victim's abduction. Having sex with a priest or nun or having sex in sacred places were but two of the sacrileges Carta had in mind when he cautioned against excessive desire.[19]

In addition to these base-level mortal sins stemming from lujuría, Carta articulated a second layer of mortal sins caused by taking morose delight (*delectación morosa*) in one's erotic fantasies. If a person lusted vicariously watching someone else in the coital act, if one fantasized about intercourse with a particular person while masturbating, or if one took pleasure recalling erotic dreams after awakening, yet another mortal sin was committed. In short, any activity that was eroticized outside the bonds of marriage, in either fact or fancy, motivated solely by the pursuit of pleasure, was sinful. Such behavior alienated the soul from God, lowered humans to the level of animals, and endangered one's personal salvation.

When Roman Catholic missionaries arrived in the Americas, they judged the sexual behavior of the indigenous peoples particularly sinful, heinous, and clearly of demonic design. The clergy always admitted baldly, at times almost gleefully, that they had been able to repress these Indian behaviors only by resorting to force, by whipping heathens to a pulp, by burning them at the stake, and by desecrating and destroying their sacred spaces. This was the sure way to extirpate the devil from the Indian body politic, or so opined the clerics of the day. Given that these stories were largely recorded by clerical quills in judicial dockets meant to regulate and punish, it is difficult to study the integrity of indigenous thought and practice regarding the relationship between the body politic and the physical body.[20]

For many of the native inhabitants of the Americas, human sexual intercourse was essential for the promotion of fertility. It assured the regeneration necessary for the continuation of life. Intercourse was deemed a symbol of cosmic harmony because it balanced all the masculine forces of the sky above with the feminine forces of the earth below. Thus were the erotic feats of the gods that had occurred at the beginning of time memorialized and celebrated. Gods that combined all masculine and feminine potentialities into one were particularly revered. In the natural world, intercourse was everywhere, from the regenerative activities of animals to the toponyms that local inhabitants gave the earth, names that translate as Clitoris Spring, Girl's Breast Point, and Buttocks-Vagina, for example. Among humans, few boundaries other than those against incest and age constrained erotic behavior and its forms. In religious ritual, the Indians sang of erotic feats and copulated openly to awaken the earth's fertility and to assure that the gods blessed them with fecundity and peace.[21]

The nexus that existed in the indigenous world between sexual intercourse and the sacred was repugnant to Catholic clerics, who had vowed themselves to lives of chastity. European descriptions of native sexual ideology and practice thus must be read with this bias in mind. There is little doubt that the Indians were really as frisky as they were described. The ribaldry of their "orgiastic" dances, the "lewdness" of their incorporation rituals that ended in intercourse, and the naturalness with which they regarded the body and its functions are all too well documented from various points of view to be dismissed as pure figments of clerical anxiety. But did the Indians live in a state of unbridled lust, as the friars constantly complained? I think not.

The goal of the Catholic missionaries was to lead the Indians to God. To keep them on that path, priests established a regime of bodily repression. They justified what they did by telling the readers of their letters, reports, and denunciations that the Indians lived in wicked debauchery in a society devoid of rules. Anthropologists attest that every society has rules governing sexual comportment, especially about such things as incest. Thus when we read the 1660 Inquisitorial denunciation by Fray Nicolás de Chavez, who stated that when Indians staged their dances they frolicked in intercourse "fathers with daughters, brothers with sisters, and mothers with sons," we must ask: What rhetorical end did such statements play in the contestation between Indians and Spaniards over the place and meaning of biological reproduction in a well-ordered society? Priests clearly believed that intercourse could only transpire within the bonds of marriage. By describing Indian behavior as wildly incestuous, priests thus gained authorization to repress native erotic activities as they deemed fit.[22]

Clerical anxiety over the "wretched" indigenous flesh had three principal foci. First, at contact most Indian groups did not wear clothing or only scantily covered their genitals. The missionaries were clearly quite disturbed by this. Asking one indigenous man why he went about naked, the man explained to the friar, "Because I was born naked." Vast amounts of energy were spent getting the Indians to wear clothes, in the hope that by so doing they would eventually develop a European and "civilized" sense of modesty and shame toward their bodies. Second was the prohibition of indigenous religious rituals, particularly those performed by women to vivify and awaken the earth's desire, that according to the missionaries were the work of the devil, characterized by lewdness, random promiscuity, and debauchery. Third, a well-ordered Christian society required chastity before marriage, fidelity within the nuptial state, and lifelong indissoluble monogamy. Indian men and women were forced to conform, men abandoning multiple wives, and if serially married, returning to their first.

THE SECULAR MODEL: THE POLITICS AND EROTICS OF POWER

The Spanish soldiers who conquered and colonized Spanish America were propelled by dreams of fame and fortune and rarely showed concern about the salvation of their souls except when they wrote their last wills and testaments. These were largely young and single Spanish men who measured their worth through military might and their honor or their social status through the spoils of war: gold, women, tribute, land, and slaves. In a society that had been fighting Moors for some seven centuries, pushing back the boundaries of Islam on the Iberian Peninsula since the year 711, by 1492 the habits of war were well entrenched.

Indian women became the alchemists who transformed labor into gold. Because of their reproductive capacities, the sexual violence of the conquistadores in short order produced illegitimate, mixed-blood children begotten only to labor and to serve. The Spanish conquest was a sexual conquest of Indian women. Through rape and rapine, through intimidation and humiliation, the Spanish soldiers subjugated native men and women, interpreting their ability to dominate others as a testament to their virility and prowess. From a reading of the clerical chronicles of the Conquest one gleans the horrors that marked the event. Fray Francisco Zamora swore before God that he had witnessed native men stabbed and knifed to death because the Spanish soldiers wanted to take their wives. "I know for certain that the soldiers have violated them [the Indian women] often along the roads," Zamora wrote. Fray José Manuel de Equía y Leronbe said that he had heard the conquistadores shouting, as they went off to their debaucheries: "Let us go to the pueblos to fornicate with Indian women. . . . Only with lascivious treatment are Indian women conquered."[23]

Whereas the clerics who toiled in the spiritual conquest of the Americas relied on the lexicon of sin and salvation to describe the process, the Spanish soldiers explained their conquests in the language of power and honor. As conquerors of the land, confirmed by royal writ, they became men of honor with all the rights and privileges of Iberia's aristocrats. Their honor had been won by acts of bravery, cunning, and brutality. Indeed, these abilities were those they needed to lord their status over others, seizing the best fruits of the land as their own, taking whatever they wanted. In public they were feared and revered for their power and might; in private it was much the same. They were masters over their domestic dominions, protecting the honor of their households and of their womenfolk, simultaneously guarding the *vergüenza* (shame) of their females from assault. The ideology of honor was contradictory in that familial protection went hand in hand with the affirmation of one's own prowess and virility, manifested by assaulting the integrity of others through violent acts. The loss of honor by one man was his adversary's gain, and so the pecking order of honor was established.

A woman's shame, intimately tied to her physical purity as a virgin, was a limited asset that could only be lost or tarnished, never restored. Since a woman's honor always reflected on that of her menfolk, women were usually under the vigilant care of fathers, husbands, brothers, and sons. Female seclusion varied significantly by class. Social ideals became norms only when material resources would allow it. In the households of the lower castes, and in households where men were not often in residence, it was always much more difficult to seclude women and, obviously, much more difficult to protect them, given the requisites of daily life. In such households it was much more difficult to fend off assaults on personal and familial honor and thus more common for women of the lower classes to be deemed *sin vergüenza* (shameless) and thus more subject to random assaults.

Men were honorable if they acted with *hombría* (manliness), which was believed to arise from basic physiology. The *miembro viril* (virile member) produced masculinity and hombría. Men were legally impotent without it. An emasculated man was *manso*, meaning meek, gentle, humble, lamblike. But manso also signified a castrated animal or person. Some Spanish men even equated penis size with virility and manliness. In 1606 Gaspar Reyes found himself sick and destitute. Hoping to secure charity from the local friars, he begged for food at their residence. A certain Fray Pedro took him in and fed him lavishly with a meal, which included even wine. Reyes recalled that when he was finished eating, the friar "stuck his hand into my pants, took my virile member and wiggled it . . . and said to me, yours is small, mine is bigger." The priest then took Reyes to his cell, where he tried to use his posterior for the nefarious sin. To be buggered was a symbolic sign of defeat equated with femininity; to bugger was an assertion of dominance and masculinity. It was thus not insignificant that it was a priest who was concerned about his penis size and actively tried to sodomize Reyes. Any man who did not assert his manhood and lived a life of abstinence and purity ran the risk of being labeled tame, assumed castrated, and thereby lacking the necessary appendage of honor. Femininity and shame in women were likewise believed to be located in the *partes vergonzozas* (shameful parts).[24]

In the initial years of Spanish America's settlement, before Spanish women arrived in significant numbers and before stable families had been formed, it was not uncommon for soldiers and settlers to rape Indian women and men with impunity. Most cases of rape were not reported, much less litigated, but when they were, the accused man usually maintained that what had transpired was an act of virility, of prowess, a simple assertion of his masculinity over a willing partner who had seduced him. For after all, as one group of soldiers in the conquest of Mexico asserted in 1601, indigenous people "have no vices other than lust."[25]

By the eighteenth century, rape in New Spain was a more openly discussed fact of life. The majority of reported rape victims in the 1700s were women under the age of nineteen who did not have a strongly knit family to protect them. Most were assaulted while home alone or while out and about on errands without a male chaperon. While women of the upper classes, of Spanish and mestizo origin, were less often victims than enslaved African and indigenous women, women of all races and status were raped. Single men between the ages of twenty and thirty who lived outside tightly integrated webs of kinship—itinerant merchants, muleteers, and seasonal day laborers—were most often accused of rape.[26]

Raping a woman was considered a repugnant, antisocial crime. Men found guilty of it, however, typically received rather insignificant punishment. Exile, public shaming in the stocks, being tied to the gibbet, and monetary compensation for the woman were the ways in which most cases were resolved by the courts. In extreme cases, corporal punishment with up to two hundred lashes did occur. Nonetheless, since a man enhanced his honor through displays of virility, the greater and more permanent dishonor belonged to the raped woman and to her kinsmen who had failed to protect her honor and physical integrity.

Female rape victims were the persons who suffered most from this crime socially. They were often publicly humiliated as loose, shameless women. Their families frequently blamed the victim for inciting the passions of strangers and kin. If the rape involved incest, the victims often were removed from their homes and placed in a house for wayward women by the authorities. It was believed that such removals would thwart a father's, brother's, or uncle's incestuous desires. In such cloistered institutions, "fallen" women were isolated from contact with their families and were all but forgotten for long periods of time—some for life.[27]

Rape pitted the erotic prerogatives of masculine honor against the Catholic Church's desire to regulate society by containing the expression of lust. Thus, when church officials were faced with a report of rape, their response focused primarily on the woman's dishonor, on minimizing the public damage that her reputation might suffer. Priests usually dealt with this sin by keeping the assault as secret as possible. Clerics feared that other young men, by hearing of it, might be emboldened to similar violence. The nature of the penances that the Church imposed on rapists illustrates clearly the fundamental conflicts between ecclesiastical theory and the ideal prerogatives of masculinity that were intrinsic to the honor code. In the eyes of the Church, only the rapist was a sinner. His penance usually amounted to prayers, corporal works of mercy, and some economic compensation for the loss of a woman's virginity and her shame, all of which were viewed as outward signs of contrition for the absolution of his sin. The raped woman was guilty of no sin. But according to the honor ideology, she and her family were the persons who remained defamed and dishonored until the assault was avenged. If the rapist prevailed in any blood feud that might result from the rape, his honor was enhanced by the sexual assault.

Enslaved Indian and African boys and men were also the victims of rape. But in the cultural lexicon of the Spanish colonists, such assaults were the prerogatives of conquest that had been practiced in Europe for many centuries and not deemed a crime, though most certainly a sin. Between men, such acts of violence were part of the physical rhetoric of humiliation by which conquered men were transformed symbolically into effeminates and dominated as "women." Raping defeated warriors was a supreme act of virility and prowess. Indeed, a whole class of defeated men known as *berdaches* existed in many indigenous societies in the Americas.[28]

European polemics on the meaning of the berdache in the Americas give us yet another instance where the lexicon of punishment that was part of war was radically at odds with that of sin. Since the times of the powerful city-states of Greece and the spread of Rome's empire, male rape was a fact of war, intended to show a defeated man that his status in the victor's world was that of an outsider, a foreigner, a slave, and worst, of a powerless and dependent woman. In medieval Islamic Spain there was an active commerce in young male slaves who were sold primarily to serve their masters as a "wife."

Indeed, the word berdache comes from the Arabic *bradaj,* meaning male prostitute. When the Spaniards arrived in the Americas, they found a host of men dressed as women, performing women's work, and offering receptive anal intercourse to powerful men in the communities in which they lived. From the ethnographic descriptions we know that these men had been captured in warfare and had their lives spared in order to serve and service their master's needs. When and where these berdaches were reported in the colonial period, they were always in the presence of men, carrying loads into battle, cooking their meals, and cooling their passions. Berdaches were found as temple adepts donning women's clothes, playing the feminine role, fellating and offering their posterior to powerful men in orgiastic rituals to the gods. In smaller towns and villages in which berdaches were observed, they offered hospitality to visiting dignitaries and were pimped out to young unmarried men who had not yet earned the right to consort with females.[29] Of course, all of these activities, in the eyes of clerics and theologians, were pure abomination, evidence that the Indians were addicted to the nefarious sin, to the sin against nature, sodomy. That such sinful behavior justified the Spanish conquest was clear enough. What was not was how extensively sodomy was practiced. And on this point there was considerable debate. Fray Bartotomé de Las Casas, the great defender of the Indians, found its existence marginal and insignificant, while his adversary Fray Gonzalo Fernández de Oviedo found it everywhere.

Spanish church and state officials believed that the only way in which social stability would be established in its colonies was by creating stable families. Today, we equate family (*familia*) with immediate kin and relatives. That which is within the family is intimate, within the private walls of the home, and excludes strangers. But if we focus carefully on the historical genealogy of the word *familia,* we find that in its antique meanings it was tied neither to kinship nor to a specific private space or house. Rather, what constituted family was the relationship of authority that one person exercised over another. Specifically, familia was imagined as the relationship of a master over his slaves and servants.

The etymological root of the Spanish *familia* is the Latin *familia.* Roman grammarians believed that the word entered Latin as a borrowing from the language of the neighboring Oscan tribe. In Oscan, *famel* means slave; the Latin for a slave is *famulus.* The second-century novelist Apuleius wrote that "fifteen slaves make a family, and fifteen prisoners make a jail." The Roman jurist Ulpian gave more precision to the term, explaining in the second century AD that "we are accustomed to call staffs of slaves families. . . . We call a family the several persons who by nature of law are placed under the authority of a single person." Family thus initially referred to the hierarchical authority relationship between people. This relationship could be based on kinship and marriage but was not limited to such situations. The family relationship is implicit in the definition of the word *pater* (father): the *paterfamilias* was the legal head of a familia, whereas a biological father was called the *genitor.* Only a man could exercise *patria potestas*—that is, the legal authority over anyone under his command—even if he himself was an unmarried man.[30]

Many of the antique meanings of familia persisted with some modifications into the seventeenth century in the Americas, undoubtedly because of the revival of Roman juridical thought in canon law and in the legal institutions of the fifteenth-century Iberian kingdoms. By the early 1600s, Sebastián de Covarrubias, in his dictionary *Tesoro de la lengua castellana o española* (1611), defined *familia* as "the people that a lord sustains within his house." Covarrubias concurred that familia was of Latin and Oscan etymology and explained that "while previously it had only meant a person's slaves," the word's contemporary meaning included "the lord and his wife, and the rest of the individuals under his command, such as children, servants, and slaves." Citing contemporary seventeenth-century usage, Covarrubias quoted the legal code known as the *Siete partidas*, which stipulated, "There is family when there are three persons governed by a lord." The 1732 *Diccionario de la lengua castellana* repeated Covarrubias's definition of familia almost verbatim.

By the seventeenth century, both in Spain and in Spanish America, familia was a jural unit based on authority relationships that were established primarily, though not exclusively, through marriage and procreation. Family was tied to a particular place, to a *casa* (house) in which the lord and his subordinates lived. The casa was a domestic realm, much as the public *real* was the king's domain. Family was thus synonymous with authority, lordship, and household.

Families were constructed through marriage, or the sacrament of matrimony, and it was through the institution of matrimony that the kings of Spain and the bishops of Spanish America hoped that the foundations of an orderly society would be built. While initially most of the Spanish men who came to the Americas did so alone, by the 1570s increasing numbers were bringing their wives. Men who were married in Spain but emigrated alone sometimes sent for their spouses after they were established. A significant number of these men also became bigamists, contracting marriages anew in Spanish America, denying that they had a wife elsewhere until clerical officials dug into the matter, usually spurred on by an abandoned wife. "Has anyone seen my husband?" these women would typically write to officials in the Americas. "His name is XYZ, a native of Andalucia, known by these nicknames, and so tall and so wide."[31] The majority of single Spanish men in the Americas were forced to turn to the local supply of women for their consorts, partners, and often for their legal brides.

Before the early 1800s, marriages were arranged by parents to advance the consolidation, protection, and expansion of familial wealth. Children could and did express their personal desires, but their opinions rarely were decisive in the selection of a mate. Starting at the Council of Elvira (ca. 300), the Catholic Church repeatedly tried to temper the power of patriarchs (paterfamilias) to expand and consolidate their wealth and cohesion by marrying off their children in calculating and economically advantageous ways. The Church opposed this practice by defining a whole set of impediments to matrimony based on concepts of incest, initially prohibiting marriage between persons related to the fourth degree of consanguinity (that is, three generations removed from the common ancestor). This prohibition was extended to the seventh degree of consanguinity at the Council of Rome in 1059. To understand how restrictive this incest law was, imagine a couple in each of six generations giving birth to two children. The consanguinity impediment to marriage eliminated 2,731 "blood" relatives of the same generation from choosing one another as mates. The intent of such consanguinity impediments was clear. As family solidarity increased, the Church tried to weaken its power by greatly expanding the consanguinity impediments or restrictions on sacramental matrimony.

The power that fathers exercised within the family over wife, children, and slaves was also a very complex and, at times, contradictory issue for the Church. The fourth commandment enjoins children to "honor thy father and mother," a scriptural injunction further elaborated in Saint Paul's Epistle to the Ephesians (5:22–6:9). Paul urges Christians to obey God as wives, children, and slaves obeyed the master of the house: "Wives, submit yourselves unto your own husbands, as unto the Lord. . . . Children, obey your parents in the Lord. . . . Servants, be obedient to them that are your masters . . . with fear and trembling . . . with good will doing service as to the Lord." According to Paul, the kingdom of heaven is governed by rules not unlike those that governed terrestrial kingdoms. But the Church also maintained a healthy skepticism about the untrammeled exercise of patriarchal power and through its theory of spiritual kinship consistently tried to limit its exercise. Biological parents were simply the earthly custodians and guardians of the children of God, or so argued clerics and theologians.

Arranged marriages remained the norm in Spanish America until the beginning of the nineteenth century, when romantic love became an equally compelling reason for choosing a particular individual as one's mate. Arranged marriages were often loveless matches, full of domestic discord, and routinely punctuated by adulterous liaisons. Married men who were unhappy often solved the problem by creating what in Spanish-speaking America is still known as the "casa grande" (big house), in which the legal wife and legitimate children lived, and the "casa chica" (small house), where the mistress and her illegitimate children resided. A form of legal separation known as "ecclesiastical divorce" was theoretically possible to dissolve particularly loveless but economically robust unions. Ecclesiastical divorces were granted only in extreme cases and then mostly to elites.[32]

Adultery was another instance where local honor codes and canon law set radically different parameters for comportment. The seduction of a woman, even if she was married, was a sign of a man's virility. A man's urge to dominate was deemed a natural impulse of the species. Adulterous women were considered shameless or sin vergüenza; their behavior shamed and dishonored their entire family. But adultery's greatest stigma fell on the cuckolded husband whose wife had not been restrained and kept from such dishonorable behavior. He had the right, still practiced in some honor-based societies to this day, of killing his wife, avenging her impurity, or sending her into exile to live the rest of her days shunned, alone, and without a husband or family to provide for her. In canon law adultery was viewed very differently. In such sinful acts both male and female were equally culpable, though it was usually only the woman who suffered its social consequences. Adulterous men were urged to return home and to make a *vida mariable* (marriageable life) with their spouse. If they continued in their philandering ways but were discreet, they could, and often did, escape the attention of the authorities. Women who desecrated the matrimonial bond were usually given penances and told to refrain from such sinful behavior in the future.

Illegitimate children were the biological byproducts of philandering husbands and of young unmarried men who exploitatively sowed their seed outside marriage. The logical result was that by the early 1700s, roughly half of New Spain's population had been born outside of wedlock, a percentage that was much higher among the offspring of Indians and African slaves. In the northern Mexican mining town of Charcas, the incidence of illegitimacy among mulattoes was 65 percent in the period 1635–39 and 75 percent in 1650–54. Between the sixteenth and eighteenth centuries, roughly similar levels of illegitimacy were the norm in Peru.[33]

How those who bore the stigma of illegitimacy were viewed and treated in society has long been a topic of debate in the historiography of colonial Spanish America. The extant evidence suggests that the stain of bad birth was not very important in the day-to-day behavior of face-to-face communities. Before the law, the case was very different. Illegitimate aspirants to educational opportunities and honorific posts were often significantly hampered because they lacked a known and honorable father of pure blood. Partly in response to the desires of such men and women for upward mobility, and largely to gather extra cash from the colonies, at the end of the eighteenth century the Spanish monarchy began selling writs of legitimacy and the cleansing of stained racial pasts known as *cédulas de gracias al sacar* (certificates of purity).[34]

These cédulas de gracias al sacar point to the fact that in the second half of the eighteenth century a whole series of social, political, and economic reforms were instituted by the crown to intensify its exploitation of the colonies and to maximize its profits therefrom. These reforms, collectively known as the Bourbon Reforms, were organized to streamline the colonial bureaucracy, heighten economic development, and subordinate the power of the Catholic Church, guilds, and hereditary groups. As part of the crown's attempt to secularize society, a whole range of activities that the Church had regulated through canon law, ecclesiastical courts, and its concept of sin gradually was replaced by civil law, secular courts, and concepts of property, degeneracy, and disease. For example, in 1700, because matrimony was a sacrament, all aspects regarding the formation of marriages were under the exclusive jurisdiction of the Church; by 1800 the state had intervened, separating out those issues related to contract and property (How had the marriage been contracted? How much dowry had been exchanged? What would be the disposition of dotal property that had been brought to a marriage?) and left issues related to the nature of the sacrament to the Church (Had it been entered into of free will? Was there any coercion involved in the promise of marriage? Were there any impediments to the sacramental state such as impotence or incest?).[35]

The tempo at which secularization occurred was particularly rapid around Indian missions. As one parish after another was taken from the control of religious orders and given to secular priests, the power the Church previously had used to dictate social behavior began to weaken and to be replaced by secular discourses of criminality, medicine, and disease. Many parishes were left without priests, and once such places were devoid of overt repression, indigenous and secular ideas and behaviors about the body and desire became increasingly important.

One gets an idea of how profound the Bourbon Reforms were in transforming personal life by examining the stated motives for marriage given in New Mexico between 1693 and 1840. When the friars asked men and women why they wished to marry, the most common responses recorded between 1693 and 1790 were religious and obligational. Individuals wanted "to serve God," "to save their souls," or to put themselves "in a state of grace." The first sign of any change in the reasons for desiring marriage appeared in a 1798 record. José García of Albuquerque averred that he wanted to marry María López "because of the growing desire [*voluntad*] that we mutually have for each other." Voluntad had previously appeared in marital investigations but only to mean volition, as in the determination that a person's free will was being exercised. María Durán gave voluntad this meaning when she proclaimed "I marry freely and spontaneously, neither counseled nor coerced, but totally of my own volition." By the end of the eighteenth century the responses, though likewise formulaic, had begun to change radically. Juan José Ramón Gallego, a resident of Jémez, wanted to marry Juana María because, he said, "I fell in love [*me enamore*]." While previously love and desire would not have been deemed acceptable justifications for seeking a marital partner, after the 1770s young men and women increasingly married for reasons of love, physical attraction, sexual passion, and personal and individual likes and dislikes. We also note a fundamental change in how the Spanish word for love (*amor*) was used. In Spanish America during the seventeenth and eighteenth centuries, the word love appeared mainly in two ways. First, it referred very broadly to Christian love and, secondly, to illicit sexual contact. Thus when men admitted to the ecclesiastical courts that they had seduced a woman or were living in adultery, they usually said that "I happened to make love to [*llegue a enamorar*]" a particular woman. After about 1800, such illicit acts were referred to as illicit friendship (*amistad ilicita*) or illicit coitus (*cópula ilicita*), and love took on meanings close to those we moderns give it today.[36]

SOCIAL TRANSFORMATIONS: THE INVENTION OF SEXUALITY

The Bourbon Reforms are often referred to as the second colonization of Spanish America, in that they led to the intensification of colonial exploitation, provoking the revolutionary movements for independence that swept the continent between 1807 and 1821. In this period all of Spain's colonial possessions in the Americas became independent save for Cuba and Puerto Rico. How independence may have transformed intimate personal lives is not well known or understood. The basic cultural transformation was that a colonial society that was hierarchically organized and viewed as holistic, in that everyone had a place in the body politic, came to be imagined as a society that was egalitarian and individualistic in organization. I use the word egalitarian here guardedly, because clearly to this day no former Spanish colony except Cuba has made any significant strides toward ending entrenched inequalities. What I mean here is that, at least before the law, the power of corporate groups—the Church, guilds, cattle breeders—evaporated and people came before the courts not as groups with privileges but as individuals. People began likewise to enter the marketplace to sell their labor and to profit, again, on the basis of their personal skills and as autonomous agents.[37] In my mind, the development of notions of personal autonomy and individualism were absolutely necessary for personal identities based on sexuality to emerge.

In the study of the Latina/o past, how sexuality was invented out of the set of former discourses about the body and its sinfulness is not yet entirely clear and needs further investigation. Nevertheless, I attempt to identify, if only in a cursory fashion, a number of areas where current research offers glimpses about the direction of changes wrought by modernity. As noted while discussing the transition from arranged marriages to those based on love, a new understanding of marriage emerged that saw it as an institution for the fulfillment of personal erotic desires and needs. If such motivations were recognized within marriage, one can only assume that similar sentiments pervaded the society more broadly, allowing for such expressions outside of marriage, be they through seduction, mutual desire, or even the purchase of commercialized sex. Sexual pleasure, while mostly documented among men in the colonial period, increasingly became an expectation among women as well, whether as a solitary activity, in the conjugal bed, in positions other than the missionary, and with the aid of instruments or toys of various sorts.

During the nineteenth century, largely as a result of the rise of export economies organized around commercial agriculture, large numbers of peasants migrated into central urban places, which often became the burgeoning hubs of industrialization. As extended households and broadly integrated kinship groups were disrupted and reformed in cities, their dimensions and domains of influence became smaller and more intense. The nuclear family increasingly dominated the social life of urbanites. Within the nuclear family women had more ability to exercise their free will. Whether patriarchal power continued to reign supreme, declined as women contested male power within and outside of the home, or intensified, we do not really yet know. Hypermasculinity, what is often called *machismo,* became a frequent symbol of the authority men exercised over women, children, and subordinates, though clearly this ability to lord it over others had a long and complex historical lineage.[38]

The power of the Catholic Church to influence behavior through its discourse of sin remained, albeit substantially weakened and no longer as hegemonic as it had been during the colonial period. Spanish America's modernizing states turned to European discourses of science, and particularly to medicine, to define the normative and the aberrant in society.[39] It was then that sexuality was born as a way of talking about bodily genital difference and about particular kinds of sexual behavior that imbued individuals with personal identities based on desire as heterosexuals and homosexuals.

The word for sex (sexo), as we saw, did not enter the Spanish language until 1809. Etymological dictionaries of the Spanish language affirm that the word *sexo* is taken from the Latin *seco*, which means "to cut or to divide," as into male and female organisms. The word sex became particularly capacious in its meanings; it denoted both a category of person (the male sex, the female sex) most readily understood as having a physiological basis in the genitals and an act (to have sex), which was believed to be an imperative of the genitals themselves. Gender ideals were tied naturally to the genitals, and how and with which genitals one got excited (different, same, both) gave rise to the behavioral identities of heterosexual and homosexual, much later to bisexual, always recognizing asexual and autosexual as alternatives realities. What was particularly new about the invention of "sexuality" in Spanish America was that it brought together a range of biological and mental possibilities—gender, bodily differences, reproductive capacity, needs, fantasies, and desires.[40]

How exactly sexuality was constructed in Latin America during the period from 1800 to 1880, we do not know. By this later date, largely from studies about how modern medicine defined social deviants in Mexico, Argentina, and Brazil, we have come to understand the extent of class anxieties about social mixing.[41] What these three countries had in common in 1880, aside from their rapid industrialization and booming export economies, was that the nation-state was being constructed and local and regional loyalties destroyed, as large numbers of migrants and immigrants flocked to Mexico City, to Buenos Aires, and to Rio de Janeiro seeking work and pleasure. It was through a new language of sex and gender that citizen-subjects were born. The nation needed strong men—active, virile, muscular, and masculine. It was out of discussions about the gendering of the fatherland (*patria*) that statesmen, politicians, and scientists debated about how the body politic would be writ on human bodies, which bodies were healthy and led to the nation's reproduction, and which were sickly and necessary to criminalize and correct.

Heterosexuals and their opposite, homosexuals, emerged out of these discussions, thus transforming the Church's and the state's older, exclusive focus on sinful and socially disruptive behaviors and giving rise to personal sexual identities. Who was normal or abnormal presupposed a sexual identity that was either heterosexual or homosexual. Homosexuals were inverts, were men and women who had made the wrong sex-object choice. The malady of the invert was that he (most of the literature is about men) was a sexually receptive, passive man and also one who did not and could not reproduce. In Spanish America, where the nationalist slogan at the time was "To govern is to populate," homosexuals were aberrant. They inverted the natural insertive and active role of men in sexual intercourse and instead were passive pederasts. Once this inversion occurred in terms of sexual desire, it was assumed that the dress, manners, and dispositions associated with the male sex were also inverted. Transvestism and prostitution were the logical results. Much of the discourse of sexual inversion borrowed the colonial Spanish American lexicon of male sodomy. The sexual postures that were coded as hombre and mujer were now conflated with *activo* (active or insertive) and *pasivo* (passive or receptive) positions of intercourse and thus associated with masculinity and femininity, respectively. In the largely male-dominated discourse of medicine, this inversion was imagined as something learned, or as a disease, a contagion that could weaken the body politic and lead to societal ruin.

By the 1600s there already existed, in the major urban centers of Latin America, a subculture among men who had sex with other men. At the end of the nineteenth century, that subculture became much more open and much more pronounced. The clinical gaze with which we read about it was particularly obvious at Carnival. Carnival, which marked the beginning of Lent, allowed men of every status and state to invert their social and sexual worlds, dressing as women if they wanted and taking it from behind. When the merriment ended, some men remained in their new roles and never looked back. The invert subculture of many cities was marked by drag shows, transvestite displays on the grand boulevards, and men sporting female names, and even speaking a feminine language of their own. Some of the inverts even formally took other men as their husbands. One Argentine physician in Buenos Aires in the early 1900s noted that "the marriage of sexual inverts is not a rare occurrence, to be sure, but this ceremony ordinarily happens only as an act of scandalous ostentation . . . with the conventional apparatus of a real wedding: *she* dressed in white, her head adorned with orange blossoms, he in tuxedo and white gloves."[42]

Eusebio Gómez, an Argentine criminologist who studied the habits of homosexuals in Buenos Aires and reported them in *La mala vida en Buenos Aires* (1908), transcribed verbatim a letter he had received from an invert named Mysotis: "I am like this because I was born like this. Anyway, this is the way I should behave because beauty has no sex. . . . I do not do anything extraordinary: I like men and for that reason I amuse myself with them. I treat them with exquisite *savoir faire*." Mysotis went on to describe the group of homosexual men he associated with and called it a *cofradía* (confraternity). Cofradias were technically religious associations of pious women and men under the supervision of the Catholic Church, but in this case clearly without ecclesiastical sanction.[43]

Much of the medical literature on inverts in Spanish America at the beginning of the twentieth century assumed that only the passive, receptive partner was a homosexual. The insertive, active partner was characterized as a seducer, who most certainly behaved against the laws of nature but was guilty only of pushing other men to invert their sexual object choice so that seducers could use them. Active, insertive men did not invert a male's correct sexual role; they were simply acting as men should. This argument was premised on the assumption that the invert had a natural predisposition to homosexuality that could be ignited by certain environments or contact with certain persons. Gymnasiums, swimming pools, segregated high schools, military barracks, seminaries, clubs all required special vigilance, criminologists of the time advised. For it was at such sites that innate tendencies, if given the slightest push, might flourish without limit. Of course, bear in mind that the etiology of homosexuality was debated endlessly not only at the beginning of the twentieth century but throughout the entire course of the century.[44]

Is homosexuality learned or innate behavior? Whatever the answer in 1900, the solution was identical: to root it out lest others learn it; to extirpate it lest its ugly head awaken latent dispositions. To this day, attitudes toward the social acceptance of homosexuality can be largely predicated on the basis of which side of this nurture/nature divide one finds most compelling. Survey research clearly shows that when most people believe that homosexuality is biologically innate, that one is born with this orientation, and that it cannot be changed or for that matter cannot be propagated and spread, social acceptance is common and with it often come beliefs that legal protections and full cultural citizenship for homosexuals are necessary and justified. When more people believe that homosexuality is learned, social responses to it are much more negative, precisely because of feelings that it can be taught by teachers in schools and by predators in the various spaces of exclusive male or female congregation. Such an understanding of homosexuality as nurtured contagion naturally requires its eradication, suppression, and criminalization.[45]

In looking at the history of Latina and Latino sexualities over the long view, what I have tried to show is how central the family was as an institution shaping colonial understandings of the ways physical desire and passion could and should be expressed in an orderly society. Clerical discourse on the sinfulness of bodily desire—in particular and on its most evil passion, lust—occupied countless pages of printed confessional guides and sermon manuals with one goal in mind: to create stable families. For this to occur clerics had to teach old and new Christians alike about the sanctity of the matrimonial vow, its dependence on marital monogamy, and premarital chastity and marital fidelity to ensure legitimate heirs to honor, fame, and property. The Spanish state endorsed or passively acquiesced in all of these church dictates until the middle of the eighteenth century, largely because it was the official patron of the Catholic Church in the Americas and by papal arrangement had defined Catholicism as the official state religion. But beginning with the Enlightenment in the early 1700s, with the rise of secular states, and with the subordination of religion to science, new discourses about the body emerged. Many of these secular discourses were rooted in older sources about the nature of power, which fit perfectly with expansionist colonial policies and the development of imperialism. Sex emerged as a discrete category in the Spanish language in 1809 out of the language of science, and it was from this language that personal identities based on sex were born.

This history of Latina/o sexualities would be much more robust, much richer in detail, more varied in geographic scope if scholars turned their attention to a number of topics. First and foremost, we know very little about African slave and ex-slave sexual ideology and comportment in the Americas. Colonial and contemporary theories of mestizaje presuppose a constant sexual mixing between dominant masters and female slaves and between persons of their own status. At the moment, these are all largely educated hunches rather than based on any sustained empirical research. The same can be said about the indigenous population of Latin America. What we know comes from a very limited perspective. Gay and lesbian scholars since the Gay Liberation movement of the 1970s in the United States have been interested in finding alternative systems of gender socialization for young girls and boys. This has led to a plethora of writing, most of it wrong-headed, on the berdache tradition, those indigenous biological males who played female roles in the aftermath of capture and enslavement. As a result, we have only a very limited understanding of indigenous sexual ideology and behavior written with a purple-colored pen. We know a great deal more about male sexual ideology, behavior, exceptions, and aberrations than we know about female, particularly when it comes to love and sex between and among women. More research is definitely needed here. Finally, our understanding of sexual identities, their genealogy, and their articulation during independence and in the period from 1800 to 1900 requires more investigation. These are some of the themes and periods that require the attention of students and scholars if we are to understand more completely the history of sexualities in Latin America and among Latinas and Latinos in the United States.

NOTES

1. Throughout this essay I use the term Latina/o, indicating both females and males. When specifically referring to males or to females exclusively, I make that gender distinction clear in the text.

2. José Vasconcelos, *The Cosmic Race: A Bilingual Edition* (Baltimore: Johns Hopkins University Press, 1979). Suzanne Bost, *Mulattas and Mestizas: Representing Mixed Identities in the Americas, 1850–2000* (Athens: University of Georgia Press, 2003). Marilyn Grace Miller, *Rise and Fall of the Cosmic Race: The Cult of Mestizaje in Latin America* (Austin: University of Texas Press, 2004). Herman Lee Bennett, *Africans in Colonial Mexico: Absolutism, Christianity, and Afro-Creole Consciousness, 1570–1640* (Bloomington: Indiana University Press, 2003). Sandra Gunning, Tera Hunter, and Michele Mitchell, *Dialogues of Dispersal: Gender, Sexuality, and African Diaspora* (Maiden, Mass.: Wiley-Blackwell Press, 2004).

3. Joan Corminas, *Diccionario crítico etimológico castellano e hispánico* (Madrid: Gredos, 1980), 7:235–236. Michel Foucault, *The History of Sexuality*, vol. 1: *An Introduction* (London: Vintage Press, 1979), 3.

4. Stephen Gudeman, "The Compadrazgo as a Reflection of the Natural and Spiritual Person," *Proceedings of the Royal Anthropological Institute of Great Britain and Ireland* (London: Royal Anthropological Institute of Great Britain and Ireland, 1971): 45–72, esp. 49.

5. Ramón A. Gutiérrez, *When Jesus Came, the Corn Mothers Went Away: Marriage, Sexuality, and Power in New Mexico, 1500–1846* (Stanford: Stanford University Press, 1991), esp. 242.

6. Clemente de Ledesma, *Confesionario del despertador de noticias de los Santos Sacramentos;* quotation on 336. Asunción Lavrin, ed., *Sexuality and Marriage in Colonial Latin America* (Lincoln: University of Nebraska Press, 1989), 72–80.

7. Alonso de Herrera, *Espejo de la perfecta casada* (Granada, Spain: Imp. por Andres de Santiago Palomino, 1636); quotation on 139–140.

8. Tomás Sánchez, *De sancto matrimonii sacramento* (Antwerp: Mart. Nutium, 1607); quotation on 37–38.

9. Gutiérrez, *When Jesus Came*, 215.

10. Judith Brown, *Immodest Acts: The Life of a Lesbian Nun in Renaissance Italy* (Oxford: Oxford University Press, 1986). Lee Penyak, "Criminal Sexuality in Central Mexico, 1750–1850" (Ph.D. diss., University of Connecticut, 1993), 290.

11. Bartolomé de Alva, *A Guide to Confession Large and Small in the Mexican Language (1634)* (Norman: University of Oklahoma Press, 1999); quotations on 105. Zeb Tortorici, "'Heran Todos Putos': Sodomitical Subcultures and Disordered Desire in Early Colonial Mexico," *Ethnohistory* 54 (2007): 35–67; quotations on 10, 1.

12. Alva, *Guide to Confession*, 105. Mary Elizabeth Perry, *Gender and Disorder in Early Modern Seville* (Princeton: Princeton University Press, 1990), 125.

13. Francisco Guerra, *The Pre-Columbian Mind: A Study into the Aberrant Nature of Sexual Drives, Drugs Affecting Behavior, and Attitude towards Life and Death, with a Survey of Psychotherapy in Pre-Columbian America* (London: Academic Press, 1971). Ramón Gutiérrez, "Must We Deracinate Indians to Find Gay Roots?" *Out/Look* 1 (1989): 61–67. Geoffrey Kimball, "Aztec Homosexuality: The Textual Evidence," *Journal of Homosexuality* 26 (1993): 7–24. Richard C. Trexler, *Sex and Conquest: Gendered Violence, Political Order, and the European Conquest of the Americas* (Ithaca, N.Y.: Cornell University Press, 1995). Pete Sigal, "The *Culoni*, the *Patlache*, and the Abominable Sin: Homosexuality in Early Colonial Nahua Society," *Hispanic American Historical Review* 85 (2005): 555–594. Sigal, *From Moon Goddesses to Virgins: The Colonization of Yucatecan Maya Sexual Desire* (Austin: University of Texas Press, 2000). Sigal, ed., *Infamous Desire: Male Homosexuality in Colonial Latin America* (Chicago: University of Chicago Press, 2003). Sigal, "The Politicization of Pederasty among Colonial Yucatecan Maya," *Journal of the History of Sexuality* 8 (1997): 1–24. Sigal, "Queer Nahuatl: Sahagún's Faggots and Sodomites, Lesbians and Hermaphrodites," *Ethnohistory* 54 (2007): 9–34. Tortorici, "'Heran Todos Putos.'" Geoffrey Spurling, "Under Investigation for the Abominable Sin: Damián de Morales Stands Accused of Attempting to Seduce Antón de Tierra de Congo," in *Colonial Lives: Documents on Latin American History, 1550–1850*, ed. Richard Boyer and Geoffrey Spurling (New York: Oxford University Press, 2000). Gutiérrez, *When Jesus Came*. Serge Gruzinski, "The Ashes of Desire: Homosexuality in Mid-Seventeenth-Century New Spain," in *Infamous Desire*, ed. Sigal. David Higgs, "Tales of Two Carmelites: Inquisitorial Narratives from Portugal and Brazil," in *Infamous Desire*, ed. Sigal. Luis Mott, "Crypto-Sodomites in Colonial Brazil," in *Infamous Desire*, ed. Sigal; De Freitas Lessa quotation on 188–189.

14. Alva, *Guide to Confession*, 105–109.

15. Mariana de San Miguel, quoted in Jacqueline Holler, "'More Sin Than the Queen of England'; Mariana de San Miguel before the Mexican Inquisition," in *Women in the Inquisition: Spain and the New World*, ed. Mary E. Giles (Baltimore: Johns Hopkins University

Press, 1999), 224. Nora Jaffary, *False Mystics: Deviant Orthodoxy in Colonial Mexico* (Lincoln: University of Nebraska Press, 2004).

16. *Tercero Cathecismo y Exposición de la Doctrina Cristiana* (1585); quotation on 81. Brian T. McCormack, "Conjugal Violence, Sex, Sin, and Murder in the Mission Communities of Alta California," *Journal of the History of Sexuality* 18 (2007), 26. Gutiérrez, *When Jesus Came.*

17. On punishments see Ward Stavig, "Political 'Abomination' and Private Reservation: The Nefarious Sin, Homosexuality, and Cultural Values in Colonial Peru," in *Infamous Desire,* ed. Sigal, 142–144; and Tortorici, "'Heran Todos Putos.'" Trexler, *Sex and Conquest.* Gruzinski, "Ashes of Desire."

18. Gutiérrez, *When Jesus Came,* 238. Albert L. Hurtado, *Intimate Frontiers: Sex, Gender, and Culture in Old California* (Albuquerque: University of New Mexico Press, 1999).

19. Juan de Zumárraga, *Doctrina breve muy provechosa* (1543), fol. h v. Gabino Carta, *Práctica de confessores: Práctica de administrar los sacramentos, en especial el de la penitancia* (1653).

20. Solange Alberro, ed., *La actividad del Santo Oficio de la Inquisición en la Nueva España, 1571–1700* (Mexico City: Instituto Nacional de Antropologia e Historia, 1982). Richard E. Greenleaf, *The Mexican Inquisition of the Sixteenth Century* (Albuquerque: University of New Mexico Press, 1969). Henry Kamen, *Inquisition and Society in Spain in the Sixteenth and Seventeenth Centuries* (Bloomington: Indiana University Press, 1985). "Notas sobre brujería y sexualidad y la Inquisición," in *Inquisición española: Mentalidad inquisitorial,* ed. Angel Alcalá (Barcelona: Ariel, 1984).

21. Serge Gruzinski, "Confesión, alianza y sexualidad entre los indios de Nueva España," in *El placer de pecar y el afán de normar,* ed. Seminario de Historia de Mentalidades (Mexico City: Editorial J. Mortiz, 1988). Guerra, *Pre-Columbian Mind.* Mariana Hidalgo, *La Vida Amoroso en el México Antiguo* (Mexico City: Editorial Diana, 1979). Alfredo López Austin, *Cuerpo humano e ideologia: Las concepciones de los antiguos nahuas,* 2 vols. (Mexico City: Universidad Nacional Autonoma de Mexico, Instituto de Investigaciones Antropologicas, 1980). María Isabel Morgan, *Sexualidad y sociedad en los Aztecas* (Toluca, Mex.: Mexico Universidad Autónoma del Estado de México, 1983). Noemí Quezada, *Amor y Magia Amorosa entre los Aztecas* (Mexico City: Universidad Nacional. Autónoma de México, 1975).

22. Nicolás de Chavez, quoted in Gutiérrez, *When Jesus Came,* 73.

23. Magnus Mörner, *Race Mixture in the History of Latin America* (Boston: Little, Brown, 1967). Karen Vieira Powers, *Women in the Crucible of Conquest: The Gendered Genesis of Spanish American Society, 1500–1600* (Albuquerque: University of New Mexico Press, 2005). Gutiérrez, *When Jesus Came*; quotation on 51.

24. Gutiérrez, *When Jesus Came,* 210.

25. Ibid., 51.

26. Carmen Castañeda, "La Memoria de las Niñas Violadas," *Encuentro* 2 (1984): 41–56. C. Castañeda, *Violacíon, estupro y sexualidad: Nueva Galicia, 1790–1821* (Guadalajara, Mex.: Editorial Hexagono, 1989). François Giraud, "Viol e société coloniale: Les Cas de la Nouvelle-Espangne au XVIII siècle," *Annales: Economies, Sociétés, Civilasations* 41 (1986): 625–637.

27. Josefina Muriel, *Los Recogimientos de Mujeres: Respuesta a una Problematica Social Novohispana* (Mexico City: Universidad Nacional Autónoma de México, Instituto de Investigacíones Históricas, 1974).

28. Will Roscoe, *The Zuni Man-Woman* (Albuquerque: University of New Mexico Press,

1991), and Roscoe, *Changing Ones: Third and Fourth Genders in Native North America* (New York: Palgrave Macmillan, 1998). Charles Callender and Lee Kochems, "The North American Berdache," *Current Anthropology* 24 (1983): 443–470. Gutiérrez, "Must We Deracinate Indians to Find Gay Roots?" Harriet Whitehead, "The Bow and the Burden Strap: A New Look at Institutionalized Homosexuality in Native North America," in *Sexual Meanings: The Cultural Construction of Gender and Sexuality*, ed. Sherry B. Ortner and Harriet Whitehead (Cambridge: Cambridge University Press, 1981). Walter Williams, *The Spirit and the Flesh: Sexual Diversity in American Indian Culture* (Boston: Beacon Press, 1986).

29. Sigal, "Politicization of Pederasty." Sigal, *From Moon Goddesses to Virgins.* Sigal, "Queer Nahuatl." Trexler, *Sex and Conquest.* Gutiérrez, "Must We Deracinate Indians to Find Gay Roots?" and Gutiérrez, "Warfare, Homosexuality, and Gender Status among American Indian Men in the Southwest," in *Long Before Stonewall*, ed. Tom Foster (New York: New York University Press, 2007).

30. David Herlihy, "Family," *American Historical Review* 96 (1991): 2–35.

31. Dolores Enciso, "Bígamos en el Siglo XVIII," in *Familia y Sexualidad en la Nueva España*, ed. Seminario de Historia de Mentalidades (Mexico City: Fondo de Cultura Económica, 1982). Richard E. Boyer, *Lives of Bigamists: Marriage, Family and Community in Colonial Mexico* (Albuquerque: University of New Mexico Press, 1995).

32. Silvia M. Arrom, *La Mujer Mexicana ante el Divorcio Ecclesiástico* (Mexico City: Secretaria de Educación Pública, Dirección General de Divulgación, 1976).

33. Marcelo Carmagnani, "Demografia y Sociedad: La Estructura Social de los Centros Mineros del Norte de México, 1600–1720," *Historia Mexicana* 21 (1972): 419–459. David J. Robinson, *Studies in Spanish American Population History* (Boulder, Colo.: Westview Press, 1981).

34. Ann Twinam, "Honor, Sexuality, and Illegitimacy in Colonial Spanish America," in *Sexuality and Marriage*, ed. Lavrin. Ann Twinam, *Public Lives, Private Secrets: Gender, Honor, Sexuality and Illegitimacy in Colonial Spanish America* (Stanford: Stanford University Press, 1999).

35. Silvia M. Arrom, "Cambios en la Condición Juridical de la Mujer Mexicana en el Siglo XIX," in *Memoria del Congreso de Historia del Derecho Mexicano* (Mexico City: Universidad Nacional Autonoma de Mexico, Instituto de Investigaciones Juridicas, 1981). Arrom, *La Mujer Mexicana.* Silvia M. Arrom, *The Women of Mexico City, 1790–1858* (Stanford: Stanford University Press, 1985).

36. Gutiérrez, *When Jesus Came*, 328–329.

37. Louis Dumont, *From Mandeville to Marx: The Genesis and Triumph of Economic Ideology* (Chicago: University of Chicago Press, 1977).

38. *Familia y Sexualidad en la Nueva España*, ed. Seminario de Historia de Mentalidades. Matthew C. Gutmann, *The Meanings of Macho: Being a Man in Mexico City* (Berkeley: University of California Press, 1996). Carrillo, *The Night Is Young.*

39. Christine Hunefeldt, *Liberalism in the Bedroom: Quarreling Spouses in Nineteenth-Century Lima* (University Park: Pennsylvania State University Press, 2000).

40. Jeffrey Weeks, *Sexuality* (London: Ellis Horwood Ltd. and Tavistock Publications, 1986), 12–16.

41. Robert Buffington, *Criminal and Citizen in Modern Mexico* (Lincoln: University of

Nebraska Press, 2000). Pablo Piccato, *City of Suspects: Crime in Mexico City, 1900–1931* (Durham: Duke University Press, 2001). Robert McKee Irwin, Edward McCaughan, and Michelle Rocío Nasser, eds., *The Famous 41: Sexuality and Social Control in Mexico, 1901* (New York: Palgrave Macmillan, 2003). James Naylor Green, *Beyond Carnival: Male Homosexuality in Twentieth-Century Brazil* (Chicago: University of Chicago Press, 1999). Jorge Salessi, *Médicos Maleantes y Maricas: Hygiene, Criminología en la Construcción de la Nación Argentina* (Rosario, Argentina: Beatriz Viterbo Editora, 1995).

42. Jorge Salessi, "The Argentine Dissemination of Homosexuality, 1890–1914," in *¿Entiendes? Queer Readings, Hispanic Writings,* ed. Emilie L. Bergmann and Paul Julian Smith (Durham: Duke University Press, 1995), 75. Green, *Beyond Carnival.*

43. Gómez, quoted in Salessi, "Argentine Dissemination of Homosexuality," 80.

44. Piccato, *City of Suspects.* Buffington, *Criminal and Citizen in Modern Mexico.* Robert McKee Irwin, *Mexican Masculinities* (Minneapolis: University of Minnesota Press, 2003).

45. Simon Le Vay, *Queer Science: The Use and Abuse of Research into Homosexuality* (Cambridge: MJT Press, 1996), 1–12.

18

GENDER STRATEGIES, SETTLEMENT, AND TRANSNATIONAL LIFE IN THE FIRST GENERATION

Robert Courtney Smith

I am not the only woman; there are a lot . . . [who] always go out alone. I don't
have a husband!

—DOÑA TALIA, speaking of her resentment about all the time her husband, Don
Gerardo, spends away from his family, including time working for the Committee

Yes, at times it bothered me. But at the same time, I said, it is good that my
husband worries about the pueblo, right?

—DOÑA SELENA, speaking proudly of how she and her family bore the sacrifice of
the absence of her husband, Don Emiliano, due to his work for the Committee

These women's diametrically opposed understandings of their husbands' absence while doing Committee work or other public work beg for explanation. Why would Doña Talia and her family come to resent Don Gerardo's absence so intensely, and to see it as a macho self-indulgence, while Doña Selena and her family regard Don Emiliano's absence as necessary for his public service, as a sacrifice accruing honor to him and to them as well?[1] My explanation lies in evolving differences in how the two men and their families think about what the sociologist Arlie Hochschild calls "gender ideology"—what people think men's and women's roles should be—and their "gender strategies" or "gender practices"—how they act on those beliefs.[2] Don Gerardo has hewed tightly to a more traditional gender ideology, eschewing household labor, treating the children as his wife's responsibility, and never involving the family in his public work or his returns to Ticuani. In contrast, Don Emiliano has adopted a more egalitarian gender ideology consistent with the views his wife and children have developed, including a more equal division of labor in the household, involvement of his children in his Committee work, and family trips back to Ticuani. These deeply differing attitudes have yielded very different family lives. The conferring or withholding of honor reflects a judgment by the families on the gender bargains adopted by each man.

Understanding the meaning of the men's absence gives us insight into the domestic consequences of Ticuani transnational political life. While the Committee imagines itself present in Ticuani politics despite its physical absence, its members are frequently absent from home: collecting funds for Ticuani public works projects places a heavy burden on them and their families. For several months or even years during a project, Committee members may spend all their weekends collecting funds, meaning that they almost never spend an entire day with their families. Whether families view this absence as positive or negative in turn affects the meaning they give to transnational life and assimilation.

Migration, assimilation, and transnational life challenge dominant forms of relations between men and women and ways of thinking about gender. The sociologists Pierrette Hondagneu-Sotelo and Jacqueline Hagan have shown that in migrating to and working in the United States, women challenge patriarchal constraints, including the unequal division of household labor, and try to renegotiate them.[3] The anthropologist Matthew Gutmann has shown that Mexican men's understanding of manhood has evolved as more men take care of children and do other "women's" work in Mexico. Contemporary Mexican men see themselves as *ni macho ni mandilón* (neither macho nor apron-wearing),[4] and instead try to differentiate themselves from these conflicting images of hyper- or compromised masculinity. The anthropologists Gail Mummert and Jennifer Hirsch have described how younger Mexican women, especially in migrant families, prefer "companionate marriages" (relationships emphasizing egalitarian companionship) to the "marriages of respect" (requiring deference to male authority) of their mothers' generation.[5] Under very different conditions from those considered by these other scholars, I show how Emiliano's and Gerardo's ideas about men's gender roles and the ways they negotiate deals with their partners affect the meaning of transnational life and assimilation for them and their families in New York.

THE MEANING OF ABSENCE

Don Emiliano and Don Gerardo offer what social scientists call a "paired comparison": because their stories run parallel much of the time but then diverge, we can assay the causes of this divergence. Both men have worked hard and steadily in Ticuani public life for more than thirty years in New York. Both describe their central identity as Ticuanense, and both are well known for their public service. Both men have worked extensively with the Committee, and Don Gerardo has also worked with other Mexican civic groups. Both have worked in restaurants in New York, where their late hours interfered with their ability to spend time with their families but paid good wages that supported a middle-class lifestyle. Both men drank heavily for years, a habit their families identified as a problem. Whereas Don Emiliano came to share this view and stopped, Don Gerardo dismissed it and still drinks heavily on weekends. Similarly, Don Emiliano changed what I call his "ranchero masculinity" during his thirty years in New York, while Don Gerardo has embraced it more strongly there.[6]

Drawing on the pioneering work of the sociologist Robert Connell, I define ranchero masculinity as one hegemonic configuration of gender practices that legitimize men's dominant and women's subordinate position:[7] in this view, men exercise authority, and women obey them. Men sometimes use physical violence to enforce their will; they must be fearless, and even violent, in the face of threats by other men; they are expected to do physically demanding work; and they drink alcohol, especially during religious feasts, as an essential dimension of male friendship. Public space and work belong to men, while private space and domestic work belong to women. By this logic, the wives and children of both Don Gerardo and Don Emiliano were not supposed to attend public events, even a picnic, while the men were collecting for the Committee, though trips to certain "female" public spaces, such as the library or the grocery store, were seen as acceptable because necessary.[8] (Many immigrant men nevertheless feel threatened in public spaces both because of potential conflict with other Mexicans or ethnic groups and because of possible exposure to U.S. immigration authorities.)[9] Ironically, it was the more progressive Don Emiliano who returned to Mexico.

An alternative image of masculinity is that of the modern migrant, who retains elements of ranchero masculinity but pragmatically adapts to the new context where his partner must also work, where the state interferes with ranchero prerogatives such as using violence, and where the man then defends such changes in a revised gender ideology. Men who live this alternative masculinity, such as Don Emiliano, participate in an ongoing critique of traditional ranchero masculinity; men who embrace the more macho image, such as Don Gerardo, engage in an ongoing defense of it.

Just as Don Emiliano and Don Gerardo had to renegotiate their notions of masculinity when they came to New York, Doña Talia and Doña Selena had to renegotiate their notions of femininity, engaging with at least four models of migrant womanhood. The first is the hegemonic Ticuani image of the ranchera, a woman who defers to her husband in all things and never shows anger toward him. She focuses her life on child rearing and domestic tasks, depends almost entirely on her husband for economic support, and spends her life in "female" spaces (that is, at home, unless engaged in domestic duties like shopping or caring for children). A ranchera never expresses what the Mexican anthropologist Federico Besserer's informants referred to as "inappropriate sentiments":[10] that is, any lack of respect for men, displayed through anger or disagreement. To express such ideas shows a lack of *vergüenza*, or shame, a primary female virtue. The second model is that of the Ticuani migrant woman who seeks to peacefully accommodate her husband's renegotiation of ranchero masculinity while both adopt new roles. Typically, she works outside the home and takes the lead in dealing with some American institutions, such as schools, while he does some housework and other "women's work." Third, there is the *pionera*, an older Ticuani woman, usually widowed or divorced (or perhaps never married), who lives independently in New York, either raising a family or living alone. The final model is the New York woman, an Americanized vision of independent womanhood who works, supports herself, and does not really need a man but would be prepared to marry one who shares her egalitarian vision. This model, however, resonates more strongly with the second generation than with the first.

Masculinity and femininity are relational concepts that acquire meaning mainly in relation to each other and in relation to other versions of themselves. Don Emiliano and Doña Selena seem to have created a more companionate marriage for themselves, emphasizing the couple's emotional intimacy and friendship while retaining elements of a "respect" marriage. In contrast, Don Gerardo wants a marriage of respect, and Doña Talia wants a companionate marriage.[11] A marriage of respect resonates with ranchero masculinity and ranchera femininity in emphasizing the man's power and honor, the woman's deference and modesty, and the separation of men and women in social space.

Vergüenza, a central element in Mexican female morality, merits more exploration. It is a quality that a woman is said to possess: *ella tiene vergüenza* (she has shame). Its fundamental feature, according to Jack Katz, is "the incapacity for action and a confession to self of moral incompetence in some regard."[12] Shame is clearly distinguished from mere embarrassment, the display of which frames error or other moral failure as situational, and hence not reflective of one's true self. I would argue that in ranchera femininity *vergüenza* is in particular the inability to respond (or at least the willingness *not* to respond) to male anger, the male gaze, or other exercises of male power. Hence, honor requires a woman to feel shame for being female in the presence of males. The ontological basis of ranchera femininity is to defer to men and to lack moral autonomy and competence in relation to men. Rancheras derive honor only from the approval of men. To exhibit sentiments such as anger toward men is to behave shamefully because one has challenged male authority; a woman who has appropriate shame would not be able to respond. For this reason, *vergüenza* fits hand in glove with the emphasis on male privilege and authority in marriages of respect.

These various notions of masculinity and femininity challenge the dominant images of a "crisis of masculinity" and "liberating femininity" in migration research.[13] In this view, men want to return to Mexico, or at least imagine they will return (a phenomenon that the sociologist Luin Goldring beautifully describes as "gendered memory"), because they lose status and power in the United States, whereas women want to stay because they gain authority and establish deeper roots. Powerless migrant men assert largely symbolic power over women to compensate for the loss of their ranchero masculinity.[14]

Among Ticuanense migrants, however, these conditions do not necessarily hold. Although women do more of the work of settlement, such as taking children to the doctor, men also participate. Moreover, men have created institutions, such as the Committee, that give them real power and status. Many men make good money in New York, send children to college, and even buy houses. Hence, they can live successful middle-class lives in New York. Their wives also gain pride and status from being married to men whose sacrifices are recognized by the community and from their own opportunities for service and honor, afforded by their husbands' work.

Moreover, the crisis-of-masculinity view presumes ranchero masculinity to persist in an unchanging, hegemonic form. But what happens when this masculinity must be legitimized—and can therefore be challenged—in the context of competing masculinities and femininities that derive from changes in Mexican society, from migration, and from American society? Such changes affect the relations men and women have with their work, with each other, and with institutions and power. By exploring the ambiguities in such relations, and the evolution of gender bargains and ideologies, I examine the dynamic and constructed character of gender in migrants' lives. In mathematical terms, my analysis attempts to move beyond discerning a reciprocal relationship, in which more American freedom means less traditional patriarchal oppression, to frame the changes as a set of simultaneous equations: things are changing both in Mexico and in the United States, and these changes are related.

This point can be clarified by contrasting my scheme with the images driving other analyses, even in quite insightful work. For example, in describing how first-generation migrant men and women negotiate their relations with their children, the sociologists Min Zhou and Carl Bankston use the metaphor of "straddling the gap," Alejandro Portes and Ruben Rumbaut use that of a "race," and Nazli Kibria adopts that of walking a "family tightrope."[15] All these metaphors portray migrants as attempting to balance the demands of the cultures of the traditional home country and the modern United States. They hope their children will succeed by retaining the virtues of the old culture before they are derailed by American culture. These metaphors do describe much of the reality and the perceived experience of immigrant parents, and I employ them in what follows. But I also focus on how gender roles are being simultaneously renegotiated in Mexico; how both Mexican and American cultures support various and internally inconsistent images of masculinity, femininity, and family life; and how these meanings have simultaneous referents in New York and Ticuani. I thus avoid, in the main, the assumption of a unitary home- or host-society culture.

One insight offered by my approach is that neither first-generation women nor second-generation men or women always prefer American culture, especially when male gender privilege is involved. For example, first-generation women often identify more closely with some aspects of Mexican culture, which they feel values the family more than the American culture that facilitates (or requires) their working outside the home. Similarly, many second-generation men who might be expected to reject Mexican culture as too much like their parents' actually embrace it because it offers them gender privileges that they feel American culture denies them. Moreover, there are larger gaps between generations, and between men and women, on such gendered issues as domestic violence than on such issues as education and upward mobility.

I offer three caveats before beginning. First, although I emphasize the dynamic nature of gender identities and analyze their performance, I stop short of the queer theorist Judith Butler's position that these identities are mainly performative and always in flux, defying categorization and stability. While Butler's position is an important corrective to the antiquated notion of fixed gender roles à la Talcott Parsons in the mid-twentieth century, I see gender identities as being performed in particular institutional and structural contexts that people (here, migrants and their children) help to create and that provide them with greater stability and offer a large, but not infinite, set of possibilities for recombination. To use a molecular metaphor, recombination of these gender ideologies, practices, and identities creates more stable rather than less stable elements, though with significant potential to recombine further.

Second, the images of masculinity and femininity outlined above all presume heterosexuality. There is little public acknowledgment of homosexuality among Ticuanenses in either Ticuani or New York. Moreover, in all my years of research I cannot recall even one reference to any Ticuanenses being lesbians.[16] Two men were said to be gay. The first was Bandolo, who was the frequent subject of jokes between men. Typically, someone would be teased about being "good friends" or "boyfriends" with Bandolo, or told that Bandolo really missed him while he was in New York. In fact, I heard about Bandolo by being teased in precisely this way, but I learned to turn the tables on anyone who seemed headed that way. For example, a Ticuanense man I did not know, who was friends with Committee members I knew, asked if I knew Bandolo, and from others' responses I knew he was trying to set me up for a joke. I told him that I did not know Bandolo, but that he should not worry, I would not steal his boyfriend. This joke was met with incredulous laughter from those who did not know me and knowing laughter from those who did. "¡El gringo te chingó!" (The gringo nailed you!) the men laughed. That I knew about Bandolo, and knew how to turn the encounter, made me, situationally at least, a fellow Ticuanense sharing in this affirmation of ranchero heterosexuality.

Another case was Yonny, who returned to live in Ticuani and run his family store after two decades in New York. Yonny was commonly called a *maricón* (faggot) behind his back but was addressed with respect in person. He participated in community affairs for the town and could be counted on for donations for projects. His status as a store owner and competent man who fulfilled his public responsibilities meant that his status as a homosexual (an identity I never heard discussed by him or in his presence) was eclipsed by his status as a competent man. I have seen similar eclipsing of homosexual status in indigenous communities, where effeminate migrant men who work hard in community service are treated with respect. When such a man's homosexuality is discussed in his absence, he is referred to as a *maricón* (or, sometimes, "homosexual") but a good man who helps in all the projects: that is, he is okay.

Finally, Don Gerardo's ranchero and Don Emiliano's mixed modern-ranchero gender strategies are not the only ones by which Committee members sought to balance their public work and home life. A third strategy—exit from public life—merits brief mention here. One of the Committee's former officers ended up leaving the Committee because it impinged too much on his family obligations. His wife complained about what she saw as excessive absences from family life—all week for work, then most of the weekend for the Committee. His exit from the Committee was a performance of gender and honor. He had told his friends on the Committee privately that he wanted to resign because it was disrupting his family life and his wife was angry. But he did not want to admit this before the whole Committee. To do so would imply that he was not ranchero enough to put his wife in her place and that he had violated the Committee's communal ethic by putting his individual interests first.

The situation was complicated by the ambiguity about which code of masculinity should be used to interpret his withdrawal. I heard comments that his wife "governed" him, that he was not man enough to continue sacrificing for the pueblo, as well as sympathetic assessments of the difficulty of balancing Committee work and family life; and others admitted they also sometimes wanted to withdraw. The Committee was adamant that he must resign in person. One said: "It doesn't matter [what his reasons are for resigning]. Whatever pretext, he has to come and present himself here to resign in front of us." Thus, the Committee denied him an easy exit; they did, however, decide to accept his resignation without subjecting him to a long and potentially shaming discussion. When he finally announced his resignation, he gave vague and mixed reasons including his work obligations as well as his family, thus invoking an external demand consistent with his ranchero masculinity. His reasons were accepted without question, he was thanked warmly for his service, and toasts were made. He and the Committee had negotiated his exit with his masculine honor intact.

UN AUSENTE NUNCA PRESENTE:
AN ABSENT ONE NEVER PRESENT

Don Gerardo's wife, Talia, and their children greatly resent his extensive involvement in Ticuani public work. Outside his job he is always working on Mexican civic events, the Committee, or sports leagues. Talia lamented her husband's absence and the lack of time he spends with their children.[17]

> Right now [a Saturday], he went to soccer. . . . I am not the only woman; there are a lot . . . [who] always go out alone. I don't have a husband! . . . This is why I always go out alone, you see, in the park when there are parties, because he does not like parties. . . . My husband does not say, Let's go, we are going to see the soccer match, I will bring the kids, no. He brings his friends . . . and for this I say, Now, on Sunday, you should bring them wherever it would be, to the park, to the library, to a museum, but no. . . . He always is doing things with the Committee or drinking or playing. . . . And we fight over this; I say to him, Look, you are always busy with your soccer.
>
> But my kids he never brings to see soccer. . . . In this moment we have a week of not talking to each other, we are mad at him. . . . It's not so much because he is not there with them, but we are fighting because he has his friends, his buddies . . . and because

he never gets to know my children. You ask them, see, when he has ever brought them to a park, or when he has brought them even to hang out on the corner—never, not the big one or the littlest one, not anyone. . . . But he believes that the money is everything. "I work like a donkey! I do this, that." I say, "No, the money is not everything! You have to know your children!" I am the one who does what you don't know, . . . to go to the school, to the meetings; I have to bring them to the doctor, to the ophthalmologist, . . . to the dentist, . . . to everything! Why?! . . . They interviewed him for the newspaper [workplace newsletter], and . . . he told them, "On my vacation I like to be with my kids," and I said to him, "You are a liar." (Spanish, translated by the author)

These impassioned words depict someone whose domestic life is far from what she wants for herself and her children. More than most migrant couples I know, Don Gerardo and Talia live in separate, gendered spheres. He spends little social time with his family and is always occupied by Mexican male public life. Talia remarks that he never even brings the children "to hang out on the corner." Given the association of "the street" with drinking and trouble, this comment implies that his interest in his children is so weak that he does not even help raise them badly! Ironically, despite his ranchero masculinity and his repeated demands, Talia and her children ignore the sanction against public socializing without the father and go to parties without him. Talia's comments indicate that she has largely rejected ranchera femininity as a model for her own life. She is clearly furious at her husband for refusing to adapt his masculinity to their new surroundings. It is significant that she openly tells him so and shares her feelings with me, a male friend of her husband who is involved with Ticuani public life.

Don Gerardo's absence from his family takes a high toll on family relations. The children are so angry at the father that they urge their mother to leave him, asking what good he brings them. Later in the interview, Talia observes that Mexican women are more long-suffering than Puerto Rican women, who readily leave their partners (she refers to one Puerto Rican friend who has had five husbands), then contrasts her stance with her second-generation daughter's open advocacy of leaving:

My aunt, she says, "You can be screwed in life [chingada], but there you are, see?" Because you have to think about your kids. Another man could abuse your kids. You have to put up with a bit, up to a certain limit. No one is obliged to live their whole life tied up, but you see that with my countrymen almost never is there a divorce. You have to put up with this until the end. . . . Now, the new generation is different. Because my daughter says to me, "Mami, why is my father so bad and always not here? Leave him!" But it is not that easy. . . . What crazy man would want me with four kids? (Spanish, translated by the author)

Talia is enacting more than one image of femininity. On the one hand, she feels bound by the requirement of ranchera or Ticuani migrant femininity that a woman stay with her husband even when unhappy. On the other, by rejecting some of her husband's demands—for example, that she enforce his will and not let their daughter date—she seems to be adopting a *pionera* or New York woman position. Then again, by hiding her actions from her husband and staying with him at all, she acknowledges his economic power and seems to act like a traditional Ticuani migrant woman. She later tells me she could not afford the house without his income, which is roughly three times hers. Her only imagined way to escape—to look for another man—is inconsistent with her values and is in any case, she says, hopeless. She is "screwed" but will endure her situation for the sake of the children. Talia's alienation from Don Gerardo extends to her colluding with their daughter to evade his assertion of masculine authority. For example, when he forbade their daughter from having a boyfriend, Talia allowed her to see him and then covered for her when Don Gerardo inquired about the daughter's activities. Talia believes that the children prefer the boyfriend to their father because the boyfriend spends time with them and gives them rides. She also believes, moreover, that Don Gerardo knows it and forbade his daughter from seeing the boyfriend partly out of jealousy.

Talia's public expressions of anger at her husband and her defiance of his proscription on going out in public show that she has rejected the ranchero concept of *vergüenza*. Moreover, she has clearly expressed "inappropriate sentiments" without compunction. In rejecting the ranchera role, she can also reject *vergüenza*. By responding angrily to Don Gerardo's treatment, she has asserted a morally competent feminine self independent of her male partner. She clearly lacks ranchera shame, but her renegotiated moral self feels no shame at this. (That both her male and female relatives support her actions suggests that women have more latitude in gender behavior than is supposed by many scholars of migration.)

Talia continued her criticisms by noting that Don Gerardo returns to Mexico regularly but never takes the family.

> He goes [to Mexico] every two years . . . but he does not bring the kids. Because they do not want to go . . . with him, no. . . . I want them to know Mexico because of the people—my husband's mother is very old, and she always faults my husband. . . . "Why don't you bring the children?" And he says he does not bring them because there are animals there and the kids don't eat. . . . But I think that he does not want to bother himself. . . . And they also say: "If my mom goes, I go. If my mom does not go, I don't go." (Spanish, translated by the author)

In Talia's view, Gerardo uses the argument that the children won't eat in Mexico, or might be bitten by scorpions, as an excuse for not taking them. Ticuani has not served for this family, as it has for many, as an important site for second-generation adolescent rituals, such as the Antorcha, the dances, or the procession, which can sometimes bridge the generation gap. In 1998, when this interview was done, the oldest child was nineteen and had never returned to Mexico. Moreover, the words of Talia and her family suggest no benefit to them from Don Gerardo's years of public work in New York and Ticuani. For them, the hours spent away from the family are all just time lost; they believe he simply does not want to spend time with them.

Don Gerardo's role as a provider is one of only two things about him for which Talia has kind words. She qualifies her harsh assessment, seeming even to defend him, or pity him as the victim of a vice he cannot control, when she explains his absence as the result of an alcohol problem and acknowledges that he has progressed at his job and provided well: "He has twenty-five years at his job. . . . He entered as a busboy . . . now he is in charge of a floor. . . . He has a good job there, [but] he goes bad because of the drink. I see him as an alcoholic before anything else; I believe this because he does not stop it, and this is bad" (Spanish, translated by the author). Also to his credit, she says, Gerardo "knows better" than to hit her, unlike some Mexican men.

Overall, Don Gerardo refuses to renegotiate the basic terms of the gender bargain, even in a context where the gender ideologies and bargains of the rest of the family are dramatically different from his. Talia's economic dependence on Don Gerardo, and her expressed belief that one can be "screwed in life" but must endure one's situation, helps preserve the relationship but compromises the quality of their family life. The father has fundamentally different expectations from the rest of the family about their collective life. In this context, it is clear why Don Gerardo's work for Ticuani public life is resented rather than revered as bringing honor to the family; they do not really consider him part of their family.

I was surprised by how openly Talia spoke to me and project researcher Sandra Lara and by the children's vigorous nods of agreement as she complained about Don Gerardo. I had thought such sentiments would be guarded as family secrets, but the material quoted above came out spontaneously, not in response to my questions. Perhaps Talia felt comfortable speaking because she too had known me for years as a friend of Ticuani, or because another woman was there. At any rate, it was clear these were not secrets but open family problems. It was also clear that Don Gerardo's gender ideology and strategy have been rejected by his family. His ranchero masculinity and his separation of home life and public life are among the most pronounced I have seen, approximating the imagined past of fully segregated private and public spaces for women and men in Ticuani. His wife and children clearly want a different gender bargain. Talia, at least, wants him to spend more time with her and the children, in Mexico and in the United States, and to do more domestic work. But Don Gerardo criticizes these positions as too "American," too far from Mexican ways, part of the reason why Mexican youth is going astray in America. The result is an unhappy and conflictive home wherein his public service is seen as a selfish indulgence and abandonment, not a noble sacrifice for the pueblo.

Talia, for her part, steers a course that takes her through various terrains of femininity. Her secret and open disobedience of her husband bumps her out of the ranchera category, but her choice to stay with him despite her unhappiness means she cannot be a pure *pionera* or New York woman. She demands that her husband spend more time with "her" children, to no avail. She also lives a life organized very much as a ranchera life would be: she spends her time mainly with her children and other adult women—though she does not restrict herself to feminine space, as her husband wishes. She is a grudging Ticuani migrant woman who, under different economic circumstances, might become a *pionera*.

UN AUSENTE QUIEN CUMPLA:
AN ABSENT ONE WHO KEEPS HIS PROMISES

The harsh meanings ascribed to Don Gerardo's absence contrast markedly with the terms of honor and sacrifice Don Emiliano's family use to describe his public work. While both his wife, Doña Selena, and their children lamented his frequent absences, they came to see them as sacrifices for the pueblo that enhanced his and their own dedication to and status in the community. Don Emiliano's evolution away from a pure ranchero masculinity, his greater involvement in raising his daughters, and their greater involvement with Ticuani resulted in the attribution of very positive meanings to his public work. Moreover, his renegotiation of masculinity involved a renegotiation of the couple's gender bargain and hence of Doña Selena's femininity as well. His greater flexibility made this possible. The end result was a modern migrant masculinity that retains elements of ranchero masculinity but in a form that was adapted to the United States context and not seen as compromising his overall masculinity.

I conducted an interview with Don Emiliano, Doña Selena, and their daughter Mia. The conversational dynamics were interesting.

ROBERT C. SMITH: *(To Doña Selena)* I wanted to ask you a question about . . . how you managed all this. Because Don Emiliano went out a lot knocking on doors, right? . . . What it was like when Don Emiliano went out so much for so many years? . . .

DOÑA SELENA: Yes, at times it bothered me. But at the same time, I said, it is good that my husband worries about the pueblo, right? With all the men who would make a plan and be concerned for the pueblo, because the pueblo had needs, for various things, Robert. So then I said, I hope that the people here in this country will support them, because all the people here have the opportunity to make a weekly wage. I believed that the people will not withhold their cooperation, no? And to do those public works. . . . There were times when it would bother me, no?—Oh God! But to this I grew accustomed. And I did not know if the people would thank them or not. . . .

DON EMILIANO: I could not think, Robert, only of my marriage or of my wife, no? . . . All of the wives . . . of my fellow Committee members,

it was the same reaction. . . . The weekends were the time that
we dedicated to go out, and sometimes we could not offer to
our wives the chance to go out and drink a cup of coffee. . . .
(Spanish, translated by the author)

Doña Selena offers a rationale for Don Emiliano's absence that Talia never advances
to excuse Don Gerardo. This contrast underlines how fundamentally different are the
gender bargains in the two families. The same behavior by Don Emiliano and Don
Gerardo assumes very different meanings. The two men also place differing constructions on the extra burden their absence imposes on their wives. While Don Gerardo
sees this burden as part of his wife's womanly duties, one she should accept without
complaint, Don Emiliano explicitly recognizes his wife's and his family's sacrifice and
acknowledges the extra work his absence has created.

In Don Emiliano's absence, not only did his family miss him, but they were prevented from attending social events without him. Unlike Doña Talia, who defies Don
Gerardo and goes out in public without him, Doña Selena and her daughters did not
attend public events unescorted, especially not Mexican events, though they could do
household errands, such as shopping or going to the library. While the use of public
space in Mexico has never been as absolutely gendered as migrants remember—women
and children do occupy the streets in Ticuani during school hours, for example—Doña
Selena took this prohibition seriously. In observing it, she was enacting a strong version
of a Ticuani migrant woman who can work to earn the money needed to live in New
York but who sees the value of maintaining some elements of traditional (remembered
or imagined) ranchero and ranchera roles. Thus Doña Selena displays a deference to
her husband appropriate to a ranchera. Although she admits that his absence bothered
her, she makes this response subordinate to the honor accruing to her husband, and
by extension to herself and her family, for his sacrifice to the pueblo. Her moral competence as a ranchera is upheld in this relationship with her husband. Despite their
daughters' desires to go to the park without their father, this Ticuani immigrant mother
enforced her version of femininity as well as her husband's masculinity.

DOÑA SELENA: This is how it was. . . . For example, if my husband was not
there, I did not go out. I was very accustomed to that if he went
out, I went with him.

SANDRA LARA: So then, the weekends when he was out, you would stay in the
house?

DON EMILIANO: Yes.

DS: In the house with my children . . . looking at movies. . . .

SL: And what did you say to your children?

DS: Well, we are not going out, now we are going to stay home.
Yes, then my children said to me: We have homework, well, we

are going to the library, and there we would spend the afternoon, we would go eat out, close by, . . . but to another place
like that we would not go.

RCS: And did they not complain?

DS: No, they did not protest, my children.

RCS: Really?

MIA: *(The daughter)* We used to get mad, too, that they would not
bring us to the park. Our only fun on Saturday and Sunday was
Prospect Park, to play volleyball with all our friends. . . .

RCS: *(To Mia)* And you guys did not go . . . ?

M: No, we did not go out of the house, [until] let's say, I think,
until Victoria was twenty, twenty-two years old. . . .

DS: Never, never did they walk around on their own, that's the real
truth. . . .

RCS: *(To Mia)* So then the sacrifice was from the whole family. And
did you understand that it was to make the pueblo better? Or
did you only get mad because you could not go out?

M: The real truth is at the beginning [we asked]: Why so much collecting? Why so much collecting? And I believe that at the end
I came to understand we made lots of things possible, as my
father says, when we saw the water, you know, with the
pipeline! Because before when we came back [to Ticuani], oh
no! . . . it was a traumatic experience for me because I had
become accustomed to bathe at any hour, and I came down
here, and it's—You have to bathe between this hour and this
hour. . . . And when I came back later and . . . there was a lot of
water, then I understood the effort my father had put out, and
Don Manuel, and all the Committee. (Spanish, translated by
the author)

During the period being discussed these young women were in their mid teens and
early twenties, an age at which most American parents let their children go out or travel
alone, and even live away at college. Don Emiliano's stance reflects the same kind of
ranchero attitude toward adolescence and freedom as Don Gerardo's. Both men forbade
their daughters to date until they were in their twenties. But the families' responses
were again different. Doña Talia colluded with the daughter to neutralize Don Gerardo's
authority and evade the limits he attempted to place on her because the family saw
him as having forfeited, by his absence, his right to control their activities. In contrast,
Doña Selena shared Don Emiliano's view and enforced it because he shared in carrying
family responsibilities and hence was entitled to wield authority. Their daughters inter-

nalized this conservative stance, joking proudly that others saw them as old-fashioned (*anticuada*).

In an interview without their parents a year later, two of Don Emiliano's daughters gave a less tolerant view of their father's absences but still rooted their understanding of it in sacrifice and service. Mia said:

> We used to get really mad. . . . But I guess that's why he's such a respected man. It was a sacrifice for the pueblo, but we didn't get it then. . . . We used to say: Why are you doing it? We're never gonna go back. You don't even have a house! There's no water. . . . But when I came back I saw changes. They were building the school—*that* explains why my father was out all weekend. It made me proud.

This quote shows anger and incomprehension yielding to an awareness of the larger meaning of their father's efforts. When they saw the new school being built, or the water coming out of the new pipes, they understood that through this work their father had become somebody in the Ticuani community. Their pride in their father's standing reflects their close relationship with him and redeems the sacrifice imposed on them by his being always busy with Committee work.

Another reason Don Emiliano came to be honored for his service while Don Gerardo was resented was what Don Emiliano describes as an "evolution" in his gender ideology, starting with his difficulty in wearing an apron while working in a New York restaurant:

> It did not worry me what they said in the pueblo, that Emiliano is frying eggs in New York and is doing the work of a woman. For us, the villagers [*pueblerinos*], to work in the kitchen is like having your pants pulled down, right? . . . The first time I put the apron on . . . I felt really bad . . . because here [in Ticuani] I worked like a man, leading an ox team, working with material. . . . From here I went and they gave me the white [cook's] uniform, and I could not put the apron on. . . . I felt humiliated, getting screwed where I came to be the one giving it. . . . I could not put the apron on the first time. And I felt that I looked like my pants had fallen down. And after that I changed my ideas and evolved. . . . I said, No, I am here to make dollars. I don't care that my hands are getting burned frying eggs, making soup, because here comes my check! [laughter]. . . . [They called me] henpecked [*mandilón*], but you know when I reacted? At the end of the week when they paid me. There is where I changed my mind: "Thanks to God, I now have seventy dollars in my first week of work!"
>
> To work in the kitchen, from here was my rotation in life, right? Because I felt ashamed that people from my pueblo knew that I was washing dishes or glasses or sweeping and mopping the floor. . . . I want to say that machismo or ignorance still applies in these pueblos, in the countryside. Yes. After that I evolved in my mentality, I said that . . . I will learn to be a really good cook, [or] at least a good enough one, right? (Spanish, translated by the author)

Don Emiliano used his desire to earn money and the need to provide for his family— also virtues in ranchero masculinity—to rationalize his crossing the line dividing men's and women's work. Earning money in amounts impossible for a peasant in Puebla enabled him to defend his gender identity against both the "machismo and ignorance" of the "villagers" and his own shame.

Unlike Don Gerardo, Don Emiliano was also active in raising his children. He and his wife described how he took care of the girls as babies, and, when they were older, got them off to school in the morning. He sometimes also brought his oldest daughter with him when he was collecting for the Committee. This more egalitarian division of labor engendered resistance from their families in Ticuani. On their first return with their two U.S.-born daughters, Don Emiliano's father objected strenuously to his son's involvement in their daily care:

DE: When I came here, my father totally did not like it. . . . I was bathing the girls in a tub [and] changed them. My wife was making the *gorditas* [fat tortillas] to eat. And my father . . . said, No, son [don't do this]. I said, No, Papa, they are my daughters and my blood. But I had taken note of the first reaction, that I should not do these things. . . .

DS: I was making the breakfast, so, well, I should not go and touch the girls because I was going to have to change a diaper. . . . So I said, Well, help me, take care of the girls while I make breakfast, no? . . . I got on very well with my husband, but . . . my in-laws saw this as weird, they did not like it. They felt that their son, no . . . (Spanish, translated by the author)

Don Emiliano's willingness to do "women's" work shows his evolution toward a masculinity different from that of his father, who, when drunk, still beat his married son. His father also charged that Don Emiliano was being "governed" by his wife, implying that he had forfeited his true masculinity in New York. Don Emiliano's response to his father was not simply to refer to the dollars he earned but was based in valuing a relationship with his daughters that he did not want disrupted by the requirements of a too-macho masculinity. Here again, Don Emiliano rejects hegemonic ranchero masculinity in favor of an emerging masculinity in the Mexican community in New York. His life in New York required him to learn to cook and care for his children while his wife worked, changes he linked with his larger evolution through migration—his "rotation in life"—and his relationship with a new kind of work in the service economy in New York, rather than in agricultural production in Puebla.

Sincerely, the change [in me] was total. I said to my wife, My father is one thing and I am another. You and I are one material, and my father is another. He follows his customs, and we are going to follow our customs, and we are going to watch as we go. For this we went [to New York], to see, to be there. I always thought this was key—to live in a super world city, you have to learn something in life. How would it do me any good . . . if I went, if one went to spend ten or fifteen years there, and I returned the same to my pueblo? Better I never went! (Spanish, translated by the author)

Don Emiliano's language indicates how he and Doña Selena jointly decided things, suggesting that he held a less rigid ranchero masculinity even before migration. They decided together to go to New York when they were *novios* (in a committed relationship) but to delay marriage until they could return to Ticuani.[18] Retrospectively, Don Emiliano even includes change as a *goal* of his migration. Don Emiliano's words do not lament lost gender privileges, as most theory would predict, but rather value what he has gained by being in New York. Instead of being *pueblerinos*, he and Doña Selena now think like citizens of a "super world city." Don Emiliano's evolution seems even clearer when we contrast his description of his basically happy marriage and family life with Doña Talia's description of hers. She complains that Gerardo "never gets to know *my* kids" (italics mine), whereas Don Emiliano and Doña Selena use team language to describe their marriage and child rearing.

Doña Selena's notion of femininity matters in this relationship too. In asking him to change the baby's diaper while she cooked, as if it were a natural thing for a father to do for his children, she stepped out of the role of a ranchera, who would in all likelihood have asked another woman but not her husband to do it. Whereas Don Gerardo has tried to impose a marriage of respect on his family while Doña Talia unsuccessfully demands a companionate marriage, Don Emiliano and Doña Selena have renegotiated a type of companionate marriage, one that retains some elements of ranchero masculinity consistent with a respect marriage.

Don Emiliano and Don Gerardo have also adopted fundamentally different stances toward alcohol that reflect different conceptions of masculinity. While both were seen by their families as drinking to excess, Don Emiliano eventually gave up drinking because his doctor urged him to and because his family demanded it; and he saw it becoming an issue between them. In contrast, Don Gerardo's family clearly and loudly disapproves of his drinking, but he dismisses their complaints, a stance facilitated by the fact that he drinks mostly while he is out with his male friends at sports events or doing public work. Interestingly, drinking is not as rigidly required a part of ranchero masculinity and male friendship as the talk about it by Ticuanense men and women, and other scholars, might lead one to believe. Although alcohol consumption is normally seen as essential to male rituals, especially among young men, other possibilities exist. Hence, even though most Committee members drank while socializing after the day's collecting was done, it was also accepted that several of these men, including Don Emiliano, did not drink. When the beer and brandy went round, these men were offered soda, without the derisive comments that I have heard in other contexts. The same kind of exception was made for some men in Ticuani and elsewhere in Mexico.

How this exception was negotiated is interesting. It was not the case, as with the male Alcoholics Anonymous members studied by Stanley Brandes in Mexico City,[19] that these men redefined manhood through their refusal to drink and thus avoid the harm drinking would do to their bodies and relationships. Rather, the group was silent on the topic. Respected Committee members had the right not to drink and not to be questioned about it because they had proved themselves by their community service. Don Emiliano renegotiated this dimension of ranchero masculinity, while Don Gerardo used it to justify his alcohol consumption.

My own experience with Ticuani and the Committee and drinking was similar. At first, I experienced pressure to drink more, no matter how much I had drunk already. I would drink one or two cans of beer during a meeting in New York, or at a party in Ticuani, and then politely accept, but not consume, the others I was offered. As I became an honorary member of the Committee and the Ticuani community, the dynamic changed. I would always be offered more beer, but when I signaled that I had had enough, I was not pressed to drink more. At the start of my fieldwork, I reluctantly drank tequila, which I found to be too strong and to cloud my ability to concentrate. But as time went on, I came to enjoy it and brought it to the meetings or dinners and other events. I found it actually helped my fieldwork by enabling me to relax. (I relaxed in many settings doing fieldwork but tried to pay special attention during the meetings.) Partaking of this male friendship ritual also facilitated my friendships. In my experience, multiple models of male friendship and alcohol consumption coexisted at such gatherings: a dominant model required that they go together, but there was also another of moderate consumption and a third of abstention, usually acceptable when the abstainer had earned respect in other ways.

Hence, three factors combined to make Don Emiliano revered for his sacrifice, whereas Don Gerardo was resented for his selfishness. First, and fundamentally, Don Gerardo demanded a strictly gendered division of labor and leisure similar to what he felt had existed in Ticuani before their migration, which included lots of time for sports, drinking, and politics with other men, but little time with his wife or family. And although Don Emiliano also spent too many hours on Ticuani work, and drank a lot, he spent a great deal more time doing the "women's work" of caring for his children and came to see the machismo of the *pueblerinos* as too limiting. Second, as a result of his greater involvement with them, his children and wife came to identify with and embrace the larger public purpose of Don Emiliano's service on the Committee. Third, because Don Emiliano's children spent more time in Ticuani and returned for adolescent rituals, they could see firsthand the results of their father's work and the family's sacrifice. These factors worked synergistically: as Don Emiliano's daughters visited Ticuani for teen rituals, they came to love Ticuani and understand the contribution their father's absences had helped to make in ways that Don Gerardo's children could not. Hence, Don Emiliano's grown children now see his absences as helping the pueblo, while Don Gerardo's children simply encourage their mother to leave their father because he has already largely absented himself from them. The end results for the two men, in terms of the kind of honor and recognition bestowed or withheld by their families, are starkly different. Don Gerardo's sacrifice is barely recognized by his family; his wife acknowledges his progress at his job, but sees him as a loser at home. Don Emiliano is revered at home, and his public honor reflects on his self-sacrificing family as well.

Ironically, given their attitudes toward gender bargains in Ticuani and New York, it was Don Emiliano and Doña Selena who returned to Mexico, while Don Gerardo's family purchased a house in New York. Don Emiliano decided to return to Mexico when the restaurant he worked in closed, his heart condition grew worse, and his doctors told him to find less stressful work. Facing the prospect of less money and equal stress at a new job in New York, Don Emiliano and Doña Selena moved back to Ticuani to build a house and open a store. They still visit New York, and their children and grandchildren, who remained in the United States, visit Ticuani. Their return was not a search for lost gender privilege by Don Emiliano. His wife pushed him to retire to Ticuani for his health, but she has also benefited from the move, as their social status has risen: they have gone from being simple peasants with little education to business owners who also work for the pueblo. Doña Selena volunteers in a charity organization for the poorest residents of Ticuani, and Don Emiliano is heavily involved in planning the yearly Feast. They own a large house overlooking the zocalo and can afford household help. Their return has been a triumph for them, a strong form of social "exit and return with voice."

Don Gerardo, who has chosen to remain in New York, asks why he would want to return to Mexico. He earned more than sixty-five thousand dollars in 1997, owned a house, and had time and money to spend on sports and politics. He has organized a privileged male world for himself. By most outward measures, he has made it as a man and as an immigrant in the United States. He has realized most of the elements of the American dream as it is commonly understood, and he is seen in the community as a successful man.

Contrary to the images of the "crisis of masculinity" and "liberating femininity," both Don Gerardo and Don Emiliano have lived a competent, and uncompromised, masculinity. As migrants, they helped create institutions (the Committee, sports leagues) that helped the pueblo in Mexico and gave them real power in Ticuani and in New York. Moreover, both were able to make good money, provide for their families, and pay for college for their children who wanted to go. Unlike the immigrants depicted in the work of Roger Rouse and Pierrette Hondagneu-Sotelo, they are not undocumented workers fearing to walk openly, and exercising only symbolic power by aggressively asserting patriarchal constraints over their wives and families. Rather, they are legal residents, and exercise power through the institutions they have created, through their economic and occupational success, and in their relations with Ticuani. However, for Don Gerardo this masculine competence is lived in rigid adherence to ranchero masculinity; for Don Emiliano it is achieved through an "evolution" and engagement with other kinds of masculinity. These different definitions of masculinity have yielded different meanings for absence and transnational life for these two families. They have also created different contexts for femininity for Doña Selena and Doña Talia.

Understood using Connell's notion of hegemonic masculinity, Don Gerardo's ranchero masculinity must compete with other, less (or differently) patriarchal visions of masculinity in the United States. His wife and children have not adopted the attitudes necessary to sustain ranchero masculinity in a strong form. Hence, although Don Gerardo lives his ranchero masculinity, he does so largely alone. In contrast, Don Emiliano lives a modified ranchero and modern migrant masculinity, and does so with the support of his wife and children.

Interestingly, the lives of Don Gerardo and his family seem to resonate more with the image of migrants' straddling a cultural gap or balancing on a tightrope than do those of Don Emiliano and his family. The responses of Don Emiliano, Doña Selena, and their children appear to be negotiated settlements to questions of how men and women, parents and children, should act. If they are straddling a gap, they are doing so more or less together, using a set of cultural tools whose choice they have negotiated jointly. Don Gerardo's strategy is clearly at odds with that of the rest of his family, and this division creates both less familial intimacy and a larger cultural gap. It is not, however, strictly a generation gap. Doña Talia sees the world through a lens more like her children's than her husband's. But, being married to Don Gerardo, she must navigate a difficult course between ranchero masculinity and other images of gender.

WOMEN'S PRACTICES OF SETTLEMENT AND TRANSNATIONAL LIFE

Ranchero masculinity and ranchera femininity also frame the experience of settlement and transnational life for first-generation women, but under very different conditions in the United States. Women see changes in relations with their men resulting from women working outside the home and the men doing "women's" work at home and in restaurant kitchens, as Don Emiliano did. These women feel that their men are less "macho" than men in Ticuani. One member of the prayer group commented:

> If we went there to Ticuani, the men would be very *machista*. . . . Here, no, because both [man and woman] work. . . . Women in Ticuani are very submissive, before they were, but now it's different, even in Ticuani . . . [things have changed in New York because] the men work in the kitchen in restaurants . . . it's more equal. Before, it hurt them to even enter the kitchen. . . . Now, many men have changed. They also take the kids to the doctor; my husband works nights, so he always did that . . . men in Mexico wouldn't help, but here, yes. (Spanish, translated by the author)

Such observations reflect the perception that in the United States it is increasingly necessary that both men and women work outside the home, which in turn requires men to work in the home and share in childcare.

In fact, economic and social changes in Mexico are also bringing about changes in relations between men and women there. Nevertheless, first-generation men and women both evaluate their present with respect to an experienced and an imagined rural *poblano* past rooted in ranchero masculinity and ranchera femininity. While discussing changing male and female roles in New York and Ticuani, one woman referred to an old joke between husbands and wives. The wife would ask, upon her husband's return at the end of the day, "Are you going to beat me first, or should we eat dinner first? Or should we eat first, and you beat me later?" All the women present laughed, and they repeated the joke to make sure I understood. So as not to offend them, I offered a small laugh. They told me several times that this was not how it was today, or with them, but they had grown up with this joke. Their laughter surprised me because they had just been talking about how much more equal relations between men and women were today, even in Ticuani.

When I repeated this joke to a group of second-generation youth in their twenties, including daughters of some of the above women, their reaction was silence, surprise, and rejection: This is a joke that they told you? It's not funny. They could not believe that the older women thought it funny either. The different generational reactions result from two factors. First, the older women at the meeting all had friends or relatives who had been hit or had themselves been hit. Making the violence into a joke and placing it in the "old days" made it easier to deal with. Second, despite changes in gender roles and ideologies, they still felt attachment to a more traditional view of the world. They derive satisfaction both from their new status and economic power in the United States as wage earners and modern women and from their "traditional" roles as mothers and caregivers (which are also valued in American society in strong and contradictory ways).[20] Rejecting the humor in this joke would come too close to rejecting their own histories and the relations with men they know who have been abusive, but whose relationships are still valued, or men who have changed their behavior.

The second generation, by contrast, has been raised to see such treatment as unacceptable, even illegal. Indeed, some among the second-generation group I spoke with had called the police to stop their fathers' abuse of their mothers. The second generation sees the world differently. They must deal with these dimensions of their own histories, which they understand as embodying ranchero masculinity and ranchera femininity, while trying to reclaim or embrace some aspects of being "Mexican" on their own terms. On this issue there is clearly a large cultural gap between the first and second generations.

GENDERED WORK IN A PRAYER GROUP IN NEW YORK

This mix of gaining greater freedom but also still needing to engage with ranchero masculinity and femininity is apparent in the most highly organized Ticuani women's group, the Prayer Group for Padre Jesús, which contributes to both settlement and transnationalization in ways different from the men's main organization, the Committee. Although it offers women authority, it is still set within a larger, male-run structure. It is common among migrant groups to have some kind of prayer group dedicated to the patron saint of their hometown.[21] The group meets monthly in the same Brooklyn basement as the Committee. Its devotional practices include buying flowers, saying the rosary, and offering special prayers. It began at the suggestion of Don Manuel, the head of the Committee, and the group's status as subordinate to the Committee is clear. When I talked with one of the group's members in 2000, I asked her its name. She first misunderstood and thought I was talking about the Committee, then said that her group had no name, and continued:

> DOÑA FLORENCIA: This is nothing more than that we pray at the end of each month . . . the señoras, we pray to Padre Jesús. Manuel [the Committee president] maintains the list of our countrymen that bring the flowers for Padre Jesús. . . . He is the one who calls them so they bring the flowers.
>
> RS: You [the women] don't call. He is the one who calls?
>
> DF: He calls them because he is the interested party [*el interesado*]. They are the ones from the Committee. . . . [It] is a prayer for Padre Jesús, who helps us and blesses us here where we are [New York]. Because you see how far we are from Him! But we don't forget about Him.

Interestingly, Doña Florencia first thinks that my question refers to the men's Committee, then does not refer to the prayer group by the name others use for it, and finally says that Don Manuel is the "interested party" who maintains the list of flower donors. The structure of the meetings reflects the group's status as subordinate to the Committee. The women sit in front of a large picture of Padre Jesús surrounded by flowers. Informal talk yields to reciting the rosary and offering direct thanks to Padre Jesús or requests for special intercessions. The men, though present, do not usually pray in the meetings. They drink beer, talk, and make jokes or talk politics in the back of the room until the prayers begin, and then stand silently. After the prayers, they eat the meal the women have prepared.

The prayer group aids both settlement and transnationalization. First, it spans the first and second generations. Five or ten Brooklyn-born preteen girls say they attend regularly for the camaraderie, to spend time with their mothers, and because they love Padre Jesús. (Indeed, devotion to Padre Jesús has emerged as a surprisingly strong dimension of many second-generation lives in New York.) Second, the basement containing the altar to Padre Jesús has become a semipublic Ticuanense site. "People come by here . . . anyone can use this space," group members tell me, explaining that people come to offer special prayers or organize their own prayer meetings. Third, although the prayer group was created at Don Manuel's behest to (in his words) give Padre Jesús a place in Brooklyn with his people, it also creates a space for female authority and power and gives its members public roles in a Ticuani-oriented institution in New York. Group members regularly serve as sponsors (*mayordomas*) for the Feast of Padre Jesús in January, helping to organize the flowers and the party after Mass. The group also offers a way for them to express their own devotion to Padre Jesús and their identity as Ticuanense women.

This mix of subordination, public honor, and women's authority in Ticuani public life, local and transnational, is illustrated by Doña Paz, the wife of Don Manuel. Doña Paz runs the prayer meetings, leads prayers, and is recognized in the community as someone with authority. When she learned that my researchers and I wanted to interview second-generation youths, she took me from table to table at the party for Padre Jesús, asking women if we could interview their teenaged children, and everyone quickly volunteered their telephone numbers. Yet when I asked Doña Paz for an interview, she responded, like other women, that it would depend on her husband. Her public role was clearly subordinate to her role as a wife, and she did not contest that subordination. Her silent perseverance in the face of the challenges his actions pressed on her was the very embodiment of the long-suffering ranchera; she never publicly expressed any "inappropriate sentiments," such as anger, disappointment, or impatience.

Doña Paz's faithful service to her sacrificing husband confers on her honor and moral virtue among Ticuanenses. For example, she and the other wives of the Committee members were strongly praised (in their absence) by their husbands in a speech by Don Manuel in Ticuani during the inauguration of the potable water system in 1993. He thanked all the wives of the Committee members

> for their patience they have with us. To abandon our children on Saturday, Sunday, instead of going out . . . with our wives, they sacrifice, getting up as if it were another work day to prepare us something to eat because they know that when we leave, we will go from nine in the morning going house to house, and we don't know what time we will return. And I believe that it is not only my wife [but] the wives of [all] members of the Committee that merit this recognition.

Despite the fact that she was absent from this and most other events in Don Manuel's public life, honor accrues to Doña Paz by her husband's acknowledgment. Indeed, the stoic Committee president's voice cracked with emotion when speaking of his wife's sacrifice.

Such public praise reinforces Doña Paz's position as a leader in the group and community and resonates with her own understanding of a woman's role. She explained that the job of a woman and wife was to always, always be there for the husband, no matter what: always cook his food, make sure he has a well-ironed shirt when he goes out, and be sure that he knows you will be there, waiting, when he gets home. To wait, cook, and clean for your husband is also to serve Ticuani. For Doña Paz these sentiments were not simple statements in an interview; they were expressed in everyday conversation, and she lived her life by them. In doing so, she manifested, more strongly than most Ticuanense women, traditional ranchera virtues of shame and deference.

Even if only in a male-dominated context, the prayer group creates a space for women's authority and leadership in Ticuani public life. It creates a formal institution dedicated to a traditionally female domain, religion, in which women are in charge. The existence of the group testifies to the importance of this "women's" work and world in Ticuanense life, and in the process helps to maintain Ticuani traditions in the first and, to a lesser extent, second generations. Moreover, the group concretely expresses a permanent Ticuanense presence in New York and a desire to create institutions to preserve special dimensions of Ticuani culture.

The different attitudes of Doña Paz and Doña Florencia show contrasting forms of renegotiated femininity in public life. Doña Paz emphasizes her duty to stick by her man in all circumstances. In contrast, Doña Florencia is almost a pure *pionera*. For decades she has lived apart from her common-law husband and has raised her children alone. She owns a house in Ticuani and conducts herself, as some Ticuanenses observed, "like a man": she expresses her opinions openly and even contradicts men, and does not give their objections much currency. She drinks beer in public without trying to hide it. She is a woman who has reached a certain age (about sixty), has no man in her life to shame by her conduct, and hence can break conventions without great penalty. Yet in the prayer group, she adopts a position much closer to the deferential ranchera or Ticuani migrant woman, ceding authority to Don Manuel; the job of the women is just to pray to Padre Jesús. The world of the Committee is a public, male one linked in people's minds directly to the male-dominated space of electoral and other public politics in Ticuani, to which the prayer group can be seen as mainly an appendage.

RETURNING TO TICUANI

First-generation men and women visit Ticuani for vacation and emotional replenishment.[22] They escape the pressures of life in New York and take a long drink of *ticuanensidad* (Ticuaniness) and *mexicanidad* (Mexicanness) at their source. Ticuanenses contrast the pace of life in New York with that in Mexico, saying: "New York is a place to work, but Ticuani is a place to live." In the small courtyard of his house in Ticuani, Tomás Maestro plays with his three-year-old son and tells me that although the work of the Committee and the political issues do matter, what really matters is time to sit in the sun, eat some good food, and play with his son. As he and I spend the afternoon trading stories about our three-year-old boys and kicking a ball around with his, I have to agree.

Returning to Ticuani places migrants and their children in a complex field of social interactions, which is intensified by unaccustomed propinquity. Gossip that runs through the Ticuanense community in a week by telephone or personal meetings in New York spreads almost instantaneously in Ticuani, as people see each other constantly. Returning for the Feast is like attending a two-week, nonstop party, engendering the sense that one is being observed and evaluated by others all the time. This sustained intensity causes returnees to experience a sense of what I call "accelerated social time," which makes relatively short stays in Ticuani feel like long periods. This phenomenon helps explain how and why Ticuani occupies such an important place in the social world of many in the second generation too.[23]

The migrants' ritual of returning to check on their houses in Ticuani embodies enduring links with the town and implies the ability to go home permanently or visit as one wishes. While most Ticuanenses and their children stay in these houses only for a few weeks or months every year or two, their visits stir up vivid memories of the Ticuani of their youth. Increasing numbers of the earliest migrants, first-generation men and women, are inheriting houses. Women migrants who have divorced or been abandoned are maintaining their houses in Ticuani and bringing their children and grandchildren back with them on extended visits. One woman migrant told me that maintaining her house in Ticuani was crucial because she never knew what would happen in the United States. Though she had applied for U.S. citizenship, having the house in Ticuani made her feel safe. If need be, she could return to live there off her Social Security benefits and a very small pension.

Women tend to stay longer in Ticuani than their male counterparts, one or two months to the men's one or two weeks. Many of these women have retired from a garment workers' union and receive a pension and Social Security benefits. Many now work as unpaid day-care providers for their own adult children in New York, often living in the same apartment or building. During the winter and summer, they take their grandchildren to Ticuani to enjoy the greater freedom and open space, offering them both a different quality of life and a chance for the third generation to learn Ticuani religious and civic traditions.

As in New York, men and women visiting Ticuani have different spheres of activity.[24] Men organize public rituals, while women participate in religious observances; they often rise for the 5 a.m. Mass, *las Mañanitas*, celebrated every day of the Feast. At public events women cook and serve the food while men do the organizational work, serve the beer and soda, and break down the tables afterward. This division of labor persists among the second generation. However, the border between the public male and private female worlds is porous. Although returning men do tend to drink and hang out in the street at night, there is a great deal of family time in Ticuani. By my estimate, many such men spend at least half their time with their families doing nothing in particular or enjoying Ticuani's traditions (cockfights, rodeos, and so on), even while attending to public Ticuanense business. Similarly, women do most of the childcare in Ticuani, but men share in it. And this responsibility is diluted by the omnipresent extended family and the greater security parents feel for their children in Ticuani.

Finally, Ticuani allows a relaxation of family bargains over issues such as drinking. Tomás Maestro at first resisted but ultimately accepted the deal his family negotiated with him in New York. He can drink heavily on the weekends if he is in their house with his friends; if he is out, he must be more careful. He cannot drink on weekdays. But in Ticuani, where every day is like a weekend, he can get drunk with his friends every night if he wants to. Yet he does not; rather, he chooses to stay home some nights with his wife and children.

CONCLUSION

These histories of first-generation Ticuanenses offer several insights into the negotiation of gender bargains and ideologies in transnational life. First, such bargains and ideologies are always context-dependent. The image of the crisis of masculinity, of disempowered men imposing hard gender bargains on their women and yearning to return to Mexico, fails to explain the situation of many Ticuanenses. A good number of Ticuanense men have succeeded economically and created institutions linked with Ticuani premised not on return there but rather on permanent settlement in New York and continued engagement with Ticuani. Rather than lose power and their links with home, they demonstrate newly created power and sustained links to a hometown to which most have no intention of returning permanently.

Though Ticuanense men may have been raised on a macho, ranchero masculinity, they can change, both in New York and in Ticuani. Just as working Ticuanense women often renegotiate their gender bargains in the United States, men too can rethink their gender ideologies. This process is aided by raising U.S.-born children, especially girls, whose gender ideologies tend to be more egalitarian than macho. Yet it would be facile to posit a dichotomy by which Mexico is seen as macho and the United States as egalitarian. While gender relations tend to become more egalitarian in the United States, they are tending in the same direction in Mexico.[25] And U.S. culture offers its own models of male privilege and female subordination. Moreover, while migration accelerates the negotiation of gender bargains, there are parts of the old gender bargain that many Ticuanense men and women wish to preserve. For example, many Ticuanense women revel in their newfound earning power and the ability to express "inappropriate sentiments" such as anger, but they also value mothering and staying home with their kids as well as pleasing their husbands. Their reality is more complex than the images of a unitary Mexican or American culture. Thus femininity, too, is renegotiated to accommodate, reject, or relate in other ways to New York and to their men's renegotiation of masculinity.

Men tend to participate more in transnational public life than women do, while women tend to do more of the everyday settlement work in New York, especially things like enrolling children in school, and private transnational life, such as caregiving for the third generation. Settlement activities can increase women's power and autonomy in the United States,[26] while public, transnational activities tend to create institutions that reproduce or create arenas over which men have power, both in Ticuani and among Ticuanenses in New York.

NOTES

1. See Artico's insightful analysis (2003) of the constructed meaning of parental absence, as abandonment or sacrifice, for stay-behind youth.

2. I benefit here from Hochschild 1989, Hondagneu-Sotelo 1994, and especially Connell 1995, as well as from Beth Bernstein's intellect and generosity.

3. Hondagneu-Sotelo 1994; Hagan 1994; Mummert 1994, 1999; Salazar Parreñas 2001; Espinoza 1998; Binford and d'Abeterre 2000.

4. The meaning of *mandilón* lies somewhere between the polite *henpecked* and the vulgar *pussy-whipped*. See Matt Gutmann's insightful 1996 book.

5. See Mummert 1993, 1994, 1999; Hirsch 2003.

6. Although in Spanish one would refer to *la masculinidad ranchera* because *masculinidad* is a feminine noun and the adjective must take a feminine ending (though the noun *ranchero* is masculine), in English I adopt the terms *ranchero* masculinity and *ranchera* femininity to simplify the issue of gender.

7. In defining hegemonic masculinity, I paraphrase closely from Connell 1995: 77.

8. Gutmann's useful critique of an early version of this chapter argued that the division of space between men and women is less rigid in Mexico than is reported in much of the research literature. He is right, but I still think that these *images* of what male and female space and conduct should be strongly influence how people act.

9. See Hondagneu-Sotelo 1994; Hagan 1994; Rouse 1995.

10. See Besserer 2000, 2004.

11. A companionate marriage emphasizes a psychologically close friendship cemented by sexual intimacy. In respect marriages, sexuality is seen as a woman's duty and is not discussed. See Mummert 1993, 1994; Hirsh 2003. Ranchera femininity resonates with the notion of *marianismo,* sometimes understood as being like the Virgin Mary—without sexual desire, deferential to one's husband and other male relatives, constant in virtue, and pure. The Mariana is often contrasted with La Malinche, the indigenous woman who became Hernán Cortés's lover—sexually voracious, disloyal, and unpredictable. See Stevens 1994; Gutiérrez 1991; Leal 1983; Bocchi 2000.

12. Katz 1999: 144.

13. "Crisis of masculinity" is Greta Gilbertson's phrase.

14. Hondagneu-Sotelo 1994; Hagan 1994; Espinoza 1998; Binford and d'Abeterre 2000.

15. Zhou and Bankston 1998; Kibria 1993; Portes and Rumbaut 2001.

16. On homosexuality, see Prieur 1998; Kulik 1997; Lancaster 1992; Cantú 2000; Almaguer 1991.

17. I have known Don Gerardo since the late 1980s and have spoken with him many times, but he always evaded my requests for a formal interview. Hence he is not quoted at length in this chapter.

18. Being *novios* literally translates into being boyfriend and girlfriend but implies a more serious commitment, assuming eventual marriage.

19. See Brandes 2002.

20. See Hays 1996.

21. On other kinds of prayer groups in New York, see Gálvez 2004 and Rivera Sánchez 2003.

22. Material from this section comes from the field notes of Sandra Lara, Sara Guerrero-Rippberger, Agustín Vecino, and myself in Ticuani in 1999.

23. See Flaherty 1999.

24. See Goldring 2001.

25. Gutmann 1996; Mummert 1994, 1999; Hirsch 2003; Binford and d'Abeterre 2000.

26. See Hondagneu-Sotelo 1994.

REFERENCES

Almaguer, Tomás. 1991. Chicano Men: A Cartography of Homosexual Identity and Behavior. *Differences: A Journal of Feminist and Cultural Studies* 3 (2): 75–100.

Artico, Ceres. 2003. *Latino Families Broken by Immigration*. New York: LFB Scholarly Publishing.

Bernstein, Elizabeth. 2001. The Meaning of the Purchase: Desire, Demand, and the Commerce of Sex. *Ethnography* 2 (3): 391–420.

Besserer, Federico. 2000. Sentimientos (in) apropiados de la mujeres migrantes: Hacia una nueva ciudadania. In *Migración y relaciones de género en México,* ed. Dalia Barrera Bassols and Cristina Cehmichen Bazan, 371–89. México, DF: Universidad Nacional Autónoma de México.

———. 2004. *Topografias transnacionales: Una geografía para el estudio de la vida transnacional.* Universita Autónoma Metropolitana Unidad Iztapalapa/Plaza y Valdés.

Binford, Leigh, and Maria Eugenia D'Abeterre, eds. 2000. *Conflictos migratorios transnacionales y respuestas comunitarias.* Puebla, México: Gobierno del Estado de Puebla/Consejo Estatal de Población/Instituto de Ciencias y Humanidades—Benemerita Universidad Autónoma de Puebla.

Bocchi, Steven. 2000. The Meanings of Marianismo in Mexico. www.lclark .edu/~woodrich/ Bocchi_marianismo.html. Accessed January 2005.

Brandes, Stanley. 2002. *Staying Sober in Mexico City.* Austin: University of Texas Press.

Cantu, Lionel. 2000. Entre Hombres/Between Men: Latino Masculinities and Homosexualities. In *Gay Masculinities,* ed. Peter Nardi, 224–46. Thousand Oaks, CA: Sage.

Connell, Robert W. 1995. *Masculinities.* Berkeley: University of California Press.

Espinoza, Victor. 1998. *El dilema del retorno: Migración, género y pertenencia en un contexto transnacional.* Zamora, Michoacán, México: El Colegio de Jalisco and El Colegio de Michoacán.

Flaherty, Michael G. 1999. *A Watched Pot: How We Experience Time.* New York: New York University Press.

———. 2004. In the Name of Guadalupe: Religion, Politics, and Citizenship among Mexicans in New York. Ph.D. diss., New York University.

Goldring, Luin. 2001. From Market Membership to Transnational Citizenship: The Changing Politicization of Transnational Social Spaces. In *Transnational Social Spaces,* ed. Ludger Pries, 162–86. New York: Routledge.

Guerrero-Rippberger, Sara. 1999. But for the Day of Tomorrow: Negotiating Femininity in a New York Mexican Identity. Senior thesis, Barnard College.

Gutiérrez, Ramón A. 1991. *When Jesus Came, the Corn Mothers Went Away: Marriage, Sexuality, and Power in New Mexico, 1500–1846.* Stanford, CA: Stanford University Press.

Gutmann, Matthew. 1996. *The Meanings of Macho: Being a Man in Mexico City*. Berkeley: University of California Press.

Hagan, Jacqueline. 1994. *Deciding to Be Legal*. Philadelphia: Temple University Press.

Hays, Sharon. 1996. *The Cultural Contradictions of Motherhood*. New Haven, CT: Yale University Press.

Hirsch, Jennifer. 2003. *A Courtship after Marriage: Sexuality and Love in Mexican Transnational Families*. Berkeley: University of California Press.

Hochschild, Arlie. 1989. *The Second Shift*. New York: Avon.

Hondagneu-Sotelo, Pierrette. 1994. *Gendered Transitions: Mexican Experiences of Migration*. Berkeley: University of California Press.

Katz, Jack. 1999. *How Emotions Work*. Chicago: University of Chicago Press.

Kibria, Nazli. 1993. *Family Tightrope: The Changing Lives of Vietnamese Families*. Princeton, NJ: Princeton University Press.

Kulik, Don. 1997. The Gender of Brazilian Transgendered Prostitutes. *American Anthropologist* 99 (3): 574–84.

Lancaster, Roger N. 1992. *Life Is Hard: Machismo, Danger, and the Intimacy of Power in Nicaragua*. Berkeley: University of California Press.

Lara, Sandra. 2000–2001. Notes from Rob Smith's Second-Generation Project. Leadbeater, Bonnie J. Ross, and Niobe Way. 1996. *Urban Girls: Resisting Stereotypes, Creating Identities*. New York: New York University Press.

Leal, Luis. 1983.Female Archetypes in Mexican Literature. In *Women in Hispanic Literature: Icons and Fallen Idols*, ed. Beth Miller, 227–42. Berkeley: University of California Press.

Mummert, Gail. 1993. Changes in the Formation of Western Rural Families: Profound Modifications. *DemoS* 6: 23–24.

———. 1994. From *Metate* to *Despate:* Rural Women's Salaried Labor and the Redefinition of Gendered Spaces and Roles. In *Women of the Mexican Countryside, 1850–1990,* ed. H. Fowler-Salamini and M. K. Vaughn, 192–209. Tucson: University of Arizona Press.

———. 1999. Juntos o despartados: Migración transnacional y la fundación del hogar. In *Fronteras fragmentadas,* ed. Gail Mummert, 451–74. Zamora, Michoacán: El Colegio de Michoacán.

Parreñas, Rhacel Salazar. 2001. *Servants of Globalization: Women, Migration, and Domestic Work*. Stanford, CA: Stanford University Press.

Portes, Alejandro, and Ruben Rumbaut. 2001. *Legacies*. Berkeley: University of California Press.

Prieur, Annick. 1998. *Mema's House, Mexico City: On Transvestites, Queers, and Machos*. Chicago: University of Chicago Press.

Rodriguez, Orlando, Emily Rosenbaum, and Greta Gilbertson. 1993. *Nuestra Nueva York: Latino Immigrants' Perspectives on Politics*. New York: Hispanic Research Center, Fordham University.

Rouse, Roger. 1995. Thinking Through Transnationalism: Notes on the Cultural Politics of Class Relations in the Contemporary United States. *Public Culture* 7: 2.

Ruggie, John G. 1993. Territoriality and Beyond: Problematizing Modernity in International Relations. *International Organizations* 47 (1): 139–74.

Ruiz Hernandez, Margarito Xib. 1993. Todo indigenismo es lo mismo. *Ojarasca,* July.

Stevens, Evelyn P. 1994. Marianismo: The Other Face of Machismo in Latin America. In *Confronting Change, Challenging Tradition: Women in Latin American History,* ed. Gertrude Yeager, 3–17. Wilmington, DE: Jaguar Books on Latin America.

Vecino, Agustín. 1999. Gangs and Crews. Notes for Rob Smith's Second-Generation Project.

Zhou, Min, and Carl Bankston III. 1998. *Growing Up American.* New York: Russell Sage Foundation.

19

"SHE'S OLD SCHOOL LIKE THAT"
Mother-and-Daughter Sex Talks

Lorena García

I was wrapping up my first interview with Carmen, the mother of seventeen-year-old Minerva, when Carmen's sister unexpectedly stopped by for a visit on her way home from running errands. Carmen introduced us, reminding her sister that I was doing interviews with Latina girls and their mothers. Taking off her winter hat and gloves as she shook off the powdery snow from her boots on a welcome mat, the sister dismissively commented to Carmen, "*¿Qué se gana uno con hablar de eso? Minerva ya hizo lo que hizo* [What does one gain from talking about that? Minerva already did what she did]."

Then, turning to me, she matter-of-factly told me, "*Yo le dije que Minerva se le iba a echar a perder si no la controlaba más* [I told her that Minerva would become ruined if she did not place more restrictions on her]." I did not know how to respond to her as I noticed that Carmen was blushing and averting her gaze when her sister made these remarks. After a brief, awkward silence, Carmen straightened her shoulders, looked me right in the eye, and assertively stated, "I've always taken care of her, but, as you see, *hace lo que le da la gana* [she does whatever she wants]. . . . And, even so, Minerva still needs my advice." In our next interview, a couple of weeks later, Carmen brought up her sister's comments: "I was so mad at her. It bothers me that she thinks like that . . . *como que si mi hija ya no vale la pena* [as if my daughter is no longer worth it (the effort)]."

Like Carmen, other mothers struggled with the judgments they encountered about their daughters' sexual behavior and, by extension, their parenting skills. Mothers frequently told me they initially felt quite embarrassed about what they understood to be their personal shortcomings and those of their daughters. For this reason, I assumed

472

it would be difficult to find mothers who would be willing to talk to me about their interactions with their daughters on the topic of sexuality, especially those that unfolded upon their discovery of their daughters' sexual activities. But mothers contacted me and expressed interest in the study, often making comments such as, "We need to talk about this topic more" and "This is something we should not be embarrassed about." Despite such assertions, most mothers were still very self-conscious at the onset of interviews, seeming almost apologetic about their parenting and about their daughters' behavior. As Betina, a stylish Mexican woman with dyed blonde hair put it while nervously wringing her hands, "*Qué vergüenza* [how embarrassing], you are probably wondering how I let this happen." But, as the interviews progressed and they became more comfortable, this initial apologetic demeanor shifted to one of determination. These Latina mothers made it clear that they were unwilling to write off their daughters as lost causes just because they were no longer virgins. Carmen exemplified this when she expressed indignation at her sister's suggestion that Minerva "was no longer worth it." Instead, mothers asserted that it was precisely because of their daughters' sexual experiences that they needed to persist in providing guidance to their daughters.

I found that mothers adopted four specific strategies to continue to offer their daughters sexual guidance after discovering their sexual behaviors. These were strategies by which they also negotiated the inequality they and their daughters faced when daughters transgressed the sexual restrictions placed on them by their families and the larger society. Mothers' strategies were (1) their continued promotion of safe sex, communicated in their redefinitions of the meanings of respect; (2) open discussion and sharing with their daughters of their own sexual experiences as a way to underscore how women's sexual biographies could exacerbate their existing disadvantages; (3) disclosure of their daughters' sexual behaviors to other women in the family and/or their husbands; and (4) making evaluative references to the sexuality of white young women. Broader cultural discourses and notions about teen sexuality, good mothers, same-sex sexuality, and race/ethnicity, as well as mothers' interactions with family members and with each other as Mexican and Puerto Rican women, significantly informed their approaches to the sex education of their daughters. As I show, their strategies were also a boundary maintenance process produced in a larger context of racialization and gender inequality, as well as heteronormativity, which refers to "both those localized practices and those centralized institutions that legitimize and privilege heterosexuality and hetero relationships as fundamental and 'natural' within society."[1]

Research on mother–adolescent daughter communication about sex suggests that in comparison to both black and white mothers, Latina mothers are more reluctant to discuss sexuality-related matters with their daughters.[2] Restrictions in Latina mother-adolescent sex communication are most often attributed to cultural values and norms, such as the often-cited stereotypical portrayal of Latinas as "culturally silent" on sexuality. Despite the limited sex communication among Latinas indicated by studies that have focused on this aspect of mother-daughter relationships, there are still instances in which the topic of sex becomes notably salient in their conversations. Two key moments that have been highlighted in the literature are Latina mothers' sexual socialization of adolescent daughters who are expected or assumed to be virgins and mothers' reactions to their unmarried daughters' unplanned pregnancy. I pick up on what occurs at the moment of mothers' discovery of the sexual behavior of their adolescent daughters (who are not pregnant) and what unfolds after this moment. I approach these occurrences as "magnified moments," which the sociologist Arlie Hochschild defines as "episodes of heightened importance, either epiphanies, moment of intense glee or unusual insight, or moments in which things go intensely but meaningfully wrong. In either case, the moment stands out."[3] Mothers' discovery of their daughters' sexual behaviors are moments that stand out because they bring to the foreground not only daughters' emerging sexuality but also mothers' approaches to the sex education of their daughters. According to Hochschild, "magnified moments reflect a feeling ideal both when a person joyously lives up to it or, in some spectacular way, does not."[4] Little is known about the interactions between nonpregnant or nonparenting Latina girls and their mothers around sexuality *after* mothers realize that their daughters are sexually active. The narratives of the Latina mothers and daughters I spoke with call into question the often-cited explanation that Latina girls have negative sexual outcomes because their mothers are "culturally silent" about sexuality. These magnified moments and ensuing interactions between Latina mothers and their adolescent daughters provide an opportunity to explore when and how Latinas rework their gender and sexual meanings and processes.[5]

FINDING OUT

About an hour into our first interview, thirty-eight-year-old Aracelia asked me to wait a minute and walked out of her kitchen. A Mexican woman who immigrated to Chicago in her teens, Aracelia took great pride in having recently obtained her G.E.D. while working as a store cashier and raising her family. For most of our first hour together, she had excitedly shared with me her desire to work at a child-care center, laying out her plans to register at a community college and obtain an associate degree. With her husband at work and her two daughters out watching a movie that Saturday afternoon, the two-bedroom apartment was fairly quiet. Aracelia reemerged a few minutes later and placed a folded-up sheet of lined notebook paper on the kitchen table as she sat back down across from me. She pushed it toward me: "Look, this is how I found out." Aracelia was ready to share with me how she came to learn about her daughters sexual behavior. I unfolded the creased and worn paper; small, neat handwriting almost filled up one side of the paper, and a few hearts embellished the outer margins. Realizing it was a personal letter written by her sixteen-year-old daughter, Soledad, I placed it back on the table. Aracelia reassured me that it was okay to read the note, but, upon seeing my hesitancy to do so, she held up the note in front of me and leaned forward, telling me, "She wrote that she was glad that she did it [sex] for the first with him [her boyfriend] and that she would never regret it, even if they were no longer together!" Aracelia explained that she found the letter in her daughter's notebook after much investigative effort.

Like Aracelia, almost all mothers became aware of daughters' sexual activities through covert searches of daughters' bedrooms, backpacks, school notebooks, or diaries or by listening in on phone calls or combing through text messages left on cell phones.[6] According to the mothers, such actions stemmed from their suspicions about their daughters' sexual propriety after they defied rules, particularly those related to curfew and/or dating, behavior that the mothers interpreted as out of character for their daughters, rather than as "normal" adolescent behavior. And, for a handful of mothers, their sleuthing activities were provoked by their discovery of a "hickey"[7] on their daughters' necks or their daughters' interest in or purchase of underwear that mothers deemed to be "too sexy," like lacy thongs or bras, as was the case for Aracelia, who was surprised when she found two animal print thongs that belonged to her daughter.

When I asked the mothers whether they had any qualms about infringing upon their daughters' privacy, they almost all emphatically responded that their actions were justified because they were tied to their efforts to protect their daughters. As Aracelia asserted, "*¿Qué tiene de malo* [what is wrong with that]? I do it for her own good! My obligation as a mother is to be on the watch for everything my daughters do, even if they don't like it." Most mothers were taken aback by my inquiries about their daughters' privacy, often responding that the idea of privacy for children and teenagers was an "*americano*" or "*güero*" notion ("American" was always conflated with "white"). "White parents always treat young people as if they should have the same rights as adults," stated Teresa, a Puerto Rican woman in her late thirties who has a great sense of humor. She continued, "I'm not saying that it is acceptable to abuse your children. . . . But privacy, no, to me it's an abuse not to know what your children are doing." When I suggested that perhaps it might be more effective to just ask daughters about their sexual activities rather than go through their personal items, Teresa made a face and quickly replied, "What young woman is going to say, 'Oh yeah, I'm having sex already'? I want to know about what my daughters are not telling me about so I can do something about it if I have to." Most mothers did indeed do something upon learning about their daughters' sexual behavior and did so in similar fashion.

Once armed with what they saw as evidence of their daughters' sexual activities, most of the mothers acted swiftly to address the matter. With initial feelings of anger and/or disillusionment, they immediately confronted daughters about their sexual behavior. The manner in which they moved forward with this information was a process that began with their construction of their daughters as victims. In seeking to make sense of their daughters' sexual behavior, mothers typically reported that they initially accused their daughters of being gullible, calling them *pendeja* (idiot) or *mensa* (stupid). Most mothers first understood their daughters' sexual behavior as a victimization of their daughters. That is, mothers accused their daughters of being naïve or having been taken advantage of by their sexual partners.

When Emma discovered some condoms in her sixteen-year-old daughter Miriam's bedroom, she immediately went to school to pick up her daughter. A full-time factory employee in her late thirties, Emma always handed me a plastic sandwich bag full of individually wrapped candy, such as caramels, butterscotch disks, and taffy whenever we met for an interview. She always seemed jovial when we talked, so it was difficult to imagine her being angry when she described her interaction with her daughter that day:

> Oh, of course, she wanted to know why I went to get her. *No le dije nada* [I did not say anything], I was quiet all the way home. When we got home, she saw the condoms on the kitchen table and when straight into her room. *Le dije, "¡¿Que no tienes vergüenza* [Aren't you ashamed]?!" She told that me that it was none of my business and I don't know what else, but I yelled at her, "*¡Qué mensa eres, Miriam* [You are so stupid, Miriam]! You think he loves you? *Se está aprovechando de ti, ya verás* [He's taking advantage of you, you'll see]!"

Likewise, Conchita, a Mexican woman in her early forties, interpreted her daughter's actions as not being taken of her own volition. When her fifteen-year-old daughter forgot her cell phone at home, Conchita decided to go through the received and sent text messages with the help of Carla's older sister. Much to her dismay, she found some of the text exchanges between Carla and her boyfriend to be overtly sexual. Later that evening, Conchita asked her about the text messages:

> I told her that I read her text messages and I wanted to know if she was having sexual relations with her boyfriend. She still denied it, at first. . . . I told her I wanted her to tell me the truth. . . . She then admitted it. . . . I told her how sad I was for her because she didn't know what she was doing and that her boyfriend was taking advantage of her.

Recently separated from her husband, Conchita wondered if her daughter would have behaved in this manner if her husband were still living at home, pointing out that her children were more "scared" of their father.

Carmen, who had been angered by her sister's suggestion that her daughter was a lost cause, was one of only two mothers who did not search their daughters' belongings. She recounted how she straightforwardly asked Minerva about her sexual experiences:

> I don't know, I just had a feeling she might be having *relaciones* [sexual relations] with her boyfriend, so I just asked her. She looked surprised at the question but then admitted it. I was so mad because she is so young, I began to tell her all kinds of things, I told her, "*¡Eres una pendeja! No sabes lo que haces* [You are a fool! You don't know what you are doing]!"

Within a larger societal context of patriarchal control over women's bodies, it was difficult for mothers to see their daughter as sexual subjects. Because girls are viewed as property that can be damaged, their sexual behaviors and activities are often not regarded as a choice they make for themselves.[8] Instead, mothers initially drew on a specific cultural frame about gendered sexuality to make sense of their daughters' sexual behavior. Their anger and concern about what they interpreted as their daughters' victimization are reflective of the prevailing dominant perspective on teenage girls' sexuality in our society, namely the assumption that, when girls participate in sexual activities, that action is not guided by their own sexual desires and curiosity. While teenage boys are readily accepted as sexual beings overrun by their hormones and/or efforts to assert their masculinity, teenage girls are generally constructed as their sexual prey, susceptible to trickery by boys and men (often in the form of promises of love and romance).[9] Rather than explain teenage girls' sexual behaviors as possibly originating in girls themselves, we tend to understand their sexual activities through the sexual agency of boys and men. Latina mothers selected this prevailing cultural frame to interpret the sexual behavior of their teenage daughters. I must underscore that when I refer to Latina mothers' use of this cultural framing, I see this frame not as unique to Latinas but rather a cultural frame that is also found and made available to them within the larger U.S. society.

The cultural frame of sexual victimization was not only applied to heterosexual-identified young women. Three of the four mothers of lesbian-identified girls also drew upon this explanation as they grappled with their daughters' sexual behavior. Martina, a Mexican woman in her late forties who worked part-time at a dry cleaner shop, was one such mother. She related how, on a fall afternoon, she came to the realization that her seventeen-year-old daughter Margarita and her daughter's best friend were more than just friends:

> I saw them walking down the street, they didn't see me, though. They were saying good-bye to each other, and you know how people sometimes give each other a kiss on the cheek when they say hello or goodbye? Well, they gave each other a kiss on the lips! ¡Me muero de vergüenza [I almost died of embarrassment]! When she got home, I told her that I saw her. I told her that I didn't want her hanging out with the girl, esa güera loca sin vergüenza [that crazy shameless white girl]! I know she put those ideas in Margarita's head.

Martina, like the mothers of heterosexual-identified girls, assumed that her daughter's partner had taken advantage of her. She attributed Margarita's violation of heteronormative expectations and unabashed public behavior to the negative influence of her daughter's partner. But Martina also specifically connected this conduct to the race/ethnicity of her daughter's partner, demonstrated in her description of her as "esa güera loca sin vergüenza." Similarly, Gina, a Puerto Rican mother of three who worked as a hairdresser, referenced race when she first learned about her sixteen-year-old daughter's relationship with another young woman:

> I overheard them in the hallway one day, talking about being in love with each other and other things. I called Imelda's friend later that night and told her I didn't want her to

come to my house anymore. I did it in front of my daughter and she started crying, that it wasn't my business, this and that. I told her that *que eso estaba muy mal y que esa blanca era una muchacha perversa* [that it was very wrong and that that white girl was a perverse young girl].

Almost all mothers discussed what they perceived to be the sexual immorality of white women, a theme I explore in more detail later in this chapter. However, the mothers of lesbian-identified girls specifically made reference to the negative influence of white young women on their daughters in their initial postdiscovery conversations with their daughters.[10] Thus, this group of mothers utilized the cultural frame of victimization to initially make sense of their daughters' same-sex attraction, but they also interpreted their daughters' actions through the lens of race/ethnicity. They found themselves having to come to terms not only with their daughters' sexual disobedience but also with their deviation from heteronormative expectations, reflecting what they took to be an undesirable assimilation to the sexual impropriety of whites. As Gina put it when I asked her why she thought that her daughter's partner was influencing her behavior, "*¿Dónde va a aprender esas cochinadas? ¡¿Con quién más, pero con esa muchacha blanca* [Where else is she going to learn such filth? With who else, but with that white girl]?!" The attitudes expressed by this group of mothers are consistent with those reported in previous studies, which found that some communities of color in the United States interpret same-sex identities, practices, and behaviors as specific to and reflective of "white culture."[11]

TALKIN' SAFE SEX WITH DAUGHTERS

All of the mothers saw themselves as the parent directly responsible for providing their daughters with sex education.[12] Prior studies of parent-child sexuality communication have found that, generally, mothers assume primary responsibility for talking to their children about sex-related topics.[13] This is not necessarily because mothers are naturally better at talking to their children about sex. One reason that mothers take on this challenging task is that they are typically the parent expected to guide their child's sexual development and the parent most blamed when a child is seen as failing to conform to normative gender and sexual expectations.

At first glance, the initial reactions of the mothers I spoke with seem to suggest that they expected their daughters to refrain from premarital sex. But most mothers insisted that virginity itself was not the overriding expectation they had for their daughters, even before learning of their daughters' sexual behaviors. In other words, the sex education they provided to their daughters prior to these magnified moments of discovery and confrontation was not limited to lessons about virginity. Despite the "victimization" reactions that affected their postdiscovery conversations with their daughters about sexuality, mothers reported that, in their prediscovery sexuality communication with their daughters, they had highlighted the importance of postponing sexual relationships until they were older and/or practicing safe sex rather than urging abstinence only. As other recent studies on Latina mothers' sexual socialization of daughters have found, in our conversations these mothers did not think it realistic to expect that their daughters would refrain from sexual activities until they were married.[14] Instead, central in mothers' accounts of their prediscovery sexuality messages to their daughters were interrelated lessons about the need to "*respetar a sí misma*" (have self-respect) and "*cuidarse*" (take care of oneself). When I asked Emma, who had found her daughter's condoms, what she meant when she told me that she instructed her daughter to have self-respect, she replied, "With so many diseases, like AIDS, I want her to be careful." She further elaborated, "I told her, 'I can't be there to watch you all the time. Sex is something normal, but very serious, nobody is going to take care of your body and your health but you. . . . That means you have respect yourself if you want people to respect you.'"

Respeto (respect) has been consistently understood as a cultural value and a familial factor that influences gender socialization practices within Latino families. Often coupled with the cultural value of *familismo* (familism), *respeto* refers to deference to the authority of elders, including parents and other adults in the family and the community. According to most cultural explanations of Latina/o sexual practices, respect is generally demonstrated in the avoidance of behavior that could bring shame to one's family; thus, there is an expectation that young women will act in a "decent and good" manner, which is tightly linked to sexual propriety. However, among the Latina mothers I interviewed, *respeto* was redefined to include the expectation of "*respetar a si misma*" (respecting one's self), emphasizing the importance of the honor that young women bestow upon themselves, particularly by taking care of their sexual and reproductive health. The sociologist Gloria González-López also found that some of the Mexican immigrant mothers she interviewed had altered the sex education lessons they provided to their daughters. As she asserts, this suggests "a new ethic of *protección y cuidado personal* that promotes sexual-moderation" for daughters.[15] According to the mothers I spoke with, having knowledge about how to prevent pregnancy and protect oneself from sexually transmitted diseases are important components of a women's respectability.

The mothers' integration of sexual safety into the meaning of respect that they imparted to daughters was informed by the prevailing discourse of teen sexuality as risky. This discourse incorporates and reinforces problematic notions about gender, race, class, and sexuality. Though teen pregnancy was not the only negative sexual outcome that concerned the mothers, they regularly mentioned it when discussing their sexual socialization of their daughters. For instance, Emma had this to say: "Latina girls now start having sex too young! I saw in the news the other night that a lot of kids of all races are having sex, but they said that it is the Latina girls that get pregnant and have babies, more than other kids." Mothers knew some young women in their communities and/or families who had experienced early motherhood, but, as evident in Emma's comments, their perception that Latina girls were more likely to become pregnant was also informed by the broader cultural treatment of teen sexuality as perilous, a dominant approach to teen sexuality that too often homes in on the experiences of Latina and African American girls as the main example of why teen sexuality is a problem. Aware of the visibility of Latina girls in representations of teen sexuality, mothers sought to protect their daughters from negative sexual outcomes. They told me that they emphasized the importance of safe sex to daughters even before finding out about their sexual behavior, when they thought their daughters were virgins, because they were concerned for their daughters' sexual well-being in what they understood to be a context of uncontrolled teenage sexual activity fraught with harmful consequences.

Even if they were uncomfortable in doing so, the mothers thought it necessary to provide their daughters with some knowledge to help them navigate what they saw to be a precarious adolescent sexuality terrain. They cited two principal resources that facilitated their ability to communicate with their daughters about safe sex: a mother-daughter program at Casa de la Mujer and the media. Emma, for example, highlighted an HIV/AIDS workshop that she and her daughter took part in as participants of *Entre Nosotras,* the mother-daughter program at Casa de la Mujer:

> I learned that it was not going to be enough for me to tell her to not have sex or not to get pregnant. There are other consequences that come with sex, like for one's health. I still tell her that I don't think she should be having sexual relations right now, but if she is, not to expect the guy she is with to protect her health—she has to do it.

The other two mothers who participated in this mother-daughter program also referred to the program as they discussed what they told their daughters about sex and how they talked to them.

The mothers who did not participate in this program mainly pointed to the media when they explained how they communicated with their daughters about sexual and reproductive health. There has been much concern about whether the media are a reliable source of information on sexuality-related issues, such as safe sex and representations of LGBTQ individuals and groups. Despite critiques of media representations of these topics, some observers have argued that certain media forms, such as TV and radio talk shows, open up opportunities for individuals and groups to have conversations about sexuality in ways that might not be possible otherwise.[16] The media forms that most of these mothers mentioned were Spanish-language TV talk shows and radio shows. They also made reference to Spanish-language newspapers and magazines, but not to the extent to which they talked about TV and radio shows. Describing an episode of *El Show de Cristina* that featured HIV-positive women, Dolores, a forty-year-old Mexican woman, said:

> The majority of them [the guests on *El Show de Cristina*] got HIV from their husbands or boyfriends, who had cheated on them with other women. They trusted them and said they felt they didn't need to use a condom or that even if they had their doubts, they felt

that their husbands or boyfriends would be offended if they asked them to put on a condom. They were devastated. I told Asucena about the show and that it is the kind of thing that can happen to anyone and that is why she needs to be very careful.

Like almost all of the mothers in this study, Dolores did not go into details about how to use a condom or STD transmission routes because she did not feel comfortable and/or knowledgeable enough to go into such specifics. But, as reflected in Emma's and Dolores's narratives, mothers still managed to use the language of safe sex, such as condom use and HIV prevention, that they drew from resources such as a mother-daughter program and/or media presentations. The cultural visibility of safe-sex promotion through such outlets in our society allowed the mothers to develop some skills to communicate sex education lessons to their daughters, particularly their integration of sexual safety into their redefinition of a woman's self-respect.

Despite the significance of media and mother-daughter workshops for what mothers said and how they talked to their daughters about sexual safety, it is important to bear in mind that their notions of gender and sexuality were not fixed before their access to these resources. Prior to arriving in the United States, these women had experienced structural changes in their homelands, such as modernity and globalization, forces that have impacted how Mexicans and Puerto Ricans understand and construct their gender and sexual identities and practices.[17] In other words, we should not assume that these women's meanings of gender and sexuality had not evolved before they arrived in the United States. For instance, in her examination of generational perspectives and practices pertaining to marriage and sexuality among members of transnational families living in rural Mexico and urban Atlanta, the anthropologist Jennifer S. Hirsch found that, even before migrating to the United States, younger Mexican women had redefined the purposes of marriage and sexuality.[18] Rather than conceive of marriage as a way for women to secure respect for themselves that required them to defer to husbands (as older women did), younger women saw this relationship as needing to be characterized by companionship. And sex within marriage, for this group of women, moved beyond serving only a reproductive purpose to being a source of pleasure and intimacy. According to Hirsch, social transformations, such as young women's increased access to media in rural Mexico and their increasing age at marriage, informed younger women's stances on marriage and sexuality.

Additionally, mothers' immigration experiences have also had implications for their daughters' approaches to gender and sexuality. Scholars who have explored the relationships among gender, sexuality, and migration processes have shown that immigrant men and women negotiate and reconfigure gender and sexual relations and arrangements as they adjust to a new context.[19] Rather than interpret gender and sexual shifts as either emancipatory or subjugating,[20] this literature illustrates that various factors, such as age, class status, marital status, place of origin (i.e., urban versus rural), and employment matter for how immigrants produce and experience gender and sexuality.

For example, González-López found that Mexican immigrant women's ability to provide economically for their families in the United States boosted their confidence and their sense of authority in the home, contributing to their perception of themselves as being capable of discussing sex with their children.[21]

LESSONS ABOUT INEQUALITY

The mothers continued offering messages about sexual safety after learning about their daughters' sexual activities. But this approach was now coupled with their explicit emphasis on the gender inequality associated with women's expressions of sexuality; they made connections among inequality, women's sexuality, and suffering. One way they accomplished this was by recounting the negative experiences of other women they personally knew. These experiences were relayed to their daughters to serve as lessons about heartbreak, unplanned pregnancy, sexually transmitted diseases, violence, and even poverty.[22] Gina, who found out about her daughter's same-sex relationship when she inadvertently overheard Imelda's conversation with her partner, highlighted violence as a consequence of expressions of queer sexuality and gender nonconformity by describing to her daughter the experience of a woman who lived in Gina's community in Puerto Rico: "We knew this woman *que era una deesas* [was one of those (implying lesbians)]. *Muy bonita* [very pretty], but didn't like men, acted and walked around like a man. She was raped and brutally beaten. . . . I told Imelda about this so that she knows what can happen to her for doing things like that." Gina's admonition to her daughter both emphasized her disapproval of Imelda's same-sex relationship and provided a warning about the physical consequences Imelda could encounter as a lesbian.

The majority of the mothers also now drew upon their own lived experiences, revealing previously guarded information about themselves in post-discovery conversations with their daughters. Such was the case for Francisca, who was the only mother who took her daughter to obtain birth control after learning about her sexual behavior. The Puerto Rican medical assistant and mother of two looked much younger than her forty years. Francisca detailed how she disclosed a painful and secret aspect of her past to her seventeen-year-old daughter, Samantha:

> I had always told her that I didn't leave my parents' house in Puerto Rico until I was married, but I decided to tell her the truth. I wanted her to know that I knew what I was talking about because *yo lo viví en carne propia* [I lived it myself in my own flesh]. I ran away from home with my first boyfriend. My mother warned me that I would suffer with him, but I didn't listen. Shortly after moving in with him, he started beating me. . . . I finally left him, but I suffered tremendously with him.

Likewise, Sara, a blue-eyed Puerto Rican woman with long black hair, recounted the information she shared with her seventeen-year-old daughter, Jocelyn:

He [Jocelyn's father] kept wanting me to live with him, and I would tell him no because I was young. So one time when he was drunk he saw my father and told him that I had already been sexually involved with him. My dad kicked me out, and I had nowhere to go, so I went to live with him. He was such a jealous man . . . he wouldn't even let me work because he did not want me to talk to any men. So I didn't work, and, when he left me, he left me pregnant with Jocelyn and no money, no job. I told Jocelyn all this so she could know that all our bad choices have consequences for many years.

Through their disclosures, the mothers worked to assert themselves as knowledgeable women because, as stated by Francisca, they had lived the consequences of sexual activity "*en carne propia*." I see the mothers' disclosures about their sexual experiences as *testimonios* (stories of lived experiences). As the Latina Feminist Group highlights, *testimonios* is a genre that has been used in a variety of ways; for example, Latin American women have employed it in their efforts to document political violence. However, the Latina Feminist Group has reconceptualized *testimonios* "as a tool for Latinas to theorize oppression, resistance, and subjectivity."[23] I utilize this conceptualization to understand the mothers' use of *testimonios* with their daughters. Mothers relied upon their *testimonios* to provide their daughters with messages about gender and sexual inequality. Thus, they also drew on the resource of their own experiences as women. They may not have had the knowledge in the "technical know-how" sense to explain the particulars of condom use or HIV transmission, but they built on the wisdom gained from their life experiences.[24] Mothers' use of *testimonios* in the postdiscovery sex education of daughters highlighted the relationship between a woman's sexual history and her life circumstances.

However, daughters made different sense of the connections between sexuality and gender inequality than that conveyed by their mothers in *testimonios*. Carefully taking sips of a hot latte, seventeen-year-old Samantha, a bright high school junior with plans to go to medical school, described how she responded to her mother upon learning of her experiences with the boyfriend with whom she ran away from home:

But, like I told her, I really wouldn't put myself in that situation because things are different now, for one, we ain't in Puerto Rico. I wouldn't be lettin' no man kick my ass! She had it rough. . . . I think she stood with that guy for as long as she did because she probably thought she had to, you know, since she lost her virginity to him and her mom had told her no other man would want her like that. But I tell her that with all my friends I know, guys and girls, it ain't like that no more, where you gotta stay with the first person you have sex with if you're a girl. It doesn't have to mean your life is over. She's old-school Puerto Rican like that.

Many young women, like Samantha, asserted that they would not encounter the types of negative experiences their mothers described because they would not tolerate them. The majority of girls reported that they identified the source of women's suffering described in their mothers' *testimonios* as women's uncritical conformity to gendered sexual scripts, rather than their failure to behave in a sexually acceptable manner. Seventeen-year-old Minerva, whose mother asked her if she was having sexual relations with her partner, explained this perspective:

> She started going off on me, you know, that I was stupid for believing everything my boyfriend told me, but it wasn't even like that! I was like, "Look, I was never going to wait [to have sex] until I was married. I'm not going to be one of those *mexicanitas* [little Mexican women, implying that some Mexican woman are very traditional] that is supposed to be all pure on my wedding day, what for?!" My cousin got married the so-called right way and her husband still treats her like shit and there she is, trying to be the good wife and mother, cooking, cleaning, while he goes out and messes around with other girls. I don't think so!

Similarly, Olivia, a slender seventeen-year-old with eyes the color of honey, conveyed a similar point as she described the violence her father often inflicted on her mother:

> My mom always tries to make excuses for my dad, "Your dad acts that way because that is how men are, jealous." So she does stuff like let him know where she is going and what time she will be back . . . but she won't leave him because she thinks my grandma will not like it. My grandma doesn't believe in divorce, she's always saying that marriage, no matter what, is forever. So my mom puts up with my dad's bullshit because she thinks that's it, there is nothing she can do about it now that she's married.

Within the *testimonios* that their mothers imparted to them and within the experiences of other women they knew, young Latinas detected the uneven terrain in which men and women negotiate and express their sexuality. As the narratives of Samantha and Minerva demonstrate, daughters understood such experiences to be testaments to the dangers embedded in gender and sexual hierarchies that privilege men and penalize women. Furthermore, Samantha's statement to her mother that "we're not in Puerto Rico anymore" and Minerva's assertion to her mother that "I'm not gonna be one of those *mexicanitas*" as they attempted to justify their behaviors to their mothers highlight the intergenerational negotiations of sexuality and gender within U.S. Latina mother-daughter relationships. Girls' narratives indicate that their second-generation status was significant in informing their adoption of gendered identities. In other words, when they considered their mothers' expectations of them, they highlighted how their social world was different from that in which their mothers grew up. Girls' responses to their mothers' *testimonios* about gender inequality suggest that they saw other possible ways to construct gendered Mexican or Puerto Rican identities for themselves. According to these Latina girls, as young women growing up in the United States, they did not want to be and could not be "old-school Puerto Rican like that" or "one of those *mexicanitas*."

However, as I discuss shortly, this did not mean that they saw themselves as more "Americanized" in their sexual attitudes and behaviors, either.

This process of intergenerational negotiations of gender and sexuality was also evident when girls challenged their mothers' accusations that they had behaved idiotically and/or been deceived by their partners. Five girls did not argue against their mothers' constructions of them as victims. Instead, they relied upon a victimization explanation to help lessen their mothers' anger or disappointment. As one young woman explained: "She was already pissed off about the whole thing, I thought she was going to kick my ass. I was just like, 'I fell for his lies.' She was still mad, but not as much. More mad at him, I think." But more than half of the girls who reported that their mothers had some knowledge of their sexual activities said that, in their initial confrontations with their mothers, they had asserted their desire and agency in their sexual decision making. Exemplifying this, sixteen-year-old Miriam (whose mother picked her up from school after discovering condoms in her bedroom) remarked, "She kept going on about how he used me and that I wasn't '*una señorita*' [a sexually innocent young women] anymore. I told her that wasn't true . . . that no one made me do anything and that I knew what I was doing. No one played me." A petite young woman with waist-length black hair, sixteen-year-old Inés made a similar point as she discussed her effort to convince her mother that she had not been duped into sexual relations: "She was, like, exaggerating, you know, crying, and saying that he [partner] wasn't gonna want me now that he got what he wanted from me. I told her, 'How do you know I wasn't the one that got what I wanted?' She slapped me . . . guess she didn't like that answer." Inés's mother's response underscores the fact that deviance from gendered sexual conformity is not only punished through verbal sanctions but is also often met with violence to secure its stability, in this case, between mothers and daughters. In these magnified moments of discovery and confrontation, the girls attempted to make visible their sexual subjectivity and also raised questions about the gendered sexual scripts they were expected to take on.

"PERO, ¡¿CÓMO EXPLICO ESTO [BUT HOW DO I EXPLAIN THIS]?!": SHAME, DISCLOSURES, AND CONCEALMENT WITHIN THE FAMILY

Teresa proudly showed me pictures of her two daughters as we sat in her living room. It was a humid August afternoon, and all the windows in her small, second-floor Humboldt Park apartment were open as a box fan sitting in a corner noisily blew some air. At one point, Teresa, who said she regularly searched her daughters' belongings, excused herself to lean out the window. A waitress with a head of tight auburn curls and skin the color of cinnamon, Teresa was checking up on her daughters, sixteen-year-old Irene and thirteen-year-old Jeanne, who were sitting on the front stairs of the three-flat red brick building talking to some girlfriends when I arrived for the interview. Spotting her youngest daughter standing on the curb and talking to two Latino boys in a black Cadillac, she yelled out the window, "*¡Jeanne! ¡¿Qué tú haces* [What are you doing]?!" With that, her daughter walked away from the curb and the car sped off, setting off car alarms along the street with the bass from the hip-hop music emanating from it. Satisfied that her youngest daughter was behaving, Teresa moved away from the living room window, disapprovingly commenting to me that her daughters wanted to act older than their actual age. As she sat down, she added, "I've been talking to them, you know, about sex *y de eso* [and that]. I'm keeping an eye on them, *no quiero ninguna sorpresa* [I don't want any surprises]," emphasizing this point by making the shape of a pregnant belly with her hands over her abdomen.

Teresa consulted with her sister when she initially learned of her sixteen-year-old daughter's sexual conduct: "I wanted to give her [daughter] *una buena paliza* [a good beating] that she'd never forget! I was so mad! I told my sister, and she made me calm down, you know? She's the one that helped me figure out how to deal with it." Like Teresa, most mothers turned to other women in the family to help them cope with their feelings of anger, disappointment, and confusion upon learning of their daughters' sexual behavior. This was typically done shortly after the mothers first confronted their daughters. But they also reached out to other women in their family to involve them in the sex education of their daughters, assistance that mothers had not actively sought out prior to their discovery. The mothers' disclosure of their daughters' behavior was not an easy task for them. Most of them described feeling shame as they revealed this information to selected women in the family, reflected in phrases such as, "*¡qué vergüenza* [how embarrassing]!" and "*¡qué pena* [what a shame]!" For instance, Emma decided to confide in her daughter's godmother, explaining, "She has daughters that are slightly older than Miriam, I thought she could advise me or give Miriam some advice. At first, *sí me dio vergüenza* [I felt shame] telling my *comadre* [daughter's godmother]." Despite their embarrassment, the mothers opened up to particular women in their families to obtain assistance for their daughters in what was interpreted as a moment of danger or crisis for them.

Several studies on gendered family dynamics reveal that, among some groups in which extended families are the norm, including Latinas/os, young women oftentimes develop important relationships with women in their families in addition to their mothers.[25] Mothers who disclosed information to other women in the family always specifically identified a woman or women that they trusted and perceived to have a close relationship with their daughters. Specifically, they involved other women so that they could provide their daughters with *consejos* (advice). For example, Lilia asked her sister to speak with her daughter Eva after her sixteen-year-old daughter admitted that she had already had sexual relations with her boyfriend. A soft-spoken Mexican woman who had the habit of pushing her oversized brown framed glasses up on the bridge of her nose, Lilia felt that her teenage daughter would be more receptive to the advice her aunt offered her: "I know Eva spends a lot of time with my sister, especially when I'm not there. Eva even told my sister first, when she got her period. My sister was the one to tell me that my daughter got her first period. So, I thought she could help *aconsejarla* [advise her]." Similarly, Luz, who volunteered as a Sunday school teacher for her Catholic parish, confided in her twenty-year-old niece after secretly reading her fifteen-year-old daughter's diary and learning about her sexual experiences. Not wanting to reveal to her daughter that she had read her diary, Luz approached her niece instead: "My niece, she's a good girl, smart, you know, going to college. . . . I told her about Iris [her daughter] and asked her if she could take her to visit her college, you know, talk to her, get her mind off the boys and back on school." Mothers' relationships with other women in the family and their daughters' relationships with these women, therefore, were a critical resource that they purposefully drew upon to offer their daughters guidance now that they were aware of some of the sexual experiences of the girls.

The mothers' strategy of revealing their daughters' sexual behaviors to specific women in their family, however, was a two-pronged tactic. Besides attempting to acquire support for themselves and their daughters, mothers also sought to perform some damage control. When talking to other women in their family, they were also certain to emphasize their proper socialization of their daughters, drawing on a larger cultural script of good mothering to deflect the blame they anticipated receiving for their daughters' sexual impropriety. Mothers generally encounter assorted scripts from various sources about the "right way to be a mother"; for instance, in terms of employment and mothering, one script can be that of a selfless mother who forgoes employment to raise her children and another script can be that of a "superwoman" who excels both as a mother and in the workplace.[26] These cultural scripts, though seemingly different, rest on the notion of an ideal mother role that women must fulfill, regardless of whether social structures actually support this expectation. By disclosing their daughters' sexual behaviors to other women in the family, the mothers I spoke with sought to demonstrate that they had not failed to be good mothers. Emma, for instance, stressed to her daughter's godmother that she had always talked to Miriam about the importance of respecting herself, explaining to her that Miriam "still did what she wanted, *siempre ha sido muy rebelde* [she's always been rebellious]." Similarly, Teresa told her sister that she had taught her daughters to behave *"como unas señoritas* [like proper young women]," pointing out that *"pero hacen lo que les da la gana* [but they do whatever they want]." Through the process of disclosure and the explanation that, despite the mothers' best efforts, the daughters did whatever they pleased, the mothers attempted to assert their respectability as good mothers.

Their effort to maintain this identity underscores the pressures felt by mothers in general within a larger cultural context of mother blaming. Since mothers are assumed and expected to be the primary caretakers of children, they are often the parents held most responsible for their children's misbehavior and failure. And, given that parents are expected to model normative gender behavior for their same-sex children, the sexual "misbehavior" of a daughter can also be read as a shortcoming of her mother's own femininity. The distance that mothers declared between themselves and their daughters' misbehavior in interactions with other women in their family indicates that they were performing a particular gendered identity, that of the good mother. This performance also reflected their internalized gendered selves. The sociologist Karin A. Martin contends that it is through such culturally constructed gendered identities that women and men are disciplined and shaped from the inside.[27] In other words, the mothers' gendered subjectivity, how they understood themselves as women, integrated a perception of themselves as mothers who had indeed fulfilled what was expected of them, unintentionally reinforcing the mother blaming that they were trying to evade.

The mothers anticipated that their husbands would also assign blame to them for their daughters' sexual behavior. To prevent the fathers from learning about their daughters' sexual transgressions, some of them decided not to consult with other women in the family about their daughters' emerging sexuality. Dolores, who discussed with her daughter the experiences of the HIV-positive women on *El Show de Cristina*, stated the following: "I don't want anyone to know about what she has done, especially her father. *Esto lo mata* [this will kill him]!" Dolores explained that her husband would react to such knowledge by blaming her for their daughter's behavior: "He's going to say that I did not take care of her." Maria, who migrated from Puerto Rico shortly after marrying her husband at the age of eighteen, expressed a similar concern about her husband's potential reaction: "I know him, he will say that it is my fault that she did this." When I asked her why she thought he would react this way, she quickly responded, "Because he always thinks that I give her too much freedom . . . *me va a echar la culpa* [he will blame me]. He is going to say that I let this happen." To avoid these interactions with their husbands, they kept the knowledge about their daughters' sexual activities between themselves and their daughters.

These mothers explained to their daughters that they would not inform their fathers about their actions because the knowledge would be especially devastating to them. Luz, who had asked her niece to reach out to her daughter, communicated this to her daughter: "I told her, you better hope your dad does not find out, you'll kill him." These three mothers described their husbands as hardworking and emotionally strong but asserted that they would not be able to handle knowledge of daughters' sexual behaviors and that they therefore felt it necessary to protect them from such news. They insisted that it was primarily their responsibility to handle such parenting challenges, especially because they were not employed outside the home.[28] They explained that, despite the financial constraints they were facing, they had decided not to work outside the home so that they could dedicate more time to their children. Like the Mexican immigrant women in the sociologist Denise A. Segura's exploration of Chicanas' and Mexicanas' meanings of the relationship between motherhood and employment,[29] almost all of the mothers that I spoke with did not feel conflicted about their employment outside the home and their ability to mother well.[30] But there were four mothers who did not work outside the home, stating that it was a voluntary nonemployment and that, like the Chicanas that Segura interviewed, they understood employment as taking away from their ability to fulfill their mothering responsibilities (rather than viewing it as part of motherhood). Holding themselves to an "idealized form of motherhood," they most likely saw themselves as failing at what they deemed to be their most important social role. These mothers, therefore, were particularly concerned that their husbands and other family members would criticize them harshly, since, as "stay-at-home" mothers, they were "supposed to be" able to be particularly vigilant about their children's activities.

However, some mothers' concerns about being perceived as bad mothers informed their decision to tell their daughters' fathers about the sexual behavior of daughters.[31] Most of these women did find that their daughters' fathers initially reacted by blaming them, a culpability that mothers rejected in heated discussions with their partners. But the mothers utilized this moment of disclosure as a way to attempt to shift some responsibility onto the fathers should their daughters encounter an unplanned pregnancy and/or develop an STD. For instance, Teresa, who was one of four mothers of heterosexual-identified girls who told her husband about their daughters' sexual activities, explained why she decided to tell her husband: "If I didn't tell him and they end up pregnant, he will ask me how come I didn't know about what they were doing. And if he finds out that I did know, he will be even more angry with me! This way, he knows what I know and we both have to be vigilant about what they are doing." Similarly, Aracelia reasoned, "I felt that, like it or not, I was going to have to tell him. He needed to know. We both needed to face this reality and think about what to do now." Most mothers did not think that the fathers would talk to their daughters about sex and did not expect them to do so, noting that the fathers would be too uncomfortable and that it was more appropriate for mothers to do so because they were the same gender as their daughters.[32] But they did expect the fathers to respond by reinforcing any rules and restrictions that both parents now placed on their daughters, such as new curfews and limits on phone use.

Additionally, mothers told their husbands because they wanted their daughters to experience shame at their fathers' expressed disappointment in them. Carmen made the following point: "Minerva *es su consentida* [is his princess/spoiled girl], and I knew that she would be very embarrassed that he knew about what she did. He told her, 'You have disappointed me. . . . I thought you were smarter than this. How could you behave like this?!' She was not talking back to him the way she did with me, she was just crying." Like other mothers I spoke with, Carmen may have communicated with her daughter about sexual safety and even opened up about her own sexual history, but this did not necessarily mean that she was completely comfortable with or condoning of her daughter's sexual behavior. These mothers invoked the relationship that daughters had with their fathers, particularly perceptions and expectations that they thought fathers had of daughters, such as fathers' views of their daughters as asexual, sexually innocent, and obedient, to reprimand the daughters and to discourage further sexual activity. Girls whose fathers did know about their sexual behavior told me that they felt "bad" or "embarrassed" about their fathers' knowledge of their behavior. Some even said they wished their mothers had not shared this information with their fathers. Sixteen-year-old Lucy, a young Mexican woman I interviewed for an exploratory study of sexual responsibility among Latina youth, expressed how she felt when her father found out that she was no longer a virgin: "I felt bad. Just it's a different relationship I have with my mom than the relationship I have with my dad. . . . He's always seen me as his little girl and I knew that at that point, he knew I wasn't his little girl anymore. I was his sweet little innocent girl."[33]

Three of the four mothers of lesbian-identified girls also told their daughters' fathers about what they had discovered. Martina, who saw her daughter kissing another girl, recounted how she demanded that Margarita tell her father about her sexual relationship with her girlfriend, "She had to tell him, because I did not want to say those words to him. I could tell that he was not expecting to hear that . . . he wanted to cry but didn't, he just kept asking her what was wrong with her. She would not even look him in the eyes because she was so ashamed." Like the mothers of heterosexual-identified girls, these mothers also relied upon the fathers' expressions of disillusionment to discourage their daughters from continuing with their sexual activities. But, unlike the mothers of heterosexual-identified girls, these mothers were also "outing" their daughters to their fathers. Fathers reacted to this information primarily as an indication of their daughter's sexual deviance or abnormality, as suggested by Margarita's father questioning what was wrong with her, rather than to their daughters' loss of virginity or sexual innocence. One of these mothers even told me that she initially hesitated to tell her husband because she was concerned that her husband might throw the daughter out of the home. This concern was based on her husband's support of a friend who had kicked his teenage son out of the home when the son came out to his parents. As scholars have noted, the repercussions for LGBTQ youth can be detrimental when they come out to their families or when they are "outed" within their families because they are vulnerable along a number of dimensions, particularly given their economic and emotional dependence on their families.[34]

Though all but one of the mothers of lesbian-identified girls told their daughters' fathers about their discovery of their daughter's same-sex attraction and sexual behaviors, all four of these mothers endeavored to conceal this knowledge from extended family members and therefore did not divulge any information to other women. Roberta, who was born and raised in a Mexican border city, was so worried that her family would find out about her daughter that she canceled our first interview three times, each time calling me back to reschedule and asking me to thoroughly explain how I would maintain the confidentiality of her and her daughter. She explained how she dealt with questions about her daughter's lack of interest in boys:

> Sometimes when we get together, like for parties, my *comadres* or sister-in-law will ask me if Barbara has a boyfriend yet. I don't know what to say, so I just tell them that she's too busy focusing on school and they tell me that I'm lucky that she's so focused on school

instead of boys. I don't want them to know, *ya me imagino el escándolo si supieran* [I could just imagine the scandal, if they knew]. This is different, it's not like when a girl gets pregnant or something like that because people can understand that sort of thing, *pero ¡¿cómo explico esto* [but how do I explain this]?!

Elsa, who had migrated from Puerto Rico with her family as a child and was a manager at a fast-food restaurant, also recounted how she addressed inquiries from relatives about her daughter Arely's participation in a gay-straight alliance club in school. One of Arely's cousins, who also attended the same high school, had told Elsa's sister about Arely's active role within the club.

> After my niece's communion, we all went to my brother's house, and my sister asked me in front of everyone if it was true that Arely was in *"uno de esos clubs en la escuela, para esos gays* [one of those school clubs, for those gay people]." I was so mad at her for asking me that like that, everyone was quiet waiting for my answer. I told them that she was in a club for young people that were gay but also for people that weren't, to support young people that are gay in dealing with discrimination and things like that. I told them that Arely was not a lesbian but that she wanted to help out with things like that. I was like, "You know how Arely is about injustice." They seemed to believe me. But I told Arely not to say anything to them, at least not yet, you know, I don't know how they are going to react or what I'm going to say when it is known. Because I know that *tarde o temprano, se van a dar cuenta* [sooner or later, they will find out].

These mothers especially struggled with figuring out how they would explain their daughters' sexual behaviors to extended family members. While mothers of heterosexual-identified girls were able to rely upon claims of victimization, mothers of lesbian-identified girls did not feel that they could frame their daughters' behavior in this way to others (although, as discussed earlier in this chapter, they did reference victimization in their initial postdiscovery interactions with daughters). Elsa emphasized this point when she exclaimed, *"Pero ¡¿cómo explico esto?!"* This group of mothers conveyed a critical awareness of the "margin of error" that is afforded to heterosexual young women but that would not be extended to their daughters because their sexual behavior defied heteronormative expectations.[35] For example, Martina pointed out that, while people would initially perceive a young girl who was pregnant or no longer a virgin in a negative manner, this reaction would not be permanent. She animatedly explained, "People will get over it because we all know that she is not the first one and she sure is not going to be the last one." Thus, their daughters' sexual behavior could be perceived as much more deliberate than that of heterosexual young women in the family whose behavior might be attributed to their victimization.

These mothers also did not feel they could readily claim that their daughters' behavior was related to their rebelliousness, reflected in the phrase *"hacen lo que les da la gana* [they do whatever they want]." They expressed concern that extended family members would view their daughters' "doing what they wanted to do" as an indication that something was inherently wrong with their daughters. When I asked Gina how she thought her family would react if they found out about Imelda's sexual activities, she quickly answered, "*Que está loca* [that she's crazy]!" Martina, when asked the same question, similarly replied, "*Van a decir que está mal de la cabeza porque no es normal lo que hace ella* [they are going to say that she is sick in the head because what she is doing is not normal]." Mothers of lesbian-identified girls were worried that, while others might accept the explanation that their daughters were acting as they pleased, their behavior would still be understood as evidence of their moral and/or psychological deficiency. Mothers based these concerns on larger public discussions about the "causes of gay behavior" in the media and on their own experiences with informal conversations about gay or lesbian individuals.[36] Familiar with the homophobic discourses circulating in U.S. culture and within their own communities and families, they expressed legitimate concerns that their daughters would be stigmatized for their identification as lesbians and about how this would reflect on them as mothers. At time of interview, these mothers were unable to articulate how they would respond to family members when information about their daughters' sexual behavior was disclosed.

This group of mothers therefore requested that their daughters assist them in their concealment efforts by performing heterosexual femininity within family contexts. For instance, both Roberta and Gina asked their daughters to conform to normative expectations of feminity at family gatherings, figuring that family members would presume that their daughters were heterosexual because their gender presentation would be read as appropriately feminine. According to both mothers and daughters, these requests were a source of conflict between them, as reflected in seventeen-year-old Imelda's comments:

> Every time we are going somewhere where my aunts, uncles, and cousins are going to be, my mom asks me to try to look more "girly," you know what I'm saying? I say no, she starts crying, big of drama, and then I just do it, just to get it over with. I wear something like a nice top or something she likes. . . . I hate when she does that shit!

As she told me this, she pinched the bridge of her nose and tightly shut her brown almond-shaped eyes, trying not to cry. Eighteen-year-old Margarita, a self-described poet, also expressed frustration at her mother's attempts to impose a heterosexual feminine presentation and script on her in front of family members:

> Sometimes she tries to make me dance with guys, you know, like at *quinceañeras* or weddings . . . they come up to ask if I want to dance and I say no, but my mom is all loud, saying, "Go dance with him!" It pisses me off because I'm already trying to be cool with her about a lot of things about who I am. . . . I know it ain't easy for her . . . but I can't pretend forever for her.

These interactions between this group of mothers and daughters indicate that the mothers' strategies were especially shaped by heteronormativity and homophobia, limiting their ability to draw on other women in the family as resources in the same manner that mothers of heterosexual girls could. Their sex education efforts were constrained, if not altogether interrupted, by their efforts to present their daughters as heterosexual to family members, a pressure that they also placed on their daughters and that their daughters deeply resented.

GENDERED RACIAL/ETHNIC BOUNDARIES AND IDENTITIES

Alongside mothers' lessons to their daughters about sexual safety were notions about race/ethnicity. One key way in which these were transmitted was through mothers' judgmental references to the sexuality of young white women. Such an "assignment of sexual meanings, evaluations, and categories to others" are what the sociologist Joane Nagel calls "sexual ascription."[37] Mothers' sexual ascription of young white women marked the racial/ethnic boundary within which their daughters needed to confine their sexual behaviors. The boundary that mothers consistently referenced was not about interracial dating or marriage but about sexual behaviors and attitudes that the mothers specifically associated with white women and girls.[38] They were adamant that they did not want their daughters "to act like white girls," indicating that any flexibility that they had regarding their daughters' emerging sexuality stopped at this border.

Almost all mothers described having warned their daughters not to behave like white young women and/or accused them of doing so, even before they became aware of their daughters' sexual behavior. For example, Sara recounted an incident in which her daughter, who was thirteen at the time, asked for permission to sleep over at a friend's house: "I told her, '¿Qué te crees?! ¿Te quieres portar como las blancas?' [What do you think?! You want to act like white girls?] Their parents let them do whatever they want and then when these girls get in trouble, the parents act like they don't know why they acting so rebellious. . . . I told her no." When I probed her about what she thought young white women acted like, she immediately responded, "Esas sí tienen mucha libertad [Now, those girls have too much freedom]! Sometimes they act like they are crazy, acting like sucias [perverted women]!" Like Sara, mothers tended to characterize white young women as having "mucha libertad [too much freedom]" and/or as being "sin vergüenzas [without shame]." Aracelia, for instance, explained, "I understand that my daughter might have questions about sex . . . but that doesn't mean she can be sin vergüenza, like white girls." Mothers had limited to no interaction with white women and girls. Those who did have limited contact with white women did so through their employment in the service sector, but, for the majority of them, the media were the basis for most of their sexual ascriptions of white women and girls.

Mothers thus also utilized a discursive strategy that specifically integrated perceptions about the sexuality of white women to talk to daughters about their gendered sexual expectations for them. This particular discursive repertoire was also indicative of "how they thought through race," which, as the sociologist Ruth Frankenberg asserts, is "learned, drawn upon, and enacted, repetitively but not automatically or by rote, chosen but by no means freely so."[39] They thought of their daughters as distinct from themselves in the sense that their daughters were coming of age in a context different from that in which they themselves had done so, but they still thought of their daughters as similar to them in terms of their gendered racial/ethnic identity. They drew upon perceptions of racial differences between white women and themselves in terms of sexual behavior and attitudes as a way to assert to their daughters the importance of maintaining a gendered identity that was grounded in their identities as Mexican and Puerto Rican women. Mothers utilized this particular discursive strategy to mark the sexual boundary for their U.S.-born daughters and to assert control over their daughters' sexual behavior through their ability to question their daughters' racial/ethnic authenticity, indicating that these mothers understood their daughters' emerging sexuality through the lens of gender and race.

Furthermore, the mothers challenged negative stereotypes about themselves as Latinas through their characterization of white women as sexually excessive and out of control. Dolores explained her perception of white women's sexual propriety in this fashion: "They are always criticizing us Latinas, saying that we are too traditional or this or that . . . but they should look at themselves first. They are the ones on TV almost naked and doing *pendejadas* [stupid/foolish things]." Like the other mothers, Dolores pointed out that, despite white women's visible presence in media, their sexual behavior was often treated as unremarkable within mainstream society. And, as they talked about how they understood themselves to be judged by the dominant society, the mothers regularly expressed a collective sense of themselves as Latina mothers through the phrase "*nosotras las latinas* [we Latinas]." Conchita conveyed this when she discussed the challenges she encountered in trying to communicate with her daughter about sexuality: "*Nosotras las latinas tenemos que seguir adelante con nuestras hijas* [We Latinas have to press forward with our daughters]." Thus, as a marginalized group in U.S. society, Latina mothers also utilized negative notions of white women's sexual propriety to distinguish themselves from them and to gain some power for themselves through their claim to sexual respectability.[40]

Latina girls, however, rejected their mothers' accusations that they were adopting the sexual behavior and attitudes of white young women, declaring that they were not like them.[41] Sixteen-year-old Juanita strongly asserted this as she discussed why she disagreed with her mother's and aunt's ideas of virginity and other gendered sexual expectations: "I guess it's different to me 'cause I grew up here, but, at the same time, it's not like I want to be like them crazy-ass white girls . . . virginity doesn't mean anything to them, it's like, 'Whatever!'" Similarly, fifteen-year-old Carla recalled that she denied wanting to be "*como las güeras* [like white girls]" in a heated argument with her mom: "She thinks I act the way I do 'cause I just want to be '*como las güeras*.' I told her, 'Not even! I ain't trying to act like that, having sex whenever with whoever, showing my boobs on TV and kissing girls so guys can just look at me. . . . I ain't a 'ho' like that!"[42] Latina girls made it clear that, although they did not fully embrace their mothers' ideas about women's sexuality, they did not identify or want to be identified with what they also perceived to be the sexual excessiveness of white young women. This also was communicated within their peer groups, which were predominately homogeneous along racial/ethnic lines). Daughters utilized the very same sexual ascriptions of young white women that their mothers communicated to them to simultaneously construct their own gendered sexual identities and challenge accusations that they were losing their racial/ethnic identities in the process.

It is worth noting that there was a general silence about the sexuality of African American women and girls in the narratives of both mothers and daughters. While most of the women and girls I spoke with lived in pre-dominantly working-class Latina/o neighborhoods, a significant number of the girls attended public schools in which Latina/o and African American students made up the majority of the student body. Thus, they had more opportunities to interact with African American girls than they did with white girls. Although I cannot offer a conclusive analysis of the invisibility of African American women and girls in these Latinas' narratives about sexuality, one possible explanation could be the pervasiveness and effectiveness of larger racial discourses that already construct African American as the "other."

"YA SABES COMO SON . . . ": ON MEXICAN AND PUERTO RICAN WOMEN

Both Mexican and Puerto Rican mothers drew contrasts between themselves and Latina mothers who belonged to other ethnic groups. Though both groups occasionally mentioned other Latina groups, such as Guatemalan or Ecuadorian women, they most often contrasted Mexicans and Puerto Ricans when talking about the challenges they faced in raising their daughters. Their perspectives on the other group were often based on their interactions with women from that group, usually as neighbors, friends, or co-workers. This was exemplified by Francisca when she discussed her efforts to talk about sex with her seventeen-year-old daughter, Samantha: "My neighbor, she's *mexicana, buena gente y todo* [nice and all], but she never talked to her daughter about *de eso* [that (meaning sex)], and now she is pregnant. *Pobre nena* [poor girl] . . . I don't know, you *mexicanas*, you can't talk about that at home *para nada, ¿verdad?* [at all, right]?"

Early in our interview process, mothers would inquire about my specific racial/ethnic identity, usually taking a guess as to which Latina group I identified with before even allowing me to answer.[43] Mexican women usually prefaced their comments about Puerto Rican women with "*tú sabes como son* [you know how they are]," while Puerto Rican women would generally initiate their commentary on the gendered behavior of Mexican women by asking me to tell them if it was true or not ("*dime si es verdad o no*") or to explain something to them (*"explícame algo"*). But, regardless of how they broached the subject, both groups of mothers expressed their ideas about the other group's socialization of its daughters. For example, discussing why she thought her daughter's friend was a bad influence, Betina criticized what she saw as Puerto Rican mothers' lack of supervision of their daughters:

> She [her daughter's friend] always wants to be out on the street. Sometimes, she tries to *sonsacarse a* [coax] Rita [her daughter] to go hang out with her on the street, but I won't let her. *La mamá la deja que haga lo que le da la gana* [Her mom allows her to do whatever she feels like doing], but I see that a lot of Puerto Rican women do that with their daughters. That's why you see the girls hanging all over the boys on the street. . . . *No les ponen las riendas a las hijas* [they don't place any restraints on their daughters].

Emma shared a similar perspective on Puerto Rican mothers when she described an argument she had had with her daughter over her unwillingness to allow her to attend a coed weekend trip organized by a local community center. The mothers of two of her daughter's friends, both Puerto Rican, had attempted to persuade her to allow Miriam to participate in the trip. As Emma explained her unwillingness to permit her daughter to participate in the weekend activity, she commented, *"Yo pienso que las puertorriqueñas les dan más libertad a sus hijas que nosotras, pero a veces es demasiado* [I think that Puerto Rican women allow their daughters more freedom than we (Mexicans) do, but sometimes it's excessive]. . . . *ya ves, a veces les vale* [but as you see, sometimes they could care less]!"

While Mexican women generally perceived Puerto Rican women as not placing enough restrictions on their daughters, Puerto Rican women tended to regard Mexican women as being too conservative in their expectations of their daughters. Maria conveyed this perception to me one day while we were watching a *telenovela* (Spanish-language soap opera) in her living room. In the *telenovela*, the protagonist, a young Mexican woman, seduced by a man discovered shortly thereafter that she was pregnant. As the protagonist dramatically cried about being taken advantage of in typical soap-opera fashion, Maria and her *comadre* loudly scoffed at her predicament, calling her a *pendeja* (an idiot). Maria then turned to me and remarked:

> Let's see, tell me if I'm right or wrong, but *las mexicanas son más cerradas sobre el tema del sexo* [Mexican women are more close-minded on the topic of sex]. I think that is why you see so many young Mexican girls having babies or getting married. Their mothers don't tell them anything. I mean, I think we [Puerto Rican women] talk to our daughters more about it.

Likewise, Francisca described Mexican women as being less willing than Puerto Rican women to talk to daughters about sex: "Sometimes, they [Mexican mothers] can be too strict with them. . . . But I think we [Puerto Rican mothers] might be more honest with our daughters about the topic, even if it embarrasses us . . . it is not fair to think that they are going to know everything they need to know about *de eso* [that (referring to sex)].

As illustrated by Francisca's comment, marriage was a topic that emerged quite often when Mexican and Puerto Rican mothers assessed each other's approaches to the sex education of daughters. Betina, who had described Puerto Rican mothers as failing to supervise their daughters adequately, discussed what she understood to be differences in Mexican and Puerto Rican women's attitudes toward marriage as we sat at her kitchen table drinking coffee and talking about her family. On that October afternoon, her fifteen-year-old daughter, Rita, was still at school. As Betina recounted how she and her sister had immigrated to Chicago in their late teens, the telephone rang, and she excused herself to answer it. After asking who it was, she visibly stiffened, and her tone changed as she replied rather curtly, "*No, Rita no está aquí ahorita. No sé cuándo va a llegar, okay? Aha, Michelle, yo le digo que llamaste. Hasta luego*" [No, Rita is not here right now. I don't know when she'll get home, okay? Aha, I'll tell her you called, Michelle. So long]. Hanging up the telephone, she shook her head and stated:

> *Esa muchacha no me gusta para nada* [I don't like that girl at all]. I already told Rita that I don't want her hanging out with her [Michelle]. *Es muy callejera* [She is always hanging out in the streets]. . . . *Y la mamá es igual de loca, ya sabes como son las puertorriqueñas* [And her mom is just as crazy, you know how Puerto Rican women are].

When I asked Betina to explain what she meant by the comment about Michelle's mother, she hesitated before she replied, thinking about how to answer my question. She explained that her mother raised her, along with her sister, to be *señoritas*. As a testament to this socialization, Betina pointed to her status as a virgin when she married Rita's father. She insisted that, while she lamented that Rita, her daughter, was no longer a virgin, she was still endeavoring to raise Rita appropriately: "I don't want her to just live with different men. . . . *todavía se puede casar bien, aunque ya no es virgen* [even though she is no longer a virgin, she can still get married properly]." She hesitated and continued, "But I don't think marriage is that important to Puerto Rican women, it's like, *se conforman con* [they are content with] just living with a man." She was quick to explain that, although she had left her husband when Rita was four years because he physically abused her, she had never lived with any man after that because that would have set a "*mal ejemplo*" (bad example) for her daughter, emphasizing that she would not live with another man unless they were married.

Betina's statement about Puerto Rican women's attitudes toward marriage was in line with comments made by other Mexican women about Puerto Rican women and marriage. For example, Aracelia was critical of what she perceived to be Puerto Rican women's inability to allow for mistakes within the context of marital relationships.

¿No sé, como que son muy exageradas para todo, ¿verdad [I don't know, it's like they make a big deal about everything, right]? The slightest thing goes wrong in their marriage and just like that [snapping her fingers], they leave their husbands or divorce them. *Como que son más rencorosas que nosotras las mexicanas* [Like they are more spiteful than us Mexicans]. I understand if there is abuse or something like that, but just because you fought *por una tontería* [because of a foolish act], you don't leave. Marriage is hard work! *No aguantan* [they don't tolerate].

Lilia made a similar comment about the inability of Puerto Rican women to tolerate the hardships that sometimes accompany marital relationships, adding that this attitude among Puerto Rican mothers negatively influences their daughters: "I think young Puerto Rican girls get pregnant and do not get married because of the example they get from their mothers. Like my neighbor, she left her husband because he would come home drunk sometimes." Rolling her eyes, she continued, "And now, her eighteen-year-old-daughter has two babies from two different men. . . . *Ellas se conforman con vivir de esa manera* [They are satisfied to accept living that way]." That Lilia herself was never married did not prevent her from asserting her evaluation of Puerto Rican women's stance on marriage.

Puerto Rican women, on the other hand, utilized the idea of *"conformando* [accepting]" differently when speaking about Mexican women and their marital situations. For example, Gina described how, unlike her Mexican friend, she left her husband rather than put up with domestic violence:

I left him like that [snapping her fingers]! . . . I don't know how some women put up with it, like my friend, *ella sí se aguanta, es mexicana* [She does put up with it, she's Mexican]. I see that Mexican women might stay married more than us, but they put up with a lot more than us *puertorriqueñas . . . se conforma con la situación* [she resigns herself to the situation].

Whereas Mexican women took on a judgmental tone in their critiques of Puerto Rican women's attitudes toward marriage, Puerto Rican women expressed a pity for Mexican women when considering their attitudes toward marriage.[44]

Teresa connected her perception of Mexican women's ethos of suffering to shame, pointing out that Mexican families relied too heavily on marriage as a solution to daughters' mishaps: "I think marriage is important, but not the answer for everything. . . . I wouldn't make them [her two teenage daughters] get married if they weren't ready just because *metieron las patas* (they got pregnant)." She paused here as she thought about how to explain why she would not demand marriage of her daughters:

Yo veo [I see] that when Mexican girls get pregnant, they want to make them get married right away. . . . *Como que la familia se conforma con que esté casada la muchacha* [Like the family can deal with it if the girl is married]. . . . I think that making them get married when they aren't ready makes it worse for them. We aren't in Mexico or Puerto Rico. Things are different here, you know what I mean?

Teresa's acknowledgment of the need to take into account how living in a U.S. context may pose different challenges in raising daughters was certainly echoed by all mothers.

Gendered racial/ethnic notions were part of mothers' strategies of action to meet the challenges of raising U.S.-born daughters, specifically in their efforts to mark for their sexually active daughters the limits of what was acceptable, as well as to set themselves apart from white women and from each other. But they also made distinctions among themselves as Mexican and Puerto Rican women, evaluating their performance as mothers vis-à-vis the performance of members of the other ethnic group. While both groups of mothers perceived white women as too sexually permissive, Mexican mothers perceived themselves to be more sexually conservative than Puerto Rican mothers, and Puerto Rican mothers thought of themselves as being less conservative with regard to their socialization of daughters. Both groups of mothers expressed an awareness of and a concern about pregnancy and about birth rates among Latinas in general, but, as evidenced in their interviews, they offered the differences in mothering between Mexican and Puerto Rican women as one explanation for these outcomes, particularly the degree to which mothers in each group were willing to discuss sexuality with their daughters and each groups' approach to marriage. Thus, while they were able to point to how some social forces, such as immigration and racialization processes, had shaped their common experiences as Latina mothers, they also maintained the boundaries between themselves as Mexican and Puerto Rican women by drawing on a repertoire of explanations for Latina girls' sexual outcomes, specifically the larger societal cultural narrative of mother blaming and the cultural distinctions they made between themselves. This form of boundary making may be a way for these two groups of Latinas to distance themselves and their daughters not only from the sexuality of white women but also from the "problem" of Latina teen pregnancy.

CONCLUSION

I do not present these mothers' strategies to evaluate how effective they are in "truly" empowering mothers and daughters or the extent to which they are "truly" reflective of a feminist consciousness. Approaching the relationship between mothering practices and empowerment in such dichotomous ways, as has often been done with women of color, distracts us from appreciating the complex and sometimes contradictory forms that resistance takes.[45] Instead, I invite readers to consider how mothers' strategies for addressing the emerging sexuality of their daughters, along with their daughters' interpretations of these strategies, provide insight into how Latinas engage and begin to rework their meanings and processes of gender and sexuality.

A larger cultural framing of adolescent sexuality as dangerous has informed Latina mothers' perceptions of their daughters as "at risk" for negative sexual outcomes. But, rather than adopt the prevailing sex education approach at the time—sexual abstinence until marriage—these mothers chose to focus on sexual safety in their conversations with their daughters. While their emphasis on sexual safety could be interpreted as a relaxing of Latinas' sexual "values" due to assimilation, it is more complex than just an indication of their assimilation. The notion that changes in sexual behavior and values among Latinas/os are a direct reflection of their "Americanization" is problematic because it suggests not only that sexuality in relation to assimilation follows a linear path in which "American" sexual values are placed at the end of the continuum but that "American" sexual values, attitudes, and behavior are somehow more liberal than those of other groups. That Latina mothers' incorporation of sexual safety lessons was not a marker of their assimilation was made especially evident in their assertions that they did not want to identify and be identified with the sexual behaviors and attitudes they ascribed to white women. Instead of focusing on the prescribed sex education of sexual abstinence, mothers decided on sexual safety as a lesson to transmit to their daughters because they wanted to be responsive to the sex education needs of their U.S.-born daughters, who are overrepresented in broader discussions of the "problem" of teen sexuality. On one level, then, the Latina mothers I spoke with wanted to protect their daughters from negative sexual outcomes and from gender inequality, continuing to emphasize the safe-sex lessons they had already been providing to their daughters while now also sharing with them some of their own experiences and recruiting other women in their family to help them. Their experiences indicate that we need to better understand how different groups of parents engage larger discourses about teen sexuality and what they consider to be responsible parenting in relation to the sex education they provide to their children.

Furthermore, the discussions that unfolded between these Latina mothers and their daughters provide some insight into how gender and sexuality among Latinas are given meaning through intergenerational interactions. Too often, it is assumed that only mothers produce and transmit cultural knowledge to their daughters.[46] It is also necessary to consider the ways in which daughters contribute to the production and transmission of meanings of gender and sexuality in these mother-daughter relationships. While many of these initial conversations between Latina mothers and daughters were fraught with tension, the interactions created opportunities for daughters to articulate their perspectives on gender and sexuality and to reconfigure gender and sexual meanings and processes with their mothers.

Mothers' sex education of their daughters after discovering daughters' sexual activities, however, were also elaborated upon in a context of gender inequality. Though they provided their daughters with lessons about safe sex, it was still quite painful for them to learn of their daughters' sexual behaviors. Mothers' construction of their daughters as victims is indicative of the broader societal negation of the sexual agency and desire of young women. And this particular reaction on the mothers' part seemed to contradict the messages of sexual safety that they were communicating to their daughters. This reminds us that we cannot lose sight of the patriarchal constraints under which women and girls negotiate and make sense of sexual subjectivity. As for most parents, it is not easy for Latina mothers to talk with their daughters about sexuality. It is undeniably a challenging task and one that mothers are primarily responsible for because gender organizes family life and parenting. And it is mothers who are typically blamed when their children deviate from gendered sexual expectations, particularly their daughters. Their daughters' behaviors also have implications for them.

Thus, on another level, mothers' strategies for responding to their daughters' emerging sexuality were also about identity and boundary maintenance for both themselves and their daughters. They were now mothers of daughters who were sexually experienced, a relationship that jeopardized their identities as good mothers, and so they were also trying to hold onto this respectable gendered identity. The significance they assigned to their identities as mothers especially emerged when they were defining themselves in opposition to each other as Mexican and Puerto Rican mothers, citing differences in their attitudes about marriage and in how they communicated with their daughters about sex. But it was also reflected in their attempts to manage knowledge about their daughters' sexual behaviors and perceptions about their parenting through their disclosures to some family members.

The mothers may have challenged patriarchal practices when they reached out to other women in their families to create more opportunities for their daughters to learn about sexuality and when they asked their daughters' fathers to share responsibility for parenting daughters. But these actions were coupled with both an emphasis on their own proper parenting and a distancing from their daughters' behaviors. Thus, these strategies also accommodated the belief that mothers are primarily to blame when their children misbehave. In other words, mothers' adoption of their specific strategies occurred in a context of patriarchal bargains that defined and shaped their options.[47]

The approaches of mothers of lesbian-identified daughters were particularly constricted not only by patriarchy but also by heteronormativity. In other words, their claims to identities as good mothers were especially jeopardized by these intersecting systems of inequality. Unlike mothers of heterosexual-identified daughters, these mothers were not able to "normalize" their daughters' sexual behavior to family members by drawing on claims of victimization or youth rebelliousness. Instead, they rejected the possibility of same-sex identities for their daughters, constructing these identities and related behaviors and desires as "foreign" to Latinas/os; their fear of stigmatization of both their daughters and themselves informed their decision to conceal this information from extended family members and to demand that their daughters cooperate with this strategy. In this way, they were able to hold on, even if briefly, to their identities as good mothers and to protect their daughters, but, in doing so, they also bolstered sexual hierarchies.

Mothers also deployed strategies to maintain an identity and a boundary grounded in gendered racial/ethnic distinctions. Mothers were teaching their daughters about sexuality, but they did so by constructing themselves and their daughters in opposition to white women and girls and to Mexican or Puerto Rican women—reflecting how race/ethnicity, sexuality, and gender are brought together in the maintenance of boundaries.[48] They may have based their assumptions about Mexican or Puerto Rican women on their everyday interactions with members of that opposite group, whereas they relied on their very limited interactions (if any) with white women to form opinions about their practices, but, nonetheless, they relied upon gendered racial/ethnic stereotypes about both groups of women to set themselves apart and to garner some power for themselves. Their strategies, then, in part, were also a response to their racialization as U.S. Latina women, demonstrating that their identities as women and mothers are constructed in relation to how others define them. Their deployment of sexualized racial/ethnic stereotypes about each other and about white women in their elaboration of strategies provides further evidence that racial, gender, and sexual identity practices are interdependent processes.[49] However, when they defined themselves on the basis of racial, class, gender, and sexual stereotypes of others—like the *"mexicana sufrida"* and the *"puertorriqueña rencorosa"*—these controlling images also limited their ability to fully see and comprehend the social forces that shaped all of their mothering experiences.

Latina mothers' responses to their knowledge of their daughters' sexual behaviors indicate that we must take into consideration the sociocultural context in which they provide sex education to their daughters. They were not "culturally silent" about sexuality in their interactions with their daughters; their approaches to sex education were related to broader discourses about adolescent sexuality, racial formations, gender and sexual ideologies, and sex education policies. In other words, we cannot thoroughly understand the content of the lessons that mothers provide to their children if we do not appreciate the social location from which they take on this challenging parenting task. By focusing on the magnified moments of mothers' discovery of daughters' sexual behaviors and the conversations between mothers and daughters that unfold after this discovery, we are able to grasp some of the ways in which they are cultural actors, rather than just understanding them as women who have culture bearing down on them.

NOTES

1. Cohen, 1997, p. 440.
2. Hutchinson, 2001; O'Sullivan, Meyer-Bahlberg, Heino, and Watkins, 2001; Meneses, 2004; Nadeem, Romo, and Sigman, 2006; Taylor, Gilligan, and Sullivan, 1995.
3. Hochschild, 1994, p. 4.
4. Ibid.
5. Magnified moments can be rich sites from which to explain the social construction of gender and sexuality. For example, by focusing on the experiences of four- and five-year-old children at a youth soccer opening ceremony as a magnified moment, the sociologist

Michael Messner (2000) demonstrates how magnified moments can provide insight into how gender is socially constructed, in this case, through various interactional, structural, and cultural processes that reinforce each other.

6. Only one mother reported that she looked through her daughter's e-mail messages, with the help of another daughter who was knowledgeable about computers and the Internet.

7. Also known as "love bites," these are marks or bruises on the skin caused by kissing, sucking, or biting the skin.

8. Alarcon, 1981; Hurtado, 1996; Trujillo, 1991.

9. This is not to deny that a culture of love and romance is marketed to young women, which may shape their interactions with sexual partners and how they make sense of those relationships. Feminist scholars have critiqued the culture of love and romance marketed to young women through films, reality shows, magazines, and novels. They point out that, given the limitations placed on young women's expression of sexuality, it is not surprising that girls refer to love as a justification for their sexual behavior. See, for instance, Asencio, 2002; McRobbie, 1991; Souza, 1995.

10. Almost all of the girls who identified as heterosexual reported the race/ethnicity of their sexual partners as Latino (only one indicated that her sexual partner was African American). Three of the eight lesbian-identified girls in this study reported the race/ethnicity of their sexual partner as white; I interviewed the mothers of these three young women.

11. See, for instance, Chan, 1989; Rust, 1996; Trujillo, 1991; Zavella, 1997.

12. In my use of the phrase "Talkin' Safe Sex," I am drawing on Patricia Zavella's term "talkin' sex." Zavella decided on this phrase to "convey the sense of awkwardness" that the Chicanas and Mexicanas she interviewed "often felt in describing feelings, experiences, sensations they rarely articulated except in occasional safe spaces" (Zavella, 2003, p. 230). Zavella argues that these women's talk of sex is contradictory in that it reflects both acquiescence and contestation.

13. Elliott, 2010; Jaccard, Dittus, and Gordon, 2000; Kirkman, Rosenthal, and Feldman, 2002; Rosenthal and Feldman, 1999.

14. See Elliott, 2010; González-López, 2005; Romo, Bravo, Cruz, Rios, and Kouyoum-djian, 2010. Note: The mothers in Elliott's study did emphasize abstinence-only to their daughters and sons, but they expressed their doubts about whether their children would wait until marriage.

15. González-López, 2003, p. 235.

16. Bonilla, 2005; González-López, 2005.

17. See, for instance, Briggs, 2002; Carrillo, 2002; González-López, 2005; Hirsch, 2003; Lopez, 2008; Suárez Findlay, 1999.

18. Hirsch, 2003.

19. See Alicea, 1997; Cantú, 2009; Espiritu, 2001; González-López, 2005; Hirsch, 2003; Hondagneu-Sotelo, 1994; Peña, 2005; Pérez, 2004; Toro-Morn and Alicea, 2003.

20. Patricia R. Pessar (2003), in her assessment of how gender has been accounted for in migration studies, notes that early work on this topic, though important, was limited in it binary treatment of women's experiences of migration as either emancipatory or subjugating.

21. González-López, 2005.

22. Other scholars have also found that immigrant mothers educate their daughters on gender and sexuality through the things they say about other women rather than by conveying messages on these issues in organized lessons to their daughters. See, for instance, Espín, 1991; Trujillo, 1991.

23. Latina Feminist Group, 2001.

24. Collins, 1990, p. 208.

25. Alicea, 1997; Collins, 1990; Segura and Pierce, 1994; Taylor, Gilligan, and Sullivan, 1995; White, 1999.

26. Douglas and Michaels, 2004; Hays, 1996; Stone, 2007; Willard, 1988.

27. Martin, 2003, p. 57

28. A total of four mothers reported that they were not employed outside the home. These mothers were all in two-parent households.

29. Addressing the limitations in the research on women of Mexican origin, Segura was interested in exploring differences and similarities among women born in the United States (Chicanas) and those who immigrated to the United States. Segura found that immigrant status informed differences in how these two groups of mothers understood motherhood and employment.

30. Segura, 1994.

31. Seven mothers (out of eleven mothers who reported being in two-parent households) stated that they also made known their daughters' sexual behavior to their daughters' fathers.

32. There is a need for further research on fathers' communication about sexuality with their children. However, one study that accounted for fathers', mothers', and adolescents' perspectives on fathers' communication with their children about sexuality found that one challenge that fathers encountered was the idea that same-gender communication was more effective. It also found that mothers communicated better than fathers and that mothers have more intimate relationships with their children (Kirkman, Rosenthal, and Feldman, 2002).

33. Garcia, 2001.

34. See, for instance, Hillier, 2002; Raymond, 1994.

35. Rich, 1980; Trujillo, 1991.

36. As in the anthropologist Patricia Zavella's (2003) interviews with Chicana and Mexicana women about sexuality, the mothers and daughters who spoke with me recounted that, while conversations about gay men did occur among family members, these were usually intended to be humorous and centered on jokes or name calling, rather than serious discussions of same-sex identities, behaviors, and desires. There was even less conversation about women's same-sex experiences.

37. Nagel, 2001, p. 124.

38. Only four mothers briefly commented on interracial dating during our interviews. They expressed greater concern about their daughters taking on behaviors and attitudes that they associated with young white women. This is not to imply that interracial dating and marriage are not discussed among Latinas/os, however.

39. Frankenberg, 1993, p. 16.

40. As Espiritu argues, the sexuality of women "is one of the few sites where economi-

cally and politically dominated groups can construct the dominant group as other and themselves as superior" (Espiritu, 2001, p. 421).

41. The young women I interviewed perceived themselves to be different not only from white young women but also from other Latina girls in their communities, such as immigrant and migrant girls and young women, whom they thought of as sexually irresponsible.

42. Latina girls construct their identities in response to racialized gender stereotypes about them that are found within the larger society.

43. It is very possible that my position not only as a researcher but as a Mexican woman (born and raised in Chicago) affected how the Mexican and Puerto Rican women in this study discussed their perceptions of each other. For instance, I wonder to what degree the distinctions they spoke of were informed by their understandings of me as a Latina.

44. In her ethnographic study of Puerto Rican transnational communities in Chicago, Gina Pérez (2003) also found that Puerto Rican women perceived differences between themselves and Mexican women in relation to marriage. Pérez noted that Puerto Rican women described Mexican women as *"sufridas"* (long suffering), while Mexican women depicted Puerto Rican women as *"rencorosas"* (spiteful, resentful).

45. See Collins, 1991; hooks, 1984; Pardo, 1998.

46. Ayala, 2006.

47. Deniz Kandiyoti defines patriarchal bargain as those rules and scripts that regulate gender relations "to which both genders accommodate and acquiesce, yet which may nonetheless be contested, redefined, and renegotiated" (Kandiyoti, 1988, p. 286).

48. As Nagel points out, ethnic boundaries fall along several dimensions, such as social, spatial, cultural, and political, but they are also sexual. According to Nagel, how sexuality and ethnicity come together, particularly "how they give power to one another" to give shape to racial/ethnic boundaries, remains underexplored (Nagel, 2003, p. 5).

49. Collins, 1991; Espiritu, 2001; Lopez and Hasso, 1998; Sandoval, 1991.

REFERENCES

Alarcón, Norma. 1981. "Chicana's Feminist Literature: A Re-vision through Malintzin/or Malintzin: Putting Flesh Back on the Object." In *This Bridge Called My Back: Writings by Radical Women of Color,* edited by Cherrie Moraga and Gloria Anzaldúa, 182–90. Watertown, MA: Persephone Press.

Alicea, Marixsa. 1997. "A Chambered Nautilus: The Contradictory Nature of Puerto Rican Women's Role in the Social Construction of a Transnational Community." *Gender & Society* 11(5): 597–626.

Asencio, Marysol. 2002. *Sex and Sexuality among New York's Puerto Rican Youth.* Boulder, CO: Lynne Rienner.

Ayala, Jennifer. 2006. "Confianza, Consejos, and Contradictions: Gender and Sexuality Lessons between Latina Adolescent Daughters and Mothers." In *Latina Girls: Voices of Adolescent Strength in the United States,* edited by Jill Denner and Bianca L. Guzman, 29–43. New York: New York University Press.

Bonilla, Dulce Reyes. 2005. "Let's Talk about *Sexo*." Color Lines: News for Action. http://www.colorlines.com/article.php?ID=35 (accessed April 16, 2010).

Briggs, Laura. 2002. *Reproducing Empire: Race, Sex, Science, and U.S. Imperialism in Puerto Rico*. Berkeley: University of California Press.

Cantú, Lionel. 2009. *The Sexuality of Migration: Border Crossings and Mexican Immigrant Men*. New York: New York University Press.

Carrillo, Hector. 2002. *The Night Is Young: Sexuality in Mexico in the Time of AIDS*. Chicago: University of Chicago Press.

Chan, Connie S. 1989. "Issues of Identity Development among Asian American Lesbians and Gay Men." *Journal of Counseling and Development* 68(1): 16–21.

Cohen, Cathy. 1997. "Punks, Bulldaggers, and Welfare Queens: The Radical Potential of Queer Politics." *GLQ: A Journal of Lesbian and Gay Studies* 3: 437–465.

Collins, Patricia Hill. 1990. *Black Feminist Thought: Knowledge, Consciousness, and the Politics of Empowerment*. New York: Routledge.

Collins, Patricia Hill. 1991. "Learning from the Outsider Within: The Sociological Significance of Black Feminist Thought." In *Beyond Methodology: Feminist Scholarship as Lived Research*, edited by Mary Margaret Fonow and Judith A. Cook, 35–59. Bloomington: Indiana University Press.

Douglas, Susan J., and Meredith W. Michaels. 2004. *The Mommy Myth: The Idealization of Motherhood and How It Has Undermined All Women*. New York: Simon & Schuster.

Elliott, Sinikka. 2010. "Talking to Teens about Sex: Mothers Negotiate Resistance, Discomfort, and Ambivalence." *Sexuality Research and Social Policy* 7(4): 310–322.

Espín, Oliva M. 1991. *Women Crossing Boundaries: A Psychology of Immigration and Transformations of Sexuality*. New York: Routledge.

Espiritu, Yen Le. 2001. "'We Don't Sleep Around Like White Girls Do': Family, Culture, and Gender in Filipina American Lives." *Signs* 26: 415–440.

Frankenberg, Ruth. 1993. *White Women, Race Matters: The Social Construction of Whiteness*. Minneapolis: University of Minnesota Press.

García, Lorena. 2001. "Sexuality and Responsibility: A Case Study of Sexual Agency among Latina Adolescents." M.A. thesis, Sociology Department, University of California at Santa Barbara

Gonzalez-López, Gloria. 2003. "*De Madres a Hijas*: Gendered Lessons on Virginity across Generations of Mexican Immigrant Women." In *Gender and U.S. Migration: Contemporary Trends*, edited by Pierrette Hondagneu-Sotelo, 217–240. Berkeley: University of California Press.

Gonzalez-López, Gloria. 2005. *Erotic Journeys: Mexican Immigrants and Their Sex Lives*. Berkeley: University of California Press.

Hays, Sharon. 1996. *The Cultural Contradictions of Motherhood*. New Haven: Yale University Press.

Hillier, Lynne. 2002. "'It's a Catch-22': Same-Sex Attracted Young People on Coming Out to Parents." *New Directions for Child and Adolescent Development* 97: 73–91.

Hirsch, Jennifer S. 2003. *A Courtship after Marriage: Sexuality and Love in Mexican Transnational Families*. Berkeley: University of California Press.

Hochschild, Arlie R. 1994. "The Commercial Spirit of Intimate Life and the Abduction of Feminism: Signs from Women's Advice Books." *Theory, Culture and Society* 11(1): 1–24.

Hondagneu-Sotelo, Pierrette. 1994. *Gendered Transitions: Mexican Experiences of Immigration*. Berkeley: University of California Press.

hooks, bell. 1984. *Feminist Theory: From Margin to Center*. Boston: South End Press.

Hurtado, Aida. 1996. *The Color of Privilege: Three Blasphemies on Race and Feminism*. Ann Arbor: University of Michigan Press.

Hutchinson, Mary K. 2001. "The Influence of Sexual Risk Communication between Parents and Daughters on Sexual Risk Behaviors." *Family Relations* 51: 238–257.

Jaccard, James, Patricia J. Dittus, and Vivian Gordon. 2000. "Parent-Teen Communication about Premarital Sex." *Journal of Adolescent Research* 15(2): 187–208.

Kandiyoti, Deniz. 1988. "Bargaining with Patriarchy." *Gender & Society* 2(3): 274–290.

Kirkman, Maggie, Doreen A. Rosenthal, and Shirley Feldman. 2002. "Talking to a Tiger: Fathers Reveal Their Difficulties in Communicating about Sexuality with Adolescents." *New Directions for Child and Adolescent Development, Special Issue. Talking Sexuality: Parent-Adolescent Communication* 97: 57–74.

Latina Feminist Group. 2001. *Telling to Live: Latina Feminist Testimonios*. Durham, NC: Duke University Press.

López, Laura M., and Frances S. Hasso. 1998. "Frontlines and Borders: Identity Thresholds for Latinas and Arab-American Women." In *Everyday Inequalities: Critical Inquiries*, edited by Jodi O'Brien and Judith A. Howard, 253–280. Malden, MA: Blackwell.

López, Nancy. 2003. *Hopeful Girls, Troubled Boys: Race and Gender Disparity in Urban Education*. New York: Routledge.

Martin, Karin A. 2003. "Giving Birth Like a Girl." *Gender & Society* 17(1): 54–72.

McRobbie, Angela. 1991. *Feminism and Youth Culture: From Jackie to Just Seventeen*. London: Macmillan.

Meneses, L. M. 2004. "Ethnic Differences in Mother-Daughter Communication about Sex." *Journal of Adolescent Health* 34(2): 154.

Messner, Michael A. 2000. "Barbie Girls Versus Seas Monsters: Children Constructing Gender." *Gender & Society* 14(6): 765–784.

Nadeem, Erum, Laura F. Romo, and Marian Sigman. 2006. "Knowledge about Condoms among Low-Income Pregnant Latina Adolescents in Relation to Explicit Maternal Discussion of Contraceptives." *Journal of Adolescent Health* 39:119.e9–119.e15.

Nagel, Joane. 2001. "Racial, Ethnic, and National Boundaries: Sexual Intersections and Symbolic Interactions." *Symbolic Interaction* 24(2): 123–139.

Nagel, Joane. 2003. *Race, Ethnicity, and Sexuality: Intimate Intersections, Forbidden Frontiers*. New York: Oxford University Press.

O'Sullivan, Lucia, F. Meyer-Bahlberg, F. L. Heino, and Beverly Watkins. 2001. "Mother-Daughter Communication about Sex among Urban African-African and Latino Families." *Journal of Adolescent Research* 16: 269–292.

Pardo, Mary S. 1998. *Mexican American Women Activists: Identity and Resistance in Two Los Angeles Communities*. Philadelphia: Temple University Press.

Peña, Susana. 2005. "Visibility and Silence: Marie! and Cuban American Gay Male Experience and Presentation." In *Queer Migrations: Sexuality, U.S. Citizenship and Border Crossings*, edited by Eithne Luibhéid and Lionel Cantú, 125–145. Minneapolis: University of Minnesota Press.

Pérez, Gina M. 2003. "Puertorriqueñas Rencorosas y Mejicanas Sufridas: Gendered Ethnic Identity Formation in Chicago's Latino Communities." *Journal of Latin American Anthropology* 8(2): 96–125.

Pérez, Gina M. 2004. *The Near Northwest Side Story: Migration, Displacement, and Puerto Rican Families*. Berkeley: University of California Press.

Pessar, Patricia R. 2003. "Engendering Migration Studies: The Case of New Immigrants in the United States." In *Gender and U.S. Immigration: Contemporary Trends*, edited by Pierrete Hondagneu-Sotelo, 20–42. Berkeley: University of California Press.

Raymond, Diane. 1994. "Homophobia, Identity, and the Meanings of Desire: Reflections on the Cultural Construction of Gay and Lesbian Adolescent Sexuality." In *Sexual Cultures and the Construction of Adolescent Identities*, edited by Janice Irvine, 115–150. Philadelphia: Temple University Press.

Rich, Adrienne. 1980. "Compulsory Heterosexuality and Lesbian Existence." *Signs: Journal of Women in Culture and Society* 5(4): 631–660.

Romo, Laura F., Magali Bravo, Maria Elena Cruz, Rebeca M. Rios, and Claudia Kouyoumdjian. 2010. "'El Sexo no es Malo': Maternal Values Accompanying Contraceptive Use Advice to Young Latina Adolescent Daughters." *Sexuality Research and Social Policy* 7: 118–127.

Rosenthal, Doreen A., and S. Shirley Feldman. 1999. "The Importance of Importance: Adolescents' Perceptions of Parental Communication about Sexuality." *Journal of Adolescence* 22(6): 835–852.

Rust, Paula C. 1996. "Managing Multiple Identities: Diversity among Bisexual Women and Men." In *Bisexuality: The Psychology and Politics of an Invisible Minority*, edited by Beth A. Firestein, 53–83. Thousand Oaks, CA: Sage.

Sandoval, Chela, 1991. "U.S. Third World Feminism: The Theory and Method of Oppositional Consciousness in the Postmodern World." *Genders* 10 (Spring): 1–24.

Segura, Denise A. 1994. "Working at Motherhood: Chicana and Mexican Immigrant Mothers and Employment." In *Mothering: Ideology, Experience, and Agency*, edited by Evelyn Naksna Glenn, Grace Chang, and Linda Rennie Forcey, 211–233. New York: Routledge.

Souza, Caridad. 1995. "*Entre la Casa and la Calle*: Adolescent Pregnancy among *Puertorriqueñas* in a Queens Neighborhood." Ph.D. dissertation, Ethnic Studies Department, University of California at Berkeley.

Stone, Pamela. 2007. *Opting Out? Why Women Really Quit Careers and Head Home*. Berkeley: University of California Press.

Suarez Findlay, Eileen J. 1999. *Imposing Decency: The Politics of Sexuality and Race in Puerto Rico, 1870–1920*. Durham, NC: Duke University Press.

Taylor, Gill McLean, Carol Gilligan, and Amy M. Sullivan. 1995. *Between Voice and Silence: Women and Girls, Race and Relationships*. Cambridge, MA: Harvard University Press.

Toro-Morn, Maura L., and Marixsa Alicea. 2003. "Gendered Geographies of Home: Mapping Second- and Third-Generation Puerto Ricans' Sense of Home." In *Gender and U.S. Immi-*

gration: Contemporary Trends, edited by Pierrette Hondagneu-Sotelo, 194–216. Berkeley: University of California Press.

Trujillo, Carla. 1991. "Chicana Lesbians: Fear and Loathing in the Chicano Community." In *The Girls Our Mothers Warned Us About*, edited by Carla Trujillo, 186–194. Berkeley: Third Woman Press.

White, Renee T. 1999. *Putting Risk in Perspective: Black Teenage Lives in the Era of AIDS*. Lanham, MD: Rowman & Littlefield.

Willard, Anu. 1988. "Cultural Scripts for Mothering." In *Mapping the Moral Domain: A Contribution of Women: Thinking to Psychological Theory and Education*, edited by Carol Gilligan, Janie Victoria Ward, and Jill McLean Taylor, with Betty Bardige, 225–243. Cambridge, MA: Harvard University Press.

Zavella, Patricia. 1997. "Playing with Fire: The Gendered Constructions of Chicana/ Mexicana Sexuality." In *The Gender/Sexuality Reader: Culture, History, Political Economy*, edited by Roger N. Lancaster and Micaela di Leonardo, 392–408. New York: Routledge.

Zavella, Patricia. 2003. "Talking Sex: Chicanas and Mexicans Theorize about Silences and Sexual Pleasures." In *Chicana Feminisms: A Critical Reader*, edited by Gabriela F. Arredondo, Aida Hurtado, Norma Klahn, Olga N. Ramirez, and Patricia Zavella, 228–253. Durham, NC: Duke University Press.

20

LONGING AND SAME-SEX DESIRE AMONG MEXICAN MEN

Tomás Almaguer

In his well-known book *Hunger of Memory: The Education of Richard Rodriguez, An Autobiography*, Mexican American writer Richard Rodriguez candidly acknowledges judging his own masculinity "against some shadowy mythical Mexican laborer dark like me, yet very different." While an undergraduate student at Stanford University, he found that it was the "Mexican-American janitors and gardeners working on campus" that he specifically positioned himself against in constructing his personal sense of gender and sexuality, eroticizing these working-class Mexican men too.

Rodriguez discloses that this latent homoerotic desire was initially ignited by the ruggedly masculine Mexican braceros who labored near his Sacramento, California, home as a child. He viewed these macho Mexican laborers with "silent envy." "I envied them their physical lives, their freedom to violate the taboo of the sun. Closer to home, I would notice the shirtless construction worker, the roofers, the sweating men tarring the street in front of the house. And I'd see the Mexican gardeners. I was unwilling to admit the attraction of their lives. I tried to deny it by looking away. But what was denied became strongly desired."[1]

I am interested here in more explicitly discussing the ways in which ethnic Mexican men construct, position themselves, and give personal meaning to their most intimate longings and same-sex desires. Where, for example, did Richard Rodriguez's homoerotic construction of dark "sweating men," the "shirtless construction worker," and the "shadowy mythical Mexican laborer" come from? How did these particular constructions of Mexican manhood ignite his desire for the men who embodied these "shadowy mythical" categories?

There is no question that the homoerotic desires and longings of ethnic Mexican men are varied and take multiple forms. All men who have sex with other men are attracted to individuals whom they have eroticized on the basis of their race, ethnicity, class, age, gender, sex, or body type. How men construct their objects of desire is not well understood. Here I want to explore only one particular way that ethnic Mexican men who have sex with other men give meaning to such acts. Of course, I am not suggesting that there is one common expression of such desire that is shared by all ethnic Mexican men. Instead, here I am primarily interested in constructions of Mexican manhood as experienced in the socialization that occurs in patriarchal families, and that in turn produces particular forms of same-sex desire.

Nettlesome issues of patriarchal power/domination, honor/shame, the privileging of masculinity, derision of femininity, eroticization of difference, and raw sexual objectification are deeply embedded in how many ethnic Mexican men structure and give meaning to their sexual lives and their intimate desires. It is here where Mexican men's fathers, uncles, brothers, and extended male kin are often erotically interpolated and deeply implicated in their most intimate constructions of desire. The homoerotic desires that often get played out in actual sexual encounters and relationships may be freely formed and consensual, with considerable agency and volition for both men. In other instances, however, they may be coercively imposed and unwelcome, riddled with elements of power that are played out in deeply disturbing ways. It is the former, rather than the latter, crystallization of homoerotic desire and longing that concerns me.

I want to explore same-sex desire in two specific ways. First, I want to approach it by sociologically problematizing homoerotic behavior among ethnic Mexican men and by exploring how the male body is erotically mapped, and how sexuality is culturally scripted through behavior. I want to draw on the life histories of three men whose personal life narratives reflect the explicit valorization and eroticization of Mexican manhood in overtly conscious and perhaps unconscious ways. Nowhere is this cultural and psychic structuring more apparent than in how they individually construct traditional Mexican masculine ideals and equate them with particular sexual roles and practices. While their preferred objects of desire and sexual behavior may vary over time, it is how these particular masculine ideals have shaped their sexual histories that is of particular interest.

HOMOSEXUALITY IN SOCIOLOGICAL PERSPECTIVE

The sociological literature on male homosexuality posits that there are four distinct patterns of same-sex behavior that can be found historically and cross-culturally. The first is age based, where older men engage in sex with younger boys as a result of personal volition, idealization of a mentor, or by force. The second model is situational, where men of any age can become objects of sexual exploitation because they are imprisoned, forced into sexual slavery through purchase, or collectively punished for their defeat in battle;

this is homosexual rape as the ultimate act of humiliation. The third model is gendered, where the insertive role in sexual acts is deemed masculine and the receptive feminine, producing an equation between masculinity and power, and femininity and powerlessness. Finally, there is an egalitarian construction of homosexuality where partners freely enter into sexual relations of their own desire, without coercion, usually on the basis of love or attraction.[2] This typology of homosexuality is, of course, a set of ideal types that vary considerably depending on the time, place, and context of deployment. These ideal types also often overlap and can coexist in a particular society simultaneously, easily producing change in the lives of individual men over the course of their lives.

For some years now historians and anthropologists have focused our attention on the fact that in Latin America homosexuality is primarily understood in gendered terms as discussed above, through the dichotomy between the *activo/pasivo* [active/passive] where the active partner is expected to be masculine and insertive, while the passive partner is feminized as orally and/or anally receptive. Bear in mind that when Latin Americans speak in the Spanish language of an *activo* or a *pasivo* in the sexual act, they are not referring to levels of activity or passivity in sex as the English cognates active/passive suggest. Among ethnic Mexicans living in Mexico and the United States, men who have sex with other men, whether they think of themselves as heterosexuals, bisexuals, or gay, most often describe their erotic partners and practices as divided into *activos* and *pasivos*. Insertive sex, either with a man or a women is deemed a great act of bravado that enhances the stature of the *activo* while the *pasivo* suffers stigma and denigration equated with the feminine, the emasculated, and the castrated.

According to anthropologist Roger Lancaster's study of sexual behavior in contemporary Nicaragua, the *activo* is deemed supremely macho for his insertive prowess. He "is not stigmatized at all and, moreover, no clear category exists in the popular language to classify him. For all intents and purposes, he is just a normal . . . male."[3] Indeed many historians of sexuality in Latin America argue that *activos* gain status among their peers for penetrating other men in precisely the same way that they derive status from seducing many women.

This cultural construction of homosexuality in Latin America confers an inordinate amount of meaning to the anus and to penetration or protection. This is in sharp contrast to the way homosexuality is viewed in the United States, where the mouth, particularly in the performance of fellatio, is highly valorized in popular culture. Indeed, Lancaster suggests that the lexicon of male insult in each context clearly reflects this basic sexual difference in cultural meanings associated with the mouth and the anus.[4] The most common derisive term used to refer to homosexuals in the United States is "cocksucker." Conversely, most Latin American epithets for homosexuals convey the stigma associated with being anally penetrated, such as *culero* and *colchón*. Mexicans like to insult with *joto, maricón,* and *puto* foregrounding the *pasivo*'s gender nonconformity and receptive sexual role, clearly marking him as effeminate and outside hegemonic constructions of Mexican masculinity, manhood, and heteronormativity.[5]

Psychoanalyst Santiago Ramirez identifies the Mexican family as the procrustean bedrock for masculinity and femininity. From early childhood young Mexican males develop an ambivalence toward women, who are less valued than men in patriarchal Mexican society. This fundamental disdain for that which is feminine, explains Ramirez, later gives way to an outpouring of resentment against women in general, and against one's wife or mistress.

Octavio Paz, the eminent Mexican cultural critic and Nobel laureate in literature, believed that the centrality of active/male–passive/female symbolism in Mexico profoundly influences the ways in which Mexicans view homosexuality. According to Paz, "masculine homosexuality is regarded with a certain indulgence insofar as the active agent is concerned. The passive agent is an abject, degraded being. Masculine homosexuality is tolerated, then, on condition that it consists in violating a passive agent."[6] Aggressive, insertive, and penetrating sexual activity was the marker of the Mexican man's masculinity. It was attained by negating and eviscerating all that is feminine and sexually subjugating it, be it in male or female bodies.

SAME-SEX BEHAVIOR AMONG ETHNIC MEXICAN MEN IN THE UNITED STATES

Let us now turn to three case studies that vividly capture the gender dynamics that operate among ethnic Mexican men who have sex with other men. These three cases are drawn from a larger qualitative study of 40 men who were interviewed for two to three hours each about their individual life histories and sexual experiences with other men. These interviews were conducted in the San Francisco Bay Area in 1998–1999 for a larger book project. These men were initially contacted through a snowball sample method or through referrals from various Latino community organizations that work with Latino gay men. All of these men were of Mexican descent but identified themselves ethnically and sexually in a variety of ways. While all were either first- or second-generation Mexican Americans, some of them ethnically identified in varied terms such as Mexican, Mexican American, Chicano, Latino, or Hispanic. Most of them deemed themselves either gay or bisexual, while others said they were primarily heterosexual but acknowledged that they occasionally had sex with other men. I have drawn from only three of these 40 interviews for this essay and want to underscore that they are not representative of all the men who were interviewed. Nor do I claim that they represent a cross-section of ethnic Mexican men who have sex with other men. Despite the differences in how they ethnically and sexually self-identified, I draw from these three life histories because of the similarities in the way they articulated their intimate longings and sexual desires for other men.

From these life histories, we can glean how these men came to define and understand their personal sexual identities and the particular erotic fantasies that led them to initiate relationships with men they chose. A recurring theme that emerges in these histories is the way they articulated their need for intimacy. Homosexuality is not only about bodies and pleasure but also about longings for intimacy and a sense of connectedness.[7] All three men spoke of longing for and desiring an older, more masculine partner, seeking intimacy, and wanting a nurturing and protective bond with a father-like figure.

None of these three men I interviewed spoke of having meaningful or close relationships with their fathers, who were often described as absent, distant, emotionless, and in some cases, even openly hostile and abusive. Consequently, the three men discussed here eloquently expressed a desire for an adult male figure who had typically eluded them in childhood. Sociologist Nancy Chodorow reminds us that "all men's and women's love fantasies, desires, or practices are typically shaped by their sense of gendered self. But this sense of gendered self is itself individually created and particular; a unique fusion of cultural meaning with a personal emotional meaning that is tied to the individual psycho-biographical history of an individual."[8]

Let us now turn to the life histories of Mario, Gustavo, and Roberto, and to what they tell us about longings and desires for other ethnic Mexican men.

MARIO: A 26-YEAR-OLD "CHICANO GAY MAN"

Mario is a 26-year-old ethnic Mexican man born and raised in Berkeley, California. He earned a Bachelor of Arts degree from a local university and was working in a midlevel white-collar position at the time of his interview in 1998. Short and muscular in stature, Mario described himself as "fairly high on the masculinity side." Mario learned about gender norms in his family by observing his father's role in the home and from other adult men in his life. He was raised with his father in the home but acknowledged that they were not particularly close or affectionate with each other. "My dad was never really open to us in expressing a lot of feelings," he recalled. "And if I were to learn something from him, it would be from observation. . . . The kind of communication that I didn't have with my father I later had with an uncle of mine."

Mario had little difficulty conforming to the male gender expectations of his family upbringing. "I was very comfortable with what a boy was supposed to do," he disclosed. "I think what made life comfortable was this freedom that I got from being a boy. I mean like not having the chores, not having the responsibility, being able to go out on the weekends with friends. These were like gifts, you know, that were sort of given to me by birth that I could like use up. These were the gifts that a boy gets because he's a boy. There was a very lax privilege and king-like comfort that I had and enjoyed."

Mario's father and other adult male relatives helped ensure compliance with the gender expectation in his family and openly patrolled these borders. His father, for example, warned him about compromising his masculinity by spending too much time with his older sisters. "I remember that I wasn't supposed to hang out that much with my sisters. I remember that he [his father] would pull me out of that circle . . . , making it clear that that's not what I should be doing. So that if it happened he would have me cut the lawn or have me go somewhere else out of the room. He made it clear that guys don't hang out with girls, you know, *los hombres no se juntan con las chavalas* [men don't hang out with the girls]." His father's brother would take this further by warning Mario that *"si te juntas con las viejas, vas a ser un maricón* [if you hang out with women, you're going to become a faggot]."

Above all, Mario stressed that the gender prescriptions he received in his family required "not showing any kind of feminine attributes. Whether it is the way you express yourself or the way you looked, whether you're holding your hand the wrong way, not sharing, not exposing any kind of emotion. Just don't express anything, just kind of keep everything in. That, I think, was the most important, that stuck to me more than anything else."

Mario candidly acknowledged that the qualities he initially found sexually attractive were ignited at a very early age, confiding that his first memory of having any sexual desire for a man occurred at the age of 10 offering his uncle massages. Mario would rub his uncle's back and stomach muscles as a way of relieving his workday stress.

While this was deemed completely innocent by family members at the time, Mario confessed being sexually aroused by his uncle's rugged Mexican masculinity, handsome dark *mestizo* features, and tall muscular body. "I would put my hand under his shirt and rub his belly and back. But I didn't see it as a massage, no, that's not the way I saw it. That was the earliest I remember having any kind of contact with another man that I enjoyed, that I saw as sexual." While there was never any explicit sexual interaction between Mario and his uncle, this titillating experience left a lasting impression.

Most of his subsequent sexual experiences during his teens and early twenties were with older white gay men who willingly offered him their sexual services. He met many of these men in a local park near his home where gay men often congregated, or "cruised" for anonymous sexual experiences. Mario's masculine demeanor and sexual preciousness immediately attracted the interests of the white gay men at that park. As a teen he circled the park on his bicycle and struck up conversations with these men, who would eventually offer with enthusiasm to fellate him. These early sexual encounters, according to Mario, were nothing more than a quick "blow and go" as he candidly put it.

Then one day he met by chance a man who embodied his sexual desire for the rugged Mexican masculinity that he remembered initially from a young age. Mario described this sexual awakening:

Then, all of a sudden, I see this Mexican man in Oakland. He was tall, had a mustache and actually reminded me of my uncle. All I knew is that I wanted to have him and I wanted him in a different way. I didn't want to just get him off. I wanted to do something more. I wanted to feel him. I wanted to be hugged. . . . I wanted to see what was under those clothes. I wanted to see his belly. So I pursued him, and guess what? I went down on him for the first time and enjoyed it. I got him off; it was a one-way scene.

You know, I never saw him again, ever. But after that I just started looking for people who resembled him. I started looking for brown faces. I started looking for black hair. I wanted to relive that again. I wanted to experience it again. . . . Now I could have sex with another man and I could blow someone off, I could kiss another man, but there were certain requirements. Yes, they had to be butch. If possible, I had to see a wedding ring. And I remember asking them before we did anything, "Are you married?" And, they would say, "Yes." And I would be like very happy. "All right, let's do it." [Laughing.]

Mario's sexuality was fundamentally transformed by this experience, and he acknowledged that he was now more open to switching sexual roles depending on the masculinity of the man he was attracted to. A constant in his life has been his primary attraction to ruggedly masculine, working-class Mexican men. While his earliest sexual experiences had been marked by his exclusively performing the *activo* role as the inserter (being orally fellated by other men), he now gradually gravitated to that role himself with men whom he deemed more masculine than himself. In gay parlance, he "flipped" his sexual roles and became sexually more versatile in enjoying the sexual pleasures of the "*pasivo*," or receptor, in his homosexual experiences with other men. Yet this new versatility was strictly limited to now being open to fellating other men; he never allowed any of them to anally penetrate him.

However, this sexual fluidity was very clearly defined and marked by mutual recognitions of their respective masculinity and the way that those differences were negotiated between him and his sexual partner. The larger, more masculine, heteronormatively defined man (who, he acknowledged, also most often had the larger penis), was deemed the *activo* in these sexual encounters. The man who was less defined in these terms became the *pasivo* who worshiped the dominant man's masculinity and submitted to offering him his sexual services. This was the tightly choreographed and scripted way that he entered into his sexual relationships with other men. There was always a mutual recognition and eroticization of their masculinity and a subsequent negotiation of the sexual roles that they would enact.

When I interviewed Mario, he had been in an ongoing three-year relationship with a Mexican man named Jorge, who was 11 years older than Mario and was a recent immigrant when they met. During their first sexual encounter, Mario recalled that Jorge "did the daddy thing, he didn't wanna touch me, nothing like that. And so, I was very careful to make sure that we would not do anything that would ruin this fantasy of mine. Yeah, that's exactly what I wanted."

Mario's initial sexual relationship with Jorge was performed in a decidedly gendered construction of homosexuality, where he secured sexual pleasure fellating Jorge, who was the *activo* in these sexual trysts, while Mario performed the *pasivo* role. For a long time, Jorge would not fellate or sexually subordinate himself to Mario. He did the "daddy thing" and would not compromise his sense of Mexican masculinity by gravitating beyond being the sexually dominant inserter. For Jorge to have done so would have compromised his masculinity and rendered him a *pasivo* and unambiguously homosexual in his own eyes. Mario, for his part, was deeply eroticized by Jorge's "one way" sexual script and increasingly found sexual pleasure in moving beyond his own initial erotic investments in that sexual role.

When I interviewed Mario, he stated that their three-year sexual relationship continued to follow carefully scripted erotic roles that both men self-consciously negotiated. While they continue to actively role play, neither has surrendered his personal sense of agency in the process. Each man retains a strong sense of sexual subjectivity and, over time, has slowly moved beyond the initial sexual roles that ignited their attraction to one another. According to Mario, "We've been together now for nearly three years, and our sex has changed. We have oral sex now, it's a two-way street, but there is still no anal sex involved from either party. But I see him hotter today than I did the first time I met him. And the first time I met him I was completely turned on by this man. I mean, he was like every wet dream that I've ever had: he's everything that I've ever wanted."

If we step back for a moment from the particulars of his sexual experiences, it becomes clear that Mario's narrative illustrates well how homosexuality is largely structured through sexual scripts that operate at the cultural, interpersonal, and intrapsychic levels.[9] For example, Mario's socialization into Mexican American family norms provided the general parameters for the gendered scripting of his adult homosexual behavior. His narrative also captures how the parameters guide and structure his intimate sexual interactions with other men along mutually recognizable erotic roles.[10]

Although Mario has always comported himself in a very masculine way, he has continually sought older, more masculine men than himself as his primary object of desire. His uncle initially embodied all of the masculine qualities that have been so central to Mario's erotic life. Despite his initial investments in the insertive, or penetrator, role, Mario eventually positioned himself in a "subordinate" way to his "dominant" Mexican immigrant partner, thus reproducing gendered *activo/pasivo* roles. Their relationship, however, is not strictly transacted on a transgender basis but rather also on a transgenerational basis in which age provided an important basis for igniting erotic difference and sexual desire. The fact that their sexuality has been so carefully scripted and negotiated in ways that sexual mutuality and intersubjectivity are now highly valued also indicates that it has been affected by modern constructions of egalitarianism that are idealized in contemporary gay relationships.

Whatever twists and turns in the fundamental form that Mario's sexual relationships have taken, their foundation is undeniably anchored in the traditional mappings of gender and sexual roles within his Mexican American family. There does exist, however, some fluidity and a degree of hybridity in the way that he has negotiated and enacted his homosexual relationships. In the end, Mario apparently found the Mexican manhood he was looking for to fulfill his erotic fantasies and now still lives with Jorge in Berkeley, California.

GUSTAVO: A 44-YEAR-OLD "BISEXUAL MEXICAN AMERICAN MAN"

Gustavo is a 44-year-old man born in Guadalajara, Mexico, who migrated with his mother and siblings to the United States at the age of five. Gustavo's father remained in Mexico and was never an integral part of his childhood socialization or upbringing. Gustavo earned an Associate of Arts degree from a local community college and was working as a station agent for one of the local transit districts at the time of his interview. Gustavo is a short, fair-complexioned man, fastidiously groomed with a soft-spoken and polite demeanor. He admits to being somewhat of a misfit as a child and being conscious of being "different" and not conforming to the expectations of manhood in his family.

> I always thought that there was something wrong with me because I wasn't aggressive or liked to fight like my older brother. I didn't like the idea that I was being viewed as feminine, but realistically I always felt like if there were two categories, feminine and butch, I'd be more on the feminine side. . . . I liked finer things, you know, like being clean shaven, and having my hair combed. I think those are characteristics usually associated with women.

Raised by a single mother, Gustavo received clear messages from her and his older siblings about the expectations of manhood in their Mexican immigrant family. His ability to conform to these cultural expectations became the template through which he would eventually assess himself as a young boy, and later as an adult man.

> I felt like they expected a man, you know, to be macho and a head of household. You go to work and come home and that's the expectation. I knew I was different; I wanted to do different things. But my mother, as far as I can remember, always said that I should be more like my brother. You know, she'd throw that up to me a lot. So, you know, I always thought that was something wrong with me because I wasn't aggressive . . . like my brother. I resented him a lot. He always like tried to boss me around and discipline me like a dad. And I used to always tell him that he wasn't my dad. I guess I was pretty rebellious because of that.

Gustavo's mother reigned in the household as the main authority figure and disciplinarian who actively policed the way he comported his gender presentation. She was a very strict woman with rigid ideas about the appropriate gender roles her children should embody. Gustavo recalled, for example, that he was expected to empty the trash and attend to extensive yard work while his older sisters took primary responsibility for chores within the home. Despite long-standing conflict with his mother because of his rebelliousness, Gustavo shouldered primary responsibility for her financial well-being and for her care as her health failed during the last years of her life. He carried these familial responsibilities with honor and respect, or so he explained.

Although Gustavo eventually married and raised three children with his wife, he eventually began to clandestinely and discreetly have sex with men. His earliest sexual experiences began in his teenage years but increased in frequency as he entered adulthood and after he married.

> I know what I like and what I don't, and I don't like anything real feminine. I've always been attracted to men who were masculine, who were macho. Because I think it was opposite of what I was, you know. I have always been attracted to older men, big, real masculine, and hairy. I like somebody else taking control and me being the submissive person. Because with girls, I've always had to take the initiative, be the aggressive person. I have always liked it, and I think it stems back to growing up without my dad, when somebody takes control of my body. It makes me feel secure and protected, you know, by somebody bigger, stronger, and more masculine. The fact that a person wants to hold me and kiss me and be affectionate with me, that excites me.

Gustavo has never been in an open homosexual relationship with a man, nor does his family or three adult children know of his same-sex behavior. He was clear in acknowledging that his sexual preference was for ruggedly masculine butch Mexican men. He has been unsuccessful in finding his idealized sexual object choice. Instead, he has had a clandestine relationship for more than 10 years with a white married man named Mark. Mark is a construction contractor who drives a large pickup truck, all of which signals the rugged masculinity that Gustavo has eroticized. While this relationship is far from personally fulfilling, it nevertheless is still satisfying and captures aspects of Gustavo's homoerotic desires that have been constant throughout his life. "It's really kind of a plus that he's [Mark is] married," he explains. "I feel comfortable having sex with him, you know. And, it's kind of a turn-on too, because he's masculine, butch, and, more or less, I guess bisexual. Hmmm, that's a real turn-on for me. He's not feminine in any way."

All of the dichotomies that circumscribe patriarchal gender relations in ethnic Mexican culture have crept in to the way that Gustavo has come to define and give personal meaning to his sexuality. He has constructed with another man an erotic relationship that is deeply inflected by binary notions of masculinity/femininity, older/younger, stronger/weaker, active/passive, protector/protected, instrumental/affective, and so forth. Gustavo's narrative also captures well how the ideals of Mexican manhood are intimately embedded in the way he has structured his sexual activities with a man. Although Mark is white and a little older than Gustavo, he nonetheless captures all the key elements that Gustavo has eroticized since childhood.

Although he was once married and played a patriarchal role in his family, Gustavo is now divorced, and subordinates himself to his idealized object of sexual desire. He is content being what he termed the "other woman" or the "mistress" in Mark's life. Yet even here some movement in and out of scripted roles has transpired over time. Gustavo explained that he has increasingly assumed the more active, penetrating and insertive role in his sexual relationship with Mark, an ostensibly heterosexual man. Although it has taken him out of the script that he prefers, Gustavo disclosed that Mark has gradually taken to wearing women's clothes when they have sex. Erotic roles, it seems, are not only far more fluid and variable among different couplings of men, but also vary considerably over time in a long-term relationship such as this one.

Gustavo initially had deep erotic investments in performing the *pasivo* sexual role with men he deemed more masculine than himself and who exhibited heteronormative masculinity. Yet over time he has negotiated that preferred sexual role with various partners, and now in his unusual long-term relationship with Mark. This fluidity is not something that Gustavo claims to have not entered into without some equivocation. He now plays the *activo* role with Mark, who has "flipped" his initial sexual role and the way they have scripted their homosexual behavior. This is something that Gustavo continues to have misgivings about but is willing to accommodate himself to because of his deep erotic desire for Mark and the pleasure he derives by providing him with sexual service. That Mark has a large penis is something that he made continued reference to, as it overshadowed whatever misgivings about the new turn in their relationship. While Mark still does not like to fellate Gustavo, he has now gravitated to a new sexual role whereby he has cast himself in a woman's role (with full accoutrements, such as a wig and lacy lingerie) and prefers being anally penetrated by Gustavo. This coupling shows that homosexual roles are far more fluid and actively negotiated than outward appearances may indicate and often involve multiple constructions of scripted homosexual behavior over the life span.

ROBERTO: A 36-YEAR-OLD "MEXICAN GAY MAN"

Roberto is a 36-year-old Mexican gay man who had lived in San Francisco for six years at the time of our interview. He completed an Associate of Arts degree at a local community college, was working part-time, and was continuing his studies toward a Bachelor of Arts degree. He also spent a fair amount of time doing volunteer work for a local Latino gay organization. Roberto was born in Tijuana, Mexico, and migrated with his family to the United States at an early age. They initially settled in the San Diego area. Roberto remembers having a difficult and strained relationship with his "emotionally distant" father while growing up. His father was verbally and psychologically abusive, and these are his most vivid childhood memories. As a consequence, Roberto rarely speaks to his father, even to this day.

Roberto's conflictual relationship with his father partially stemmed from his inability to fully embody the male gender roles that were expected of him. He recalled that his father was "very tough on me, very tough on my brother and me, but more on me, it never seemed like I could do anything right." Particularly painful was "being humiliated in front of other children by my own father. It was really painful to the point where that I started crying sometimes . . . *porque me maltrataba verbalmente* [because he verbally mistreated me]. . . . If I didn't do something right, my father would be like *ay, no vas a ser nada, vas a terminar barriendo la calle* [oh, you're going to amount to nothing, you'll end up as a street sweeper] or something like that, something really menial and mean."

Roberto recalled that his earliest sexual attraction for men was a yearning for protection and intimacy. He always wanted "to be close to men . . . sort of clinging on them without necessarily having sex with them."

> I love to kiss and I love . . . to wrap my arms around another man and have him wrap his arms around me. *Envuelto como papel* [wrapped up like paper], I love that. That's like the best feeling in the world. I find myself if I'm really comfortable, putting my hand on his chest, like protect me, protect me, because that's how I feel. That's one of the reasons why when I was first out I do, to a certain degree, am attracted to older men, because I want to be protected. And being that I'm 5'5", most men are taller than I am. I like them to be stocky, but I like them to be taller too. I can wrap myself around them, but kind of be protected. And that's a big issue for me.

Although Roberto identifies as Mexican and is perfectly bilingual in Spanish and English, he particularly enjoys having sex with Latino men who speak Spanish. He occasionally plays into the colonial fantasies of white gay men who are sexually attracted to him in this intimate and endearing way as well:

> This one guy I remember saying can you speak to me in Spanish and I'm like what? Then I got into it and I started touching him and I kissed him on the neck and said, *Aqui quieres que te bese? Como quieres que te bese? Ay, papi dime como!* [Do you want me to kiss you here? How do you want me to kiss you? Oh, daddy, tell me how!] It was really like a *telenovela* [television soap opera], *papi dime como* [daddy, tell me how] and the guy really got aroused.

But it is with ruggedly masculine and hairy[*velludo*] Latino men that Roberto most enjoys this type of sexual intimacy. He recalled with great fondness one particular Latino man who embodied these special qualities:

> It was a guy from Argentina . . . *me encanta tu acento* [I love your accent]. . . . We started talking in Spanish, and then I kissed his neck. He wanted me to kiss his shoulders. . . . He was a great kisser. Oh, yeah. He kissed me in the back of the neck while I was sitting on the side of him and he was behind me, and he started to kiss the back of my neck and I just let him have it. I was in the moment. I put my head back and listening to the music that they were playing. I closed my eyes and *como que estaba flotando en una nube* [like I

was floating on a cloud]. That's how I get. When I make love with somebody, I listen to the music in my head. I listen to the music.

Roberto continues to be sexually attracted to men he deems more masculine than himself and gravitates to a sexually subordinate, scripted role. Roberto prefers to orally fellate and be sexually penetrated by his sexual partners. He casts himself as the *pasivo* in his relationships with these masculine men who performed the *activo* role (and may or may not be homosexually identified). Yet these erotic investments have remained fairly constant throughout his life, and he is certainly far more committed to this preferred sexual role than the other two men whose life histories are drawn upon here.

At the time of his interview, Roberto had not been in a long-term, committed relationship with another man. Although he had dated a number of men while living in San Francisco for six years, and had had six sexual partners in the past year, he remained unattached. Although he was sexually active and looking for a partner, he stressed that sexuality was more than simply a matter of pleasure-seeking bodies. According to Roberto, "You should have some sort of connection with somebody even if it doesn't necessarily have to be a heart-to-heart connection. There should be some sort of connection that kind of goes beyond the physical sense." In describing what he ideally sought in a relationship with another man, Roberto said it was a need for a male protector in his life:

> I'm happy that this person is attracted to me, I'm happy that this person sees me as a sexual being and wants to be with me. We both smile, and we both are very gentle with each other. It's a great feeling and even for the moment. What I do is I sometimes hold people, and I put my head on their chest. I do that a lot. I feel protected. I feel like no one's going to hurt me.

The romantic storyline and need for male intimacy that Roberto articulates, like the *telenovelas* he refers to, come with a well-crafted script and orchestrated soundtrack (that is, of course, sung in Spanish). Roberto has idealized the object of his most intense homosexual desire and has carefully constructed any future relationship as well.

Here, too, is the familiar cultural world replete with the traditional binaries that underlie constructions of gender and sexuality in Mexican American culture. There are protective fathers (who are big, strong, tall, and hairy chested) who "wrap their arms around" and protect their loved ones from the ravages of a cruel, heartless world. Roberto has clearly positioned himself as a protagonist in this drama and constructed a homoerotic world with deep roots in the Mexican cultural world in which he was raised. At the present time, he continues to look for the longed-for construction of Mexican manhood in his life. He continues to search for the elusive *activo* in his life with whom he can perform the sexually submissive, *pasivo* role that he prefers. Yet, as he has strongly stressed, this idealized object of desire also provides the equally elusive intimacy and bonding that he seeks from these masculine men.

DISCUSSION AND CONCLUSION

The three men discussed here carried a gendered sense of self that was deeply rooted in their childhood socialization in ethnic Mexican family norms. In different ways, each man negotiated and reconciled his gender identity in light of the way that masculinity and manhood was defined in his family. Each man not only positioned himself differently in relation to these cultural ideals but also incorporated them consciously and unconsciously into his sexual practices and erotic fantasies. The experiences captured here were consensual and freely entered into. However, other men interviewed for this project articulated different experiences that were marked by sexual coercion, not only in gendered ways but also in terms of age. These men were often subjected to unwelcome sexual coercion and rape by family members and neighbors during childhood and later in their lives.

When asked to describe their most intimate objects of sexual desire, Mario, Gustavo, and Roberto wanted ruggedly masculine, "*muy macho*" Mexican men who had "brown faces" and "black hair," and who were "older," "bigger," "stronger," "taller," "stocky," "hairy," "aggressive," "butch," "real masculine," and "married." They also disclosed being particularly attracted to men who had large, brown uncircumcised penises.

The life histories discussed here also capture the undeniable way in which the gender role binaries in their ethnic Mexican families found expression along parallel lines in their homoerotic lives. While this often occurred in unexpected ways, it does not obscure the agency involved in how these men deployed and scripted their sexual activities with other men. More often than not, they gravitated toward scripted erotic roles in the sexual fantasies and experiences that they so vividly described.

The narratives Mario, Gustavo, and Roberto offer us reflect a powerful underlying need for intimacy and longing for an adult male figure. This quest for intimacy generally found expression in their desire to surrender themselves to an older, more masculine man who could offer them "protection" from the ravages and cruelties of their daily lives. In so doing, these men entered into a variety of sexual relationships with other men that were transacted in carefully scripted sexual roles anchored in different cultural constructions of homosexuality. Some of these relationships were clearly transacted in a transgender way, whereby the relationship was scripted along an *activo/pasivo* axis. In other cases, these men gravitated to sexual relationships that were inflected in these terms, but also cast along age-based differences that provided erotic currency. In still other cases, these relationships often began in these terms and then slowly moved into a more egalitarian homosexual relationship where sexual mutuality and intersubjectivity are highly valued.

These differences notwithstanding, the ways in which these men structured their homoerotic desires raises nettlesome issues for those of us committed to gender and sexual egalitarianism in ethnic Mexican culture on both sides of the U.S.-Mexico border. How we come to live and experience our sexuality is not something that we simply choose at will. I have tried to suggest how larger social structures and cultural world views are embedded in how ethnic Mexican gay and bisexual men give personal meaning to their sexuality.

It would be naïve to think that homoerotic desire and longing does not involve some association with one's Mexican father or adult male relatives. I have tried to illustrate that the structuring of homoerotic desires and practices has deep cultural moorings in familial gender socialization. How this is personally constructed, individually deployed, and experienced in the lives of men of Mexican descent who have sex with other men refracts in different ways for each man.

Sociologist Nancy Chodorow's view of men and women as "object-seeking" beings helps us make sense of Mario's, Gustavo's, and Roberto's desires for sexual intimacy with other men. Relationality and love, rather than primal aggressiveness and libidinal drives as postulated by Sigmund Freud, are the driving force in Chodorow's "object relations" approach to sexuality.[11] Sexuality is experienced as a longing to not only be with but to become one with a desired object, which is most often a person or part of a person who has been eroticized. So imagined, our sexuality becomes intimately bundled up with a lifelong quest for human connectedness rooted in the preoedipal relationship between mother and child. We incessantly and irrepressibly seek to recapture the original state of oneness and total satisfaction that we experienced in our mother's arms.

Following the logic of this argument, this state of oneness finds expression in different ways for Mario, Gustavo, and Roberto. For Mario, for example, having another man's penis in his mouth and fellating him to orgasm while murmuring, as he put it, "*dame tu leche*" [give me your milk] captures this preoedipal moment. The total satisfaction he attained while fellating the man who reminded him of his uncle is a good example of this "oceanic bliss." For Gustavo and Roberto, on the other hand, it is a far less sexualized relationality that propels their homoerotic desires. Their bliss involves little more than resting their heads softly on their partner's chest while in the arms of his tender embrace.

While this need for intimacy and human connectedness may be a universal feature of our existence and have roots in maternal childrearing, it has apparently taken male rather than female form in the case of these homosexual men. While heterosexual Mexican men seek this elusive connectedness with women who embody qualities that they associate with their mothers, Mexican and Chicano gay men seek the same thing, but do so with men as their object of sexual desire. It should come as no real surprise, therefore, that aspects of Mexican men's sexual desire for other men would reflect an unconscious longing associated with their fathers or another important male relative. Homosexuality is, ultimately, about both sexual desire and emotional longing for other men.

Perhaps Chicano gay writer Raul Coronado has put this best when he noted that "it is time for men to explore how men become the men that we are, how our relationships with the men in our family have shaped and formed our sense of masculinity, how our sexual and emotional desires impact and are shaped by other aspects of our identity. One way we, as men, can begin to engage in this dialogue may be by returning to our own sense of loss during these formative years."[12]

NOTES

Note: This essay draws from two previously published articles that have been woven together here for inclusion in this anthology: "Chicano Men: A Cartography of Homosexual Identity and Behavior" (published in 1991); and "Looking for Papi: Longing and Desire among Chicano Gay Men" (published in 2007).

1. Richard Rodriguez, *Hunger of Memory: The Education of Richard Rodriguez, An Autobiography* (Boston: Godine, 1982), p. 126. I am grateful to Ramón Gutiérrez for reminding me of the importance of this particular passage in Rodriguez's book.

2. See, for example, David F. Greenberg, *The Construction of Homosexuality* (Chicago: University of Chicago Press, 1988); Stephen O. Murray, *Homosexualities* (Chicago: University of Chicago, 2000); and Stephen O. Murray, *Latin American Male Homosexualities* (Albuquerque: University of New Mexico Press, 1995).

3. Roger N. Lancaster, "Subject Honor and Object Shame: The Construction of Male Homosexuality and Stigma in Nicaragua," *Ethnology* 27, no. 2 (1987): 113.

4. Ibid. p. 111.

5. Ibid.

6. Octavio Paz, *Labyrinth of Solitude: Life and Thought in Mexico* (New York: Grove, 1961) p. 40.

7. See Rafael M. Díaz, *Latino Gay Men and HIV: Culture, Sexuality, and Risk Behavior* (New York: Routledge, 1998).

8. Nancy Chodorow, *Masculinities, Femininities, Sexualities: Freud and Beyond* (Lexington: University of Kentucky Press, 1994), p. 78. Chodorow argues that "we experience and enact our sexuality in a gendered way that is both consciously and unconsciously inscribed." She perceptively reminds us that "men and women love as psychologically and culturally gendered selves, with gender identities and sexual desires that they consciously and unconsciously experience and enact."

9. See John H. Gagnon and William Simon, "Sexual Scripts: Permanence and Change," *Archives of Sexual Behavior* 15, no. 2 (1986): 97–120.

10. See John H. Gagnon and William Simon, *Sexual Conduct: The Social Sources of Human Sexuality* (Chicago: Aldine, 1973).

11. Chodorow, *Masculinities, Femininities, Sexualities*.

12. Raul Coronado, "Bringing It Back Home: Desire, Jotos, and Men," in *The Chicana/o Cultural Studies Reader*, ed. Angie Chabram Dernersesian (New York: Routledge, 2006), p. 239.

PART 7

LATINO POLITICS

The word "politics" in the popular imagination most often conjures up elections; listening to candidate platforms; endless radio, television, and Internet ads vaunting the merits of this candidate over that one; election day workers rushing you to the ballot box, followed by the results; and eventually all the promises kept and those conveniently forgotten. But politics is much more. It does indeed include all the formal institutional rules that govern elections and the procedures that dictate how legislation is fashioned, passed, and forged into law by our elected representatives, but it is also about the social activism of ordinary women and men who come together for a variety of reasons that have nothing to do with governing and everything to do with their quality of life. These politics stem from local issues and concerns: the parent-teacher elementary school association seeking more-effective learning outcomes for their children, a church's congregation debating the need for more-effective policing, or service workers and unauthorized immigrants seeking ways to better their wages and working conditions and, ultimately, to regularize their immigrant status. These informal, nongovernmental politics often are not given the same attention that electoral politics get. In part 7 of *The New Latino Studies Reader*, we explore both types of politics, as well as the burning issues that preoccupy Latino lives.

Lisa García Bedolla's essay in chapter 21, "Latina/o Politics and Participation: Individual Activity and Institutional Context," delves into the numeric presence and rising political influence Latinos could have in American politics if they only became citizens, if they voted more regularly, if their disparate political interests could be coalesced in unified form, and if the formal electoral system itself were not as deeply and historically biased against the participation of minorities. There is no such thing as a unified Latino electorate, much less a political identification all Latinos share. They do not all speak Spanish. They are not all Catholics. They are not all citizens. They do not all hold the liberal political values mostly espoused by the Democratic Party, as ignorant national pundits say they do. Women and men behave differently at the ballot box and in nongovernmental politics. Latinos vary enormously by age, education, income, and nativity, and whether an individual decides to expend the energy and resources to vote is mostly determined by his or her socioeconomic status. "We cannot assume that a common 'Latino' political identity exists," García Bedolla writes. For such a cohesive *Latinidad* to develop into a sense of communal unity, it requires a contentious give-and-take about a burning issue of concern that animates both upper-class Cuban Americans and dirt-poor Guatemalans, where they each put aside their differences to act together to advance their common cause. That is politics.

David E. Hayes-Bautista, Werner Schink, and Jorge Chapa's essay in chapter 22, "Young Latinos in an Aging American Society," which they first published in 1984, looks at the future of Latino politics and offers us a dystopian scenario that is produced by population growth in the United States, accelerated by high levels of immigration and female fertility. The authors predict a young, undereducated Latino population largely relegated to low-paying work and vilified for their race. Whites occupy the older end of society's age pyramid, enjoy much longer longevity, have negligible fertility rates, and experience almost no in-migration. As these white baby boomers, born in the 1950s and 1960s, start to retire and to depend on social insurance programs, the population that is expected to pay higher taxes to support these retirees consists of Latinos, precisely the group least financially able to do so. "Sixty-six percent of the population under 16 will be minorities, while only 32 percent over 65 will be minorities." Hayes-Bautista, Schink, and Chapa postulate a rather fractious future, with a society sharply stratified by race and age. Under such conditions will the United States remain intact as a polity or fracture into warring factions? The authors postulate the latter, and advance a number of policy proposals to achieve a more utopian future than the dystopian one the population statistics portend.

Hayes-Bautista, Schink, and Chapa update their essay in chapter 23, "Afterword: Thirty Years Later, 2016." Today, the lives of Latinos are routinely marked by violence and harassment. Indeed, for the past two decades, hate crimes against Latinos have risen significantly, in direct proportion to their rates of immigration.[1] They suffer from high assault rates and see their homes burglarized more often than do whites.[2] Because of racial profiling and police and popular stereotypes about their criminality, they get arrested at much higher rates than their numbers would predict. When Latinos become ensnared in the criminal justice system because of poverty, lack of adequate representation, inability to speak English, or undocumented immigrant status, they fare dismally. They get incarcerated at much higher rates than whites do. Along with African Americans, they are much more likely to remain jailed while awaiting trial because they lack the money to post bail. The average bail Latinos have to raise—$53,031—is almost twice the average of $28,430 that whites post. If convicted of a crime, Latinos often receive mandatory sentences, despite sentencing discretion. These stark outcomes help explain why, since 2007, almost 40 percent of all federally sentenced offenders have been Latinos. Between 1991 and 2007, Latinos accounted for more than half (54 percent) of the growth of federally sentenced offenders. The number incarcerated in Federal prisons represents only a small fraction, 8.6 percent, of the 2.3 million women and men housed in state and locally run prisons. The Pew Hispanic Center estimated in 2008 that one out of every fifty Latinos in the United States was incarcerated, compared to one out of every thirty African Americans, and less than one out of every hundred whites.[3] At present some 300,000 Hispanics are incarcerated, a number scholars deem a gross underestimate, mainly because most prison populations remain enumerated by race only as black and white.[4]

These statistics bring into sharp focus the future ex-convicts face when they are freed from jail and attempt reintegration into society. Martin Guevara Urbina's essay in chapter 24, "Life after Prison for Hispanics: Ethnic, Racial, and Gender Realities," describes the almost insurmountable obstacles these individuals face. Because prisons are no longer deemed places of rehabilitation, few prisoners are released with enhanced educations or employable skills. If they were addicted to drugs on entry, many still are on exit. Once they have a criminal conviction record, few employers will hire them, communities will ostracize them, family and kin will shun them, public housing and most forms of social insurance, including food stamps, will be denied, even their right to vote will be stripped from them. These are the reasons why almost 75 percent of all prisoners released at the end of a sentence or on parole soon return to prison.

The barriers to immigrant integration in American society are many, and in the Southern Poverty Law Center's report in chapter 25, "Climate of Fear," we learn of the vicious ways in which the white residents of Suffolk County (Long Island) in New York have been treating Latinos. The prejudice chronicled here is systemic and pervasive, exhibited by young men in brutal acts of violence; encouraged, indeed even fomented by elected county officials; enforced by the police; and celebrated by local anti-immigrant organizations such as the Sachem Quality of Life, and by the nationally powerful Federation for American Immigration Reform. In this report we learn of the daily forms of aggression Latinos have endured since the late 1990s: how they are pelted with rotten fruit, with full bottles and cans of beer as they walk along the streets; how their houses are spray-painted with racist epithets; how the immigrants themselves are attacked with BB guns, with bats, with knives. When Latinos report physical attacks such as being run down by cars while on their bikes, being spit on and pelted in public, being chased and beaten by baseball-bat-swinging white thugs, the police rarely investigate and instead immediately blame the victims, demanding their identification documents. The explicit message is that all Latinos, whatever their legal status, are unauthorized immigrants who have no human rights in Suffolk County.

On November 8, 2008, Marcelo Lucero, an Ecuadorian immigrant working in Suffolk County was stabbed to death by a gang of white teens who were out for a night of "beaner-hopping." The police half-heartedly investigated. On October 5, 2010, José Fermín Sánchez, an immigrant from El Salvador, was found dead, while his companion, Antonio Tum from Guatemala, was severely beaten and rectally sodomized with a large piece of wood. Again, the police moved slowly. Four years after the murders and assault, the police still had no leads. In the aftermath of the August 9, 2014, police shooting of Michael Brown in Ferguson, Missouri, the U.S. Justice Department issued two reports about the behavior of the police and municipal courts in that city. The "Ferguson Municipal Court has a pattern . . . focusing on revenue over public safety, leading to court practices that violate the 14th Amendment's due process and equal protection requirements. Court practices exacerbating the harm of Ferguson's unconstitutional police practices and imposing particular hardship upon Ferguson's most vulnerable residents, especially upon those living in or near poverty. Minor offenses can generate crippling debts, result in jail time because of an inability to pay and result in the loss of a driver's license, employment, or housing."[5]

Latinos in Suffolk County complained of similar police and court practices. A routine and unwarranted police traffic stop could easily cost them $400: a $185 fine, a car impound fee of $150, and then $25 a day for holding the vehicle. Enriching Suffolk County's coffers at the expense of Latinos was just the tip of the iceberg brought to light when Latinos enjoined the U.S. Justice Department to intervene. On April 29, 2015, twenty-one Suffolk County residents filed a federal class-action lawsuit against their police, charging widespread racial discrimination, harassment, and the systematic cover-up of crimes against Latinos. Named in the suit were Police Commissioner Edward Webber and Sergeant Scott A. Greene. Sergeant Greene was accused of frequently harassing Latinos, frisking them without cause, and routinely taking whatever cash and valuables they had, facts fully documented and digitally recorded.[6]

We turn next to informal, nongovernmental politics, using the example of the immigrant rights movement that exploded onto the national stage in the spring of 2006, with massive rallies in New York, San Francisco, Chicago, Los Angeles, and many smaller cities. In chapter 26, "What Explains the Immigrant Rights Marches of 2006? Xenophobia and Organizing with Democracy Technology," Pierrette Hondagneu-Sotelo and Angelica Salas show that what immediately precipitated the marches was the introduction of the Border Protection, Antiterrorism and Illegal Immigration Control Act of 2005 (HB 4437), authored by Congressmen James Sensenbrenner (R-WI) and Peter King (R-NJ). The bill, had it passed, would have been draconian in its reach, not only ordering the border between Mexico and the United States fortified with seven hundred miles of additional fence, but also criminalizing unlawful entry, ordering automatic deportation for legal residents found guilty of minor crimes, and even making it illegal and punishable for individuals to offer immigrants basic humanitarian aid in the form of food and water. Pro-immigrant advocates rose in opposition, staging rallies that gathered millions, which were made possible by three developments. The most immediate was the use of Spanish- and English-language radio, where DJs were particularly instrumental in telling their immigrant and working-class audiences just what was contained in the proposed legislation and how they could do something about it, and specifically urging listeners to attend the planned protest rallies.

A second development is that the marches of spring 2006 were fundamentally the culmination of years of organizing by labor unions, religious leaders, and civil rights organizations that had been working intensely to curb the impact of xenophobic laws aimed against immigrants. And a third development factoring in to this political mix was an emerging immigrant rights movement that had been taking shape since the 1980s in direct response to the emergence of radical nativist vigilantes and repressive state legislation that was limiting access to driver's licenses and social services, enacting housing restrictions, and authorizing local police to enforce immigration laws, thus abrogating federal jurisdiction. Hondagneu-Sotelo and Salas explain how, through grassroots organizing reaching bigger and broader networks of activists sharing a common concern for the rights of immigrants, a national, muscular movement was born.

The lesson this essay imparts is how groups with distinct visions and organizational structures can coalesce for purposes of social change. This is but one potential model Latinos have created to allow a broader sense of *Latinidad* to emerge as a political force.

In 1966 President Lyndon B. Johnson signed into law the Cuban Adjustment Act to grant expedited residency, a host of generous government benefits, and eventually expedited citizenship to those Cubans who fled the island and successfully placed a foot on American soil. This is the topic of Ann Louise Bardach's essay in chapter 27, "Wet Foot, Dry Foot . . . Wrong Foot." For close to fifty years, Cubans of mostly white, middle-, and upper-class standing have been admitted freely into the country while refugees from war-torn Central America are denied entry because the United States has refused to admit its involvement in anti-Communist covert operations in Central America. The policy of favoring Cubans while deporting others has been most extreme during the presidency of Barack Obama, when the government has routinely apprehended and deported nearly 400,000 undocumented immigrants yearly, while enthusiastically welcoming Cubans who manage to make the ninety-mile trek to Miami. Such differences in state policies clearly pit Latinos of various nationalities against one another, and further explain why these Cubans—who have been so highly reliant on federal welfare, job training programs, home and small business loans—have advanced economically and become particularly enthusiastic supporters of the Republican Party.

NOTES

1. Bureau of Justice Statistics, "Household Burglary, 1994–2011" (Washington, DC: NCJ 241754, 2013).

2. Mark Hugo Lopez and Michael T. Light, *A Rising Share: Hispanics and Federal Crime* (Washington, DC: Pew Research Center, 2009), p. iii.

3. The Sentencing Project, "Hispanic Prisoners in the United States," http://www.sentenc ingproject.org/doc/publications/inc_hispanicprisoners.pdf (accessed May 15, 2015).

4. Ibid.

5. Manny Fernandez, "Guilty Verdict in Killing of Long Island Man," *New York Times*, April 19, 2010; Kirk Semple, "4 Years Later, Still No Answers in Killing of a Long Island Laborer," *New York Times*, July 28, 2014; Liz Robbins, "Latinos, in Class-Action Case, Accuse Suffolk County Police of Bias and Harassment," *New York Times*, April 29, 2015.

6. National Institute of Justice, "Research Briefing: Understanding Trends in Hate Crimes against Immigrants and Hispanic-Americans" (Washington, DC, 2011); M. Stacey, K. Carbone-López, and R. Rosenfeld, "Demographic Change and Ethnically Motivated Crime: The Impact of Immigration on Anti-Hispanic Hate Crime in the United States," *Journal of Contemporary Criminal Justice* 27 (3), 278–98.

21

LATINA/O POLITICS AND PARTICIPATION

Individual Activity and Institutional Context

Lisa García Bedolla

LATINO POLITICAL ENGAGEMENT

In the 2000 presidential election, for the first time the Republican candidate, George W. Bush, exceeded his Democratic rival, Al Gore, in the amount his campaign spent on Spanish-language advertising targeting Latino voters. The Bush campaign hired veteran political strategist Lionel Sosa to develop a sophisticated and well-run Spanish-language outreach campaign. This effort is credited with significantly increasing Latino support for Bush in comparison to support for the 1996 Republican candidate, Bob Dole. In 2007, candidates competing for the Democratic presidential nomination participated, for the first time ever, in a bilingual presidential debate televized on the most popular Spanish-language channel, Univisión. Similarly, during the 2012 presidential campaign, both major-party presidential candidates—Barack Obama and Mitt Romney—appeared in presidential forums on Univisión. In addition, actress Eva Longoria and wealthy San Antonio businessman Henry Muñoz founded the Futuro Fund, a Latino-focused fundraising effort for the Obama campaign that raised $32 million to help Obama woo the Latino vote.[1] Due to the fund's success, in 2013 Muñoz became the first Latino to be selected as Finance Chairman of the Democratic National Committee. Why are we seeing increased attention being paid to Latino voters by both political parties at the national level? The answer is simple: demographics.

DEMOGRAPHICS

According to the U.S. census, in 2012 there were just over 53 million Latinos currently living in the United States, making Latinos 16.9 percent of the total U.S. population and the nation's largest minority group.[2] From 2000 to 2010, the Latino population grew 48 percent.[3] Much of this population growth has been among U.S.-born Latinos, who made up 64 percent of the Latino population in 2011. Future estimates of population growth in the U.S. suggest that the Latino population will double by 2060; that year, an estimated one in three Americans will be of Latino origin. In terms of the national-origin distribution of the U.S. Latino population in 2011, individuals of Mexican origin constituted by far the largest group, at 65 percent. They were followed by Puerto Ricans (9.3 percent), Central Americans (8.4 percent), South Americans (5.7 percent), Cubans (3.6 percent), and Dominicans (3 percent).[4] Thus, although there is substantial national-origin diversity within the Latino population in the United States, it is important to keep in mind that almost two-thirds of U.S. Latinos are of Mexican origin.

The Latino community varies from the U.S. population at large along a number of parameters that include age, income, and education, and that, we will see below, are important when considering the factors driving their participation patterns. Table 21.1 compares Latinos to the American population along several dimensions. We can see that the Latino population is significantly younger than the U.S. population overall. Relative to Americans in general, more Latinos are under the age of 18 and fewer are over the age of 65. Latinos earn significantly less than other Americans, although, interestingly, there is less of a gender gap in earnings among Latinos than there is among the total U.S. population. The poverty rate among Latinos is more than twice that of the general population, and is particularly high among children (those under 18). Latino households also tend to be larger, which means that household income for the Latino population is expected to support a larger number of people than income for the rest of the population. Latino educational attainment is also lower on average: many more Latinos than other Americans have less than a 9th-grade education, and the number of Latinos with a college degree is less than half of that found in the general population.

This demographic information is important not only in terms of getting a snapshot of the community, but also in terms of how it may affect Latino public policy preferences. Given the relative youth of the community, one can imagine educational attainment and educational quality being very important issues, along with policies aimed at decreasing poverty rates among children. On the other hand, given the small number of Latinos over the age of 65, issues such as social security and retirement may not be as immediate. Because of these demographic differences, it is unlikely that voters from the general U.S. population will have the same political concerns and policy preferences as Latinos. That is why it is important that Latinos have a voice in the political process that is equal to their demographic numbers. As we will see below, there are a number of reasons why that has yet to be established.

Not only do Latinos differ from the general U.S. population, they also differ on a number of important parameters across national-origin groups. Table 21.2 summarizes age, nativity, income, and educational attainment across the Latino national-origin groups we will be studying in this book. In terms of age, Cubans stand out as the oldest

	Latinos	Total U.S. population
Age		
Median Age	27	37
Population under 18	35.1%	22.4%
Population aged 65 and over	5.7%	14.2%
Nativity		
Foreign population	36%	7.9%
Income and Poverty		
Median annual earnings for men 25 and older	$26,497	$37,653
Median annual earnings for women 25 and older	$18,765	$23,395
Percentage of overall population living in poverty	26.6%	12.9%
Population under 18 living in poverty	35%	18%
Household Size		
Population living in household with 2 people or fewer	39.2%	64%
Population living in household with 5 people or more	22.7%	8.3%
Educational Attainment		
Population with less than a 9th-grade education	20.7%	2.7%
Population with a high school diploma or more	64.3%	91.1%
Population with a college degree or more	14.1%	32.9%

Source: American Community Survey, 2011.

national-origin group, with a median age of 40, more than 10 years higher than any other national-origin group. Mexicans have the largest under-18 population, and Salvadorans and Guatemalans have the smallest over-65 group. More than two-thirds of Guatemalans and over 60 percent of Salvadorans are foreign born. Among the foreign-born populations, Mexicans, Salvadorans, and Guatemalans have the highest rates of noncitizenship. In terms of income, Puerto Ricans and Cubans have the highest median incomes, and Salvadorans and Guatemalans the lowest. This is likely a reflection of low levels of educational attainment among Salvadorans and Guatemalans—over half of individuals over the age of 25 from these two countries have less than a high school diploma. Salvadorans and Guatemalans also have much lower levels of college degree attainment than the other national-origin groups.

An awareness of these differences is important because they demonstrate that the

TABLE 21.2 Age, Nativity, Income, and Education by Country of Origin

	Mexican	Puerto Rican	Cuban	Dominican	Salvadoran	Guatemalan
Population Size	33,557,922	4,885,294	1,891,014	1,554,819	1,977,657	1,214,076
Female	48.6%	51%	49.3%	53.3%	49.6%	43.3%
Male	51.4%	49%	50.6%	46.7%	50.4%	56.7%
Age						
Median Age	25	27	40	29	29	27
Population under 18	36.6%	33.3%	21.2%	29%	29.5%	29.2%
Population 65 and over	4.4%	6.6%	16.7%	6.3%	3.2%	2.6%
Nativity						
Percent foreign born	35.6%	NA[a]	58.8%	56.5%	62.4%	67%
Entered U.S. before 1990 (% of foreign-born)	34.8%	NA[a]	48.3%	36.9%	35.5%	27.1%
Entered U.S. 2000 or later (% of foreign-born)	34.5%	NA[a]	32.3%	33.5%	36.2%	48.7%
Non-citizen (% of foreign-born)	77%	NA[b]	45%	53.1%	72.7%	76%
Income						
Median income (year-round full-time workers)	$27,000	$35,100	$33,300	$28,000	$25,000	$23,000
Educational Attainment						
Pop. over 25 with < high-school diploma	43.4%	25.5%	24%	34.5%	53.1%	54.4%
Pop. over 25 with high-school diploma	26.2%	30%	28.7%	26.5%	24.1%	22.1%
Pop. over 25 with college degree or more	9.4%	16.3%	23.7%	15%	7.3%	8.5%

[a] Since Puerto Rico is a U.S. territory, no Puerto Rican is "foreign-born," although those born on the mainland have a different legal status from those born on the island

[b] All Puerto Ricans are U.S. citizens

Sources: 2011 American Community Survey, 1-year estimates, and Pew Hispanic Center's National-Origin Statistical Summaries, 2010.

Latino community is not monolithic, but rather is made up of disparate national-origin groups that are situated within varied economic and social opportunity structures. Each of those groups has a unique history and a distinct set of social, political, and economic challenges. Those differences can and do affect the kinds of public policies each group supports, their partisan attachments, and their political engagement.

Since the 1960s, political scientists have been studying American political behavior—which factors explain why individuals turn out and vote, or why they engage in other kinds of political activity such as contacting elected officials, contributing to campaigns, engaging in political protest, and so on. This work, which has focused mainly on the general U.S. population, has found that a person's socioeconomic status (SES)—their education, income, and occupation—is the best predictor of their likelihood to vote. In other words, those who are more educated, have higher incomes, and come from professional occupations (versus more blue-collar jobs) are more likely to vote than those who are less educated, poorer, or do manual labor. This is intuitively logical. Higher SES individuals have more resources in terms of personal capacity, time, and flexibility they can use to help toward paying the "cost" of engaging in politics.

Yet when this work has been extended to minority communities, it seems not to be able to explain all the aspects of their engagement. Political scientist Katherine Tate finds that education and income are only occasionally related to African American participation, and studies of Latinos have found that SES can explain only part of the gap between Latino and Anglo electoral and nonelectoral participation.[5] Scholars attempting to find other explanations have turned to psychological resources—feelings of efficacy, trust in government, and civic duty—as the explanatory factors. Studies using these approaches have found that levels of political interest and efficacy have a significant effect on participation. These models center around the idea that feelings of "linked fate," "political alienation," "group identity," and "group conflict" have an impact on minority groups' political attitudes and behavior.[6] In other words, individuals feel (or do not feel) connections to particular groups, and their political attitudes and levels of participation are influenced in important ways by those feelings.

But, the fact that feelings of group attachment are important to participation does not mean we can assume that Latinos automatically feel a particular attachment to "Latinos" as a social group. As political scientist Cristina Beltrán points out in *The Trouble with Unity*, Latino-oriented collective engagement in the United States is a *political* product, rather than something that simply exists outside the realm of politics and history.[7] The varied national-origin groups discussed here have engaged in a variety of political movements, campaigns, and other collective organizing efforts. Each of those efforts was a product of a particular moment in historical time, a unique set of political circumstances, and the specific experiences of that local community. Therefore, we cannot assume that a common "Latino" political identity exists. Instead, to understand Latino politics, we need to consider where, historically, a "Latino" (or national-origin-focused) identity might come from and under what circumstances that identity can (or cannot) translate into political action.

It is also important to consider how nativity can affect ethnoracial groups' participation within U.S. electoral politics. Figures 21.1 to 21.5 summarize Latino registration

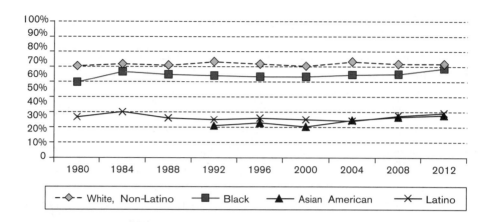

FIGURE 21.1

Registration in Presidential Elections as Percentage of Total Population, 1980–2012
Source: U.S. Census Bureau, Current Population Survey, November 2012 and earlier report.

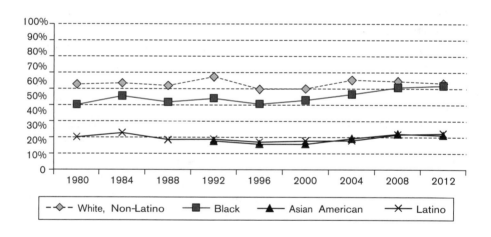

FIGURE 21.2

Voting in Presidential Elections as Percentage of Total Population, 1980–2012
Source: U.S. Census Bureau, Current Population Survey, November 2012 and earlier report.

and voting rates from 1978 to 2012 in comparison to those of other U.S. ethnoracial groups. What is clear from these figures is that nativity is a big issue for the two largest immigrant groups in the United States: Latinos and Asian Americans. If one looks only at the citizen population, their registration and voting rates are somewhat similar to those of whites and Blacks, albeit still lower. Yet when these rates are compared to those of the general population, we see that the proportion of individuals over 18 who are registered and voting within these groups represents a significantly lower percentage than

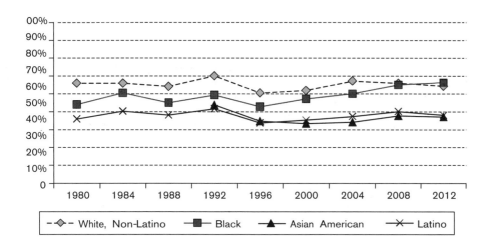

FIGURE 21.3

Voting in Presidential Elections as Percentage of Citizen Population, 1980–2012

Source: U.S. Census Bureau, Current Population Survey, November 2012 and earlier report.

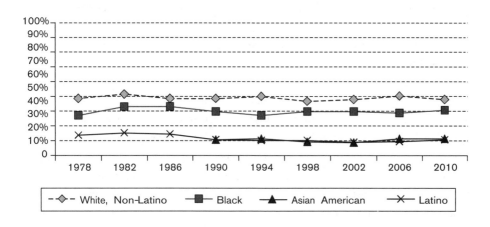

FIGURE 21.4

Voting in Midterm Elections as Percentage of Total Population, 1980–2012

for the U.S. population as a whole. In figure 21.2, we see that, in presidential elections, which are the highest turnout elections in the United States, only about 30 percent of the Latino population overall actually votes. That is compared to about 60 percent for whites and Blacks. Compared to other advanced industrialized nations, those numbers are low across the board. For Latinos, it means that only a very small proportion of the overall population is able to have an electoral voice during even the most high turnout elections. Figure 21.4 shows that, in midterm elections, the proportion of the total Latino

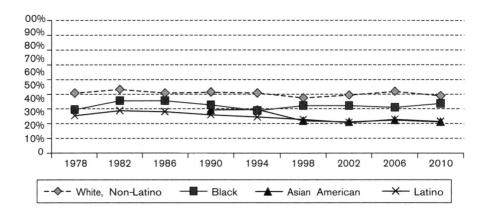

FIGURE 21.5

Voting in Midterm Elections as Percentage of Citizen Population, 1980–2012

Source: U.S. Census Bureau, Current Population Survey, November 2012 and earlier report.

population voting goes down to about 20 percent, while for whites it remains at about 50 percent. This means that, relative to whites, Latinos have even less electoral influence in low turnout elections.

These differences are due to the fact that Latinos have lower registration rates than whites or Blacks, combined with the fact that about 40 percent of the community consists of non-citizens, which means that they are ineligible to vote. As we saw in table 21.2 above, Mexican, Salvadoran, and Guatemalan immigrants have low rates of naturalization among their foreign-born populations.[8] Latinos also are, on average, younger than other U.S. ethnoracial groups, meaning that fewer Latinos are over age 18, as a proportion of the population, than is true for other groups. Thus a smaller segment of the population is eligible to vote than in other populations. Only about 43.9 percent of Latinos are eligible to vote, and a smaller proportion of that eligible group chooses to register and vote than is true among whites or Blacks. The result is that Latino voters do not come close to representing the demographic power of the Latino population as a whole.

These national-origin groups vary in terms of their group histories and of the kinds of political activity they have chosen to engage in. According to the 2012 Current Population Survey, 11.2 million Latinos voted in the presidential election in November 2012, comprising about 48 percent of Latino eligible voters. The highest rate of turnout was among Cubans (at 67.2 percent) and the lowest among Mexicans (at 42.2 percent). Puerto Ricans fell somewhere in the middle, at 52.8 percent turnout. Although some of this variation is attributable to differences in SES among the groups, it also highlights important differences in the kinds of political activities each national-origin group chooses to engage in. Historically, Mexicans and Puerto Ricans have been more likely to engage in protests than Cubans. Cubans, in turn, tend to engage in voting more than other types of political activities. These differences are due to history, geography, and the U.S. institutional context. When thinking about the Latino electorate, we also need to keep in mind that Latina women register and vote at higher rates than Latino men across all national-origin groups. Nationally, Latina registration rates are about 10 points higher than those of men; turnout rates vary in similar ways. Therefore there are many cross-cutting factors that affect Latinos' propensity to go to the ballot box on Election Day.

INSTITUTIONAL CONTEXT

When Latinos decide to incorporate themselves into the U.S. political system, they must do so within the context of a specific set of electoral and legislative rules that affect how much power a minority group will be able to muster within that system. These rules fall into two broad categories: *electoral rules* and *legislative rules*. We will explore each in turn.

ELECTORAL RULES

Electoral rules are the rules that underlie the American electoral system. The most important rules with regard to Latinos are: majority rule; rules surrounding voting rights; and citizenship requirements for voting.

Majority rule   The most basic electoral rule underlying the American political system is the idea of majority rule: if you can get more than 50 percent of the vote, you win the election. That is why scholars describe the American political system as majoritarian—you must have a majority in order to win. Other democracies around the world are not organized this way. Some have proportional representational rules that guarantee a certain number of parliamentary seats, for example, to a particular minority group or party. Others have quota systems to ensure the representation of women or minority groups. The fact that the United States' electoral rules are majoritarian places important structural constraints on the electoral participation of minority groups like Latinos.

Since Latinos constitute a minority community within the United States, majority rule significantly affects their ability to express their interests through voting. Nationally, Latinos make up about 17 percent of the total U.S. population. Yet, because of the demographic issues discussed above—namely the community's significant non-citizen population, large under-18 population, and low registration and voting rates—the 2012 Current Population Survey estimates that Latinos made up only about 8.4 percent of the voters in the 2012 presidential election. The story is similar at the state level. In California, for example, Latinos make up 38 percent of the state's population, yet only about 16 percent of likely voters. Similarly, in New Mexico—the state with the largest Latino population, 46.3 percent of the state total—Latinos make up 35 percent of voters. Of course, at the municipal level, in cities with a population over 75 percent Latino, Latinos can and often do make up the majority of voters. But that is rare. In most places and in most electoral races, for Latino voters to meet the 50 percent threshold they must build coalitions with like-minded groups in order to ensure the success of their chosen candidate or of their preferred policy proposal. This means that, in the electoral arena, Latinos are not in complete control of their destiny. As a minority group within a majoritarian system, they can win elections only if they join coalitions large enough to surpass the 50 percent threshold. This, of course, means that they must compromise with those groups regarding their policy preferences and their choice of candidate. Thus majority rule makes it difficult for U.S. minority groups like Latinos to win elections.

The Voting Rights Act Voting rights are important because, within a republican democracy, voting is the main way citizens may express their political preferences. Voting is also substantively important because it has instrumental value: it is an instrument that citizens use in order to determine who gets to make the laws and what kinds of public policies are put into place. For most of American history, the majority of the country's population—women and people of color—was denied the right to vote. This is why achieving the ability to exercise that right was a centerpiece of the civil rights movement. One of the greatest successes of the civil rights movement was the passage of the Voting Rights Act (VRA) in 1965. This Act was designed to outlaw the mechanisms— direct intimidation, poll taxes, literacy tests—that had been used to suppress African American voting in the south. The VRA, although originally conceived to address the African American case, positively affected the Latino community's ability to exercise the right to vote and to elect Latino candidates to public office.

In addition to outlawing the voting restrictions listed above, the VRA also made a number of counties with histories of excluding minority voters subject to federal electoral supervision. That supervision included "preclearance" of county districting rules and other electoral logistics. Initially, these rules targeted largely African American jurisdictions. Yet when Congress renewed the VRA in 1970, the number of counties subject to federal supervision expanded. As a result, for the first time, counties with significant Latino populations were included under the preclearance rules, which provided important protections to Latino voting rights. In 1975 the VRA was renewed again, and this marked the first time when Latinos were included directly under its provisions. From 1975 forward, the VRA was expanded so as to cover the protection of "language minorities," which included Latinos, Asian Americans, Alaska natives, and Native Americans. Under the 1975 rules, jurisdictions with a language-minority population of 5 percent or more were eligible to request federal election observers. The law also required that jurisdictions meeting this population threshold provide bilingual ballots to language-minority voters. Latinos were not included under the law by accident—these changes were the direct result of political organizing on the part of Mexican Americans and Puerto Ricans in the late 1960s and early 1970s.

The VRA has had an important impact on Latino political activity and representation. First, it removed the most overt structural barriers to voting. It outlawed things like direct intimidation of voters, capricious changes in voting rules and/or polling places, English-language requirements for registration and voting, lengthy residential requirements for voter registration, the manipulation or control of the Latino vote by economic elites, and the drawing of district lines so that they diluted the minority vote—a practice known as racial gerrymandering. Requirements of long-time residence for voter registration were especially detrimental to migrant workers, many of whom are Latino, because of their need to move regularly for their employment. Most of these barriers existed for Mexican Americans in Texas, but variants of them were used also to exclude Puerto Ricans from voting in New York City.

Second, the VRA significantly increased the number of Latino elected officials across the country. Although Latinos, unlike African Americans, were never excluded from public office entirely, because of racial gerrymandering Latino officeholders were relatively rare before 1975. In 1973 there were 1,280 Latino elected officials serving in the six most heavily Latino states: Arizona, California, Florida, New Mexico, New York, and Texas. By 2013, there were 5,263 Latino elected officials serving in those states—more than four times the number in 1973. Across all states in 2013, there were 6,011 Latinos serving as elected officials at the national, state, and local levels; 95 percent of those serve at the local level where it is easier for minority candidates to meet the majoritarian threshold necessary for election.[9] This dramatic growth in the number of Latino elected officials in the United States was largely due to legal changes in districting practices that occurred under the VRA. By 1982, the federal courts and Congress had established that states and localities with large and concentrated minority populations had an affirmative responsibility to create districts from which minority groups could elect the candidates of their choice. The VRA urged the creation, when possible, of majority–minority districts, which in practice guaranteed the election of minority representatives from a particular area. The downside to this move, however, was that it only allowed for minority representation from areas with high levels of racial segregation. That being said, even though African American candidates still find it difficult to be elected in majority white districts, Latino candidates generally need over 35 percent of the majority party's voters to be Latino in order to have a strong chance of taking that seat. This is a big change, which is due in large measure to the VRA.

In June 2013, the U.S. Supreme Court, in *Shelby County* v. *Holder*, fundamentally changed the VRA. Section 5 of the VRA laid out the preclearance requirements for covered jurisdictions. Section 4(a) laid out the formula that would be used to determine which jurisdictions would be covered under Section 5.[10] In 1965, the formula standard under Section 4 had two parts: (1) if a jurisdiction, on November 1, 1964, had a "test or device" (such as literacy tests, moral character requirements to register, etc.) in place to restrict voting access; and (2) if fewer than 50 percent of eligible voters were registered to vote, and/or less than 50 percent of eligible voters had voted in the 1964 presidential election. If both items were found to be true, the jurisdiction was made subject to Section 5. In 1970, the formula was adjusted to reference the 1968 election. In 1975 the relevant election date was changed to 1972 and the definition of "test or device" was expanded to include the practice of providing any election information, including ballots, only in English in states or political subdivisions where members of a single language minority constituted more than 5 percent of the citizens of voting age. The 1975 change resulted in many Latino-heavy jurisdictions now being covered by the VRA.

In the *Shelby* decision, the Supreme Court ruled that the Section 4 formula, because it was based on 1972 electoral information, was too old and therefore not reflective of current practice. Subjecting covered jurisdictions to preclearance under that formula was thus deemed unconstitutional. The Supreme Court left open the possibility that Section 4 could be made constitutional by updating the VRA formula. Given the current make-up of Congress, however, it is highly unlikely that Congress will act in the near term to make this change. The result is that Section 5 is moot; no jurisdictions in the United States will be subject to preclearance under the old rules.

This constitutes a huge change in the power behind the VRA. Jurisdictions are still, after *Shelby*, subject to Section 2 requirements not to discriminate against ethnoracial and language—minority voters. But Section 2 challenges must occur *after* the election, and, even in cases where the plaintiffs win, they do not change the outcome in that election. Some legal analysts believe that it may be possible to make jurisdictions subject to preclearance under the VRA by "bailing in" jurisdictions under Section 3, rather than Section 5, under specific conditions of demonstrated intentional discrimination. Legal scholars call this a "pocket trigger" that would create a dynamic preclearance regime that could pass constitutional muster because it would be based on evidence from current practices.[11]

This is what many are considering attempting with the state of Texas. Since 1975, the Justice Department has found the state of Texas and its jurisdictions in violation of the VRA 207 times.[12] Within hours of the *Shelby* ruling, Texas Attorney General Greg Abbott announced that its voter identification law would take effect immediately, as would the state's 2012 redistricting plan, despite the fact that both had been struck down by the courts based on evidence of the state's discriminatory intent. Texas' current voter identification law is expected to affect the over 600,000 registered Texas voters who do not possess valid identification, a large proportion of whom are Latino. Similarly, the redistricting plan was shown to significantly dilute Latino voting strength in the areas of the state with the highest rates of Latino population growth. E-mail from state officials, which were made public during the trial, showed that Latino vote dilution was a specific goal in how the maps were drawn. The Texas Attorney General contended that the *Shelby* ruling freed the state to do what it wished in both these instances because it was no longer subject to Section 5 preclearance. In July 2013, U.S. Attorney General

Eric Holder announced the federal government's plan to "bail in" Texas under Section 3's pocket trigger based on this evidence of discriminatory intent. At the time of this writing, the outcome of this move is still unclear.

After *Shelby*, it remains to be seen whether the progress that occurred under the VRA will be reversed or Section 3 will be used to create a dynamic preclearance system that can satisfy the current Supreme Court. What is clear is that legal changes under the VRA were an important structural change that had a positive impact on Latinos' ability to exercise the right to vote and to be represented by Latino elected officials. How the VRA is interpreted after *Shelby* will have an important impact on the kinds of structural obstacles Latinos face at the polling booth in years to come.

Citizenship and voting rights   About 40 percent of the Latino population in the United States is foreign born. This means that the Latino community continually has a large percentage of non-citizens. Since citizenship is, in most places in the United States, a requirement for voting, this means in turn that a large proportion of the population has no formal say in the U.S. political system. Yet, for much of U.S. history, citizenship was not a requirement for voting; this is a fairly recent phenomenon. During the nineteenth century, over twenty states and territories had alien voting rights. During the colonial era, non-citizens voted and held public office throughout the colonies. These policies were maintained after independence. Instead of citizenship, the key criteria for granting voting rights were race, gender, property, and residence. As the country expanded westward, states used non-citizen voting rights to encourage white immigrants to settle in their areas. For example, Congress approved non-citizen voting in Illinois, Indiana, Kansas, Kentucky, Michigan, Minnesota, Missouri, Nebraska, Nevada, North Dakota, Ohio, Oklahoma, Oregon, South Dakota, Washington, Wisconsin, and Wyoming. The year 1875 marked the height of non-citizen suffrage in the United States, with twenty-two states and territories granting white immigrants the right to vote. Most of these states only required that voters be white, male, and express an intent to naturalize. States saw the provision of non-citizens' voting rights as a way to teach civic ideals to future citizens.

Around the end of the nineteenth century, concerns arose regarding the power and influence exercised by immigrant groups. As anti-immigrant sentiment grew, states began to retract their support of non-citizen suffrage. Many states passed constitutional amendments limiting the franchise to United States citizens. By the late 1920s, most states required that individuals must be citizens in order to vote. But non-citizen voting is not illegal. Currently a number of municipalities allow non-citizen voting. One of the most liberal statutes exists in Takoma Park, Maryland, where, since 1992, non-citizens have been allowed to vote in local elections and hold municipal office regardless of their migration status.

For the Latino community, the issue of non-citizen voting is not simply an academic one. Because non-citizens tend to be concentrated in particular geographic areas, their formal exclusion from the political process raises questions about democracy and representation in the United States. For example, the state of California has at least twelve municipalities where the non-citizen population makes up more than 50 percent of the adults living there.[13] These individuals work, pay taxes, have children in school, and yet have no formal say in who represents them in government. This is why many scholars and activists have called for non-citizen voting to be allowed at the local level, particularly in school board and municipal elections. They argue that this helps to teach non-citizens about participation and democracy and ensures that their voices are heard in matters that affect them or their children directly. Given that Latinos make up such a large share of the non-citizen population in the United States, any changes in this direction would have an important impact on their participation rates and ability to influence the political process.

Nonelectoral participation Yet political participation is not solely about voting. There are many other ways in which individuals and groups can engage in the political process. These form what is called nonelectoral participation, which can include activities such as engaging in political protest, working for a community-based organization, contacting elected officials, signing petitions, boycotting a particular company or product, and so on. Any sort of collective activity aimed at addressing a political problem can be defined as nonelectoral activity. Other than giving contributions to elected officials (which may only be done by U.S. citizens or permanent residents), non-citizens can engage in any of these types of activities. Thus nonelectoral participation is an important way through which non-citizen Latinos can express their political views. Nevertheless, the factors that determine who engages in nonelectoral participation have been found to be the same as for electoral participation: those who have higher incomes, higher levels of education, and are older are more likely to participate in these kinds of activities than those who are young, less educated, and have lower income levels. Since the Latino community in the United States is younger and less affluent than non-Latino whites, Latinos are less likely than whites to engage in these kinds of political activities, even though there are no legal barriers (such as citizenship status) to their participation.

Table 21.3 summarizes Latino political interest and engagement in some nonelectoral activities. As we have seen with electoral participation, there are differences among Latino national-origin groups in terms of their preferred forms of engagement. Salvadorans are the least likely to report interest in politics in general, while about two-thirds of the Mexicans and Puerto Ricans say they find politics interesting. Cubans seem to be the group most interested in politics. Puerto Ricans are the most likely to report contacting an elected official and Guatemalans are the least likely. Just under a third of the respondents from all the groups prefer to use existing organizations to solve problems. All the group members seem slightly more likely to prefer to resolve problems informally, except for Salvadorans and Guatemalans. Thus, not all Latinos are the same in terms of their attitudes toward politics and the kinds of activities they choose to engage

TABLE 21.3   Political Engagement by National Origin among the Total Population

	Mexican	Puerto Rican	Cuban	Dominican	Salvadoran	Guatemalan
Somewhat interested to very interested in politics	66.2%	68.6%	73.3%	63.9%	47.7%	51.0%
Have contacted public official to express concerns	30.3%	45.1%	38.8%	29.0%	22.9%	17.4%
Prefer to resolve problems through existing organizations	27.5%	28.6%	24.0%	28.1%	30.2%	28.2%
Prefer to resolve problems informally	31.1%	29.4%	30.0%	32.5%	26.3%	21.5%
Total Number	5,704	822	420	335	407	149

Source: 2006 Latino National Survey.

in. These differences reflect individual-level preferences combined with structural factors such as organizational density, local electoral rules, and the group's political history.

Therefore, the US political system operates under a set of electoral rules that either limit or facilitate minority participation and representation. When considering the political incorporation of a minority group like Latinos, it is important to keep these rules in mind and to understand the consequences they may have on the strategies groups choose to employ in order to express their political interests and on the chances that these tactics may enjoy success.

LEGISLATIVE RULES

Legislative rules are the rules that govern decision-making within legislative institutions such as the United States Congress or the state legislatures. As with electoral participation, the emphasis on majority rule is very important within legislatures and dictates how decisions are made at the committee and floor vote levels. Party agendas and leadership are much more important within legislatures than they are within American politics at large, and they affect elected officials' abilities to serve their constituents' interests.

Committee rules   Most legislative bodies rule through committees. This means that the responsibilities of a body in terms of policymaking are divided up across a number of standing committees. Each legislator serves on a few committees that are in charge of issues under its jurisdiction. For example, at the federal level, the Education and Workforce Committee is responsible for all legislation related to educational and workplace issues. Those legislators who serve on that committee have more of an impact on drafting legislation related to such issues than do legislative members who do not serve on that committee. The committee system is meant to streamline the law-making process. If all the members were able to have a say on every piece of legislation, the law-making process would be unmanageable. Instead, the proposed law is brought before the relevant committee, amended as the committee members see fit, and then voted on by the committee, which has to determine whether or not the revised legislation should be subject to a vote by the entire legislative body.

The committee system is an important part of the legislative process and is what makes law-making possible. However, for representatives of minority communities, it does have some important negative effects on their ability to pursue their political agenda. As we have seen with the electoral system in general, majority rule makes it difficult for minority communities to cross the 50 percent threshold necessary to win elections. This limitation is only compounded when majority rule is applied within the legislature itself. For example, in the 113th Congress (2013–15), there were 28 Latinos serving in the U.S. House of Representatives, which contains a total of 435 members. In order to get any legislation passed, a Latino member first has to obtain the support of the majority of the relevant committee. Then they have to persuade 217 other representatives to support their proposal for the floor vote. We saw above how majority rule in the electoral system often makes coalition-building necessary for being elected. Once representatives are elected, coalitions become an absolute requirement in order to get legislation passed. Thus crossing the majority threshold in an election is only the very first step in the multiple levels of majority rule that affect the policymaking abilities of Latino elected officials.

Party influence and agendas   Majority rule is important not only within legislative bodies, but also within the two major political parties. For most Americans, political parties and their platforms have little relevance to their day-to-day lives. Within legislatures, however, parties are very important. In the United States, the political party system was created within Congress during the eighteenth century in order to help politicians to muster the number of votes necessary to pass legislation. This imperative remains valid today. To be successful, parties need their members to stick together and support the bills that the party leadership wants passed. Thus party loyalty is very important within legislatures, and this is something that party leaders spend a great deal of time working to develop. They do it through carrots and sticks—incentives and disincentives for following the party line.

On the side of incentives, the strongest one that party leaders have at their disposal is committee assignments. Who gets to sit on what committee is determined by the leaders of each party. And some committee assignments are much more popular than others. For example, within the U.S. House of Representatives, the Appropriations Committee is responsible for all the appropriations (that is, spending) that go through the House.

For obvious reasons, this is a very powerful committee and one that members want to join. If a member does what the leadership asks and votes with the party, the party leaders can reward him or her with a seat on a coveted committee. Conversely, if members do not vote with the party on an important issue, their leadership can punish them by removing them from a particular committee or by denying them the committee assignment they want. Another incentive the parties can muster is support for a particular member when the time comes for reelection. Both political parties have national and statewide committees whose job is to raise money for the party's candidates. A loyal party member is more likely to receive this kind of financial support than a disloyal member. This is another way parties can encourage their members' support in legislative voting. Conversely, party leaders can deny these benefits to uncooperative members to discourage them from voting against the party line.

The question then arises: what are the members actually supporting? Individual representatives are focused on responding to the needs of their particular district or constituency. Party leaders, on the other hand, represent their districts but also have to consider the needs of the party in general. Because of the majoritarian electoral requirements both in electing representatives and in the legislatures themselves, party leaders need to develop policy proposals that appeal to the broadest possible number of people. Remember, any proposal must get over 50 percent of the vote. This often makes parties reluctant to take positions that can be seen as targeting the needs of a specific group. They would rather be seen as being as broad and inclusive as possible. The kinds of proposals that have this sort of broad appeal tend to represent the ideological center—to be not too extreme either in the liberal or in the conservative direction. Yet, from a political ideology standpoint, Latinos in general, and Latino elected officials in particular, tend to hold policy positions that are more liberal than those of Americans generally. For example, Latinos are more likely than other Americans to say they support increased government programs, particularly for education and health-related services. Thus, from a policy standpoint, the kinds of proposals Latino representatives are likely to advocate often fall to the left of the political center in the United States. Since party leaders want to put forward proposals that will be successful, the kinds of policy proposals advocated by Latino representatives will often not be included in the final legislation, or will be watered down so as to appeal to a broader number of people. In other words, the ability of Latino representatives to influence the party's agenda depends on the degree to which their policy preferences coincide with what will appeal to the party leadership and to a majority of the legislative members as a whole. Again, we see how having political influence can be difficult for minority group members within majoritarian legislative bodies.

REPRESENTATION

The issue of party leaders, elected officials, and their policy agendas raises the question of representation. When the founders were writing the U.S. Constitution, the only democracies they had as models were those of ancient Greece and Rome. Both of those systems allowed all citizens to engage in decision-making.[14] Yet, in a country the size of the United States this approach was not feasible. Instead, our founders developed a representative system of government—one in which citizens choose representatives to uphold their interests in the decision-making process. If the citizens do not agree with their elected representatives, they can remove them in the next election. Yet the founders never truly answered the question of what representation means within a majoritarian context. James Madison in *Federalist* argued that the tyranny of the majority—the tendency of the majority to impose their will on the minority—could be avoided if the majority shifted continually.[15] In other words, a particular individual may be in the majority on religious issues, but in the minority on economics; and, as long as the majority is made to shift across issues, this form of tyranny can be avoided.

Yet this formulation does not address the question of what a democratic system might do in a situation where a particular population, like Latinos, could potentially have different economic or educational preferences from the majority population. How can such a minority have its interests represented? And, more importantly, what happens if those interests can never be represented? Does that affect the legitimacy of the system? The VRA is meant to address this question by ensuring a minimal level of *descriptive representation* for minority groups—representation by an individual who shares the same race, gender, class, or national origin as the voter. But is this all that matters? Can we assume that a poor female representative can represent the interests of all poor females? The fact of the matter is that, at the state and federal levels, our elected representatives are predominantly male and much richer than the general population. Does that mean that they cannot represent the majority's interests?

This remains an open question—which is why some scholars argue for the idea of *substantive representation*: representation by someone who agrees with the voter ideologically and in terms of their public policy interests. The idea is that the voters have a representative with congruent policy views acting as their advocate. Yet how do we know what a voter's policy views are? And which voters should have their policy views represented? Any representative at any level of government will have constituents with opposing views. How should that representative decide which views "matter"? Also, is an elected official's job simply to echo her constituents' opinions, or should she vote according to her own judgment? These are important, and to a large extent unanswerable, questions. Yet they go to the heart of the problem of defining and measuring "representation." It is likely that most voters want their representative to represent their substantive interest, and they use descriptive representation as shorthand, on the basis of the assumption that, if an individual has had similar life experiences, they probably have similar policy preferences. But it is important to point out that this is not always the case and that continually questioning representation and what it means is crucial within the context of a representative democracy.

For minority groups, the issue of representation also raises a number of other questions, in particular about authenticity and accountability. In terms of authenticity, the pertinent question is: how often do minority voters get represented by the people they want (that is, how often does the candidate they support win?)? If the minority group votes as a bloc and continually loses, this threatens democratic legitimacy. As Madison pointed out, avoiding the tyranny of the majority requires that everyone should win every once in a while. This is why one of the factors taken into consideration in VRA litigation is the presence of racial bloc voting in a particular jurisdiction. This reflects authenticity, but accountability is equally important. If a politician has a very "safe" seat, how driven will he be to protect his constituents' interests? This is a growing problem in American politics in general, as the political parties regularly draw district lines that ensure very little party competition within legislative districts. For example, of the 435 seats up for election every two years in the U.S. House of Representatives, only about 40 are truly competitive. This issue is only exacerbated in majority-minority seats. Since most of the minority groups subject to VRA scrutiny (African Americans, Latinos, Asian Americans, and Native Americans) vote overwhelmingly for the Democratic Party, creating a majority-minority seat often means creating a safe Democratic Party seat. This means, further, that those representatives are elected easily and have little competition for reelection. In addition, many of their constituents, for important historical reasons, are not as engaged politically as the general population. Within this context, who ensures that those representatives truly are accountable to the people that they represent? This remains one of the major challenges within U.S. democracy and a particular problem for members of minority groups.

Minority representation also raises the problem of institutional compromise. To get their issues on their party agenda, minority representatives often need to make compromises in order to build coalitions. Yet many Americans, in the majority and in the minority alike, complain that their representatives forget them, or forget their promises, when they achieve political office. How much should minority representatives be willing to compromise? Democracy is built on the principle of compromise; yet is there a point, if they compromise too much, at which elected leaders cease to be "representative"? This too is an open question, and one that applies to all U.S. representatives. But in the case of individuals who represent groups that have continually been the "losers" in terms of their public policy agendas, like Latinos, these questions take on additional salience.

LEVELS OF GOVERNMENT AND REGIONAL DIFFERENCES

The previous discussion was not meant to imply that all government is created equal. The scale required for election, funding, and success at the national level is exponentially greater than at the local level. This is one of the reasons why the majority of Latino elected officials is found at the local level. In general, it is easier for minority groups to be represented at the local level because it takes a smaller number of people to surpass the 50 percent threshold. From a districting standpoint, the creation of majority-minority districts at the local level still encourages segregation, but the size of the overall community can be smaller and yet still have representation. Thus it is much easier for minority groups to be represented, and have political influence, at the local level. Local governments, in turn, through their provision of basic services like putting up stop signs, fixing sidewalks, picking up trash, and establishing zoning rules, can have huge direct effects on individuals' lives. For minority groups, the municipal level is the level where they are most likely to have a direct influence on political decision-making. Yet, ironically, most Americans, including Latinos, do not vote in their municipal elections.

In addition, not all governments across the United States are organized the same way. The structure of state and local governments in the United States varies significantly by region. The regional distribution of Latino populations varies as well. According to the 2010 census, 41 percent of Latinos in the United States live in the west, 36 percent live in the south, 14 percent live in the northeast, and 9 percent live in the midwest. National origin concentrations vary by region as well, and are summarized in Table 21.4. About two-fifths of Salvadorans and Guatemalans live in the west. Over half of Mexicans live in California and Texas. More than three-quarters of Cubans live in the south; 68 percent of those are concentrated in Florida. About half of Dominicans live in New York state, as do just under a quarter of Puerto Ricans. Most of the western Latinos live in the southwest, which, by and large, is made up of "post-reform" cities—cities whose government structures were reorganized after the progressive movement in the early twentieth century. The progressive movement arose out of concerns about the corruption that characterized many of the party machines that ran cities in the northeast, such as Tammany Hall in New York City. Progressives wanted to reduce the power of those machines and of the immigrants who ran them. To do so, they advocated the bureaucratization of city government; this included the use of civil servants instead of political appointees, the enlargement of city council districts, and the weakening of city mayors (so they could not use the office to appoint their friends, or use city resources to support their pet projects).

The progressives were highly successful, and most local governments in the southwest remain organized according to their ideals. Their reforms did diminish political corruption. But they had *en susto* run for public office and to have larger numbers of people supporting them. This situation has some negative effects. First, it makes it very difficult for a candidate to be successful without personal wealth, party backing, or corporate support. Second, voters are more distant from their representatives because they represent a larger number of people, which makes it nearly impossible for elected officials to have personal contact with a significant proportion of their constituents. For example, each Los Angeles County Supervisor represents about 2 million people, and it costs more than $5 million to run for a seat on the board. This clearly makes it difficult for constituents to feel connected to their government or to have any personal contact with their supervisor. It also puts the cost of running for a supervisorial seat outside of the reach of most people. The need to raise large amounts of money to run for office and

National origin	Total	Rank				
		First	Second	Third	Fourth	Fifth
Mexican						
Area	U.S.	California	Texas	Arizona	Illinois	Colorado
Population	31,798,258	11,423,146	7,951,193	1,657,668	1,602,403	757,181
Percent of total	100%	35.9%	25%	5.2%	5%	2.4%
Puerto Rican						
Area	U.S.	New York	Florida	New Jersey	Pennsylvania	Massachusetts
Population	4,623,716	1,070,558	847,550	434,092	366,082	266,125
Percent of total	100%	23.2%	18.3%	9.4%	7.9%	5.8%
Cuban						
Area	U.S.	Florida	California	New Jersey	New York	Texas
Population	1,785,547	1,213,438	88,607	83,362	70,803	46,541
Percent of total	100%	68%	5%	4.7%	4%	2.6%
Dominican						
Area	U.S.	New York	New Jersey	Florida	Massachusetts	Pennsylvania
Population	1,414,703	674,787	197,922	172,451	103,292	62,348
Percent of total	100%	47.7%	14%	12.2%	7.3%	4.4%
Salvadoran						
Area	U.S.	California	Texas	New York	Virginia	Maryland
Population	1,648,968	573,956	222,599	152,130	123,800	123,789
Percent of total	100%	34.8%	13.5%	9.2%	7.5%	7.5%
Guatemalan						
Area	U.S.	California	Florida	New York	Texas	New Jersey
Population	1,044,209	332,737	83,882	73,806	66,244	48,869
Percent of total	100%	31.9%	8%	7.1%	6.3%	4.7%

Source: Sharon R. Ennis, Merarys Ríos-Vargas, and Nora G. Albert, "The Hispanic Population: 2010," Census Brief (Washington, DC: U.S. Census Bureau, 2010) tab. 4. Percentages calculated by author.

to have large-scale name recognition also privileges incumbents. This makes turnover for elected officials very low, which decreases representational accountability.

Another local-level factor of importance is whether or not a locality has at-large or single-member districts. At-large districts mean that a city is defined as one large district, and a certain number of individuals are elected "at large" to serve on the city council. In an at-large election, all qualified voters within a particular district are able to vote. The exact mechanisms for choice can vary, but in general the candidate(s) who receive the highest number of votes win the election. A single-member district system means that the jurisdiction is broken up into a set number of districts, with non-overlapping geographic boundaries. Voters from that geographic area then select one representative to serve that representational unit. Studies have shown that cities with single-member districts are much more likely to elect minority representatives, because it is easier for the latter to surpass the 50 percent threshold within a small district than to do it within the city at large. As a result, under the VRA, courts have often ordered cities to adopt single-member districting when there is a geographically concentrated minority community that consistently supports candidates who lose under an at-large districting system. That being said, this remedy again requires residential segregation in order to ensure minority representation.

CONCLUSION

We have seen in this essay that the Latino community in the United States is not monolithic in terms of its socioeconomic status, age, nativity, or political propensities. We have also seen that Latino registration and voting rates are lower than those of other groups even after controlling for nativity and age. When looking at the total population, only a very small portion of Latinos (about 30 percent in presidential elections) regularly engages in the electoral process.

Latinos' limited electoral voice has consequences. Voting is important because this is how we choose our representatives. Those representatives, in turn, make public policy. Electoral rules have a significant effect on which groups are able to win elections and therefore on which groups are able to have the representatives (and thus policies) of their choice. Once in office, legislative rules affect those representatives' ability to represent their constituents' interests. But how do we know if these representatives are doing a good job? "Representation" is one of the most difficult ideas to define or to measure. What exactly does it mean to be represented? It is likely that all members of the polity feel that their elected representatives reflect their interests on some issues but not on others. Looking from the outside, how can elected officials know what a particular constituency favors in terms of public policy? We cannot have ongoing surveys of every community in the United States. And, even if we did, the ranking of issues in order of importance would probably vary from month to month. In any case, even if representatives have perfect information about their constituents' preferences, they may choose to vote in a different way, according to their conscience. Are these representatives supposed simply to echo the beliefs of their constituency or to take principled positions based on their own political preferences? Is a representative still "representing" her community if she supports a minority position on the basis of a moral principle? These are very difficult questions to answer. Given that fact, many analysts use descriptive representation as a proxy for substantive representation, on the basis of the assumption that individuals with similar life experiences are better able to represent one another. On the descriptive side, Latinos remain significantly underrepresented at all levels of government, relative to their population. This is due to the fact that U.S. institutional structures, with their majoritarian rules and historical exclusion of people of color and women, make it difficult for minorities to get elected. It is unlikely that the situation will change in the future. The question is: to what extent does the U.S. political system represent Latino substantive interests? The answer to this question varies across time, national-origin group, and geographic context.

NOTES

1. For a description of the Futuro Fund, see www.nytimes.com/2013/03/08/us/ politics/3-fund-raisers-show-latinos-rising-clout. html?_r=0 (last accessed November 30, 2013).

2. U.S. Census Quick Facts, http://quickfacts.census.gov/qfd/states/00000.html (last accessed July 12, 2013).

3. Pew Hispanic Center, "Hispanic Population Trends" (based on the 2011 American Community Survey): www.pewhispanic.org/2013/02/15/hispanic-population-trends/ph_13–01–23_ss_hispanics1/ (last accessed July 12, 2013).

4. Population numbers for all groups other than Dominicans based on the U.S. Census Bureau, "The Hispanic Population in the United States: 2011," tab. 2, "Hispanic Population by Sex, Age, and Hispanic Origin Type: 2011," available at: www.census.gov/population/hispanic/data/2011.html (last accessed July 12, 2013). Dominican population figures found at the Pew Hispanic Center, "Hispanic Population Trends."

5. Katherine Tate, *From Protest to Politics: The New Black Voters in American Elections* (Cambridge, MA: Harvard University Press, 1993); F. Chris García, Angelo Falcón, and Rodolfo de la Garza, "Ethnicity and Politics: Evidence from the Latino National Political Survey," *Hispanic Journal of Behavioral Sciences* 18(1996): 91–103; and John A. García, "Political Participation: Resources and Involvement among Latinos and the American Political System," in F. Chris García, ed., *Pursuing Power: Latinos and the Political System* (Notre Dame, IN: University of Notre Dame Press, 1997), 44–71.

6. For linked fate, see Michael C. Dawson, *Behind the Mule: Race and Class in African American Politics* (Princeton, NJ: Princeton University Press, 1995); for political alienation, see Marvin E. Olsen, "Two Categories of Political Alienation," *Social Forces* 47(1969): 288–99; for group identity, see Tate, 1993, and Carol Hardy-Fanta, *Latina Politics, Latino Politics: Gender, Culture and Political Participation in Boston* (Philadelphia, PA: Temple University Press, 1993); for group conflict, see Henri Tajfel and J. Turner, "The Social Identity Theory of Intergroup Behavior," in Stephen Worchel and William Austin, eds., *Psychology of Intergroup Relations* (Chicago: Nelson-Hall, 1986), 7–24.

7. Cristina Beltrán, *The Trouble with Unity: Latino Politics and the Creation of Identity* (New York: Oxford University Press, 2010), 256.

8. The other U.S. immigrant group least likely to be naturalized is that of Canadians,

which leads scholars to suggest that geographic proximity may have a negative impact on immigrants' decision to naturalize.

9. NALEO Educational Fund, *National Directory of Latino Elected Officials, 2013* (Los Angeles, CA: NALEO Educational Fund, 2013).

10. For more detail on the law, see www.justice.gov/crt/about/vot/intro/intro_b.php. Sections 4(e) and 4(f) contain provisions specific to the protection of language minorities: www.justice.gov/crt/about/vot/misc/sec_4.php (website last accessed February 23, 2014).

11. Travis Crum, "The Voting Rights Act's Secret Weapon: Pocket Trigger Litigation and Dynamic Preclearance," *Yale Law Journal* 119(2010): 1992–2038.

12. www.justice.gov/crt/about/vot/sec_5/tx_obj2.php (last accessed February 23, 2014).

13. They are the cities of: San Joaquín, 63.5%; Maywood, 59.5%; Cudahy, 58.9%; Bell Gardens, 56.5%; Huron City, 55.9%; Huntington Park, 55.9%; Bell, 53.9%; Arvin, 53.8%; Mendota, 53.5%; King City, 52.3%; Santa Ana, 51.9%; Orange Cove, 51.6%. From Joaquín Avila, "Political Apartheid in California: Consequences of Excluding a Growing Noncitizen Population," in *Latino Policy and Issues Brief* (Los Angeles: UCLA Chicano Studies Research Center, 2003).

14. Granted, both systems were quite exclusionary in terms of who was accorded "citizenship," particularly in terms of gender and class, and both systems allowed for slavery; but they did, despite their flaws, allow all their "citizens" to have a say.

15. The full text of *Federalist* 10 can be found at: http://thomas.loc.gov/home/histdox/fed _10.html (last accessed February 23, 2014).

REFERENCES

Acosta-Belén, E., and C. E. Santiago. 2006. *Puerto Ricans in the United States: A Contemporary Portrait*. Boulder, CO: Lynne Rienner.

Aparicio, Ana. 2006. *Dominican-Americans and the Politics of Empowerment*. Gainesville: University Press of Florida.

Baver, Sherrie. 1984. "Puerto Rican Politics in New York City: The Post–World War II Period," in James Jennings and Monte Rivera, eds., *Puerto Rican Politics in Urban America*. Westport, CT: Greenwood Press, pp. 43–59.

Beltrán, Cristina. 2010. *The Trouble with Unity: Latino Politics and the Creation of Identity*. New York: Oxford University Press, 2010.

Caro-López, Howard, and Laura Limonic. 2009. "Dominicans in New York City, 1990–2008," Report 31, *Latino Data Project*. City University of New York, Center for Latin American, Caribbean, and Latino Studies.

Carter, Susan B., Scott Sigmund Gartner, Michael R. Haines, Alan L. Olmstead, Richard Sutch, and Gavin Wright, eds. *Historical Statistics of the United States: Millennial Edition Online* (New York: Cambridge University Press, 2006), available at http://hsus.cambridge .org/HSUSWeb/HSUSEntryServlet (last accessed March 2, 2014).

Falcón, Angelo. 1984. "A History of Puerto Rican Politics in New York City: 1860s to 1945," in James Jennings and Monte Rivera, eds., *Puerto Rican Politics in Urban America*. Westport, CT: Greenwood Press, pp. 15–42.

Fernández, Raúl E., and Gilbert G. González. 2003. *A Century of Chicano History: Empire, Nations, and Migration*. New York: Routledge.

García, Alma M. 1997. *Chicana Feminist Thought: The Basic Historical Writings*. New York: Routledge.

García, María Cristina. 1996. *Havana USA: Cuban Exiles and Cuban Americans in South Florida*. Berkeley: University of California Press.

———. 2006. *Seeking Refuge: Central American Migration to Mexico, the United States, and Canada*. Berkeley: University of California Press.

García Bedolla, Lisa. 2005. *Fluid Borders: Latino Power, Identity, and Politics in Los Angeles*. Berkeley: University of California Press.

García Bedolla, Lisa, and Melissa R. Michelson. 2012. *Mobilizing Inclusion: Transforming the Electorate through Get-Out-the-Vote Campaigns*. New Haven: Yale University Press.

Gómez-Quiñones, Juan. 1990. *Chicano Politics: Reality and Promise, 1940–1990*. Albuquerque: University of New Mexico Press.

Grasmuck, Sherri, and Patricia R. Pessar. 1991. *Between Two Islands: Dominican International Migration*. Berkeley: University of California Press.

Hardy-Fanta, Carol. 1993. *Latina Politics, Latino Politics: Gender, Culture and Political Participation in Boston*. Philadelphia, PA: Temple University Press.

Moreno, Darío. 1996. "The Cuban Model: Political Empowerment in Miami," in F. Chris García, ed., *Pursuing Power: Latinos and the Political System*. Notre Dame, IN: University of Notre Dame Press, pp. 208–26.

NALEO Educational Fund. 2013. *National Directory of Latino Elected Officials, 2013*. Los Angeles, CA: NALEO Educational Fund.

Navarro, Armando. 2004. *Mexicano Political Experience in Occupied Aztlán*. Lanham, MD: AltaMira Press.

Omi, Michael, and Howard Winant. 1994. *Racial Formation in the United States: From the 1960s to the 1990s*. New York: Routledge.

Passel, Jeffrey S. and D'Vera Cohn. 2011. "Unauthorized Immigrant Population: National and State Trends, 2010." Washington, DC: Pew Hispanic Center, available at: www.pewhispanic.org/files/reports/133.pdf (last accessed July 24, 2013).

Passel, Jeffrey S., D'Vera Cohn, and Ana Gonzalez Barrera. 2013. "Net Migration from Mexico Falls to Zero—Perhaps Less." Washington, DC: Pew Hispanic Center, available from: www.pewhispanic.org/files/2012/04/Mexican- migrants-report_final.pdf (last accessed July 22, 2013).

Pycior, Julie Leininger. 1997. *LBJ and Mexican Americans: The Paradox of Power*. Austin: University of Texas Press.

Rose, Margaret. 2004. "Dolores Huerta: The United Farm Workers Union," in Eric Arnesen, ed., *The Human Tradition in American Labor History*. Wilmington, DE: SR Books.

Ruiz, Vicki L. 1998. *From Out of the Shadows: Mexican American Women in Twentieth Century America*. New York: Oxford University Press.

———. 2005. "Luisa Moreno and Latina Labor Activism," in Vicki L. Ruiz and Virginia Sánchez-Korrol, eds., *Latina Legacies: Identity, Biography, and Community*. New York: Oxford University Press, pp. 175–92.

Ruszczyk, Stephen. 2012. "How Do Latino Groups Fare in a Changing Economy? Occupation in Latino Groups in the Greater New York Area, 1980–2009," Report 48, Latino Data Project (City University of New York, Center for Latin American, Caribbean, and Latino Studies).

Sagás, Ernesto, and Sintia E. Molina, eds. 2004. *Dominican Migration: Transnational Perspectives*. Gainesville: University Press of Florida.

Sánchez, José Ramón. 2007. *Boricua Power: A Political History of Puerto Ricans in the United States*. New York: New York University Press.

Sánchez-Korrol, Virginia. 1994. *From Colonia to Community: The History of Puerto Ricans in New York City*. Berkeley: University of California Press.

Tate, Katherine. 1993. *From Protest to Politics: The New Black Voters in American Elections*. Cambridge, MA: Harvard University Press.

Torres, Andres, and José E. Velásquez, eds. 1998. *The Puerto Rican Movement: Voices from the Diaspora*. Philadelphia, PA: Temple University Press.

U.S. Census Bureau. 2001. "The Hispanic Population: Census 2000 Brief," May.

Voss, Kim, and Irene Bloemraad, eds. 2010. *Rallying for Immigrant Rights: The Fight for Inclusion in 21st Century America*. Berkeley: University of California Press.

22

YOUNG LATINOS IN AN AGING AMERICAN SOCIETY

David E. Hayes-Bautista, Werner Schink,
and Jorge Chapa

The aging of American society is a phenomenon that appears to be well documented and unavoidable. Much current discussion focuses on the society-wide policy implications of the unprecedented growth of the elderly population, which may double in the next 30 to 50 years. Somewhat neglected in this debate are serious policy questions about minorities. What has not been fully recognized is that there are significant changes occurring in the minority population, changes directly linked to policy discussions regarding the elderly and the aging of American society.

One basic change is the rapid growth of the minority population, which appears to be the greatest for Latinos* and Asians. Because of continued immigration and the high fertility rate of Latinos, some states, such as California, are rapidly developing an age-race stratified population, in which the older segment will be composed almost exclusively of a white, non-Latino population, while the working-age segment will increasingly be made up of Latinos and other minorities.

This essay examines the age pyramid of California, to identify the dynamics that are creating an age-race stratified society. Since we do not have sufficient data to make nationwide projections, the data presented are all based on changes in the California population. These findings, however, have implications for the rest of the country, since the same age-race stratification appears to be working at different speeds from state to state.[1]

SOCIAL FORCES THAT CHANGE THE POPULATION

The size and composition of a population are affected by three social forces: deaths, births, and migrations. These three forces act differently in the Anglo and Latino populations, and will yield very different demographic results over the next 50 years.

Deaths   The basic fact of demographic transition is that among the Anglo population mortality has been very low for some time, and longevity is increasing. While data for the Latino mortality rates are not readily available, evidence from Mexico indicates that the mortality rate is decreasing. The longevity rate is less than for Anglos, although it is rising slowly. There are, and will continue to be, fewer Latinos in the elderly age brackets.

Births   It is in fertility behavior that the Latino population differs from the other major groups in California. The replacement level of completed fertility is 2.1 births per woman. If each woman gives birth to 2.1 children, the population would neither grow nor shrink in size. The fertility rate for Anglo women falls quite a ways below replacement level, at 1.4 births per woman.[2] Blacks and Asians are also somewhat below replacement, at 1.8 births per woman in each group. The Latino population, however, is significantly above the replacement level. Those Latinos born in the United States have a fertility rate of 2.6 and those Latinos born in Latin America have a total completed fertility rate of 3.2.[3] The fertility rate for Latina women is connected to the high fertility rates of the sending countries, notably Mexico. It should be noted that, due to fertility alone, the Latino population will grow while other populations, especially the Anglo, will shrink.

Migrations   The third force that changes population size is migration. California experiences a yearly net gain of in-migrants, that is, more people enter the state than leave it. It is difficult to know exactly how many in-migrants arrive each year in California because of the unknown, but presumably large, numbers of undocumented in-migrants.[4]

The Anglo population is aging, increasing in longevity, and is not replacing itself by births. Its declining numbers are offset only by constant in-migration from other parts of the country. The Latino population is much younger, has a higher fertility rate, and is added to by constant in-migration from sending areas (such as Mexico) that have an even younger population and higher fertility rates. The other minority populations, the Blacks and Asians, occupy a middle ground in terms of population growth, but represent far smaller percentages of the state's total population. Thus, demographic changes in the state's population are not evenly distributed over the entire population, but are concentrated in certain groups.

AGE-RACE STRATIFICATION

The long-range effects of these different demographic behaviors will result in the emergence of a population stratified by age and race. Due to the growth in the younger, minority, and largely Latino population by the year 2010, the result will be that the elderly population of 65 and over will be largely Anglo, while the younger population will be largely Latino. In 1980, for example, while 33.4 percent of the state's total population was minority, minorities made up over 47 percent of the population under 16, while they comprised only 16 percent of the population 65 and over. By the year 2010, the year that the "baby boom" population begins to enter retirement age, minorities will comprise 52 percent of the total population. Sixty-six percent of the population under 16 will be minorities, while only 32 percent over 65 will be minorities.

The group that has traditionally been cast in the role of supporting the under 15 and over 65 age groups is the working-age population, from 16 to 64. The proportion of this group that is minority grows from 32 percent in 1980 to over 50 percent in 2010 to 61 percent in 2030.

California, therefore, is likely to become a highly age-race stratified population within the next 30 to 50 years. The burden of support of the large elderly population may fall on the shoulders of a smaller working-age population. The perception of this burden is likely to be more sharply focused when it is considered that the younger workforce is likely to be composed largely of Latinos and other minorities.

In large part, the growth of the Latino population in California is linked to the growth and welfare of the populations of Mexico and Latin America. The median age in Mexico is 16.2 years,[5] nearly half the median age of 33 of white California.

As recently as 1960, the vast majority of the Latino population of California was of Mexican origin. Gradually, the Latino population is beginning to include sizeable elements from other Latin American countries. Currently, about 80 percent of the Latino population is of Mexican origin.

These projections are based on the assumptions of political and economic stability in Mexico and Latin America, especially in Central America. A political or economic collapse could easily accelerate the rate of age-race stratification by creating a rapid infusion of young, foreign-born Latinos. Today, prospects for economic and political stability for Mexico and Central America do not look good. Thus, there is likely to be a sudden, discontinuous leap in the Latino population at some unknown date in the near- to mid-future.

THE SUPPORT BURDEN AND THE YOUNG LATINO POPULATION

Some of the long-range projections for the financial future of support programs for the elderly depend upon the number of retirees in relation to the number of workers.[6] In addition to absolute numbers of workers, one must also look to the ethnic composition of the workforce, its present and future preparation, its place in the workforce, and its abilities and desires to be taxed rather heavily to support the elderly.

There is no question that an increase in the number of older persons will mean an increase in the support that the working-age population will have to provide in one form or another.[7] A straightforward projection is that if there are proportionately fewer working-age persons, they will have to carry a heavier burden than is currently the case when there are relatively more workers per retiree.[8] Currently, the Latino population in California has a lower educational attainment than does the overall population. Nearly

57 percent of all Latino adults have less than a high school education, while 22 percent of non-Latinos have such a similar low educational level. At the upper end, nearly 22 percent of the non-Latino population has graduated from college, while only 6 percent of the Latino population has been able to do so. This lesser educational attainment is directly related to much lower earning power. In 1980, the median income for Latinos was $16,140, while for whites it was $22,689.

Unless there is some major change in educational and job policy and achievement, it seems likely that the working-age population of the future, being increasingly composed of Latinos and other minorities, will have a lower total wage base upon which to make income support contributions to the elderly. If the current levels of benefits are to be maintained, it would cause such high tax burdens that a projected largely Anglo workforce with high education and high income might feel resentful; the resentment could be much greater if the tax rate had to be increased even more to offset the much lower earning capabilities of a largely Latino workforce. That the income transfer would be taking place between racial and generational groups might only increase future resentment. Clearly, such a society could become subject to some serious strains and fractures. The development of policy for the support and care of the aged must be done in conjunction with policies for the preparation of the Latino and minority workforce to provide such care.

POLICY CONSIDERATIONS

The double division lines of age and race will be a fact of social life in the future. Can such a society, with such great potential chasms separating one group from another, become a single, unified society? Will difficult policy decisions regarding the care of the elderly and the participation of the younger working-age population be made without having the reactions of one group or another tear society apart?

There are at least three policy areas that need attention in order to achieve a smoothly functioning society of the future. Within each area, different policy choices may be made. The constellation of decisions in all three will greatly determine the type of society that will emerge from the age-race shift.

HUMAN RESOURCES INVESTMENT

This is a useful paradigm for making policy decisions, which conceptualizes the population of the state as a natural resource that has to be invested in and developed thoughtfully to develop a maximized, sustained yield.[9] The yield, in this case, may be defined as labor force participation and productivity. As with any resource, short-range policies designed to extract maximum yield for the present may deplete the resource, making future yields much smaller. The growing minority population, which will make up the bulk of the labor force 30 to 50 years from now, may be seen as a human resource, which will require some investment now for greater societal benefits tomorrow.

Education is a critical area, particularly as the California economy moves further out of manufacturing and into the service industries. Brainpower, not manufactured products, may become the principal American export.[10] The level of education of the population will be one of the principal determining factors in this movement from manufacturing to services. One might easily surmise that if current policies are followed, there will be a lowering of the general educational level in the workforce by 2030[11] as the proportion of Latinos increases, although the "baby boom" generation will continue to benefit from its very high level of educational achievement.

The health of the labor force is another important characteristic to consider in calculating the productive capacity of a group: a workforce in poor health is less productive than one with good health. There are few reliable health statistics for Latino populations. This lack is being corrected by the Hispanic Health and Nutrition Evaluation Survey, currently being conducted to provide a nationwide data base of health status of three different Latino groups—Chicanos, Puerto Ricans, and Cubans. Some spotty information indicates that the Latino population suffers from infectious diseases to a greater extent than the general population. Such diseases are the ones most affected by cutbacks in public health programs.

SOCIAL COHESION

Social cohesion is the product of members of a society feeling that they have a stake in the outcome of events, and subsequently some urge or obligation to participate in them. When many feel little or no desire to participate in society, low social cohesion results, and the possibility of social breakdown becomes real. With high social cohesion, difficult policy choices may be made without certain groups feeling "left out," even though the changes might mean a decrease in the social benefits they might otherwise feel should be theirs. Social cohesion may be measured and achieved in a number of dimensions: economic and political participation and immigration.

Economic participation is possibly the most important way to effect social cohesion. Full economic participation would occur in those situations where Latino and other minorities are fully integrated into all segments of the economy: research and development, administration, policy, marketing, in the service industry, as well as in manufacturing and extraction. Low economic participation would occur when Latino and other minorities are confined to the assembly lines in manufacturing and the harvesting and processing lines in agriculture.

In the public sector, political participation determines the presence or absence of social cohesion. Currently, Latino and other minorities do not participate fully in the political process, and often feel that decisions are being made at their expense. With full political participation, these feelings could be diminished, as the decisions would belong to everyone, not to just a perceived few.

Immigration may also affect statewide social cohesion. Certain immigration policy proposals would put at risk nearly all Latinos and Asians, who are racially distinct from the mainstream population, by forcing employers to require proof of citizenship before hiring. Rather than go through the trouble of verifying such status, employers might find it easier simply to be reluctant to hire from those two groups. The necessity to carry identification, and the burden of being asked for it when others are not, could well create the feeling of division and separateness that could lead to low social cohesion.

CULTURAL PLURALISM

In addition to human resources and social cohesion, policy makers should consider cultural pluralism. Cultural pluralism is a situation in which various cultures are given equal importance and the contribution of each to the societal whole is recognized. Cultural pluralism recognizes the different histories, languages, and experiences that comprise the cultural mosaic known as the California and United States population. Within the borders of the state, a policy that emphasizes cultural pluralism will most likely lead to a situation in which no group feels that it has to give up any significant part of itself in order to participate in the economic and political life of the state. All groups might then feel more attached to the overall society, and more willing to participate in some difficult decisions ahead.

There are cultural pluralistic considerations that go beyond the borders of this country, however. In particular, the California economy stands poised at the brink of the larger Pacific Rim economy consisting of Mexico, Central and South America, the South Pacific, and Asia. In order to compete successfully, it will have to be able to understand and work with these other economies and cultures. As minorities from these areas are to make up the bulk of the labor force in the future, if cultural pluralism is seen as a value and cultivated, the work of this economy with other Pacific Rim economies will be easier.

In order for this to occur, a policy of cultural homogenization would have to be reversed, otherwise the advantage of having so many Latinos and other minorities in the workforce will be lost: a totally assimilated minority would be as inept in the Pacific Rim markets as a culturally unaware non-minority. The trick is to conceive of achieving social cohesion through a process of cultural pluralism: the positive affirmation of cultural differences may add up to greater overall social cohesion.

TANDEM POLICY ISSUES

As policy makers become aware of the aging of American society, discussion about the care and support of the elderly—Social Security, Medicare, pension plans, medical care income maintenance, and other issues—is much in vogue, with an eye not only to the immediate future, but to the mid- and long-range future. Yet, it should be apparent that by the projections presented earlier, the policy future of the aging American society is very much intertwined with the policy future of Latinos and other minorities. Policy discussions about the aged have to be carried on in tandem with policy discussions about Latinos and other minorities, for they are the ones, demographically speaking, who will be asked to shoulder the burden of the aged "baby boom" generation.

Given the seemingly inexorable demographic dynamics, it is no longer necessary to be prodded by a social conscience to be concerned about the plight of the elderly or of the poorer Latinos and other minorities: all of us shall be older some day, and the poor Latinos and other minorities will be called upon to support the older generation. The future cohesion of society could easily depend upon choices made today, during the relatively short-lived "policy window" from the present to about 2000. To wait until the year 2010, when the "baby boom" begins to retire, to become concerned about the education and earning capacity of the younger Latino and other minority population, will be to wait until it is too late—certain negative social dynamics will have already been set in motion, the productive capacity of the workforce will have already been lowered, and the age-race stratification will have become solidified into a barrier against social cohesion.

The projections presented here are intended to bring attention to an area that is being overlooked during the current, very real concern about the plight of the elderly. Much more work remains to be done in the linkages of the policy areas of the elderly and minorities.

NOTES

* Data used in this study come from different sources, which not only utilize different terms (e.g., Mexican-American, Spanish surname, Chicano, Hispanic, Spanish origin), but, to a certain extent, different methodologies to determine who is included and excluded from the group in question. The term "Latino" is used to refer to those of Mexican, Central American, South American, and Spanish-speaking Caribbean descent. All data reported will be cast in terms of "Latino," even though the terminology used by the different sources might be different.

1. Center for the Continuing Study of the California Economy, *Projections of Hispanic Population for the United States: 1985–2000* (Palo Alto, Calif., 1982).

2. California Department of Health Services, *Vital Statistics of California, 1980.*

3. California Department of Rehabilitation, *California Disability Survey, 1978.*

4. Wayne A. Cornelius, Leo R. Chavez, and Jorge Castro, *Mexican Immigrants and Southern California: A Summary of Current Knowledge* (San Diego: Center for U.S.-Mexican Studies, University of California, 1982). The in-migration figure is assumed to be 250,000, of which 78,440 are foreign-born Latinos. These figures are derived from projections made by the California State Department of Finance, which projects the total net population gain,

and by a backward cohort analysis, comparing the 1970 and 1980 census data to get rates of growth by cohort for the different racial and ethnic groups.

5. Consejo Nacional de Población, *México Demográfico: Brevario, 1978.*

6. Peter G. Peterson, "No More Free Lunch for the Middle Class," *The New York Times Magazine,* January 17, 1982a; Peter G. Peterson, "The Coming Crash of Social Security," *The New York Review of Books,* vol. 29, no. 19 (1982b), pp. 34–38.

7. Eric R. Kingson and Richard M. Scheffler, "Aging: Issues and Economic Trends for the 1980s," *Inquiry,* vol. 18 (1981), pp. 197–213.

8. Peterson, op. cit., 1982a.

9. Theodore W. Schultz, *Investing in People: The Economics of Population Equality* (Berkeley: The University of California Press, 1981).

10. Eugene T. Kelley, "America's Economic Future: The Key Is Brains and Services." Presented at the Commonwealth Club, San Francisco, 1981.

11. Richard C. Carlson, "Threat to the State's High Technology Leadership." Presented at the Commonwealth Club, San Francisco, 1982.

23

AFTERWORD
Thirty Years Later, 2016

David E. Hayes-Bautista, Werner Schink,
and Jorge Chapa

In 2014 Latinos became the largest single population group in California, composing 39 percent of the state's population, overtaking non-Hispanic whites, who compose 38.8 percent.[1] The Demographic Research Unit of the California State Department of Finance estimates that by 2039, Latinos will constitute 50 percent of the state's entire population. The population dynamics we described in 1984 have worked their way through the state's population for the past 30 years pretty much in the way we laid out: by 2030 Latinos will compose nearly 50 percent of the young working-age population (48.6 percent of the age 25–50 group), while non-Hispanic whites will compose nearly 50 percent of the elderly (47.5 percent of age 65-plus group).[2]

And nearly 30 years after our article was published, a huge chasm still separates Latinos' educational attainment from that of non-Hispanic whites: in 2013, while 40.5 percent of non-Hispanic whites complete college, only 11.2 percent of Latinos manage to do so.[3]

Over the past 30 years, the biggest game-changing policy event in the state was the passage of Proposition 187 in 1994, the first of the "get tough on undocumented immigrants" measures to sweep the country, championed by the Republican governor Pete Wilson. The public discourse supporting the measure managed to demonize nearly all Latinos (most of whom historically have been U.S.-born and not immigrant, much less undocumented). Rather than stunning Latinos into political silence, Proposition 187 galvanized Latinos' electoral participation. The number of Latino voters exploded, and the number of Latino elected officials at all levels has grown enormously. The measure so polarized the Latino electorate that in the 2014 election, not one single Republican candidate was elected to state-level office.

What does the Latino electorate want out of California state policy? Upon taking office as Speaker of the California State Assembly in 1996, Cruz Bustamante responded to a reporter's inquiry about a supposed "Latino agenda" that he and other Latino elected officials might pursue. Happy to oblige, Bustamante listed the main points of the "Latino agenda" that he had in mind: good schools, safe streets, and good jobs for everybody.[4] As Bustamante pointed out 20 years ago, the "Latino agenda" is really a reinforcement of the American agenda, and its achievement will benefit all Californians, especially the baby boom generation, whose investments (public and private) will increasingly depend upon the productivity of an increasingly Latino labor force.

NOTES

1. State of California, Department of Finance, *Population Projections for California and Its Counties, 2010 Baseline Series* (Sacramento, CA, January 31, 2013), p. 1

2. State of California, Department of Finance, *Population Projections by Race/Ethnicity, Gender and Age for California and Its Counties 2000–2050* (Sacramento, CA, May 2004).

3. U.S. Census Bureau, American Community Survey using American FactFinder, January 20, 2014, http://factfinder2.census.gov.

4. Hayes-Bautista, David E., *La Nueva California: Latinos in the Golden State* (Berkeley: University of California Press, 2004), pp. 142–43.

24

LIFE AFTER PRISON FOR HISPANICS
Ethnic, Racial, and Gender Realities

Martin Guevara Urbina

America is the land of the second chance—and when the gates of the prison open,
the path ahead should lead to a better life.

—GEORGE W. BUSH

When it comes to criminal defendants, the focus of the criminal justice system, research and publication, and those vested in community safety or social justice has been on formal proceedings, from arrest to once people are released from prison. In the current era of law and order, though, over 50,000 people leave prison every month, and more than 630,000 inmates are released from state and federal prisons every year, the biggest number in the history of the U.S. penal system. Further, in the twenty-first century, prisoners who are being released are serving longer sentences than inmates of earlier decades, and they are less likely to have received an education or job training behind bars and less likely to be rehabilitated. During the 1980s and 1990s, as jails and prisons filled to overcrowding and a tough-on-criminals movement prevailed, states significantly reduced rehabilitation programs. As such, prisoners typically return home carrying their *old* liabilities, like addictions, limited education, unskilled, and poor work habits, in addition to new ones, like a damaged relationship with family and friends, a criminal stigma, and often no place to go. Worse, since most exiting inmates are Latino or African American, minority prisoners must also *confront the influence of being Latino or African American.* Together, the central question becomes, how do ex-prisoners fare on the outside, in the community? And, by extension, how do communities fare in incorporating former-prisoners?

This essay, then, provides a discussion of "life after prison" for the typical adult male and female offender, which involves not only the experience of Latinas/os and African Americans but Caucasians as well. After noting the methods of release, the major roadblocks to community reentry are detailed, followed by an analysis of the significance of community integration and the importance of building *bridges* between prison and society. It is argued that the most crucial gap to the establishment of social control remains to be bridged: from prison to the community. Otherwise, with limited resources, a chaotic environment, and a hostile community, released inmates are likely to return to prison. Then, recommendations for breaking state and federal *legal barriers* for reentry are provided, followed by propositions for community reentry of both male and female offenders as well as a series of steps for *making it outside* upon release. The essay concludes with a discussion of major challenges facing reformers in the twenty-first century, as we seek to create a more understanding, tolerant, and forgiving society, while securing public safety.

METHODS OF RELEASE

To begin, the combination of tougher sentences has led to a drastic increase in the incarceration of both male and female offenders, and inmates are serving longer prison terms for a wider array of criminal activity. Yet, most prisoners are eventually released back into the community because the majority of offenders are incarcerated for non-violent crimes, normally drug offenses. With the exception of those serving life or death sentences, incarcerated people are released from prison to the community, usually under parole supervision through various means, depending on federal or state laws. These categories include discretionary release, mandatory release, expirational release, or some other form of conditional release. A very small percentage of people are "removed" from prison as a result of escapes, executions, or deaths (Urbina, 2012).

Once offenders have been punished for their crimes, served their sentences, and released from prison, they are back in the community, normally in their "old" neighborhoods, to begin a new life, with the expectation that they will never return to prison. Nonetheless, about 75 percent of inmates return to prison. In this context, there are several essential questions that must be addressed to facilitate *reentry planning* for those who are still in prison to avoid recidivism upon release, and thus reduce the probability of inmates returning to prison. Morally, what will become of male and female offenders once they are released from prison? Will inmates be able to find legal employment with the skills they learned while incarcerated? Considering the wide range of problems facing both male and female offenders, will they be able to pay for their basic needs, like healthcare, and not return to illegal activities like drugs or prostitution? If inmates do not have the necessary skills, will they be able to acquire credentials and qualifications that will allow them to survive in a highly competitive and technological job market? Will ex-prisoners be able to reunite with their children, partner, spouse, friends, or other loved ones? Will released prisoners be accepted by the community? Or, will they be treated with mistrust, disdain, rejection, or hostility? Ultimately, what is the probability that those released from prison will end up back in the correctional system?

LEGAL ROADBLOCKS TO COMMUNITY REENTRY

As noted above, more than 630,000 people are released from state and federal prisons every year, a population equal to that of most major cities, and hundreds more are released from local jails. Critically, though, rather than helping released inmates successfully transition from prison to the community, many current state and federal laws have the opposite impact, legal barriers which are significantly interfering with the obligations, rights, and expectations of full citizenship in nearly every aspect of people's daily lives. In effect, current state and federal laws diminish rehabilitation efforts, community reentry and stability, and public safety, and they undermine the presumed commitment to equality and justice. Together, as designed and applied, existing laws are creating legal roadblocks to basic necessities for thousands of people who are trying to rebuild their lives, support their families, and become productive members of their communities.

Further, while legal barriers to community reentry have only recently been critically analyzed, for more than 30 years the federal government and various states have drastically increased the range and severity of civil penalties for people with criminal convictions, and, in some cases, applying legal barriers to people who have never been convicted of a crime (Urbina and Kreitzer, 2004). In fact, for 3 decades Congress and state legislatures have created new restrictions for the eligibility of various necessities, including public assistance, food stamps, public housing, drivers' license, and student loans, while further expanding legal barriers to crucial social issues, such as parenting, employment, and voting.

Consequently, as a result of such explosive increase of legal roadblocks during the last three decades, successful reentry into society after inmates have been released is much more difficult for people who have been arrested or convicted of crimes, especially for drug offenses, and those who have multiple convictions or incarcerations, even if they can demonstrate that they are rehabilitated, qualified to work, and willing to participate in society. As for ethnic and race variation, because Latinos and African Americans are arrested, indicted, prosecuted, convicted, and sentenced to prison at significantly higher rates than Caucasians, minorities are disproportionately harmed by these state and federal legal barriers, leading to widespread social, economic, and political disenfranchisement of Latinos and African Americans. In effect, a two-year study by the Legal Action Center (2004:7) found that "people with criminal records seeking reentry face a daunting array of counterproductive, debilitating and unreasonable roadblocks in almost every important aspect of life." While obstacles are numerous and complicated, the following are ten of the most influential legal barriers facing released prisoners when they attempt to reenter society and become law-abiding and productive citizens.

PUBLIC HOUSING

Considering that the majority of male and female offenders are indigent, with many of them having spent years behind bars, the most immediate concern upon release is a place to stay, especially if they are no longer allowed in their old house or apartment. If released prisoners are not able to stay with family or friends, they either seek public or low-income housing, or live in the streets. Federal laws, though, give local housing agencies leeway in most situations to decide whether to bar people with criminal convictions from public housing premises, even if arrests never led to conviction, creating a difficult situation for inmates who have no other place to stay. National data show that:

- In a majority of states, public housing authorities make individualized determinations about an applicant's eligibility that include considering the person's criminal record, as well as evidence of rehabilitation.
- Many public housing authorities consider arrest records that did not lead to conviction in determining eligibility for public housing (Legal Action Center, 2004:16).

PUBLIC ASSISTANCE AND FOOD STAMPS

Along with shelter, released prisoners must also cope with actual survival, and if they do not have a place to stay, they are also likely to lack money and food, especially those who are unable to quickly find employment. As such, released prisoners often look for public assistance. The 1996 federal welfare law, however, prohibits people convicted of drug-related felonies from receiving federally funded food stamps or cash assistance (known as Temporary Assistance for Needy Families, TANF). Further, considering that drug offenses have become the focal target of the criminal justice system, most states now also restrict people with drug convictions from being eligible for federally funded public assistance, including food stamps and cash (Legal Action Center, 2004). As a lifetime ban, applied even if people have completed their sentence, overcome addictions, earned a certificate of rehabilitation, or been employed but gotten laid off, such prohibition significantly hinders community reentry for thousands of released prisoners.

EMPLOYMENT

Upon being released from prison, people are confronted with multiple expectations, like obeying the conditions of parole, not engaging in criminal activity, and quickly finding employment. In effect, employment is not only one of the most crucial expectations, but one of the most essential in that it signifies social and economic stability, it provides people a physical address, it enhances the chances of securing housing, and it enables people to afford basic necessities, like clothing and food. This expectation, though, is hindered with employment obstacles in that:

- Employers in most states can deny jobs to people who were arrested but never convicted of any crime.
- Employers in most states can deny jobs to, or fire, anyone with a criminal record, regardless of individual history, circumstances, or "business necessity."
- States have the power to offer certificates of rehabilitation but few issue them (Legal Action Center, 2004:10).

ACCESS TO CRIMINAL RECORDS

While released prisoners have spent their time behind bars for the crime they committed, upon being released they are not immune from the stigma or legal obstacles of a criminal record. Officially, states have the authority to allow the sealing or expungement of arrest records that never led to conviction as well as conviction records after the elapse of an appropriate period of time. Yet, considering the influence of a criminal record on housing, public assistance, employment, and other social, economic, and political activities, national data show that:

- Most states never expunge or seal conviction records but do allow arrest records to be sealed or expunged when the arrest did not lead to a conviction.
- Virtually anyone with an Internet connection can find information about someone's conviction history online without his or her consent or any guidance on how to interpret or use the information (Legal Action Center, 2004:15).

DRIVER'S LICENSES

Possibly more than any other formal document, a driver's license has become a necessary element for *everyday functioning*, ranging from driving to opening a bank account. To further complicate matters for released prisoners, many inmates have no place to stay and thus no physical address. In 1992, Congress enacted legislation withholding 10 percent of highway funds unless states enact laws revoking or suspending driver's licenses of people convicted of drug offenses for at least six months after the date of the conviction. More recently, in addition to federal legislation restricting the limits of driver's licenses to people with criminal records, states have passed or attempted to pass laws restricting, revoking, or suspending driver's licenses for undocumented people, targeting Latinas and Latinos, especially Mexican immigrants. In 2011, for instance,

New Mexico Governor Susana Martínez tried to repeal a law granting driver's licenses to undocumented people. In fact, some states have attempted to restrict the limits of driver's licenses to *legal immigrants,* including Texas under Governor Rick Perry. Truly, if implemented, these laws lead to consequential obstacles for both illegal and legal immigrants who are being released from state or federal prisons. In short, restricting the ability to drive makes it more difficult to be employed, participate in addiction treatment, obtain an education, get job training, and it restricts people in many other areas of everyday life. In all, national statistics show that:

- 27 states automatically suspend or revoke licenses for some or all drug offenses; 23 states either suspend or revoke licenses only for driving-related offenses or have opted out of the federal law.
- Many states make restrictive licenses available so individuals whose licenses would otherwise be suspended can go to work, attend drug treatment, or obtain an education (Legal Action Center, 2004:17).

SURVEILLANCE

In addition to monitoring inmates released on parole to ensure that they meet the conditions of parole, the criminal justice system indirectly or directly monitors those who have committed felonies, even if the offenses are not classified as violent, as well as immigrants waiting for their immigration status to be determined by immigration officials. However, in the aftermath of the September 11, 2001, terrorist attacks on the United States and the continued international war on drugs, constant surveillance on those suspected of terrorist or narcotics connections is now being conducted by state and federal law enforcement agencies, a critical situation for Latinos who are already associated with narcotics trafficking and even terrorism. While surveillance monitoring seems to make sense in ensuring public safety, intrusive surveillance adds to the legal barriers facing released prisoners, as the criminal stigma of being under constant surveillance makes it more difficult to reintegrate into society and live a *normal* life.

DEPORTATION

In the current era of law and order, immigrants, particularly Latinos, are once again a primary target of anti-immigrant legislation, politicians, law enforcement officials, and immigration hawks. As such, when released from prison, people who are not U.S.-born citizens face the possibility of deportation, this includes undocumented people, legal residents, people who legally reside in the country with some type of visa, and even naturalized U.S. citizens. Realistically, the impact is not only on those who get deported, but also on their families, as young children might be left in the United States if they are U.S.-born, creating chaos, fear, and uncertainty for many people and, in a sense, the entire Latina/o community.

STUDENT LOANS

The typical male and female offender is impoverished and uneducated, making it difficult to obtain education and training that enables them to compete in the job market. As such, those who wish to pursue an education or specialized training are forced to seek financial assistance. However, here too, ex-prisoners are confronted with yet another formal obstacle in that the Higher Education Act of 1998 makes students convicted of drug-related offenses ineligible for grants, loans, or work assistance. Consequently, since this federal legal barrier cannot be altered by states, and the fact that the majority of offenders are convicted for drug-related offenses, the great majority of all released prisoners are not eligible for education financial assistance, significantly impacting Latina/o offenders. In effect, while the range of criminal offenses is wide, no other offense results in automatic denial of federal financial assistance.

ADOPTIVE AND FOSTER PARENTING

To further complicate reentry, long-term community reintegration, and the opportunity of living a normal life, released prisoners who wish to be law-abiding citizens, be productive members in their communities, and have a stable family are confronted with an additional obstacle in that the federal Adoption and Safe Families Act of 1997 impedes people with certain convictions from being foster or adoptive parents, impacting the everyday life of not only ex-prisoners, but also of children in need of a family. Though, national statistics show that most states do make individualized determination on the applicants' suitability to be adoptive or foster parents, while considering people's criminal record and evidence of rehabilitation.

VOTING

Beyond the daily legal obstacles confronting released prisoners, states have absolute power to decide whether people with a criminal record are allowed to vote, impacting not only individual ex-inmates but the entire community, particularly Latino and African American communities. In fact, all but two states place restrictions on people with felony convictions regarding the right to vote.

In sum, these ten legal barriers not only hinder reentry, long-term community reintegration, and stability and continuity over time, but these obstacles counteract the very purpose of the criminal justice system, rehabilitation, public safety, and justice. Worse, the great majority of those who get detected, arrested, indicted, prosecuted, convicted, sentenced to jail or prison, and placed on death row are either Latino or African American. The inability to engage in civil activities, like voting, pushes ethnic and racial minorities further into the margins of society, ultimately silencing the entire minority community. Together, the central question of the current model of arrest, incarceration, and release becomes: are ex-prisoners actually being integrated into the community? Or, are they simply being *placed* back to survival days?

COMMUNITY INTEGRATION OR BACK-TO-SURVIVAL DAYS?

Theoretically, male and female offenders should be able to *regain* their lives once they are released from prison; arguably inmates should not be worse off than when they entered the prison system. In fact, if inmates took advantage of *available resources* while in prison, they should be in a better position (than those who did not) to begin the community (re)integration process. Practically, though, "life after prison is more a reflection of 'back to survival days,' than it is of 'community (re)integration'" (Urbina, 2008:189).

Released prisoners are in fact not provided with a smooth transition from prison to their next living shelter. Likewise, the existing mechanisms do not provide a smooth transition back into the community. To begin with, when inmates are released, often in the middle of the night, the typical ex-prisoner is confused, scared, has no belongings, and has little idea about what lies ahead. Normally, offenders express concerns as to whether they will be able to turn their lives around after being released, especially if they spent several years behind bars. For female offenders, the situation is even more complicated in that stable housing and employment are essential to regain custody of their children, as is a permanent address and transportation for legal employment to avoid the temptations of the streets, continuation of healthcare, and substance abuse treatment after release. In effect, the majority of women not only suffer from health conditions like depression, but 60 to 70 percent of women released from prison have nowhere to go. In essence, the typical male and female offender "leaves prison economically, politically, socially, and morally bankrupt" (Urbina, 2008:191).

Economically, upon release, the typical inmate has no place to go, limited resources, and little knowledge of whatever resources might be available in the community. Independent of how long they were in prison, their level of education remains low, lacking the skills to compete in a highly competitive and technological job market. When unemployment is high, the situation is even more drastic for ex-prisoners who are perceived by society as undeserving, threatening, and unwanted in the community. For minority parolees, Latinos and African Americans, the situation is even more devastating in that they are not only being marginalized for breaking the law, but for supposedly taking the few jobs available.

Politically, the typical male or female ex-prisoner has no ties to appointed or elected officials or to America's main institutions. Consequently, either because their right to vote has been taken away as a result of a criminal conviction or because they simply fail to exercise their vote, ex-prisoners are *strategically* forgotten or neglected by local, state, and federal politicians. As a general rule, politicians' main objective is to address the concerns of the "voting class," and thus the views and concerns of ex-prisoners are not likely to be addressed in a proper and efficient manner, as illustrated by the various legal barriers to reentry. In the case of minority ex-prisoners, Latinas and Latinos, the situation is further complicated in that their friends and relatives cannot vote if they are not U.S. citizens.

Socially, ex-prisoners typically have no social support when they are released from prison. To the contrary, former prisoners are usually viewed as undeserving people who should not be entitled to voice their experiences, views, or concerns. Further, as people who have violated the law or community norms, or challenged the status quo, released prisoners are viewed and treated as third- or fourth-class citizens. In the case of women and minority ex-prisoners, the post-prison experience is normally more consequential if they do not have friends or relatives to rely on for social support, like cultural understanding, appreciation, and, ultimately, reintegration. For instance, studies show that weak family ties or complete separation from their children creates a severe problem for reintegration and stability (Urbina, 2008).

Morally, male and female prisoners typically leave the prison system energized and motivated to start their new lives. However, for the typical offender, the prison experience is in fact disheartening, demoralizing, and damaging. Once released, inmates are scared and uncertain about having to interact with a judgmental society, and, for female and minority offenders, susceptible to diverse and punitive gender, ethnic, or racial stereotypes. Even though the United States is often characterized as a sensitive, understanding, ethical, and moral society, the community is not very forgiving of those who are considered strangers, outsiders, different, or threatening (Urbina, 2011, 2012). In a sense, ex-prisoners continue to pay, economically, politically, socially, or morally, for their criminal acts long after they are released from prison.

Evidently, having a population of ex-prisoners that is absolutely bankrupt carries high consequences in that it leads to the very same problem that we are arguably trying to solve: crime. In effect, studies show that recidivism is partially attributed to economic need as well as discriminatory policies and lack of community support (Urbina, 2008). Consider, for instance, the experience of one released female prisoner:

> I really tried to stay out of trouble, but its very difficult, you know. Like once you're into a routine and the people you're hanging about with and everything, and plus you're always getting hassled by the police . . . It was about this time that I left home . . . and I was on the streets for a very long time . . . because I was homeless, I couldn't get a . . . job . . . but I still had . . . fines that I had to pay . . . So I am stuck in this rut. I've got to pay these fines or go to jail, and I've got to live as well. So I was committing more crimes, going back to court and getting more fines, and it was just a vicious circle. So the next thing I ended up back in prison again. (Maruna, 2001:71)

In sum, all inmates are older when they are released from prison. If inmates have served lengthy sentences, they might experience additional difficulties, like more severe health problems. More fundamentally, since the typical inmate leaves prison economically, politically, socially, and morally bankrupt, most offenders will return to prison. Unfortunately, each time people return to prison, their situation becomes more devastating and consequential. For example, their chances of obtaining a legitimate job are further tarnished with an increase in apprehensions, prosecutions, convictions, and incarcerations. Of course, reentry also presents a critical situation for the prison system in various areas of daily prison life, like management, service delivery, and rehabilitation. For instance, reentry makes it difficult to maintain a reliable medical history, which is vital for community treatment. Still, while the majority of inmates wish to stay out of trouble and become productive members of society, their actual reality is closer to back to survival days than community integration (Urbina, 2008).

BUILDING BRIDGES BETWEEN PRISON AND SOCIETY

Understanding male and female offenders requires that we explore their lives by the totality of circumstances, experiences, events, and situations. This includes the investigation of not only life while incarcerated, but life before, during, and after incarceration (Urbina, 2008). In the context of the prison system, a central objective is to "rehabilitate" inmates for community reentry upon release, so that they can be productive members of society. However, too often, policymakers, politicians, social activists, and others with vested interest in "prison reform" concentrate on offenders who are entering prison and pay little attention to inmates who are about to be released, and essentially isolating inmates who are just released from prison, neglecting reintegration, public safety, and the conditions that originally led to criminal behavior and that will once again place people back in prison, resulting in a never-ending cycle.

As noted above, once inmates are released into the community, they are disconnected from conventional society. As such, without well-established bridges between prison and society, *the typical offender is prone to "fail" as a citizen*, reoffend, and end up in prison for a minor crime, or simply breaking parole conditions, with Latinos, African Americans, and Native Americans being prone to experience greater challenges (Díaz-Cotto, 1996; Oboler, 2009; Urbina, 2008). In essence, as documented by Raymond Michalowski (1985:240),

> Prisons in America exist as a kind of distorted mirror image of American society. Like the mirrors in a carnival funhouse, prisons exaggerate and expand some of the characteristics of the society they reflect. Yet, like fun-house mirrors, what they show is based in the very real object they are reflecting. The parallel between free society and prisons exists at both the organizational and the social level.

Exploring the female experience, Barbara Owen (1998:192) reports that

> Women in prison represent a very specific failure of conventional society—and public policy—to recognize the damage done to women through the oppression of patriarchy, economic marginalization, and the wider-reaching effects of such shortsighted and detrimental policies as the war on drugs and overreliance on incarceration as social control.

In all, the penal system, with its priority on security and control, places little emphasis on treatment and rehabilitation while inmates are incarcerated, with limited planning for community reentry upon release. Successful reintegration, though, involves proper planning prior to their release, as they are being released, and shortly after their release into the community. The focus should be immediately upon release and not after they have engaged in illegal behavior, and thus the challenge is trying to find ways to keep them in the community and not send them back to prison, especially for issues that can be addressed in the community. In effect, some of the most detrimental issues facing male and female prisoners are best addressed in the community and not behind bars. For instance, substance and alcohol abuse, domestic violence, employment skills, healthcare (like stress and depression), and parenting responsibilities are best addressed outside the correctional setting. However, under current penal policies, these problems are often deferred to the correctional system by a society unable, but mostly unwilling, to confront the problems of marginalized and neglected people, with the majority being Latinos, African Americans, women, and impoverished whites.

In sum, a well-established bridge between prison and society must be developed to avoid fear, chaos, ruptures, and recidivism. With a sharp increase of prison rates, the penal system is becoming a "way of life" for thousands of people in the United States, and for this very same reason the United States must realize that isolation and detachment is contributing to the very same problem we are trying to solve. Therefore, instead of neglecting, isolating, and marginalizing released prisoners, the criminal justice system, community agencies, and conventional society should work together, share resources, and exchange information to create a *road map* for inmates so that they have realistic established planning, goals, and continuity during reintegration.

COMMUNITY PROGRAMS

The main objective of community-based programs is for ex-prisoners to resolve their legal and social issues without risking future arrest, prosecution, conviction, or incarceration, while keeping the community safe. In fact, considering that the typical male and female offender suffers from a series of complicated problems, including childhood abuse, addictions, and health issues, community-based programs are probably the single most essential element in the creation of proper and lasting bridges between prison and the community. Upon release, people typically end up in the same physical environment where they grow up, which is plagued with physical contamination, air pollution, drugs, guns, violence, and crime. This time, however, ex-prisoners are burdened with a criminal record and few social, political, and economic resources to rely on while they find a legal job to survive, while trying to meet the requirements of parole.

Unfortunately, even though community programs have proved to be an effective and beneficial mechanism for the reintegration of ex-prisoners into the community, these programs have not been a priority, and thus they have struggled to keep their doors opened because of limited funds, lack of volunteers, and social and political unwillingness to support these agencies. As agencies that are arguably helping criminals, community programs do not get proper recognition by the media, making it difficult to convince the community, policymakers, and criminal justice officials that reintegration is vital for controlling recidivism and fear, and for community stability. In the current era of crime and punishment, the biggest challenge facing community programs will continue to be lack of resources and resistance by the warriors of law and order. Community-based programs must be made a priority in order to slow down the *cycle of crime, prison,* and *release.*

BREAKING STATE AND FEDERAL LEGAL BARRIERS FOR COMMUNITY REENTRY: RECOMMENDATIONS

Together, a well-planned and established bridge between the penal system and mainstream society is missing, and, by extension, there is a huge disconnect between prison and local communities, impacting not only reentry upon release but long-term community reintegration. To begin, there are numerous consequential legal barriers; that is, as reported by the Legal Action Center (2004:23):

> Without a job, it is impossible to provide for oneself and one's family. Without a driver's license, it is harder to find or keep a job. Without affordable housing or food stamps or federal monies to participate in alcohol or drug treatment, it is harder to lead a stable productive life. Without the right to vote, the ability to adopt or raise foster children, or access to a college loan, it is harder to become a fully engaged citizen in the mainstream society.

Therefore, along with the establishment of a well-planned bridge between prison and society to facilitate reentry upon release and ensure long-term community reintegration, the state and federal governments should amend existing laws to eliminate legal barriers so that laws will in fact protect public safety, while making sure that people with past criminal records successfully reintegrate. As recommended by the Legal Action Center (2004:22), the following principles are vital for the establishment of strategic reform:

1. Maximizing the chance that people with criminal records can successfully assume the responsibilities of independent, law-abiding citizens is a critical component for guaranteeing and reinforcing the community's legitimate interest in public safety.

2. An arrest alone should never bar access to rights, necessities, and public benefits. Doing so denies the presumption of innocence, the value of our legal system, to millions of Americans. Employers, housing authorities, and other decision-makers should not be permitted to consider arrest records.

3. A conviction should never bar access to a citizen's right to vote or to basic necessities such as food, clothing, housing, and education.

4. Eligibility for employment, housing, adoptive and foster parenting, or a driver's license should be based on the community's legitimate interest in public safety and the particulars of an individual's history and circumstances. Blanket bans on entire categories of people, such as everyone convicted of a felony, are neither wise nor fair; they do not take into account such important factors as the nature of the circumstances of the conviction and what the person has done since the commission of the offense, including receiving an education, acquiring skills, completing community service, maintaining an employment history, or earning awards or other types of recognition.

5. States should enact legislation to provide for the automatic sealing or expungement of any arrest that never led to conviction, and of conviction records after an appropriate amount of time has elapsed. States also should issue certificates to qualified people with criminal records that acknowledge rehabilitation and lift automatic bans.

6. Given the potential for misuse, conviction information should not be publically accessible on the Internet. Access should be restricted to those agencies, such as law enforcement, that need to retrieve criminal records to perform their duties.

RECOMMENDATIONS FOR COMMUNITY REENTRY OF MALE AND EX-FEMALE OFFENDERS

Exploring the experience of female offenders before, during, and after incarceration, Urbina (2008:203–204) notes the following recommendations, which are not politically appealing but they can serve as a significant step in breaking the *revolving door cycle of prison admissions and discharges*, which tends to get more vicious and consequential every time a female or male re-enters the prison system.

1. As the prison population continues to increase, expansion of service delivery among existing programs and the development of additional programs are

essential to avoid chaos, reduce medical and rehabilitation deficiencies, and secure a smooth transition from prison into the community.

2. Community programs should be given the highest priority and authorities should be sensitive to the specific needs of the various populations being released from prison. Female offenders, for instance, need better service delivery because they are the ones with the greatest demand for basic healthcare, education, job-seeking skills, and pre-release planning. As for undocumented mothers, they also face the possibility of losing their children. Further, in the case of those who do not have the necessary documentation to obtain a social security number, they are further confronted with additional barriers for service delivery and legal employment.

3. Community programs often discriminate against indigent people through examinations, by withholding information about available resources, or negligence. Therefore, male and female offenders should be fully informed of the programs in their communities long before they are released from prison. Also, for those who are released on parole, parole officials should ensure that people continue to receive information regarding resources in the community.

4. A transition team, including correctional staff, community agencies, community organizers, and volunteers, could provide advice, counseling, services, and referrals.

5. Local governments, the media, and the community should advocate for a volunteer program in which people from the community would offer mentoring and one-on-one or group assistance to released prisoners.

6. The implementation of a realistic educational and employment program must be a priority, as a sound education and successful employment reentry strategy can increase public safety, can reduce spending on costly jails and prisons, reduce poverty for some of the most disadvantage citizens, and develop social and economic prosperity of racial and ethnic communities. Further, education and employment for reentry can also promote family stability and provide a more stable future for millions of children who have parents in jail or prison.

LIFE AFTER PRISON: STEPS TO MAKING IT OUTSIDE

The latest national data indicate that about two-thirds of released prisoners are re-arrested within three years, illustrating the significance of joint reentry efforts and well-designed mechanisms. In effect, successful reentry upon release not only requires the elimination of legal barriers and the establishment of a well-designed bridge between prison and the community, but also strategic steps by the released prisoners themselves, if they are to make it on the outside. Imagine life after prison after being physically, socially, and politically disconnected from the community for years, often spending years in state prisons far from their hometown or in federal prisons in a different state. After years behind bars dreaming of freedom, inmates are normally unprepared for life after prison. As noted herein, along with a criminal record, the typical inmate has minimal education and work experience, shackled by addictions, chronic depression, or mental illness, haunted by the criminal stigma, under pressure to quickly find legal employment, and other pressing factors, like managing housing issues, drug or alcohol treatment needs, and family relationships (Urbina, 2008).

In fact, while inmates spend years behind bars waiting for the day of their release, *prisoners have little knowledge about the practicalities of street survival after prison*. To begin, seldom do prisoners realize that they are likely to have their parole revoked within the first forty-eight hours, and thus it is essential that they know, *through education while in prison*, and have the necessary steps in place before they are released. For instance, inmates must know that life after prison is not simply getting a job quickly upon release, and, of course, staying out of trouble. Inmates should *learn* that life after prison is more than simply rebuilding a new life, but seeking to break the cycle of crime, arrest, imprisonment, and release, while setting the foundation so that future generations will not follow the same path, the road to prison. As such, through education while incarcerated, inmates should learn the following 11 rules for making it outside after being released from jail or prison.

1. SUPPORT: WHO CAN HELP?

In terms of supporting themselves financially, both men and women leave prison with no money and often with hundreds of dollars in debt, and thus they are unable to sustain themselves. As such, inmates should know that the single most important step is the one they start inside prison, a support group of people they can contact while in prison, people they can call, visit, or work with upon release. In fact, one of the biggest mistakes the majority of inmates make when leaving prison is not identifying or locating a safe support group. Prisoners need to know that they need to develop a network of people that do not have a criminal past. Sometimes the first thing inmates want to do is get laid, drunk, or high (Visher, Yahner, and La Vigne, 2010). However, inmates must learn that if they are serious about making it, they must give themselves time to resocialize, with a focus on a lifetime of freedom and not one to two days of excitement that will land them right back in prison.

In the context of building bridges between prison and conventional society, identifying friends and family who can help is essential to prevent recidivism. One recent study found that family members were a key housing resource for most men, sometimes providing cash, food, and emotional support (Visher, Yahner, and La Vigne, 2010). Further, lack of family ties can result not only in detachment from society, but create difficulties for inmates while they are incarcerated, and make it difficult to be reintegrated into the community upon release. In fact, inmates who come out of prison with a committed relationship, and those who form one soon after release, are more likely to stay out of prison, revealing the significance of social support.

2. THE FIRST FORTY-EIGHT HOURS AFTER RELEASE

Since the majority of people who are released from prison have their parole revoked within forty-eight hours, inmates must learn about the significance of the first two days, the time when people are most vulnerable, when they are experiencing their weakest point. Inmates must realize that along with following the rules of their parole, they need to hang out with their support group. Prisoners should know that they need to have all of their faculties to do this, instead of being drunk, stoned, or preoccupied with other irrelevant matters. At this point, their *main* worry should be on the conditions of parole and any other requirements, staying away from "old" influences, and avoiding jeopardizing the reentry process.

3. ILLEGAL ACTIVITIES AND CRIMINAL ASSOCIATIONS

Before leaving prison, inmates must be well aware that getting out of prison early may take months or years of work, counseling, treatment, and the cooperation of various programs, only to be thrown away by associating with people with a criminal past, associating with people who are engaged in illegal activities, or simply being in the wrong place. Prisoners must know that when they are on parole they cannot just watch themselves, but they have to be careful of others too and realize that parole is like defensive driving; they should not only follow the rules of the road, they also need to watch what the other drivers are doing to avoid an accident.

4. DEALING WITH DRUG AND ALCOHOL ADDICTIONS

Since many prisoners suffer from addictions and depression, inmates must learn the significance of attending, and the consequences of not attending, Alcoholic Anonymous (A.A.) or Narcotics Anonymous (N.A.) after their release from prison. Of course, this includes all inmates with addictions, not only those who are released on parole. In fact, alcohol and drug addictions are among the most common reasons that people get involved in crime and, eventually, arrested, indicted, prosecuted, convicted, and sentenced to prison. As such, without proper treatment after prison, people are likely to get reinvolved in crime and sent back to prison.

5. CONFRONTING LIFE SITUATIONS UPON RELEASE

Before leaving prison, inmates should also be educated on ways of confronting difficult and unexpected situations that might arise during the first few months after their release, especially during the first month, which is the most difficult time after release, as they will have to walk away from temptations. In fact, the whole first year is very difficult, but the first forty-eight hours and the first month set the groundwork for successful community reintegration. Then the focus is on doing what is effectively working, while making adjustments for leaving a criminal past behind and gaining employment, family, and community stability.

6. PROVINCIAL OR FEDERAL HALFWAY HOUSES

Prisoners should also be familiar with provincial and federal halfway houses before they are released to reduce chaos, uncertainty, and ruptures, establishing continuity. A halfway house, for instance, can offer them a place to stay, food, and a little money to survive during the first few weeks. In effect, tracking the experience of male ex-prisoners returning to Chicago, Cleveland, and Houston, researchers Christy Visher, Jennifer Yahner, and Nancy La Vigne (2010) found that housing was a major challenge and that housing stability diminished over time for many released male prisoners, resulting in recidivism, rearrests, and reimprisonment.

7. UNDERSTANDING THE NATURE OF THE OFFENSE COMMITTED

While the high majority of inmates probably understand that they in fact committed a crime, inmates do not necessarily understand the nature or significance of their behavior. Therefore, prisoners must fully understand the nature of their crime if they are to become responsible, accountable, and able to make it on the outside. In fact, inmates will never make it on the outside unless they understand the nature and consequences of their acts. Simply, if prisoners do not know *exactly why they did what they did*, there is a good chance it will happen again. Worse, not only are inmates doomed to fail, but they will be in and out of prison their entire life. The biggest problem, however, is that many prisoners are often too medicated to be educated on these issues. Yet, the mere fact of having inmates medicated, and, by extension, making it difficult for them to comprehend, indicates the *global importance* of treatment during incarceration.

8. THE PRISON CODE: HONOR AMONG CRIMINALS

Prisoners must also learn that if they are living by the *criminal code* once they are released from prison, they will not be out for very long, will not only lose everything they gained but will be in a worse position than before. Inmates must realize that they cannot follow the code on the outside and be *normal* law-abiding citizens. Prisoners need to fully understand that the code they live by to survive inside prison is the *same* thing that will send them back to prison, normally within the first three years.

9. EMPLOYMENT UPON RELEASE

Before being released into the community, prisoners must also be educated on the realities of employment upon release. Under pressure, quite often when inmates get out of prison, they try to find employment fairly quickly. In truth, one of the biggest mistakes is trying to be *too normal*, because in fact they are not, yet, as illustrated herein. In fact, most of us have problems with just basic functions of everyday life as well as difficult or unexpected life situations that arise. To begin, many inmates face challenges seeking legal employment not only for the existence of a criminal record, but for lack of photo identification, a driver's license, a social security number, a physical address, an impressive resume, or references. Further, depending on the individual, it normally takes 6 to 12 months before inmates are ready to handle the stress, duties, and responsibilities of a full-time job. In all, combined with various other issues, a job can result in more stress, depression, and eventually lead to a breaking point if inmates try to move too quickly. Prisoners should learn that the focus must be on making themselves better, while participating in required programs and following the rules of parole and the halfway house, and cautiously progressing to a point where they can function in a day-to-day society. Eventually, the more people work, the more detached they will be from their criminal past and criminal associations, and the greater their chance for becoming socially and economically stable and thus taxpayers instead of a tax burden to society.

10. EDUCATION AFTER BEING RELEASED

Over the years penal institutions have established educational programs for prisoners to enhance rehabilitation while incarcerated and better prepare inmates for reentry. Upon release, however, the educational component is abandoned by both inmates and the correctional system, impacting community reintegration and the long-term economic, political, and social stability of inmates and the community at large. Therefore, both inmates and the penal system must realize and acknowledge that continued education after prison is, in a sense, the *secret* to making it on the outside, with the ultimate objective of breaking the cycle of crime, imprisonment, and release.

11. POST-RELEASE MONITORING, COUNSELING, AND MENTORING

As a final step, both the penal system and prisoners must realize that *successful long-term reintegration involves post-release monitoring*, counseling, and mentoring. Specifically, because of changes in sentencing laws, more inmates are now serving full terms. As such, prisoners are being released with no parole, and they have no official contact with state or federal authorities. Therefore, since no officers are monitoring their behavior, it is difficult to evaluate the *reintegration process*, determine the magnitude of specific legal barriers they are confronting, or provide a *needs-assessment* of their basic necessities. Achieving successful reintegration, then, requires well-planned and unintrusive post-release monitoring, counseling, and mentoring to help men and women not only address the issues mentioned herein, like addictions, traumas, and negative family and neighborhood influences in their lives, but also to establish a *solid foundation* for the betterment and well-being of inmates and society at large.

In sum, these steps should constitute an educational blue book for the penal system and prisoners, where inmates are well-versed in these areas of survival before being released from prison. As for successful reentry, instead of neglecting prisoners, especially as they are about to be released, the penal system should expand the availability and quality of in-prison programming. Once released, the initial weeks after release from prison are a high-risk period for relapse and reoffending. Therefore, exiting prisoners need to have access to programs and service immediately upon release, continuing for several months to ensure that people can transform their desire for successful reentry and long-term reintegration into pro-social activities and behavior. As repeatedly reported by U.S. Attorney General Eric Holder, out-of-prison programming, including job training and substance abuse programs, for released prisoners can improve public safety and reduce spending not only on prisons but also policing and the judicial system. In all, if we are in fact vested in stopping the cycle of crime, imprisonment, and release, reintegrating prisoners back into society should be a priority.

A TWENTY-FIRST CENTURY CHALLENGE

For the twenty-first century, critical questions remain to be answered, from a theoretical, research, and policy perspective. Likewise, the correctional system, the male and female offender population, and conventional society are likely to confront serious challenges. Globally speaking, though, the biggest challenge boils down to one question: How do we change the public opinion of Americans, particularly the "voting class," so that they can be more tolerant to a population that historically has been perceived and treated with *indifference* (Urbina, 2008)?

A question of such magnitude, of course, will not be resolved overnight in that it will require restructuring of the American society. What follows are a few recommendations that can serve as a road map for a more inclusive America (Urbina, 2008). First, we must come to the realization that from whatever angle the situation is analyzed (cost-benefit, economically, politically, morally, ethically, or legally), we cannot continue to marginalize, discriminate, manipulate, subjugate, isolate, neglect, and silence male and female offenders. Second, we must acknowledge the "true" logic and utility of the prison system in the context of those who are being arrested, indicted, prosecuted, convicted, sentenced to prison, or placed on death row. In the words of one critic,

What to do with those whom society cannot accommodate? Criminalize them. Outlaw their actions and creations. Declare them the enemy, then wage war. Emphasize the difference—the shade of skin, the accent in the speech or manner of clothes. Like the scapegoat of the Bible, place society's ills on them, then "stone them" in absolution. Its convenient. Its logical. It doesn't work. (Rodriguez, 1993:250)

Third, we need to be more sensitive to the experiences and realities of male and female offenders in the context of society as a whole. As reported by some investigators, "... the disturbing expansion of prisons and jails as a means of social control for the poor ... Now, all of these crises—the crises of class, the crises of race, the crises of prisons and the crises of education—are all interconnected ... the have-nots are disproportionately black and brown" (Marable, 1999:41). Taken together, U.S. prisons are vast warehouses for the impoverished, the unemployed, the poorly educated, and, most particularly, for minorities. Fourth, the American society must acknowledge and accept responsibility for the implications and ramifications of neglecting the "undeserving" members of society or simply warehousing them in prison. In the same way that an alcoholic must accept the "problem and responsibility" before an effective treatment takes its course, we must acknowledge that the prison system yields very few benefits at the cost of many negative consequences. Fifth, in a highly judgmental and prejudicial society, prison-based education must be made a high priority. The fact that states like California are spending more money on corrections than education, and states like New York are sending more minorities to prison than to universities has long-term consequences. Realistically, education is not only significant to compete in the job market, but it influences the level of ignorance in the general public, which in turn governs the level of stereotypes and fears about certain members of society. Sixth, male and female offenders must have better access to employment opportunities. As part of the restructuring process, policymakers must keep in mind not only the implications of low wages and highly advanced job requirements, but that jobs in the areas where the typical offender lives (who most likely lacks transportation) are scarce. As noted earlier, rearrests are tied to failures in economic support, including employment. It is ironic that the prison system is adopting some of the latest "safety technologies," yet advanced educational and vocational training for people in prison is minimal or nonexistent. As we enter the twenty-first century, how can it be possible that when it comes to quality and up-to-date technology, safety technologies stand on one end of the spectrum and innovations that will prepare men and women for after release stand on the other end of the spectrum? Last, fueled by notions of colonialism, conquest, imperialism, slavery, stereotypes, hate, and threat perceptions, the history of race and ethnic relations in the United States continues to be vicious, vindictive, and bloody (Acuña, 2010; Almaguer, 2008; Bosworth and Flavin, 2007; Urbina, 2011, 2012). Yet, "no single historical element has been more influential in unjustifiable behavior, beliefs, apathy, and feelings than 'indifference'" (Urbina, 2008:206). In this context, as reported by Urbina (2008), the educational system, starting in preschool, must play a more active role in advocating and developing more tolerance for indifference, if we are to achieve tranquility, equality, and justice.

CONCLUSION

Invariably, both male and female offenders are not only confronted with great uncertainty and confusion, they are economically, politically, socially, and morally bankrupt when they are released from prison. What will become of male and female inmates once they are released from prison? Will they be able to find legal employment with the skills they learned while incarcerated? Considering the wide range of problems facing prisoners, especially female offenders, will they be able to pay for their needs, like healthcare, and not return to illegal activities, like prostitution or narcotics trafficking? If inmates do not have the necessary skills, will they be able to acquire credentials and qualifications that will allow them to survive in a competitive job market? Will they be able to reunite with their children, partner, spouse, friends, or other loved ones? Will they be accepted by the community? Or, will they be met with looks of mistrust, disdain, rejection, or hostility? What is the probability that those released from prison will end up back in the correctional system?

Clearly, there is a big disconnect between prison and community reentry, hindering long-term community reintegration. If released prisoners cannot find legal employment, they are unable to obtain an education, they are not allowed to participate in community civic functions, they cannot find a mate for stability, and they cannot get help with basic necessities, what's left? What's left, especially for young Latino and African American men, is the pharmacy on the streets: selling drugs or stealing.

In a sense, like offenders, the prison system as well as conventional society lack significant "rehabilitation." In effect, to promote and guarantee public safety, the federal government and all 50 states must adopt policies and practices that facilitate successful reintegration, judging people on their individual merits instead of racial, ethnic, or gender stereotypes, stigma, or prejudice. For the well-being of society as a whole, there seems to be increasing support in various states and Congress for the repeal of oppressive and counterproductive laws. In fact, a number of initiatives are currently underway that will help ex-convicts who have spent their time behind bars become independent and law-abiding citizens, thereby strengthening community safety and stability. Globally, instead of creating further isolation and detachment, the prison population, the correctional system, and conventional society should work together to create a more inclusive, understanding, and safe America. Above all, society must take steps toward the creation of a more tolerant and forgiving society, while advocating public safety and justice.

REFERENCES

Acuña, R. (2010). *Occupied America: A history of Chicanos*. 7th edition. Upper Saddle River, NJ: Prentice Hall.

Almaguer, T. (2008). *Racial fault lines: The historical origins of white supremacy in California*. Berkeley: University of California Press.

Bosworth, M., and J. Flavin, eds. (2007). *Race, gender, and punishment: From colonialism to the war on terror*. Piscataway, NJ: Rutgers University Press.

Díaz-Cotto, J. (1996). *Gender, ethnicity and the state: Latina and Latino prison politics*. Albany, NY: SUNY Press.

Legal Action Center (2004). *After prison: Roadblocks to reentry*. Available at: http://www.lac.org/roadblocks-to-reentry/upload/lacreport/LAC_PrintReport.pdf.

Marable, M. (1999). The politics of race. In Conference summary and action plan. *Money, education, and prisons: Standing at the crossroads*. Milwaukee, WI: The Benedict Center.

Maruna, S. (2001). *Making good: How ex-convicts reform and rebuild their lives*. Washington, DC: American Psychological Association.

Michalowski, R. (1985). *Order, law and crime*. New York: Random House.

Oboler, S., ed. (2009). *Behind bars: Latino/as and prison in the United States*. New York: Palgrave Macmillan.

Owen, B. (1998). *In the mix: Struggle and survival in a women's prison*. New York: State University of New York Press.

Rodríguez, L. (1993). *Always running: La vida loca: Gang days in L.A.* New York: Simon & Schuster.

Urbina, M. (2007). Latinas/os in the criminal and juvenile justice systems. *Critical Criminology: An International Journal* 15: 41–99.

Urbina, M. (2008). *A comprehensive study of female offenders: Life before, during, and after incarceration*. Springfield, IL: Charles C. Thomas, Publisher.

Urbina, M. (2011). *Capital punishment and Latino offenders: Racial and ethnic differences in death sentences*. New York: LFB Scholarly Publishing.

Urbina, M. (2012). *Capital punishment in America: Race and the death penalty over time*. El Paso, TX: LFB Scholarly Publishing.

Urbina, M., and S. Kreitzer (2004). The practical utility and ramifications of RICO: Thirty-two years after its implementation. *Criminal Justice Policy Review* 15: 294–323.

Visher, C., J. Yahner, and N. La Vigne (2010). *Life after prison: Tracking the experiences of male prisoners returning to Chicago, Cleveland, and Houston*. Urban Institute, Justice Policy Center.

25

CLIMATE OF FEAR
Latino Immigrants in Suffolk County, N.Y.

Southern Poverty Law Center

INTRODUCTION

On November 8, 2008, Marcelo Lucero, an Ecuadorian immigrant, was murdered in the town of Patchogue, N.Y. The killing, police say, was carried out by a gang of teenagers who called themselves the Caucasian Crew and targeted Latino residents as part of a sport they termed "beaner-hopping." It highlighted a growing national problem— violent hatred directed at all suspected undocumented immigrants, Latinos in particular. Officials in Suffolk County, N.Y., where Patchogue is located, minimized the tragedy, with the county executive even suggesting that it would have been a mere "one-day story" if not for earlier publicity about his and other residents' anti-immigrant activism over the prior decade.

But the reality was that nativist intolerance and hate violence had been festering for years in Suffolk County, fostered by some of the very same officials who were now wishing the story away. The situation in Suffolk County, in fact, is a microcosm of a problem facing the entire United States, where FBI statistics suggest a 40% rise in anti-Latino hate crimes between 2003 and 2007, the latest numbers available. The number of hate groups in America has been rising, too, climbing more than 50% since 2000, mainly by exploiting the issue of undocumented non-white immigration.

In the aftermath of the Lucero murder, the Southern Poverty Law Center (SPLC) sent a Spanish-speaking researcher to Suffolk County to interview Latino residents, both documented and undocumented, over a period of months. What SPLC found was frightening. The Lucero murder, while the worst of the violence so far, was hardly an isolated incident. Latino immigrants in Suffolk County are regularly harassed, taunted, and pelted with objects hurled from cars. They are frequently run off the road while riding bicycles, and many report being beaten with baseball bats and other objects. Others have been shot with BB guns or pepper-sprayed. Most will not walk alone after dark; parents often refuse to let their children play outside. A few have been the targets of arson attacks and worse. Adding to immigrants' fears is the furious rhetoric of groups like the now-defunct Sachem Quality of Life, whose long-time spokesman regularly referred to immigrants as "terrorists." The leader of another nativist group, this one based in California, was one of many adding their vitriol, describing a "frightening" visit to an area where Latinos are concentrated in Suffolk: "They urinate, they defecate, [they] make sexual overtures to women."

Fueling the fire are many of the very people who are charged with protecting the residents of Suffolk County—local politicians and law enforcement officials. At one point, one county legislator said that if he saw an influx of Latino day laborers in his town, "we'll be out with baseball bats." Another said that if Latino workers were to gather in a local neighborhood, "I would load my gun and start shooting, period." A third publicly warned undocumented residents that they "better beware." County Executive Steve Levy, the highest-ranking official in Suffolk, is no friend of immigrants, either. When criticized by a group of immigrant advocates, for example, Levy called the organization a den of "Communists" and "anarchists." At the same time, immigrants told the SPLC that the police were, at best, indifferent to their reports of harassment, and, at worst, contributors to it. Many said police did not take their reports of attacks seriously, often blaming the victim instead. They said they are regularly subjected to racial profiling while driving and often to illegal searches and seizures. They said there's little point in going to the police, who are often not interested in their plight and instead demand to know their immigration status.

Although Suffolk County is not unique—many communities across the United States are undergoing similar racial conflicts and rapid demographic changes—there are several concrete measures county officials could take to remedy what has been a worsening problem there for a decade:

- First, local politicians should halt their angry demagoguery on the issue of immigration. There is abundant evidence that Suffolk County officials have contributed substantially to an atmosphere conducive to racial violence.
- Second, the county and state legislatures should mandate that crime victims and witnesses not be asked their immigration status during criminal investigations. As long as they are, immigrants will be unwilling to come out of the shadows to report crimes against themselves and others.
- Third, law enforcement officials should train officers to ensure that they take seriously cases of hate-motivated crime. Until they do, Latino residents will continue to distrust law enforcement officials and avoid cooperation.

- Fourth, the county should maintain accurate hate crime statistics that are readily available to the public. Doing so will help guide county leaders and residents in confronting the problem of hate-motivated violence.
- Fifth, the county should promote educational programs in the public schools to encourage respect for diversity and opposition to hatred. In the end, educating the next generation is the only permanent antidote to hate.

If these measures are taken to combat an increasingly volatile situation, it's likely that angry passions in Suffolk can be cooled and a rational debate on immigration and its consequences begun. The alternative is that the county continues to foster a dangerous growth of violent racial intolerance and nativism—a climate of fear.

CLIMATE OF FEAR

SUFFOLK COUNTY, N.Y.—The night of Nov. 8, 2008, seven teenage males gathered in a park in Medford, N.Y., to drink beer and plot another round of a brutal pastime they called beaner-hopping. It consisted of randomly targeting Latino immigrants for harassment and physical attacks.

Five days earlier, three of them had gone on the hunt and beaten a Latino man unconscious, they later told police. "I don't go out and do this very often, maybe once a week," one of them said.

Two of the youths in the park had started their day just after dawn by firing a BB gun at Latino immigrant Marlon García, who was standing in his driveway. García was hit several times.

After leaving the park, the pack of seven drove around Medford. Unable to locate a victim, they set off for Patchogue, a nearby seaside village. Both communities are in Suffolk County, which occupies the eastern, less urban half of Long Island. In Patchogue, they caught sight of Hector Sierra walking downtown. They ran up to Sierra and began to punch him, but Sierra was able to flee.

Then, just before midnight, according to prosecutors, they spotted Ecuadorian immigrant Marcelo Lucero walking with a friend, Angel Loja. Lucero, 37, had come to the United States in 1992. He worked at a dry cleaning store and regularly wired money home to his ailing mother.

The seven teenagers jumped out of their vehicles and began taunting the two men with racial slurs. Loja fled, but the attackers surrounded Lucero and began punching him in the face. Trying to defend himself, Lucero removed his belt and swung it, striking one of the teens in the head. Enraged by that blow, 17-year-old Jeffrey Conroy, a star high school football and lacrosse player, allegedly pulled a knife, charged forward and stabbed Lucero in the chest, killing him.

All seven attackers were arrested a short time later. Conroy was charged with second-degree murder and manslaughter as a hate crime. The other six were charged with multiple counts of gang assault and hate crimes.

The local and national media gave the murder of Lucero extensive coverage. This was in part because it occurred less than four months after the highly publicized slaying of a Mexican immigrant in Shenandoah, Pa. Luis Ramírez, 25, was beaten to death by drunken high school football players in a case that sparked a national discussion and heightened awareness of the rising tide of anti-immigrant violence.

In few places is that trend more viciously evident than in Suffolk County, where anti-immigrant sentiment has long run deep, and where a fast-growing Latino immigrant population has been victimized by a continuing epidemic of anti-immigrant hate crimes since the late 1990s.

In recent months, Southern Poverty Law Center (SPLC) researchers interviewed more than 70 Latino immigrants living in Suffolk County, along with more than 30 local religious leaders, human rights activists, community organizers, and small business owners. Their accounts are remarkably consistent and demonstrate that although Lucero's murder represented the apex of anti-immigrant violence in Suffolk County to date, it was hardly an isolated incident.

Latino immigrants in Suffolk County live in fear. Low-level harassment is common. They are regularly taunted, spit upon, and pelted with apples, full soda cans, beer bottles, and other projectiles. Their houses and apartments are egged, spray-painted with racial epithets, and riddled with bullets in drive-by shootings. Violence is a constant threat. Numerous immigrants reported being shot with BB or pellet guns, or hit in the eyes with pepper spray. Others said they'd been run off the road by cars while riding bicycles, or chased into the woods by drivers while traveling on foot. The SPLC recorded abundant first-hand accounts of immigrants being punched and kicked by random attackers, beaten with baseball bats, or robbed at knifepoint.

Political leaders in the county have done little to discourage the hatred, and some have actively fanned the flames. County Executive Steve Levy, Suffolk's top elected official, has made hostile policies targeting undocumented immigrants a central theme of his administration since he was first elected in 2003. Others have done worse, with public statements that all but endorsed violence. At a public hearing on immigration in August 2001, County Legislator Michael D'Andre of Smithtown said that if his own town should ever experience an influx of Latino day laborers like that of nearby communities, "We'll be up in arms; we'll be out with baseball bats." In March 2007, County Legislator Elie Mystal of Amityville said of Latino immigrants waiting for work on street corners, "If I'm living in a neighborhood and people are gathering like that, I would load my gun and start shooting, period. Nobody will say it, but I'm going to say it."

Most immigrants said they do not dare travel alone at night. Few let their children play outside unattended.

"We live with the fear that if we leave our houses, something will happen," said Luis, a Mexican who migrated to Suffolk County three years ago. "It's like we're psychologically traumatized from what happens here."

Like all but two immigrants contacted by the SPLC, Luis spoke for this report on the condition that, to avoid retaliation, he would be identified only by his first name and country of origin.

At best, the immigrants said, the police seem indifferent to their plight. At worst, the police contribute to it, in the form of racial profiling, selective enforcement, and outright bullying. A detailed account provided by Agosto, a Guatemalan immigrant, was typical. Agosto said that in early 2008, he was waiting for work at *la placita* (little plaza), a day labor pick-up point in Brentwood, when a police car pulled up. The two officers inside told him he wasn't allowed to stand there and demanded to see his identification. When he replied that he didn't have his I.D. with him, the officers told him to get in the back of the squad car. "I thought they were giving me a ride home," he said. But when they arrived at his residence, the police officers got out of the car and told Agosto to find his I.D. When he unlocked the front door, he said, the officers barged in without asking permission to enter. The police ransacked his living quarters, rifling through drawers and knocking items off shelves.

"I was very nervous," Agosto said. "They kept pushing me and telling me to hurry up. I got even more nervous so it took me a while to find my I.D. When you are undocumented, you get scared." When Agosto finally located his *cédula de identidad*, a Guatemalan government-issued I.D. card, the police looked it over then left. "I felt bad, like they were treating me like I was less than they were," he said. "It felt racist."

No immigrants reported serious physical abuse at the hands of Suffolk County law enforcement authorities. But time after time, they gave similar accounts of being pulled over for minor traffic violations and then interrogated, or being questioned harshly at nighttime checkpoints after watching Anglo drivers being waved through. A few said they'd been arrested for driving under the influence or for refusing to take a breathalyzer test even though in fact they'd submitted to the test and registered well below the legal limit.

Evidence suggesting unequal enforcement of the motor vehicle code in Suffolk County is easily observed in the local courts that handle minor offenses. Latinos account for roughly 14% of Suffolk County's population, but on a typical day in a Suffolk County justice court, they make up nearly half the defendants appearing for motor vehicle violations. A review of the police blotters printed in Suffolk County daily newspapers yields similarly suggestive demographic evidence: almost every day, around 50% of the drivers listed as having been fined for a motor vehicle violation have Latino surnames.

The most common violation that Latino immigrants are tagged with is violation 509, for unlicensed driving. It carries a $185 fine on top of a $150 vehicle impound charge and $25 a day for vehicle storage. Failure to appear in court or to pay a fine leads to arrest warrants.

Law enforcement officers in Suffolk County tend not to exhibit the same enthusiasm for investigating hate crimes against Latinos as they do writing them tickets, according to immigrants and other county residents interviewed for this report.

Immigrants in Suffolk County don't trust the police. They say there's no point in reporting bias-motivated harassment, threats, or assaults, even severe beatings, because from what they can tell, the police take the report and then do nothing. They say that when the police arrive on the scene of a hate crime, they often accept the version of events given by the assailant or assailants, even to the point of arresting the true victim in response to false claims that the immigrant started a fight. And they say that officers discourage hate crime victims from making formal complaints by questioning them about their immigration status.

In the days following the murder of Marcelo Lucero, the Congregational Church of Patchogue invited immigrants to the church to speak about hate crimes. In all, more than 30 Latino immigrants in Suffolk County came forward with detailed accounts of their own victimization. In response, the Suffolk County Legislature formed a task force to investigate the sources of racial tension in the county. To date, the task force has held one of at least four planned hearings.

Prosecutors, meanwhile, have announced new indictments that accuse the defendants in the Lucero murder of assaulting or menacing a total of eight other Latino immigrants.

On June 24, 2008, according to prosecutors, the teenagers set upon Robert Zumba, kicking him and pinning his arms while Conroy, the alleged knife-wielder in the Lucero slaying, sliced Zumba with a blade. Members of the group repeatedly victimized another man, José Hernández, in December 2007, prosecutors said. During one attack, Conroy allegedly held a pipe in one hand and smacked it against his opposite palm, threatening, "We're going to kill you."

Immigrants who have been the victims of hate-crime violence in Suffolk County report that in most cases the attackers are white males in their teens or 20s. A few reported being attacked by African-American males, or being lured by a white female to a nearby "party" where assailants lay in wait. Almost always, the reported attackers were young.

All seven youths accused of participating in the attack on Lucero reside in Patchogue or Medford—predominantly middle-class towns whose strip malls and pizzerias appear in sharp contrast to the lavish wealth on display elsewhere in the county. Suffolk County has one of the steepest wealth gradients in the country. Six of its ZIP codes are among the 100 wealthiest in the United States. The village of Sagaponack, one of a group of seaside communities collectively known as the Hamptons, is the most expensive ZIP code in the nation, with a median home sale price in 2005 of $2.8 million. It's home to investment bankers and real estate tycoons.

The parents of the alleged Lucero attackers include a teacher, a butcher, a store clerk, a deli owner, and a former K-Mart operations manager. Latino immigrants may find work in Suffolk County's rich seaside communities, but they live in the more affordable inland towns, alongside middle- and working-class American families who are more likely to view the brown-skinned newcomers as competitors for jobs than hired help.

Immigrant advocates say that the violence committed by high school students and their slightly older peers is fueled by the immigrant-bashing rhetoric they absorb in the hallways and classrooms at school, in the news media, or in conversations at home.

Demographic change in Suffolk County has been rapid over the previous two decades. Some towns have gone from being practically all white to having a 15% Latino population, made up mostly of immigrants from Central America and Mexico, according to the latest census statistics. In Patchogue and Medford, the Latino population is 24%.

Although this influx has slowed since the U.S. economy faltered last year, the nativist backlash continues. It began in earnest in the late 1990s, when about 1,500 Mexican workers showed up over the course of a few years in the small, majority-white, middle-class hamlet of Farmingville. The hamlet's central location made it ideal for contractors looking to hire day laborers for jobs throughout the county. That in turn made it attractive to immigrants drawn to the area by then-abundant employment opportunities in the landscaping, restaurant, and construction industries.

In 1998, a militant nativist group called Sachem Quality of Life formed in Farmingville and began disseminating propaganda that accused undocumented Latino immigrants of being inherently prone to rape, armed robbery, and other violent crimes. Although Sachem Quality of Life is now defunct, the group, along with the Federation for American Immigration Reform and a smaller nativist group called American Patrol, heavily influenced the tone for public discourse on immigration in the area.

Nativist ideology now permeates many levels of society and government in Suffolk County. County Executive Levy in June 2006 mocked activists demonstrating against hate crime violence and the mass eviction of Latino immigrants based on the selective enforcement of zoning laws. "I will not back down to this one percent lunatic fringe," he said. "They evidently do not like me much because I am one of the few officials who are not intimidated by their politically correct histrionics."

That same year, a school board member in the Hamptons distributed an online petition to parents, teachers, and a school principal calling for undocumented immigrants to be prevented from receiving any "free services" in the U.S.

"Look, we need you to continue sending this around. . . . [G]et as many viable names on here so that someone hears our voices," the e-mail read. "It seems the only voices they hear are the illegal immigrants who say 'foul play,' or the agencies backing them. We need to stop this and stop it in the bud!"

Also in 2006, the same official distributed an e-mail containing a "hilarious" mock description of a doll called Brentwood Barbie. "This Spanish-speaking only Barbie comes with a 1984 Toyota with expired temporary plates & 4 baby Barbies in the backseat (no car seats)," it read. "The optional Ken doll comes with a paint bucket lunch pail & is missing 3 fingers on his left hand. Green cards are not available for Brentwood Barbie or Ken."

In a February 2007 public hearing on proposed legislation, County Legislator Jack Eddington of Brookhaven singled out two immigration advocates who were speaking from the podium in Spanish and demanded to know if they were in the country legally. Eddington also warned undocumented immigrants, "You better beware" and "Suffolk County residents will not be victimized anymore."

Later in 2007, Levy was reelected with 96% of the vote.

Over the years, immigrant advocates have built an energetic movement in Suffolk County. Earlier this year, on the six-month anniversary of Lucero's murder, the Long Island Immigrant Alliance and The Workplace Project organized a vigil at the site of the killing. The event featured speakers from an array of groups, including the Fundación Lucero de América (Lucero Foundation America), along with Marcelo Lucero's brother, Joselo.

A few months before the vigil, some residents of eastern Long Island formed Neighbors in Support of Immigrants, in part to counter what they perceived as a takeover of local town council and community meetings by anti-immigrant zealots. In Patchogue, residents formed the Unity Coalition with the help of the New York Division of Human Rights to work to ease tensions in that community. A more established grassroots organization, Farmingdale Citizens for Viable Solutions, runs La Casa Comunal, a community center that serves Latino day laborers. The group also documents hate crimes.

Immigrant advocates cheered the news earlier this year that the Department of Justice had begun a criminal investigation into hate crimes against Latinos in Suffolk County. The federal agency also launched a probe into the way the Suffolk County Police Department, the main law enforcement agency in the county, has handled such crimes.

Nevertheless, the Latino immigrants interviewed for this report expressed little optimism that attitudes will change. If anything, they said, their situation is growing more perilous by the day. The weak economy means that more residents are out of work and looking for someone to blame. And many of the jobs for immigrants have dried up, forcing day laborers to spend more time traveling to and from their residence or waiting for work on street corners, making them all the more vulnerable.

Although most of the Latino immigrants who are victimized in Suffolk County are undocumented, their attackers have no way of knowing their immigration status. "They don't know if I'm legal or not so it must be because we're [Latino]," said Orlando, a Guatemalan immigrant who came to Suffolk County in 2005. "The racist people aren't going to change just because we get papers."

FUELING THE FIRE

Immigrant-bashing in Suffolk County, N.Y., dates back at least a decade to the founding of Sachem Quality of Life (SQL), a trendsetting anti-immigrant group whose militant tactics inspired later nativist extremist groups like the Minutemen and Save Our State.

SQL took its name from a Long Island school district. Most of its members lived in

Farmingville, a small hamlet of 15,000 residents that, like much of Suffolk County, experienced an influx of Latino immigrants beginning in the mid-to-late 1990s.

After forming in 1998, Sachem began a generalized campaign to rid Farmingville of Latino immigrants. The efforts included harassment and verbal abuse of laborers and contractors at day-labor pickup sites. Members called for the U.S. military to occupy Farmingville so that soldiers could assist in rounding up immigrants for mass deportation. SQL spread defamatory anti-immigrant propaganda laden with bogus data purporting to show that Latino immigrants were responsible for a nonexistent rise in sexual assault, burglary, manslaughter, and other serious crimes in the area.

The group worked to thwart the establishment of a day laborer hiring center that was authorized by the Suffolk County Legislature but ultimately vetoed by then-County Executive Bob Gaffney. Its ranks swelled to 400 members after the powerful Federation for American Immigration Reform, a national anti-immigrant hate group based in Washington, D.C., dispatched a field organizer to assist SQL's recruiting, street actions, and propaganda campaign. SQL referred to Latino immigrants as "invaders," and branded any American who advocated for immigrant rights a traitor to the country.

As SQL's influence grew, racial tensions ratcheted up. Incidents of verbal harassment and violence multiplied. They included rocks and bottles being thrown at Latino immigrants, BB gun snipers firing at Latinos from rooftops and passing cars, vandalism and window breaking at houses and apartment complexes where immigrants lived, and Latinos being accosted on the street by groups of white youths.

In September 2000, two local racist skinheads posed as homebuilding contractors to lure two Mexican day laborers to a warehouse where the white supremacists stabbed and nearly beat the immigrants to death. One of the assailants was tattooed with swastikas. The other had a tattoo on his stomach of a skinhead menacing a kneeling Jew.

Shortly after the skinheads were arrested for attempted murder as a hate crime, Paul Tonna, a moderate Republican and presiding officer of the Suffolk County Legislature, helped organize a rally for racial unity in Farmingville. In response, SQL held a rally outside Tonna's home. Picketers hurled racial slurs at his adopted children, four of whom are Mexican American and one a Native American.

Two weeks after the attack, SQL held a "Day of Truth" forum that featured guest speakers from several hate groups, including Glenn Spencer, head of California-based American Patrol.

At the forum, SQL President Margaret Bianculli-Dyber said that she was inspired to form the group one spring day when she witnessed "hundreds" of Latino men loitering on a corner outside her house. "I called the police. I said, 'There are hundreds of men standing on the corner. Send a patrol car.' They said, 'You mean the Mexicans waiting for work? We're not sending a car. You're a racist.'"

Also at the Day of Truth, SQL member Dave Drew said his group's ultimate goal was the deportation of all undocumented immigrants. "Some say, 'There are millions of illegal aliens. That's a big job to deport.' Is it really? How many planes and cars are on the road as we speak? Not that big a deal to deport a couple million people. Farmingville is a one-day job, that's Farmingville! If the INS [U.S. Immigration and Naturalization Service] wanted to do it, they'd come in the morning with buses, with document people, and remove them all, repatriate them. One-day job. Farmingville would be restored."

A few days after the forum, a member of SQL was arrested for threatening a local immigrant family. The targeting of Latinos in Suffolk County has continued since. On July 5, 2003, when SQL was still active, five teenagers used firecrackers to set fire to the Farmingville home of a family of five Mexican immigrants. The family narrowly escaped death as flames melted the house's aluminum siding and kept spreading, scorching the trees outside. After speaking with the teenagers, the local district attorney reported that they showed no remorse over burning down the house, for the simple reason that "Mexicans live there."

In 2004, SQL divided into competing factions and gradually disintegrated. It's now defunct. But its hateful legacy remains.

VOICES FROM THE SHADOWS

SUFFOLK COUNTY, N.Y.—Orlando, a 23-year-old immigrant from Guatemala, arrived in Suffolk County in 2005. He earns $11 an hour building tennis courts "for rich people," he says. He lives in a tiny rented room in Riverhead that he shares with his pet guinea pig, Sarita María. It contains his bed, a small television, and Sarita María's cage. On top of the cage, Orlando's toothpaste, toothbrush, and dental floss are lined up in a neat row on a folded towel. The room is immaculate.

Orlando moved to this tiny room after a white neighbor assaulted him outside his previous residence on Oct. 3, 2008. Orlando was celebrating his birthday with a group of friends around a barbecue. Around 10 p.m., he recalls, the man who lived down the street came over to complain about the music and the smoke from the grill.

Here is Orlando's account, related to an investigator for the Southern Poverty Law Center (SPLC) in Spanish, of what happened next:

> The man was drunk, and he came to cause trouble. One of my friends went to talk with him so there would not be any problems but [the neighbor] started to offend us, saying we were immigrants and we should not be in America, because we were stealing work from Americans, a lot of things like that. One of my friends tried to hold him back, and [the neighbor] hit him in the head with a flashlight. My friend's head opened up in a wound. I went to try and help him and [the neighbor] then hit my head as well. Then he ran.
>
> The police came, and he did not want to come out of his house. He said that we had started it. He lied. He said that we were looking for trouble and we would not let people sleep. Even the neighbors in the house right next to us supported this man and said it was our fault.

Orlando said the police asked him if he wanted to file charges and he said no because he did not want to cause any trouble.

> There is a lot of discrimination [in Suffolk County]. They say, excuse the word, "Fucking immigrant, you should return to your country, you're just here to rob us." But we're the ones getting beaten and robbed, and the police do nothing. There are many Latinos here that work more than Americans, but there are a lot of Americans here that treat Latinos like garbage. Like we are worth nothing.
>
> Because these Americans know that Hispanic people stay quiet, they make fun of us, they attack us, they steal from us, and they get away with it.

The great majority of Latino victims of hate crimes interviewed for this report said they were too fearful of retribution—from their assailants, local authorities, or both—to speak without assurances that they would be identified only by first name and country of origin.

Carlos Morales, a Latino immigrant community organizer in Suffolk County, was one of only two victims who agreed to give their full names. Morales, 30, came from Mexico City in 1998. When he first arrived, he was homeless. He slept outside in cardboard boxes, often behind a church in Farmingville. In 1999, when the immigrant-bashing organization Sachem Quality of Life was at the height of its power, Morales was run over by a car and beaten in one of the area's first anti-immigrant attacks.

Here is how he tells his story:

> The laundromat where I worked closed at 10:30, and around 11 at night, I was riding home on my bike. I was crossing the street and there was a car coming. First, they stopped for me to cross the street, and then, when I am crossing, they ran me over. When I fell on the ground, they got out of the car and kicked me. They took baseball bats out of the back of their car. They hit me on my knees, in the face, on my back. One of them put his foot on my mouth and said, "You should go back to where you come from, you dirty Mexican." And he continued to hit me.
>
> There is a bar nearby, and the people at the bar heard the noise and came running out. The [attackers] got in their car and drove away. They left me in a bad state—on the ground, really beaten. The people that came out of the bar called the police and the ambulance came and got me.
>
> I remember when I was in the ambulance, the [paramedic] who was putting the sheet on me, he said to me: "This happened to you because you are here. If you were not here, this would not have happened." He said it in a sarcastic way because he did not like that I was a Mexican. I remember his face because he was laughing at me. It is something I will never forget because I could not say anything. I was hurt, and he was the one with the ambulance. When I was learning English, I could understand a lot of things but I couldn't speak well, I couldn't say what I really wanted to say.

The ambulance brought me to the hospital. I was there with a dislocated shoulder and fractured knees, both knees fractured. I still have knee problems. When it is really cold, I have a lot of pain in my knees. Also, I lost my two front teeth when they hit me in the mouth with a baseball bat.

That was my first experience of racial hate. I had heard of other attacks. I knew people who had been attacked but I didn't think it would happen to me, especially not in this way. I had experienced other incidents, like customers in the laundromat giving me looks where you know you're not welcome. But I never thought it would reach this level, that people could have so much hate, to beat you so much, so hard.

No one was ever arrested.

In the beginning, it affected me in a negative way because I felt a lot of anger. I started to feel like all Americans are bad people. You cannot trust them. It changed the way I was. I was always ready to fight. I turned into a very defensive person with other people. I was like that for about two years, I think, really angry with people, always thinking to do the same to other people that they had done to me. But after two years, I started working in the community, and I began to get better. Now, whenever I am walking or riding my bike, I always try to stay alert and see if there are witnesses around or not.

I try to convince people who are attacked to come forward with their own stories, but it's hard to bring them out. The majority of people don't tell these stories outside of the [immigrant] community. Inside the community, you hear the new stories that are happening almost every day, constantly, in one form or another. For someone that does not know what it's like for us, they would think that all the stories were invented, but these are the things that happen to people every day.

Here are the accounts of four other Latino victims of violence in Suffolk County, in their own words:

DAVID (FROM PERU): There's one house I walked by and someone was standing at the front door. He was saying, "Hey," and started throwing rocks at me. He pointed up to the top floor where a man was leaning out the window with a rifle pointed at me.

David and his brother also reported being menaced by black youths armed with chains and samurai swords who made anti-immigrant comments, and working at a factory where the manager regularly shoves immigrant employees and uses racial epithets.

DIEGO (MEXICO): It was dusk a few weeks ago [mid-May 2009], and I was riding my bike through town. A car pulled over and a few kids got out and started shooting me with rubber pellet guns from about 10 feet away. They shot me repeatedly. I held up my backpack to protect my face, and they stole my bike. I didn't report it or anything. It's not worth missing a day of work to go and report a crime when [the police] won't do anything about it. . . . During the day, we all feel better, safer, but at night I walk with two or three friends to be protected.

"SANTOS" (MEXICO): I was driving through Brentwood April 11 [2009], and a car pulled out into the road and hit my car. Two [white] passengers got out and started yelling, "Stupid Mexican!" When I got out of my car to talk with them, they pushed and kicked me until the cops arrived. The police let them go even though I complained about their assaulting me. Two weeks later, I received a police report saying the accident was my fault. The report says nothing about them hitting me.

"FRANCISCO" (ECUADOR): One evening in the summer of 2006, I was leaving a deli when I was confronted by four kids, all about 16 years old. They said, "Fucking immigrant," and told me to go back to Mexico." They grabbed me and threw me against the building. I fell down and they started kicking me and they left me there. It was around 5 p.m., still light outside. The police came and took a report but I never heard from them again. My shoulder was injured and cost me $1,200 in hospital bills. I paid the bills myself. Now, I never go outside alone.

An SPLC investigator also recorded the description by Aníbal, a 22-year-old immigrant from Mexico, of an attack by his former employer. This happened on Nov. 23, 2008, his medical records show. Aníbal says that when he showed up 30 minutes late for a flooring job, his boss started punching him as soon as he stepped out of his car at the job site, breaking his nose with the first blow.

Here's what he says happened next:

My boss continued the attack. Then he said that if I went to the police, he would go to immigration and get me deported and also he would not pay me the $2,500 I was due, so I better shut up. I went to Sister Margaret [Smyth, a local nun and immigrant advocate], and she encouraged me to report what happened to the police and go to the hospital. So I did, even though I was afraid of being deported.

One week later, I went to the police station to get a copy of my report for my records. They said they couldn't just give me one, that I had to fill out an application, send it in, and I would have the report in about three months. I filled it out, but I have received nothing from the police. My hospital bills total about $4,800. I don't spend much time in the streets anymore. I'm afraid.

Javier Monroy, 56, is another immigrant who understands the twin pressures of constant fear and looming hospital bills. Early one morning in March 2008, Monroy was throwing a coffee cup into a garbage can outside a 24-hour pharmacy in Farmingville when a passing car pulled into the parking lot. He remembers hearing a door slam. Then something struck him in the head so hard it knocked him nearly unconscious. He says he fell to the ground and couldn't defend himself. He was hit at least 10 times, he says, by something harder than a fist—most likely a chunk of wood or a metal pole, he thinks. The attackers stole his wallet and continued to beat him.

Bleeding heavily from a head wound, he was taken to a hospital, where he remained for five days, waiting to see if he needed surgery. It took eight staples to close his wound, and his badly bruised arm still hurts a lot in cold weather.

Monroy says he remembers giving a report to a police officer, but says nothing ever came of it. When he went to the hospital to have the staples removed, the hospital staff demanded that he pay $300 up front. He didn't have the money, so his cousin extracted them at home after soaking the staples in hot water and soap.

Last November, just after the murder of Marcelo Lucero, Monroy was invited to attend a gathering at a church in Patchogue with Father Dwight Wolter. He was invited into a room to speak with someone who introduced himself as a detective. Two other people were present, and all wore suits; Monroy thought maybe they were police or city employees but he wasn't sure—they did not identify themselves. He asked for names and business cards, and they said they had run out. They asked to hear his story, so he told them what happened when he was attacked. They asked a few questions and said they would call him back. Monroy has not heard from them since, or from the police. But he's hounded by collection agencies demanding payment of his hospital bills, which exceed $30,000.

When he lived in Mexico, Monroy recalls, he liked to watch police-glorifying reality shows from the United States, and he remembers being impressed by the police, especially by their eloquent squad-car soliloquies about how they'd joined the force to help regular people. He is disillusioned with the reality in Suffolk County.

Orlando, the Guatemalan immigrant, shares Monroy's disappointment with the apparent priorities of at least some Suffolk law enforcement officers.

For example, he says, one night in April 2008 he went to pick up his girlfriend, who's from the United States, to take her out to dinner. He parked his car just past her house, in front of another house, locked it, and walked up to his girlfriend's residence. When they returned together a short time later, four police cars had surrounded his car, and officers were walking around. Orlando pressed the unlock button on his remote control as he approached the car, and the police officers, perhaps startled by the *beep-beep* sound of the alarm deactivating, reached for their guns, but did not pull them out of their holsters.

Orlando asked what was wrong in his limited English, but the officers shoved him against his car and patted him down. They demanded his license and registration. They said that someone had called in a report of a suspicious vehicle. Several times, they asked him how many times he'd driven through his girlfriend's neighborhood before parking. Just once, he kept saying. When they started asking him about where he worked and where he lived, his girlfriend yelled at them in fluent English to leave him alone, and they left.

Orlando says this kind of law enforcement interaction is typical for undocumented immigrants in Suffolk County, which is why they're reluctant to file charges or even report hate crime assaults and ethnic intimidation.

To illustrate his point, he recounts this incident from May 2009:

I was in my car at a traffic light and I saw about four white high school kids, about 16 or 17 years old, harassing two Latino men in the parking lot of a Walgreens. The white kids were yelling and pushing the Latinos. They had encircled them. They were humiliating them, insulting them. I was about five meters away in my car when I parked, so I could see and hear what happened.

One of the high school kids started to push one of the Latinos like he wanted to fight. But the Latino guy, he did nothing, because, this is what I'm telling you—Latinos here are afraid. They are afraid if they defend themselves they'll get put in jail or deported, because the police are not fair.

Next, I saw all four of the high school kids start to kick one of the Latino men. I got out of my car. I told them, "Why are you doing this?" They said they were just playing. I told them they were racists. I told the Latinos they were stupid. I said, "Why are you letting them do this?"

I told them, "Defend yourselves!" But they said no. They were too worried about the police.

It's like what I said. Too many Latinos are terrified. They are terrified to know that if they defend themselves, they get taken away in handcuffs.

Practically, as an immigrant, you don't have any rights here.

Because we're just "the illegals."

THE ENABLER

As misguided young men have engaged in violent attacks on Latino immigrants in Suffolk County, N.Y., some local politicians on the sidelines have been playing the role of cheerleaders. Far from acting as peacemakers, they have fed the atmosphere of hostility with rhetorical attacks of their own.

County Executive Steve Levy isn't the only public official engaging in the verbal immigrant-bashing, or the most extreme. But he is the highest-ranking, and since he was elected to his first term in November 2003 after promising a crackdown on illegal immigrants, Levy has been acting like the enabler-in-chief.

Soon after taking office, Levy proposed that Suffolk County police officers be empowered to detain Latinos solely on suspicion of being undocumented immigrants and turn them over to federal authorities for deportation. Police unions blocked the proposal, arguing that it would compromise public safety by making immigrants all the more wary of providing information about criminal activity.

In June 2005, Levy oversaw zoning violation raids on 11 houses in Farmingville and the eviction of 200 Latino day laborers and their family members. He then refused to meet with immigrant-rights advocates. "I'm not one who's going to be intimidated by their antics or marches," he said. "Bring it on."

Later the same month, Levy mocked demonstrators who protested the raids. "I will not back down to this one percent lunatic fringe," he said. "They evidently do not like me much because I am one of the few officials who are not intimidated by their politically correct histrionics."

At a forum in 2006, he said that women crossing the border to give birth in the United States "free of charge" were having "anchor babies," and he asserted that Southampton Hospital was on the verge of closing its maternity ward because of the births. The ward remained open.

In 2007, Levy was interviewed by the *New York Times* about his championing of local ordinances designed to drive undocumented immigrants out of the county. "People who play by the rules work hard to achieve the suburban dream of the white picket fence," Levy told the newspaper. "If you live in the suburbs, you do not want to live across the street from a house where 60 men live. You do not want trucks riding up and down the block at 5 a.m., picking up workers."

As part of his efforts to protect the suburban dream, Levy co-founded Mayors and Executives for Immigration Reform, a national group that promotes immigrant-cleansing ordinances. He described critics of the organization as "Communists" and "anarchists."

In the days after the Nov. 8, 2008, slaying of Marcelo Lucero, Levy at first minimized the significance of the hate-crime murder. Had it happened elsewhere, he said, it would have been just a "one-day story."

That comment outraged Latinos and Suffolk County activists, among others, and Levy backpedaled. He apologized about a week later.

But Levy also denied any link between Lucero's death and his administration's targeting of undocumented Latino immigrants. "Advocates for those here illegally should not disparage those opposed to the illegal immigration policy as being bigoted or intolerant," he said.

It wasn't long before Levy was back to making flippant comments about Lucero's murder. While speaking to a gathering of business people, he compared the difficulties he was having in dealing with the fallout of the killing to the discomfort of undergoing a colonoscopy.

26

WHAT EXPLAINS THE IMMIGRANT RIGHTS MARCHES OF 2006?
Xenophobia and Organizing with Democracy Technology

Pierrette Hondagneu-Sotelo and Angelica Salas

During the spring of 2006, millions of people, most of them Latino immigrants of various nationalities and ages, took to the streets to raise their voices and placards demanding justice in immigration reform. The marches were in favor of immigrant inclusion and civil rights—specifically, the right to legal status. Among the protestors were many people without legal, authorized immigration status. Cries of "Hoy marchamos, manana votamos" (Today we march, tomorrow we vote), and placards demanding "Full Rights for Immigrants!" but also "We Love U.S.A. Too!" filled the streets. Many of the marchers wore white, to symbolize peace, and carried American flags. Hundreds of marchers in Los Angeles wore a t-shirt featuring the imprint of El Cucuy, a popular Spanish-language DJ who was instrumental, along with a few of his DJ colleagues, in disseminating the call to get out in the streets. The t-shirt succinctly summarized the rationale behind the marchers' claim to legalization: "This nation was built by immigrants! And that's it!" New immigrants were claiming the right to legal status, and ultimately American citizenship, not on the basis of existing laws but on the basis of their economic contributions as immigrant workers.

These largely Latino mobilizations peaked on April 10, 2006, with "The National Day of Action for Immigrant Social Justice," when immigrant rights marches and rallies occurred in over sixty cities. The mainstream media was taken aback by the dimensions of the marches and by the simultaneity of large demonstrations in New York City, San Francisco, Chicago, and many smaller cities. In fact, not only the English-language media but also political pundits, social movement observers, and political scientists were caught by surprise. But this movement did not drop out of the sky overnight. The marches were not spontaneous. These had been quietly brewing, nurtured by key grassroots leaders and organizations for many years.

We argue that three themes explain the development of this massive immigrant rights mobilization. First, different tributaries flowed into the immigrant rights marches of spring 2006. A long process of organizing by people in many sectors, including organized labor, legal advocates, traditional civil rights leaders, different religious organizations, and an emerging sector of immigrant rights activists allowed for these manifestations to emerge. Bringing the different strands together into a finely coordinated national effort was a long-term process. Second, the immigrant rights movement developed in reaction to growing restrictionism. It emerged in reaction not to growing immigration but, rather, in response to the urgencies posed by racialized nativism (directed largely, but not entirely, against Mexicans), xenophobia, and restrictionism. Third, national coordination and mobilization of the masses hinged on the harnessing of communications technology for democracy. These included Spanish-language radio broadcasts and the dedicated efforts of a handful of Los Angeles–based but nationally distributed DJs, themselves Mexican and Central American immigrants, and the dissemination power of communications technologies. Telephone conference calls and the long arm of Spanish-language radio emerged as the new democracy technology, as important disseminators of information. At the local level, cell phones and internet technology helped bring youth to the streets. These tools enabled networking and tightly coordinated collective action, allowing for the mass, nationwide mobilizations for immigrant rights.

THE LEGACY OF IMMIGRANT EXCLUSION AND RESTRICTIONISM

The burgeoning immigrant rights movement has emerged in tandem with and in response to restrictionist immigration laws and legislation. For this reason, we begin by noting the legal legacies and dimensions of contemporary immigration to the United States. Our starting point is this: The United States is a nation of immigrants with a long legacy of anti-immigrant and blatantly racist exclusion laws. In fact, the nation's first major federal immigration law was one of explicit racial exclusion, the Chinese Exclusion Act of 1882. With a few exceptions, U.S. immigration laws have been more about promoting exclusions, barriers, and quotas rather than integration, social cohesion, and inclusion.

Still, there are distinctive periods of immigration legal history. The period from about 1965 to 1980 was one of liberal reform in immigration law in the United States. That liberal era was inaugurated by the 1965 Immigration Act, which ended racial exclusions for Asians and promoted family reunification and a new quota system as the basis for obtained legal entrance and permanent residency. This was followed by the 1980s

Refugee Act, which sought to uncouple U.S. foreign policy from decisions about who to admit as refugees.

Since the 1980s, we have seen a barrage of anti-immigration legislative effort and administrative decisions, and the new immigrant rights movement emerged in response to these efforts. In this time, new immigrants to the United States have faced hostility in workplaces, talk radio, newspaper editorials, and the legislative corridors of political power. This hostility has been codified in immigration laws. Beginning in the 1980s, a steady stream of immigrant restrictionist legislation has been enacted. Highlights of key restrictionist legislation of recent decades include the Immigration Reform and Control Act (IRCA) in 1986, with its attempt to diminish the undocumented immigrant population through the implementation of employer sanctions; California's Proposition 187, which sought to control and diminish undocumented immigrants by denying public education and health services to undocumented immigrants and their children (this ultimately proved unconstitutional); and the federal 1996 Illegal Immigration Reform and Immigrant Responsibility Act (IIRIRA), which curtailed the rights of both unauthorized immigrants and legal permanent immigrants.

Immigration law remains the jurisdiction of the federal government, but in recent years we have also seen the emergence of anti-immigrant vigilante groups, such as the Minutemen and Ranch Rescue. Simultaneously, we have also witnessed efforts by state governments to restrict immigrants by denying driver's licenses to undocumented immigrants. Municipalities have joined the restrictionist bandwagon by passing laws against renting residential units to undocumented immigrants and by authorizing local law enforcement authorities to enforce federal immigration laws. Mexicans and Latino immigrants have become the favored targets.

While racialized nativism, xenophobia, and restrictionist efforts have been many faced, multipronged efforts, the mass marches in favor of immigrant rights during the spring of 2006 were in direct response to one particular proposed national bill, H.R. 4437, introduced in December 2005, and colloquially known as the Sensenbrenner bill. H.R. 4437 included provisions for fortifying 700 miles of fence at the U.S.-Mexico border; new fines and fees for legal residency applications; the imposition of a minimum sentence of ten years for those using fraudulent documents; deportation for legal immigrants convicted of DUI; and criminalization of anyone assisting undocumented immigrants, potentially even priests or social workers who teach English classes or offer food and water. While H.R. 4437 galvanized both the restrictionists and the immigrant rights advocates, it is important to acknowledge that it was only the latest in a long line of anti-immigrant legislative efforts.

By the spring of 2006, an estimated 12 million immigrants were living in the United States without authorized legal status. The majority of them were people embraced by U.S. labor markets and employers but legally excluded through immigration law. The immigrant rights movement of spring 2006 focused on this fundamental flaw in the

U.S. immigration system: the subordination, disenfranchisement, and partial inclusion of millions of immigrants. The primary demand centered on gaining front-door legal status for 12 million people. Below, we detail how this unfolded.

IMMIGRANT RIGHTS ADVOCACY IN THE 1980S: PROVIDING LEGAL SERVICE

Advocates have been working for immigrant rights for many years. These advocates and activists, drawn from ethnic communities, legal services, labor organizing, and religious sectors, have generally found themselves reacting to legal and policy assaults on immigrants. The first big formation and national coordination of immigrant rights efforts came in response to legislation of the 1980s that intended to deter illegal immigration by imposing employer sanctions at the workplace on employers who hired immigrants unauthorized to work legally and that included an amnesty-legalization provision.[1]

With IRCA, the undocumented immigrant population was cast into two groups: those who would qualify for legalization and those who would be criminalized at the workplace. In response to these new uncertainties and opportunities, legal service providers, advocates, and community organizers responded with services, outreach information, and advocacy. And as communities across the country grappled with similar issues, immigrant rights coalitions cropped up in all major U.S. cities.[2] In California, the Coalition for Humane Immigrant Rights in Los Angeles (CHIRLA) emerged, bringing together many different organizations. Similar coalitions devoted to promoting immigrant rights and services emerged in San Francisco, New York State, Massachusetts, Chicago, and Texas.

These citywide and statewide coalitions worked with national organizations like the National Network for Immigrant and Refugee Rights (NNIRR) and the National Immigration Forum. The National Network, based in Oakland, California, served as a grassroots think tank, providing leadership on organizing around immigrant issues, and it served as a forum through which the citywide immigrant and refugee rights coalitions could share information and develop strategies to advance their cause. The National Immigration Forum provided policy updates, organized national lobby days, and directed legislative advocacy in Washington, D.C.

The period of the 1980s was marked by responding to the urgencies and contingencies of IRCA. For the first time, "immigrant rights" entered the lexicon. These organizations and their leaders were involved in some lobbying efforts, but providing services for amnesty-legalization needs consumed most of their time. As soon as IRCA was signed into effect in November 1986, community centers and churches in undocumented-immigrant neighborhoods were filled with lawyers and service providers explaining the barrage of documents, forms, and fees that successful applicants for legalization would need. Groups such as U.S. Catholic Charities, the International Institute, One Stop

Immigration, and Hermandad Mexicana used both paid staff and volunteers to help Mexican immigrants navigate the confusing federal instructions required by amnesty-legalization provisions. There were some efforts at organizing the undocumented immigrants, who would not qualify for amnesty legalization.

Meanwhile, civil rights organizations such as the Mexican American Legal and Educational Defense, American Civil Liberties Union, and National Association of Latino Elected and Appointed Officials (NALEO) sought to document and deter the most egregious employment discriminatory outcomes of IRCAs I-9 forms. To reiterate, most immigrant rights efforts during the 1980s, however, were directed at providing legal services.

THE 1990S: TOWARD AN ORGANIZING MODEL

Organizing for immigrant rights as a strategy took off in the mid-1990s. This was largely in response to the devastating effect of IIRIRA and Welfare Reform in 1996. Both pieces of legislation demoted undocumented immigrants, as well as legal permanent residents.[3] Before this moment, much of the effort around immigrant rights had been toward providing services with sporadic mobilizing, as was the case against Proposition 187 in California.

In the 1990s, more efforts were directed at organizing immigrants to become involved in the public sphere around particular issues. One arena that galvanized momentum in the 1990s was the citizenship movement. In the 1980s, IRCA allowed 3.1 million persons to obtain legal status, and when California's Proposition 187 placed undocumented immigrant relatives of those newly legalized people in jeopardy, many newly legalized people opted to naturalize as U.S. citizens. "Citizenship USA," a national campaign to streamline the naturalization process, was supported by Democrats such as President Bill Clinton, and the philanthropist George Soros supported citizenship efforts by funding new campaigns.

The 1990s also witnessed an upsurge in innovative labor organizing for immigrant workers toiling on the margins, usually in low-wage, highly exploitative jobs in informal-sector labor markets. In Los Angeles, the Garment Workers Center spurred organizing among immigrant workers toiling in sweatshops, and the Justice for Janitors campaign successfully organized janitors, mostly Latino immigrants; in addition, the Service Employees International Union (SEIU) organized nearly 100,000 mostly immigrant homecare workers into the union as Local 434B. Meanwhile, CHIRLA became a staging ground for labor organizing among immigrants working as day laborers and domestic workers. A national organization of day laborers was eventually established.

On the other side of the country, the Long Island Workplace Project brought undocumented immigrant workers together to fight for fair wages, dignity, and safe working conditions. From Los Angeles to Long Island, undocumented domestic workers and day laborers won job improvements and new social recognition.

2000: ORGANIZED LABOR MOVES FROM EXCLUSION TO INCLUSION

Organized labor's turn toward an inclusive immigration politics also contributed mightily to the growing immigrant rights movement. After decades of declining rates of unionization, a revitalized labor movement emerged in the United States at the turn of the millennial century. Spearheaded by progressive leaders working at the grassroots level and in the AFL-CIO, the movement gained momentum with the rise of service sector unions; the concerted cultivation of community allies; and a new commitment to organizing women, minorities, and immigrant workers.[4]

The decision to support immigrant workers and to strive to organize them represented a 180-degree turn in labor's approach. Overnight, immigrants went from being seen as organized labors' nemesis and lower-wage competitor to becoming part of organized labors winning card.[5] As established labor unions sought to organize hotel and restaurant cooks, housekeepers, and janitors, they achieved major success. We have seen this new face of the labor movement and its organizing and integration of immigrant workers chronicled in newspaper headlines, weekly newsmagazines, and even a docudrama style movie, *Bread and Roses*.

Part of organized labor's new strategy involved the concerted cultivation of community support, such as the support of clergy, laity, and students. Building these new alliances allowed organized labor to meet with immigrant rights organizers. This was quite significant. Immigrant rights organizers and community activists had been working for immigrant rights for years, but until then, and with a few notable exceptions, the union leaders had remained tone deaf. When organized labor began singing the tune of immigrant rights, new coalitions emerged among people from community groups, religious organizations, and the labor movement.

Then, to promote a new amnesty legalization and build momentum for repealing employer sanctions, the AFL-CIO sponsored a series of public, regional forums in New York City, Atlanta, Chicago, and Los Angeles, where immigrants gave testimonies. On June 10, 2000, some 20,000 people packed the Los Angeles Sports Arena to participate in this event. Unions, community organizations, and church congregations supported the forums, bringing their respective constituencies together and building momentum for an immigrant rights movement. Students, congregation members, and rank and file workers came together to voice their support for a massive legalization program. The unions also sparked a national postcard campaign, recruiting 1 million people to sign and send postcards to Washington in favor of legalization, just before 9/11. Other sectors joined in this effort, including the Roman Catholic Church and Mexican hometown associations.

Labor organizers with connections to Latino immigrant communities proved to be central players in this new movement. Organizers such as Miguel Contreras, Fabian Núñez (then with the Los Angeles County Federation of Labor), Eliseo Medina, and

María Elena Durazo came from Mexican immigrant families and had been influenced by the Chicano movement and the United Farm Workers.

Durazo, for example, emerged as a strong leader who helped bring "immigrant rights" to the core of the AFL-CIO. The child of Mexican immigrants, and one of ten siblings who had worked in California's agricultural fields, she stems from roots that are strikingly similar to those of César Chávez. Durazo, trained as a lawyer, began her labor-organizing career in garment sweatshops and then moved on to organizing hotel and restaurant workers.[6] As she later testified before Congress, when she began as an organizer with Local 11 she witnessed not only unfair treatment of the immigrant workers by the employers but also by the union:

> I got hired as an organizer at Local 11 in 1983 and for 4 years I witnessed a Union deteriorate right before my very eyes. The leadership of that Local had a policy of exclusion. 70% of the members are immigrants from Mexico and Central America. The meetings were held in English only; the publications were sent out in English only and members rarely attended meetings. The office closed down at 4 p.m.—the time most members were getting off their shifts.[7]

Durazo led a rank and file effort to change union leadership and policies. The cooks, dishwashers, and housekeepers she organized were, like those in the garment industry, predominantly Spanish-speaking, Latino immigrant workers. Under her leadership, Local 11 emerged as a union at the forefront of the struggle for Latino immigrant worker rights, a union not shy about using aggressive tactics, such as strikes, boycotts, and fasts.

It was under Durazo's HERE (Hotel Employees and Restaurant Employees International Union) leadership and influence that the national AFL-CIO undertook the ambitious Immigrant Workers Freedom Ride campaign in the fall of 2003. Inspired by the "freedom riders" of the civil rights movement of the 1960s, this campaign involved busloads of union supporters traveling from ten cities throughout America to converge on Washington to lobby Congress and show broad support for immigrant civil rights. Designed also to teach Latino immigrant workers about African American civil rights struggles, the bus riders descended on the city to push for amnesty legalization. Initiated by HERE, the freedom ride won support and participation from religious groups and leaders, community groups, immigrant rights activists, and local and national politicians.

RELIGIOUS SUPPORT FOR IMMIGRANT RIGHTS

Religion has provided a wellspring of support for immigrant rights advocacy in the contemporary United States. Consider these facts. All of the major, mainline religions have issued statements in favor of antirestrictionist reform. Among the most prominent are the pastoral letters issued by the U.S. Conference of Catholic Bishops. In 2000, they issued a statement declaring. "We advocate for just policies that respect human rights of immigrants," and stated opposition to policies that attempt to stem migration but do not "adequately address its root causes."[8]

In 2003, together with the Mexican bishops, they issued a historic joint statement, "Strangers No Longer: Together on the Journey of Hope." Citing New and Old Testament and Catholic social teachings, the statement focused primarily on the world's largest and longest-running labor migration, US.-bound Mexican migration. While recognizing the right of a sovereign state to control its borders, the statement's declaration is unabashedly in favor of migrant rights. If people are unable to find employment in their home societies, the bishops declared, then "they have a right to find work elsewhere in order to survive. Sovereign nations should provide ways to accommodate this right."[9] Building on this earlier momentum, in June 2004, the U.S. Conference of Catholic Bishops launched the Justice for Immigrants campaign, laying a moral foundation for comprehensive immigration reform.

Consequently, religious leaders were visible and vocal in the immigrant rights marches of 2006. Cardinal Roger M. Mahony, the leader of the nation's largest archdiocese in Los Angeles, garnered national media attention when he denounced the Sensenbrenner bill as "un-American." He publicly stated that he would urge priests to resist orders to ask immigrants for legal papers, and during Lent he asked Catholics to fast and pray for social justice in immigration reform. He and his organization cosponsored an immigrant rights march on May 1. In the marches of spring 2006, the Catholics were joined by Presbyterians, Muslims, Lutherans, and Episcopalians, among others. The National Hispanic Christian Leadership Conference, an organization of Latino Evangelical ministers led by the Reverend Samuel Rodriguez also threw their support behind immigrant rights and even pushed the National Association of Evangelicals to issue a statement in support of immigration reform.

COMPREHENSIVE IMMIGRATION REFORM AND THE FAIR IMMIGRATION REFORM MOVEMENT (FIRM)

The Coalition for Comprehensive Immigration Reform (CCIR) was formed by national and local immigrant rights, labor, and community leaders and policy makers in 2004. The board of directors included immigrant rights activists from different sectors—labor unions, such as SEIU and UNITE HERE!, as well as immigrant rights coalitions from Los Angeles, New York, and Illinois and law centers and policy groups such as the Asian American Justice Center and the National Council of La Raza. Based in Washington, D.C., CCIR's goal was to pass progressive immigration legislation.

The New American Opportunity Campaign (NAOC) was launched as a legislative campaign for comprehensive immigration reform and as an alternative to the purely punitive and restrictionist proposals. The key organizing principles for NAOC include the following commitment to immigration reform:

1. Encourage comprehensive reform
2. Provide a path to citizenship
3. Protect workers (U.S.-born and immigrant workers)
4. Reunite families
5. Restore the rule of law and enhance security
6. Promote citizenship and civic participation[10]

The Fair Immigration Reform Movement (FIRM) was launched in May 2000 as the campaign of the Immigrant Organizing Committee (IOC). The IOC was a coming together of over thirty immigrant and nonimmigrant organizations from across the nation whose priority was organizing immigrants to change workplace conditions and reform immigration policy. The IOC prioritized building alliances with other antipoverty groups.

The participants involved in CCIR and FIRM were scattered across the country. While spatial distance could potentially hinder nationally coordinated efforts among so many disparate organizations, the geographical distribution of these organizations was also an asset, assuring greater outreach. But this would require close communication and coordination, and new communications technology facilitated this. Bimonthly telephone conference calls allowed key leaders in Washington and in the major cities where immigrant rights activism was more developed to discuss the issues. This allowed advocates in more distant, smaller immigrant communities located in places like Nebraska, Rhode Island, and Connecticut to listen in and become informed of the rapidly changing political context, and then to coordinate commensurate strategies. This resulted in a tight web of communication among community-based organizations, unions, advocates, and policy makers.

From the period of December 2004 to May 2005, the strategy was to develop a strong bipartisan bill on immigration reform. Community-based organizations, labor, religious, and business sectors were all involved, and this effort resulted in the Kennedy-McCain Bill (S. 1033, the Secure America and Orderly Immigration Act), with specific provisions for legalization. Delicate negotiations were brokered among different sectors and communities. Advocates targeted legislators to gain their support and endorsements.

Advocates for comprehensive immigration reform had planned to introduce the bill in the Senate, but Hurricane Katrina and two U.S. Supreme Court nominations garnered attention first. Things seemed to be moving smoothly until Senator Sensenbrenner introduced his bill, which he had been working on for about a year, before the immigrant rights advocates introduced theirs. Once again, immigrant rights organizers were put on the defensive. This new urgency to the immigrant rights cause prompted the flurry of immigrant rights marches and rallies.

THE MARCHES AND RALLIES OF SPRING 2006

Immigrant rights activists needed to show strong public support against the Sensenbrenner bill. On March 7, 2006, the National Capitol Immigrant Coalition organized a march of 40,000 in Washington, D.C. On that same day, NAOC announced a National Week of Action around immigrant rights for March 20–27. Through conference calls, organizers around the country were urged to mobilize rallies and protests in favor of progressive immigration reform. Both the NAOC and FIRM, for example, organized bimonthly and weekly conference calls that included as many as 300 simultaneous participants listening in as organizers shared reports from their cities.

Massive marches and protests in favor of immigrant rights ensued in late March and on April 10 and May 1. In Los Angeles, 500,000 took to the streets on March 25. On April 10, "The National Day of Action for Immigrant Social Justice," marches and rallies took place in more than sixty cities around the United States. And on May 1, more than 1 million people gathered in protest rallies throughout the country. While professional advocates and organizers from community-based groups, unions, and religious congregations had laid the groundwork, and had used conference calls and face-to-face meetings to coordinate their efforts, an unlikely group of advocates stepped to the fore at the last minute to bring out the masses: Spanish-language DJs on commercial radio.

HOW THE BOGEYMAN, TWEETYBIRD, AND THE BABOON GOT PEOPLE TO THE STREETS

Commercial radio, either in English or Spanish, does not usually promote protest or social justice advocacy. But in the spring of 2006, that changed when three enormously popular Spanish-language DJs in Los Angeles adopted the immigrant rights cause. "El Cucuy" (the Bogeyman, also known as Renán Almendárez Coello), "El Piolín" (Tweetybird, Eddie Sotelo), and "El Mandril" (the Baboon, Ricardo Sanchez) are three extraordinarily popular morning DJs. They are all immigrants from Mexico and Central America. Sotelo says he entered the country illegally in the trunk of a car in 1986 before getting legal status in the 1990s. After they were approached by organizers of the March protests, they put their weight behind the cause and even tried to outdo one another, promoting the protest, featuring immigrant rights advocates on the air, and hosting audience call-ins on all sorts of immigration legal matters.

Latino immigrant workers do watch Spanish-language television and read newspapers, but radio is a form of media that is particularly important to this community. This is a population that is hyperemployed, with many adults holding two or three jobs. Radio is easily accessible to people traveling to work in cars and trucks or listening at work places. The DJs also enjoy a kind of rapport with their listeners that TV news broadcasters and newspaper writers do not. These DJs come from similar immigrant backgrounds as their listeners, and they have a particularly close rapport with their audiences. Not surprisingly, Arbitron reports have consistently shown that the shows of these DJs are the highest-rated radio programs in *any* language in Los Angeles. In recent years, as Mexican and Central American immigrant workers have fanned out to fill labor demands in poultry processing plants, furniture factories, construction, and services in new destinations in the Southeast and Midwest, these DJs' radio programs have been broadcast throughout the nation.

Ethnic media is important in immigrant communities, but most ethnic media is taken up with entertainment and advertisements. This was true of their radio shows, which typically featured, until spring of 2006, a mix of ribald, sexually picaresque humor on the Cucuy show and music, skits, and humor on the Mandrill show. These were and largely remain talk-entertainment shows with call-ins, loud gags, and recorded laugh tracks. In March, a group of immigrant rights organizers in Los Angeles (including Jesse Diaz, Gloria Saucedo, Angela Sanbrano, Angelica Salas, and Javier Rodriguez) went on El Piolin's morning show to tell the public about the proposals of the Sensenbrenner Bill. El Piolin, Eddie Sotelo, decided to call a summit with his rival DJs to urge them to get the word out. By March 16, 17, and 18, 2006, the DJs were telling their listeners to call the offices of Senator Dianne Feinstein and to join in solidarity for the March 25 immigrant rights march.

Immigrant rights organizers made regular appearances on the Spanish-language DJ shows. Angelica Salas, executive director of the Coalition for Humane Immigrant Rights in Los Angeles, found herself appearing as a regular guest, through a call-in, on the 6 a.m. El Piolin show, answering immigration questions from listeners, providing legislative updates, and urging people to attend the upcoming marches. Public service announcements on Spanish-language television followed.

These radio shows expanded from purely commercial entertainment venues to constituting nothing less than a big democratic town hall meeting on immigration reform. Listeners called in with questions about how the proposed reforms would affect them and their families, were educated about the legislative proposals, and received, quite literally, their marching orders. While the DJs broadcast out of Los Angeles, their shows and information reached Latino immigrant listeners in Houston, Las Vegas, Minnesota, and Idaho.

WHAT EXPLAINS THE MASS MARCHES?

The efforts of organizers working from different sectors, the urgency of responding to restrictionist legislation and sentiment, and the democracy technology explains why rallies in favor of immigrant rights occurred in over sixty cities on May 1, 2006. While the goal of a nonpunitive, comprehensive immigration reform that will feature legalization has not yet been reached, the manifested groundswell of support for immigrant rights is unlikely to wither. All of the conditions that gave rise to it are still in place. The commitment to organizing for immigrant rights is still visible among professional advocates in the Washington beltway and among grassroots organizers in labor, churches, and community-based organizations around the country. These groups are now better networked and better acquainted with one another, although there have been the inevitable conflicts that come with coalition work. The harsh restrictionism exemplified by the Sensenbrenner bill has not disappeared. And finally, not only is the technology of conference calls, radio airwaves, and cell phones still with us, but the organizers have learned the power of mobilization through this communications technology. The celebrity DJs have discovered their power as leaders and have used this to further an agenda of democracy, civil engagement, and legal inclusion.

Social movement scholars always want to know why collective moments for social change emerge when they do. As we have shown in this essay, the immigrant rights movement already had several decades of traction before the massive street debut in the spring of 2006. The union leaders, clergy and laity, professional advocates, and grassroots community leaders who laid this foundation are still working in the trenches. So what explains the marches?

More than resource mobilization, political opportunity structures, or new creative framing of grievances, the massive immigrant rights mobilizations of spring 2006 are best explained by the confluence of three factors. This includes long-term organizing from many sectors, the urgency of reactively responding to proposed legislation, and the powerful communications technologies (conference calls, cell phones, and the airwaves). In an effort to search for explanations, and to understand why and how this was possible, we should not overlook the most stunning fact: this was an instance of people at various stages of legality and partial inclusion demanding full inclusion for themselves and for their communities. While the meaning of citizenship is changing in the context of globalization and transnationalism, it is clear that millions of immigrants are not consigned to remaining in legal limbo and partial inclusion. For them, immigrant rights is nothing less than citizenship rights.

NOTES

1. Simpson-Mazzoli legislation, with employer sanctions at its centerpiece, was introduced in the 1980s. It subsequently morphed into the Simpson-Rodino Bill, which eventually became the Immigration Reform and Control Act (IRCA) of 1986. IRCA mandated employer sanctions but also provided provisions for amnesty legalization for those immigrants who could prove they had resided continuously in the United States for five years or who could prove they had worked a certain amount of time in agriculture.

2. These groups came out of efforts to respond to the legal and service needs of the some 3.1 million immigrants who were able to qualify for legal status under IRCA's new amnesty-legalization provisions.

3. IIRIRA created devastating losses for new immigrant communities and, for the first time, rolled back the rights of legal permanent residents. The main advocates in Washington, D.C., such as the National Immigration Forum and the National Council of La Raza, responded directly by trying to safeguard the rights of legal permanent residents, asylum seekers, and immigrants with temporary legal authorization. This was something of a triage system. While the needs of legal resident immigrants received attention, the needs of undocumented immigrants were ignored.

4. On the contemporary resurgence of labor and efforts to mobilize immigrant workers, see Hector L. Delgado, *New Immigrants, Old Unions* (Philadelphia: Temple University Press, 1995); Ruth Milkman, *L.A. Story: Immigrant Workers and the Future of the U.S. Labor Movement* (New York: Russell Sage Foundation, 2006); Immanuel Ness, *Immigrants, Unions, and the New U.S. Labor Market* (Philadelphia: Temple University Press, 2005).

5. Organized labor, with the exception of the International Workers of the World (the Wobblies), has a long legacy of immigrant and racial exclusion in the United States. In fact, the unions were key in promoting anti-immigrant exclusionary laws. Samuel Gompers built the American Federation of Labor as an organization reserved for white, male, U.S.-citizen workers, and the AFL steadfastly opposed immigrant workers, especially Chinese immigrant workers in the late nineteenth century. Similarly, Dennis Kearney's Workingman's Party advocated exclusion of Chinese immigrant workers and promoted vigilante violence against them. Later, the United Farm Workers Union, under César Chávez, initially viewed Mexican immigrant workers as a threat and a wage-cutting competitor to U.S.-born Mexican migrant farm workers. Later, the UFW changed this policy and organized both U.S.-born and Mexican-born farmworkers. For most of the twentieth century, however, organized labor continued to see immigrant workers as a threat, not as a potential source of solidarity.

6. By 2006 Durazo was the executive secretary-treasurer (the leader) of the Los Angeles County Federation of Labor, representing 850,000 union members and 350 local unions.

7. María Elena Durazo, *Public Testimony to the Subcommittee on Employer-Employee Relations Committee on Education and the Workforce U.S. House of Representatives*, Wednesday, July 21, 1999, at http://www.house.gov/edworkforce/hearings/106th/eer/ud72199/durazo .html (accessed May 24, 2006).

8. U.S. Conference of Catholic Bishops, *Welcoming the Stranger among Us: Unity in Diversity*, Pastoral Statement, November 15, 2000, at http://www.usccb.org/mrs/welcome.shtml (accessed May 24, 2006).

9. U.S. Conference of Catholic Bishops and Conferencia del Episcopado Mexicano, *Stranger No Longer: Together on a Journey of Hope*, Pastoral Letter Concerning Migration from the Catholic Bishops of Mexico and the United States, January 22, 2003, at http://www .usccb.org/mrs/stranger.shtml#1 (accessed May 24, 2006).

10. Coalition for Comprehensive Immigration Reform, *CCIR Principles*, at http://www .cirnow.org/content/en/about_principles.htm (accessed November 4, 2006).

27

WET FOOT, DRY FOOT . . . WRONG FOOT

Ann Louise Bardach

Every Cuban knows the wet-foot/dry-foot drill: risk fleeing to the United States and get caught at sea, and you will be sent back to the island; but if you wangle just one toe onto dry land, you're home free. From there, it's a fast track to permanent residency, eligibility for all manner of benefits (from green cards to welfare), then onto citizenship—all compliments of the Cuban Adjustment Act of 1966. Indeed, for a half century, Cubans have been the most privileged immigrants in the United States.

The repeal of this Cold War relic of immigration policy is long overdue. In January 2015—on the same day that the highest-level American diplomat in almost 40 years arrived in Cuba, the Miami-Dade County Commission unanimously voted to petition Congress to revise the act. Should the commission get its wish, the wet-foot/dry-foot policy, devised in 1995, would likely also be upended.

Most Americans are under the impression that the Republican Party is unequivocally opposed to amnesty for immigrants. In fact, the GOP has long backed a blanket amnesty—but only for Cubans. For every other hopeful immigrant, the party's message has been clear: "Deportations, deportations, deportations," to quote Jorge Ramos, the Walter Cronkite of Spanish-language television. "Why?"

One answer is that the 2.1 million Cuban Americans have been, until quite recently, a rock-solid GOP constituency. There is also a race and class issue. Unlike most of Central and Latin America, Cuba does not have an indigenous population (the Spanish slaughtered almost all the native Indians of the island). When the Cuban Adjustment Act was created in the 1960s, those fleeing the Castros' island fiefdom were almost entirely white, educated, and middle or upper class—a demographic that did not change substantially until the 1980 Mariel exodus.

In 2014 the number of Central and Latin American migrants sharply declined; for Cubans, however, it was a record year. About 30,000 migrants took to the Florida Straits or arrived via Mexico (the preferred route for those who can afford the flight). In 2015 even more fled Cuba for the United States. Not since the *Balseros* (Rafters) crisis of 1994 have so many Cubans attempted the crossing. But unlike the Mexicans, Guatemalans, Salvadorans, and Haitians—all of whom received the heave-ho—each Cuban is welcome.

Word has spread that the two pieces of legislation that make up the Cuban Privilege might not be around much longer. Since December 17, 2014, when President Obama reestablished relations with Cuba, the waters between the two countries have been swarming with migrants.

Not all Cuban stories have a happy ending. The year 2015 began with a makeshift craft tossing four Cubans into the roiling sea. Three young men miraculously made it to shore, but a fourth companion drowned. Almost every week, there is a similar story, often with higher casualties. Some migrants try five or 10 times before they successfully cross the 90 miles of water. How many have not made it? Thousands for sure over the past 50 years—making the Florida Straits the world's largest aquatic graveyard (at least, since the end of the slave trade).

Fidel and Raúl Castro have long demanded an end to the Cuban Adjustment Act, claiming that the policy causes a brain drain. (Of course, they never acknowledge why more than a million Cubans have risked their lives to escape.) The January vote in Miami, however, stemmed from different motivations: Commissioner Bruno Barreiro, whose family were beneficiaries of the act, argued that the Castro brothers have long exploited the law to ship out dissidents and to infiltrate spies into the exile community of South Florida. Moreover, *el exilio histórico* (the old guard, who are generally older, wealthier, and whiter), have long complained that the new arrivals from Cuba are economic migrants, not political refugees fleeing Communism—the law's raison d'être— and thus should not be awarded their coveted status. Worse, they fume, many of them turn out to be virtual commuters scuttling between the two Cubas: Miami and Havana.

While all this is true, there are more compelling reasons to end the Cuban Privilege. One of them is fairness. Are Cubans seeking a better way of life really more deserving than, say, refugees fleeing death squads or drug cartels?

Another is its enablement of a veritable crime syndicate: according to a 2014 series in the *Sun Sentinel* (Broward County, Florida), a small cadre of Cuban crooks specializing in Medicare and insurance fraud have bilked American tax payers and businesses out of more than $2 billion since 1994. Even when caught and prosecuted (many flee back to Cuba before capture or prison), they cannot be deported, because Cuba flatly refuses to accept them. (Note to State Department negotiators: make sure that loophole gets closed.)

It is not at all clear if these two relics of immigration policy will be scotched; the State Department has said they are not on the table. Much depends on the Hispanics in Congress, whose colleagues expect them to take the lead. But the three serving in the Senate happen to be, yup, Cuban American: Marco Rubio, Ted Cruz, and Robert Menéndez, and none have expressed any enthusiasm for revoking the Cuban Exception.

And herein lie some savory ironies.

Contrary to Beltway conventional wisdom, none of the three senators have particularly strong bona fides among Latinos. Indeed, being second-generation white Cuban exiles puts them at odds with the overwhelming majority of Latinos in the United States, who are of mixed-race/indigenous descent. In 2012 an anti-Rubio commercial that ran on Spanish-language TV ended with the punning tag *"No Somos Rubios,"* meaning "We are not Rubios" but, more importantly, "We are not blondes [whites]." Such is the price for Rubio's failure to back the Dream Act.

The issue has been worse for Ted Cruz, whose Latino credentials—being the son of a Cuban father, an Anglo mother, and famously born in Canada—have been challenged as anemic. "Ted Cruz is as much Hispanic as Tom Cruise," declaimed Gilberto Hinojosa, the chairman of the Texas Democratic Party, and a former county judge. "There is nothing, not an ounce, about the way he thinks and the way he has led his life that in any way is similar to Hispanics in the state of Texas and all across America."

No one expects virtue to prevail in politics. But if Mr. Rubio and Mr. Cruz are serious about their White House ambitions, they will need the votes of Latinos. That means they might want to see to it that fairness dictates immigration reform. And that means the end of the Cuban Adjustment Act and wet foot/dry foot. Imagine, three Cuban Americans—members of a group that enjoys an unprecedented, coveted status—get to decide the fate of millions of their less fortunate Hispanic brethren. Now that's rich. Only in America.

CONTRIBUTORS

TOMÁS ALMAGUER is Professor of Ethnic Studies and former Dean of the College of Ethnic Studies at San Francisco State University. His areas of specialization include the sociology of race and ethnicity, gender and sexuality studies, Latino gay studies, historical sociology, and Latino/a studies. He is the author of *Racial Fault Lines: The Historical Origins of White Supremacy in California* (2009).

FRANCES R. APARICIO is Professor of Spanish and Portuguese and Director of the Latina and Latino Studies Program at Northwestern University. She is author of *Listening to Salsa: Gender, Latin Popular Music and Puerto Rican Cultures* (1998), and co-editor of various critical anthologies, including *Tropicalizations: Transcultural Representations of Latinidad* (1997).

ANN LOUISE BARDACH is a journalist who has done extensive research on Cuban history and social relations. She is the author of *Without Fidel: A Death Foretold in Miami, Havana and Washington* (2014) and *Cuba Confidential: Love and Vengeance in Miami and Havana* (2003).

GINETTA E. B. CANDELARIO is Associate Professor of Sociology and Latin American and Latina/o Studies at Smith College. She is the author of *Black Behind the Ears: Dominican Identity from Museums to Beauty Shops* (2007) and editor of *Miradas desencadenantes: Los estudios de género en la República Dominicana al inicio del tercer milenio* (2005).

JORGE CHAPA was Professor of Latina/Latino Studies and Institute of Government and Public Affairs at the University of Illinois at Urbana-Champaign. He passed away in 2015. He wrote extensively on diversifying higher education, Latinos in the Midwest, quantitative methods, and racial disparities in health. He was the co-editor of *Implementing Diversity: Contemporary Challenges and Best Practices at Predominantly White Universities* (2010) and *Apple Pie and Enchiladas: Latino Newcomers in the Rural Midwest* (2004).

NICHOLAS DE GENOVA is Reader in Urban Geography in the Department of Geography at King's College London, where he is the Director of both the Cities Research Group and the Group on Spatial Politics. His research focuses on the conjunctures of racialization, labor subordination, and the politics of immigration and citizenship in the United States. He is the author of *Working the Boundaries: Race, Space, and "Illegality" in Mexican Chicago* (2005), and, with Ana Y. Ramos-Zayas, the co-author of *Latino Crossings: Mexicans, Puerto Ricans, and the Politics of Race and Citizenship* (2003).

G. WILLIAM DOMHOFF is formerly Professor of Psychology and Sociology and currently Research Professor at the University of California, Santa Cruz. His publications include *Who Rules America? The Triumph of the Corporate Rich* (7th ed., 2014), *The Myth of Liberal Ascendancy: Corporate Dominance from the Great Depression to the Great Recession* (2013), and with Richard L. Zweigenhaft, *The New CEOs* (2011).

JORGE DUANY is Professor of Anthropology in the Department of Global and Sociocultural Studies in the Steven J. Green School of International and Public Affairs at Florida International University and Director of the Cuban Research Institute. He is the author of *Blurred Borders: Transnational Migration between the Hispanic Caribbean and the United States* (2011) and *How the United States Racializes Latinos: White Hegemony and Its Consequences* (2009).

LUIS RICARDO FRAGA is the Arthur Foundation Endowed Professor of Transformative Latino Leadership and Professor of Political Science at the University of Notre Dame. He is the co-author of *Latinos in the New Millennium: An Almanac of Opinion, Behavior, and Policy Preferences* (2012) and *Latino Lives in America: Making It Home* (2010).

LORENA GARCÍA is Associate Professor of Sociology at the University of Illinois, Chicago, with theoretical and methodological interest in the intersection of gender, sexuality, and race/ethnicity. She is the author of *Respect Yourself, Protect Yourself: Latina Girls and Sexual Identity* (2012) and currently at work on a book on Latina/o families, focused on partnering and parenting.

LISA GARCÍA BEDOLLA is the Chancellor's Professor of Political Science and a faculty member of the Graduate School of Education at the University of California, Berkeley. Her research focuses on how marginalization and inequality structure the political and educational opportunities available to members of ethnoracial groups, with a particular emphasis on the intersections of race, class, and gender. She is the author of *Latino Politics* (2014) and co-author of *Mobilizing Inclusion: Transforming the Electorate through Get-Out-the-Vote Campaigns* (2012).

LILLIAN GUERRA is Professor of Cuban and Caribbean History at the University of Florida, and the author of several books, among them *Visions of Power in Cuba: Revolution, Redemption and Resistance, 1959–1971* (2012) and *The Myth of José Martí: Conflicting Nationalisms in Early Twentieth-Century Cuba* (2005).

DAVID G. GUTIÉRREZ is Professor of American History at the University of California, San Diego. His research focuses on the history of citizenship and civil rights in the United States, comparative immigration and ethnic history, and the history of Mexican America. His publications include *Walls and Mirrors: Mexican Americans, Mexican Immigrants, and the Politics of Ethnicity* (1995), and *Between Two Worlds: Mexican Immigrants in the United States* (1996).

RAMÓN A. GUTIÉRREZ is Preston and Sterling Morton Distinguished Service Professor of American History at the University of Chicago. His research and publications focus on race and ethnic relations in the Americas from 1492 to the present, religion and spirituality in the hemisphere, ethnic Mexican culture and politics on both sides of the border, immigration and adaptation in the United States, and inequality and diversity in American society. He is the author of several books, among them *When Jesus Came the Corn Mothers Went Away: Marriage, Sexuality, and Power in New Mexico, 1500–1846* (1991) and co-editor of *Mexicans in California: Emergent Challenges and Transformations* (2009).

DAVID E. HAYES-BAUTISTA is Distinguished Professor of Medicine and Director of the Center for the Study of Latino Health and Culture at the David Geffen School of Medicine at the University of California, Los Angeles. His research focuses on the dynamics and processes of the health of the Latino population using both quantitative data sets and qualitative observations. His publications include *El Cinco de Mayo: An American Tradition* (2012), *Nueva California: Latinos in the Golden State* (2004), and, with Werner Schink and Jorge Chapa, *The Burden of Support: Young Latinos in an Aging Society* (1990).

PIERRETTE HONDAGNEU-SOTELO is Professor of Sociology at the University of Southern California, where she also serves as Associate Director at the Center for the Study of Immigrant Integration. Her research examines how Latino immigrants negotiate challenges with informal sector work, varied legal status, and changing gender, family, and community relations. She is the author of several books, among them *Paradise Transplanted: Migration and the Making of California Gardens* (2014) and *God's Heart Has No Borders: Religious Activism for Immigrant Rights* (2008).

FRANCES NEGRÓN-MUNTANER is Associate Professor of English and Comparative Literature at Columbia University. She is the editor of several books, including *Puerto Rican Jam: Rethinking Nationalism and Colonialism* (1997), *None of the Above: Puerto Ricans in the Global Era* (2007), and *Sovereign Acts* (2009).

VILMA ORTIZ is Professor of Sociology at the University of California, Los Angeles. She is the co-author (with Edward Telles) of *Generations of Exclusion: Mexican Americans, Assimilation, and Race* (2008) and co-editor (with Mary Romero and Pierrette Hondagneu-Sotelo) of *Challenging Fronteras: Structuring Latina and Latino Lives in the U.S.* (1997).

MANUEL PASTOR JR. holds the Turpanjian Chair in Civil Society and Social Change and is Professor of Sociology and American Studies and Ethnicity at the University of Southern California, where he also serves as Director of USC's Program for Environmental and Regional Equity and Co-director of USC's Center for the Study of Immigrant Integration. His research focuses on urban poverty and regional economies, Latinos in the urban United

States, labor markets and low-wage workers, and social movements and social justice. He is the author of many publications, including *Just Growth: Prosperity and Inclusion in America's Metropolitan Regions* (2012) and co-author of *This Could Be the Start of Something Big: How Social Movements for Regional Equity Are Reshaping Metropolitan America* (2009).

ANA Y. RAMOS-ZAYAS is the Valentín Lizana y Parragué Chair of Latin American Studies in the Black and Hispanic Studies Department at Baruch College of the City University of New York. Her work focuses on U.S. Latino communities, race, migration, transnationalism, and the anthropology of affect. Her books include *Street Therapists: Race, Affect and Neoliberal Personhood in Latino Newark* (2012) and *National Performances: Class, Race and Space in Puerto Rican Chicago (2003)*.

ANGELICA SALAS is Director of the Coalition for Humane Immigrant Rights of Los Angeles. As an organizer and social activist, she has spearheaded several ambitious campaigns to win in-state tuition for undocumented immigrant students and to establish day-laborer job centers that have served as a model for the rest of the nation. She also led efforts to allow all California drivers to obtain a driver's license and is a leading spokesperson on federal immigration policy.

WERNER SCHINK is President of Community and Local Neighborhood Research, a consulting firm specializing in research and technical support for nonprofit organizations in low-income communities. He has collaborated with David Hayes-Bautista and Jorge Chapa on numerous professional publications beginning in 1980. While working for the State of California he was Chief of Research for the Social Services Department during the welfare reform era in the 1990s and was Chief Economist for the Employment Development Department during the 1980s.

ROBERT COURTNEY SMITH is Professor in the School of Public Affairs at Baruch College, and a member of the Sociology Department at the Graduate Center of the City University of New York. He is currently working on a book project that ethnographically follows the paths of 100 children of Mexican immigrants through adolescence into early adulthood, seeking to explain their differing life outcomes. He is author of *Mexican New York: Transnational Worlds of New Immigrants* (2006).

EDWARD TELLES is Professor of Sociology at the University of California, Santa Barbara. He is the author of *Pigmentocracies: Ethnicity, Race, and Color in Latin America* (2014) and (with Vilma Ortiz) *Generations of Exclusion: Mexican Americans, Assimilation, and Race* (2008).

MARTIN GUEVARA URBINA is Professor of Criminal Justice at Sul Ross State University/ Rio Grande College. His research focuses on race and ethnic relations, capital punishment, law and society, and social justice. His most recent books include *Latino Police Officers in the United States: An Examination of Emerging Trends and Issues* (2015), *Twenty-First Century Dynamics of Multiculturalism: Beyond Post-Racial America* (2014), and *Ethnic Realities of Mexican Americans: From Colonialism to 21st Century Globalization* (2014).

PATRICIA ZAVELLA is Professor and Chair of the Latin American and Latino Studies Department at the University of California, Santa Cruz. Her research focuses on family, poverty, sexuality, reproductive justice, social networks, transnational migration of Mexican women and men, women's paid and domestic labor, Chicana/o-Latina/o studies, feminist studies, and ethnographic research methods. She is the author of numerous publications, among them *"I'm Neither Here nor There": Mexicans' Quotidian Struggles with Migration and Poverty* (2011) and co-editor (with Ramón A. Gutiérrez) of *Mexicans in California: Transformation and Challenges* (2009).

RICHARD L. ZWEIGENHAFT is Charles A. Dana Professor of Psychology at Guilford College. He has co-authored, with G. William Domhoff, *The New CEOs: Women, African Americans, Latinos, Asians Americans Leaders of* Fortune 500 *Companies* (2014), and *Diversity in the Power Elite: How It Happened, Why It Matters* (2006).

CREDITS

PART 1: HISPANICS, LATINOS, CHICANOS, BORICUAS: WHAT DO NAMES MEAN?

Ramón A. Gutiérrez, "What's in a Name? The History and Politics of Hispanic and Latino Panethnic Identities." This essay was written for this volume.

Frances R. Aparicio, "(Re)constructing *Latinidad*: The Challenge of Latino/a Studies," in *A Companion to Latino Studies*, ed. Juan Flores and Renato Rosaldo, 39–49 (Malden, Mass: Blackwell Publishing, 2007). Reprinted with permission of John Wiley & Sons.

Frances Negrón-Muntaner, "Celia's Shoes," in *Archipelagos of Sound: Transnational Caribbeanities, Women and Music*, ed. Ifeona Fulani, 119–42 (Kingston, Jamaica: University of the West Indies Press, 2012). Reprinted with permission of University of the West Indies Press.

PART 2: THE ORIGINS OF LATINOS IN THE UNITED STATES

Ramón A. Gutiérrez, "The Latino Crucible: Its Origins in Nineteenth-Century Wars, Revolutions, and Empire," in *American Latinos and the Making of the United States: A Theme Study* (Washington, D.C.: National Park Service, 2013).

David G. Gutiérrez, "A Historical Overview of Latino Immigration and Demographic Transformation of the United States," in *American Latinos and the Making of the United States: A Theme Study* (Washington, D.C.: National Park Service, 2012).

Lillian Guerra, "Late-Twentieth-Century Immigration and U.S. Foreign Policy: Forging

Latino Identity in the Minefields of Political Memory," in *American Latinos and the Making of the United States: A Theme Study* (Washington, D.C.: National Park Service, 2013).

PART 3: THE CONUNDRUMS OF RACE

Jorge Duany, "Neither White nor Black: The Representation of Racial Identity among Puerto Ricans on the Island and in the U.S. Mainland," in *The Puerto Rican Nation on the Move: Identities on the Island and in the United States* (Chapel Hill: University of North Carolina Press, 2002), 236–60. Reprinted with permission of University of North Carolina Press.

Ginetta E. B. Candelario, "Hair Race-ing: Dominican Beauty Culture and Identity Production," *Meridians* vol. 1, no. 1 (August 2000), pp. 128–56. Copyright, 2000. Reprinted with permission of Indiana University Press.

Tomás Almaguer, "Race, Racialization, and Latino Populations," in *Racial Formation in the Twentieth-First Century*, ed. Daniel Hosang, Oneka Bennett, and Laura Pulido, 143–61 (Berkeley: University of California Press, 2012). Reprinted with permission of University of California Press.

PART 4: WORK AND LIFE CHANCES

Patricia Zavella, "The Working Poor," in *I'm Neither Here nor There: Mexicans' Quotidian Struggles with Migration and Poverty* (Durham, N.C.: Duke University Press, 2011), 89–122. Copyright 2011. Duke University Press. All rights reserved. Republished by permission of the copyright holder. www.dukeupress.edu

Nicholas de Genova and Ana Y. Ramos-Zayas, "Economies of Dignity: Ideologies of Work and Worth," in *Latino Crossings: Mexicans, Puerto Ricans, and the Politics of Race and Citizenship* (New York: Routledge, 2003), 57–82. Reprinted with permission of Routledge Publishing.

Manuel Pastor Jr., "Not So Golden? Latino Fortunes and Futures in California's Changing Economy." This essay was written for this volume.

PART 5: CLASS, GENERATION, AND ASSIMILATION

Luis Fraga, et al., "Trying for the *Americano* Dream: Barriers to Making the United States 'Home,'" in *Latino Lives in America*, 28–52 (Philadelphia: Temple University Press, 2010). Reprinted with permission of Temple University Press.

Edward Telles and Vilma Ortiz, "Conclusions," in *Generations of Exclusion: Mexican Americans, Assimilation, and Race* (New York: Russell Sage Foundation, 2008), 264–92. Reprinted with permission of Russell Sage Foundation.

Richard L. Zweigenhaft and G. William Domhoff, "Latinos in the Power Elite," in *Diversity in the Power Elite: Have Women and Minorities Reached the Top?* (New Haven: Yale University Press, 1998), 118–39. Reprinted with permission of Rowland & Littlefield.

Richard L. Zweigenhaft and G. William Domhoff, "Postscript: Latinos in the Power Elite, 2016." This essay was written for this volume.

PART 6: GENDER AND SEXUALITIES

Ramón A. Gutiérrez, "The History of Latino Sexuality," in *Latina/o Sexualities: Probing, Powers, Passions, Practices, and Policies*, ed. Marysol Asencio, 13–37 (New Brunswick, N.J.: Rutgers University Press, 2010). Reprinted by permission of Rutgers University Press.

Robert Courtney Smith, "Gender Strategies, Settlement, and Transnational Life in the First Generation," in *Mexican New York: Transnational Lives of New Immigrants* (Berkeley: University of California Press, 2006), 94–122. Reprinted with permission of University of California Press.

Lorena García, "'She's Old School Like That': Mother and Daughter Sex Talks," in *Respect Yourself, Protect Yourself* (New York: New York University Press, 2012), 19–56. Reprinted with permission of New York University Press.

Tomás Almaguer, "Longing and Same-Sex Desire among Mexican Men." This essay was written for this volume.

PART 7: LATINO POLITICS

Lisa García Bedolla, "Latina/o Politics and Participation: Individual Activity and Institutional Context," in *Latino Politics* (Cambridge, MA: Polity Press, 2014), 15–44. Reprinted with permission of Polity Press.

David E. Hayes-Bautista, Werner Schink, and Jorge Chapa, "The Young Latino Population in an Aging American Society," *Social Policy*, vol. 15, no. 1 (Summer 1984), 49–52. www .socialpolicy.org.

David E. Hayes-Bautista, Werner Schink, and Jorge Chapa, "Afterword: Thirty Years Later, 2016." This essay was written for this volume.

Martin Guevara Urbina, "Life after Prison: Ethnic, Racial, and Gender Realities," in *Hispanics in the U.S. Criminal Justice System: The New Demography* (Springfield, Ill.: Charles C. Thomas Publisher, LTD), 291–314. Reprinted with permission of Charles C. Thomas Publisher, LTD.

Southern Poverty Law Center, "Climate of Fear: Latino Immigrants in Suffolk County, N.Y.," Montgomery, Alabama (Special report, September 2009). Reprinted with permission of Southern Poverty Law Center.

Pierrette Hondagneu-Sotelo and Angelica Salas, "What Explains the Immigrant Rights Marches of 2006? Xenophobia and Organizing with Democracy Technology," in *Immigrant Rights in the Shadow of Citizenship*, ed. Rachel Ida Buff, 209–25 (New York: New York University Press, 2008). Reprinted with permission of New York University Press.

Ann Louise Bardach, "Wet Foot/Dry Foot . . . Wrong Foot" (appeared in shortened form in the *New York Times* [January 21, 2015], p. A17). Reprinted with permission of the author.

INDEX

Abad y Lasierra, Iñigo, 68–69

Abbott, Greg, 546

acculturation, 315, 317, 331, 336, 340–41, 343, 352. *See also* assimilation; cultural assimilation; integration

activism, 46–48. *See also specific topics*

Adams, John Quincy, 29

Addison, Oscar M., 97

adolescents. *See* teen pregnancy

Adoption and Safe Families Act of 1997, 577

adoptive parenting, 577

adultery, 431–33

advertising, 46–47

affirmative action, 2, 46, 308, 407; in corporations, 44, 406; in universities, 345, 348, 365, 402, 406

Affordable Care Act (ACA), 302, 307

African American CEOs, 381, 400, 401

African-American Civil Rights Movement, 214

African American women, beauty regimes, and beauty shops, 189, 193, 194, 196, 198–200, 203, 205, 206. *See also* "black hair"/"black women's hair"

African Americans: "American"-ness and, 283; "blackness" and, 217, 219, 220; Celia Cruz and, 70; demographics, 213–14, 288; Dominicans and, 189, 193, 199, 200, 203, 205, 206; education, 306, 341, 355; income and poverty among, 292, 294, 300; labor market and, 301, 309n12, 355, 376, 402, 402t; Mexicans and, 219–20, 282, 284, 341, 355; political participation, 539, 544, 545, 577; prison and, 530, 571, 573, 577–78, 580; Puerto Ricans and, 164–66, 167t, 173, 221, 266–67; race mixing and, 25; racialization, 217, 219–21; racialized, 217; racialized terms referring to, 219, 220; sexuality and, 220, 438, 480, 495; skin-tone variation and, 358, 382–83; stereotypes of, 186. *See also* African American CEOs; blacks; slaves: African/black

African ancestry: Dominicans and, 186, 187, 218; Mexicans with, 217–19; Puerto Ricans with, 223; and the term "Latino," 156. *See also* "one-drop rule"/"one drop of blood rule"

African-diaspora hair. *See* "black hair"/"black women's hair"

undocumented immigrants. *See* illegal immigrants

unemployment rates: in California and its regions, 290, 291f. *See also* labor market

United Farm Workers Union (UFW), 247–49, 258n39, 621n5

United Fruit Company, 133, 134

United Press International (UPI), 379

United States Refugee Act of 1980, 610–11

universities: affirmative action in, 345, 348, 365, 402, 406. *See also* education

University of California (UC), 305–6

Univision, 48, 379, 385, 535

urban context and assimilation, 352–55

Urrely, Maggie, 77

U.S. Conference of Catholic Bishops, 616

U.S. Immigration Act of 1965. *See* Immigration and Nationality Act (INA) of 1965

U.S. Immigration and Customs Enforcement. *See* Immigration and Customs Enforcement (ICE)

U.S.-Mexican War. *See* Mexican-American War

U.S.-Mexico War (1846–1848). *See* Mexican-American War

"us" vs. "them," 37. *See also* other

Valentín-Escobar, Wilson, 73

Vásquez, Tiburcio, 100

vecino, 29

Velasco, Carlos, 36

vergüenza. See shame

Villagrá, Gaspar Peréz de, 22

Villarejo, Don, 248

virginity: Christianity, the Catholic Church, and, 418, 423; of daughters, 412, 413, 473, 474, 478, 480, 483, 490, 494, 497; marriage and, 483, 497; pregnancy and, 474; rape and, 426, 428; shame around the loss of, 412, 428, 473, 483, 490, 491

voter registration, 539–42, 540f

voting, 577–78; in midterm elections, 541–42, 541f, 542f; in presidential elections, 539–42, 540f, 541f

voting rights: citizenship and, 547–48; racial/ethnic discrimination and, 546–47

Voting Rights Act of 1965 (VRA), 544–47, 552, 553, 556

Walker, Madam C. J., 205–6

War of 1836. *See* Texas Revolution

War of 1846. *See* Mexican-American War

War of 1898. *See* Spanish-American War of 1898

war rape. *See under* rape

Waters, Mary, 365–66

Watsonville, California, 235, 240–42, 243f, 244, 245, 247, 248, 250

Webber, Edward, 532

"welfare," 266–70, 281, 282, 284; discourses of, 266, 269, 272–73; the moral economy of, 272–76; the racial economy of work and, 281–84; scope of the term, 268; stigma of, 266–68, 272, 273, 275, 276, 281–82

"welfare dependency," 266–67, 269–70, 272, 284. *See also* "welfare"

welfare programs, 268–69, 272

"Welfare Reform" law of 1996. *See* Personal Responsibility and Work Opportunity Reconciliation Act (PRWORA) of 1996

White, Tony, 381

"white" looks, 199, 203, 203t, 204t

white privilege, 223

white supremacy, 37, 165, 186, 198, 202, 205, 206, 217, 281, 601. *See also* hate groups; Hispanophobia/anti-Spanish sentiment

"White"/"white," 215; "American" conflated with, 475; Latinos identifying as, 172, 178, 214, 215, 221; Mexicans as, 156, 212–13, 218; Puerto Ricans as, 158, 164, 166, 172, 178, 215, 221; Spanish terms for, 154, 217

"whiteness": honorary whiteness/"honorary white" status, 187, 212, 217; Mexicans and, 218; writs of, 25. *See also* "White"/"white"

whitening/"bleaching" *(blanqueamiento),* 162, 163, 168–69, 175, 177, 193

Wilson, Pete, 569

Winant, Howard, 210–11, 223

womanhood, migrant, models of, 445–46

women: as the agents who diffuse and cement *Latinidad* as lived experience, 45; Mexican American, 356. *See also* pionera; *specific topics*

women's practices of settlement and transnational life, 461–67

Wood, Elizabeth Jean, 147n34